PREACHING THROUGH
THE CHRISTIAN YEAR

PREACHING THROUGH THE CHRISTIAN YEAR

Year A

A Comprehensive Commentary on the Lectionary

Fred B. Craddock *Gospel*
John H. Hayes *Psalms*
Carl R. Holladay *Epistles & Acts*
Gene M. Tucker *Old Testament*

Trinity Press International   Philadelphia

First Edition 1992

Trinity Press International
P.O. Box 851
Valley Forge, PA 19482

Cover design by Brian Preuss

Library of Congress Cataloging-in-Publication Data

Preaching through the Christian year. Year A / Fred B. Craddock . . .
   [et al.].
      p.   cm.
   Includes index.
   ISBN 1-56338-054-4 (v. 1) :
    1. Bible—Homiletical use. 2. Bible—Commentaries. 3. Common
lectionary (1992) 4. Lectionary preaching. I. Craddock, Fred B.
BS534.5.P7272 1992
251—dc20   92-25860
                                        CIP

Printed in the United States of America on acid-free paper.

95 96 97   6 5 4 3

CONTENTS

LENT

HOLY WEEK

TRINITY SUNDAY

PROPERS AFTER PENTECOST

SPECIAL DAYS

Introduction

The Consultation on Common Texts issued the *Common Lectionary* in 1983, inviting the churches to use it and then offer suggestions for amendments and modifications. That trial period is now ended, and in December 1991 a final draft of the calendar and table of readings was completed. No further changes in this lectionary are anticipated.

The present volume—one of three to appear in a series—is based on the newly revised *The Common Lectionary: The Lectionary Proposed by the Consultation on Texts* (1992).

The now finalized *Common Lectionary* more fully converses with the lectionaries of the Episcopal, Lutheran, and Roman Catholic churches than did the 1983 edition. Readers will notice the influence of these three traditions in both calendar and readings. For example, Holy Saturday with its appropriate readings is offered for those who observe liturgically the Saturday between Good Friday and Easter. At some points, this greater inclusiveness has meant embracing the selected texts in the Roman, Lutheran, or Episcopal lectionaries. In other instances, the texts of these three traditions are offered as alternate readings. In every case, it has been our decision to comment on all the texts, hoping to make this commentary useful to as wide an audience as possible and as helpful to as many pulpits as possible.

In 1989, the New Revised Standard Version of the Bible was published. The present work follows the NRSV as its primary translation. In addition, two other widely used translations, the New English Bible and the Jerusalem Bible, have been used in their new revisions. Other translations are also quoted occasionally.

This commentary series will treat all the readings for each year in a single volume. Having in one volume a full year's calendar, table of readings, and commentary gives the preacher and others who work with the liturgy a clearer sense of continuity and greater ease of reference within a year and of cross reference among the three years. A commentary is a reference book, most at home on a study desk.

As an aid for focus and direction, each of the volumes in the series will provide a brief introduction to the readings for each service.

We think it important that the reader understand the perspectives and convictions that will inform our work throughout the three volumes. We offer these under the following three headings.

The Scripture. There is no substitute for direct exposure to the biblical text, both for the preacher in preparation and for the listener in worship. The Scriptures are therefore not only studied privately but also read aloud as an act of worship in and of itself and not solely as prelude to a sermon. The sermon is an interpretation of Scripture in the sense that the preacher seeks to bring the text forward into the present in order to effect a new hearing of the Word. In this sense, the text has its future and its fulfillment in preaching. In fact, the Bible itself is the record of the continual rehearing and reinterpreting of its own traditions in new settings and for new generations of believers. New settings and new circumstances are properly as well as inescapably integral to a hearing of God's Word in and through the text. Whatever else may be said to characterize God's Word, it is always appropriate to the hearers. But the desire to be immediately relevant should not abbreviate study of the text or divorce the sermon from the biblical tradition. Such sermons are orphaned, released without memory into the world. It is the task of the preacher and teacher to see that the principle of fidelity to Scripture is not abandoned in the life and worship of the church. The endeavor to understand a text in its historical, literary, and theological contexts does create, to be sure, a sense of distance between the Bible and the congregation. The preacher may grow impatient during this period of feeling a long way from a sermon. But this time of study can be most fruitful. By holding text and parishioners apart for a while, the preacher can hear each more clearly and exegete each more honestly. Then, when the two intersect in the sermon, neither the text nor the congregation is consumed by the other. Because the Bible is an ancient book, it invites the preacher back into its world in order to understand; because the Bible is the church's Scripture, it moves forward into our world and addresses us here and now.

The Lectionary. Ever-increasing numbers of preachers are using a lectionary as a guide for preaching and worship. The intent of lectionaries is to provide for the church over a given period of time (usually three years) large units of Scripture arranged according to the seasons of the Christian year and selected because they carry the central message of the Bible. Lectionaries are not designed to limit one's message or restrict the freedom of the pulpit. On the contrary, churches that use a lectionary usually hear more Scripture in worship than those that do not. And ministers who preach from the lectionary find themselves stretched into areas of the canon into which they would not have gone had they kept to the path of personal preference. Other values of the lectionary are well known: the readings provide a common ground for discussions in ministerial peer groups; family worship can more easily join public worship through shared readings; ministers and worship committees can work with common biblical texts to prepare services that have movement and integrity; and the lectionary encourages more disciplined study and advance preparation. All these and other values are increased if churches share a common lectionary. A common lectionary could conceivably generate a communitywide Christian conversation.

However, to the nonlectionary preacher also we offer this commentary as a helpful tool in sermon preparation. An index of Scriptures on which comments are made is provided in each volume. By means of this index, any preacher or teacher will find easy access to commentary on hundreds of biblical texts.

This Book. This volume is not designed as a substitute for work with the biblical text; on the contrary, its intent is to encourage such work. Neither is it our desire to relieve the preacher of regular visits to concordances, lexicons, and commentaries; rather, it is our hope that the comments on the texts here will be sufficiently germinal to give direction and purpose to those visits to major reference works. Our commentary is an effort to be faithful to the text and to begin moving the text toward the pulpit. There are no sermons as such here, nor could there be. No one can preach long distance. Only the one who preaches can do an exegesis of the listeners and mix into sermon preparation enough local soil so as to effect an indigenous hearing of the Word. But we hope we have contributed to that end. The reader will notice that, although each of us has been aware of the other readings for each service, there has been no attempt to offer a collaborated commentary on all texts or a homogenized interpretation as though there were not four texts but one. It is assumed that the season of the year, the needs of the listeners, the preacher's own abilities, as well as the overall unity of the message of the Scriptures will prompt the preacher to find among the four readings the word for the day. Sometimes the four texts will join arm in arm; sometimes they will debate with one another; sometimes one will lead while the others follow, albeit at times reluctantly. Such is the wealth of the biblical witness.

A final word about our comments. The lections from the Psalter have been treated in the same manner as the other readings, even though some Protestant churches often omit the readings of the psalm or replace it with a hymn. We have chosen to regard the psalm as an equal among the texts, primarily for three reasons. First, there is growing interest in the use of psalms in public worship, and comments about them may help make that use more informed. Second, the psalms were a major source for worship and preaching in the early church, and they continue to inspire and inform Christian witness today. And third, comments on the psalms may make this volume helpful to preachers in those traditions that have maintained from earliest times the use of psalms in Christian services.

A brief word about the relation of this commentary to our earlier work, *Preaching the New Common Lectionary*. From the comments above, it is already apparent why those volumes could not be given a new introduction and offered again to you. Changes in appointed texts, revised translations of the Bible, additions to the liturgical calendar, and attention to texts appearing in Lutheran, Anglican, and Roman Catholic lectionaries necessitated much new writing. The new writing in turn called for a reappraisal of the comments on texts that remained unchanged, prompting additions, deletions, and modifications. The result is a new, larger, and, we hope, improved commentary to aid those who preach and teach.

> Fred B. Craddock (Gospels)
> John H. Hayes (Psalms)
> Carl R. Holladay (Epistle and Acts)
> Gene M. Tucker (Old Testament)

First Sunday of Advent

Isaiah 2:1–5;
Psalm 122;
Romans 13:11–14;
Matthew 24:36–44

On this day that is the turning point of the year, all of the assigned texts direct the attention of the church to the future. They begin the preparation for Christmas, to be sure, but they also stress the eschatological dimensions of the coming of Jesus. A new age is dawning, already present but not yet consummated. The Old Testament lesson is a vision of peace for all peoples, that peace on earth announced by the angelic host to the shepherds in Luke's account of the birth of Jesus (Luke 2:13–14). The responsorial psalm sets the tone for celebration of that peace which has its center in Jerusalem. The reading from Romans reminds the faithful that they are living between the ages and should be prepared at all times for the end of the present age. The Gospel likewise calls for watchfulness, for only the Father knows the day and hour. The expectation, mystery, and celebration of the reign of God are the leading themes for the day.

Isaiah 2:1–5

These words here attributed to Isaiah of Jerusalem appear in virtually identical form in Micah 4:1–4. There is no way of determining which prophet depends upon the other. Indeed, it is quite likely that both occurrences are either citations from an older tradition, known at the temple in Jerusalem, or later additions to the words of the two eighth century prophets. The liturgical dimensions of the passage lend support to the view that the tradition is older than Isaiah and Micah, but the particular eschatology expressed in the poem is more consistent with perspectives of the exilic or early postexilic eras.

Our reading contains three distinct parts, a superscription in verse 1, the announcement of salvation in verses 2–4, and a call to the congregation to respond in verse 5. The superscription, similar in many respects to the one in Isaiah 1:1 and the others that begin prophetic books, is the heading for a collection of prophetic addresses, and not simply the passage before us. Its presence indicates that some part of the Book of Isaiah that begins here—either through the end of chapter 4, through 9:7, or perhaps as far as the end of chapter 11—once circulated independently. The call to the congregation (v. 5) applies the good news of the announcement to the addressees.

It is the lines in verses 2–4 that attract our attention, and with good reason. Although there are liturgical allusions and even hymnic features—the implicit praise of Yahweh, his temple, and Zion—the passage is not a hymn but an announcement or promise of salvation. The words are not addressed to God, but are indefinite, to any who listen. Nor is God the speaker, but a prophetic voice announces what will happen and what Yahweh and others will do. The sequence of events is important. First, "the mountain of the Lord's house," that is, Zion, will be elevated and exalted (v. 2ab). Second, there will be a pilgrimage of all peoples to the holy mountain (vv. 2c–3a). Third, as they approach, the people will sing a call to pilgrimage that expresses their reasons for coming to Zion, namely, that the God of Jacob may teach them his ways (v. 3b). Fourth, the motivation for the pilgrimage, or the attraction of Zion, is stated: instruction (or the law) and the word of Yahweh go forth from Jerusalem (v. 3c). Finally, the results of all that has transpired thus far are specified: Yahweh shall "judge between the nations," who will turn their instruments of war into farming tools, inaugurating a permanent reign of peace (v. 4).

Note that some of the events are characterized passively and others actively. The mountain "shall be established . . . , raised" (v. 2), and instruction and the word of the Lord "shall go forth" (v. 3). The only actors in the drama of peace are Yahweh and "the nations," or "many peoples" (vv. 2, 3, 4). Yahweh takes on the role of teacher or instructor (v. 3) that traditionally was held by the priests in ancient Israel, and the duties of judge and administrator of justice (v. 4). The role of the nations is crucial. They come to Zion seeking instruction and revelation, and they—not God—destroy the weapons of war. Consequently, their acknowledgment of and trust in God is the basis for peace.

What is the role of the people of God, those people of Judah and Jerusalem mentioned in the initial verse? At some stage in the transmission and liturgical use of our text—if not when it was originally composed—that same question arose and was answered with the lines that stand in verse 5. The announcement is a vision of peace for all peoples, in which the foreign nations come to Jerusalem to learn the ways of justice. Having heard that proclamation, the congregation of the faithful in Jerusalem is called to "walk in the light of the Lord." The point seems clear: those who already live in the presence of God are admonished to take the first steps on the path that all the nations will tread one day. "The light of the Lord" thus refers to the vision of God's reign just announced. The appropriate response to this vision is to be guided by it.

The reading is rich in themes for theological and homiletical reflection. (1) Above all, there is the announcement of the future reign of God. This is good news in the Old Testament prophetic sense. The time is not specified—indeed, the poem is vague on this point—but the announcement is concrete. The poem is not a prediction, but a statement of the certainty that history will reach its goal, its culmination. That goal is the reign of God that will involve the utter transformation of existing conditions, from nationalism and conflict to unity and peace. Resources will be turned from weapons to tools for harvesting food. (2) This vision has international political if not universalistic dimensions. The expectation is that all nations will come to Jerusalem to know the one true God, and the result will be peace. (3) Especially important in this hope is the understanding of God as judge (v. 4a). This is not the typical image of the Lord as judge, handing out punishment after establishing guilt or innocence. Like that image, the view here has deep roots in the view of Yahweh as just and in the prophetic calls for justice and righteousness. But the divine judge here is the one who settles the disputes among the nations, resolving their differences so that peace can be established and maintained.

It is tempting for us, in an era of military conflict, nationalism, and international mistrust, simply to write off such an announcement as this one, either as unrealistic or as applying to an era only beyond history and not within it. It probably is unrealistic to expect peace among all nations in the immediate future. Should one then capitulate to such harsh realities? Our reading, like so much of the Bible, holds forth the assurance that God will one day reign, and in peace. Moreover, the passage brings home to us the power of expectation. Who can read or hear these lines and not have his or her hope for peace kindled? Surely such a reign of God could not come among us unless we have—and keep alive in each generation—a vision of that reign.

Psalm 122

Psalms 120 to 134 form a collection in which each of the psalms bears the heading "a song of ascents." Although the meaning of the term "ascents" has been previously much debated, it is now widely agreed that the expression (literally, "going up") refers to pilgrimage. Thus these are pilgrim songs. (Other interpretations include "a song of going up" [from exile], "a song of graduated vocalization," "a song of graduated expression," "a song for the temple steps" [the ascents], and so on.)

This collection of fifteen psalms may once have existed as a small songbook for use by pilgrims on their way to Jerusalem. Some of the psalms appear to have been adopted secondarily for use on pilgrimage, some having initially been composed for other occasions. (Psalm 130, for example, is a lament that may have been written for use in some specific time of trouble.) After the move by kings Hezekiah and Josiah to close all sanctuaries except for Jerusalem (see 2 Kings 18, 22–23), pilgrimages would have become more important in the life of the people. If they were to worship in a temple, some had to travel long distances on foot to get to the capital city.

The tractate *Bikkurim* ("First Fruits") in the Mishnah tells us about features involved in going on pilgrimage. The persons in a district would assemble in the main village/town in the area, sleep outside the night before departing (to avoid becoming unclean through contamination, such as the presence of a corpse, which could make one unfit to enter the sanctuary), move out together (men in one group, women in another) under the supervision of a pilgrimage director (see Ps. 42:4; see Luke 2:43–44), and make their way to the temple.

There are many ways of thinking of a pilgrimage and its symbolism. The Book of Hebrews, for example, conceives life as a pilgrimage. The pilgrimage reflected in Psalm 122 was a periodic and repeatable pilgrimage, a recurring event fraught with meaning, like Advent.

The thought of a pilgrimage conjures up many images—the movement from the periphery to the center, from the ordinary to the holy, from the mundane to the meaningful, from the normal to the highly symbolic, from the loosely organized to the highly concentrated, from obsession with the present to the wellsprings of memory, from the low voltage of the everyday to the high voltage of celebration, from the famine of the ordinary to the festivities and feasting of the special. To return to a holy place on pilgrimage is like homecoming or reunion time, a return to the roots, to the source, to the "mother" who still sustains and nourishes.

Now to the psalm. Like many of its companions in Psalms 120–134, this composition gives indication of being sung on the way to the temple. Antiphonal singing, with individual and group participation (the director-pilgrims' participation?), is suggested by the movement from first person singular ("I") to first person plural ("our"). The rapturous joy of departing on pilgrimage is expressed in the opening lines. Verse 2 anticipates the joy of arriving at the object of pilgrimage—two totally different sets of emotions, departure and arrival, but related sentiments nonetheless. The arrival is anticipated by recalling a previous experience of standing in Jerusalem. In addition to the joy of the experience of visiting Jerusalem, three things should be noted about this psalm's content.

1. First, the psalm stresses the unity that is symbolized by the city (vv. 3–4). This is done in two ways: (a) with reference to the city's architecture and (b) with reference to the city as the object of tribal pilgrimage. In antiquity, every major city was compactly built, nestled atop some defendable elevation, and no doubt gave the impression of houses stacked one upon another. Such towns, surrounded by a defense wall, were frequently no more than ten to twenty acres in size. Streets within the towns were merely passageways for humans and an occasional beast of burden. Intimacy and communal knowledge, familiarity and gossip were characteristics of every such town, but also there were sharing and a sense of common fate. Not only was Jerusalem compactly built and thus knit together, but also the city was the central goal of pilgrimages for the various components (the tribes) of Israelite society. A common place of worship manifested and helped create a sense of national unity. In going on pilgrimage, the people were fulfilling the divine command (see Exod. 23:14).

2. Jerusalem is also the place of judgment (v. 5). The Davidic family who ruled in Jerusalem was responsible, like all kings in antiquity, for seeing that justice prevailed in the land. (Note Jer. 21:11–12 where the prophet reminds the ruler of this ongoing royal responsibility.) The reference in the plural to the "thrones for judgment," "the thrones of the house of David" has baffled scholars. The plural is perhaps best understood as referring to the throne of the king and to the throne of the queen-mother who, instead of a wife of the reigning monarch, served as first lady of the realm. This had the practical effect of eliminating competition for the post by the various wives of the king. The importance of the queen-mother and her possible role in the administration of justice in Jerusalem are suggested by two facts. For all the Judean kings, with only two exceptions, the biblical historian has provided us with the name of the king's mother. (This is not given for the northern or Israelite kings.) First Kings 2:10 reports that Bathsheba had a throne alongside that of her son Solomon, and it may have been she who was the first Judean to assume the role of queen-mother. (Note 1 Kings 15:9–13 with regard to the importance of the queen-mother.)

3. The peace of Jerusalem is a burning concern of the psalm (vv. 6–9). It is widely assumed that the name Jerusalem is built on the Hebrew word for peace, *shalom,* and as such incorporates in its very name a plea for or an affirmation about peace. The opening line of verse 6 reads in Hebrew *shaalu shelom yerusalayim,* and such assonance suggests that it may have been a proverbial expression—"ask about [or pray for] the peace of Jerusalem." Jerusalem, a city sacred to all three of the world's monotheistic religions (Judaism, Christianity, and Islam) and a symbol of peace, has proven throughout history to be one of the most fought over cities in the world. One scholar has calculated, for example, that between 323 BC (the death of Alexander the Great) and 63 BC (the capture of Jerusalem by the Roman general Pompey), over two hundred major military campaigns were fought in and across Palestine and against or in the vicinity of Jerusalem. Almost one per year! In modern times, the city is still frequently a battleground. As in days of old, so today too we should remember and pray for the peace of Jerusalem, the mother of us all.

As we move into Advent, we also can see it as a pilgrimage, as a journey back to the center, to a place of meaning, to the manger where kings bring their gifts and human hearts are wrapped in swaddling clothes.

Romans 13:11–14

Advent themes are boldly stated in this arousing call to vigilance. We are reminded "what time it is" (v. 11, NRSV), "that this is the hour of crisis" (REB), that "the time has come" (NJB). The text confronts us with the eschatological *kairos*—the impending Day of God when salvation comes. Elsewhere Paul reminds his readers that the *kairos* has grown very short (1 Cor. 7:29).

Such reminders reflect the widespread early Christian expectation of the speedy return of Christ (1 Cor. 7:26, 31). The death and resurrection of Christ had ushered in the period of the "last days" (Acts 2:17), the new era of God's reign. In one sense, this new period could be understood as calendar time, but it was more than that. It was a different era qualitatively, for salvation was now possible in an unprecedented manner. For Paul, the Christ-event now confronted everyone with "the acceptable time . . . the day of salvation" (2 Cor. 6:2). In Johannine Christianity, this new time was understood as the ushering in of "eternal life" (John 5:24). This time was often regarded as "the hour" that was at hand (John 5:25; 1 John 2:18; cf. John 4:23).

The call to "wake from sleep" is a call for us to be awake to this new set of realities. As one age dawns, another age is eclipsed. An age of darkness gives way to an era of light (cf. 1 John 2:8). The light of God's new revelation has broken through time, with the Christ-event as the dawning moment (2 Cor. 4:6). Our options for living are sketched in dualistic terms typical of early Jewish apocalyptic, well attested in the Qumran community and shared by many early Christians. It is a choice between light and darkness, day and night, good and evil (1 Thess. 5:4–8). Such dualism reflects the common notion that evil flourishes at night but flees before the coming day. The metaphor is graphic but should not lead us to the naïve view that light and darkness are to be equated with day and night. It is rather the case that good and evil cut across all time—through the day and into the night.

The call here is to "lay aside the works of darkness" (v. 12; cf. Eph. 5:11). Instead, we are to "put on the armor of light" (v. 12; cf. Eph. 6:11–17; also 2 Cor. 6:7; 10:4). The metaphor of donning new clothing is continued in verse 14 as we are urged to "put on the Lord Jesus Christ" (cf. Gal. 3:27; Eph. 4:24; Col. 3:12–14). It is a charge to clothe ourselves in the new being of Christ. So clothed, we are warmed, protected, and adorned.

The text does not leave us guessing as to the profile of the new life in Christ. "To live honorably as in the day" means eliminating certain vices from our lives (cf. Matt. 15:19; Rom. 1:29–31; 1 Cor. 5:10–11; 6:9–10; 2 Cor. 12:20; Gal. 5:19–21; Eph. 4:31; 5:3–5; Col. 3:5, 8; 1 Tim. 1:9–10; 6:4–5; 2 Tim. 3:2–4; Titus 3:3; 1 Pet. 4:3; Rev. 9:21; 21:8; 22:15). Three pairs of vices are listed: no "reveling and drunkenness" (NRSV) or "drunken orgies" (REB); no "debauchery and licentiousness" (NRSV) or "sexual immorality and debauchery" (NIV); no "quarreling and jealousy" (NRSV). We should note that social sins, or sins against the community and the common good, are here included alongside various forms of personal indulgence, or sins against the self.

Today's text is a challenge to develop a Christian sense of time. This entails more than knowing the time of day, the season of the year, even more than making good use of the time we have (cf. Eph. 5:16). It certainly requires more than the art of circling the calendar and trying to predict the exact time of Christ's coming. This is a misguided venture not only because it is bound to fail but mainly because it misconstrues the true nature of Christian time. The New Testament is fairly uniform in urging us to be alert, always prepared for Christ's coming, not because we know *when it is* but because we know *what it means*. Living with an eye toward Advent is living preparedly and expectantly.

To develop a Christian sense of time is to live with a new understanding of time. Christ's first coming allows us to see that time is not just a matter of clocks and calendars. It is to sense the tension between the divine will and human ways, the ongoing struggle between good and evil that goes on around us and within us. It is to recognize that Christ's coming has begun to make a difference in this conflict between light and darkness. Things may be dark but not as dark as they might have been otherwise. The light of Christ has provided significant illumination. This is not only true on the grand, historical scale of human history; it is also true within us as communities of believers and as individuals. The Christian sense of time finally translates into a way of life whose contours are clear, and for that reason offers a clear set of options for those of us who have experienced within ourselves the tension between good and evil, day and night, light and darkness.

Matthew 24:36–44

Advent is not a period of Christmas preliminaries but a season in itself, with its own integrity and its own announcement. Advent proclaims the coming of the Lord, but that is not the same as saying that Christmas is coming. Lest Advent melt too easily into the birth stories, the first Sunday of this season calls upon biblical texts that are not at all associated with the nativity. In fact, they are most usually understood as pointing to the "Second Coming." The preacher would do well to disengage from thinking first coming or second coming and announce that which all Scripture affirms: our God is the one who comes to the world. The question is, How shall the day of the Lord be? Will it be darkness or light, joy or dread, judgment or redemption? It is this thought that stirs the people of God and reminds us that not only joy and anticipation but also repentance mark the observance of Advent.

In all three cycles of the lectionary, the Gospel for the First Sunday of Advent is drawn from Jesus' apocalyptic discourse (Mark 13:5–37; Matt. 24:4–36; Luke 21:8–36). However, unlike the readings from Mark (Year B) and Luke (Year C), which describe the nature of the Lord's coming along with the attendant cosmic and historical signs, today's lection contains only the closing verse of Matthew's version of the discourse (24:36). The verse is joined to an extended call for watchfulness in view of the uncertain time of the Lord's coming (vv. 37–44). It could well be that Matthew intended verses 37–44 to be included as a part of the apocalyptic discourse. The reasons for this judgment are two. First, Matthew has taken material (vv. 37–44) that Luke has scattered through the travel narrative (17:26–27, 34–35; 12:39–40) and placed it here immediately after declaring that only God knows when the Son will come (24:36). As we will see, the calls to watchfulness are appropriate to this setting. Second, Mark's ending to the discourse (13:33–37), which Matthew does not repeat, is a call for watchfulness. Although Matthew depends heavily on Mark's account (Matt. 24:36 is almost an exact following of Mark 13:32), he replaces Mark's concluding exhortation to be alert with his own version of essentially the same message.

Matthew 24:36–44 consists, then, of two statements: the uncertain time of the Lord's advent (v. 36) and the behavior of the faithful in view of that uncertainty (vv. 37–44). That the time of the Lord's appearing is not known by angels or even by the Son, but by God alone, is a statement congenial to other words of Jesus to the effect that some matters are hidden within God's own purposes. "It is not for you to know the times or periods that the Father has set by his own authority" (Acts 1:7). In fact, Matthew states elsewhere that Jesus regarded not only the time of the Parousia as God's own business but also the granting of place in the kingdom (20:23). Some scribes, however, found it offensive to their Christology to speak of what the Son did not know, and so they deleted "nor the Son" from 24:36. And throughout church history there have been those unwilling to permit times and places to remain in the knowledge of God alone and who, therefore, have arranged certain texts so as to create a calendar of the last days.

The call for watchfulness (vv. 37–44) consists of three parts with different images and emphases. Verses 37–39 employ the catastrophe of the flood as an analogy. However, it is not the wickedness at the time of the flood (Gen. 6:5–7, 12–13) but rather the lack of preparedness that is Matthew's concern. In verses 40–41, the theme of an all-encompassing destruction is dropped and replaced by the image of the one taken, the one left. Here the accent is on the suddenness and the finality of the two fates that will occur "then"; that is, at the coming of the Son of Man (v. 39). The form of the third part of the exhortation to watchfulness (vv. 42–44) is that of a parable. If the householder had known when to be alert, his house would not have been burglarized. The image here is the much-used one of the thief coming in the night (1 Thess. 5:2–9; Rev. 16:15).

A flood, a kidnapper, a thief: all are sharp, intrusive, disturbing images with which to begin Advent. But they are effective in instructing us in alertness, in making preparation for uncertain certainties. Watch, stay awake; the Lord is coming.

Second Sunday of Advent

Isaiah 11:1–10;
Psalm 72:1–7, 18–19;
Romans 15:4–13;
Matthew 3:1–12

Preparation for Christmas continues with readings that kindle hope for the future reign of God in all the world, a reign of justice and righteousness. The Old Testament reading is one of the classic announcements of a future king in the line of David, one who will inaugurate a rule of peace with justice, especially for the poor. Psalm 72, a petition to God that the king rule with righteousness and justice, continues the same themes. A major motif in the epistolary lection, which cites Isaiah 11:10, is hope, based on the confirmation of the Old Testament promises by the coming of Jesus. The apocalyptic dimensions of the season are dramatized in the Gospel lesson, the account of the appearance of John the Baptist with his announcement of the kingdom of God.

Isaiah 11:1–10

Advent, the time of expectation, is a good season for Old Testament texts, and especially those that anticipate the future reign of God. All of the Old Testament readings for Advent and Christmas itself in Year A are from the Book of Isaiah. Today's selection continues the vision of the future expressed in last week's reading (Isa. 2:1–5) and is a direct extension of the text used in all years on Christmas, First Proper, the announcement of the birth of the messianic king in Isaiah 9:2–7.

When we recognize the parts of Isaiah 11:1–10 and their relationship to one another, the meaning and implications of our reading become more clear. Although everything in it concerns the future, three distinct parts comprise the passage. The first section, verses 1–5, is an announcement of the birth or ascension of a new king from the Davidic line. Verses 6–9 contain an announcement of peace and tranquillity in the natural order. It is possible that these two units arose independently or that verses 6–9 were composed after the first section. There are actually very few internal links between the two parts. In the context in which these two elements are juxtaposed, however, the cosmic peace of the second unit is viewed as the consequence of the rise of the king in the line of David. Verse 10 is yet another announcement concerning the descendant of David, in this case that he will be an ensign around which all nations will unite. The fact that this final verse is prose, whereas the preceding lines are in poetry, supports the conclusion that it is secondary to the original unit or units, serving the purpose of linking 11:1–9 to what follows in 11:11ff.

The question of the authorship and date of this passage has been the subject of considerable debate and disagreement. Does the passage, or any of its parts, come from Isaiah in the eighth century BC or from a later hand? The answer, at least for verses 1–5, turns primarily on the interpretation of "the stump" (or "stock," NEB) of Jesse in verse 1. Those commentators who take the passage to be late see this as an allusion to a time when the Davidic dynasty had been cut down, that is, in the exilic or postexilic era. Although that is the meaning that would have been heard in those later times, the language more likely refers simply to the lineage—the family tree—of David. Nothing in verses 1–5 in particular is inconsistent with the thought or language of Isaiah of Jerusalem. The vision of cosmic peace in verses 6–9 may be later, but even that could have come from Isaiah.

In ancient Israel, confidence in the reign of a Davidic king in Jerusalem was based on the promise expressed in 2 Samuel 7 and celebrated regularly in worship (see Pss. 2, 45, 110, etc.). Prophets such as Isaiah saw the Davidic monarchy as Yahweh's means of implementing his will first for Judah and Jerusalem, and then for the world as a whole. In later centuries, the hope for such a messiah ("anointed one") was linked more and more to the culmination or fulfillment of God's will for human history.

Verses 1–5 of our reading announce a new Davidic king (v. 1) and then describe him and his rule (vv. 2–5). The lines do not comprise an oracle, for the words are not attributed directly to Yahweh. Instead, a prophetic voice proclaims what will happen in accordance with the divine will. The character of the ruler (vv. 2–3a) will be shaped by the "Spirit" of Yahweh. This spirit (Hebrew *ruah*) represents the active and creative divine presence known at creation (Gen. 1:2) and in the inspiration of prophets (2 Kings 2:9; Mic. 3:8) as well as kings (1 Sam. 11:6) and other leaders (Judg. 6:34). Here that divine spirit provides the king with the gifts necessary for just rule and evokes from the anointed one true piety ("fear of the Lord"). The description of this king's administration (vv. 3b–5) concentrates on his establishment of justice. As one who sees and hears deeper than the surface, he will ensure that the "poor" and the "meek," that is, those least able to protect themselves, have full rights before the law. The character and administration of the king here are those that the people hoped for—but never fully realized—as each new descendant of David took the throne in Jerusalem.

Whereas the first five verses characterize the rule of justice in human society, verses 6–9 picture a transformation in the natural, cosmic sphere. Natural enemies in the animal world will live together in peace. There are echoes of a return to a world without violence among creatures, such as that assumed in Genesis 1:29–31. The goal of this transformation is for human beings to live without fear (vv. 6, 8). The "little child" (v. 6), the "nursing child," and the "weaned child" (v. 8) represent children generally, human beings at their most vulnerable stages, and not any particular individual. The center of the peaceful cosmos is the same as that in Isaiah 2:1–5, Yahweh's "holy mountain," that is, Mount Zion in Jerusalem. And as a consequence of the rule of justice and the transformation of nature, "the earth will be full of the knowledge of the Lord" (v. 9).

The juxtaposition of verses 1–5 and 6–9 evokes reflection on the relationship between justice, mercy, peace, and harmony in the natural order. Thus the preacher may be moved to remind the congregation, as Reinhold Niebuhr and many others have said, "If you want peace, work for justice." That would not be inconsistent with John the Baptist's call for repentance in today's Gospel lesson. However, one should not lose sight of both the contents and the mood of these powerful lines. They bring unqualified good news. Whether in this world and history or beyond, they cry joyfully that God wills—and will one day bring about—justice and peace for the world and all its living creatures.

Psalm 72:1–7, 18–19

This lection forms part of an intercessory prayer offered by the community on behalf of the king at his royal coronation. Thus it is a royal psalm expressing aspects of the theology of kingship—what the people believed, expected, and hoped for the ruling Davidic monarch—and forming the basis for messianic speculations about the future—what might be expected from the ideal ruler in the future, the messiah to come.

The component features and actions in the coronation of the Judean king can be partially reconstructed from 1 Kings 1 (the account of Solomon's coronation) and 2 Kings 11 (the account of the coronation of the young boy king Jehoash). We cannot be certain, however, about the exact sequence of events (compare 1 Kings 1:38–40 with 2 Kings 11:9–12).

1. A significant feature was the *anointment,* or the "messiahing," for the messiah was the anointed one, a title that would have been used for the reigning king. The anointing with holy oil set the new king apart from normal humanity and transferred the ruler to the realm of the divine, the holy.

2. The *acclamation,* with trumpet blowing and public shouts, affirmed the population's support. These two events, the anointment and acclamation, occurred either at the pool of Gihon (thus with Solomon), the sacred water source for the city of Jerusalem, or in the temple (so with Jehoash whose life, however, was in danger, which might explain why there was no excursion to Gihon).

3. The *procession* to the throne marked the king's assumption of power.

4. The *homage* of the officials may have been offered in the throne room. These events formed the skeleton of the ritual. No doubt, spoken components formed significant parts of the ceremony.

Psalm 72 would have been one of the spoken parts of the coronation liturgy. Perhaps after the new king was enthroned, the community offered prayer on his behalf. The petitions in Psalm 72 reflect many of the basic beliefs associated with the Davidic ruler, the reigning messiah. (1) The king was considered the representative of God's justice and righteousness (v. 1). (2) He was responsible for ruling over the people with equity (v. 2). (3) The new reign was hailed as the dawn of a new era in which prosperity was expected (vv. 3, 6–7). (4) The king was the special custodian of the poor, the defender of the powerless, and the opponent of the unscrupulous and the oppressor (vv. 4, 12–14). (5) The king was Yahweh's representative (God's son; see v. 1*b*) on earth and thus was the potential ruler of all of creation, a dominion extending from sea to sea (vv. 8–11, 15).

The extravagant imagery and idealistic expectations associated with the Davidic monarchy almost exceed the bounds of normal life and illustrate the flowery speech and language used at the royal court. (Note the sort of speeches and the claims made at presidential inaugurations in the United States.) Long life is requested for the king in totally unrealistic terms—"while the sun endures, and as long as the moon," "until the moon is no more" (vv. 5, 7).

Verses 18 and 19 are not an integral part of Psalm 72. They constitute a doxology to the collection found in Psalms 42–72. In the final editing of the Psalter, the work was divided into what the rabbis called the "five-fifths" of the Psalter of David paralleling the "five-fifths" of the Law of Moses (the Pentateuch). As noted in such translations as the NRSV, Psalms 1–41 constitute book I of the Psalter, 42–72 book II, 73–89 book III, 90–106 book IV, and 107–150 book V. These books of the Psalms were probably read consecutively in some early synagogues as parallel readings to consecutive readings of the Torah or Penta- teuch in a three-year lectionary. (The end of book IV may have originally been Psalm 118, and Psalm 119 the beginning of book V.) Book I was read with Genesis, II with Exodus, III with Leviticus, IV with Numbers, and V with Deuteronomy. (Ps. 72:20 probably once con- stituted the conclusion to a collection that began with Psalm 2 or 3.)

Verses 18 and 19 are appropriate to Advent, for they praise God who does wondrous things and request that the divine glory will universally fill the world.

Romans 15:4–13

Advent is above all a time of hope. As we reflect on the Lord's coming in its many dimensions, our mood is expectant. Our eyes are cast forward as we lean into the future, and we see the future as a time of promise.

Today's epistolary lection sounds the note of hope. It opens by reassuring us of our hope (v. 4) and closes by anchoring human hope in "the God of hope" (v. 13).

We all realize how fragile hope can be. We wonder whether it is an illusion. What might be competes with what never will be. Hope dances on the edge of wishing, comes close to expecting, but retreats to wishing. We do not want to be disappointed, so we wish instead of hope. The one flirts with the future; the other flings itself toward the future. On what, then, can we rest our hope? Two things, according to Paul in today's text.

First, we can rest our hope on "whatever was written in former days . . . the scrip- tures" (v. 4). We are reminded that these "scriptures written long ago" (REB) were written for our benefit—to instruct us. In view here, of course, are the Jewish Scriptures, which later came to be called the Old Testament. These were the Scriptures early Christians had at their disposal. They were the church's bibliography, as it were. The writings that later came to be called the New Testament were still being composed at this period. Paul's writings were among the earliest of these. Because Judaism provided the setting in which early Christian- ity originated and took root, it was understandable for the earliest Christians to look to the Jewish Scriptures for guidance and instruction. It was their conviction that these writ- ings were written "for our sake" (1 Cor. 9:10; Rom. 4:23–24; cf. 1 Cor. 10:11). Accordingly, these inspired writings provided guidance for righteous and obedient living before God (2 Tim. 3:16).

One of the chief values of the sacred Scriptures is "the encouragement they give us" (v. 4, REB; cf. 1 Macc. 12:9). The stories they tell help us "maintain our hope with perse- verance" (v. 4, REB) or give us examples of "how people who did not give up were helped by God" (v. 4, JB).

Early Christians read the Jewish Scriptures in terms of promise and fulfillment. Here they saw unfolded the story of God's promises to Israel and the fulfillment of those promises. What moved the story along was the promise God gave and the hope that it would be ful- filled. It was God's fidelity in keeping promises that provided the source of encouragement.

But it was not a story without breaks. Sometimes Israel proved unfaithful to the covenant. Sometimes fulfillment took a while. The singular virtue turned out to be "steadfastness" (v. 5, NRSV), or "endurance" (NIV). To receive the promise can mean to wait, and wait patiently.

Second, our hope is rooted in "the God of steadfastness and encouragement" (v. 5, NRSV), "the God of hope" (v. 13). Paul insists on "God's truthfulness" (v. 8, NJB), or the absolute fidelity of God, and in doing so stands firmly within the Old Testament tradition (cf. Ps. 88:3; Mic. 7:20). Elsewhere, Paul insists that the "gifts and the calling of God are irrevocable" (Rom. 11:29; cf. 2 Pet. 1:19).

Even though some of Paul's detractors thought that God's integrity had been called into question by the mission to the Gentiles, he insists that God's fidelity to the divine promise remained intact. True, God had given promises to the patriarchs, but the fact that Christ was a Jew merely confirmed that God kept the promise. The Jews thus remained part of God's saving work. But God's promise had not been one-sided. It had also extended to the Gentiles, and Paul cites several Scripture quotations to clinch this point (vv. 9–12; Ps. 18:49; Deut. 32:43; Ps. 117:1; Isa. 11:10; also cf. 2 Sam. 22:50). It was just as important for God to keep faith by extending salvation to the Gentiles as it was to keep the promise made to the patriarchs. Paul's mission to the Gentiles attests God's truthfulness.

If our hope is predicated on God's record in fulfilling divine promises, we can be reassured by the way in which God has extended salvation to both Jews and Gentiles. What God has done in the past, in the arena of human history, gives substance to our hope. It is not as if our hope is rooted only in who God is, or whom we believe God to be, but also in what God has done. The being of God is rooted in the acts of God.

Our text, then, confronts us with a hope previewed in Scripture and embodied in God, two reasons for us to "abound in hope" (v. 13).

In conclusion, we might note that our common conviction and expression of hope has a unifying force (vv. 5–6). What results from our common hope is a genuine sense of community, which in its best form is harmonious as it, with one voice, glorifies God (cf. Rom. 12:16; 2 Cor. 13:11; Phil. 2:2; 4:2; 1 Cor. 1:10; 1 Pet. 3:8). Concretely, this manifests itself in forms of genuine hospitality (v. 7; Rom. 14:1; Philem. 17). Hope turns out not to be ethereal but practical as it binds us into a community where we extend our love to one another, as we learn to "accept one another as Christ accepted us" (v. 7, REB).

Matthew 3:1–12

On the second Sunday of Advent, the Gospel reading each year treats the person and work of John the Baptist. All four Evangelists deal at some length with John, not primarily because he was a significant religious leader who had disciples (Mark 2:18), who suffered martyrdom (Mark 6:14–29), and who became the central figure in a continuing sect (Acts 18:24–19:7), but because the church understood John's function to be one of preparing for the Advent of Christ. He was the one of whom Isaiah spoke (Matt. 3:3; Isa. 40:3); he was the returned Elijah (Matt. 11:14; 17:13; Mal. 4:5–6) who was to prepare the people for "the great and terrible day of the LORD." But the preacher will not want to rush past John to Jesus. There is yet time. The accents of last Sunday continue in our text today; the time of the Lord's coming is near, and preparation for that event is of primary importance. If one is true to today's lection, Jesus is not yet introduced as the

Coming One. Matthew leaves Jesus a child in Nazareth (2:23), and we do not learn he is now an adult until 3:13. There is no indication at 3:11–12 that John knew at that time the identity of the One to come who was mightier than he.

For his presentation of John the Baptist, Matthew had access to Mark 1:1–8 and had in common with Luke a source of information about the content of John's preaching (Matt. 3:11b–12; Luke 3:16b–17). Much briefer than Mark or Luke is Matthew's introduction of the narrative: "In those days" (v. 1). The phrase is chronologically vague but is used later by Matthew as a reference to the last days (24:19, 22, 29) and, therefore, may have eschatological overtones here. John comes announcing the last days, the messianic age, the time that is ushered in by the Advent of Christ.

Matthew introduces John in verses 1–6, and he does so in this way: (a) by name and location; (b) by activity and message; (c) as the one fulfilling the prophecy of Isaiah 40:3 (Matthew omits Mark's awkward use of Mal. 3:1 in connection with Isa. 40:3); (d) by description of personal appearance, on the model of Elijah (2 Kings 1:8); (e) by the public response to John. By this brief sketch, Matthew makes it clear that, although he assumes that the readers already know of John the Baptist, it is important that they see him as introducing the messianic age and, therefore, as the eschatological prophet of Isaiah and the returned Elijah. He functions as preparer of the way through the preaching of repentance and baptism.

Both Matthew (vv. 7–10) and Luke (3:7–9) at this point present a summary of John's preaching of repentance. They use a common source, but Luke has John address the multitudes (all Israel together), whereas in Matthew's account John directs his words to the religious leaders, the Pharisees and Sadducees. The sermon is a strong indictment of a "brood of vipers" (Isa. 11:8; 14:29; 30:6) and a compelling call for the bearing of good fruit. The bearing of good fruit is a familiar image from the Gospels (Matt. 7:16–20; 12:33–37) implying the demand not only for conduct and activity appropriate to repentance and faith but also for integrity; that is, the tree and its fruit should be of the same kind. Before the searching and judging word of God, neither ritual (John does not seem eager to see how many he can baptize) nor genealogy (God is able from stones to raise up children to Abraham) provides valid claim or ground for exemption from the wrath to come (v. 7; 1 Thess. 1:10; Amos 2:4–16).

Matthew concludes his presentation of John with a brief summary statement of his messianic preaching (vv. 11–12).

John does not identify this person to come by name (we are thinking "Jesus," but the narrative asks us to exercise restraint and let the story unfold in its own time) or by title but rather as "he who is coming after me" and as "more powerful than I." The identification of the One whose Advent is near is sharpened by contrast with John's person ("I am not worthy to carry his sandals") and John's baptism (water, as distinct from the Holy Spirit and fire).

Whereas Mark speaks only of a promised baptism with the Holy Spirit (1:8), Matthew has the stronger image of judgment in the phrase "with the Holy Spirit and fire." Verse 12 makes it clear that "wind and fire" are judgment images in the sense of making distinctions between wheat and chaff. The Advent of the Messiah means that the differences among persons and their futures will become evident.

John's preaching makes it abundantly clear that one aspect of the Lord's Advent is the full revelation of the kind of persons we are and of the consequences of character and conduct that await us.

Third Sunday of Advent

Isaiah 35:1–10;
Psalm 146:5–10 or Luke 1:47–55;
James 5:7–10;
Matthew 11:2–11

As the church anticipates celebrating the Incarnation, the readings for the day highlight eschatological themes. The effect is to recall that the birth of a particular baby is an event of the end times, of the culmination of God's will for the world and human history. Except for the Epistle and the Magnificat (the alternative response), the texts have in common the healing of the sick as signs of the new order. Isaiah 35:10 celebrates the transformation of the wilderness into a fertile land; the healing of the blind, the deaf, the lame, and the dumb; and the restoration of Zion. The psalm is a song of praise to the God who sets prisoners free and opens the eyes of the blind. Similarly, Luke 1:47–55 praises God for acts of salvation. James 5:7–10 affirms that the coming of the Lord is at hand, and counsels patience. In the Gospel lection, John the Baptist is confirmed as the one who prepared the way for Jesus, and Jesus is confirmed as the Messiah through his healing of the sick and preaching of good news to the poor.

Isaiah 35:1–10

Last week's Old Testament reading from Isaiah 11:1–10 left us with a vision of nature transformed, especially of the natural enemies of the animal kingdom and human beings living together in peace. Today's lesson complements that one vision of the reign of God, but now it is the land, and especially the wilderness, that has become a supportive environment for human beings. In Isaiah 11:1–10, Zion was the center of the peaceful kingdom; in Isaiah 35, Zion is the goal of a pilgrimage of the elect through lands that once were hostile.

Because of the chapter's similarities to the poetry in Isaiah 40–55, some commentators have attributed Isaiah 35 to the same prophet, Second Isaiah, who wrote those words in 539 BC. On closer examination, however, it appears that the author of Isaiah 35 knew and depended upon Second Isaiah. He frequently cites but often reinterprets expressions from that prophet of the end of the Babylonian Exile: "highway" (v. 8) from 40:3; "streams in the desert" (v. 6) from 43:19; the appearance of the "glory of the Lord" (v. 2) from 40:3, 5; and more. However, where Second Isaiah had announced the return of the Judean exiles from Babylon along a highway in the desert, the poet of chapter 35 expects more. The dispersed of Israel from throughout the world shall return to Zion, and the desert will become a fertile garden. The vision in our passage is even more cosmic and eschatological than that of Second Isaiah. Because it depends upon Second Isaiah, the chapter can be dated to the postexilic age, and perhaps relatively late in the Persian period.

The question of the place of this chapter in its context in the book is closely related to the issue of its date of composition. Isaiah 35 stands in sharp contrast to the immediately preceding chapter, a harsh prophecy of judgment with almost apocalyptic overtones against Edom, Judah's neighbor. Isaiah 36–39 is an appendix to the prophetic collection containing narrative accounts concerning Isaiah of Jerusalem. It thus seems likely that at one stage in the growth of the book, our chapter stood either as the conclusion to the work of Isaiah of Jerusalem or as the transition to the words of Second Isaiah in chapters 40–55.

The poem before us today closely resembles a prophetic announcement of salvation, but its themes and language are more apocalyptic in character. Its two main parts, linked by their attention to wonderful changes in nature, present distinct but closely related themes.

1. Verses 1–6a, with all the language about the transformation of the desert, concerns the coming of "the glory of the Lord" (v. 2). The words actually seem to be addressed to the Lord's messenger or messengers, urging them to call for the wilderness to celebrate and the desert to bloom (vv. 1–2). The messengers also are to encourage the weak (vv. 3–4). There are echoes here of the old tradition about the theophany, the arrival of God and the dramatic and terrifying effect his coming has on nature; but here nature is transformed by the coming of God's glory, and then the sick are healed (vv. 5–6).

2. Verses 6b–10, on the other hand, concern the return of the redeemed, that is, the dispersed people of Israel, to Zion. Here, too, nature is transformed, made into a well-watered land, and fitted with a highway called "the Holy Way" (v. 8). The familiar threats to travelers in the desert—dry land, wild beasts, and enemies—no longer exist. The final lines (v. 10) catch the tone of the entire poem—joy and gladness, for "sorrow and sighing shall flee away." And that is the contribution of this text to the preparation for the coming of Jesus: those who experience their lives as exile, those who pass through a wilderness, those who are weak may shout for joy, for God will transform all things.

Psalm 146:5–10

The Old Testament lection from Isaiah 35:1–10 holds out hope for a grand and glorious transformation of world orders and a reversal of fate for both human beings and the world of creation. As one of the Hallelujah psalms (Pss. 146–150), Psalm 146:5–10 breathes the air of praise and trust in the divine. In its descriptions of the qualities and acts of God, the psalm shares many of the hopes and expectations of Isaiah 35:1–10.

The psalm is structured around two opposites. The negative, cast as a warning, in verses 3–4, admonishes the audience not to trust human leadership, princes or mortals, who cannot aid and whose efforts and plans are destined to sleep with them in the same tomb. (The NJPSV translates v. 3 as "Put not your trust in the great, in mortal man who cannot save.") The best laid plans, the highest hopes, the grandest designs die with their architects; they dissipate with their discoverer's demise. The one who trusts and hopes in such is doomed to disappointment because the mortal (*adam*) always returns to earth (*adamah*).

The opposite end of the spectrum is viewed in verses 5–8. Over against the human, the transitory, the disappointing, the inadequate, stands the Divine, the eternal, the satisfying, the sufficient.

Verse 5 declares "happy" anyone whose help and hope lie with the Deity. The term *happy* denotes a state of well-being and contentment but not necessarily a state of extravagance and luxury. Beginning in verse 6, a series of four characteristics of God are presented as supporting the contention that happy is the one whose help and hope is in God. (1) First, appeal is made to God as creator. As the one who made heaven, earth, and sea—that is, the totality of the universe—God is not bound by the structures and limitations of creaturehood. As creator, God is owner and ruler. (2) Second, appeal is made to the fidelity and constancy of the Creator "who keeps faith forever." Unlike humans, whose plans and programs die with them, God and divine help endure forever. Unlike humans, God is not threatened by the possibility of nonbeing. (3) God is the one who is not only concerned for but also executes (guarantees) justice for the oppressed. In this affirmation and throughout verses 7–9, one finds a consistent emphasis of the Old Testament: God takes a special interest in and acts in behalf of the downtrodden, the powerless, and the despairing. (4) The satisfaction of physical needs is also the concern of God, who "gives food to the hungry." As the maker of heaven and earth, God does not will that humans be oppressed or that they should suffer from hunger.

Following these four divine characteristics, the psalmist speaks of seven activities of God in which the Divine acts to alleviate human distress and to defend those without rights. Most of those noted as the object of God's care are persons without full authority and potential to assume responsibility for and to exercise rights for their own welfare: the prisoners (at the mercy of the legal system or perhaps in slavery), the blind (at the mercy of the seeing), those who are bowed down or with bent backs (in debt or oppressed by others, thus carrying burdens not their own), the righteous (the innocent in the legal system who however were at the mercy of the upholders of justice), the sojourners (foreign settlers or visitors, not members of the native culture, and thus aliens), and the widow and fatherless (who were without the support of a male patriarch in a male-dominated culture). God is declared to be committed to the care of all those, while at the same time God sees to it that the wicked come to their just reward—ruin.

The psalmist here obviously presents the basic nature and character of God but does not claim that conditions and circumstances conform to this idealized divine will. In the list of attributes, God is primarily contrasted with human leaders (vv. 3–4 over against 5–9). Verse 10 adds an eschatological note to the text and points to the future as the time when the intervention of God in behalf of society's rejects and subjects will occur. In this forward-looking thrust, the psalm participates in and contributes to the expectations of Advent.

Luke 1:47–55

The alternate reading to Psalm 146:5–10 is not another psalm of David but the song of Mary, the so-called Magnificat, whose title is derived from the opening words of the song in the Latin Vulgate. Luke has given the song the following setting: Elizabeth, the barren wife of the priest Zechariah, has been blessed with a pregnancy in her old age (1:5–25) and is visited by her relative Mary (1:36), now carrying the infant Jesus. In an unnamed Judean hill-country village, the two women meet, and Elizabeth's child, later to be called John the Baptist, leaps in her womb at the presence of the pregnant Mary (1:39–41*a*). Elizabeth offers praise to Mary (1:41*b*–45), and the song follows.

Three general factors should be noted about the Magnificat. (1) A few ancient manuscripts have Elizabeth, not Mary, as the speaker of the hymn. This ascription to Elizabeth is probably a scribal mistake, based on the context, rather than Luke's original ascription of the song. (2) Some scholars have argued that the song was originally a general Jewish-Christian hymn that Luke appropriated and placed in this context. There is some cogency to this argument, for the psalm does not focus specifically on Mary's pregnancy and the birth of a child. (3) The text's placement and its content allow the Gospel writer to highlight positions that later play important roles in the gospel—the special significance of women in the Christian movement and salvation as reversal of fate for the poor and lowly in society.

The song has its Old Testament intertextual counterpart in the song of Hannah in 1 Samuel 2:1–10 offered at the time of her delivery of Samuel to the sanctuary at Shiloh in fulfillment of her vow. (The story of Hannah in 1 Samuel 1 should be read as background to the story of Mary in preparing to preach on this text. Some contrasts between Mary and Hannah are obvious: Hannah is old and barren and pleas for a child, whereas Mary is a young virgin chosen to give birth; Hannah's child is an extraordinary son who will serve God in the tabernacle at Shiloh, whereas Mary's child is the Son of God through whom God will tabernacle with the Lord's people.)

Mary's joy is the joy reflective of Advent. This joy is expressed, first, in Mary's recognition of her role in the history of salvation (vv. 47–49). But God's mercy and grace are shown not just in the choice of Mary but in the manifestation of God's mercy from generation to generation (v. 50). Verses 51–53 emphasize the reversal of fortune that comes with divine action: divine opponents, the proud, the powerful, the rich are made the victims, but the lowly and the hungry are rewarded, elevated, and fed. All of this is proclaimed as divine fidelity to promises made long ago (vv. 54–55). The lowly but obedient—like Mary—are assured of divine aid and a share in God's work.

James 5:7–10

In the setting of Advent, today's epistolary text emphasizes the Lord's future coming. By the third week of Advent, we may find that our thoughts have begun to shift toward the Lord's first coming, the Incarnation. Today's other lections lay special stress on the healing miracles that accompany the coming of the Lord. Our text, however, moves in another direction. Its orientation is still eschatological, reminding us that "the coming of the Lord is near" (v. 8). In a similar mood and tone, we are warned that "the Judge is standing at the doors" (v. 9). These are salutary reminders that throughout Advent the eschatological note is present. It may be dominant, it may be recessive, but it is always there.

The fundamental message of our text is a call to patience. Twice we are told, quite straightforwardly, "Be patient" (vv. 7 and 8). Even though patience was especially necessary in view of the return of Christ, it was recommended as a standard feature of Christian exhortation (1 Thess. 5:14; cf. 2 Cor. 6:6; Gal. 5:22; Eph. 4:2; Col. 1:11; 3:12; 2 Tim. 3:10). As a natural outgrowth of love (1 Cor. 3:14), patience was seen to reflect the very nature of God (Rom. 2:4; 9:22; 1 Pet. 3:20; 2 Pet. 3:9, 15) and the work of Christ (1 Tim. 1:16). It was the special capacity by which the patriarchs distinguished themselves. Only after Abraham "patiently endured" did he receive the promise (Heb. 6:15).

Our text recognizes that awaiting the Lord's final Advent requires an extra measure of patience. To be sure, the coming of the Lord was an event expected in the near future (1 Thess. 2:19; 3:13; 4:15; 5:23; 2 Thess. 2:1, 8). Because the interim was seen to be short, some Christians became anxious and apparently stopped working, deciding instead to remain inactive during the remaining time (1 Thess. 5:14; 2 Thess. 3:10). Others became troubled when relatives and friends died during the interim, wondering what was to become of them (1 Thess. 4:13–18).

With so much uncertainty, it is easy to see how grumbling could become the order of the day (v. 9). In similar circumstances, where the future was unknown, the Israelites turned to grumbling (1 Cor. 10:10; cf. Exod. 16:2; 17:3; Num. 14:2; Ps. 106:25). Paul also recognizes that those who are unable to wait patiently tend to become factious (Rom. 2:7–8). The antidote to grumbling is a stern reminder that we stand under God's judgment (cf. 4:12; Heb. 12:12; 2 Tim. 4:8). Indeed, the Judge stands at the door (v. 9; cf. Matt. 24:33; Rev. 3:20).

We are given two examples of those who know how to wait. First is the farmer who plants the seed and waits patiently for the rains, then the harvest (cf. Deut. 11:14; Jer. 5:24; Hos. 6:3). The essence of farming is to "plow in hope . . . thresh in hope" (1 Cor. 9:10). For those who must have immediate results, farming is the wrong profession. Second are "the prophets who spoke in the name of the Lord" (v. 10). Not only did they wait; they suffered while they waited (cf. Matt. 5:12; 23:31; Acts 7:52; Heb. 11:33–38). Yet the essence of their prophetic task was to speak in hope, even if they did not live to see their promises fulfilled.

Being patient means that we must "strengthen our hearts" (v. 8, NRSV), or be "stouthearted" (REB). Ultimately this comes as God's gift to us (1 Thess. 3:13) but expresses itself in our capacity to maintain equanimity in the face of anxiety. We all will be impatient at one time or another, for one reason or another, but if impatience becomes an ingrained pattern of behavior, it is a sure mark of weakheartedness. The true test of strength is to wait before the Lord and let the Lord come when the Lord wills.

Matthew 11:2–11

The Gospel lection for today continues last Sunday's attention on John the Baptist, but now his ministry is over and it is being seen in retrospect. What did that man and his ministry mean for the Advent of Jesus Christ? John deserves a second look, not because he was a fascinating figure, but because he prepared minds and hearts for the One whose coming meant the end of John's era, standing as he did at the doorway of the new. Through the words of Jesus our text offers us the early church's understanding of the one who prepared the way.

Matthew 11:1 concludes a discourse of Jesus with the repeated formula "when Jesus had finished" (7:28; 11:1; 13:53; 19:1; 26:1). Our lection follows immediately that transition and constitutes a portion of Jesus' conversation about John, first with John's disciples (vv. 2–6) and then with the crowd (vv. 7–19). This material is absent from Mark but is shared with only slight alterations with Luke (7:18–28). That John is in prison at the time (v. 2) is information shared with the reader casually and without explanation. Because this is the first mention of it in Matthew (Luke tells his readers as early as 3:19–20; Matthew supplies details later at 14:3–12), we can only assume that Matthew knew that his readers knew enough not to be stalled at this point in the narrative.

Verses 2–6 consist of a question from John to Jesus and the reply to be carried to John by his disciples. The question "Are you the one who is to come, or are we to wait for another?" (v. 3) is not at all clear, either in what is being asked, or why. John does not ask if Jesus is the Messiah. Earlier John had announced that one was to come after him who would be mightier (3:11), but even then he did not identify that one as the Messiah, but only that he would baptize with the Holy Spirit and with fire. Perhaps he had in mind Elijah, who would return in the last days to turn people again to God (Mal. 4:5). Jesus said John himself was the Elijah to come (11:14), but according to the fourth Evangelist, John did not claim that role (John 1:20). But our uncertainty about John's question does not explain John's uncertainty about Jesus. Matthew says that when Jesus came for baptism, John recognized him as greater and without need of baptism (3:13–15), and following the baptism, John (and others?) was told from heaven, "This is my Son, the Beloved" (3:17). How, then, are we to understand the question? That even the revelation at the baptism was not clear to John? That John, for all his courageous preaching, is now pressed by prison, persecution, and the prospect of death into doubt and uncertainty? That the difference between John's image of the One to come and the actual style and nature of Jesus' ministry was so radical as to generate this question to Jesus?

Perhaps in all these answers there is some truth. Certainly this text prompts in an Advent community the reflection: As we await the coming of Christ, what kind of person, what kind of ministry, what kind of relation to us are we anticipating? Christ disappoints the expectations of some.

Jesus' reply to John is a summary of Jesus' ministry, leaving John to arrive at his own conclusion based on what is heard and seen (vv. 4–6). This summary echoes Isaiah 29:18–19 and 35:5–6. Healing lepers and raising the dead are not in Isaiah but are added from the accounts of Jesus' activity. Scholars are divided on the interpretation of the beatitude in verse 6. Does it or does it not imply a criticism of John?

Whatever one's interpretation of verse 6, verses 7–11 leave no doubt about Jesus' estimate of John. He was, said Jesus, no weather vane, turning with the wind, nor was he a fashion setter. John was not just a prophet but more than a prophet. "More than a prophet" apparently refers to John's introduction of the One toward whom the other prophets pointed and to John's unique place at the door of the messianic age. Yet even John's greatness pales before that great life which belongs to even the least among us who are Jesus' disciples.

Through public sermon and private doubt, John has introduced us to the One who is to come. And like John, we will have to respond on the basis of what we hear and see.

Fourth Sunday of Advent

Isaiah 7:10–16;
Psalm 80:1–7, 17–19;
Romans 1:1–7;
Matthew 1:18–25

As Christmas approaches, the Gospel accounts of the birth of Jesus command our attention more and more. Today's reading from Matthew, with its report of Joseph's marriage to Mary, who is "with child of the Holy Spirit," is the most obvious selection for the last Sunday of Advent. The Old Testament lesson contains the lines quoted by Matthew, Isaiah 7:14. The verses from Psalm 80, a petition of the people for help from their enemies, anticipate the Gospel's reference to Joseph and present the situation of need to which the coming of Jesus responds. The key lines of the epistolary lection for this day are those of the christological confession in Romans 1:2–6 that set the coming of Jesus in the context of God's activity in history.

Isaiah 7:10–16

Texts such as this one, when read in the context of Christian worship, sharpen the tension between the historical meaning and the homiletical or theological interpretation of the Bible, and of the Old Testament in particular. What Isaiah 7:10–16 meant in its original context and what it means in the shadow of Matthew 1:18–25 may be quite different. Matthew quotes Isaiah 7:14 as a prophecy of the conception and birth of Jesus, whereas Isaiah himself almost certainly had in view a particular woman and child in his own time. Because the church's commitment to the Bible includes the Old Testament, we should seek to allow the words from Isaiah to be heard in their own terms first, and to consider not only how the New Testament interprets the Old, but also how the Old Testament enriches the New.

Some of the literary and historical questions concerning our passage can be answered with relative certainty. It is one of a number of reports of encounters in Jerusalem between Isaiah and King Ahaz at a particularly critical moment in the history of Judah. The historical situation is summarized in Isaiah 7:1–2 and spelled out further in 2 Kings 16:1–20. When the Assyrian king, Tiglath-pileser III, began to move against the small states of Syria and Palestine, the leaders of those states responded by forming a coalition to oppose him. Apparently because Ahaz of Judah refused to join them, the kings in Damascus and Samaria moved against Jerusalem (about 734 BC) to topple Ahaz and replace him with someone more favorable to their policies. In the passage that immediately precedes our reading (7:1–9), Isaiah counseled nonresistance based on faith in the ancient promise to David that one of his sons would always occupy the throne in Jerusalem.

Seen in that historical situation, Isaiah 7:10ff. is an announcement of salvation to the king and the people of Judah concerning the immediate future. Within a short time ("before the child knows how to refuse the evil and choose the good," v. 16), the threat from "the two kings"—that is, Rezin of Damascus and "the son of Remaliah" of Israel—will be ended. The passage is one of a number of sign acts or symbolic action reports in the context, and it is not even the only one to see the birth of a baby as a symbol of hope (see Isa. 9:1–7). When Ahaz refuses Isaiah's invitation to ask for a sign, the prophet gives one. The birth of a child is a sign of salvation, of deliverance from a specific political and military threat. The good news is carried by the child's name, "Immanuel," (v. 14), that is, "God is with us." Deliverance will come, not through alliances or military might, but through divine intervention, by a God who keeps promises.

Also clear are the reading and translation of the Hebrew text of verse 14. The Hebrew word is 'almah, correctly rendered by the NRSV and almost all other modern translations "young woman." The term is neutral with regard to her marital status. It was the Greek translation of the Book of Isaiah, the Septuagint, that read "virgin" (Greek parthenos), thus setting the stage for the particular messianic interpretation expressed in the New Testament. The bridge between the eighth century and the early church is thus yet another historical and theological context, the translation of the Hebrew scriptures for Jews in a Hellenistic, pre-Christian culture.

Other aspects of the unit are less clear, including the point where it ends. Is verse 17 a part of the original sign act or a later addition, and what does it mean? It is not even clear whether that verse expresses good news or bad. Highly disputed is the identity of the child and his mother. In view of a context that stresses the significance of the Davidic dynasty, many commentators have taken the child to be the crown prince, and the woman as the wife of Ahaz. Others, seeing the passage in some ways parallel to Isaiah 8:1–4, have argued that the woman was the wife of the prophet, and the child his son. It is quite likely, however, that the "young woman" was simply an unnamed pregnant woman whom Isaiah saw as he was addressing the king.

Regardless of the extent and limits of our understanding of the passage in its own literary and historical context, it is hardly possible for a Christian congregation to hear the Immanuel prophecy without thinking of the birth of Jesus. What, then, are we to do with the tension between the ancient and the Christian meanings? It is difficult, but essential, to sustain the tension, to refuse to resolve it quickly by choosing the one while rejecting the other. Even a typological interpretation that sees the woman and her son as a model of Mary and Jesus should be attentive to what it is that has been reinterpreted.

Living with Isaiah 7:10–16 itself keeps our feet on the ground of history and human experience. The particular kind of good news proclaimed here by the ancient prophet should not be forgotten. It is a message that sees pregnancy and birth—even when not understood as miraculous—as signs of God's concern for God's people. That good news comes into a world with such concrete problems as international politics and threats of war. The fact that the prophet and his message are so directly involved in political events may move us to ask if such expectations as his—along with the message of the coming of

Jesus—are legitimate hopes for the people of God. Is the coming of Jesus related to international politics or not?

Psalm 80:1–7, 17–19

This is a communal lament. Such prayers were offered by the community in the context of a national fast after some calamity had threatened its existence or dissipated its life. On such occasions, the people broke with the normal routine of life, assembled at sanctuaries, offered sacrifice, lamented their distress, and entreated the Deity to intervene in their behalf.

The first seven verses of this psalm have been selected for Advent reading because of the material's description of distress and the plea for restoration. These verses ought to be studied and understood in light of the entire psalm, or else they will appear as only a truncated part of the whole. The integral relationship of the entire psalm, which is addressed to the Deity, is substantiated by the threefold repetition of the refrain in verses 3, 7, 19, which is almost identical in all three. Perhaps in the service of communal lamentation, these refrains represent the part of the liturgy spoken by the entire congregation while the rest of the psalm was voiced by the priest or person in charge.

An outline of the entire psalm makes for a better understanding of the opening verses. The following are the component parts: (a) address to the Deity with an initial plea (vv. 1–2), (b) the initial refrain (v. 3), (c) a description of the distress (vv. 4–6), (d) the second refrain (v. 7), (e) a second description of the distress (vv. 8–13), (f) a plea for God's help (vv. 14–17), (g) a vow or promise of loyalty to the Deity if salvation is forthcoming (v. 18), and (h) the concluding refrain (v. 19).

Two primary images of the Deity appear in the psalm. At the beginning, God is addressed as the Shepherd of Israel (v. 1), a very common way of speaking of the Deity in the ancient Near East, where sheep raising and the importance of shepherds were widely understood. In verses 8–13, God is portrayed as the viticulturist, or vineyard keeper. Both images imply a God who must oversee the items under divine supervision—the sheep and the vineyard—with great care, concern, and tenderness.

Now let us focus more closely on the verses of today's lection. The opening address to the Deity would suggest that the psalm originated in the Northern Kingdom of Israel. The use of the name Joseph for the people as well as the reference to the northern tribes of Benjamin, Ephraim, and Manasseh (the last two were names of the sons of Joseph; see Gen. 48:1) point in this direction. Also the reference to God as "thou who art enthroned upon the cherubim" was a divine epithet used of God's sitting enthroned upon the ark, which contained cherub decorations. (Cherubs were considered semidivine figures probably depicted with an animal body, human head, and bird wings; in the ancient world, they were not depicted as in medieval times as fat little winged angels!) This epithet was used at the old ark shrine in Shiloh (see 1 Sam. 4:4). All of this implies that the distressful situation requiring a lament had to do with a calamity involving the northern state of Israel. What the calamity was is unknown, perhaps defeat in some military campaign.

In the description of the distress, the people complain that God is angry with their prayers, that is, unresponsive to their pleas for help (v. 4). Unlike a good shepherd, who provides the flock with sustaining food and good water, God is depicted as feeding them with bread of tears and giving them tears to drink in full measure. That is, God is accused of bringing misery and suffering on them and failing to function as a good shepherd (v. 5). Instead of protecting them from their enemies, God becomes their enemy. Their plight is so bad that their neighbors make fun of them and their adversaries hold them up to ridicule (v. 6). It is, indeed, the dark side of the Divine that the people have experienced. Just as they see that their hope is in God, so they attribute their misery to the same source.

The refrain in verse 7 is an appeal for God to help. If only God's face would shine forth, that is, if the divine disposition would change, then the people would be saved.

Verse 18a petitions God to remember and support the "one at your right hand," that is, Israel the elect, which occupies the place of honor at the right hand of the Divine. God is reminded in verse 17b that Israel is, after all, Yahweh's creation and thus a responsibility of the Divine. On its behalf, the community vows to offer fidelity and worship as thankful response (v. 18).

Just as Israel gave thought and expression in this psalm to its need for God's help and saw its situation as desperate without divine aid, so we in the Advent Season think of the misery of human existence and look forward to the shining of God's face in the coming of the Redeemer. Advent, like Israel's lamentation services, should be a time to ponder the conditions of life under the wrath of the Divine and life's futility without the presence of God's shining face.

Romans 1:1–7

With the Fourth Sunday of Advent, we edge closer to the celebration of Christ's coming in the Incarnation. This is seen especially clearly in the Old Testament and Gospel readings, both well-known incarnational texts. In the epistolary lection, it is verse 3 that figures most prominently in this regard. With our ears attuned to Advent themes, we are especially eager to hear "the gospel concerning his Son."

As the Gospel reading calls attention to the Davidic lineage of Christ (Matt. 1:20; also 1:1), so our text stresses that Christ was "descended from David" (v. 3). Deeply embedded in the Old Testament was the expectation that a descendant of David would establish another kingdom (2 Sam. 7:12; Ps. 89:3–4; Jer. 23:5). Early Christian faith saw Jesus Christ as the descendant of David who fulfilled these expectations (Matt. 22:42; John 7:42; Acts 13:23; 2 Tim. 2:8; Rev. 22:16).

Our text also echoes incarnational themes with its insistence that Christ was descended "according to the flesh" (v. 3). Like the Gospel text, this places Christ squarely within human history and guards against all forms of Gnosticism that deny or de-emphasize the humanity of Christ (cf. 1 John 4:2–3). It also conforms to the recurrent New Testament emphasis on Christ's full participation in humanity (Rom. 8:3; 9:5; Eph. 2:14–15; Col. 1:22).

Even though these incarnational themes are especially prominent in this Fourth Sunday of Advent, they by no means exhaust the text. We should note first the unusual form of the text. It is an epistolary greeting; but unlike most opening greetings in the Pauline Letters, it is lengthy and does far more than identify the author and addressees (cf. 1 Cor. 1:1–3; 2 Cor. 1:1–2). At the center of the passage is a summary of the early Christian faith in which Paul traces God's activity from the time of the prophets down to his own apostolic ministry. The language is clearly confessional, with each phrase virtually echoing early Christian worship. It is generally agreed that the language is pre-Pauline, which suggests that Paul is citing earlier Christian tradition that he had received. This was an especially appropriate move, because Paul had not visited the Roman church. By aligning himself with a widely accepted Christian creed, he commended himself and his gospel to those who knew him only by reputation.

Several features of the confessional summary are worth noting. First is the emphasis on the gospel as expressing the age-old purpose of God (Rom. 16:25–26; Titus 1:2). The promise was expressed through the prophets whose message became embodied in the Scriptures (cf. Luke 1:70). Second is the resurrection as the point when Jesus is certified as Son of God (v. 4; cf. Acts 13:33; 1 Tim. 3:16). A Pauline note is sounded in the emphasis on the Holy Spirit as that which mediates the power of the resurrection (Rom. 8:11).

Apart from these more formal features, the text is also revealing for what it tells us about Paul. He identifies himself as a servant of Christ (cf. Phil. 1:1; Gal. 1:10; also James 1:1; 2 Pet. 1:1; Jude 1) who was called to be God's apostle. The language Paul uses to describe his "setting apart" by God is reminiscent of Old Testament prophetic calls, suggesting that he understood his apostleship in terms of prophetic vocation (cf. Isa. 49:1; Jer. 1:4–5; also Gal. 1:15; 1 Cor. 15:10). The object of his commission was "the gospel of God" (cf. Rom. 15:16; 2 Cor. 11:7; 1 Thess. 2:2, 8; cf. Mark 1:14; 1 Pet. 4:17). His specific mission, of course, was to extend the gospel to the Gentiles (v. 5; cf. Rom. 15:18; 16:26; Gal. 2:7–8). Those who respond obediently are called by God to affiliate with Christ (v. 6; cf. Rom. 8:28; 9:24; 1 Cor. 1:9).

The final verse of our text is the greeting addressed to the saints in Rome (v. 7). Unlike the first part, it conforms to the standard Pauline form of greeting (cf. 1 Cor. 1:2; 2 Cor. 1:2; Gal. 1:3; Eph. 1:2; Phil. 1:2; Col. 1:2; 1 Thess. 1:1; 2 Thess. 1:2; Philem. 3).

Homiletically, the most natural point of entry to today's text will be verse 3, with its emphasis on the Davidic descent of Christ and his coming in the flesh. But because the overall framework of the epistolary text is much broader than this, extending from prophetic times to the time of Paul, it may serve to balance the more narrow focus of the other readings. In this sense, the epistolary text is helpful in sketching the larger story within which the single event of Christ's incarnation is set.

Matthew 1:18–25

For two Sundays, the question of who Jesus is has been answered by John the Baptist: "the one to come" and "he who is more powerful than I" (3:11). Now Matthew in four stories expands on that answer: Jesus is descended from Abraham and David (1:1–17); Jesus is the child of the virgin Mary, wife of Joseph (1:18–25); Jesus is king of the Jews and hope of the nations (2:1–12); Jesus is God's Son called out of Egypt (2:13–23). The reader who is left with many questions of historical details unanswered needs to remember that the Evangelist is concerned only to give the Christian community's response to the question, Who is Jesus, founder and Lord of the church? Today's lection is the second of these four stories.

Notice how much Matthew assumes is already known by the community. The conception and birth are very briefly and only indirectly told. That Jesus was born in Bethlehem of Judea is not mentioned until later (2:1) in connection with the cycle of Herod stories (2: 1–23) and the circumstances under which Jesus of Bethlehem came to be Jesus of Nazareth. (Notice this is the reverse of Luke's concern to show how Jesus of Nazareth was actually from David's town of Bethlehem, 2:1–7.) From what Matthew records in this brief account, it seems that he wanted to respond to three questions that were prompted by the church's claims about Jesus: How can Jesus be the son of David when his genealogy is traced through Joseph (1:16), who was not his father? In what way can it be claimed that this unusual birth was of God's doing? And where does this child fit into the divine scheme of promise and fulfillment? Our discussion will pursue these three questions.

The Evangelist places upon himself the burden of explanation when he states, "and Jacob the father of Joseph the husband of Mary, of whom Jesus was born, who is called the Messiah" (1:16). That is, Joseph is the son of David (1:20), but how can Jesus be? The answer is twofold. First, at the time of Jesus' conception, Joseph is betrothed to Mary (v. 18) and, therefore, is her husband (v. 19). Betrothal was not an engagement to be married in the modern sense. Betrothal was a legal bond that could be broken only by divorce (v. 19). A woman betrothed, if bereaved of her "husband," was considered a widow, and if she, during her betrothal, had an affair with another man, it was regarded not as fornication but as adultery. Second, Jesus is the son of David because at the time of his birth Joseph is Mary's husband (v. 24) and, therefore, the legal father of Jesus.

The second question is, How can the Christian community claim that this unusual birth was God's doing? The response of the Evangelist is fourfold. First, he simply asserts that the conception was "from the Holy Spirit" (1:18). That expression is rather restrained and does not provide historical detail. However, Mary is a virgin (vv. 23, 25), and God is the giver of children (Gen. 18:10–12; 25:21; 29:31; 30:2, 22–23). Second, Matthew uses the passive voice to speak of the conception (vv. 18, 20), the traditional way of referring to divine activity. Third, Matthew appeals to Joseph's character, "a righteous man and unwilling to expose her to public disgrace" (v. 19). "A righteous man" in that tradition should not be translated "a nice guy" in ours. And finally, God is related to these events by means of revelation. An angel of God, coming to Joseph through a dream (vv. 20, 25), explains Mary's condition, calms Joseph's fear, directs him to marry her, and gives the name for the child (Jesus-Joshua-salvation from the Lord).

And the final question, Where does this child fit into God's divine plan? is answered by the use of Isaiah 7:14. The quotation formula concerning "what had been spoken by the Lord through the prophet" (1:22) is found about twelve times in Matthew (among them 2:6, 15, 17, 23) and is important for the Evangelist not simply as a proof pattern but as a declaration of God's faithfulness. Isaiah 7:14 was in its original context a promise and a fulfillment, and so is it here in a new setting. Here, however, the fulfillment is more broadly understood than in its context in Isaiah, for here the word "Emmanuel" capsules the central meaning of Jesus as son of David and Son of God: "God with us." That is the promise containing all promises, the fulfillment containing all fulfillments.

Christmas, First Proper
(Christmas Eve/Day)

Isaiah 9:2–7;
Psalm 96;
Titus 2:11–14;
Luke 2:1–14 (15–20)

The texts for all the Christmas services are the same every year, but the story never grows old. The Lucan account of the birth of Jesus, the shepherds, and the angels concludes with Mary pondering all these things in her heart and the shepherds glorifying and praising God for what they had heard and seen. Isaiah 9:2–7 sings of good news that accompanies the birth of one to sit on the throne in Jerusalem, and the responsorial psalm is an exuberant song of praise for God's reign. The epistolary text speaks of living between the times, between the appearance of the glory of God in the Incarnation and the return of the Lord.

Isaiah 9:2–7

This poem, so distinctive in many ways, closely resembles the thanksgiving songs in the Book of Psalms (e.g., Pss. 18:5–20; 32:3–5). There is an account of trouble and the deliverance from it, and a thanksgiving service in celebration of that deliverance. But the song also is similar in important respects to prophetic announcements of the future. Although it concerns events that have happened and are happening, at the end it announces the implications of those events "from this time onward and forevermore." In effect, the deliverance from trouble is a sign of what God intends for the future.

Although many commentators in the late nineteenth and early twentieth centuries took the present passage to be a postexilic addition to the Book of Isaiah, it is now widely accepted that it comes from Isaiah in the eighth century BC. The precise date is difficult to establish. There doubtless are historical allusions within the poem itself, but they are obscure. Isaiah 9:1 refers to the territories taken by Tiglath-pileser in 733–732; but this verse probably was added when the book was compiled, and in any case the poem speaks of events after the Assyrian invasion. Some scholars have seen the poem as part of the coronation ritual for a particular Judean king, most commonly identified as Hezekiah in 725 BC. However, it is more likely that the prophetic hymn was composed to celebrate the birth of a new crown prince some time after 732. The sign of God's deliverance is the birth of a new descendant of David.

In terms of literary and grammatical structure, the poem has two major parts. Verses 2–3 present an account of release from trouble and the accompanying celebration. Verses 4–7 give three reasons for that celebration, each introduced by "for." Those reasons are the deliverance from an oppressor (v. 4), the destruction of the gear of battle (v. 5), and the birth of the special child (vv. 6–7). Most of the verbs are properly translated as present or past tenses, but the final lines are future.

One may also analyze and interpret this passage as a series of graphic images, each with its accompanying moods and tones. First there are the contrasting images of darkness and light (v. 2). Darkness is a metaphor for depression and death. The NEB makes that explicit in the final line: "dwellers in a land as dark as death" (compare Ps. 23:4). Light symbolizes life and joy.

Second, in the language of prayer the prophet sketches a scene of celebration. One can almost see and hear the festivities. People shout and sing to their God as if it were the thanksgiving festival at the end of a good harvest or the spontaneous expression of joy when a war has ended and a time of peace begun.

Third, contrasting images again come to the fore—the harsh pictures of the instruments of war and oppression and a gathering lighted by a fire in which those instruments are burned. The mood of joy and celebration from the previous images continues. What begins as the immediate deliverance from a particular oppressor—doubtless the heel of Assyria—becomes a vision of perpetual peace: war boots and bloody uniforms are burned.

Fourth, there is the image of a messenger emerging from the royal palace with the good news that a son—a crown prince—has been born. This birth announcement image is the central scene of the poem. Like the symbolic action reports in the immediate context in the Book of Isaiah (7:10–16; 8:1–4), the birth of a baby is a sign of God's saving activity in behalf of the people of God.

Finally, and with no dramatic transition, the scene moves to the throne room of the king and even beyond. The newborn baby is now seen as the righteous and just king, sitting on the throne of David. This son of David will administer justice, establish righteousness, and inaugurate a reign of peace, all of which corresponds to the will of God and thus will extend forever.

One way for the preacher to proclaim the good news of this passage is simply to present these graphic images to the congregation. Good news is preached not only by what is said but also by establishing a mood of celebration, and these scenes do just that. Or one could explore the specific contents of the passage. Those would be God's deliverance from oppression, the establishment of peace, and the reign of justice and righteousness. Any or all of these would carry forward the message of Christmas.

Psalm 96

The psalms for the three propers of Christmas are the same throughout the three years of the lectionary, namely Psalms 96, 97, and 98. All of these psalms belong to the same genre or type. They are hymns proclaiming and celebrating the kingship of Yahweh, the Hebrew Deity. To be more specific, they celebrate the enthronement of God. As such they may be seen as proper responsorial psalms to the arrival of Jesus, the Messianic-Davidic king. Christmas is a time when "heaven and nature sing," and these psalms call upon the whole of nature to join in the celebrative chorus.

Psalm 96 actually contains two extended calls to praise and proclamation (vv. 1–3 and 7–9), and two series of imperatives characterize each of the calls: sing, sing, sing, tell, declare (vv. 1–3), and ascribe, ascribe, bring an offering and come, worship, tremble (v. 7–9).

One of the early rabbis said the following about the first three of these imperative verbs: "The three times that the word *sing* is used in this psalm correspond to the three prayers during which the children of Israel sing praises every day to the Holy One, blessed be He. Thus *sing* in O *sing to the Lord a new song* corresponds to the morning prayer during which the children of Israel sing praises to the Holy One . . . because He renews daily the work of creation; *sing* in *Sing to the Lord, all the earth* corresponds to the afternoon prayer, because during the day all the inhabitants of the earth enjoy the sun and its beams; and *sing* in *Sing to the Lord, bless his name* corresponds to the evening prayer when the Holy One . . . is praised because He brings in the evening twilight" (*Midrash Tehillim* on Ps. 96).

The center of this psalm is verse 10*a*: "Say among the nations, 'The Lord is king!'" Here we have the shout or acclamation (perhaps better translated, "Yahweh has become king") that proclaimed the enthronement of God probably celebrated in an annual enthronement ritual.

Preceding verses 4–6 declare the impotency of other gods and extol the greatness of Yahweh. Other deities are merely idols (the products of human handiwork and thus of no ultimate value to humans), whereas Yahweh is the creator of the heavens (hardly the consequence of someone else's creation). Yahweh is the one "to be feared above all gods." (The NJPSV here translates: "He is held in awe by all divine beings.")

The proclamation of praise and ascription of the honor due Yahweh terminate in submission. Recognition of Yahweh's status as reigning king should, according to the psalm, eventuate in submission to God. This is the emphasis of verses 8*b*–9, which the NJPSV translates: "bring tribute and enter His courts. / Bow down to the Lord majestic in holiness; / tremble in His presence, all the earth!"

The verses following 10*b* speak of the conditions and consequences of Yahweh's reign as king. Verses 10*b* and *c* may be seen to embody both present and eschatological affirmations. The present is described as secure, for Yahweh has established (or reestablished) the earth (10*b*). Again the NJPSV provides a translation that brings out the emphases of the text: "The world stands firm; it cannot be shaken." Human lives are thus not at the whim of irrational forces, not at the mercy of senseless powers, not the pawn of some cosmic game between divine beings, not the object of some supercilious deity. The belief that Yahweh was in control meant for the ancient Hebrew that life could make sense, that life could be lived in some consistency and hope, and that even consolation could be found in calamity. The eschatological or future dimension can be seen in 10*c*: "He will judge the peoples with equity."

The consequences of these conditions are that heaven and nature should sing and rejoice: the heavens, the earth, the sea, sea creatures, the field, wild animals, and the trees of the forest.

Titus 2:11–14

This passage is an appropriate Christmas text because of the prominence of the "appearing" motif. In fact, two "appearings" are mentioned. The first "appearing" occurred when God's grace was manifested to everyone in the sending of Christ (v. 11). The second "appearing" lies in the future when Christ will come again as the God and Savior of the redeemed people of God (v. 13). Here we see the dual themes of Advent interlocked—the Incarnation as the First Coming and the Parousia as the Second Coming. This serves as a reminder that even when our attention is centered on the birth of Christ as the moment of incarnation, we are never far removed from that future moment of God's revelation.

This epistolary reading is not a Christmas text in the same sense as the Gospel reading, which makes explicit reference to the birth of Christ. Rather than seeing God's coming into the world as a single event in the life of Jesus, it views the entire life and work of Christ as a time of divine visitation. Taken as a whole, it was nothing less than a demonstration of divine grace (v. 11). Nor was it merely for the sake of God's making an appearance in the world. The purpose was salvific—"to save the whole human race" (v. 11, NJB).

We should note the force of this claim. This divine epiphany, or appearance of God, was not a moment of private revelation. Such was the case when God was revealed to Jacob, an epiphany memorialized in the name El-bethel (Gen. 35:7). Similar appearances occurred with other Old Testament figures, including Abraham, Moses, and others. We also know of other instances where a dramatic appearance of God occurred, localized in a particular place (cf. 2 Macc. 3:30). But today's text places the appearance of the grace of God through the coming of Christ in a different category. It was not merely a moment of private revelation, limited to one person at one place and time. It was universal in scope. It is for everyone (1 Tim. 2:4; 4:10).

The redemptive work of Christ receives special emphasis in today's text: he "gave himself for us that he might redeem us from all iniquity" (v. 14). This, of course, is a reference to the sacrificial work of Christ (Gal. 1:4; 2:20; Eph. 5:2, 25; 1 Tim. 2:6; 1 Pet. 1:18). It recalls last week's Gospel reading and its reference to Jesus, who would "save his people from their sins" (Matt. 1:21). In this respect, Christ the Savior now fills the role of Yahweh as the one who redeems us from all our iniquities (cf. Ps. 130:8). His sacrifice also has a purifying effect. The promise that God's people would be cleansed and purified is now fulfilled in Christ (Ezek. 37:23).

The final effect of the redemptive work of Christ is to create a people for himself. A people for God's own possession is a frequent Old Testament hope (Exod. 19:5; Deut. 7:6; 14:2). It is now realized in the people of God redeemed by Christ. The moral effect of Christ's redemptive work is to create a people "zealous for good deeds" (v. 14; 3:8, 14; 1 Pet. 3:13; Heb. 10:24).

In a sense, the real test of how we appropriate God's grace is the life we lead. As our text suggests, God's grace has an educative function. It actually trains us in a form of life that renounces "impiety and worldly passions" and instead enables us to be "self-controlled, upright, and godly" (v. 12). Standing, as we do, between the two moments of God's "appearing"—the First Coming in the Incarnation and the Second Coming in the Parousia—we are urged to adopt a form of life that befits divine grace. If Christ sacrificed himself to redeem and purify us, we are expected to extend his salvific work into our own being. It is in this posture that we face the future and await "the blessed hope" (v. 13).

Even though today's epistolary text is not a Christmas text in the narrow sense, it is in the truest sense. Seen through Christian eyes, the birth of Christ is nothing if not a manifestation of divine grace.

Luke 2:1–14 (15–20)

The Gospel lesson for Christmas each year is the ever-familiar, ever-new story in Luke 2:1–20. Notice that the preacher is given the option of concluding at verse 14. This option does not follow the natural division of the text, but neither does it violate Luke's message. The advantages of attending only to verses 1–14 are two. First, concluding at verse 14 highlights the twofold significance of the birth of Jesus, glory to God and peace to the earth. Second, if an additional Christmas service is planned, attention can there be given to verses 15–20 with minimal repetition of content. For our purposes, however, the natural folds of the entire story will be observed.

The account consists of two parts, verses 1–7 and verses 8–20, the former stating quite simply the event, the latter announcing its significance. The two units together reveal a common trait of Lukan writing: a straightforward narration that could have been written by a disinterested historian joined to material highly confessional that hides nothing of the writer's worldview and faith. (As other examples, see 3:1–9 and Acts 23:1–11.)

To say that verses 1–7 read as lines composed by a disinterested historian is not to say that this brief record is free of historical problems. Every serious commentary on Luke struggles with the chronological difficulties spawned by the reference to a census under Quirinius, governor of Syria. Luke sets his nativity story in the days of Herod, king of Judea (1:5), and yet it was not until after the reign of Herod's son Archelaus (AD 6) that Judea was placed under the governor of Syria. Added to that is the whole question of whether a Roman tax decree required subjects to return to ancestral homes. Those two questions hang over the text. But Luke, having done his research (1:1–4), writes as a historian, providing an event with time, place, principal characters, and circumstance. No angels, no wise men, no stars invade the story, alerting the reader to its peculiarly Christian promptings. Not even the manger scene is given any special halo. The census enrollment had crowded the city, the inn was full, a manger had to suffice; it was as simple as that.

However, to say that verses 1–7 have the style of a disinterested historian is not to say that the writer has pulled from the account the interests of faith. On the contrary, within the historian's style are to be found many Christian affirmations. In addition to answering the question, How could Jesus of Nazareth qualify as the prince to be born in David's city? (Mic. 5:2), the passage is full of allusions to the Old Testament (Mic. 5:2; Isa. 1:3; Jer. 14:8). Likewise, the reference to Caesar Augustus and Quirinius is more than a method of dating; it is also a way of affirming that God uses emperors, governors, and kings to carry out the divine will even though those authorities are unaware of their roles in God's purposes. (Acts 23–28 dramatically illustrates this perspective in Paul's arrest, official protection, and voyage to Rome.) And finally, the description of the baby in the manger is Luke's way of affirming what Matthew says with "Emmanuel" (1:23), what John says with "the Word became flesh" (1:14), what Paul says with "born of a woman, born under the law" (Gal. 4:4), and what the writer of Hebrews says with, "In the days of his flesh . . . he learned obedience through what he suffered" (5:7–8).

Less subdued and more openly confessional are verses 8–20, which announce the significance of the event in verses 1–7. But even here amid angelic choirs and excited shepherds there is a sad silence. At the annunciation that she would bear the Christ Child, Mary had an angel visitor (1:26–38), and in the home of Elizabeth, Mary had her place in God's purpose confirmed (1:39–56). But now, away from home, in a stable, in the pain of labor and birth, there is no angel, there is no heavenly confirmation. She hears of heaven's shout from the shepherds (vv. 15–20), to be sure, but one still would have wished for her that night one angel of her own, just for reassurance. But faith is usually one angel short, left to ponder these things in the heart (v. 19).

The messages of verses 8–20 are both stated and implied. The messages stated are many: Jesus is Lord, son of David, Christ, and Savior; his birth ushers in a time of joy in the good news of God's favor and a time of peace among those who please God; the good news of Jesus Christ is for "all the people" (v. 10); the sign of God's favor is not in heavenly voices or in visions of angels but in the "child wrapped in bands of cloth and lying in a manger" (v. 12); and appropriate responses to the child's birth are wondering, praising God, glorifying God, rejoicing, and pondering these things in the heart. Implied but no less important are other messages: God has been faithful to a promise (Mic. 5:2); as with David the shepherd (2 Sam. 7:8), God visits with favor the least likely and lifts up those of low degree (1:52); the story previews the first sermon of Jesus in his home synagogue: "He has anointed me to bring good news to the poor" (4:18; Isa. 61:1–2). Both the angels of heaven and the poor of the earth will reappear often throughout this Gospel and Acts.

Christmas, Second Proper
(Additional Lessons for Christmas Day)

Isaiah 62:6–12;
Psalm 97;
Titus 3:4–7;
Luke 2:(1–7) 8–20

A note reverberating through the lessons for today is that of proclamation, the making known of the good news embodied in the birth of the Christ Child. The reading from Isaiah recalls weary but alert sentries who herald the coming news of salvation. The psalm affirms that God has become king, a kingship proclaimed by heaven and earth. The reading from Titus testifies to the experience of responding to the good news. The Gospel reading—Luke's birth story—focuses on the proclamation of good news first heard by the shepherds at Bethlehem—good news that leads the shepherds to praise, people to wonder, and Mary to ponder.

Isaiah 62:6–12

Many of the Old Testament readings for the season concern the dramatic transformation of Jerusalem, the Holy City, into the center for the people of God in a new era of salvation. The motif is taken up in various ways, but usually as part of a prophetic announcement of salvation that ultimately affects not only all peoples but even nature itself (Isa. 2:1–5 on the First Sunday of Advent; Isa. 11:1–10 on the Second Sunday of Advent). Even the other texts that are more explicitly messianic have Jerusalem and Zion in the background, as the center from which God will reign through the descendant of David.

The Old Testament text for this occasion likewise looks to the restoration and elevation of Jerusalem, but the angle of vision is somewhat different, and the range a bit more limited. Instead of announcement of salvation, the reading begins with prayers for restoration. Only in the final verses does it turn confidently to the future, but even those lines serve to remind Yahweh of the promises he has made. The perspective from which these words emerge, therefore, is quite sober. The prophetic poet knows that the present reality of Jerusalem is far from that anticipated in the ancient promises concerning the city. The city and its people are in trouble, and it is time to pray for deliverance.

Isaiah 62, as part of the collection of material identified as Third Isaiah (Isa. 56–66), does indeed come from a troubled time, especially for the city of Jerusalem. Precise dates for the units in these chapters are difficult to establish, mainly because they do not come from a single prophet. Rather, Isaiah 56–66 is a collection of prophetic and liturgical materials from the postexilic era, many of them depending upon and extending the message of Second Isaiah (chaps. 40–55). Many of the sections, including the one before us now, appear to assume the situation in the first decades after the exiles began to return from Babylon to Judah, that is, 538–516 BC.

Most of our evidence for the circumstances of Judah and Jerusalem in those years comes from Ezra 1–6, Haggai, and Zechariah 1–8. Haggai and Zechariah, like Isaiah 62, are concerned with the restoration of Jerusalem, and the rebuilding of the temple in particular. Serious construction work on the new building began in 520 BC, and it was completed in 516 BC. During this period—in fact, for the two centuries from 538 to 333 BC—Judah was a province of the Persian Empire. In the first years after the return, the former exiles found the city and the temple in ruins, experienced conflicts among themselves and with those who had remained in the land, and faced threats from the outside, including from former enemies such as the Edomites. They also faced more than one crisis of faith when the new life in the Holy City fell far short of what the prophets had given them to expect.

Although a central motif in Isaiah 62 is prayer to God for the salvation of the city, it is not easy to identify the various speakers and addressees in the passage. Is the "I" of verse 1 a prophetic voice that will not be silenced, or Yahweh himself who affirms that he will now speak up? The initial speaker probably is a prophetic one, for in verse 6 that same voice speaks first to Jerusalem, appointing sentries for her walls, and then commissions them to remind Yahweh of his promises concerning the city, giving him no rest until he fulfills them. The image of "sentinels" is indebted to a tradition such as the one found in Ezekiel 33; but in that case the prophet was to warn the people, and here the prophetic sentries are to be in continuous prayer to Yahweh.

In the concluding section (vv. 10–12), the prophetic figure now addresses the people of Jerusalem, exhorting them to prepare "the way for the people," that is, for all who will come to the Holy City. The image of a highway is familiar from Second Isaiah, but there it involved God's transformation of the dry wilderness trails into a level road with water along the way. Here those who stayed in Jerusalem and those who have already returned are urged to go out and "build" the road and "clear it of stones" (v. 10). They are to work hard in behalf of other returnees.

The good news is that the Lord himself is coming to Zion, bringing "salvation," "reward," and "recompense" (v. 11). Throughout the entire chapter it is clear that God is asked for—and will grant—a renewal of the covenant with Jerusalem and its inhabitants. In that covenant the people themselves will be renewed. The new relationship is like a marriage (vv. 4–5). Moreover, the transformation will be effected by giving the city, the land (v. 6), and the people themselves new names that embody the new reality: "Holy People," "The Redeemed of the Lord," "Sought Out," and "A City Not Forsaken" (v. 12).

Psalm 97

Like Psalm 96, this text focuses on the kingship and reign of God and on the consequences of God's coming in judgment.

The psalm opens with a statement that "Yahweh reigns," "is king," or "has become king," and that the whole earth and the coastlands (the islands to the west) should rejoice and be glad. Such an announcement assumes the existence of a new state of being, a new reality that can only be greeted or announced but not humanly brought into being or created.

The qualities or effects of God's reign are described, in verses 2–5, using the metaphorical language of a thunderstorm (see Ps. 29). With some simplification, the reign and presence of God as king may be said to reflect the following conditions (using the NJPSV): *mystification* ("Dense clouds are around Him, / righteousness and justice are the base of His throne"), *purgation* ("Fire is his vanguard, / burning His foes on every side"), *illumination* ("His lightnings light up the world; / the earth is convulsed at the sight"), *transformation* ("Mountains melt like wax at the Lord's presence, / at the presence of the Lord of all the earth"), and *proclamation* ("The heavens proclaim His righteousness / and all the peoples see His glory").

Two human responses are noted (in verses 7–8). Shame and dismay overtake the idol-worshipers, who are exposed as practicing futility in their worship (because even the other gods must bow to Yahweh; verse 7c). Shame is the consequence of being discovered as something other than what we have claimed to be. On the other hand, Zion and the daughters (=towns) of Judah can rejoice in God's judgments (v. 8). Here the idea of rejoicing in judgment is based on the fact that judgment, which vindicates by revealing the truth, is salvation. The people proclaim their readiness to be judged with confidence in the outcome.

The final section of the psalm (vv. 10–12) concentrates on God's preservation of those who belong to the people of God. They have nothing to fear. Note the three actions of God emphasized: the Lord loves, preserves, and delivers. The opening line of verse 10 has no hesitancy in declaring that God loves those who hate evil. Ancient Israel had no qualms about affirming hatred if it was hatred of that which God did not condone. The righteous and the upright in heart in verse 11 are probably synonymously used terms. The righteous were those declared in the right in judgment. Because in biblical thought the heart was the center of the will and the intellect, being upright in heart was being consistent in thought and action. (The heart's association with the intellect has been preserved when we say we memorize things "by heart.") Though the psalm closes with a call to rejoice—that is, a call to let human emotions be given free rein—it also closes with a call to worship and give thanks to God.

Titus 3:4–7

Several preliminary observations are in order. First, as to the literary form of the text, some scholars see behind these verses an ancient baptismal liturgy. The strophic arrangement of these verses in Greek editions of the New Testament (e.g., Nestle-Aland, 26th ed.) reflects this judgment, even though most other translations print these verses as straight prose (NRSV, REB, NJB, NIV). The suggestion is plausible not only because of its context but because of its content as well. The previous verse depicts life before conversion, following the pattern of "once we were . . . ." In such a context, one might reasonably recite the words of a baptismal service to depict the change that occurs in conversion. Besides the context are the explicit references to the "water of rebirth" (v. 5) and the renewing and receiving of the Holy Spirit (vv. 5–6), both of which point in the same direction.

Second, we should take note of what immediately precedes these verses. In verse 3 we have a vivid depiction of life apart from Christ as both self-indulgent and self-destructive.

Today's text presents the other side by showing us how the work of God has made a decisive difference. Taken alone, verses 4–7 appear to provide merely a capsule summary of salvation history, but when seen in their context they are far more than this. They depict the saving work of God as a dramatic response to the human condition. It is one thing to rehearse the story of God's saving work, quite another to see it as the answer to our own human dilemma. Today's text does the latter. This is well worth remembering at Christmas, when we may find ourselves proclaiming the gospel as mere story, not as saving story. We may tell the story of an accident vividly and excitedly, but we will tell it differently if it is an accident in which *we* were involved, and one we lived through.

Third, our text speaks primarily of God's work. It is God's "goodness and loving kindness" that has appeared; it is God who is "our Savior" whose uncalculated mercy has saved us and has been lavishly poured out on us. To be sure, all this has been achieved through the saving work of "Jesus Christ our Savior" (v. 6), but the lead actor in today's story is God. This too is worth remembering at Christmas, when the primary focus is Christ. And well it should be, but not if the prior work of God is eclipsed. We might note even further that the Holy Spirit figures centrally in our passage—another reminder that the Trinitarian God remains focal even in the context of celebrating the work of Christ.

Having made these preliminary observations, we might note the way in which today's text focuses on certain crucial "moments" or "events." God's saving work through Christ is taken as a whole, as that which happened at a point in time. God's goodwill "appeared" (aorist) as an event in time, notably in the person and work of Christ. In this respect, it was a decisive, visible, identifiable event that made a difference. The "moment" envisioned here is a historic moment, cosmic in scope yet historically specific.

But another moment is envisioned—our own salvation. God "saved us" (v. 5). This is not a moment out there, beyond us, but in here, within us. It is the salvific moment of the individual. We should notice this because the text does not imply that God first saved humanity corporately, as if each of us receives his or her respective share. The moment in view here is our own salvation when we experienced God's rescue through baptismal regeneration and spiritual re-creation.

The tone here is thoroughly Pauline in the insistence that God's saving work had not occurred in response to, or because of, "works of righteousness that we had done" (v. 5). Our text reminds us what a serious mistake it is to think that our actions—even our good actions—prompted God to act in our favor. Salvation is not a quid pro quo where God presents us with the gift of salvation in response to, or in exchange for, our own righteous deeds. What we have done or achieved does not commend us to God. God's saving work is prompted instead by uncalculated mercy. It is not as if God rewards us because of our religious acts, but rather that God extends grace to us in spite of our irreligious nature. In the one case, plus meets plus; in the other, plus meets minus. The one can be construed as the divine responding to the human, the other as the divine rescuing the human. One is an act of reward, the other an act of mercy. What distinguishes the two is motive. To reward is to acknowledge goodness and achievement. To be merciful is to recognize need.

In the context of Christmas, today's text can prompt us to probe both the nature and mystery of our own salvation. The Gospel text can provide the christological focus, whereas the epistolary text can provide the theological focus. Both clearly have a soteriological focus.

Luke 2:(1–7) 8–20

This additional lesson for Christmas has as the Gospel lesson a portion of the reading (Luke 2:1–20) offered as the First Proper for Christmas. Luke 2:8–20 is the second of two parts of Luke's nativity story, both of which were discussed in the preceding lesson. There is no need to repeat that here. If in the Christmas Season there will be a need for this additional service, it would be appropriate to use verses 1–7 as the Gospel for one occasion and verses 8–20 for the other. As we have seen, the natural division of the text welcomes such an arrangement, and both parts are certainly rich enough in thought, imagery, and proclamation so as to provide amply for different messages at the services. In fact, the preacher might welcome a briefer text, given the fact that restraint often serves to release one's faculties of thought and imagination.

Christmas, Third Proper
(Additional Lessons for Christmas Day)

Isaiah 52:7–10;
Psalm 98;
Hebrews 1:1–4 (5–12);
John 1:1–14

Today's readings combine to produce a symphony of various compositions centering upon the theme of redemptive good news. In the Old Testament reading, Deutero-Isaiah, the anonymous prophet of the Exile, extols the glory of the messenger who brings good news to Zion. The psalm calls for the singing of a new melody making known the victorious triumph of Israel's God. The Epistle lesson proclaims both the unique and the fulfilling quality of the coming of Christ. In the Gospel reading, the redemptive word that becomes flesh in Jesus is identified with the word that existed with God from the beginning.

Isaiah 52:7–10

Second Isaiah, the prophet of the end of the Babylonian Exile (539 BC), again both establishes the mood for our celebration and articulates the good news of the day. In fact, the contents of the reading concern the proclamation of good news to people in trouble. Although this very familiar poem is hymnic in tone and substance, and it alludes to cultic matters, it is not itself a hymn. By the time we reach its conclusion in verse 10, it is clear that it is a particular kind of announcement of salvation, one concerning the triumph of Yahweh.

The prophet, although actually in Babylon, describes a scene in distant Jerusalem. It is a powerful and captivating portrayal of a messenger arriving at the city with good news. The report of the message is overloaded with terms indicating just how positive the news is: "good news," "peace," "salvation" (v. 7). The actual contents of the messenger's proclamation is, however, a single line: "Your God reigns." It is the triumph of God as king that amounts to such good news.

Then (v. 8) attention shifts to the sentries ("sentinels") on the walls of the city, shouting out that Yahweh is returning to Zion (see Isa. 40:9–10). Either the prophet himself or the sentries on the walls call for the city in ruins to sing for joy (v. 9). Here the language closely resembles a hymn of praise, typically beginning with a call to praise and then citing reasons for that praise. The reasons, introduced by "for" (*ki*), are that Yahweh has comforted his people (see Isa. 40:1) and redeemed Jerusalem. Finally (v. 10), those reasons for praise are extended to include the entire world. The Lord has displayed power and authority before "all the nations," so that all can see "the salvation of our God."

These four verses set before us a festival of sights and sounds, alternating from one to the other. First there is the sight of the messenger arriving with good news, seen as in a prophetic vision (v. 7*a*), and then as we look we hear the messenger's news (v. 7*b*). Next we hear the sentries on the city wall singing (v. 8*a*), and then are shown the reasons for their joy (v. 8*b*). Note the mixture of images: the city stands in ruins, but there are walls with sentries stationed on them. This picture is followed by the sounds of the song of praise (v. 9) and concluded with the most dramatic sight of all, the Lord's saving power revealed to the entire world.

A number of the words and expressions in the passage call for comment. Earlier translations had read, somewhat awkwardly, a single word in verse 7: "Him who brings good tidings" (RSV). The term is more accurately read "herald" (NEB, NJPSV) or "messenger" (NRSV). The Hebrew *shalom* (v. 7) is read variously "peace" (NRSV), "happiness" (NJPSV), and "prosperity" (NEB). In this context it does not refer so much to the absence of war as the presence of well-being. The word translated "salvation" in the NRSV (vv. 7, 10) could be taken as "deliverance" (NEB) or "victory" (NJPSV). In any case, it characterizes the concrete activity of Yahweh in behalf of God's people.

The central themes of the passage concern the kingship of Yahweh, his return to Zion, and the revelation of his saving power before all the world. As is usually the case in Second Isaiah, the themes are closely related to one another. Yahweh's reign is the good news; he manifests that reign by returning to Zion; in returning to Zion and redeeming his people, the divine king displays his authority and power.

The kingship of Yahweh is an ancient tradition, celebrated in the temple in Jerusalem. The three psalms for Christmas (Pss. 96, 97, 98) all come from such celebrations, as do a great many others (e.g., Pss. 47, 93). The expression translated here "your God reigns" (v. 7, NRSV) could just as well be read "your God is—or has become—King."

That God returns to Zion raises questions about the presence and absence of God, and the meaning of holy places. The particular motif here is known also in Ezekiel and elsewhere. With the destruction and the Exile, Yahweh was believed to have abandoned the Holy City, and even the chosen people. With the release from captivity and the return, the divine presence comes back. The announcement in this passage, then, is addressed to persons who have experienced the absence of God. Behind this understanding, moreover, stands a deep sense of Zion as a holy place, a location where God is more present than elsewhere. Various biblical traditions attempt to understand the meaning of such beliefs. In the Book of Deuteronomy, Jerusalem is the place where Yahweh chooses for his "name" to dwell, that is, the place where he is known and addressed. In Priestly and other traditions, the temple in Zion is the site of God's holiness (e.g., Isa. 6).

Is this a scandal of particularity, that the God who transcends all places should be present in a special way—and even "return"—to a particular place? Here that particular presence is for worldwide visibility, for revelation, and what is revealed to all the world is that the God who reigns is the one who saves. That, it appears, is not unlike the event celebrated on this day in the Christian year, the Incarnation.

Psalm 98

Psalm 98 is the third of our trilogy of enthronement/kingship psalms (along with Pss. 96 and 97). Throughout these psalms, we find the motifs of Yahweh's kingship, the judgment of the earth, the control and stabilization of the world's orders, and the universal rule of God.

The opening stanza (vv. 1–3) shows the following three characteristics. (1) The verses are filled with the imagery and metaphors of battle, warfare, and the exercise of power. Note the threefold reference to "victory." The right hand (the "clean" hand used in greeting and eating but also the symbol of favoritism and power) and the holy arm are representative of militant force. (These images may appear a bit out of order at Christmastime, when attention is focused on a babe, shepherds, a family, and monarchs on a peaceful mission. Only Matthew in the birth stories speaks in violent imagery and then only with regard to the frustrated Herod, whose paranoia hardly achieves anything approximating a victory.) (2) The use of the verb "to save" or "to deliver" occurs three times in these verses. Yahweh's exercise of power is saving power. (3) Many of the central theological terms of the Old Testament appear in these verses (just as many Christian theological terms get employed in speaking of Christmas). Among these are "vindication," "steadfast love," and "faithfulness."

A special feature of these first three verses is related to the Christmas theme and has probably influenced the selection of this text (and the other enthronement psalms) for the nativity season. Here we refer to the universalism of the psalm. Note the references to "in the sight of the nations" and "all the ends of the earth." But even in light of this universalism, the particular still plays its role; God's love and faithfulness are shown to "the house of Israel."

The central section (vv. 4–6) is a lengthy summons to praise addressed to all the earth. Here it is clearly the world's human audience that is addressed, because the musical instruments noted are human in origin and usage. (These verses would suggest that much of the cultic, celebrative quality of Christmas has been caught best by street-corner Salvation Army bands!)

The final stanza (v. 7–9) continues the summons to praise, but now the address is to the world of nature—the sea and its occupants, the earth and its inhabitants, the floods, and the hills. The reasons for such praise are found in the promise that God will come to judge and that God will judge with righteousness and equity. The animals—representing the world of nature—have their place at the manger!

Hebrews 1:1–4 (5–12)

Today's epistolary text is the opening section of the Epistle to the Hebrews, an anonymous writing at one time thought to have been written by Paul. Like the epistle as a whole, which may be regarded as a lengthy, sustained christological argument, these introductory verses have Christ as their central focus. They represent a lofty meditation on Christ as the preeminent Son of God, without rival or peer either in heaven or on earth.

In verses 1–4, we are presented with a series of contrasts: "long ago . . . but in these last days," "to our ancestors . . . to us," "by the prophets . . . by a Son." The first contrast signals a temporal shift, a turning point in time when one era gives way to a new era.

It reflects the early Christian conviction that the coming of Christ had marked the end of one age, the beginning of a new age (cf. 9:26; 1 Pet. 1:20; Jer. 23:20). The second contrast marks a shift in the recipients of God's revelation. In former times, God had appeared to patriarchs such as Abraham (Luke 1:55), but now both author and readers constitute a new audience. The third contrast marks a shift in the mode of revelation. Previously, God had used prophets and other representative figures as speakers and interpreters of the divine will (Hos. 12:10–14). God no longer speaks through a chorus of human voices but through the solo voice of the chosen Son.

With the mention of the sonship of Christ, there follows an avalanche of christological claims: Christ as the legitimate heir of God, God's assistant in creation, a reflection of God's glory, the very imprint of divine essence, the one who sustains the whole universe through his powerful utterances, the high priest who offers sacrifice on behalf of the people, and the one exalted to the right hand of God (vv. 2–4). This set of claims is treated more fully in our remarks on this passage in Years B and C.

These various claims about Christ gradually move toward a final argument for his superiority to angels (v. 4). This in turn is supported by a form of midrashic argument in which various Old Testament passages are cited to show precisely how and why Christ is so superior to angels (vv. 5–14). Specifically, his status exceeds that of angels because he bears the incomparable name Son of God (cf. Eph. 1:21; Phil. 2:9). The name itself reflects his exalted status as the one who was raised from the dead and is now seated at God's right hand (cf. Eph. 1:20; 1 Pet. 3:22; Ps. 113:5).

Even though the Old Testament quotations in this second section (vv. 5–14) focus specifically on Christ's superiority to angels, they are not unrelated to the various christological claims made in verses 2–4. We would suggest the following scheme of interpretation:

First, *Christ in the preexistent state* (v. 5). Psalm 2:7 and 2 Samuel 7:14 are cited in the conviction that their references to "Son" apply to Christ. This is taken to mean that in his preexistent state Christ enjoyed a relationship with the Father that was uniquely his. No angel was ever honored by being called "Son."

Second, *the incarnate Christ* (v. 6). We are told that God "brings the firstborn into the world," an apparent reference to the Incarnation. To speak of Christ as the "firstborn" is to underscore his preeminent status, not to imply that he was the first thing created (cf. Col. 1:15; Rev. 3:14). In words reminiscent of the Lukan birth narrative (Luke 2:8–20), we are told that the angels worshiped him at his birth (Deut. 32:43). It is not the angels who are worshiped; it is they who worship.

Third, *the resurrected Christ* (vv. 7–9). We next find Psalm 104:4 (v. 7) and Psalm 45:6–7 (vv. 8–9) being applied to Christ. So understood, these psalms appear to envision his enthroned status as God's anointed, which would presuppose his resurrection. By contrast, the angels are but "winds . . . and . . . flames of fire" (v. 7). His role is to rule forever, theirs to provide accompanying signs of his exalted reign.

Fourth, *the creator Christ* (vv. 10–12). Here Psalm 102:25–27 is applied to Christ, who is addressed as "Lord" and given credit for creating the heavens and the earth. In contrast to the created order, however, Christ neither changes nor perishes, but remains the same (cf. 13:8).

Fifth, *the reigning Christ* (v. 13). Finally, Psalm 110:1 is applied to Christ to underscore his interim reign. He sits exalted at God's right hand but waits until all his enemies are destroyed. Presumably, this envisions the period of the present between his resurrection and the final consummation.

Within the context of Christmas, the part of this second section that relates most directly to the birth of Christ is the claim made in verse 6: God "brings the firstborn into the world." As noted above, the reference to God's angels worshiping him (v. 6b) also echoes familiar Christmas themes. The homilist may wish to focus on this narrow slice of the passage by relating its view of the Incarnation to that of the Gospel text for today. But if one wishes to approach the text more broadly, other possibilities exist, especially in the first section. For one thing, there are several points of convergence between the Christology of this passage and that expressed in the Johannine prologue: the finality of God's revelation through Christ (vv. 1–2), Christ as God's agent of creation (vv. 2–3), the sustaining force of Christ's "powerful word" (v. 3).

Part of today's epistolary text (Heb. 1:1–4) also serves as one of the epistolary texts for Proper 22 in Year B. The reader may want to consult our comments on this text in the volume on Year B.

John 1:1–14

So significant for Christian history and Christian faith is John 1:1–14 that the minister might choose to alternate this lection with Luke 2:1–20 as the primary Gospel reading for Christmas. If that is the case, then it would be well to underscore in a message based on John 1:1–14 those affirmations that are not found in Luke's story.

Before proceeding to focus on the major themes in this text, the preacher may want to make a decision about verses 6–8. A choice not to treat these three verses in the sermon could be justified on several grounds other than the fact that there is more than enough to occupy the preacher in verses 1–5 and 9–14. Practically speaking, verses 6–8 concern John the Baptist, whose person and message were treated the second and third Sundays of Advent. Literarily speaking, these verses are an insert into the hymn to the Word as a part of the writer's polemic against the sect of John the Baptist and can be extracted without loss to the central affirmation of the passage. In fact, the move from verse 5 to verse 9 is noticeably smooth. And theologically speaking, the message of the lection without verses 6–8 is God's act in Jesus Christ, the word for this and every season.

Because John 1:1–14 has been otherwise treated in cycles B and C, let us here simply call attention to five major affirmations of this text that are especially appropriate for this season.

1. John 1:1–14 reminds us that the central subject of the Bible and therefore of our faith is God. Eight times in this brief passage that fact is stated. Some christologies tend to forget that God sent the Son; some pneumatologies tend to forget that God sends the Spirit. God through the Word is creator (vv. 2–3), and God through the Word is redeemer, the end being for us to become children of God (vv. 12–13). At Christmas, the spotlight is properly on the Word made flesh, but the glory that faith sees in Bethlehem's child is that of "a father's only son" (v. 14).

2. The larger context for the Christmas story is creation. Two important faith statements proceed from that observation. First, because the One through whom we are redeemed (vv. 12–13) is the same One through whom all things were created (v. 3), then salvation is not to be understood as over against the world or out of the world, as though the created order were evil and alien to the life of God's children. There is evil in the

world, to be sure, but by choice not by nature. Second, all creation is involved in God's redemptive effort. Although only implied here, this theme is elsewhere developed at some length (Rom. 8:18–25; Col. 1:15–20; Eph. 1:10, 20–23).

3. The Word becoming flesh does not represent a sole and single effort of God in behalf of the world. God has continually been life and light to the world, even though the reception of God's life and light has not been universal (vv. 4–5, 9–13). Ecclesiasticus (Sirach) 24 offers a beautiful portrayal of the Word (Wisdom) seeking to find a home in which to dwell on earth.

4. The eternal Word *became* flesh and dwelt among us (v. 14). That statement of identification with us is too strong and clear to be handled by analogies about being clothed as we are, or dressing as one of us, or taking on a human disguise. John 1:14 implies all the vulnerability that one finds in Luke's baby in a manger. The glory that "we" behold is that which the community of faith sees but which is not and was not openly obvious to all casual passersby. The glory of God in Jesus of Nazareth was not and is not evident to the world (14:17, 22–24). Those who will not see cannot see.

5. The birth imagery, so central to the Christmas Season, in Johannine literature is applied to all who believe. To embrace God's Word is to be born of God, to become a child of God (1:13; 3:3; 1 John 3:9; 5:18). The line in the carol that petitions "be born in us today" is a proper extension of the meaning and the good news of Christmas. He became as we are that we might become as he is.

First Sunday After Christmas

Isaiah 63:7–9;
Psalm 148;
Hebrews 2:10–18;
Matthew 2:13–23

The Gospel lesson for this Sunday narrates the story of the holy family's flight to Egypt to escape the wrath of Herod, and then their settlement in Nazareth. The Old Testament lesson, although addressing an earlier situation, speaks of a savior as well as a protecting angel and thus shows analogies to the Gospel reading. The psalm is a powerful psalm that has all the cosmos as well as the heavenly hosts praising God, whereas the Epistle reading focuses on the descendants of Abraham who, like the patriarch himself, went down to and came out of Egypt.

Isaiah 63:7–9

Read out of context, these three verses from Isaiah 63 extol God by recounting the history of his saving events in behalf of the chosen people. Read with the other texts for the First Sunday After Christmas, the links with the Gospel lesson become obvious. Both mention angels or divine messengers (Isa. 63:9; Matt. 2:13, 19), and Matthew's account of the flight of the holy family to Egypt and their return parallels the Old Testament reading's allusions to the Israelite exodus from Egypt.

Understood in this way, the main theme of Isaiah 63:7–9 is the saving, redemptive activity of God in history, particularly in behalf of the elect. Such an understanding of the passage from Isaiah is not only legitimate, especially in the framework of Christian worship, but accurate if the verses are read alone. However, our interpretation and proclamation of the text can be both broadened and deepened by considering its literary and historical context.

Although it is not immediately obvious, Isaiah 63:7–9 is the first part of a prayer, an act of worship, that is not concluded until Isaiah 64:12. It is not immediately obvious because the prayer language—that is, direct address to God—is not explicit until 63:14. The first part of the prayer instead refers to Yahweh in the third person. Nevertheless, the structure, contents, and purpose of the prayer closely parallel a particular type found in the Book of Psalms (e.g., Pss. 44, 74, 79) and the Book of Lamentations, the complaint song or lament by the community.

All the major elements of such complaint psalms are present: (1) Affirmations of God's capacity to respond. Here, as elsewhere, that takes the form of praise of God in terms of his actions in the past. Psalm 89, which like our text begins with an announcement of the intention to praise, is a close parallel. (2) Confession of sin. (Some individual complaints have instead a confession of innocence; cf. Ps. 17.) In this case, the confession is part of the historical recital (63:10ff., 16; 64:5ff.), the rebellion of the people contrasting with Yahweh's saving acts. (3) Accounts of the trouble or distress. The community reminds the Lord of their present difficulties (63:18–19; 64:7, 10–11), in this case, the destruction of the city of Jerusalem and the temple. (4) Complaints against God and petitions for his help. The community asks the Lord to intervene in their behalf (63:15, 17; 64:1ff., 9, 12).

In this framework, praise of God for God's historical activity in behalf of the people undergirds petition. The God addressed by a people in trouble is the God who has saved the people in the past and is capable of doing it again. Moreover, God's disposition to act in mercy is revealed by history. There is yet another point to this recital as a part of prayer: When the history of salvation is told as part of petition, it quickly leads to confession of sin. If complaint and petition are in view, then praise and confession must go hand in hand. Part of penitence is to recall what God has done in one's behalf.

Historically, most of the materials in Isaiah 56–66 stem from the postexilic period. They are not the work of a single author, but amount to a collection of prophetic and liturgical units from the era. The song (Isa. 63:7–64:12) of which our reading is a part appears to be an exception in that it presumes the situation of the Exile. It must have originated in worship services among either the exiles in Babylon or those who remained in the ruined land of Judah. Like many of the psalms, it would have found its place in the liturgical life of the community far beyond the time of its origin.

The text is rich in the language of the history of Israel's election and of the covenant. "Steadfast love" (from *hesed*, v. 7) characterizes the ideal relationship of both parties in a covenant and may be interpreted, if not translated, as "covenant loyalty." In this verse, however, it is plural and in parallel to "praises" in the next line. Thus a more accurate translation would be: "I will recount the loyal deeds of Yahweh, and Yahweh's praiseworthy actions." Verse 8 contains a paraphrase of the fundamental formula for the conclusion of the covenant between God and people "Surely they are my people." The full formulation contains two parts "You shall be my people and I will be your God" (cf. Exod. 6:2–8; 19:3–6; Lev. 26:12; Hos. 1:8–9). The address to the people as "children" recalls the language of Hosea 11:1ff. and Isaiah 1:2. Although there are textual problems, verse 9 certainly alludes to the exodus from Egypt (cf. Exod. 12:1–32). The problem of text and translation concerns "It was no messenger or angel but his presence that saved them," which at points follows the Septuagint (NRSV). The REB is similar: "No envoy, no angel, but he himself delivered them." The RSV, following the Hebrew text closely, reads: "In all their affliction he was afflicted, and the angel of his presence saved them."

Isaiah 63:7–9, containing words of praise that recall saving events parallel to those in the Gospel lesson for the day, enables us to confess our faith in the God who does such things. But also, as part of a prayer of complaint and petition, it may enable us to confess our corporate sins as well.

Psalm 148

Psalms 146–150 constitute a small collection of hymns of praise. All begin and conclude with the cultic shout "Hallelujah" that calls upon the community to "praise Yahweh," "praise the Lord."

Psalm 148 consists of two types of genres: two extended calls to praise (vv. 1–4, 7–12) and two statements giving the reason or rationale for praise (vv. 5–6, 13–14).

The psalm is an exuberant summons for the whole of creation to join in shouting out and celebrating the name and glory of Yahweh. Practically no aspect of creation is omitted in the call to praise: angels, heavenly hosts, sun and moon, shining stars, highest heavens, waters above the heavens, sea monsters and all deeps, fire and hail, snow and frost, stormy wind, mountains and hills, fruit trees and all cedars, wild animals and all cattle, creeping things and flying birds, kings, princes, rulers, young men and women, old and young. What a chorus!

How different this psalm is from the Epistle and Gospel readings for today! The Letter to the Hebrews talks about the suffering of the Redeemer, and the Gospel of Matthew recounts the attempt of Herod to exterminate the infant Jesus. Psalm 148 breathes not a word of pain and suffering, of life's shortcomings and disappointments, nor of ruthless abuse of power and the personal Egypts to which all flee in despair and depression at some stage in life's pilgrimage.

In spite of its tone, Psalm 148 should not be faulted for a Pollyanna perspective on life. There are times when unbounded jubilation should reign and carry us to the limits of celebration, to the borders of insanity, and to the heights of self-transcendence. Few are the times when the whole world is a chorus and the music of the spheres invades every nook and cranny of existence. Their scarcity should only endear their occurrence. It is only in such moments that we can spiritually and sensually realize the truth that modern ecology has taught us. We are all—from shining star to slithering snake—in this together, and we need to sing, at least occasionally, the same song and join in a common medley.

The psalm offers two sets of reasons undergirding such praise. The first (in vv. 5–6) declares that Yahweh is the creator of all, who has established everything and set a law that cannot pass away (NRSV margin). The created order is divine handiwork in which every part serves its function within a created natural order (see Jer. 5:22–24; 31:35–36). The second (in vv. 13–14) alludes to the rule of the Davidic monarch, the horn raised up for the people of Israel. (On the horn as the symbol of strength and royalty, see 1 Sam. 2:10; Pss. 75:4–5; 89:17, 24; 92:10; 112:9; 132:17; Lam. 2:3, 17.) The psalm thus anchors praise in the divine rule in the universe and the messianic rule over the chosen people.

Hebrews 2:10–18

It is fully appropriate on this First Sunday After Christmas to concentrate on how Christ in the Incarnation fully identified with us—wholly, unexceptionally, unreservedly. Few New Testament texts press this point more forcefully than today's text from the Epistle to the Hebrews, where we are assured that Christ "had to become like his brothers and sisters in every respect" (v. 17). Our text suggests that Christians have not always found it easy to believe that the Son of God actually became "flesh and blood" (v. 14) in a fully human sense. Knowing ourselves as we do, we find it hard to conceive of Christ looking at life through our eyes. When we look inward, we see frailty, flaws, and gross imperfection. We know only too well that flesh and blood humanity carries with it limitations far too great, far too severe to befit the Son of God.

Today's text responds to this resistance of ours, this reluctance to believe in a Christ who was and is one of us. First, we are assured that God willed it this way. It is the God "for whom and through whom all things exist" (v. 10) who thought it fitting for Christ to be perfected through suffering. Christians confess God as the source, means, and object of all things, the one from whom, through whom, and for whom all things exist (cf. Rom. 11:36; 1 Cor. 8:6; also Col. 1:16–17). However much we may see the Incarnation as a mystery, the God we confess is surely able to reveal the mystery to us. To wonder whether incarnation is possible is to doubt God's preeminent power.

Second, our text stresses the common origin we have with Christ. The one "who sanctifies [Christ] and those who are sanctified [we] all have one Father" (v. 11). Literally, the text reads that the "consecrator and consecrated" (NJB) are "all of one" (*ex henos pantes*). Most likely this means that both we and Christ are "of God," perhaps even "of the one God" and hence "of the same family" (NIV), "of the same stock" (NJB; similarly, REB), or "form a single whole" (NJB, note). The emphasis here is not that Christ owes his origin to God in the sense that we do, for this would suggest that Christ was created, and thus that "there was a time when he was not." The emphasis is rather that just as Christ cannot be understood apart from God, neither can we. In this sense, we are his "brothers and sisters," members of God's family.

Third, our text extends this point further by stressing Christ's solidarity with us as "brothers and sisters" or "children of God." This is achieved by several Old Testament quotations attributed to Christ. The first is Psalm 22:22, in which the psalmist praises God and proclaims the divine name to his fellow worshipers. We have no record in the Gospel tradition where Christ quotes this particular passage, although Christ on the cross utters the more famous opening line, "My God, my God, why have you forsaken me?" (Ps. 22:1; Mark 15:34). Perhaps through this association, the entire psalm was read as a prayer of Christ, in which case its use here would make sense. We may hear an echo of this sentiment in John 17:6: "I have made your name known to those whom you gave me from the world." We should also recall the other times when Christ is closely identified with his "brothers and sisters" (Matt. 12:48–49; 25:40; 28:10; Rom. 8:29).

The other Old Testament quotation is Isaiah 8:17–18, where the prophet confesses his trust in God (v. 13; also Isa. 12:12; 2 Sam. 22:3) and acknowledges the "children" God has given him. Here again these words are understood as an utterance of Christ who, like the prophet, had implicit trust in God and finds himself before God with a company of fellow believers.

Both of these texts have the force of identifying Christ with us as his "brothers and sisters," the fellowship of those who belong to God and are at God's disposal. Accordingly, Christ entered fully into the human family, sharing "in flesh and blood" (v. 14; cf. Rom. 8:3). That he did so completely is signified by plunging into the ultimate act of humanity—death (v. 14). This is the suffering of which our text speaks (v. 10; cf. 9:13–14; 13:12). Yet his death was unique in that it overcame death. By dying, he killed death (cf. 2 Tim. 1:10; 1 Cor. 15:55; Rev. 12:10).

This was another aspect in which Christ differed from angels (v. 16). His ultimate concern was with the "descendants of Abraham," his own family, the children of God. This was where his full identity lay. Consequently, his priestly work was concentrated with the human family, with whom he became completely identified as the great high priest (3:1; 4:14; 5:5, 10; 6:20; 7:26; 8:1; 9:11; 10:21). In this capacity, he demonstrated absolute fidelity as God's priest (cf. 1 Sam. 2:35), making expiation for the people (5:1; 1 John 2:2).

He achieved full identification through being tested and suffering (v. 18; cf. 4:15; also Matt. 4:1–11; 26:41; Luke 22:18; Rom. 8:3). Consequently, he can be fully sympathetic with us in our own human struggles.

It may seem that the heavy emphasis on Christ's suffering in today's text carries us too quickly to Good Friday. As a result, the homilist may find it difficult to relate this text to the time immediately following Christmas. But surely the post-Christmas period is the time for us to think of the implications of the Incarnation: our commonality with Christ in God's family, his full identification with us in the human arena where praise and suffering go hand in hand, our common fidelity to the task set before us.

Matthew 2:13–23

It is appropriate, after reading and hearing again Luke's nativity story, to return to Matthew, not simply because Matthew is the Gospel for this year but because Matthew has stories about the child Jesus. One clearly gets the impression that Matthew's accounts concern a child but not necessarily an infant, as in Luke. The flight to Egypt (vv. 13–15) and Herod's slaughter of children "two years old or under" (v. 16) imply that we are here dealing with "post-Christmas" stories. We begin at verse 13 because the account of the visit of the Magi (2:1–12) is always the Gospel reading for Epiphany. The text falls naturally into three parts, each concluding with a statement of a prophecy fulfilled: the flight to Egypt (vv. 13–15); Herod's slaughter of Bethlehem's children (vv. 16–18); the exodus from Egypt (vv. 19–23).

First, let us locate our lection for today. The reader knows at 2:1–2 that the record to follow will be one of threat and clash. "In the time of King Herod, after Jesus was born in Bethlehem of Judea, wise men from the East came to Jerusalem, asking, 'Where is the child who has been born *king* of the Jews?'" (italics added). One does not ask a king the address of the new king, nor does one country comfortably accommodate two kings. The sky darkens and lowers. That which follows is a cycle of Herod stories as one would find among a suppressed minority who looked to the new king for relief from the old. These Herod stories are typically anti-institutional, charting the almost comical frustration and fall of a tyrant on the occasion of the birth of a deliverer from tyrants. The stories are as follows:

Herod the king	verses 1–2
Herod the troubled king	verses 3–6
Herod the deceptive king	verses 7–8
Herod the deceived king	verses 9–15
Herod the vengeful king	verses 16–18
Herod the dead king	verses 19–23

The narrative of Matthew 2:13–23 is carried along by the use of easily discernible Old Testament materials. One hears the clear echoes of stories involving Old Testament heroes and heroines, and there is the direct use of the promise/fulfillment motif. The revelations from God by means of dreams, especially to Joseph (1:20; 2:12, 13, 19, 22), recall the stories of Joseph as dreamer and as interpreter of dreams (Gen. 37–41), and the rescue of the favored child from the murderous designs of a wicked and threatened ruler brings to mind the beautiful stories about the young Moses (Exod. 1:1–2:10). The brief account (vv. 16–18) of the slaughter itself is built around a quotation from Jer. 31:15, a lament for the nation of Israel that recalls the tragedy of Rachel, who died in childbirth and was buried near Bethlehem (Gen. 35:16–20). The use of the Old Testament in Matthew's promise/fulfillment formula, "to fulfill what has been spoken by the Lord through the prophet," occurs at verses 15, 17, and 23. "Out of Egypt I have called my son" has a clear source (Hos. 11:1; also Exod. 4:22), but "he will be called a Nazorean" has an uncertain origin. A corruption of the word "nazirite" (Judg. 13:7) is a possibility. The commentaries will argue the issue.

But Matthew has more in mind than telling Herod-versus-Jesus stories or tracing the early itineraries of Joseph, the Child, and his mother. Matthew is concerned here, as in the genealogy (1:1–17) and the birth narrative (1:18–25), to tell the reader who Jesus is. And what does today's lection supply in answer to the question, Who is Jesus? Several affirmations can be made.

First, Jesus of Nazareth is indeed Jesus of Bethlehem, but he came to be the Nazorean by the clear guidance and providence of God, who makes even wicked rulers such as Archelaus serve the divine purpose.

Second, Jesus fulfills the role and purpose of Israel in that, like Israel, he was called of God out of Egypt. This theme of being God's obedient and faithful Israel will continue through the experience of baptism and the wrestling with temptation in the wilderness (3:13–4:11).

Third, Jesus' escape from the wrath of a wicked ruler not only recalls the story of Moses, but prepares the reader to hear Jesus as one like Moses, whom God has raised up (Deut. 18:18). This Moses likeness will reappear strongly when Jesus speaks with authority from the mountain (chaps. 5–7).

Fourth, Jesus appears here as a providentially favored child in a cycle of Herod stories, but the fact is, his identity is clearly stated: Jesus is God's son (v. 15). Matthew makes room for this declaration throughout the narrative in the way he refers to the holy family: Joseph is addressed by the dream angel, and Joseph is the obedient servant, but the subject is "the child and his mother" (2:11, 13, 14, 20, 21). "The child and his mother" is a clear and beautiful way to make reference, in a very human story, to One who is beyond all doubt, even in infancy, the Son of God.

January 1
(Holy Name of Jesus: Solemnity of Mary, Mother of God)

Numbers 6:22–27;
Psalm 8;
Galatians 4:4–7 or Philippians 2:5–11;
Luke 2:15–21

Celebrating the beginning of the new year on January 1 goes back to the mid–first century BC, when Julius Caesar restructured the civil calendar. Prior to that time, March 1 marked the beginning of the new year. From the outset, it was a festive celebration that easily gave way to excesses of various kinds. In response, the Roman church called on Christians to open the new year with prayer, fasting, and penitential devotions. Another way to provide an alternative to raucous festivals was to designate January 1 as a time for honoring Mary, the Mother of God. In the Roman calendar, the day was designated *Natale Sanctae Mariae*, the Feast of Saint Mary.

Even though the particular emphasis given to January 1 has shifted through the centuries, in modern times, and especially in the Roman church, this day has received a dual emphasis. First, it is a time to recall the naming of Jesus, hence the designation the "Holy Name of Jesus." This aspect of its celebration is closely related to the custom, going back at least to the sixth century, of celebrating the Feast of the Circumcision of the Lord on this day. Second, it is an occasion for commemorating Mary, hence the designation the "Solemnity of Mary, Mother of God."

The selection of readings for this day echoes these themes. The Old Testament reading is chosen because of its emphasis on the bestowal of the divine name on the people Israel. Psalm 8 is the response because its initial and concluding lines praise the name of the Lord. The epistolary readings in different ways pick up on both themes: the Galatians passage embodies a pre-Pauline tradition in which Christ is confessed as one "born of woman, born under the law," whereas the Philippians reading lays stress on the exalted name that God bestowed on the risen Lord. The Gospel text, of course, combines both themes: the central role of Mary as the one who pondered the divine mystery in her heart and the circumcision of Jesus as the occasion when he received the holy name.

Numbers 6:22–27

Within the Pentateuch as a whole, Numbers 6:22–27 is part of the laws given to the people of Israel through Moses at Mt. Sinai. The context is the history of the salvation of the people from Egypt and the establishment of a covenant at Mt. Sinai. The section of which it is a part began with Exodus 19 and will end in Numbers 10. In terms of literary source, this unit, like most of the laws given at Sinai from Exodus 25 to Numbers 10, comes from the Priestly Writer (sixth century BC). Specifically, the stress on the priesthood of the sons of Aaron (6:23) reveals that writer's point of view. However, in the great body of legislation, this passage stands out for its poetic style, suggesting that the blessing itself is much older than the source in which it is found. Its style and contents clearly reflect its repeated cultic use, doubtless by the priests in the Jerusalem temple, but probably in other contexts as well.

The unit consists of the Aaronic blessing surrounded by a brief narrative framework. The narrative (6:22) simply but significantly indicates that what follows is a divine speech to Moses. The benediction as a prayer for God's blessing was itself a gift from God. In effect, God tells Moses to instruct Aaron and his sons—that is, all future priests in the line, down to the writer's day—to bless the people of Israel, gives them the words of the blessing, and then (6:27) states the meaning of the act of blessing.

The blessing contains three sentences, each with two parts and each one longer than the one before. Every sentence begins with the divine name, Yahweh, followed by verbal forms that indicate wish or hope, for example, "[May] the Lord bless you. . . ." They are then prayers for the well-being of those addressed. Because the form of address is second person singular, the blessing may apply equally to individuals or the group as a whole. The contents concern God's protection (v. 24), gracious care (v. 25), and gift of peace. "Peace" (*shalom*) is a comprehensive term, a fitting greeting, that includes wholeness. Priests are to pronounce the blessing, but, as verse 27 expressly states, the Lord is the one who blesses.

What does it mean that by pronouncing the blessing the sons of Aaron thus put the divine name upon Israel? One hardly need stress the importance of names in the Old Testament. When a covenant was made with them, Abram and Sarah were given new names (Gen. 17). After struggling through the night, Jacob was given the new name Israel, but the one with whom he struggled would not reveal his name, for in the name is power (Gen. 32:27–29). Yahweh was to be worshiped at the place where he would choose "to put his name . . ." (Deut. 12:5). To "put the name" of the Lord over the people of Israel is to indicate that they are known, and know themselves by that name. They are thereby identified with this God, and this God with them.

Psalm 8

This hymn was composed in praise of God the creator, whose name and handiwork pervade all the earth. This is made evident in the prologue and epilogue verses (vv. 1a, 9). The second person speech—direct address to God—that appears throughout the psalm is unusual in hymns that are normally human speech to a human audience intent on instilling and enriching faith. (Ps. 104 supplies another example of such a second person hymn.) The hymn could have been spoken in worship by the Judean king who, it appears, may have referred to himself circumlocutionarily as "son of man" (v. 4b; see also Pss. 80:17; 144:3).

Two aspects of human existence are highlighted in this psalm. There is, first, the human sense of insignificance when confronted with the awesome reality of the created order. Whoever penned verses 3–4 must have viewed the heavens on some clear, crystal, Palestinian night and wondered, like many of us who have beheld the earth as televised from some silently sailing spaceship, where humans—invisible from such heights—fit into the scheme of things. This is the feeling in the psalm that viewed matters from the human side looking upward.

A second set of anthropological affirmations center on humankind's high status in the created order—"a little less than God" with "dominion over." Humans are thus the intermediates between the heavenly and the nonhuman world. The positions in this psalm should be compared with Genesis 1, the Priestly account of creation. In the latter, human are made, unlike any other part of the earthly order, in the image of God (1:26) and are granted dominion over the other orders of creation—fish, fowl, and land animals (1:28). As a little lower than God, humans are thus affirmed as related and akin to the divine order. The other side of this affirmation is seen in the role of humans as supreme in the world of creation. Domesticated animals, wild beasts of the field, fowl of the air, and fish in the sea are all seen as subservient and subordinate to the human world. Such a claim and understanding allowed the Israelites, with a sad conscience nonetheless, to slaughter and consume other living beings, only returning the blood (symbolizing life) in sacrifice or burial to God as an apology for killing (see Lev. 17:1–13).

In this psalm there is only a tinge of that anthropological ambivalence that has occupied the thought of philosophers, the concern with humanity's double quality of greatness and depravity. (For the Yahwist, the first human was viewed as a divinely animated clod—Gen. 3—that preserves the twofold quality of human existence.) There is little of that ambivalence one sees, for example, in the description of humankind by the French philosopher-mathematician Blaise Pascal (1623–62): "What a chimera then is man! What a novelty! What a monster, what a chaos, what a contradiction, what a podigy! Judge of all things, feeble earthworm, depository of truth, a sink of uncertainty and error, the glory and the shame of the universe."

The elevated, exalted state of man in this psalm and its employment of the phrase "son of man" made it possible for the early church to use this text in expounding an understanding of Jesus, who as "Son of Man" reigns over God's order (see Matt. 21:16; 1 Cor. 15:27; Heb. 2:6–9) and bears the name that is above all names (Phil. 2:9).

Galatians 4:4–7

The phrase from this epistolary passage that makes it a suitable text for this special day is "born of woman" (v. 4). Although Mary is not mentioned by name, she is clearly in mind in what appears to be a pre-Pauline kerygmatic summary. What makes it remarkable is that it is one of the few times that Paul refers to the tradition of Jesus' birth (cf. Rom. 1:3). In fact, in none of Paul's writings does he ever refer to Mary, the mother of Jesus, by name (cf. Rom. 16:6). For that matter, she is referred to by name only once outside the Synoptic Gospels (Acts 1:14).

Even so, this single reference achieves a prominence, if for no other reason than that it is exceptional. The preacher's task on this occasion is to highlight its significance within this Pauline passage rather than treat it as Paul's slighting Mary.

Given the prominence of this phrase, and its companion phrase "born under the law," within this passage, we should observe first that Paul anchors the Incarnation in time and history. In this respect, he shares Luke's view of the Christ-event as an event that is part of world history (cf. Luke 2:1–3; 3:1–2). In this respect, the epistolary reading nicely complements the Gospel lesson from Luke, with its distinctive interest in the role of Mary in the birth and infancy story (cf. Luke 1:26–56; 2:5–7, 16, 19, 22–35, esp. vv. 34–35, 48, 51).

By focusing on Mary, the preacher might explore her role in the following respects:

1. As the one through whom "the fullness of time" occurred (v. 4). One of the characteristic ways of interpreting the Christ-event was to see it as the end of one era and the beginning of a new era. Because the "time" of the old era came to an end with the coming of Christ, the story of Jesus begins with the announcement, "The time has arrived" (Mark 1:15, REB; cf. 1 Cor. 10:11; Eph. 1:10; Heb. 1:2; 9:26; 1 Pet. 1:20).

2. As the one through whom the sending of God's Son occurred (v. 4). We might compare this metaphor with others used of the Incarnation. "Sending" suggests a commissioning for a particular task (Rom. 8:3; cf. John 5:36; 1 John 4:9), whereas "giving" suggests a sacrificial image (Rom. 8:32; cf. John 3:16).

3. As the one through whom liberation from the law occurred (v. 5). This must be understood within the context of Paul's special agenda in the Epistle to the Galatians, where he emphasizes Christ's role as rescuing us from the curse of the law (3:13). The image is rendered especially well in the REB: "to buy freedom from those who were under the law" (v. 5; cf. 1 Cor. 6:20; 7:23; 1 Pet. 1:18–19).

4. As the one through whom our adoption as children occurred (v. 5). Earlier Paul has insisted that our becoming "children of God" was made possible in Christ (3:26). But the contrast here is between being slaves and being children (v. 7; 3:29; Rom. 8:16–17). The crucial difference, of course, is that being a child means being an heir (3:29). We should note that the designation "children of God" was already applied to Israelites in the Old Testament (cf. Deut. 14:1). Thus it is not as if Christians are given this name, or are entitled to this status, for the first time. But by stressing that Christians become children by adoption (v. 5), Paul is emphasizing that Christ's "Sonship" comes to be extended to those who are not "children" in the strictest sense. The status that belongs to Christ alone ("Son") is granted to those who are incorporated into Christ. What was uniquely Christ's now becomes the possession of those "in Christ."

5. As the one through whom our status as children is validated by the Spirit of Christ (v. 6). Our text speaks of two sendings: God's sending of the Son and God's sending of the Son's Spirit. The one sending has occurred in the world, the other within our hearts. The role of the Spirit receives particular definition as the one who utters the words of Jesus in Gethsemane, "Abba, Father" (Mark 14:36). It is Christ's Spirit who utters within us the words of filial obedience that continually confirm our status as children.

Obviously, each of the above claims is true primarily with reference to Christ. The one danger of this way of appropriating the text is that the role of Christ may easily become subsumed under the role of Mary. And yet none of this would have been possible had Christ not been "born of woman."

It should be noted that Galatians 4:4–7 also serves as the epistolary reading for the First Sunday After Christmas in Year B. The reader may want to consult our remarks in the volume on Year B.

Philippians 2:5–11

The fuller version of this well-known Pauline text (2:1–13) serves as the epistolary reading for Proper 21 in Year A. Today's text (2:5–11) also serves as the standard epistolary lesson for Passion/Palm Sunday in all three years. The reader may want to consult our remarks on these texts in their other liturgical settings.

This passage opens with an exhortation (v. 5) that, in turn, introduces what many scholars regard as an early Christian hymn (vv. 6–11). In spite of this emerging scholarly consensus about the form of the passage, there is not a similar consensus among biblical translators. These verses are printed strophically in NRSV, NIB, and NJB, but not in REB.

Various structural arrangements for the hymn have been suggested. Two of the most well known are presented in the NRSV and the NJB. In the NRSV, it is printed with two main parts, verses 6–8 and verses 9–11, each part consisting of three subsections that correspond to the numbered verses. In the NJB, by contrast, it is printed as six separate stanzas, each corresponding to a numbered verse.

Regardless of the structural arrangement one adopts, what is clear is that verses 6–8 depict the descent of Christ to the earth, whereas verses 9–11 depict his ascent and exaltation. Accordingly, the hymn is sometimes said to depict a "V-shaped" Christology.

There are two motifs in the hymn that make it a fitting text for this liturgical setting. First, the reference to Christ's "being born in human likeness" (v. 7) provides a meaningful focus for reflecting on Mary's role as Mother of God. Second, the double reference to "the name" in verses 9–10 makes it an especially appropriate text for the day set aside for honoring the Holy Name of Jesus.

With reference to the first motif, our remarks above on Galatians 4:4–7 provide some suggestions for further reflection. Thus here we provide some remarks on the second motif.

The "name that is above every name" is doubtless a reference to "Lord." This is made clear in the confession in verse 11: "Jesus Christ is Lord" (cf. 1 Thess. 1:1; Eph. 1:21). This name is bestowed as a result of Christ's resurrection, here referred to as his exaltation and in other texts rendered even more vividly as an enthronement at God's right hand (cf. Acts 2:33; 5:31). Elsewhere the exalted name is "Son of God" (Rom. 1:3), which according to the Epistle to the Hebrews is incomparably superior to the name of angels (Heb. 1:4–14).

Yet the Lord is clearly identified with the historical figure Jesus, for it is "at the name of Jesus" that the universe bows in submission (v. 10). The language is doubtless supplied by Isaiah 45:23, where Yahweh calls on the nations of the earth to recognize him as the only God, the One before whom there is none other, promising, "To me every knee shall bow, every tongue shall swear." This universal recognition of Yahweh's preeminent status equalizes our status (Rom. 14:11). In our text, however, the name of Jesus has replaced the name of Yahweh as the name of universal recognition and submission.

Bowing before the name of Jesus finally expresses itself as confession (v. 11). The confession that embodies the sum and substance of the Christian faith in its simplest terms, which at one time defined earthly loyalties (Rom. 10:9; 1 Cor. 12:3; 2 Cor. 4:5; Col. 2:6), now reconfigures heavenly loyalties.

There are several exegetical problems in this text, some of which are treated in our other remarks on this passage. To some extent, the preacher must grapple with these questions in deciding how to use this text on a day honoring the name of Jesus. What should not be ignored, however, is the honorific tone of this passage and the central claim of the ultimate preeminence of Christ's name.

Luke 2:15–21

The tradition that calls for this special service on January 1 carries with it a double focus, either one of which may be central to the liturgy and sermon for any given year of the lectionary. Primary attention may be given to Mary, or it may be given to the child upon the occasion of circumcision and naming. In either case, it means for the preacher a return to the Lukan text treated earlier as the Gospel (along with John 1:1–14) for the season of Christmas. Only verse 21 is added to the earlier reading. This return will be no strain either on the familiar text or on the preacher's imagination if the special focus of this service is kept in mind. We will here discuss Luke 2:15–21, with attention first upon Mary and then upon the eight-day-old child, leaving to the preacher the choice of accent. For the recovery of the whole narrative (Luke 2:1–20), the reader may wish to review the comments on the Christmas lection.

In Luke 2:15–20, Mary is in the unusual position of hearing from strange visitors, the shepherds, the testimony about her son's significance in God's gracious purpose for "all the people" (v. 10). The shepherds receive from heaven's messenger the good news of a Savior; the shepherds hear the angelic choir; the shepherds are given a sign for confirmation. Mary, the child's mother, hears all this, not directly, but through their testimony—not that there is anything wrong with hearing it the way the whole world receives it (24:47–48; Acts 1:8). But his young mother, in pain, away from home, uncomfortably housed in a stable, would surely have been cheered and encouraged by a brief return of the angel who visited her nine months earlier. Nine months is a long time; in fact, plenty of time to doubt one's own experience, plenty of time to wonder about the adequacy of one's answers to inquiring relatives and friends.

But our quiet wish for Mary is not her own wish. She keeps these things in her heart, pondering, remembering (v. 19). The witness of the shepherds confirms what Gabriel had said (1:26–38) and what her kinswoman Elizabeth had told her (1:39–45). Soon Simeon would add to this testimony, as would Anna, and the child himself at age twelve, causing Mary to ponder further the meaning of all this (2:22–51). Mary was not, however, only a ponderer. She believed God's word and was obedient to it (1:38, 45); she had strong confidence and hope in God (1:46–55); and she became a disciple of her firstborn, joining his other followers in Jerusalem as they prayerfully waited for the Holy Spirit he had promised (Acts 1:5, 14). No fear of an excessive adoration of Mary should blind us to Luke's portrayal of her as a true disciple.

Verse 21 provides the second perspective in today's lesson, the naming of Jesus. Luke, who alone among the Evangelists records this moment in Jesus' life, conveys three messages in the one sentence devoted to it. First, there is the name itself. Jesus is a form of the name Joshua, which means "salvation from Jehovah." Luke has already called Jesus "Savior" (2:11), but it is Matthew who states more directly the choice of the name: "you are to name him Jesus, for he will save his people from their sins" (1:21).

Luke's second point is that the naming of Jesus both fulfills and confirms the word of God delivered by the angel (1:31). To say that the word was fulfilled is to acknowledge a pattern of promise/fulfillment very important to Luke both in the Gospel (4:16–21; 24:44) and in Acts (2:17–36). More consistently in Luke than in any other New Testament writer, the theme of continuity between the Old Testament and the New is developed. To say that the word of God was confirmed is to say that the event of naming the child Jesus confirmed the divine revelation. The same was true in the case of John. The name was given to Zechariah in a revelation (1:13), and so the child was called John, much to the surprise of relatives and neighbors (1:57–63). Both John and Jesus are of families that hear, believe, and obey the word of God.

And finally, Luke wants it understood that there was nothing about Jesus and his followers that violated the law of Moses. In chapter 2 alone, Luke cites repeated observances of the law: circumcision, dedication at the temple, purification of the mother, journey to Jerusalem at age twelve for the Passover. Luke's Jesus worships regularly in the synagogue (4:16), and following his death, the disciples continue to worship God in the temple (24:53). Jesus and his disciples do not represent a breach of ancient law and covenant but rather continuation and fulfillment of God's gracious purpose as revealed in the law, the prophets, and the writings (24:27, 44–47).

January 1
(When Observed as New Year's Eve or Day)

Ecclesiastes 3:1–13;
Psalm 8;
Revelation 21:1–6a;
Matthew 25:31–46

All these texts focus attention on time and the passing of time. The Old Testament reading is highly appropriate for a new year, emphasizing the rhythms of time and meditating on the human response to the passing of time. The psalm calls forth praise apropos of a new beginning and identifies the place of that time-bound human being in God's order. The Epistle reading envisions a new and eternal heaven and earth and a new and eternal Jerusalem. The newness of a new year that gives us the taste of beginning again, of leaving behind, also raises the yearning for the totally and permanently new. The Gospel text preserves for us the association, so common in Judaism, of the new year with judgment.

Ecclesiastes 3:1–13

Read as a whole and in its literary context, this is not a cheerful text. The author, Qohelet, begins his book with the declaration that "all is vanity" (1:2) and throughout reflects on the futility of all human endeavor. In the text before us at the beginning of the year, he meditates on the meaning of time and the times, and is drawn to a somber conclusion.

The lection consists of two major parts, each with its subdivisions. The first part is the poem on times and seasons (vv. 1–8). Verse 1 is an introduction that states the general thesis: "For everything there is a season, and a time for every matter [or "experience," NJPSV] under heaven." Verses 2–8 then develop that thesis in detail by means of fourteen opposites. These in turn begin with the most comprehensive opposites of all, at least with regard to human life: "a time to be born, and a time to die" (v. 2). All the other opposites have to do with human activities or experiences, and a progression of thought is difficult to discern: hostility and violence along with their opposites frame verses 3–8: killing—as in warfare or executions—and healing (v. 3a); love and hate, war and peace (v. 8). The other pairs concern a wide range of human activities, including construction (v. 4), speaking (v. 7), and acts of affection (v. 5b), as well as the extremes of human emotions and their expression (v. 4). The point is conveyed not only by the contents but also by the style and mood. The steady rhythm and the repetitious pattern suggest the thesis itself: everything has its regular time, and time moves on.

The lines of the poem on time—apart from their present context—can be heard in many different ways. They can affirm an orderly creation, not only in terms of space but of time as well. The wisdom of that understanding, common in Old Testament wisdom literature, would be patience: Endure whatever you face, for its time will end. War and peace, love and hate all have their time. And the wisdom teachers stressed the importance of study and learning in order to know the right time for each thing:

> To make an apt answer is a joy to anyone,
> and a word in season, how good it is! (Proverbs 15:23)

The wise person has good timing, whether in knowing when to speak or in when to plant particular crops. Or one could take the rhythm of time as a gift, as in Yahweh's promise to Noah following the flood:

> "As long as the earth endures,
> seedtime and harvest, cold and heat,
> summer and winter, day and night,
> shall not cease." (Genesis 8:22)

But none of these is the conclusion that Qohelet draws from the poem on time, which he probably did not write but is quoting from the wisdom tradition. His response is presented in the second part of our reading, verses 9–13, and probably continues through verse 15. There are three movements to that response. In verse 9 he poses a rhetorical question that at first glance appears discontinuous with the poem: "What gain have the workers from their toil?" Answer: None. Second (vv. 10–11), as often in his reflections, the Preacher cites his experience—"I have seen. . . "—of human life ("business . . . to be busy with") that have led him to conclusions about God. God has, he agrees, "made everything suitable for its time," and has put a sense of time ("past and future," NRSV, or "eternity," RSV) in the human mind. But that leads to frustration, for it is impossible for human beings to comprehend God's ways. Third (vv. 12–13), given that situation, Qohelet offers his advice. Human beings should "be happy and enjoy themselves as long as they live," for the capacity to eat and drink and have pleasure in their work is a gift of God. In the verses that follow our reading (vv. 14–15), there is a note of awe in the presence of God's design and knowledge of all times, but there is resentment as well that, although what God does endures forever, human times come to an end.

Reflection on the times, the appropriate times for human activities, has led the Preacher to meditate on time itself and has brought him face to face with human limits. Finally, it is not the difficulty of knowing the right time to do something that produces the frustration and resentment, but the fact that all human times come to an end, that there is the inevitable "time to die" (v. 2). That awareness of death as the final human boundary is the key to the Book of Ecclesiastes. That "time" which God has appointed for all—both the righteous and the wicked, and for the animals—is the day of death (see 3:16–22). "Again I saw that under the sun the race is not to the swift, nor the battle to the strong, nor bread to the wise, nor riches to the intelligent, nor favor to the skillful; but time and chance happen to them all" (9:11).

Awareness of human finitude leads our author to frustration, but it also focuses his attention on life as a gift of God. The advice in 3:12–13 is repeated frequently throughout the book. In spite of the presence of evil, "whoever is joined with all the living has hope, for a living dog is better than a dead lion. The living know that they will die, but the dead know nothing" (9:4–5). Make the most of your life, especially before you grow old and weak, and "desire fails," and finally "the silver cord is snapped, and the golden bowl is broken at the fountain . . . and the dust returns to the earth as it was" (12:5–7).

The beginning of a new year is the best time to meditate on time and the times. So first we can follow the example—if not the advice—of Qohelet and reflect on the times and the limits of human life under God. His is a sober realism that is bracing if not refreshing, and it encourages us to acknowledge the limits of our knowledge and of our lives. No one can count on an infinite supply of New Years. It is certainly possible to hear the Preacher's specific advice in view of that sad reality as stressing physical pleasure: eat and drink and enjoy yourself. But it does call attention to the importance of living in the present tense. To take time seriously is threatening, but to do so can also emphasize that every day of every new year and every moment of every day is precious.

Psalm 8

The contents and emphasis of this lection are almost completely the opposite of Ecclesiastes 3:1–13. The latter presents humanity almost at the mercy of divine determinism. Psalm 8, however, stresses the exalted position of humanity in God's created order, although it too can speak of the human sense of insignificance when confronted with the created universe. Both of these emphases, the greatness and glory of humanity and yet its sense of insignificance when viewed in light of the divine might and majesty, can be combined in a sermon, and the minister can have the two lections dialogue with each other, recognizing the truth in both positions.

Although it is true that Psalm 8 sees humanity in a more exalted status than practically any other biblical text, nonetheless, the focus of the psalm is praise of a God who created the world and conferred on humanity a position of honor and responsibility exceeding that of any other created being. (Note that Eccles. 3:19 declares that humans have no real advantage over animals in that both end up with the same fate.) This praise of God as the purpose of the psalm can be seen (1) in its hymnic quality, (2) in the fact that it is a hymn directly addressed to the Deity, which is a very rare feature of biblical hymns (for another example, see Ps. 104), and (3) in the use of identical praises in the prelude and the postlude. Thus, what the psalm has to say about both the insignificance and the status of humanity is a way of praising the Deity.

Verses 1b–2 present innumerable problems both to the translator and the exegete, although the sense of the text seems to be that babes and infants recognize and testify to the greatness of God (see Matt. 21:16) and that their testimony puts at rest any enemy or avenger. Babes see the truth that others miss.

Verses 3–4 give expression to that universal feeling of humanity's inconsequential status when confronted with the broad sweep of the night skies dotted with the moon and the stars. (One should note that in antiquity, when pollution was so much less and artificial lighting was nil, the skies at night must have been even more splendid and awesome than they appear today.) Confronted with the lighted canopy of the heavens, humans almost naturally sense their littleness and wonder why God could be concerned for something so small. If the ancients felt this way, how much more should we moderns, who have seen the earth from outer space and are aware of the vastness of the regions beyond our solar system. (With a universe so large, does it ultimately matter if we ordered English peas and instead were served green beans?)

Over against the sense of human insignificance, Psalm 8 affirms the high status of human existence. Humans are created only a little lower than God, who has placed the whole of creation under human dominion. The works of God's hands are placed beneath the feet of humankind. Humanity thus serves as God's vice-regent over the whole of creation.

In preaching from Psalm 8, and especially when combined with Ecclesiastes 3:1–13, the preacher should focus on the paradoxical nature and situation of humans in the world. Opposite poles—human lowliness and human heights—are held in tension because both reflect realities of the true situation. Humankind, this mortal creature of insignificance, overshadowed by the vastness of the sky's canopy, nonetheless possesses dominion over the whole of the divine creation and shares in the divine dignity.

An ancient rabbi taught that we should all carry two rocks in our pockets to be withdrawn depending on the situation. On one rock should be written, "I am but dust and ashes," and on the other, "For me was the world created." Such is the character of human existence.

Revelation 21:1–6a

This text also serves as the epistolary lesson for All Saints Day in Year B, as well as the Fifth Sunday of Easter in Year C. The reader may want to consult our remarks on these texts in the other volumes.

The use of this text in such varied liturgical settings provides an excellent example of how a single passage will be read and heard differently in different contexts. On All Saints Day, it serves as a reminder of the heavenly hope to which God's people aspire and for which they have lived and died. In the post-Easter season of Year C, it serves as one of several semicontinuous readings from the Johannine Apocalypse. Bracketed by texts from the same canonical writing on preceding and succeeding Sundays, it will be heard as part of the continuous revelation of John. In its post-Easter setting, its triumphant note will be especially apparent. But heard in the context of New Year's, the same text is bound to evoke yet another set of responses.

What strikes us first is the recurrent refrain of the new—new heaven, new earth, new Jerusalem—all finally culminating in the bold declaration by the enthroned God: "See, I am making all things new" (v. 5). We are hearing again the voice of Yahweh, who spoke to the disconsolate exiles, urging them: "Do not remember the former things, or consider the things of old," declaring instead, "I am about to do a new thing" (Isa. 43:18–19a). If they felt locked into the slavery of exile and alienation, they are now reminded that God can break through the old and inaugurate the new. Things need not remain as they have been. Dramatic change is possible when God decides to let "new" shatter "old."

Similar sentiments are echoed when Paul declares Christ to be the arena of new creation (2 Cor. 5:17). He too calls attention to this new reality, inviting us to open our eyes: "Everything old has passed away; see, everything has become new!" If Yahweh had broken through Israel's fixation on the past by reminding them of the divine capacity for renewing, Christ now becomes for Paul (and us) the agent of divine renewal. Through him the old era gives way to the new. In this new age, moral renewal is possible: we can now walk in "newness of life" (Rom. 6:4). Conforming our will to the divine will results in a "renewing of the mind" (Rom. 12:2), which doubtless entails both a renewal of the intellect as well as the will. How we think changes along with why we act. What ultimately matters is not how well religious acts are performed, but whether they are indicative of genuinely moral and spiritual renewal—whether they are expressive of the "new creation" (Gal. 6:15).

To be sure, the vision of the Seer in today's text is an eschatological vision, one of several visions with which the Book of Revelation closes. The collapse of the old order is seen in the passing of heaven and earth, or the world as we know it (v. 1). The vanishing of the earthly order is often depicted in apocalyptic thought as earth, mountains, and sky fleeing away (cf. 6:14; 16:20; 20:11; 2 Pet. 3:7; also Ps. 114:3, 7). Into this cosmic vacuum there descends a new order, the heavenly city of Jerusalem (cf. 3:12; Gal. 4:26; Heb. 11:16; 12:22). With its descent comes the presence of God, radically new in the way it redefines the people of God. The new presence enables the new relationship of which the prophets spoke (Jer. 31:31; Isa. 8:8, 10). To dwell with God is to know God in a radically different way. The pressures, anxieties, and pains of the old order are no more (v. 4).

Even if the vision is eschatological, should it be any less compelling? Is it not usually the vision of what can be that forces us to question what is and what has been? It was the future that beckoned the exiles to forget the old and look to the new. It was the Christ-event that shattered the old with the utterly new. It is the hope of a future totally defined by God that shatters our reliance on the past and moves us along toward a new time, a new day.

Matthew 25:31–46

The Gospel reading for today prompts the observance of New Year by reflecting on rather than forgetting the past. The "new" in our text is the new age, the time of final reward and punishment, launched by the coming of the Son of Man, who pronounces judgment entirely on the basis of past behavior toward persons in need.

Before looking at this lection, let us locate it in the scheme of Matthew's Gospel. Jesus' apocalyptic speech delivered from the Mount of Olives details the end of the temple, Jerusalem, and this present age, and envisions the coming of the Son of Man (24:1–36). This discourse is followed by a stern call to vigilance in view of the uncertain time of that certain event (vv. 37–44). The call to vigilance is followed by three parables concerning behavior during a possible delay in the Lord's coming: the parable of the slave supervisor (24:45–51, "My master is delayed"), the parable of the ten maidens (25:1–13, "As the bridegroom was delayed"), and the parable of the talents (25:14–30, "After a long time"). At this point Matthew places our reading, as if to say, "But when the Lord does come, late or soon, it will be as follows." With 25:31–46, an account without parallel in the other Gospels, Matthew concludes the public ministry of Jesus.

Matthew 25:31–46 is not a parable but a prophetic vision not unlike the throne scene of Revelation 20:11–15, in which the final judgment occurs. The enthronement of the Son of Man occurs elsewhere in Matthew 19:28, but the uses of Psalm 110:1 (the Lord seated at the right hand of God) are many and varied in the New Testament. In fact, the image in Psalm 110:1 lies at the base of the early Christian confession "Jesus is Lord" (Rom. 10:9; Phil. 2:11), which replaced "Jesus is the Messiah" as the church moved into cultures where a messiah was not expected.

There is no question but that for Matthew the one enthroned in power and glory is Jesus, but the passage draws upon titles from Jewish literature that Christians applied to

Jesus. Daniel 7:13–14 provides a scene of one like a son of man coming with the clouds of heaven to be presented before the Ancient of Days, who grants to this one dominion, glory, and kingdom. The image is, as in Matthew, that of a cosmic ruler. The term "Son of Man" shifts to "king" (Zech. 9:9; Ps. 89:18, 27) at verse 34 as well as to "son of God" (implied in "my Father," v. 34). In addition, there is a variation of the picture of the shepherd dividing sheep and goats from Ezekiel 34. But regardless of the various sources for the imagery, for Matthew the scene is that of the Parousia, the coming of Jesus as Lord and judge of all people, Jews and Gentiles, church and nonchurch alike.

Several features of the judgment are most striking. First, there is the Lord's identification with the poor, lonely, hungry, sick, and imprisoned (vv. 35–36, 40, 42–43, 45). At Matthew 10:40–42 and 18:5 in the instructions about giving the cup of water and practicing hospitality, Jesus says such activity is ultimately toward himself and toward God. But there is nothing there or elsewhere in the Gospels that approaches the complete identification expressed in "I was hungry . . . , I was thirsty . . . , I was a stranger." Nor is there any indication that the text refers only to the poor and neglected within the church; before him are gathered "all the nations" (v. 32).

A second striking feature of the vision is that judgment is not based on heroic deeds or extraordinary feats but on the simple duties, the occasions for expressing care for other persons that present themselves every day. In fact, some students of Matthew have expressed concern over the absence of major Christian themes such as faith, grace, mercy, and forgiveness. That those matters are important to Jesus and to Matthew is beyond question; they are well documented elsewhere, as in 20:1–16, but not every parable or vision emphasizes every truth. To do so would blur all truth. However, it should be said that the Christian's concern for faith and grace should not replace attention to fundamental human obligations that, as this vision reminds us, are a primary concern of him who is Lord of all people of the earth. One does not cease to be a member of the human race once one joins the church.

A third and final unusual feature of the judgment is that both the blessed and the damned are surprised. Those banished to eternal punishment apparently miscalculated on what it takes to gain eternal bliss. And those rewarded had attended to the needs of others with such naturalness and grace that they were surprised that their behavior received heaven's attention. Saints are always surprised to hear their deeds recounted.

Second Sunday After Christmas Day

Jeremiah 31:7–14 or Sirach 24:1–12;
Psalm 147:12–20 or Wisdom of Solomon 10:15–21;
Ephesians 1:3–14;
John 1:(1–9) 10–18

The early church proclaimed that, in the coming of the Christ, the Old Testament prophecies and predictions were fulfilled. The Old Testament lesson from Jeremiah speaks of the redemption to come, when the scattered of Israel would be gathered from the farthest corners of the earth and when merriment, gladness, and feasting would signal the status of the new affairs. The reading from Sirach describes Divine Wisdom, which like the Word in the prologue to the Gospel of John, is said to have existed with God from the beginning and to have become implanted like a tree in Israel. The psalm praises God for his great gifts but above all for the fact that God has not dealt with any other nation as with his own people. The reading from The Wisdom of Solomon, with its emphasis upon the holy people and divine wisdom, is a fitting response to either Old Testament lection and is a fitting anticipation of the Gospel lesson. The Epistle contributes its melody to the theme of the Incarnation and the dwelling of God among humans.

Jeremiah 31:7–14

Jeremiah 31:7–14, which has few direct links with the other lessons for the day, is appropriate for the occasion because it expresses the mood and spirit of the continuing celebration of Christmas. The passage is filled with announcements of salvation—that the Lord has saved, gathered, consoled, and ransomed a people from sorrow to joy.

Because it is so similar to the perspective of Isaiah 40–55 and Isaiah 35 (see the comments for the Third Sunday in Advent in this volume), many commentators have taken this passage, along with most of the other materials in Jeremiah 30–31, the so-called Book of Consolation, as additions to the book from the time of the Babylonian Exile. In that case, the song of gladness anticipates release from Babylon and return to Judah. However, the references to "Jacob," "Israel," "Ephraim," and the "remnant of Israel" could very well mean the inhabitants of the Northern Kingdom who had been carried off by the Assyrians. In that case, Jeremiah here announces the return of those captives, and "the land of the north" (v. 8) would have been the far reaches of the Assyrian Empire in the seventh century BC.

Although the passage is hymnic in tone and in some of its contents, it is part of a prophetic announcement. The call to sing and praise (v. 7) is like the beginning of many hymns, and there are allusions to a ceremony of praise and thanksgiving (vv. 12, 13); but the unit is framed by messenger formulas and oracle formulas that mark it as prophetic address. Throughout, the prophet quotes the words of Yahweh concerning the future. Thus the text is a prophetic announcement of salvation concerning the return of exiles. It is good news that God has "ransomed" and "redeemed" (v. 11) people from captivity.

The context of this reading contains both joy and sorrow concerning the Northern Kingdom. The immediately preceding section (Jer. 31:1–6) is a distinct unit, another prophetic announcement of salvation. The prophet announces not only the return of the exiles from Samaria, but also the reunification of all the tribes at Zion. The passage that follows (Jer. 31:15–22) is the poignant lament of Rachel, mother of Benjamin and Joseph, for her children; that is, for the tribes descended from them.

The passage itself consists of two parts that likely arose as two separate prophetic speeches, verses 7–9 and verses 10–14. The addressees of the first part are not specified, but the prophet hears God announcing that those who are scattered will be returned. Even the ones least able to travel—the blind, the lame, pregnant women, and women in labor (v. 8)—will make the journey. The language of care and concern is particularly strong, as seen in Yahweh's affirmation that he is Israel's "father" (v. 9; see also Deut. 32:6 and Hos. 11).

In verses 10–14, the prophet addresses the (foreign) nations with a summons to hear. They are to hear the news that the one who scattered Israel will gather them, and Israel will come and sing in Zion (v. 12). Mourning will be turned into joy (v. 13), and celebrations will break out. Faces will shine in the presence of the Lord's goodness, and food will be abundant (v. 12). The prophet's point of view is Jerusalem, and even the temple on Mt. Zion. He seems to envision a reunion of the long-divided people in the Holy City.

The central motif of our reading is the redemption of a lost people. In verse 11, redemption and ransom are used as synonymous expressions. Both refer to the practice of reclaiming a possession or a person left in pledge for a debt or from slavery. The people are assumed to be owned by another, a foreign nation. Only Yahweh can ransom or redeem them, although there is no reference to a price paid. Yahweh, like a loving father (v. 9), will reclaim his firstborn. The view is a corporate one, with the firstborn standing for the people. What is their response? They are only to return when released and join in the joyful celebration of their reunion.

Sirach 24:1–12

Few biblical books give us more information about its author than the The Wisdom of Jesus the Son of Sirach, also called the Book of Ecclesiasticus. The author, Ben Sirach, was a wisdom teacher who conducted a school in Jerusalem in the early second century BC. On the basis of information that he gives us, as well as the report by his grandson, who translated the book into Greek (see the Prologue), the original composition of the book can be dated shortly before 180 BC. This places the author and his audience in the Hellenistic period, before the Maccabean wars, but in a time when there must have been conflict between Jewish and Greek ideas and religious practices. The somewhat polemical tone at points, insisting that divine wisdom belongs to his people in Jerusalem (24:8–12), should be read in the light of that conflict.

Ecclesiasticus is wisdom literature, similar both in style and point of view to the Book of Proverbs. It includes a great many sayings like those in Proverbs 10–31, and a number of more extended discourses similar to the ones in Proverbs 1–9, Ecclesiastes, and Job. Although sayings and discourses on similar topics are grouped together, attempts to discern the organization of the composition have been less than satisfactory. The author considers wisdom in many different ways—as practical knowledge gained from experience and tradition, and as an abstract and universal phenomenon.

The reading for the day is selected from an extended discourse on the nature of wisdom that includes 24:1–25:11. The immediate context is Sirach 24:1–22, in which personified wisdom herself is the speaker.

Wisdom's speech, rich in allusions to Old Testament traditions, gives an account of the relationship between wisdom and the world in general and Israel in particular. It combines history of salvation motifs with attention to nature and creation, as Ben Sirach frequently does throughout the book.

Verses 1–2 introduce the speech itself and the speaker, personified wisdom. Such personification of wisdom, always as a female figure, is well-known in both earlier and later literature (Prov. 8:22–36; Wisd. of Sol. 6:12–20; 8:1ff.). Her intention here is to praise herself. She is pictured as standing before and addressing two audiences at once: "her people," that is, Israel; and "the assembly of the Most High." That assembly is mentioned elsewhere in the Old Testament as well as in other ancient Near Eastern literature. The scene pictured is the divine throne room, with the lesser deities or messengers in the presence of God (Isa. 6; Ps. 89:6–7; 1 Kings 22:19–23).

Wisdom's speech itself recalls her cosmic origins (vv. 3–6), her special relationship to Israel (vv. 7–12), her growth like every good plant (vv. 13–17), and concludes with an appeal to follow her (vv. 18–22).

Particularly important when this passage is considered along with the Prologue to John is the language of verse 3. That wisdom "came forth from the mouth of the Most High" suggests a parallel to the word (Greek *logos*) of God present before creation. Elsewhere in the book, God is said to have accomplished by his words what is attributed here to wisdom (42:15). The background of this passage certainly is to be found in the accounts of creation in both Genesis 1 and 2, where God creates by word. The "mist" is an allusion to Genesis 2:6. A more fully developed view of personified wisdom as God's activity in the world is found in Wisdom of Solomon 7:22–8:1. In that same book, the identification of wisdom and the word of God is quite explicit (9:1–2).

Verses 13–17 give a virtual catalogue of good plants as analogies for the growth and development of wisdom in the good soil of the people of Israel. This series of metaphors picks up on the motif of planting in verse 12 and sets the stage for wisdom's call in verse 19 to "eat your fill of my fruits."

Whereas verses 3–6 emphasize the cosmic presence of wisdom, verses 7–12 affirm that she found her true home among a particular people, Israel, and in a specific place, Jerusalem. The point of that claim is not reached until after wisdom's speech is concluded: "All this is the book of the covenant of the Most High God, the law that Moses commanded us" (24:23). That is, wisdom and the law amount to the same. Thus the major concern of the passage is divine revelation. How is God present and known in the world by human beings? God is known in and through wisdom present in creation, and specifically through the revealed law. Through faithfulness to the law of Moses one knows God.

Psalm 147:12–20

Psalm 147 is comprised of three sections that give the impression of being distinct units (vv. 1–6, 7–11, and 12–20). In fact, the ancient Greek translation treats the psalm as two compositions (vv. 1–11 = Ps. 146; vv. 12–20 = Ps. 147). The themes of the return to and restoration of Jerusalem are so persuasive in the psalm that the Greek translators associated it (or both) with the prophets of the return, namely, Haggai and Zechariah.

The blessing and restoration of Zion (Jerusalem) or the creation of a new Jerusalem run as themes throughout most of the reading for this Sunday. A second theme is God's sending of the word (or wisdom) into the world. We can analyze Psalm 147:12–20 around these two themes.

1. Verses 12–14 call upon Zion to praise God (v. 12) and then offer reasons for that praise (vv. 13–14). The city is divinely protected (v. 13*a*), and amid her streets the children play (v. 13*b*). Although these two ideas may not seem to go together, they do, because security for the present provides assurance for the future, for the children to have a chance to grow to maturity. Verse 14*a* parallels verse 13*a*, and verse 14*b* does the same for verse 13*b*. God provides peace throughout Jerusalem's realm (as well as protection for the city) and fills the land with wheat (so that its children may eat and grow).

2. Verses 15–20 speak of the word, its sending forth, and its residency with Jacob. God's word (or command/utterance) is described as an active agent. Along with the snow, the frost, the ice, the cold, God gives his word, which has the power to melt the frozen; God breathes and the waters flow. The world of nature is at the mercy, is the active respondent, to the divine word.

But to Israel, God has acted in a unique way: to Jacob/Israel God has given his statutes and ordinances, the embodiment of the word. One of the psalm's fragments found among the Qumran (Dead Sea) Scrolls has the following reading for verse 20*ab*: "He has not dealt thus with any other nation; nor made known to them the ordinances." In the word, God came and comes unto God's own.

Wisdom of Solomon 10:15–21

The Wisdom of Solomon was composed in Greek, probably in the Egyptian city of Alexandria, by a pious Jewish intellectual living in the Diaspora. Its date is uncertain, although the late first century BC has been suggested by many scholars. More philosophical than most of the other wisdom books, it finds its closest parallels in Proverbs 1–9, especially chapter 8.

In The Wisdom of Solomon 10:1–11:4, the examples of eight lives are treated—seven positively and one negatively—to illustrate how wisdom, understood as a female cosmic figure, brought salvation and the good life: Adam (10:1–2), Cain (10:3), Noah (10:4), Abraham (10:5), Lot (10:6–8), Jacob (10:9–12), Joseph (10:13–14), and Moses (10:15–11:4). The last of these biographical vignettes provides the context for this lection.

In this version of the Exodus, it is wisdom that plays the role of redeemer and guide for the Israelite people. She delivers from oppression, enters the soul of Moses, and performs the task of leading the people from bondage and through the wilderness. Wisdom tends to assume the place occupied by the Deity in the Exodus account of the events. Verse 20, with its reference to "O Lord," suggests that wisdom and God, however, are not completely identified in this text.

That this book may have been intended for apologetic purposes in defense of Judaism in an alien Hellenistic climate is indicated by two factors. (1) Israel is described in extraordinarily glowing terms: a blameless race, a holy people, and the righteous. (2) None of Israel's faults—murmuring, and so forth—that characterize the Exodus account are even referred to in this particular section.

Wisdom in this text, like the Word (Logos) in John's prologue, is the guiding, unifying principle emanating from and doing the work of God.

Ephesians 1:3–14

This text also serves as the epistolary reading for Proper 10 in Year B. Related portions of the passage serve as epistolary lessons at other points in the liturgical year: Ephesians 1:11–23 for All Saints Day in Year C and Ephesians 1:15–23 for Ascension in all three years. The reader may want to consult our remarks in these other settings.

Even though today's Gospel and Epistle readings differ in many respects, they agree in one fundamental respect: the story of Christ began before the world began. If John's Prologue focuses on the person of Christ "in the beginning," this epistolary prayer sees the saving work of God as having begun before time. We are told that even "before the world was made, [God] chose us in Christ" (v. 4, NJB). This can easily be understood as a further development of Paul's theology of election (Rom. 8:29; cf. 2 Thess. 2:13). Here our own calling, or election, by God becomes an extension of Christ's own vocation. Elsewhere in John's Gospel, Christ claims to have been given God's glory even before the world was founded (John 17:24). It is a theme later echoed in the early Christian confession that Christ was "destined before the foundation of the world, but was revealed at the end of the ages for [our] sake" (1 Pet. 1:20).

In an important sense, the Epistle to the Ephesians pushes beyond the Johannine Prologue to insist not only that the story of Christ, but the story of our own salvation as well, began before the world began. How we experienced this blessing from heaven is spelled out through the use of several images and metaphors.

First, as already noted, our salvation is viewed as divine election. Naturally, the notion of election is thoroughly grounded in Old Testament thought, but here it is not the election of a people on earth but of a people in heaven before the beginning of time.

Second, our salvation is viewed as sacrificial purification: God chose us to be "holy and blameless" (v. 4; cf. 5:27; Col. 1:22).

Third, our salvation is viewed as being incorporated into God's family. We were destined even from the beginning to be the children of God (v. 5; cf. John 1:12; Gal. 3:26; 1 John 3:1). To be sure, ours is an adopted status (v. 5, NIV, JB), made possible "through Jesus Christ," God's beloved Son through whom God lavishly bestowed divine grace.

So construed, our salvation gives us access to "blessings in the heavenly places" (v. 3). Put another way, God "has blessed us with all the spiritual blessings of heaven in Christ" (v. 3, NJB). Everything that was theoretically possible in heaven became actual through Christ. For this reason, God is the object of our prayers of thanksgiving. Hence the prayer opens with a prayer of blessing: "Blessed be God" (v. 3). It is a form of prayer deeply rooted in Jewish thought and practice, reminiscent of prayers offered by David (1 Kings 1:48; 1 Chron. 29:10–19), Hiram (1 Kings 5:7; cf. 2 Chron. 2:12), Solomon (1 Kings 8:15), the psalmist (Pss. 18:46; 28:6; 106:1; 144:1, etc.), Daniel (Dan. 2:20–23), Tobias (Tob. 8:5), Tobit (Tob. 13:1–17), Sarah (Tob. 3:11–15), Raguel (Tob. 8:15–17), and later, of Zechariah (Luke 1:68). It becomes a standard form of epistolary prayer (2 Cor. 1:3; 1 Pet. 1:3).

Especially worth noting in this prayer is the recurrent emphasis on what God has done. This is seen in the numerous actions attributed to God in our behalf: God has blessed us (v. 3), chosen us (v. 4), foreordained, or "pre-selected" us (v. 5; cf. v. 9), bestowed grace on us (vv. 6 and 8), revealed to us the contents of the divine mysytery (v. 9), energized us (v. 11), and finally sealed us through the Holy Spirit (v. 13). These generous acts of God performed in our behalf prompt this prayer of praise; and rightly so, because praise is the appropriate way for us to acknowledge what God has done.

Although this opening prayer of praise abounds in language about God's activity, in a post-Christmas setting its emphasis on Christ as the locus of God's activity can well be appropriated. One way of grasping this is to note the number of times the phrase "in Christ" occurs (vv. 3, 4, 6, 7, 9, 11, 13; also cf. vv. 5, 12). In one sense, the prayer unfolds the story of how God's actions, even from the beginning of time, were moving in the direction of Christ.

John 1:(1–9) 10–18

All of today's readings proclaim God's visiting us with favor, but the Prologue to John's Gospel is of central importance to Christian history, Christian doctrine, and the understanding of the life of faith. The Gospel lesson for Christmas, Third Proper (second additional lesson) was John 1:1–14, and the preacher is referred to those comments for use here, especially if that lection was not treated in a Christmas service. We will here add to the earlier discussion only comments on verses 14–18, which constitute a unit that concludes the Prologue as a literary piece distinct from the narrative beginning at verse 19.

Before proceeding, however, the preacher will want to decide whether to treat verses 1–9 as optional. If John 1:1–14 was used at Christmas, avoiding some repetition would justify exer-cizing such an option. Omitting verses 1–9 would also allow for moving away from the pre-incarnational work of God's Word (vv. 1–5) and the preparatory work of John the Baptist (vv. 6–8) in order to focus on the incarnation of the Word and its benefits for the world. Or more simply, one might use only verses 10–18 in order to attend to a more manageable portion of Scripture. Some preachers avoid John 1:1–18 altogether because its theological and philo-sophical sweep of thought is so intimidatingly immense. As stated above, we refer the reader to the earlier treatment of verses 1–14 and here focus only on verses 14–18.

Verses 14–18 make the following three statements:

1. "And the Word *became flesh*" is a christological affirmation of a radical nature with far-reaching implications for our thinking about God, life in the world, and what it means to be Christian. Analogies about changing clothes, as in the stories of a king who wears peasant clothing in order to move among his subjects freely, are not adequate for clarifying John 1:14. The church has always had members who wanted to protect their Christ from John 1:14 with phrases such as "seemed to be," "appeared," and "in many ways was like"

flesh. Whatever else John 1:14 means, it does state without question the depth, the intensity, and the pursuit of God's love for the world.

2. John 1:14–18 is a confessional statement. Notice the use of "us" and "we." The eyes of faith have seen God's glory in Jesus of Nazareth, but not everyone has. At the time of this Gospel, the Baptist sect (v. 15) and the synagogue (v. 17) were viable religious groups, and they did not see the glory. Faith hears, sees, and testifies, but faith is not arrogant or imperialistic, as though its view were so obvious as to be embraced by all but the very obstinate. Faith involves a searching (Rabbi, where do you live? 1:38), a response to an offer (Come and see. 1:39), a hunger (14:8), a willingness to obey (7:17). Nothing about Jesus Christ is so publicly apparent as to rob faith of its risk, its choice, and its courage. Faith exists among alternatives.

3. The observation above in no way means that faith must be tentative and quiet about its central affirmation that the God whom no one has seen (v. 18) is both known and available in Jesus Christ. Jesus reveals God (v. 18) and makes God available to us (v. 14) in gracious ways (v. 16). Believing in Jesus is not simply adding another belief to one's belief in God; it is also having one's belief in God modified, clarified, and informed by what is seen in the person and work of Jesus. Jesus' statement "Whoever has seen me has seen the Father" (14:9) does not simply tell us what Jesus is like but what God is like, and to know God is life eternal (17:4).

Epiphany

Isaiah 60:1–6;
Psalm 72:1–7, 10–14;
Ephesians 3:1–12;
Matthew 2:1–12

Epiphany themes dominate these classic texts that have come to be used for this day. Images of light, glory, and brightness are introduced in the Old Testament reading from Isaiah, and they are counterbalanced by the double reference to darkness in verse 2. Isaiah 60:6 is the background for the Gospel account of the gifts of the Magi. Universal manifestation of God's glorious light is also indicated by the reference to the nations who would come to see the light. In the psalm, it is the universal recognition of the righteous king's dominion that especially commends the text for this day. The manifestation of God's revelation to the Gentiles is the key theme sounded in the epistolary reading. The Gospel lesson, which records the visit of the Magi, has become the Gospel reading most closely associated with the Epiphany. In narrative form, we see the impact of the Christ Child reaching to the distant East, thus symbolizing his manifestation to the Gentiles.

Isaiah 60:1–6

Our reading begins a major section in the collection of prophetic and liturgical materials commonly identified as Third Isaiah. Chapters 60–62 contain a series of promises and announcements of Jerusalem's salvation and restoration. They are addressed to or concern the inhabitants of Judah and Jerusalem, and probably stem from early in the postexilic period, not long after exiles began to return from Babylon. The temple is either under construction or recently completed. As Haggai 2:1–9 indicates, the community that began to reestablish itself on the ruins of Jerusalem soon became discouraged that the restoration was not all they expected, especially given the dramatic vision of Second Isaiah (Isa. 40–55). Isaiah 60 seems to be addressed to that discouragement, proclaiming the future glory of Jerusalem.

The entire passage, indeed virtually all of chapter 60, is addressed to Jerusalem. The verbs of the initial verse, "arise," "shine," are feminine singular, appropriate for addressing the city personified as a woman. Thus the "you" throughout is Zion, standing also for its inhabitants. It is not so easy to identify the speaker of the lines. In verses 7, 10, and 15–18, the one who says "I" surely is Yahweh. However, in verses 1, 6, and 9, Yahweh is mentioned in the third person, suggesting a prophetic speaker. This alternation of speaker probably is not evidence for multiple authorship, but rather the relatively free movement from direct to indirect account of Yahweh's message for the people.

In terms of literary genre, the poem is a particular kind of announcement of salvation, one with strong eschatological overtones and contents. It does not concern the last things in the narrow sense, but does anticipate a dramatic transformation in historical circumstances. Attention does not focus upon a particular event, as in Second Isaiah's announcement of the end of the exile and the return of the captives, but on a new set of circumstances in and for Jerusalem.

The two parts of the passage correspond generally to the two major themes associated in Christian liturgical tradition with Epiphany. Verses 1–3 proclaim the manifestation of God's presence, the appearance of God at a particular time and place in history, thus contributing to reflection on the Incarnation. Verses 4–6—the original unit goes at least through verse 7 and more likely through verse 9—picks up and develops the motif already introduced in verse 3, the pilgrimage of the Gentiles to see the appearance of the Lord. Epiphany came to be associated with the visit of the Magi, and then in some traditions with the proclamation of the Gospel to the nations.

Images of light and darkness dominate the first three verses. "Light" symbolizes life, salvation, and joy, where darkness represents death (see Isa. 9:2; Ps. 23:4). The theme of the arrival of light is stated in verse 1 and repeated in verse 2, against the background of the darkness. In verse 3, nations now are seen to come to Jerusalem's light. The appearance of the light is the same as the arrival of "the glory of the Lord." Unusual here is that this glory, or the Lord himself (v. 2), "has risen," "will arise." More typically, in the accounts of the appearance of the Lord the imagery speaks of his coming down. The metaphor clearly is that of the rising sun. But, lest one identify Yahweh with any heavenly body, the concluding part of the poem is quite explicit in insisting that Yahweh—and not the sun or moon—will be "your everlasting light" (60:19).

The light of God's presence will shine on Jerusalem, and it will then be the light that attracts nations from their darkness (v. 3). This picture seems indebted to Second Isaiah's proclamation that the servant Israel will become a "light to the nations" (Isa. 42:6).

In verses 4–6, Jerusalem is called to behold all those streaming to her. The nations are coming, and they are bringing her children back. She will rejoice like a mother reunited with her sons and daughters. Moreover, the nations will bring their material wealth to Jerusalem. "Abundance of the sea" (v. 5) doubtless means goods brought by ship. Verses 6 and 7 concern goods brought by land, especially from Arabia. Midian and Ephah would have been traders from Northern Arabia. Sheba was further to the south. All this reference to material wealth is hyperbole, to be sure, but it is quite specific. Many of the items mentioned were important to the temple, either for decoration (gold), for rituals (frankincense), or for offerings (flocks, rams). Jerusalem becomes a world center, and not just for religious observances. There are economic and political dimensions as well.

Epiphany is a time of light, the light of the Lord's presence. This text suggests two directions for meditation on the appearance of that light in the darkness. One is simply to celebrate and give thanks. The other is to consider how those upon whom the light has shined are to enlighten the darkness around them in the world.

Psalm 72:1–7, 10–14

A portion of this psalm was the responsorial psalm for the Second Sunday of Advent. Today's verses are also the psalm selection for Epiphany during all three years of the lectionary cycle.

Epiphany, in the Western tradition, commemorates several themes: the visit of the Magi, the first manifestation of Jesus to the non-Jewish, Gentile world represented by the Magi, and the church's missionary work in the modern world. Psalm 72 shares in this universal perspective and in seeing an interrelationship of the Jewish people with non-Jewish nations.

Psalm 72 was no doubt written as the community's intercessory prayer offered on behalf of the Davidic king at his coronation and/or the annual celebration of the king's rule. Perhaps no other text in the Old Testament gives such an elevated and yet humane portrayal of (or perhaps longing for) the ideal Davidic ruler. The monarch is depicted in this text as the embodiment of justice and compassion, as the inaugurator of a new era.

As an intercession, the psalm requests and petitions the Deity for many things, all mediated through the monarch. One of these, and thus the psalm's use on Epiphany Sunday, is the request for a universal rule, for a dominion that extends throughout the inhabited world (vv. 8–11). A number of geographical expressions are employed to speak of this dominion: "from sea to sea," "from the River to the ends of the earth," "Tarshish and of the isles," and "Sheba and Seba." The first two expressions are mythological in background and are used metaphorically to denote the entire world. The last two refer to the regions to the distant west of Palestine and to the distant lands to the east, respectively. The basis for such cosmic claims on behalf of the Judean monarch was the belief in God as creator. As creator of the world, God could make his earthly representative ruler of the world. Thus the doctrine of creation undergirded the extravagant claims of the Davidic monarch and gave birth to the hope of a universal rule for the Messiah.

Three actions by the nations are requested in the prayer, all expressing and demonstrating subordination to the Davidic ruler. Although all three are practically synonymous, one may detect a difference in the sources of the imagery. One (v. 9) is drawn from the area of warfare and denotes the surrender of a foe and the submission of an enemy. The one representation we possess of an Israelite king appears on the Black Obelisk of the Assyrian king Shalmaneser III (858–824 BC). On this inscription, the Israelite king Jehu (in about 841 BC) is shown kissing the ground ("licking the dust") at Shalmaneser's feet. We know from the accompanying inscription that Jehu surrendered to the Assyrians. The second image (in v. 10) is that of paying tribute and bringing gifts to remain on peaceful terms. Throughout history, subordination to a superior state was always shown in the Middle East by the (generally annual) giving of gifts by the inferior. Finally, verse 11 draws on the practice of common protocol at the royal court. Bowing was the appropriate posture to greet the appearance of the king. Is it any wonder that the New Testament describes the veneration of the Magi with the story of their bringing gifts?

Ephesians 3:1–12

E piphany is a time when we celebrate the manifestation of the gospel to the nations. Indeed, the word *epiphany* means "manifestation." It suggests that something obscure becomes manifest. What was veiled is now unveiled; what was hidden is now revealed. Ignorance gives way to knowledge, darkness to light, hiddenness to openness.

It may be obvious to us that Gentiles should be a part of the people of God, but this was not always the case. Nor was it inevitable that the church would include both Jews and Gentiles as equals. It only looks obvious and inevitable to us now because the controversy over this question has come and gone, the agonizing conflict is over. It may be difficult for us to believe that it ever occurred.

Such complacency is foreign to today's text. True, the inclusion of the Gentiles is viewed as an event of the past, a conflict the church had already absorbed into its history. But rather than being viewed as a routine event, it is seen as a matter of wonderment. How the Gentiles came to be a part of the people of God is viewed here as nothing less than a miracle of cosmic proportion.

We should note, first, that the language of mystery is used to capture the true significance of these events. That the Gentiles should be incorporated into the people of God is "the mystery hidden for ages in God" (v. 9). In Jewish apocalyptic, it was common to depict the will of God as hidden behind a veil, enshrouded in mystery, locked up, as it were, until the appropriate time for unveiling occurs. Conceived in this way, the "mystery" could be presented as hidden from human eyes in previous generations (v. 5; cf. Rom. 16:25; 1 Cor. 2:7; Col. 1:26). It was known to God but hidden from human view.

But the mystery has now been unveiled. What was once hidden and unknown "has now been revealed to his holy apostles and prophets by the Spirit" (v. 5). The time has come in the divine economy (*oikonomia*, vv. 2, 9) for God to uncover what has been hidden. The use of the term *oikonomia* should be noted. It is an expression difficult to render in English: "plan" (NRSV), "administration" (NIV). The term suggests a planned order, an organized scheme for accomplishing a specific purpose (cf. 1:9–10; Col. 1:25; 1 Cor. 9:17; also 4:1). The point is that God's decision to include the Gentiles in the plan of salvation was not an afterthought. It was part of God's overall purpose and scheme from the very beginning. It was "according to the plan which he had formed from all eternity in Christ Jesus our Lord" (v. 11, NJB).

We should also note Paul's relationship to this mystery. According to verse 1, he is imprisoned for Christ on behalf of the Gentiles. His special vocation was to preach the gospel to the Gentiles (v. 8; cf. Gal. 1:16; 2:7; 1 Tim. 2:7; Acts 9:15). He has been charged with this task even though his previous record as the church's archenemy made him the least likely candidate. Accordingly, he was the "very least of all the saints" (v. 8), the "least of the apostles" (1 Cor. 15:9–10; 1 Tim. 1:15). Yet he had received an unusually generous measure of God's grace in being selected as a minister of the gospel (v. 7; cf. Rom. 1:5; 12:3, 6; 15:15–16; 1 Cor. 3:10; Gal. 2:9; Col. 1:25). It was grace bestowed "by the working of his power" (v. 7). For this task he strove "with all the energy that [God] powerfully inspires within [him]" (Col. 1:29; also Phil. 4:13).

All this suggests that Paul was seized by the power of God to make known the mystery of salvation to the Gentiles. For him it was not volunteer work. He did not come to the task as a seeker. Rather, God had sought him out, and he had responded involuntarily. It was not a matter of choice, but compulsion (1 Cor. 9:16–17). His insight into this mystery came as the result of revelation (v. 3; Gal. 1:12). In this respect, he stands in the succession of his predecessors, the "holy apostles and prophets" (v. 5; cf. 2:20).

The essence of the mystery was that the Gentiles now had a full share in God's blessing. Along with the Jews, Gentiles were now full heirs of the divine promise (Gal. 3:29). They were no longer stepchildren, but children with all the privileges of heirs (Rom. 8:17). No longer were they outside the body; they were now organically related to the body of Christ

(2:16–18). No longer aliens, they were citizens with all the rights and privileges of full membership.

With this newfound status as full members of the people of God comes full access to God's promises (v. 12; 2:18; also John 14:6; 1 John 3:21). This makes it possible to come to God with "boldness and confidence" (v. 12; cf. Heb. 3:6; 4:16; 10:19, 35).

In retrospect, we can hardly believe that it should have been otherwise. What was once hardly imaginable now appears obvious. In commenting on a theory that had received the Nobel Prize, one observer noted, "What first is thought to be wrong is later shown to be obvious." That pagans should be included in God's plan was first thought by some to be impossible, indeed morally wrong. Now it appears to be obvious. The conviction of to-day's text is that through the church it is now possible to see "how comprehensive God's wisdom really is" (v. 10, JB). In God's plan there has emerged a new humanity, a form of fellowship that knows no inequities, no barriers. At least, this is the vision. In reality, it remains an unfulfilled promise, and this is why Epiphany is still celebrated. We need to be reminded of the profound impact the gospel has had in, and on, the world. But we also need to be reminded that its impact is still not fully realized. Thus the message of Christ must continue to have manifest witness among all peoples.

Matthew 2:1–12

The Season of Epiphany is the time of the church's proclamation of the appearance or manifestation of Christ to Israel and to the nations. The word *epiphany* transliterates a Greek verb meaning "to be manifest, to appear openly" (Titus 2:11). Antiochus, a pre-Christian Syrian ruler, impressed with his own power, assumed the name Antiochus Epiphanes as a declaration that he was the appearance of a god on earth. During this season, the church proclaims Christ Epiphanes, and appropriately enough, the Gospel lesson to launch this season each year is Matthew 2:1–12. In this text, Matthew says that even in infancy the Christ Child stirred a capital city, disturbed a reigning king, and attracted foreigners to come and worship.

It is clear that Matthew intends 2:1 to begin a new cycle of stories (ending at v. 23) rather than continue the birth story of 1:18–25. Literarily speaking, the birth story has its own conclusion (v. 25), and the account of the visit of the wise men (NRSV; "astrologers" in REB) has its own introduction (2:1). This separation of the two stories is important lest there be frustrating and futile attempts to interweave and harmonize Luke's nativity (2:1–20) and Matthew's story of the Magi. Chronologically speaking, Matthew 2:1–12 carries clues that this is not a nativity but a childhood story. The REB has "after his birth" instead of the more vague "after Jesus was born" (NRSV). Add to this the time needed for traveling from the East, the fact that Mary and the child were in a house (v. 11), and the age of children to be killed in Herod's attempt to destroy the child (v. 16), and one gets the clear sense that Matthew's Magi and Luke's shepherds do not arrive in Bethlehem at the same time. The Eastern church has long stressed the Feast of Three Kings and Epiphany as distinct from Christmas. In fact, Epiphany is the greater festival, to which Christmas is prelude. Such a distinction between the festivals sets the church and the preacher free to attend to the different emphases in Luke and Matthew, to leave Luke's stable and shepherds and to see the Christ Child among the powerful and rich. One cannot miss the echoes of the Moses story, the child who found himself among the powerful and rich of Egypt (Exod. 2) and who later became the deliverer of God's people.

Matthew 2:1–12 carries within it more echoes than simply those from Exodus 2. The general culture, religious and secular, contained many stories to the effect that the birth of a great ruler would be accompanied by celestial signs. In the Old Testament, a strange seer from the East, Balaam, spoke of a star arising out of Jacob (Num. 24:17). Isaiah 60:1–6 announced the coming of kings from distant lands with gifts of gold and frankincense, paying homage to Israel's God. All this is to say that Matthew had available the threads with which to weave the rich tapestry of this much-loved story.

But Matthew is not simply telling a beautiful story; he is making several theological statements. First, by the use of his familiar quotation formula "so it has been written by the prophet" (v. 5), Matthew shows that Jesus qualifies as the Davidic ruler to be born in David's city of Bethlehem (Mic. 5:2). Jesus is the one who fulfills God's promise to Israel.

Second, Jesus not only is the one to "govern my people Israel," but he also is the one to draw all nations to Israel's God. Some readers of Matthew are so struck by the use of Matthew's promise/fulfillment pattern that they forget that the promise in the Old Testament included Gentiles as well as Jews. Ruth, Jonah, Isaiah (2:1–3; 9:1–2), and other texts declare this plainly, and Matthew picks up on this theme of the mission to the nations (4:14–16; 28:18–20). In today's reading, the coming of the wise men to worship the Christ Child symbolizes the coming of the nations. This story functions for Matthew as the story of the coming of the Greeks does for the Fourth Evangelist (John 12:20–32); that is, as a symbolic announcement of the mission to the nations.

A third theological statement made by Matthew in this story is that these events are providentially guided. We are not here reading of good fortune, happy coincidences, and historical accidents. Jesus is the son of God, king of the Jews, and Davidic ruler. It is no surprise, then, that his life is not only divinely begun (1:18–25), but announced with extraordinary signs and preserved providentially from the threats of a jealous tyrant. Matthew thereby creates in the reader a sense of praise and gratitude, along with high expectation for the story that will now unfold.

Baptism of the Lord
(First Sunday After the Epiphany)

Isaiah 42:1–9;
Psalm 29;
Acts 10:34–43;
Matthew 3:13–17

The Old Testament reading is provided by the first Servant Song from Isaiah, which has long been recognized as informing the Synoptic account of the baptism of Jesus. Its emphasis on the bestowal of the Spirit on God's chosen one is clearly echoed in Matthew's account of Jesus' baptism, the Gospel lesson for today. Compared with the parallel accounts in Mark and Luke, the Matthean account is quite distinctive, with its more extended dialogue between John and Jesus. Psalm 29 is used for this day in all three years because of its repeated emphasis on the voice of the Lord and the various ways it breaks through the natural order to be heard. It provides an excellent background against which to interpret the heavenly voice confirming the identity of Jesus as God's chosen one at his baptism. The second lesson for this day is provided from the Book of Acts in all three years. Today's selection is Peter's sermon to the household of Cornelius, remarkable as a rare mention of the baptism of Jesus outside the Gospels.

Isaiah 42:1–9

This text is also the Old Testament reading for Monday of Holy Week. At that point in the Christian year, it serves to characterize the obedience of Jesus as God's servant and to set the events of that week in an eschatological context, the ultimate reign of God. On this day in the year, celebrating the baptism of the Lord, the emphasis will be upon the designation and confirmation of the servant of God.

Isaiah 42:1–9 consists of two originally independent units, the first of the Servant Songs in verses 1–4 and a distinct prophetic speech in verses 5–9. Both parts were composed by Second Isaiah shortly before the end of the Exile in 538 BC. The combination of the two units addresses one of the perennial problems in the interpretation of the Servant Songs, namely, the identity of the servant. Although the answer to that question is unclear within the song itself, the following verses interpret the servant as the people of Israel (vv. 6–7).

The Servant Song in verses 1–4 is the first of four such poetic passages in Second Isaiah; the others are Isaiah 49:1–6; 50:4–11; 52:13–53:12. It has the form of a public proclamation in which Yahweh is the speaker, introducing the servant. The audience is not identified; it may have been Israel as a whole, the nations, or the heavenly council presumed in Isaiah 40:1–8. The answer depends to some extent upon the identification of the servant. The proclamation has the force of ordination, indicating first that God has chosen this particular one, and second, the purpose for which he was chosen. Thus the form and the contents make it explicit that the servant's role is an extension or embodiment of the divine intention. Designation by conferring God's spirit applies to leaders, including kings, and to prophets. What the servant does and how he accomplishes it have the divine blessing, authority, and power to accomplish God's purposes.

This servant has a particularly intimate relationship to the one who has chosen him. The only reason given for the election of this servant is God's love: "in whom my soul delights" (v. 1). The Hebrew word for "soul" here refers simply to the self, so REB accurately translates, "in whom I take delight." He is characterized as gentle, perhaps in contrast to the ancient prophets or the kings of Israel and Judah, and persistent in the pursuit of his responsibilities.

Although debate about the identity of the servant is likely to continue, there is no doubt about his role. It is stated three times that he is to "bring forth justice" (vv. 1, 3, 4). "Justice" (*mishpat*) is one of the most fundamental categories in the prophetic tradition. It characterizes the fair and equitable behavior of human beings in society, established with due process in law, administered without discrimination, and based on the just will of Yahweh. To establish justice is to establish the reign of God. The word in the present context refers primarily to the administration of justice, the promulgation of a just order in society. NJPSV translates in all three instances "true way."

Another key term for understanding the role of the servant is "law" (v. 4), the traditional translation of the Hebrew *torah*. The concept was deeply ingrained in Israel's view of its relationship to its God. In one sense, it is the instruction in covenant responsibilities given by the priests. Thus the NEB, REB, and NJPSV read here "teaching." Eventually it came to mean the whole body of divine revelation, embodied in the first five books of the Bible. Instruction in and the interpretation of the covenant stipulations are necessary for the establishment of justice. Consequently, whereas the servant's role is similar in some ways to both priests who were responsible for instruction and prophets who proclaimed God's word, the role is most like that of a king who administers the law.

The ordination of the servant looks to a time when all people will live in the same just order. The song does not seem to envision a dramatic day when all things will be transformed suddenly, but a gradual promulgation of justice until it includes the world.

The second unit (vv. 5–9) is introduced by a prophetic messenger formula ("Thus says God, the Lord"), elaborated by means of a series of participial clauses characterizing the Lord (v. 5), who then speaks (vv. 6–9). Yahweh speaks directly to an audience in the second person. That audience is the people of Israel, shown here to have roles and responsibilities quite like those given to the servant of the Lord in the previous unit. The style of the passage is both hymnic and persuasive, even somewhat argumentative at the end. There are points to be made, and it is assumed that the hearers need to be convinced.

These verses organize the main theological themes of Second Isaiah almost systematically. Yahweh is introduced as the creator of the earth and all who dwell in it, giver of the breath of life (v. 1). Then there is the election and redemption of Israel (v. 6a), with allusions to both the past and to the coming release from Babylonian captivity. Next, the chosen people are reminded of their role and responsibility toward the rest of the world

(vv. 6b–7). Belief in creation by a single God and in the election of a particular people lead our prophet to the obvious conclusion that those chosen people are called to be "a light to the nations." Israel's call is not laid out as duty, but as the response to gifts received. Then the prophet returns to the initial concern with the authority of Yahweh, with polemical asides against "idols" (v. 8). The section concludes with the reminder that this God is doing new things, and one can believe in the promise of new things because in the past God had announced the future through his prophets, and it happened as God said it would.

One of the most critical expressions in the passage is also enigmatic. What does it mean that Israel is given as "a covenant to the people" (v. 6)? The words may be read "covenant-people" (NJPSV). The term (berit) could refer to the stipulations of the covenant, that is, the laws that stipulate the right human behavior. Thus the role of Israel would parallel that of the servant in verse 4, the establishment of justice based on the law. It could indicate that through Israel God establishes a worldwide covenant, including all humankind. Given the fact that "covenant to the people" parallels "light to the nations," it seems likely that both of these meanings are intended. Israel, teaching the will of God and thereby bringing all peoples into a covenant with the one creator, enlightens the world.

Psalm 29

The open heavens, the voice of God, and the imagery of water are all features in the narratives of Jesus' baptism and play roles in this event depicted as the affirmation of his messiahship. A similar set of images is found in Psalm 29 and explains the choice of this psalm for this Sunday throughout the three years of the cycle.

When the ancient rabbis read this psalm, they noticed the eighteen occurrences of the divine name Yahweh ("the Lord" in the NRSV) and saw these as paralleling and even providing the basis for their eighteen benedictions used in synagogue worship and private devotions.

The repetitive quality of the psalm is further evidenced in the sevenfold repetition of the term "voice" (of the Lord). Such repetitions indicate an artistic effort and a desire to overwhelm the hearer with a certain emotional impact, an emotion focused on God and the divine voice.

The hearer of this psalm, like the listener to the account of Jesus' baptism, is not asked to become a part of the scene or a participant in the account. The significance of the action asks that the worshiper simply affirm what has been said and then live in the certainty of what has been affirmed.

Acts 10:34–43

Originally, Epiphany was a celebration focusing on the baptism of Christ. This was especially the case in the Eastern church from the third century onward. It eventually came to rank with Easter and Pentecost as one of the three major feasts of the church. In the West, Epiphany came to be associated less with the baptism of Christ and more with Christ's manifestation to the Gentiles, as symbolized in the visit of the Magi. Consequently, the observance of Epiphany in the West saw the disappearance of the consecration of the baptismal water that characterized the celebration of Epiphany in the East.

The Common Lectionary now clearly acknowledges this historical development in which the celebration of the Epiphany became separated from the celebration of the Lord's baptism. Today's texts concentrate exclusively on the latter. In each of the three liturgical years, the Second Reading is taken from the Book of Acts and relates to a significant baptism from the early church: Cornelius (Year A), the twelve disciples from Ephesus (Year B), and the Samaritans (Year C).

Today's second lesson consists of the summary of Peter's sermon to the Roman centurion Cornelius. This same text serves as the first option for the First Reading or the second option for the Second Reading for Easter Sunday in all three years. The reader may wish to consult our remarks on the text in its Easter setting.

What makes today's text especially appropriate in the context of celebrating the Lord's baptism is its explicit reference to "the baptism that John announced" (v. 37). Though it does not specifically say that Jesus was baptized by John, this is implied in the following phrase: "how God anointed Jesus of Nazareth with the Holy Spirit and with power" (v. 38). This is one of the few references outside the Gospels to Jesus' baptism (cf. Acts 1:21–22). The baptism of Jesus was regarded as the moment when God's Spirit was bestowed on him, as the narrative accounts of this event in the Gospels make clear (cf. Matt. 3:13–17; Mark 1:9–11; Luke 3:21–22). It was an anointing in the sense that Jesus received a measure of God's Spirit as a chrism that was poured out (cf. 4:27). As such, it was a bestowal of power.

It is common for the receiving of God's Spirit to be understood as an anointing. When Samuel anointed David with oil, he received a powerful infusion of the Lord's Spirit (1 Sam. 16:13). Similarly, at his Nazareth inaugural, Jesus applies Isaiah 61:1–2 to himself as he claims that the Lord's Spirit has anointed him to launch his prophetic mission (Luke 4:18). The Lord's baptism, then, is regarded as a singular moment of divine anointing, when God acknowledges Jesus as the beloved Son and signifies this by bestowing the Spirit.

This sermon summary, attributed to Peter, conforms to the story line of the Synoptic Gospels in seeing Jesus' baptism as the inauguration of his ministry. Even though it was widely recognized that the story of Jesus was a continuation of the Old Testament story and could be told as another chapter in the saga of significant figures, such as Abraham and Moses, here the first peg to be driven down is his baptism by John the Baptist. It is after this that Jesus embarks on his ministry of "doing good and healing" (v. 38). It is truly the inaugural event of his life and ministry, and for this reason was often seen in the early church as the moment when he really became the Son of God.

Today's text invites us to ask about the significance of the Lord's baptism. We see that it was above all an inaugural event, a time of beginning, which not only sets Jesus' ministry apart from the work of John the Baptist but also marks a beginning in its own right. This moment of ordination launched his ministry of good works and healing through which the power of God was manifested: it became clear that "God was with him" (v. 38). It was the beginning of the era in which the "good news of peace" was proclaimed (v. 36). Its essence was his universal Lordship: "He is Lord of all" (v. 36). It also inaugurated a new era in which forgiveness of sins was made possible through his name (v. 43).

Matthew 3:13–17

One of the accounts of Jesus' baptism serves each year as the Gospel lesson for the First Sunday After the Epiphany. Matthew's record of the event (3:13–17) is especially appropriate as an Epiphany text because in this Gospel the voice from heaven publicly proclaims Jesus as the son of God (v. 17).

Both Matthew and Luke (3:21–22) follow Mark (1:9–11), but each has its own accents. Matthew is most concerned to explain or to clarify matters open to misunderstanding in Mark, who seems unconcerned that questions would arise as to the reason for Jesus' baptism. That Jesus was baptized is a historical certainty; the church would never have created such a story. After all, why would Jesus go for baptism by a preacher who called for repentance and forgiveness of sin? This puzzle occupied many in the early church. Jerome cited a certain gospel according to the Hebrews in which Jesus responds to his mother's suggestion that they be baptized by saying, "In what have I sinned that I should go and be baptized by him? Unless, perhaps, what I have just said is a sin of ignorance." Matthew enlarges upon Mark to deal with this problem as well as address the issue of Jesus' relation to John the Baptist.

On the question of why Jesus was baptized, Matthew makes three statements. First, he says that Jesus went to the Jordan "to be baptized" by John (v. 13). In other words, his act was intentional; he was not simply caught up in John's preaching and his movement. Second, John recognized that Jesus did not fit the image of those coming in repentance, seeking forgiveness. Jesus transcended John's baptism (v. 14). And third, Jesus states his reason for being baptized: "to fulfill all righteousness" (v. 15). This is to say, it is what God wills; it is an act of fidelity to the commands of God (as in 5:20).

As stated earlier, this passage also addresses the question of Jesus' relation to John. Because John had disciples (Luke 11:1) and a movement arose around him (John 1:6–8, 15; Acts 18:24–19:7), that John baptized Jesus could have been (and probably was) used by John's disciples to argue his superiority over Jesus. All the Gospel writers deal with John and his movement. Matthew inserts in the baptismal scene a polemic to the effect that John himself recognized Jesus' superiority and was hesitant to baptize him. In fact, said John, Jesus should be the one baptizing (vv. 14–15).

In addition to these two concerns of Matthew, the account is offered as a prototype of Christian baptism, an act of the church that carried the authority of Jesus' own example. It is especially important to notice in this regard that the writer offers not a word about Jesus' feelings, his internal state, or any messianic self-consciousness, if such a condition were present. On the contrary, the focus of attention is upon what God announced at Jesus' baptism.

That Jesus' baptism was an epiphany event has in all three Synoptics triple attestation: the heavens were opened, a sign associated with divine revelation (v. 16: Ezek. 1:1); the Holy Spirit descended upon Jesus, empowering him for the ministry before him (v. 16; 4:17); and the voice from heaven declared, "This is my Son, the Beloved, with whom I am well pleased" (v. 17: Ps. 2:7; Isa. 42:1). It is not, then, with the baptism itself that Matthew is most concerned but with the divine proclamation that immediately followed. Because Matthew has earlier offered the virgin birth as a statement that Jesus is son of God (1:18–25), it is not appropriate to use Matthew in support of the adoptionist Christology that holds that Jesus became son of God at his baptism.

Two words about the voice from heaven: (1) the expression "this is" rather than "you are" (Mark 1:11; Luke 3:22) means that for Matthew the declaration was not to Jesus but to John and perhaps the others present; in other words, it was a public announcement; and (2) the voice joins Psalm 2:7 and Isaiah 42:1, the former being a coronation proclamation (the king is God's son) and the latter a reference to God's suffering servant. Sovereignty is joined to sacrificial service, a theme that was to characterize both Jesus' teaching and his life.

Second Sunday After the Epiphany

Isaiah 49:1–7;
Psalm 40:1–11;
1 Corinthians 1:1–9;
John 1:29–42

The Old Testament lesson for today is provided by the second Servant Song from Isaiah, a fitting complement to last week's Old Testament reading. Its emphasis on the calling of the servant and his special vocation as a "light to the nations" makes it especially appropriate in this Epiphany setting. The psalm and the epistolary reading are similar in that both contain prayers of thanksgiving. In the psalm, thanksgiving finally prompts the psalmist to tell abroad the good news of deliverance. Of course, the epistolary reading has not been selected to relate thematically to the other readings, because it is the first of several semicontinuous readings from 1 Corinthians 1–4 that continue for seven weeks. The Gospel lesson consists of the Johannine account of the baptism of Jesus. Because John's account of this event is not used in any of the three years for the baptism of the Lord, it occurs here. Actually, it is not an account of the event in the strict sense, but more or less presupposes it. In the context of the Epiphany, its emphasis on John's role as one who bore witness should be noted.

Isaiah 49:1–7

This same reading, including the second of the Servant Songs, is also assigned for use on Tuesday in Holy Week. There, as here, the passage from Second Isaiah is heard in the context of Christian worship as a prophecy fulfilled by the coming of Jesus. On the Second Sunday After the Epiphany, the call and designation of the servant is linked with the baptism of Jesus by the Holy Spirit (John 1:32ff.). However, the text requires it to be heard in other ways as well, including in its own literary and historical context. It may turn out that Second Isaiah's servant is not only a type of Jesus, but may also be a model for understanding the vocation of the church.

The Servant Song ends with verse 6. Verse 7 begins a new unit, an announcement of salvation to Israel, that runs through verse 12.

In the first Servant Song (Isaiah 42:1–4; see the commentary on last week's Old Testament lesson), Yahweh was the speaker, designating his servant. Here the servant himself speaks. The song has many of the features of a typical prophetic address, including a summons to attention at the outset and direct quotation of the words of God (vv. 3, 6), and there is a very expansive messenger formula in verse 5. The song also has some of the features of a thanksgiving psalm, with an account of trouble and the report of deliverance from it.

However, in important ways the passage is like prophetic vocation reports found in other prophetic books (Isa. 6; Jer. 1:10–17; Ezek. 1–3; cf. Isa. 40:1–11). The main theme is the call of the servant and his response to that call. There is a dialogue on the subject between the prophet and the one who has called him. Like Jeremiah, the servant reports (vv. 1, 5) that he was designated while he was "in his mother's womb" (Jer. 1:5), and like Jeremiah (Jer. 1:16), Isaiah (Isa. 6:5), and Moses (Exod. 3–4), he responded with a sense of unworthiness (v. 4). In this passage, the note of inadequacy seems to stem from frustration with the results of work already in progress. Likewise, as with others, the Lord reacted with reassurance. As in other vocation reports, the task of the servant is spelled out, and it concerns his "mouth" (v. 2).

Thus, although the emphasis in the first Servant Song was upon the royal, administrative responsibility of the servant, here the role is more prophetic. The servant was given powerful words to speak, but he held back until the appropriate time. That is the meaning of the metaphors of the weapons in verse 2, and it seems to stand in contrast to the gentle servant of Isaiah 42:2–3, at least until it becomes clear how these weapons are to be used.

In short, the servant reports that he has been called to a task that involves words, that he came to believe that his work was in vain (v. 4), but then was confident of God's approval. Whether this reflects stages in his work or ambivalence is not clear. The call is reiterated and the duties spelled out (vv. 5–6). The servant is to "bring Jacob back to him." This responsibility corresponds to the central message of Second Isaiah; that is, that Yahweh will set the captives in Babylon free and bring them back to Jerusalem. Then there is a second role. In addition to raising up the tribes of Jacob, the servant is to be "a light to the nations," toward the end that the Lord's "salvation may reach to the end of the earth" (v. 6).

Thus the servant has both a national and a worldwide vocation. As in Isaiah 42:5–9, the redemption of Israel by the one God is a step toward making the glory of that God known to all humankind. In our passage, that concern was indicated from the very outset, for the addressees of the speech are "the coastlands," the "peoples from afar" (v. 1). This probably does not anticipate what we would call missionary activity to the Gentiles, but rather the display of the glory of God and the establishment of the universal reign of the Lord of Israel.

The roles of the servant are clear, but the identification of the servant is difficult. Verse 3 states explicitly that the servant is Israel. But how can the servant then have a role *toward* Israel? Moreover, the language is highly individualistic. Some commentators, stressing the parallels to the vocation accounts of the prophets, see the servant as Second Isaiah himself. It is possible that the ambiguity here and in the other songs is intentional.

Modern hearers of this passage may find it possible to identify with any or all of the human parties. As individuals and as a church, we experience vocations and may experience unworthiness or frustration as well. In such cases, there is the divine reassurance in verses 4b and 5b. As servants of God, we may hear a call to set captives free and to make the reign of God visible throughout the world. We may recognize ourselves in captive Israel, and then for us there is the proclamation of the message of release, the good news that God intends restoration (vv. 5–6a). Or we may even be able to see ourselves in those other nations, to whom the good news comes.

Psalm 40:1–11

Psalm 40, portions of which are used as one of the readings for the Annunciation, is a thanksgiving psalm, but a thanksgiving psalm that moves into petition and lament (following v. 10). Today's reading picks up the plea or appeal in verse 11. The thanksgiving portion of the psalm is completed in verse 10.

The structural components of the thanksgiving ritual can be seen in this psalm if one pays attention to the contents and to the changes in the person being addressed. Verses 1–3 have the worshiper, who is celebrating some event that produced well-being, address a human audience offering testimony to God's saving action. The impersonal statement of verse 4, which sounds like a beatitude, probably represents the priest's affirmation of the worshiper and his or her confessional thanksgiving. With verse 5, the worshiper turns to address the Deity directly and continues to do this, except in verse 17a, throughout the psalm.

From what we can deduce about thanksgiving services, it is clear that the liturgy was divided into two distinct phases. One was oriented to a human audience (friends, family, the congregation). In this phase, the worshiper gave testimony to the new status that God has created, reiterated the conditions of trouble from which he or she had been rescued, and sought to convince the hearers to have a similar type of faith in God's ability to redeem. This part of the service probably occurred before the direct thanksgiving to God. The latter was the central focus of the second phase of the worship service.

Verses 1–3 describe briefly the worshiper's earlier sentiments at the time of trouble (v. 1a) and testify to the fact that God responded (v. 1b). Much of this section, however, is devoted to the consequences, to the new status the person has, to the new condition of life. The imagery is well reflected in the NJPSV's rendering of verse 2 (v. 3 in the Hebrew):

> He lifted me out of the miry pit,
>   the slimy clay,
> and set my feet on a rock,
>   steadied my legs.

The new status is declared to produce a new song, a song of praise, a turn from lament to hymn, from petition to praise (v. 3a). Verse 3b suggests the public character and the public benefit to be derived from the worshiper's (the king's?) testimony. Others will see, stand in awe, and participate in a similar faith and trust.

The priestly blessing in verse 4 in itself contains some preaching and proclamation. While affirming the experience of the worshiper, it simultaneously invites others to test the proposition that "happy are those who . . . ."

The opening word by the worshiper to the Deity (v. 5) repeats, in direct address and with different words, the sentiments of verses 1–3. In verses 1–3, the before and after conditions of the individual worshiper were stressed. In verse 5, two slightly different slants are given to the thanksgiving: (1) the material is less personalized and is presented in general terms—"wondrous deeds," "your thoughts," "them"; and (2) the public quality of the sentiments receives attention. Along with personal pronouns referring to the speaker (seven times in vv. 1–3, twice in v. 5), the worshiper now speaks of an "us" that is the recipient of God's actions and thoughts. (This could suggest that the speaker was either the king or some other leader.) This shift to the more general produces a reduction in the passion but simultaneously incorporates the audience in the ritual.

Verses 6–10 comprise the worshiper's statement of fidelity to God and a rehearsal of what the person believes, feels, and does as response to the Divine.

Verse 6 suggests that conventional, habitual religious practices—four different kinds of sacrifices are referred to—are not seen as the only or the necessary components in religion. The writer gives expression to the commitment of one's self in what must have been a popular saying indicating one's hearing of and submission to another—"You have dug ears for me" (NRSV marginal reading). For the worshiper, what God desires and requires is first of all, a faithful hearing—receptivity.

The hearing response leads to voluntary obedience (vv. 7–8). In terms somewhat reminiscent of the prophet Isaiah (see Isa. 6), the person volunteers—"Here I am." The second half of verse 7, with its reference to the book, could denote that (1) in the book of the psalmist's life it is written (and preordained) that the psalmist will make the will of God the delight of living; (2) the record of the person's life kept in the divine world demonstrates that the psalmist is one delighting in obedience; (3) the book of the law, the Torah (the Pentateuch?) was written as if speaking of the psalmist, or (4) to say "it's in the book" was a way of affirming something's and someone's truthfulness. However one understands the particulars, the affirmation is clear. The psalmist claims a complete submission to and obedience to God. "Your law is within my heart" is an affirmation of the internalization of the law; one's inward being, the conscience, the heart, one's ultimate commitments are devoted to the will of God.

Verses 9–10 affirm the public testimony of the commitment. This affirmation is stated twice positively and three times negatively: "I have told," "I have spoken," "I have not restrained my lips," "I have not hidden," and "I have not concealed."

The psalmist thus delineates an action sequence pattern; sincere hearing leads to responsive commitment, which leads to public exuberance, the testimony in the congregation.

Verse 11, in the NRSV, appears as an appeal. It is possible to translate the verse as an affirmation as is done in the NJPSV: "O Lord, You will not withhold from me Your compassion; Your steadfast love will protect me always."

1 Corinthians 1:1–9

On the Sundays immediately following Epiphany and the Baptism of the Lord (First Sunday After the Epiphany), the epistolary readings for all three years are taken from First Corinthians. In Year A, 1 Corinthians 1–4 provides the readings for the second through the eighth Sundays after the Epiphany. In Year B, 1 Corinthians 6–9 provides the readings for the second through the sixth Sundays, with 2 Corinthians providing the epistolary reading for the following Sundays after the Epiphany. In Year C, 1 Corinthians 12–15 provides the readings for the second through the eighth Sundays after the Epiphany.

We should also note that today's text overlaps with the epistolary reading for the First Sunday of Advent in Year B (1:3–9). The reader may want to consult our remarks on the text in that setting.

As noted above, today's epistolary reading marks the beginning of the semicontinuous reading of 1 Corinthians 1–4 that occurs over these seven Sundays. Accordingly, some words of introduction to this epistle are in order here.

First Corinthians divides into three sections. After the initial greeting and prayer of thanksgiving, chapters 1–4 contain an extended exhortation. Here Paul urges the church to be unified in its mission and outlook as it lives out the message of the cross. It is to embody the unity of purpose exemplified in the work of Paul and Apollos. Chapters 5–6 treat two topics: the proper response to sexual immorality within the church and the proper response to internal conflicts. In each case, the Corinthians had been lamentably deficient in conduct, even though some were claiming to have superior wisdom. In this section, Paul reminds them that there are still a number of things they do not know. Chapters 7–16 may be regarded as instructional. They contain what appear to be Paul's answers to a list of questions that the Corinthian church had submitted to him. In serial fashion, he treats a variety of topics, including marriage (chap. 7), eating sacrificial meat (chaps. 8–10), worship (chap. 11), spiritual gifts (chaps. 12–14), resurrection (chap. 15), the collection, and miscellaneous matters (chap. 16).

As to the situation prompting the letter, it appears that some within the church had pretensions to wisdom that posed a threat to the church. In some cases, they exhibited arrogant behavior that was insensitive to the needs of other members in the church. Rather than developing a sense of corporate solidarity where individual preferences were giving way to the common good, some members were exhibiting a robust individualism that emphasized personal freedom more than collective responsibility.

In response to this situation, Paul urges the Corinthian church to become more united in its fellowship. He calls on individuals to seek the common good rather than their own personal good, to be willing to make concessions in the interest of others. The letter also imposes limits on spiritual enthusiasm. Although recognizing the Spirit as an energizing force within the church and its ministries, Paul also sees the excesses of spiritualism. If spiritual pursuits threaten domestic stability, they should be curbed. If they threaten to undermine meaningful worship, they should be balanced with more edifying spiritual behavior. On the whole, what emerges in the letter is a set of exhortations and instructions designed to make congregational life a meaningful form of fellowship.

Today's epistolary lesson consists of two parts: the opening greeting (vv. 1–3) and the opening prayer of thanksgiving offered on behalf of the church (vv. 4–9).

The Greeting (vv. 1–3). The greeting is typical in many respects of other Pauline greetings (cf. Rom. 1:1; 2 Cor. 1:1; Eph. 1:1; Col. 1:1; 2 Tim. 1:1). Paul identifies himself as an apostle called through the will of God (v. 1). It is not only he who is called, however, but the Corinthians themselves who are "called to be saints" (v. 2; Rom. 1:7). As such, they stand solidly with Christians everywhere who "call on the name of our Lord Jesus Christ" (v. 2). They are in solidarity with those everywhere who confess Christ as Lord and pray to God through Christ (Acts 2:21; 9:14, 21; 22:16; Rom. 10:12–13; cf. Ps. 99:6; Joel 2:32; 2 Tim. 2:22).

We should note that the letter is addressed quite specifically to the congregation at Corinth—a single, local church (v. 2). This reminds us that the letter was first addressed to someone else before we became its readers. In one sense, we are reading someone else's mail. We are overhearing a conversation between Paul and his church. But even if we stand outside the original conversation, because we have been sanctified in Christ and call upon the name of the Lord, their conversation enlightens us as well. As a result of the canonical process, the church decided that the letter was instructive to later readers as well.

The Prayer of Thanksgiving (vv. 4–9). Typically, Paul's opening prayers set the mood of the letter and preview some of its central concerns. In this sense, it does what we expect a pastoral prayer for the congregation, or an opening prayer in a worship service, to do: it articulates the church's needs and matters of immediate concern.

The mood of this opening prayer is above all reassuring. The readers are reminded that they are "not lacking in any spiritual gift" (v. 7). If some of the church members were claiming spiritual superiority, it is not difficult to see how other members would feel deficient. Here Paul addresses a common concern in all churches: the strong tend to get stronger, the weak weaker. To combat this debilitating tendency, Paul reminds them (and us) that each has been endowed by the Spirit in some way, with some gift. They should not allow the heroic spiritualists to intimidate them and leave them feeling spiritually depressed.

Not only does the prayer reassure us about our own spiritual endowments, it reaffirms the Lord's fidelity: "God is faithful" (v. 9; cf. 10:13; 2 Cor. 1:18; 1 Thess. 5:24; 2 Thess. 3:3; also Heb. 10:23; 11:11; 1 John 1:9; Rev. 1:5). The God who promises also delivers. The One who called us into fellowship will make good on the promises made. We are promised that the Lord Jesus Christ will sustain us to the end (v. 8). It is not as if Christ has left us orphaned, with no direction and sustenance for the interim, much less that he will leave us stranded as we gaze into the future. Instead, he will present us "blameless" before God in the final day, the "day of our Lord Jesus Christ" (v. 8; 2 Cor. 1:14; Phil. 1:6, 10; 2:16; also Acts 2:20).

Besides this generally reassuring tone, the prayer signals themes later developed in the letter: the proper role of wisdom and rhetorical ability (chaps. 1–2), the right attitude toward spiritual gifts (chaps. 12–14), and the proper view of the end time (chap. 15).

John 1:29–42

John 1:29–42 is very much an Epiphany text, for in it Jesus is declared publicly to be the Lamb of God, the one who baptizes with the Holy Spirit, the Son of God, and the Messiah. Testimony to Jesus is given first by John the Baptist (vv. 29–34) and then by one of his disciples (vv. 35–42).

In this Gospel, the role of John is that of a witness to Jesus Christ. He has been so portrayed in the Prologue (1:6–8), and so he is subsequently described (1:19, 32; 5:33). This identification of Jesus as God's Christ and Son of God is unparalleled in the Synoptic accounts of John's ministry. In those Gospels, John preached about one coming, a stronger one, who would baptize with the Holy Spirit (Matt. 3:11–12; Mark 1:7–8; Luke 3:15–18), but John has no direct association with Jesus and does not identify Jesus as this messianic figure. Matthew (3:13–17), as we saw in last Sunday's lesson, does say that John recognized Jesus as greater and heard the voice from heaven declare him God's beloved Son. Both Matthew (11:2–6) and Luke (7:18–23) report that the imprisoned John sent to Jesus asking, "Are you the one who is to come, or are we to wait for another?" but in none of these Synoptic references to John is he characterized as a witness to Christ in the manner of the text before us.

The first section of the Gospel of John immediately following the Prologue (1:1–18) begins with an expression that could serve as a title for what follows: "This is the testimony [witness] given by John" (v. 19). John's testimony consists of two parts: his witness about himself (1:19–28) and his witness about Christ (1:29–34). To this second part we give our attention here.

The first question is, How did John know who Jesus was? John says that the point of his own ministry of baptism was that Christ would be revealed to Israel (v. 31), but first Christ had to be revealed to John. Already John had said to the Jews, "Among you stands one whom you do not know" (v. 26); now he acknowledges, "I myself did not know him" (vv. 31, 33). John can therefore witness only after he has received the revelation about Jesus. This perspective is supported elsewhere in the New Testament. Knowing the Son is by revelation (Matt. 11:27); God, not flesh and blood, has made him known (Matt. 16:17); only by the Holy Spirit can anyone say Jesus is Lord (1 Cor. 12:3).

John the Baptist says the revelation occurred in this way: "The one who sent me to baptize with water said to me, 'He on whom you see the Spirit descend and remain is the one who baptizes with the Holy Spirit'" (v. 33). John saw the Spirit descend as a dove (v. 32; agreeing with Matthew, who says John witnessed heaven's attestation to Jesus, 3:16–17), and he knew. We assume that the Evangelist is reporting on an occurrence at Jesus' baptism, but no account of Jesus' baptism is actually given. This event is simply omitted by the Fourth Evangelist except for this reference to what John saw.

Although it may seem minor at this point, it is important to notice that twice the Evangelist says the Holy Spirit "remained" (vv. 32–33) on Jesus. To remain or to abide is a favorite expression of the Fourth Gospel to express the relationship between Christ and God and between Christ and his followers (e.g., 15:1–11). Here the point is that Jesus and the Holy Spirit have no "come and go" relationship, as though he were a charismatic prophet. He is the permanent bearer of the Spirit, and his life carries the quality, knowledge, and power which that implies. And Jesus gives the Holy Spirit to his followers (1:33; 20:22). According to this Gospel, true Christian spirituality is not an alternative to the life of obedient discipleship; it does not distance one from Jesus of Nazareth but rather ties one inseparably to him.

A final word: John the Baptist hails Jesus as "the Lamb of God who takes away the sin of the world" (v. 29). The preacher will want to resist being drawn immediately to all the lamb images in the Jewish sacrificial system. The allusions are plentiful: the sin-offering lamb, the Passover lamb, the warrior lamb of apocalyptic literature, but which is in the writer's mind? In what sense does Jesus take away the sin of the world? More atonement doctrines are found in Paul and Hebrews than in the Fourth Gospel. For this Evangelist, Jesus lays down his life for the sheep (10:15) and dies as the true Passover Lamb (19:31–37). Whether 1:29 relates to either of those interpretations of Jesus' death or adds a third is not clear. Sermons that focus on this statement can share with the congregation the rich plenitude of symbolism and Old Testament associations without seeming to be certain about the writer's specific focus. Churches appreciate honest caution.

Verses 35–42 remind us that in this Gospel and unlike the Synoptics, John and Jesus have parallel ministries in Judea, and Jesus' first disciples come to him from John's following. This shift from John to Jesus dramatizes the writer's understanding of the relation of John to Jesus. Perhaps more significant for us, however, is the model of witnessing provided here. John bears witness to Jesus; two of his disciples are pointed to Jesus; these two learn firsthand by staying (abiding; see above) with Jesus; one of the two witnesses to his brother about Jesus as Messiah; the brother comes to Jesus. Thus the circle of faith widens. The language is simple yet profound: What are you looking for? Where are you staying? Come and see (the invitation to faith; see also v. 46 and 4:29); They stayed with him; We have found the Messiah. One further note of interest: at the time that this Gospel was written, Simon Peter is well known, so that even though Andrew introduces Simon to Jesus, it is Simon who introduces Andrew to the reader; he is Simon's brother.

Third Sunday After the Epiphany

Isaiah 9:1–4;
Psalm 27:1, 4–9;
1 Corinthians 1:10–18;
Matthew 4:12–23

Light shining in darkness is the central theme of the Old Testament reading from Isaiah. Its depiction of the messianic king has become a symbol of hope. The image of light is also the note on which the psalm opens, with its declaration "The Lord is my light and my salvation." In the epistolary reading we hear Paul exhorting the Corinthians to realize the unity that has eluded them. The Gospel reading from Matthew begins the semicontinuous reading of this Gospel, which runs through the next five weeks. Even so, Epiphany themes are dominant in the prophetic announcement taken from Isaiah 9:1–4, the Old Testament reading for today.

Isaiah 9:1–4

Except for the first verse, this passage is included in the Old Testament lesson for Christmas, First Proper. For a more extensive commentary, the reader may want to consult our remarks in that setting. Isaiah 9:1–2 has been assigned for this occasion because the first two verses are cited in the Gospel lection as a particular prophecy that Jesus fulfills.

The lesson includes two parts. The first is a narrative introduction (v. 1) that locates and dates the events. The second (vv. 2–4) contains the initial parts of a prophetic announcement concerning the rule of God through the designation of a new descendant in the line of David. Thus the reading is incomplete. The proclamation that light has shined upon those in darkness (v. 2) is followed by an account of celebration (v. 3). Then the reasons for celebration are given, with our lesson including only the first of the three reasons. Ending the text with verse 4 puts the emphasis upon the dramatic contrasts between light and darkness, the joyful celebration, and God's intervention to release the people from oppression (v. 4).

Psalm 27:1, 4–9

The overall structure of the psalm is as follows: (1) an affirmation of confidence addressed to a human audience (vv. 1–6); (2) a petition addressed to God requesting help (vv. 7–12); (3) a confessional statement by the worshiper to a human audience (v. 13); and (4) a response by the priest (or other cultic official) to the worshiper (v. 14).

The psalm lection for this Sunday contains (1) the worshiper's opening statement of confidence addressed not to God but to a human audience, perhaps the official in charge of the sacrificial service, or maybe friends and family or even opponents assembled at the sanctuary for religious services or for some ordeal (vv. 1, 4–6), and (2) the beginning portion of the petition addressed to God (vv. 7–9).

The psalm opens with a statement of great confidence. Three metaphors are used to describe God, the source of confidence: light, salvation, and stronghold. The two affirmations in verse 1 are followed, however, by two rhetorical questions: "Whom shall I fear?" "Of whom shall I be afraid?" The rhetorical questions help raise the issue of fear in such a way that the worshiper can answer "no one." Their function, of course, is to reinforce courage. Whoever wrote this psalm (and we should think of some cultic official associated with the temple) knew that courage is a fragile vessel lightly floating upon an abyss of fear and uncertainty. Thus every effort is made to sustain courage.

Verse 4 has the worshiper say that the one thing desired is to live in the temple "all the days of my life." In ancient Israel, those who lived in the temple precincts were either fugitives fleeing from opponents or persons given to the temple. (One should beware of spiritualizing such an expression as "live in the house of the Lord all the days of my life" to mean "go to heaven" or "be with God.") That a fugitive could take refuge in the sanctuary is evident in Deuteronomy 16:1–13, and 1 Samuel 1 tells how Samuel was given to the temple to abide there forever. Whether refuge in the temple is what the psalm has in mind is not certain but seems probable (note the references to witnesses in v. 12).

Verses 5–6 reaffirm the worshiper's confidence and contain the vow to offer sacrifice and worship after God has aided the supplicant. Three images of shelter are used in verse 5: a shelter (in Hebrew a *sukkah*, a lean-to, which offered shade and cool in the fields), a tent, and a rock. The worshiper's confidence of God's favor leads to a boast in verse 6a. The supplicant claims not only escape from the adversary but triumph over all enemies round about! This section closes with a vow, publicly announced, that sacrifices and songs would be offered in the temple. Courage and confidence would culminate in celebration.

Verses 7–9 begin the worshiper's petition to God, requesting not only a hearing but also a favorable response. Appeal is made to the Deity to react to the petition as the Divine had done on previous occasions.

1 Corinthians 1:10–18

The opening exhortation of the Epistle of First Corinthians is an appeal for unity (v. 10). Paul had received a report from "Chloe's people" that there was quarreling among the Corinthian brothers and sisters (v. 11). The word used here (*eris*) suggests attitudinal divisions and interpersonal bickering rather than doctrinal or ideological schisms. It is often closely associated with jealousy and petty strife (cf. 3:3; Gal. 5:19–20). His hope, of course, is that these would not develop into full-scale divisions (*schismata*, v. 10), which is always the danger. Petty disagreements become the occasion for more serious doctrinal cleavages, and often the latter become the justification for the former.

It is difficult to ascertain clearly the nature of the internal differences or strife within the church. Paul elaborates in verse 12 that the members were defining their loyalties around various personalities, such as himself, Apollos, Cephas (Peter), and even Christ. What did it mean for them to claim to belong to each of these figures? Most likely, these were the figures being suggested as the ultimate poles of authority and sources of guidance for Christian life and practice. Thus some preferred Paul because he was their founding missionary (2:1–5), even though he was now living across the Aegean carrying on his apostolic work in Ephesus (16:8). Others preferred Apollos, the minister who had been there most recently and whose intellectual ability, rhetorical eloquence, and knowledge of the Scriptures especially commended him (3:4–6, 22; 4:6; 16:12; Acts 18:24; 19:1; also Titus 3:13). Still others preferred to look to one of the original apostles for guidance, and thus offered Cephas as their polestar (9:5). Still others, eschewing all human teachers, preferred to look to Christ alone for guidance, contending that they were "of Christ" (3:23; 2 Cor. 10:7; cf. Mark 9:41) and remembering perhaps that the risen Lord had promised to be with them and instruct them in the ways of truth (Matt. 28:20; cf. Luke 12:11).

As admirable as each of these viewpoints might have been, the underlying assumption of each had a debilitating effect on the life of the church. It meant that the unity they all shared in Christ was being dissolved in favor of human loyalties. What should have been holding them together—their common life in Christ—was evaporating before their very eyes.

What was at stake, according to Paul, was the nature of existence in Christ. Thus, he asks rhetorically, "Has Christ been divided?" (v. 13). How can Christ's body be dismembered? A divided Christ is a destroyed Christ. Yet this is what happens when we define Christian existence in terms of human loyalties. Paul insists that he was neither crucified for them nor were they baptized in his name (v. 13). Because no human being fills this role, they can belong to no one in the sense they are claiming.

The exegetical question, of course, is in what sense some were claiming to belong "to Christ" (v. 12), and why this would be objectionable, if indeed it was. The gist of Paul's remarks suggests that all four groups are being reprimanded for false loyalties or for identifying their loyalties wrongly. Those claiming to belong to Christ are perhaps being censured because they are as divisive and exclusive in their claims as the rest, in which case they would be party to dismembering the Body of Christ. Even the right title, or the right cliché, is meaningless if it becomes the occasion for arrogant and exclusive claims.

Paul is aware that such loyalties are often the result of our relationship with the one who baptized us or who introduced us into the faith. It is understandable that we should feel strong attachment to the person who baptized us. Even Paul recognized his special relationship to those whom he baptized or taught personally (4:17; Philem. 10, 19). Yet he also recognized the inherent danger that those whom he baptized could mistakenly construe their relationship with Christ as essentially a relationship with Paul (v. 15). Accordingly, he stresses how few people he actually baptized: Crispus (Acts 18:8), Gaius (Rom. 16:23; cf. Acts 19:29), and the household of Stephanas (16:15, 17).

It was Paul's primary task to preach the gospel, not to baptize people (v. 17; cf. Rom. 15:15–16; Gal. 1:16). Even when his task was defined this way, there were hazards, because the effectiveness of his preaching could be laid to his rhetorical ability. He is all too aware that preaching could be packaged in such a way that it derived its power not from the message itself but from the messenger and the messenger's way with words. Paul saw this as emptying the cross of its power (v. 17). Ultimately, it is the message of the cross that is the source of power (v. 18).

The overall appeal in this section is for Christian unity—for the congregation to be one in its mind, or outlook, its purpose, and its life (v. 10; cf. Rom. 12:16; 15:5; 2 Cor. 13:11; Phil. 2:2; 4:2; 1 Pet. 3:8). We should not confuse unity with uniformity. To agree and to be of the same mind and judgment does not require us to formulate our theology in identical terms. Indeed, the true test of Christian unity is the ability to disagree in our formulation of the truth, even in our convictions about the truth, without compromising our ultimate loyalty to Christ—and to each other.

Historically, today's text has served as a crucial text for Christian unity. Even though the focus of the passage is congregational and the divisions that were occurring pitted individuals against each other, its scope is naturally much broader. As such, it speaks to all situations where the Body of Christ is being dismembered, whether the nature of the division is congregational, confessional, denominational, or religious in the broadest sense.

One of the fundamental insights worth noting is that our unity in Christ is something that exists by virtue of our incorporation into Christ through baptism. It is already present, waiting to be realized rather than something that has to be created by human effort. It is something implicit within the Christian fellowship. Whether it becomes explicit in congregational life depends on the way we relate to each other. In mediating church squabbles or even denominational differences, perhaps it is more constructive to begin conversation by emphasizing what we already have in common in Christ, the unity we already share, rather than assuming that our experience of Christ—either our personal experience or our church's experience—is wholly ours and is radically different from that which others claim to be true Christian experience.

Matthew 4:12–23

Today's lesson is appropriate for the Season of Epiphany not only in the general sense of relating the beginning of Jesus' public ministry but in the particular sense of providing an announcement to the nations, "The people who sat in darkness / have seen a great light, / and for those who sat in the region and shadow of death / light has dawned" (v. 16).

There are in Matthew 4:12–23 four discernible parts: the beginning of Jesus' public ministry in Galilee (vv. 12–16); a summary statement of Jesus' message (v. 17); the call of the first four disciples (vv. 18–22); a summary of Jesus' travels and the nature of his ministry (v. 23).

In the first unit, Matthew follows Mark (1:14–15) both in locating the account immediately after the temptation story (Matt. 3:1–11; Mark 1:12–13) and in the description of Jesus launching his ministry. (Luke 3:14–15 has the same order but abbreviates the account to introduce the rejection in Nazareth, 4:16–30.) The record as Matthew provides it says that Jesus withdrew into Galilee upon hearing of John's imprisonment (v. 12). Whether the withdrawal from Judea was prompted by concern for his own safety, or to avoid having his ministry construed as merely a continuation of that of the now silenced John, or to use John's imprisonment as a natural turning point providing opportunity to begin his own separate work, we do not know. Once in Galilee, Jesus moved from Nazareth to Capernaum (v. 13; implied in Luke 4:23). Whatever may have been the practical considerations prompting such a move, Matthew interprets it as the fulfillment of the prophecy in Isaiah 9:1–2. This fulfillment formula, familiar in Matthew, has no parallel in the other Gospels. Luke refers to Jesus' work in Capernaum (1:21–28), but no connections are made to prophecy. Mark's account of Jesus' message says, "The time is fulfilled" (1:15), but for Matthew the *place* is fulfilled, "Galilee of the Gentiles" (v. 15). Attention to the Gentile mission continues this theme from the visit of the wise men from the East (2:1–12). In its own context,

Isaiah 9:1–2 refers to the march of the army of Assyria westward to the Mediterranean and the promise of a deliverer to free the besieged people. Matthew (or his source) applies the passage to the Sea of Galilee and to the coming of Jesus as Messiah.

As for Jesus' message (v. 17), it was essentially a continuation of John's preaching. Here Matthew reworks Mark 1:15, changing "kingdom of God" to his more characteristic "kingdom of heaven" and omitting "and believe in the good news." The phrase "has come near" is a translation of the perfect tense, which may also be translated "is near" or "is here." The whole of Jesus' message is needed to determine if he announced the approaching end of this age and the soon arrival of the age to come (this age and the age to come is a distinction provided by Jewish apocalyptic eschatology) or if Jesus was saying that his arrival marked the presence ("is here") of the reign of God. Scholars are divided on the matter but generally tend to speak of God's reign being both present and future in the work and words of Jesus. Jesus announces, then, both a hope and a warning: in view of God's new activity, the people must prepare through repentance.

The third unit, the call of the first four disciples (vv. 18–22), follows closely Mark 1:16–20. (Luke's account is somewhat different, and later, 5:1–11. In John, Jesus calls his first disciples in Judea from among the followers of John, 1:35–43.) There is no evidence here of an earlier meeting, nor any basis to discuss the psychology of conversion. The suddenness of the call prompted E. Lohmeyer to call this an epiphany story. The metaphor "fishers of men" is more familiar than clear. When pressed to yield details descriptive of the church's mission, the image becomes rather unattractive. Even though the image has continued to live in the church, it did not fare so well in New Testament writings. The shepherd analogy became more popular.

And finally, verse 23 provides a summary of Jesus' travels (all Galilee; for some strange reason, Luke has Judea, 4:44) and his activity: teaching in the synagogues, preaching, and healing. Mark has preaching and exorcising demons (1:39). Matthew follows verse 23 with an elaboration of Jesus' fame (throughout all Syria, verse 24), his healings (v. 24), and his gathering of crowds from Galilee, Decapolis, Jerusalem, Judea, and beyond the Jordan (v. 25). Very likely, verses 23–25 are Matthew's preparation for the Sermon on the Mount, which is delivered not only to "the crowds" but to people gathered from everywhere. In other words, Jesus' teaching is for everyone.

Fourth Sunday After the Epiphany

Micah 6:1–8;
Psalm 15;
1 Corinthians 1:18–31;
Matthew 5:1–12

One of the most famous Old Testament passages supplies the first lesson for today—the text from Micah that speaks of justice, kindness, and humility as the essence of doing God's will. Psalm 15, also well known, reflects an entrance liturgy similar in many respects to Micah 6:6–8 in that the worshiper asks what is required to be in the presence of God and is given instructions in the will of God. The epistolary reading is Paul's classic statement of his theology of the cross, in which he pits God's foolishness against human wisdom. In the Gospel reading, we have the most familiar version of the Beatitudes, in which we have sketched a profile of life in the kingdom of God. This collection of passages combines four classic biblical texts, each in its own way has earned its rightful place as memorable and compelling.

Micah 6:1–8

This reading, which includes some of the best-known lines of the prophetic literature, consists of two distinct units of speech, verses 1–5 and 6–8. As the Book of Micah has come down to us, the two are meant to be heard as part of a larger collection, but because each unit is in a different genre and conveys its own message, they are best analyzed individually.

Micah 6:1–5 is the beginning of a prophetic lawsuit against Israel. First the prophet speaks (vv. 1–2), and then Yahweh addresses the people directly (vv. 3–5). In formal legal language similar to that found in Micah 1, the prophet utters on behalf of Yahweh a series of summons to the people of Israel (vv. 1–2). They are called to present their case before the mountains and hills, and then commanded to hear Yahweh's "controversy" (better, "suit," "case" [NJPSV], or "lawsuit"). The prophetic speeches of judgment generally resemble the pattern of the legal process, with accusation and then pronouncement of punishment. Here, however, the specifically covenantal background is more obvious, reflected in the formal legal terminology and in the call to natural phenomena, such as mountains and hills or—elsewhere—heavens and earth. The contents and form of this section are familiar from other prophetic literature (Isa. 1:2–2; 3:13–15; Hos. 4:1–6; Jer. 2:4–13). The unit is a prophetic covenant lawsuit.

It is different, however, from others in that a specific accusation or indictment does not follow the summons. Instead, Yahweh begins with a self-defense, asking what he has done to weary Israel, and then recites the history of his saving actions in behalf of the chosen people (vv. 3–5). These actions are familiar from the first six books of the Bible: the exodus from Egypt, the designation of leaders (the reference to Miriam with Moses and Aaron is remarkable), the preservation in the wilderness, and the entrance into the promised land (Shittim and Gilgal).

Such a recitation of the history of salvation frequently serves as the basis for prophetic accusations against Israel (see Amos 2:6–16). Here, however, the purpose is summarized in the last line of verse 5: "that you may know the saving acts of the Lord." If an indictment is implied, it is that Israel has forgotten what Yahweh has done, and therefore whose she is.

Micah 6:6–8 is in the form of a question and answer, with a worshiper speaking in verses 6–7 and another voice responding in verse 8. The form borrows from priestly and liturgical practice. When a layperson wished to enter the temple for worship or proposed to offer a sacrifice, there was a ritual of inquiry and instruction. A religious specialist, generally a priest, answered the questions about appropriate worship or sacrifice. Our text is thus a priestly or prophetic torah or instruction (see Pss. 15; 24; Isa. 1:10–17; Amos 5:21–24; Hos. 6:1–6). As in the other prophetic uses of the instruction, Micah has changed the contents of both the question and the answer. Specifically, cultic inquiry has been turned into the question of what the Lord "requires," that is, what it takes to restore and maintain one's relationship with God, given the acknowledgement of sin (v. 7b). Moreover, a cultic pattern has been used to reject reliance upon cultic activity.

The worshiper's question concerns sacrifices and offerings. With the use of hyperbole it moves from the normal practice ("burnt offerings," "calves a year old") to exaggerated proposals ("thousands of rams," "ten thousands of rivers of oil") to climax with the possibility of child sacrifice ("my firstborn"). There is irony in the tone, suggesting already that what is not possible is not necessary or right. If one relies upon sacrifices, how many does it take? There is, at least theoretically, no limit. Israel knew that its neighbors practiced or had practiced child sacrifice, but the prophet considers it ridiculous to think that Yahweh would require it (cf. Gen. 22).

The answer ignores the question; the prophet does not even bother to reject these proposals, as Amos did (5:21–24). Instead, he states what God does require (v. 8). It is clear that no new expectations are introduced. The Lord has already shown what is "good" and what he requires. The three "requirements" summarize the responsibilities of the nation and of individuals in the covenant relationship; all of them have to do with human activity in society and under God. "To do justice" (*mishpat*) concerns the establishment of law in the courts, the care for equity in all human relationships. "To love kindness" (or "mercy," "steadfast love," *hesed*) is to be faithful in covenant relationships, to maintain solidarity with others, including those in need or trouble. "To walk humbly with your God" is not an additional expectation, but a summary of the others. It means to acknowledge the Lordship of God, to submit one's will to the will of God. Genuine piety is seen in doing justice and loving mercy.

Psalm 15

This psalm provides an excellent counterpart to the other readings for this Sunday. All are concerned with ethical behavior. Psalm 15 was originally used as an entrance liturgy by pilgrims entering the sanctuary. It offers a series of qualities characteristic of the ideal worshiper.

The psalm opens with a question, perhaps asked by pilgrims as they reached the temple gates: Who can enter the sacred precincts? It is asked here in a graphic and metaphorical form as if access was to be permanent (v. 1). Admittance to the courts of the temple is the concern of the question.

The remainder of the psalm is an answer to the question, probably spoken by cultic officials (the Levites? the priests?) inside the precincts. The requirements for entry are given in a series of ten characteristics. It should be noted that, in antiquity, temples did not operate on the principle "Everyone welcome, all come." Certain persons (cripples and the deformed, those with improper parentage) and persons at certain times (when unclean from contact with some pollutant, women during menstruation, persons with certain skin ailments) were not admitted into the sanctuary (see Deut. 23:1–8).

The characteristics of those who might enter were probably proclaimed to the worshipers as the proper qualities of life; pilgrims could not be checked on an individual basis, and some of the characteristics noted are as much attitudes as action. Two features about the requirements in the psalm are noteworthy. (1) The requirements articulated all fall into the category of what we would today call moral qualities and interpersonal attitudes. None of the characteristics would fit into the category of purity laws and regulations, such as having recently touched a dead body or eaten unkosher food. (2) The qualifications given in the psalm are ten in number. (Ten was a round figure, and a list of ten could be memorized by ticking off the list on one's fingers. The Ten Commandments may once have been used in such gate or entrance liturgies, perhaps being written on two stone slabs or the posts of the temple gates.)

The following is a listing of the ten requirements:

1. Walk blamelessly and do what is right (behave according to the accepted mores and standards of the society).
2. Speak truth from the heart (show integration of the internal will and external actions; do what one says and say what one thinks).
3. Do not slander with the tongue (do not attack others verbally and falsely so as to destroy them).
4. Do no evil to a friend (do not physically harm one's fellow human beings).
5. Do not take up a reproach against the neighbor (do not participate in or perpetuate gossip or spread rumors).
6. Despise a reprobate (dislike those who turn their back upon God or society).
7. Honor those who fear God (the positive counterpart to the preceding negative).
8. Stand by an oath even when it hurts (one's word and oath are to be kept, even if keeping them brings injury and cost to oneself).
9. Do not lend money at interest (do not use another person's need to one's advantage; see Deut. 23:19–20).
10. Do not take a bribe against the innocent (do not do wrong even if paid; see Exod. 23:8; Lev. 19:15; Deut. 16:19).

Those who live up to such standards are declared blessed, unshakable, immovable (v. 5c). This final formulation is interesting. The focus of the conclusion is no longer on such a person who has access to the holy place but on such a person who has the quality of life and integration of social characteristics that make for stability and integrity in life.

1 Corinthians 1:18–31

The vital importance of today's text is seen in its frequent use in the *Common Lectionary*. It serves as the epistolary reading for Tuesday in Holy Week in all three years. The first section of this text (1:18–25) provides the epistolary lection for the Third Sunday of Lent in Year B. Yet another portion of the text (1:18–24) serves as the epistolary lection for the celebration of Holy Cross (September 14) in all three years. The reader may want to consult our remarks on this text in these other settings.

Because today's epistolary text occurs as part of the semicontinuous reading of First Corinthians, we will pay special attention to how it relates to its immediate context (chaps. 1–4). Last week's lesson concluded by noting that Paul's primary task was to preach rather than baptize. As a clarifying remark, he insists that he does not preach "with eloquent wisdom," fearing that this will somehow empty the cross of its power. This mention of his preaching the cross prompts today's text, a rather extended treatment of "the message about the cross" (v. 18). In fact, verse 17 is perhaps best understood as introducing this section rather than concluding the former section (NJB). Our text begins, then, with Paul's insistence that the cross can be compromised by rhetorical display. Preaching the cross can actually be robbed of its true power if it derives its force from "eloquent wisdom," the preacher's ability as a wordsmith.

Here Paul already begins to respond to a way of thinking in the church that he regards as not only unproductive but sinister. Some of the members held human knowledge in such high regard that it had become the sole measuring rod of all things, even things religious. Recognizing that knowledge inflates whereas love edifies, Paul later reminds the Corinthians that knowledge must be counterbalanced with love (8:1).

It appears, then, that some were beginning to measure the Christian message by the standards of human reason. Why did God choose to work through a crucified Messiah? How can an event of desperation—the crucifixion—become an event of salvation? How can a moment of powerlessness be a display of divine power? These are the questions human reason puts to God. Before we know it, humans have placed God in the dock, as if God must be defended in the court of human wisdom! Paul sees this as the beginning of unbridled arrogance. Today's text is his response.

First, he recognizes that the "message about the cross" (v. 18) has a radically polarizing effect. Its preaching inevitably creates two groups: "those on the way to destruction" and "those on the way to salvation" (REB). The former, "those who are perishing" (NRSV), are those for whom Christ is a "deadly fume that kills" (2 Cor. 2:16, REB; cf. 2 Cor. 4:4; 2 Thess. 2:10). The latter, "us who are being saved" (NRSV), are those for whom Christ is "a vital fragrance that brings life" (2 Cor. 2:16, REB; cf. Acts 2:47; Luke 13:23). Later, Paul concedes that it is "those who are the called" (v. 24) who are able to see in the cross divine power and divine wisdom.

The cross is best understood, Paul insists, when it is properly experienced. To "understand" the cross, one must experience it as saving event. In this sense, Paul concedes that seeing the cross as saving event is a subjective experience. Once we have experienced the divine summons, the call of God, through the cross, then we see the event as insiders.

And from inside the event, we see divine power at work, primarily because it has transformed the way we construe reality.

Second, we should note the way in which Paul pits divine wisdom and power against human presumption. His response is thoroughly informed by Old Testament thought, not only the direct quotation from Isaiah 29:14 (v. 19), but other reminiscences as well (Ps. 33:10; Isa. 19:12; 40:13; 44:25; Job 12:17). The preacher would do well to look up these references, for each in its own way relates to a common theme: God cannot and will not be judged in the court of human wisdom. The history of God's dealings with Israel and other peoples has shown that Yahweh has often made a mockery of human wisdom. Humans have often prided themselves on their wisdom while remaining oblivious to God's true purposes. To presume that God needs our advice and counsel is not only the mark of arrogance but illusion. It reflects a profound misunderstanding of God as well as ourselves. Elsewhere Paul insists that human reasoning left to itself results in darkened hearts rather than enlightened minds (Rom. 1:21).

Paul cuts through this rational misunderstanding by the use of irony, asserting that it is really "through folly" that God has chosen to save us (v. 21). In a similar vein, Jesus reminded his disciples that God had hidden certain things from the wise and revealed them instead to babes (Matt. 11:25; Luke 10:21). Elsewhere Paul insists that the ways of God are ultimately inscrutable (Rom. 11:33–34). At its worst, divine folly is superior to human wisdom; divine weakness exceeds human strength (v. 25). To pit ourselves against God is a mismatch from the start.

Third, the cross is presented as a novel way for God to communicate with us. According to Paul's view, there are essentially two ways of demonstrating divine presence: through signs and wisdom. Morever, each of these ways of authenticating divine activity within the world characterizes Jews and Greeks respectively (v. 22). The one looks for dramatic demonstrations of the presence of God (cf. Matt. 12:38; 16:1–4; Luke 11:16, 29–32; 23:8; John 2:23; 4:48; 6:30; 7:31; 11:47; 12:37; 20:30–31). The other looks for logical explanations (cf. Acts 17:18). Thus miracles and wisdom are seen here as the major ways of determining whether God is speaking or acting in the world.

Paul insists that neither of these "epistemological" methods properly "gets at" God. Instead, there is a third option—the cross—through which the true character of God is more clearly revealed to us. Unlike miracles, the cross is not a grand display of power and strength. It is, in fact, raw powerlessness. Unlike wisdom, the cross does not conform to our ways of reasoning. Rather, it runs against the grain of the way we think. It confounds us. In both respects, the cross radically calls into question the way we ordinarily construe God. For this reason, it tends to be a stumbling block rather than a stepping-stone (v. 23; Gal. 5:11; Rom. 9:32–33; 1 Pet. 2:8; also Matt. 16:23; Isa. 8:14).

Fourth, our text lays stress on the primacy of God—on who God is and what God has done. In this way, Paul undercuts human presumption. In the second section (vv. 26–31), he insists that it is God who is finally responsible for creating Christian existence. The Corinthians had little to commend themselves (v. 26). Note the threefold refrain: "God chose . . . God chose . . . God chose" (vv. 27–28). They came into existence as a result of God's actions, not their own. Because they did not generate themselves, "no one [can] boast in the presence of God" (v. 29). We should note the force of verse 30. Even though it is christologically rich, with all its claims about Christ, it is fundamentally a statement about God. The opening words may be paraphrased as follows: "It is of, and from, God that you are what you are in Christ Jesus; it was, after all, as a result of God's action that Christ became our wisdom, our justification." If we must boast, we can only boast of what God has done (v. 31; cf. Jer. 9:23–24; 2 Cor. 10:7; Gal. 6:14; Phil. 3:3).

Matthew 5:1–12

Today is the first of four consecutive Sundays that have as the Gospel lesson a portion of Matthew, chapter five. In fact, the four Sundays provide the occasion for treating that entire chapter in the sequence of its own material. Because Matthew 5 is a portion of the Sermon on the Mount (Chaps. 5–7), we should take time now to introduce ourselves anew to that body of teaching.

The Sermon on the Mount is the first of five major sections of Jesus' teachings provided by Matthew. All five sections conclude with the same formula (7:28; 11:1; 13:53; 19:1; 26:1), giving the impression of careful structuring. Some scholars consider the choice of five to be a deliberate paralleling of the five books of Moses. That Matthew draws on the Moses story to tell about Jesus has already been seen in the child's rescue from the wicked tyrant (2:13–23) and appears again in today's reading: like Moses, Jesus brings God's instruction from the mountain. However, the depth and breadth of subject matter in the Sermon on the Mount, plus the fact that portions of it have parallels scattered rather than gathered in Mark and Luke, persuade one to believe that the "Sermon" is really a compilation of teachings of Jesus delivered at different times and places during his ministry. Such a view does not rob any of the sayings of their meaning or authority, but it does free the interpreter from trying to discover or having to construct a single audience for all the material. Were a subject or title to be given to this collection of sayings, it could well be "Life Under the Reign of God" or "The Law of Christian Society."

It is not altogether clear to whom Matthew has Jesus address these teachings. In 4:23–25, a crowd gathers from all the regions of the land to hear Jesus, and at 5:1, "When Jesus saw the crowds, he went up on the mountain." Likewise, at 7:28 the section concludes with the observation that "the crowds were astonished at his teaching." However, Matthew says at 5:1, "and after he sat down, *his disciples* came to him" (italics added). Does this mean he taught those from the crowd who were his disciples or that he taught the crowds? Luke, who places the sermon "on a level place" (6:17) and provides a partially different and greatly abbreviated version, helps us here very little. He says there was with Jesus "a great crowd of his disciples and a great multitude of people" (6:17). Luke concludes by saying that Jesus had spoken "in the hearing of the people" (7:1). Luke's version of the Beatitudes is given specifically to his disciples (6:20). The question of audience is very important, however inconclusive the evidence. Perhaps it would be safe to say that the Sermon on the Mount was not offered as a way of ordering society as a whole regardless of faith or relationship to Jesus. Rather, these teachings are for the community of his disciples, but not first for his immediate disciples during his ministry. The presence of the crowds keeps the invitation open; "whosoever will" is still true. And speaking to his followers in the presence of the crowds keeps all of them honest about who they are and where their commitments lie. The church is a community but not a ghetto; meetings are open to, and aware of, the world.

The Sermon on the Mount begins with blessings, or beatitudes. To preface instruction with blessing is as appropriate here as prefacing the Ten Commandments with the recital of God's deliverance of Israel from Egypt (Exod. 20:1–2). In other words, God's imperative is couched in and surrounded by grace. The obedience demanded by the Sermon on the

Mount must be understood as response to, not an effort to gain, God's favor. The beatitude says, "Blessed are those who"; that is, it gives its blessing, it is not an urging or an exhortation to be this or that. The preacher will want to be careful not to give the impression that Jesus said, "We ought to be poor in spirit" or "Let us be meek." He pronounces his blessing, and the language is performative, conferring its blessing in the saying of it.

The preacher cannot possibly give in one sermon detailed word studies and exegetical analyses of each beatitude. There will be occasions for that task. In this sermon, however, it would be helpful to give attention to the background of the blessing in Judaism (Pss. 84:5–6, 12; 128:1; Ecclus. 25:7–10) and to call attention to the powerful dynamic of saying the blessing and receiving the blessing. Second, notice that these blessings completely reverse the values of most societies, including our own. No doubt many in Jesus' audience, zealous to take the kingdom into their own hands, were infuriated by these beatitudes and the behavior called for in the teachings that followed. Third, attention needs to be given to the types of persons who receive Christ's blessing. Commentaries will help with words such as meek, poor in spirit, peacemakers, and those who mourn, but it will be important to get an overview. These blessings elaborate upon the description of those to be visited with God's favor in Isaiah 61:1–3. And finally, the preacher would do well to distinguish between Jesus extending his blessing upon the victims in society and Jesus calling persons to be victims. The former he does; the latter he does not do. Even victims do not have to have a victim mentality. Victims hear Christ's beatitude and then take the initiative to claim a life appropriate to that beatitude. Those who give the coat, love the enemy, turn the cheek, and go the second mile are no longer victims. They are kingdom people.

Fifth Sunday After the Epiphany

Isaiah 58:1–9a (9b–12);
Psalm 112:1–9 (10);
1 Corinthians 2:1–12 (13–16);
Matthew 5:13–20

I n today's Old Testament reading we hear a compelling cry for justice and kindness—a valuable reminder that God's light shines no more brightly than when we serve humanity. Epiphany is the form of service. Similar themes are echoed in today's psalm in its insistence that light shines through the lives of the righteous. Here too righteous living is living committed to others. In the epistolary reading, we hear Paul clarifying the nature and essence of his missionary preaching and congregational teaching, insisting that both derive their power from God and not from human sources. The Gospel lesson is provided by the Matthean version of Jesus' teaching concerning the salt of the earth and the light of the world. The second image carries through themes from the Old Testament reading and the psalm as it presents disciples as the means of God's manifestation.

Isaiah 58:1–9a (9b–12)

T his reading continues the major theme of Micah 6:6–8 from last week's lesson, the definition of genuine piety, and the relationship between religious practices and the moral life. Micah 6:6–8 addressed the question of sacrifices and offerings. Isaiah 58 considers fasts and fast days.

Our passage is part of the so-called Third Isaiah (Isa. 56–66) and very likely stems from the years soon after the return of the exiles from Babylon. The reading reflects some of the religious practices that developed during the Exile and afterwards, and also indicates some of the divisions that were emerging in the newly reconstituted community of faith in Judah. The mood of disappointment and frustration with the new life in Jerusalem is similar to that reported in Haggai 2:1–9 and Zechariah 7.

The reading is part of a composite unit of literature (Isa. 58) concerned with the general topic of cultic activity. Verses 1–12 concern fasts; verses 13–15 turn to the issue of proper observance of the sabbath.

In some ways, the form of the passage is similar to the prophetic torah or instruction in Micah 6:6–8 (see also Amos 5:21–24 and Isa. 1:10–17), with a question from the laity answered by a religious specialist. But the dialogue here is more like a dispute than a request and an answer. It is clear that the addressees are the people in general, but the role of the speaker is not so obvious. Generally, he speaks with prophetic authority, on behalf of God. It is quite possible that the setting for such a discourse was the sort of community of worship and teaching that later became the synagogue.

In verses 1–2, Yahweh speaks to instruct the unidentified speaker in what he is to say to the people. He is told to be bold and direct, proclaiming to the people their "rebellion" and "sin." Those violations are not specifically identified, and it is presumed in verse 2 that those same people have regularly inquired of the Lord and his will.

Next (v. 3ab) this speaker responds to the divine instructions by quoting the words of the people. They complain to God because their fasts have not been effective. The assumption is that fasts are a form of prayer, probably of penitence. Fasts in ancient Israel, along with the use of sackcloth and ashes (v. 5), generally were associated with rituals of mourning, but they were also used as part of petition and intercession (2 Sam. 12:16, 22). Public fasts became important in the exilic and postexilic periods, and several such days were known (Zech. 7). The rituals for the Day of Atonement must have included fasts (Lev. 16:29–31; 23:27–32; Num. 29:7).

Then (vv. 3c–4) our speaker responds with an indictment of the people for their attitudes and their behavior on fast days. Business as usual, and oppressive business at that, continues on such days (v. 3c). People are contentious when—verse 4 implies—the public fast should be a reverent expression of solidarity before God.

To this point the author has said, in effect, that fasts are not effective because the participants do not take them seriously, do not devote themselves reverently to fasting. In verses 5–7, however, he begins to question the very idea of fasts (v. 5) and then to state what kind of "fast" would evoke the desired response from God (vv. 6–7). In a series of rhetorical questions, each expecting the answer "yes," an answer is spelled out in four points: "loose the bonds of injustice," "undo the thongs of the yoke," "let the oppressed go free," "break every yoke" (v. 7).

It turns out that these four metaphors refer to one activity—to care for the poor, to set them free from oppression, from the bonds of their poverty. Verse 7 states the point in very practical terms. Those complaining should see that the ones in need have food ("share your bread"), housing ("bring the homeless poor into your house"), and clothing ("when you see the naked, to cover them"). The final line of the verse is best read "And not to ignore your own kin" (NJPSV), that is, your fellow Judeans. This catalogue of social responsibilities is similar to that in Zechariah 7:8–10 and is an echo of Isaiah 1:10–17, which advocates justice and righteousness, especially for widows and orphans, as the necessary prerequisite for genuine worship.

Verses 8–9a promise that when these conditions are fulfilled, the people will live in the light of God's presence, and God will hear their prayers. That point is extended in detail in verses 9b–12: If the people will abide by that "fast" described in verses 6–7, then God will indeed be their guide. They will be like "a spring of water whose waters never fail," and the ruins will be rebuilt (v. 12). It is possible to take this promise as a form of works righteousness, that good works will earn salvation. Good works would then only replace fasting as a means of earning God's favor. Doubtless many heard—and many will continue to hear—these words in that way. However, the more fundamental meaning is that those who attend to justice and righteousness thereby live in the presence of the just and righteous God, they are part of God's people. Moreover, when the people attend to the needs of the hungry, the homeless, and the naked, they have their own reward: the solidarity of the community is strengthened, their "light" breaks forth, their "healing" springs up, and their "vindication" (v. 8, NRSV footnote) goes before them.

Psalm 112:1–9 (10)

This psalm consists of human-to-human address that seeks to instruct and offer advice about the art of living. This text is an alphabetic psalm having twenty-two lines (omitting the opening, "Praise the Lord"), each beginning with a successive letter of the alphabet.

The symmetry and order of the psalm, reflected in its alphabetic structure, are also characteristic of its thought. It assumes a morally oriented and governed world in which the righteous and blessed enjoy well-being and in which the wicked (noted only in v. 10) receive the opposite.

Verses 2–3 promise great and elevated status to those who delight in God's commandments. They will possess status in life as well as wealth and riches in their houses.

In the central section of the psalm, the righteous (see v. 1) are described. Three characteristics of the righteous are expounded. (V. 4 is difficult to translate. It could read: "He [the righteous] rises in darkness like a light for the upright ones, gracious, merciful, and righteous.")

1. The righteous deals equitably and generously, lending money and giving to the poor (vv. 5, 9). In ancient Israel, it was forbidden to charge interest on a loan to one's countryman. This prohibition against lending money at interest is found in all sections of the Hebrew Scriptures (Exod. 22:25; Lev. 25:35–38; Ps. 15:5; Ezek. 18:8). One should not make a profit by trafficking on the misery of others' problems. At the same time, goodness is relational; it is what one does to and with others.

2. The righteous life can withstand adversity and can confront existence with serenity (vv. 6–8). The righteous is not shaken (not a reed blown back and forth by every wind), can withstand evil tidings or bad news, is stronghearted and firmly planted, unafraid. Constancy in life is the principle advocated and the personality trait being praised.

3. The righteous are remembered (v. 6b). Not only the person but the acts of righteousness are lasting. Verse 9b can be translated "an act of charity endures for ever," because the word for righteousness also meant charity.

1 Corinthians 2:1–12 (13–16)

Whether one adopts the longer or the shorter form of today's epistolary lection, it basically consists of two parts. In the first section (vv. 1–5), Paul recalls the circumstances of his original visit when he founded the Corinthian church. The focus here is on his own work and preaching, as seen by his use of the past tense and the first person singular. The second section (vv. 6–16) is variously construed: as a single unit (NJB, REB), as two units consisting of verses 6–13 and verses 14–16 (NRSV), and as two units consisting of verses 6–10a and verses 10b–16 (NIV). Regardless of how it is divided literarily, there is a noticeable shift in both tense and person. With the present tense dominating in verses 6–16, these remarks appear to deal less with past missionary preaching and more with Paul's typical practice of providing instruction. The first person plural is also prominent in this section, although it is not altogether clear who "we" refers to, whether to Paul and Apollos as the teachers of the Corinthian church (cf. 3:4–9; 4:6), or to Christian teachers, apostles, and prophets generally.

We might note at the outset that ending the lection at verse 12 is justifiable, given the exegetical difficulty of verse 13b.

Paul's missionary preaching (vv. 1–5). In this opening section, Paul develops themes introduced earlier in last week's reading. Having noted that the Corinthians could not take credit for their own existence apart from the mighty work of God, Paul now makes a similar observation about his own preaching. Ultimately, he wants to emphasize that the power of his preaching derived not from his facility with words but from God's power (v. 5). Neither the Corinthians' existence as a church nor his message as a preacher could be attributed to human generation or ingenuity. They both serve as living proof of divine power. The gospel Paul preached was the power of God (1:18, 24; Rom. 1:16; 15:19; 2 Cor. 12:9; 1 Thess. 1:5).

The heart of his preaching was "Jesus Christ, and him crucified" (v. 2). This was the "message about the cross" (1:18), the message whose content was the proclamation of Christ's crucifixion (Gal. 6:14). In these verses Paul insists that his manner of preaching conformed to the message he preached. In his ministerial life-style, he came to them as one who was "weak, nervous, and shaking with fear" (v. 3, NEB; 2 Cor. 10:10; 11:30; Gal. 4:13). He made no attempt to package the gospel in "plausible words of wisdom" (v. 4, NRSV); he did not "sway [them] with clever arguments" (v. 4, REB). His own testimony here squares with the charges of his opponents that his manner of speaking was not especially impressive (2 Cor. 10:10).

Rather than deriving its power from well-turned phrases, Paul's preaching convicted because of its "spiritual power" (v. 4, REB). The preached word was nothing if not an occasion through which God's Spirit bore testimony (2 Cor. 6:7; cf. Matt. 10:20; John 14:26; Acts 4:8). As Paul insists elsewhere, preaching is not a matter of mere words. Done properly, it becomes a sacramental act through which God's power is mediated through the Spirit (1 Thess. 1:5). It is a channel of God's Spirit.

Wisdom for the mature (vv. 6–16). In his earlier remarks, Paul has given wisdom a diminished role in the work of God. At this point, he changes tactics and concedes that there is, in fact, a form of Christian wisdom reserved for those who are suitably mature to appropriate it. It looks as if he envisions a two-tiered form of Christian teaching, a lower wisdom for the young and inexperienced, a higher wisdom for the more advanced Christian. This distinction became much more full blown in later Christian thought, especially in Alexandrian thinkers such as Clement and Origen. The Gnostics drew the line even more sharply.

Paul's distinction here has a particular point. He wants to assure the Corinthian "gnostics" (those placing a high premium on human knowledge) that there is a form of higher wisdom. But it is reserved for the mature (*teleioi*; cf. 14:20; Phil. 3:15; Col. 1:28) and hence has eluded them because of their conspicuous lack of spiritual maturity (3:1, 18). It is characterized by its secrecy and hiddenness. According to the Synoptic tradition, Jesus had stressed to his disciples that God's revelation was "hidden from the wise and revealed to infants" (Matt. 11:25; 13:35; Luke 10:21; cf. Ps. 78:2; Col. 1:26).

Especially blind to this hidden wisdom were "the rulers of this age" (v. 6), which is likely a reference to the heavenly powers inimical to the purposes of God (Eph. 1:21; 2:2; 3:10; 6:12; also Rom. 8:38; 1 Cor. 15:24; Col. 1:13, 16; 2:10, 15; 1 Pet. 3:22). They are the minions of *the* ruler of this age, Satan (John 12:31; 14:30; 16:11; 2 Cor. 4:4), whose work is carried out through such earthly rulers as Pilate and Herod. Had these figures perceived this hidden wisdom, they would not have acted to thwart the purposes of God by crucifying Christ (v. 8).

As it is, God's purposes are enshrouded in a mystery oblivious to human eye, ear, and mind (v. 9; cf. Isa. 52:15; 64:4; 65:16; Jer. 3:16). They are available to those who love God

(v. 9b). The contrast implicit here should be noted: God's wisdom is not for those who *know* God, but for those who *love* God (cf. 1 Cor. 8:1). Being privy to the divine secrets occurs as divine revelation. Such "knowledge" is revealed by God through the Spirit (v. 10; cf. Matt. 11:25; Dan. 2:22). It is, after all, the spirit of a person who knows the interior of the person (v. 11; cf. Prov. 20:27; Zech. 12:1). By analogy, it is God's Spirit who probes the depths of God (v. 10; Rom. 11:33; Job 11:7–8). Once again, we are reminded that as human beings, we are not privy to the innermost thoughts of God. Nor can we discern the mind of God and serve as God's counselor. Rather, we receive God's revelation as a gift.

The latter part of this passage (vv. 13–16) further stresses that access to the mind of God does not occur through human wisdom (v. 13). As noted above, verse 13b is especially problematic: "interpreting spiritual things to those who are spiritual." Variant translations are offered in the NRSV notes: "interpreting spiritual things in spiritual language" and "comparing spiritual things with spiritual." On this difficult phrase, it is advisable to consult the various translations, as well as critical commentaries. What seems to be implied is that comprehending what God reveals through the Spirit involves a distinctive form of discourse, a kind of spiritual grammar, a language that makes sense only in the world of faith.

Those who are not tuned in to these dimensions of the Spirit are "unspiritual" or "natural," and consequently cannot participate in the conversation (v. 14). They are two-dimensional figures living in a three-dimensional world. By contrast, those who are "spiritual" (v. 15) see the third dimension, and, insofar as they see what others do not see, they are answerable only to themselves (v. 15b). The real irony, of course, was that the Corinthians against whom Paul is arguing were apparently insisting that they had achieved the status of "spiritual persons" (3:1), but their childish behavior belied their claim.

Among the several homiletical possibilities presented by this passage, one of the most intriguing is to explore what Paul means by "wisdom for the mature." One way of proceeding might be to note that the ordinary route to wisdom is through knowledge, whereas Paul insists that the point of entry is love (v. 9). How then does love become the qualifying norm for Christian wisdom?

Another possibility is to explore the way in which divine wisdom normally eludes this age and the rulers of this age (v. 6). Here it might be worthwhile to contrast the ways in which "human wisdom" and "divine wisdom" construe reality.

Matthew 5:13–20

This is the second of four consecutive Sundays that draw upon Matthew 5 for the Gospel lesson. Because this is the first chapter of the Sermon on the Mount, the reader may wish to review the introductory comments on Matthew 5–7 in the commentary for last week. Today's lection contains two distinct units: verses 13–16 and 17–20.

Verses 13–16 take up the subject of discipleship by means of two metaphors, salt and light: these two images govern the text. However, before proceeding with the discussion, the preacher might entertain the suggestion that the unit begins at verse 11. It is at verse 11 that the Beatitudes in the third person shift to the second person. Verses 11–12 address the reader (listener) directly: blessed are you, revile you, persecute you, against you, your reward, before you. This direct address continues into verses 13–16. If a natural break occurs at verse 11, what difference would be made in the interpretation of verses 13–16? One major difference is that the theme of persecution (vv. 11–12) would serve as a backdrop for understanding the salt and light sayings. To be more specific, if the pressure of persecution causes you to lose your saltiness, you are of no more value to anyone. Or, if persecution causes you to hide or to put your witness under a bushel, you become an absurd denial of your purpose. Or, by your good works the persecutors may be silenced and caused to glorify God. The possibility of this perspective should certainly be considered. Now to verses 13–16, our lesson for today.

Disciples of Jesus are not *urged* to be salt and light: they are *defined* as being salt and light. The urging or the imperative comes in being shown the absurdity of denying that role or trying to deny it. What could be more useless or meaningless than saltless salt and hidden lamps? Nor should the interpreter lose sight of the common and basic elements involved here. Salt, light, bread, water, flesh, blood, and breath; these essentials provide Christ and the early church with descriptions of the life of discipleship.

The salt saying (v. 13) has parallels at Mark 9:50 and Luke 14:34–35 and is, judging by its different contexts, a floating saying. The metaphor of salt carries not only its common and plain sense, drawing upon the basic functions of salt in all societies, but also religious and symbolic meaning. Salt was involved in Israel's covenants with God (Lev. 2:13; Num. 18:19) and in the purification of sacrifices (Exod. 30:35; Ezek. 16:4). "Sharing the salt" also came to be a way of referring to table fellowship (Acts 1:4, translated "staying with them" in the NRSV). Whether any or all of these associated meanings were stirred in the minds of Jesus' hearers is only conjecture. It is also conjecture to assume that Jesus meant for the salt metaphor to emphasize some particular quality of salt, such as preserving, or flavoring, or purifying. But one thing is not conjecture: the quality of saltiness gives salt its identity and purpose. Likewise, the quality of following and obeying Jesus, even under hardship, gives a disciple identity and purpose. Remove that and such phrases as "was once a disciple" or "still has the appearance of a disciple" are of no more value than saying "but it still looks like salt."

The metaphor of light is carried in three sayings (vv. 14–16). The first, using the analogy of a city on a hill, has no parallel in the other Gospels, even though light is a metaphor common to many religions. For Christians, Christ's claim "I am the light of the world" (John 8:12) is so central that the use of the image of light to describe the disciples is understood only in a derived and dependent sense. Still the obligation, implications for mission, the exposure and vulnerability in a hostile world are no less present in this definitive image of who we are in the world (Phil. 2:15). The second saying (v. 15) has parallels in Mark (4:21) and Luke (8:16; 11:33) but in other contexts, again indicating a saying for which we cannot recover an original setting. Variations in the saying occur: under a bushel, under a bowl, in the cellar. There may be some significance to the difference between Matthew's "light to all in the house" (v. 15, all the church) and Luke's "that those who enter may see the light" (8:16; 11:33, guidance for new members). But why would anyone hide a light? Persecution perhaps; fear of the lamp going out, perhaps; pride and embarrassment because of the cross, perhaps; making the church into a secret sect of the elite (Gnostics), perhaps.

The last saying (v. 16) is in Matthew alone and makes an extraordinary demand upon disciples. Their life and work is for all the world to see, but to be offered with such humility and grace that not they but God will be praised. That is a most difficult assignment.

Verses 17–20 are regarded by many as the thematic center of Jesus' teaching in Matthew. They contain four sayings of Jesus that probably existed earlier in different contexts but have been drawn together here by Matthew. Of the four, only the second (v. 18) has a parallel elsewhere (Matt. 24:35; Mark 13:31; Luke 16:17; 21:23). The passage as a whole offers Jesus' relation to Judaism, the church's relation to the synagogue, the Gospel's relation to the law of Moses.

All the Gospels testify that the Christian movement was under attack for violating the sabbath, being lax about observance of fasts, not keeping the rituals of the faith, and in general eroding morals by associating with sinners and saints without proper discrimination. According to Matthew, Jesus refutes these charges against himself and his followers by a statement of complete fidelity to the law of Moses (v. 17). "The law and the prophets," the first two of the three divisions of the Hebrew Scriptures ("the writings" being the third), here are taken in the sense of commandments and not as prophecy of the messianic era, as in Luke 24:27, 44. In other words, Jesus and his disciples are no less serious than Judaism about matters of moral and ethical behavior. But the very statement "Do not think that I have come to abolish" indicates an ongoing debate on the relationship between law and grace. Paul's letters to the Galatians and the Romans and Acts 15 carry two perspectives on the issue. The point here is that following Christ does not mean being careless about conduct, nor does grace mean permissiveness. On the contrary, the very opposite is the case, as verse 20 makes clear.

The last of the four sayings calls for a righteousness that exceeds that of the scribes and Pharisees (v. 20). Scribes and Pharisees are not synonymous terms. One is a profession; the other is a party. Pharisees were a lay group concerned primarily with interpreting and obeying the law of Moses. Because scribes were experts in the sacred texts, they naturally were associated with the Pharisees. The two groups were the persons most conscientiously committed to observance of the law. For Jesus to mention them was to say that his disciples were to exceed the best, not the worst.

Sixth Sunday After the Epiphany

Deuteronomy 30:15–20 or Sirach 15:15–20;
Psalm 119:1–8;
1 Corinthians 3:1–9;
Matthew 5:21–37

Here as always during the liturgical year, the Gospel is primary, gathering to itself the other readings. Matthew's Jesus is the new Moses, giving the authoritative teaching for his followers. Foundational for Matthew is the Mosaic law. The reading from Deuteronomy, as well as the lection from Sirach, recalls that Moses' word was God's word, which to obey was life, to neglect was death. Psalm 119 pronounces a blessing on those whose obedience to the law draws them near to God. The epistolary text is Paul's explanation why he could not offer the strong word of the Lord to the Corinthians; their immaturity was such that milk, not meat, was called for. Throughout today's texts the word of God is central.

Deuteronomy 30:15–20

This passage is itself a powerful sermon, and appropriately so, for both in terms of its location in the book and its substance it is a summary statement of the message of the Book of Deuteronomy. It contains the final words of a lengthy speech attributed to Moses on the plains of Moab (Deut. 29:1–30:20), introduced as "the words of the covenant that the Lord commanded Moses to make with the Israelites" (29:1). Immediately following our reading, the narrative resumes, leading finally to the report of the death of Moses. In substance, these six verses state the major points of the book: obedience to the law, establishment of the covenant, the conditions for life in the promised land, and responsibility laid upon the hearts of the people.

Opinions vary considerably concerning the antiquity of this paragraph. As it now stands, it has been incorporated into the edition of the book prepared by the Deuteronomistic Historian who wrote the account of Israel's past from the time of Moses to the Babylonian Exile (Deuteronomy through 2 Kings). When that work was written about 560 BC, Israel no longer lived in the land, so words such as these provided interpretation of the disaster of the Exile and guidance for a future return. But the lines are characteristic in every respect of the heart of the Book of Deuteronomy, from the seventh century BC, before the Exile, but still centuries after the time of Moses. In that context, the words were addressed to a people who had experienced the fulfillment of the promise of the land. Moreover, there are elements of the most ancient covenant tradition itself, going back to Israel's earliest days. Centuries of use and reinterpretation underscore the grave importance of the matters addressed in this text.

The context of the passage is the conclusion of the covenant between Yahweh and Israel. The reference to "heaven and earth" (v. 19) as witnesses reflects the background of this covenant in the ancient Near Eastern treaty tradition, in which the gods were called upon to witness the agreement and its stipulations, and to verify violations (cf. Isa. 1:2 and the comments on Mic. 6:1–5 given for the Fourth Sunday After the Epiphany). This covenantal context means that the speech is addressed to the people of Israel, that the focus of attention is corporate, not only for the sake of the present group, but also for the community that extends through time (v. 19).

Obedience to the law is a matter of life and death: that is the central point of the address. In language that is repetitious and hortatory, this point is urged upon the audience, laid upon the hearts of the hearers. The law is not perceived as a burden, but a gift, for it leads to life, the good life that the Lord wishes for his people. "Life" means the long and abundant life in the good land. "Life" parallels well-being or "prosperity," and "death" parallels "adversity" or misfortune (v. 15).

"Statutes" (or "decrees") and "ordinances" are used together in Deuteronomy to signify the law as a whole, the stipulations of the covenant (Deut. 4:1; 5:31; 6:1; etc.). One should not be misled by the repeated reference to such requirements in the plural, for although there are many laws, they all rest upon and amount to one prohibition and one commandment. That one prohibition is not "to bow down to other gods and serve them" (v. 17). During the centuries when the Book of Deuteronomy was developed, the prospect of serving gods other than Yahweh was not an abstract or vague possibility, but a concrete and practical temptation. In the land there were the deities of the Canaanites; in Babylon there were the gods of the dominant culture, including the heavenly powers (cf. Deut. 4:19). We may appropriately see this issue as the conflict between faith and culture. To what extent can one acknowledge the authority of the forces the culture considers as "gods" or make use of the culture's symbols of faith? Deuteronomy is clear: Do not bow down to them at all.

The single commandment on which all the individual laws rest is the positive side of the prohibition: Love the Lord your God and cleave to him (v. 20). This love is parallel to that of a child for a parent, a love entailing respect and obedience (Deut. 6:5; 8:5). It amounts to devotion to a single God (Josh. 22:5; 23:6–8). How can one command an attitude, a feeling? It can only be in response to God's love (Deut. 7:7, 13; cf. Hos. 11:1ff.), expressed in the history of election and salvation.

If there is but one requirement, with a negative and a positive side, then why are there so many statutes and ordinances and laws? Ancient Israel knew, as we do, that in practice the meaning and application of that loyalty to God are complex. Precisely what does it mean to avoid the worship of other gods and to love God in various circumstances? The multitude of laws and their frequent reinterpretation through time testify to the understanding that those who intend to obey the command to love only one God must work at learning and applying the meaning of that love. The rabbinical tradition developed a practical criterion for applying the law that stems from the theology of this passage. The law leads to life. If one interprets the law and finds that it leads to death, then that interpretation is wrong.

Sirach 15:15–20

For a discussion of the book The Wisdom of Jesus the Son of Sirach (or Ecclesiasticus) as a whole, see the comments on the texts for the Second Sunday After Christmas Day.

Our reading is part of a discrete unit that begins in verse 11 and concludes with verse 20. The passage is a disputation in the wisdom style, a debate concerning a fundamental theological issue. The teacher begins by quoting the point of view of his opponents (v. 11), but he does not give the arguments for their side. He makes his own case through the use of logic (would God act contrary to his nature? vv. 11, 12), by alluding to Scripture (vv. 14, 17), by stating commonly accepted doctrine (v. 18), and even by reducing the alternative to the absurd (v. 16). He concludes with a summary statement of his answer to the question at issue (v. 20).

The question at stake is the subject of one of the most persistent of all theological debates, the existence of free will. However, in Ben Sirach's time the debate was not quite an argument over free will and predestination. Rather, it had a particular, limited focus on the question of the source of—and hence the responsibility for—human sin. It was believed that there was an evil impulse (Hebrew *yeṣer*) in human beings. If God created that impulse, then some could say, "Because of the Lord I left the right way" (v. 11), "It was he who led me astray" (v. 12).

Ben Sirach's answer is unequivocal. God does not act contrary to his nature. God did indeed leave human beings with their own inclinations (v. 14)—here Ben Sirach uses the term *yeṣer* to mean freedom of the will—and God set choices before them (v. 15). Although God made both fire and water, God is not to be blamed if you decide to put your hand into the fire (v. 16). Ben Sirach reminds the hearers of the ancient choice between life and death, alluding to Deuteronomy 30:19 (see above). God does indeed have the power and wisdom to see every human act and will hold individuals responsible (vv. 18–19). Not only has God not commanded anyone to be ungodly; God has also not given anyone permission to sin (v. 20).

That would seem to settle the matter, but the other side of the argument must not be written off too quickly. Ben Sirach's vigorous rhetoric itself indicates that the controversy was a real one, with two sides. Do not the Scriptures more than once report that Yahweh "hardened the heart" of someone to do evil (e.g., Exod. 14:4)? Moreover, because God created human beings, God must be responsible in an indirect if not direct manner for all that they are. Elsewhere Ben Sirach himself seems to take a point of view different from the one expressed here. He bewails the creation—by whom?—of the "evil imagination" (33:3) and suggests that good and evil, the sinner and the godly, are created by God (33:14–15). Later rabbinic reflection will conclude that the evil impulse (*yeṣer*) was created by God, and the Torah was given as a means to overcome it (Babylonian Talmud *Kiddushin* 30b).

However, the disputation in Ecclesiasticus 15:11–20 does not mean to consider all aspects of the problem of the freedom of the will and evil impulses. In effect, it addresses the question of responsibility for sin. Here the sage's answer is consistent with the Hebrew Scriptures in general. God, who indeed gave human beings freedom of choice, is not responsible for the wrong choices. Whatever the ultimate source of the possibility of sin, human beings are held accountable for their decisions. In short, theological reflection cannot be the excuse for irresponsibility.

Psalm 119:1–8

The 176 verses of this psalm divide into twenty-two stanzas of eight lines each. In each individual stanza, all eight lines begin with the same Hebrew letter, working through the alphabet in order. In each of the stanzas there is a play on a series of synonyms for the law or the will of the Deity. Generally, there are eight such synonyms per stanza, and generally the same eight are used throughout the entire psalm. In verses 1–8, the eight terms referring to the Torah are these: law, decrees, ways, precepts, statutes, commandments, ordinances, and statutes (repeated).

The Old Testament readings (Deut. 30:15–20 and Sirach 15:15–20) speak of two ways—life and death, good and evil, fire and water, obedience and disobedience (to the commandments)—and challenge the hearer to choose the one over the other. Psalm 119 is praise of the law and praise of the one who has chosen the path of obedience, the way of law-piety. As such, it revels in the law and rejoices in the commandments.

Verses 1–8 reflect a rather interesting pattern insofar as speaker-audience is concerned. Verses 1–3 contain two benedictions pronouncing blessedness upon the obedient. The benedictions are thus composed to be addressed to a general human audience. Verses 4–8 are a prayer addressed directly to the Deity. The prayer, running throughout the remainder of the psalm, is thus the response to the benedictions.

In the prayer of verses 1–8, the worshiper asks to be obedient and observant of God's Torah. Running through these verses are both negative and positive strands. The positive aspects are reflected in references such as "be steadfast," "keep," "eyes fixed," "praise," "learn," and "observe." The negative aspects, that is, the inability to keep the law and obey the commandments, is also present. The worshiper prays "not to be put to shame" and that God "forsake me not utterly." On the human level, the fear is that of failure; on the divine-human level, it is the fear of being forsaken by the Divine.

Shame, which is noted frequently in the Bible, is a common human emotion. It is often, as here, associated with the failure not to measure up, the failure to be what one aspires to be, the failure to achieve one's goal. Shame is, however, an emotion that does not necessarily arise from public awareness or disclosure. One doesn't have to be found out in order to suffer shame. The ancient rabbis noted that "it is the heart which puts a person to shame because the heart knows what it has done and is ashamed of itself."

1 Corinthians 3:1–9

There can be little doubt that some of the Corinthian Christians placed a high premium on spiritual pursuits. Later Paul devotes three chapters (chaps. 12–14) to the question of "spiritual gifts" (*pneumatika*, 12:1) or possibly "spiritual persons." That the Spirit and the things of the Spirit set the Corinthian agenda is seen by the sheer frequency with which these terms occur in the letter. In the Second Epistle to the Corinthians, Paul refers to his readers as a "letter . . . written not with ink but with the Spirit of the living God" (3:3).

The desire to be "spiritual people" (3:1) can be a worthwhile aim, but some of Paul's readers had seriously miscontrued what this entailed. They were exhibiting a form of spiritual superiority that manifested itself in arrogant behavior (4:6–7, 19; 5:2). This no doubt gave rise to Paul's warnings against human boasting (1:29–30; 3:18, 21; 4:7). In particular, some members were being insensitive to the needs of others who were not as advanced spiritually (cf. chaps. 8–10). Consequently, Paul reminds the church that even though certain forms of behavior are permissible, they may not be edifying (6:12–13; 8:7–13; 10:23–30).

What unfolds, as Paul responds to this situation in the First Epistle to the Corinthians, is an extended critique of those with spiritual pretensions. Thus it is the "strong" who are admonished to be mindful of the "weak" (8:7–13). Those who claimed that they were already filled, rich, and reigning (in God's kingdom) are reminded that true spiritual existence is life that is deprived, poor, and humiliating (4:8–13).

Today's text contains an important part of this critique because it points up the potentially deceptive character of spiritual pursuits. We think we are spiritual; we see ourselves as spiritual; we may even call ourselves spiritual, all the while behaving in ways that are comically unspiritual. Paul's critique of such persons is that in spite of their pretensions to being spiritual, they were, in fact, "people of the flesh" (v. 1). The term "flesh" (*sarx*) in the New Testament almost uniformly has a negative connotation, signifying an outlook that is essentially centered on the self and pursues one's own interests. Its orientation is human in that it is driven by the desire to fulfill human wants and needs. Though Paul uses a different word in verse 14 (*psychikos*), he insists that the "unspiritual" person is the one who is unable to discern spiritual things.

Paul follows up on this in verse 4, when he insists that those who define themselves and their religious life by human loyalties, even in relation to prominent religious leaders such as Paul or Apollos, are behaving as "merely human" (v. 4) or "ordinary people" (JB). This is a sure sign that they are "all too human" (v. 4, REB).

Our text warns us that the quest for spirituality may produce an illusion. Our practice may not measure up to our pretension. We may pretend to be mature when we are actually spiritual infants (vv. 1–2; cf. Heb. 5:12–13; also 1 Cor. 13:11).

And what is one of the sure signs of unspiritual behavior? Jealousy and strife (v. 3; cf. 1:10–11; Gal. 5:19–20; James 3:14). One mark of spiritual immaturity is the inability to get along with one another. No matter what we claim, we are not spiritual if our behavior toward other members of the fellowship is marked by petty jealousies and strife.

In the second part of our text (vv. 5–9), Paul goes ahead to clarify the true nature and status of Christian leaders, in this case, himself and Apollos. Do they deserve to be the defining points of Christian existence? No. They are "servants" through whom the Corinthians had come to faith (cf. Acts 18:4, 11, 24). The proper way of viewing God's messengers is as instruments in the hands of God, doing the work the Lord had assigned them (cf. 2 Cor. 4:5).

In this discussion, we hear again a theme Paul mentioned earlier—the primacy of God in the work of salvation. True, Paul planted and Apollos watered, but the growth was God's (vv. 6–7). Consequently, the only proper way for defining ourselves is in terms that relate us to God: "God's fellow workers . . . God's field, God's building." We should not overlook this heavy emphasis on the role of God. It is Paul's remedy for human presumption. We finally must recognize that church growth, even spiritual growth, occurs at God's initiative: "*only* God . . . gives the growth" (v. 7, italics added).

We might also note Paul's emphasis on his solidarity with Apollos: "The one who plants and the one who waters have a common purpose" (v. 8). Their work together "as a team" (v. 8, REB) should be exemplary to the Corinthians, who seem bent on strife.

The true mark of spirituality, then, is to recognize that we identify ourselves properly only when we do so in relation to God. Becoming fixated on human leaders, however prominent or dear to us, misdirects us and finally causes us to operate on a purely human level.

Today's text offers numerous possibilities for sermons. It may serve as a way to explore the true nature of spirituality—the illusion, the pretension and the reality, the signs. Or it may be read as a commentary on the opening description of the Corinthians as the "church *of God*" (1:2, italics added). Then again, the graphic metaphors employed in verse 9 have their own possibilities. What does it mean for us to be "God's fellow workers" (v. 9, NIV), those who "share in God's work" (v. 9, NJB; cf. 2 Cor. 1:24; 6:1; 1 Thess. 3:2; also 3 John 8)? The church as God's field, or more literally as "God's farm" (v. 9, NJB; "God's garden" REB), calls up images from Jesus' parable of the sower (Matt. 13:3–9, 18–23), as well as the other parables of growth. The image of God's building also has rich connotations (cf. 3:16–17; 6:19–20; Eph. 2:20–22).

Matthew 5:21–37

In this the third of four lections from Matthew 5, we are introduced to specific examples of what it means to practice the higher righteousness mentioned in verse 20. In verses 21–48 there are six antitheses framed on the formula "You have heard that it was said . . . but I say to you." In each case, following the basic antithesis there are one or more elaborations on Jesus' teachings representing Matthew's or the early church's attempts to apply Jesus' teachings to new and very real situations. This means that the teaching on each of the six subjects will consist of the word of the law, the word of Jesus, and the interpretation and application of the teaching to a particular circumstance. In this lection we consider four of the six antitheses. The preacher may regard this as too much for one sermon. However, all four can be embraced in one message if one remembers that not only these four but all six antitheses focus on a common theme—the primary importance of personal relationships.

In verses 21–26, we have, then, the basic antithesis (vv. 21–22*a*), an elaboration (v. 22*b*), a second elaboration (vv. 23–24), and a third (vv. 25–26). The basic antithesis states that the higher righteousness extends beyond the act of murder to the condition of anger that prompts it. To this has been added a pattern of instruction based on the idea of increasing seriousness of offense calling for increasing severity of punishment. To be angry with a brother places one before the judge; to insult a brother (literally, to say "Raca," an Aramaic term of derision) places one before the council (the Sanhedrin, the supreme court); and to say, "You fool!" (moron, stupid, worthless) places one before the final judgment, the hell of fire. The second and third elaborations picture strained human relations in two very important settings, the sanctuary and the courtroom, and stress the urgency of reconciliation. The negative mood of punishment earlier (vv. 21–22) is now balanced with instructions on taking the initiative to restore good relations. In the one case, reconciliation takes precedence over ritual (vv. 23–24); in the other, over legal settlement (vv. 25–26). Note: in both cases it is assumed that the disciple of Jesus is neither the offender ("your brother has something against you") nor the plaintiff ("make friends quickly with your accuser"). The teaching addresses victims but calls on them to take responsibility to restore the relationship. Evil is overcome with good.

The antithesis on adultery (vv. 27–30) states the seventh commandment and then sets over against it Jesus' expectation that his disciples not harbor adulterous thoughts (vv. 27–28). To this Matthew attaches two sayings on the right eye and right hand (vv. 29–30), variations of which are found in Mark 9:43, 45, 47, and later in Matthew 18:8–9. These additional sayings were not to be taken literally, for self-mutilation would hardly immunize a sinful heart. Rather, they represent a forceful statement on the urgency of a life spiritually disciplined. In fact, one could argue that rather than blinding the eyes, one would do better opening the eyes to see and learn more about the person who might be an object of inordinate desire. Lust is usually toward strangers or pictures in a book, but once those persons have names, families, dreams, plans, fears, and concerns—in other words, once one knows personally the other—the nature of the attraction is radically altered and takes on a wholeness of which sex is only a part. In the antithesis itself, it is assumed that the woman at whom a man "looks lustfully" is married, because the issue is adultery. The law forbids coveting the neighbor's wife (Exod. 20:17), and the words "covet" and "lust" translate the same Greek word. The point is, a woman is not a thing, a property to be coveted so as to possess, but a person to whom one relates with care and respect.

The antithesis on divorce (vv. 31–32) is really an extension of the one on adultery. The issue of divorce was a thorny one for the early church, as evidenced by Matthew's return to the subject in 19:2–9, paralleled with variations in Mark 10:2–12 and Luke 16:18. Mark's version speaks also of a woman divorcing her husband, indicating a non-Jewish context, for that was not a possibility in Judaism. Paul struggles with the question of divorce in yet another setting (1 Cor. 7:10–16). The law involved in this teaching was Deuteronomy 24:1–4, which assumed that a man could divorce a wife in whom he found something unseemly, indecent, disturbing. Conservative Jewish teachers (school of Shammai) defined "unseemly" as unchastity, whereas the liberals (school of Hillel) said it could mean anything, from a wart to inability to cook to constant talking. Matthew's phrase "except on the ground of unchastity" (v. 32) puts him in the conservative camp. However, most believe that phrase is Matthew's and is not from Jesus, who would not have opened doors to divorce. Matthew 19:3–9 offers a fuller treatment in which Jesus appeals to creation as the ground for indissoluble marriage. Here the contrast is with Deuteronomy 24:1–4, which forbids the divorced woman, once remarried, from returning to her first husband. Jesus says she is not to be passed around at all, putting her in the position of becoming an adulteress and making whoever marries her an adulterer. Again, at the heart of the matter is the disregard for a person who was by ancient law treated as property to be moved about.

The antithesis on swearing (vv. 33–34a) concerns one's relation to oneself; that is, integrity, developed in a rather detailed elaboration (vv. 34b–37), an echo of which appears in James 5:12. The laws back of this teaching regulated perjury (Lev. 19:12) and failure to perform vows (Num. 30:2–15; Deut. 23:21–23). Under Judaic law, swearing was not only permitted but commanded (Deut. 10:20). Jesus' teaching, in contrast, is predicated on strength and integrity of character, which needs no scaffolding of an oath to persuade others of one's truthfulness. (Care must be taken to ensure that the listeners do not confuse swearing with cursing or profanity. Popular usage is not careful to distinguish.) Jesus' teaching here says there is no need for a structure of oaths to support one's word, as though one were assumed to be a liar and hence had to have one's word guaranteed. If I am and know myself to be truthful, then self-respect demands that I offer my yes as yes and my no as no. Truth does not need to call in outside help.

Seventh Sunday After the Epiphany

Leviticus 19:1–2, 9–18;
Psalm 119:33–40;
1 Corinthians 3:10–11, 16–23;
Matthew 5:38–48

Given the varieties of human relationships, pleasant and painful, friendly and hostile, the community of faith needs a polar star, a governing principle for any and all relationships. Matthew 5 concludes with Jesus reminding his hearers that neither friend nor foe determines behavior; rather we are to love as God loves. In a similar vein, Leviticus holds before all relationships the constant of Israel's faith: I am the Lord your God. The psalmist understands this and prays for understanding and strength to please God through obedience and trust. Paul uses the image of a foundation in Jesus Christ, whose temple we are and who relates us all to God.

Leviticus 19:1–2, 9–18

Because readings from the Book of Leviticus are exceedingly rare in Christian lectionaries, the contents of this lesson may come as a surprise to hearers familiar with the book mainly by its reputation. It is commonly assumed that Leviticus is concerned only with obscure matters of priestly ritual practice. Most of the book does indeed deal with the practice of worship, including sacrifices, the priesthood, the ritual calendar, the distinction between clean and unclean, and the definition of holiness. However, as this passage reveals, the book is concerned with the proper ordering of all of life before God, including life in society as well as in the cult. Leviticus, like ancient Israel in general, did not distinguish between religious and secular requirements.

Within the Pentateuch, the Book of Leviticus is part of the account of what transpired at Mt. Sinai. That report includes all of the material from Exodus 19 through Numbers 10:10, reporting the covenant, the law, and the initiation of Israel's life of worship, all through the mediation of Moses. The narrative framework of Leviticus comes from the latest of the pentateuchal sources, the Priestly Writer in the time of the Babylonian Exile or later, but most of the legislation itself is somewhat older in its literary formulation and in many cases goes back to ancient oral tradition. Our reading comes from a distinct body of legislation, the so-called Holiness Code in Leviticus 17–26. This code includes instructions for both laity and priests. There are detailed regulations concerning diet, sexual relations, gifts and offerings, rituals, and ceremonies of worship.

Chapter 19 addresses the laity in general and mainly concerns activities of everyday life outside the cult as such. Verses 1–2 give the narrative introduction to the chapter as a whole, stating the general command to the congregation and its reason: "You shall be [or "are"] holy; for I the Lord your God am holy."

The purpose of the regulations, then, is to define what it means for Israel to "be holy." Holiness is fundamentally a divine attribute and refers basically to what is distinct, radically different from the ordinary. Then it refers to holy places and things, such as cult objects, priestly attire, and offerings, sacred because of their proximity to God. Sacredness is contagious, so one must take care to maintain the proper distinctions between sacred and profane. The holy can also be dangerous, as the accounts of the calls of Moses (Exod. 3–4) and Isaiah (Isa. 6) reveal. Here, the people of Israel are holy because they are God's people, and they are to live out that holiness in all of life.

After the introduction, the instructions themselves appear as an almost random collection. Some are in the second person singular and some in the plural, and most are formulated like the apodictic laws of the Decalogue (Exod. 20). A refrain echoes no less than twelve times throughout the chapter: "I am the Lord." or "I am the Lord your God" (vv. 3, 10, 11, 14, 16, 18, 25, 30, 31, 32, 34, 37). Thus the instructions are given in order to define what it is to behave as the people of God.

Verses 9–10 give some specific regulations for the harvest. Fields are not to be reaped all the way up to the border; what falls at random is not to be picked up, nor are vineyards to be stripped bare. Rather, something is to be left for those who have no fields or vineyards. Verses 11–12 contain a series of prohibitions, some of which are related to the laws in the Decalogue: theft, lying, and false oaths profane the name of Yahweh. Verses 13–14 prohibit oppression of the neighbor, including the day laborer, who should be paid quickly, and the blind. Verse 15 concerns justice in the law court. Because all Israelite citizens participated in the legal process, it requires that no one should show partiality, either to the powerful out of fear or the weak out of pity. Verse 16 forbids slandering or profiting from the blood of the neighbor. (This second expression may refer to endangering the life of the neighbor through a curse.)

Verses 17–18 turn to the emotions and feelings that determine actions in society toward the neighbor. Instead of hating the brother, one should reason with him; instead of taking vengeance or bearing a grudge, one should love one's neighbor.

These final lines, "you shall love your neighbor as yourself," are neither vague nor unrealistic. Read in their context, they have a very specific and concrete force. All of the instructions in today's reading in effect define what it means to love one's neighbor. They concern the fair and equitable behavior that expresses concrete concern for the needy and the sort of justice that establishes and maintains a community of neighbors. The criterion for this love of neighbor is one's love of self. The refrain that runs through this chapter, "I am the Lord your God," already had laid the foundation for the combination of this command with the injunction to "Love the Lord your God" (Deut. 6:5; etc.) as the summary of the law, a summary that was already known in the rabbinic tradition when it was cited by Jesus (Mark 12:31; Matt. 22:34–40; Luke 10:25–28). Each part defines the other. Love of neighbor rests upon and expresses love of God, which in turn is possible because God has chosen—and thereby expressed his love—for a people.

Psalm 119:33–40

These verses, like the psalm reading from last Sunday, come from the longest and most complex of the psalms. Psalm 119, generally in prayer form, offers thanks and praise to God for the gracious gift of the "law."

In these verses, the eight lines of the text repeat eight of the synonymous terms used for law throughout the psalm: statutes, law, commandments, decrees, ways, promise, ordinances, and precepts. (Elsewhere in the composition, "words" and "judgments" are also used.) This multiplicity of terminology leads to two basic conclusions: (1) The psalm is speaking about more than we normally include when we refer to "law" or Old Testament law. Law (or torah) is thus not just the Mosaic legislation or even the Pentateuch. It denotes the whole of what was considered the revelation of God and thus clearly included Torah or the law of Moses in the narrower sense. One should think of the psalmist as writing about the written laws, about what might be called customs, rules, and practices of everyday living and about divine judgments and decisions seen as reflected in the ongoing course of life—what we might call fate or what life hands us. In all of these areas, the law, however, is seen as good, as a beneficent possession of people and thus as a gift, not a burden, from God. (2) The diverse terminology indicates that the author was looking at the "law," the total revelation of God, from a wide angle of vision so as to stimulate thought and interest.

Each of the lines of this section provides interesting metaphors and highlights particular concerns that can be developed in preaching.

1. Verse 33 recognizes that "law" is not a natural possession of a person; it is not instinct, but must be taught. God as teacher occurs in other texts (Job 36:22; see Pss. 25:4, 9; 27:11; 86:11). Others could teach as representatives of God (see Deut. 24:8). The law is thus not identified with conscience or natural inclination but with something requiring study—study being the dominant characteristic of the informed good person in later Judaism.

2. Understanding (v. 34) has always been seen as going beyond the intellectual grasp. A person needs knowledge/wisdom, but he or she also needs understanding, the ability to use profitably what one knows. The ancient rabbis described this as follows: "He that has wisdom but no understanding is like a man with bread in his hand but nothing to eat it with. And he that has understanding, but has no wisdom, is like a man with a savory dish in his hand but no bread to eat with it. But he that has both wisdom and understanding is like a man with bread and a savory dish in his hand, who eats both and is full-fed."

3. Verse 35 concerns the need for continued guidance (see Prov. 4:11–19) and sees the commandments making life into a (marked-out and delineated) path, not a road with uncertain shoulders and no signposts.

4. The heart (v. 36), the intellect, the will, the goal-setting organ, needs to be inclined toward the law. The heart must be shaped or tilted, disposed toward a particular life-style. The psalmist realizes that God's torah and gain (or "covetousness," "unjust gain") are contrary goals.

5. Life and eyes are brought together (v. 37; see Matt. 6:22–23). Visual imagery feeds the soul and thus tilts the heart's inclination. Here the psalmist asks that his or her eyes not look at vanity (either the materially unsubstantial or the morally corrupt).

6. The promise (or word) asked for in verse 38 may refer to either what is given to those who fear God or that which leads to fear of God. At any rate, it asks for assurance that God's way is the right way.

7. Verse 39 provides some problems: Does disgrace refer to the psalmist's troubles, to the fear of failure, to judgment for failure, or to the scorn that may come from adherence to the law? Probably the latter. "Ordinances" here may mean judgments and refer to the judgment upon the scorners.

8. The final line of this stanza closes, like most prayers, with a request but also with an affirmation.

1 Corinthians 3:10–11, 16–23

The first part of today's epistolary lection picks up one of the three metaphors from the previous verse—God's building—and amplifies it. At least three facets are worth noting.

Paul as a skilled architect (v. 10). When Paul received his apostolic call, he experienced it as a moment of divine grace (Rom. 1:5; 12:3, 6; 15:15; 1 Cor. 15:10; Gal. 2:9; also Eph. 3:2, 7–8; Col. 1:25). Accordingly, "the grace of God given to me" probably refers to his apostolic commission.

What is striking here is Paul's description of himself as a "skilled master builder" (v. 10, NRSV, REB; "expert builder," NIV). The adjective used is "wise" (*sophos*), which suggests the idea of being accomplished or highly skilled. The same phrase (*sophos architekton*) is used in Isaiah 3:3 of one of the various functionaries whom the Lord would remove from Jerusalem. It is rendered in the NRSV as "skillful magician." Here, however, the image is clearly that of a builder who lays the courses of a foundation. It is not clear why he designates himself as a *wise* builder (cf. 2 Pet. 3:15), especially in light of his critique of wisdom in the earlier sections. Perhaps he is stressing that as their founding missionary and first minister he proceeded deliberately and methodically as he laid the groundwork for the church.

In any case, he now recognizes that his successor is adding another course to the foundation. His word of caution is that each successor should give careful attention to the quality of work that is done (v. 10*b*).

Christ as the foundation (v. 11). Even if Paul and Apollos have worked with the church at different stages (3:6), they are not to be seen as the originators or as the foundation. This role can only be occupied by Jesus Christ himself (v. 11). The foundational role of Christ is presupposed in Paul's advice to the Colossians to be "built up in [Christ] and established in the faith" (Col. 2:7). The image of the foundation is slightly altered in Ephesians 2:19–22, where the church is said to be "a holy temple in the Lord" whose foundation consists of "the apostles and prophets." But within the foundation, Christ is the cornerstone holding the whole structure together. The confession that Jesus is the Christ also serves as foundational (Matt. 16:18).

Paul's insistence that Christ is the only foundation has the same effect as his earlier claim that God was ultimately responsible for the church's growth (3:6–7). In each case, human work is given an ancillary role, important but ultimately derivative and subordinate. The substructure is provided by Christ, or God; the superstructure by human beings. It is a crucial difference.

The church as God's temple (vv. 16–17). Paul's remarks here render the image of "building" in verse 9 more specific. The church is God's sanctuary (*naos*). The metaphor is introduced later in the epistle (6:19), but there it is applied to the individual. Here the use is corporate: the church, or congregation as a whole, should be seen as the sanctuary in which God dwells (cf. 2 Cor. 6:16).

Once this is recognized, members of the church should be more judicious in their behavior. The warning in verse 17 is quite stern: the one whose behavior is responsible for bringing down the church, or who is intent on obstructing the work of the church, must be willing to confront the judgment of God. In this "sentence of holy law" we are reminded that the one who destroys God's work will be destroyed by God. To tamper with the sacred is to invite disaster.

The concluding section of our text returns to themes introduced earlier. Those who claim superior wisdom are addressed with slight irony: "If there is anyone among you who fancies himself wise . . ." (v. 18, REB). The only solution to pretended wisdom is acknowledged folly. Echoing his sentiments in 1:18–24, Paul again insists that God looks at this world's wisdom and smiles (Job 5:12–13; Ps. 94:11). Human pretension is transparent to God, who sees us for what we are and for who we really are.

Consequently, trust in human beings is misplaced trust. "So let no one boast about human leaders" (v. 21). All such boasting is excluded (1:29, 31; Rom. 3:27; Eph. 2:9). And why? Because it confuses being with the Source of all being. The hierarchy of being sketched in verses 21–23 is critically important. Granted, "all things are ours" in the sense that God's workers work in our behalf and all of reality is at our disposal. But finally, because we belong to Christ we are Christ's (Gal. 3:29; Rom. 14:8; cf. Mark 9:41). And because Christ is who he is because of God (1:30–31), Christ is God's (1 Cor. 15:28). To be Son of God is to recognize that Christ is God's (cf. Luke 3:38).

At the top of the cosmic hierarchy is God. Like Christ, we ultimately define ourselves with respect to God. Our existence is ultimately derivative from God. Whether we are God's workers, God's farm, God's temple, we are above all God's. It is God who is source of all being, the ground of being.

Once again, we find our text redefining human wisdom and human values. True wisdom consists in recognizing God as the One who knows us and finally judges us. To boast of anything, or anyone else, is utter folly.

Matthew 5:38–48

Matthew 5:21–48 contains six specific teachings of Jesus making concrete the general instruction of verse 20: "For I tell you, unless your righteousness exceeds that of the scribes and Pharisees, you will never enter the kingdom of heaven." The form of these six teachings is that of the antithesis: "You have heard that it was said . . . but I say to you." In each case, Matthew provides the command to Israel and the command of Jesus to his followers, to which is attached an elaboration showing how the early Christians applied Jesus' word to their situations. Today's lection consists of the last two of these antitheses: on retaliation (vv. 38–42) and on relating to one's enemies (vv. 43–48).

The *lex talionis*, the law of "retaliation in kind," is found in Exodus 21:22, with additional applications in Leviticus 24:19–20 and Deuteronomy 19:16–21. The law was for the due process of administering justice and not for private indulgences in getting even. Jesus states his demand as though the old law were individually carried out, and against such vengeful behavior he calls for actions free of revenge and free of attempts to even the score. The conduct of Jesus' disciples is in no way to be determined by that of the one who harms and hurts.

The principle "Do not resist an evildoer" (v. 39) is given four applications: when someone strikes you, when someone takes you to court, when someone forces you to go a mile, and when someone seeks a loan from you. In each of these it is assumed that the other person has taken the initiative to harm or victimize, but the disciple takes the initiative to act in kindness, without hostility. The teaching does not call simply for nonretaliation or passivity, but rather for positive acts of good. One may be victimized, but one is not to think and act like a victim. Jesus was not a victim; he gave his life. So Jesus' followers take intentional steps of healing and helpful behavior toward those who are violent and abusive. The Mosaic law prohibited taking as a pledge the cloak of the poor (Deut. 24:10, 12–13), but Jesus says that to the one suing for your cloak, give your coat as well. Paul told the Corinthians it is better to be wronged, to be defrauded, than to be entangled in litigation (1 Cor. 6:7). Going an extra mile involved not Jewish but Roman law by which soldiers could force noncitizens into service for one mile. The application of the principle to situations of begging or seeking loans is different from the other instances both because no "resisting an evildoer" is involved and because Jesus' teaching really continues rather than alters the law of Moses. Moses wrote that loans to the poor were to be made, and without interest (Exod. 22:25; Lev. 25:36–37). Of these four applications, Luke's sermon on the plain contains three (6:29–30).

In the teaching on relating to one's enemies (vv. 43–48; see Luke 6:27–28, 32–36), the statement of the law of Moses is here offered differently. The law required love of neighbor (Lev. 19:18) but not hatred of the enemy; that was an interpretation of the law's silence. If one is to love neighbors, then surely one must hate enemies. Jesus rejected such distinctions: one is to love all regardless of friendliness or hostility. The behavior of Jesus' followers is not in response to, not a reaction to, the conduct of another. Neither friends nor enemies dictate the life-style of disciples. The faithful take their pattern from the God who never reacts on the grounds of others' attitudes and behavior but who acts out of God's own nature, which is to love and to bless both good and evil, the just and unjust. God is even kind to the ungrateful and selfish (Luke 6:35). To be determined by the conduct of others is to be as tax collectors and Gentiles.

Behavior that loves without distinction or reaction is perfect because it is behavior like that of God, who is perfect (v. 48). "Perfect" can also be translated "complete" or "mature." It is not here referring to moral flawlessness but to love that is not partial or immature. Partial and immature love embraces those who embrace us and rejects those who reject us. To be perfect is to love in the manner of our God, who is without partiality.

Eighth Sunday After the Epiphany

Isaiah 49:8–16*a*;
Psalm 131;
1 Corinthians 4:1–5;
Matthew 6:24–34

In the Old Testament lesson, the prophet of the end of the exile announces the continual restoration of God's people, always in comfort and compassion, like that of a mother to a nursing child. The psalm, an expression of humble trust in God, echoes the metaphor of the nursing child from Isaiah 49:15. Paul reminds the Corinthians that it is God with whom we have to deal; hence we do not judge ourselves or one another. We belong to God. The Gospel reading concerns the singleness of devotion to God in the context of confidence in God's care.

Isaiah 49:8–16*a*

The lesson resumes where the Old Testament text for the Second Sunday After the Epiphany left off. The original unit of speech probably was 49:7–12, preceded by the second Servant Song (49:1–6). As the first of the Servant Songs (42:1–4) was followed by a passage that interprets the servant as the people of Israel, so this unit is an interpretation of the second Servant Song in a similar fashion.

The reading contains three parts, verses 7–12, verse 13, and verses 14–16*a*, which in turn is not concluded until at least verse 18. Isaiah 49:7–12 is a prophetic announcement or proclamation of salvation, like a great many others in Second Isaiah, addressed to the people of Israel. The messenger formulas ("Thus says the Lord," vv. 7, 8) introduce the direct quotation of the words of God concerning what he is doing or is about to do. These words are, without exception or qualification, good news for the people in exile in Babylon and for the entire world. The glorious future is so certain that it even can be reported in the past tense.

"I have answered you" (v. 8) assumes that the people have been in prayer for deliverance. Their prayers would have been complaints or laments of the community such as those in Lamentations and Psalms 44, 74, 79, and so forth. The prayers would have been part of ceremonies of petition such as reflected in Joel 1–2, in which the community reminded Yahweh of their troubles and asked why he did not answer. Now, says Second Isaiah, God has answered.

Even before describing the salvation in store for the people, the prophet reminds Israel of the larger divine purpose, namely, that they are to be "a covenant to the people" (v. 8; see also 42:6). The redemption of the people of Israel from Babylon and their restoration in the land are not ends in themselves, but initiate the awareness of the lordship of Yahweh over the entire world, and implicitly ("covenant") the solidarity of all peoples.

The announcement of what is in store for Israel draws deeply upon the old salvation history. Yahweh will apportion the heritages, that is, divide up the land among the people, as in the time of Joshua. Prisoners will be released (v. 9), as the people of Israel were brought out of Egypt. They will be led through the desert, as Moses led them through the wilderness. The new miraculous preservation will be even more dramatic than the old, for the wilderness will be transformed into pastures (v. 9) with ample food and water (v. 10) along smooth highways (v. 11). The summary description of the return (v. 12) appears to include far more than the exiles in Babylon, for people will come from north and west and as far as the southern part of Egypt ("Syene").

The second part of the reading is verse 13, a hymnic response to the proclamation of salvation. It begins with a call to praise, addressed to heavens, earth, and mountains, and then states the reason for praise—that the Lord has comforted his people (cf. Isa. 40:1).

If the people are heard to express praise in verse 13, verse 14 begins a dialogue between personified Zion and the Lord. First, the city speaks to complain that Yahweh has forsaken and forgotten her. In his response, Yahweh argues that he could not and has not forgotten his chosen place. There is a powerful and remarkable reversal of roles: Yahweh could no more forget the city than a mother could forget "her nursing child" or fail to have compassion for "the child of her womb" (v. 15). Typically, in the prophetic tradition it is the city that is personified as a woman, but in this metaphor the mother stands for Yahweh. God's "compassion" for the chosen city—and for its people—is like that of a mother for her children.

It is tempting for the preacher to look for a "lesson" in every text, to find instruction or guidance for the congregation. Often, to be sure, that is the appropriate and responsible proclamation of the text in Christian worship. This reading, however, contains no instructions for the life of faith. Even the allusion to the people of God as "a covenant for the people" makes it clear that divine, not human, action is in view. It is God who will give such a covenant. The text is good news and requires only that it be proclaimed. God intends to set the captive people free, to transform the hostile environment of the desert into a highway. God's love endures like the love of a mother for her baby. The only response is to tell that story and to sing a song of praise, accepting the gifts of God.

Psalm 131

One of the psalms of pilgrimage (Pss. 120–134) sung as worshipers made their way to Jerusalem for a festival, Psalm 131 allowed the pilgrims to give expression to a childlike humility and confidence. Verses 1–2 are addressed to God as an individual's confessional prayer, probably sung by one group of pilgrims or the pilgrimage leader. Verse 3 is addressed to Israel, calling the community to hope in Yahweh, and is probably sung as an antiphonal response to verses 1–2.

The confessional aspect stresses the lack of arrogance ("my heart is not lifted up"), contentment with conditions as they are rather than looking for those beyond one's grasp ("my eyes are not raised too high"), and satisfaction with one's understanding, which does not seek to ply the mysteries of life nor plunge headlong into the incomprehensible nor grasp the unattainable ("I do not occupy myself with things too great and too marvelous for me").

As a consequence, the psalm can speak of being quieted and resting contented like a weaned child beside its mother.

The elements of self-satisfaction and passivity that permeate this psalm may tend to turn off the modern reader. Three factors should be noted that can help alleviate such negativity. (1) The tone of the psalm fits well alongside the Gospel lesson, with its emphasis on taking no thought for the morrow. (2) The psalm was sung on pilgrimage, somewhere between home and sanctuary, in that in-between state. To express confidence here is not passivity toward the world but confidence in one's course. (3) The image of the weaned child is that of one who has been released from the last vestiges of infancy, from a dependent state of reliance on the mother for succor. The trauma of giving up the security of being breast-fed to stand alongside the mother should not be underplayed. The humility of the psalmist also veils a sense of achievement, a soul that has been "calmed and quieted" and that now must be an individual.

1 Corinthians 4:1–5

How should ministers be regarded? As reference points for defining our religious loyalties (1:12–13)? As those whose preaching attracts us because of well-chosen words and well-turned phrases (1:17; 2:1–4)? As those about whom we boast (3:21)?

For Paul, the answer is none of the above. For him, ministers (*diakonoi*) such as himself and Apollos were best regarded as "servants of Christ and stewards of God's mysteries" (v. 1). Earlier he has stressed the servant role of ministers (3:5). They are those through whom the Word of God does its work: "God's agents in bringing you to the faith" (3:5, REB). Throughout, he has stressed the subordinate role of ministers as God's servants, those discharged to an assigned work by their superior, doing the work the Lord has assigned them (3:5).

A steward (*oikonomos*) is someone entrusted with a particular responsibility, a trustee given charge of something that belongs to someone else. In this case, ministers are "those entrusted with the secret things of God" (v. 1, NIV). Earlier Paul has spoken of the higher wisdom that had been hidden from the world that is now revealed to those who have received God's Spirit (2:6–13). As the recipient of God's revelation, the steward's primary responsibility is to be faithful in proclaiming God's will (cf. Luke 12:42; 16:1).

The important thing to note in both cases is that the minister's work is defined with respect to someone else—Christ and God. Ministers are not their own. They serve on behalf of Christ to whom they belong (2 Cor. 10:7). They unfold mysteries of the faith that derive from God, not from themselves.

Our text implies rather strongly that Paul is being judged negatively by some in the Corinthian church. He says as much later in the epistle (9:3). We are not quite sure of the precise nature of these negative judgments. In the Second Epistle to the Corinthians, the tone of the polemic is sharper as Paul mentions the unfavorable assessments of his preaching and personal demeanor (2 Cor. 10:10–12; 11:6). This may already be foreshadowed in his remarks earlier (1:17; 2:1–5).

Whatever the nature of the criticisms he was receiving, Paul's response is instructive even now. First, he insists that the opinions of outsiders matter very little to him because he does not judge even himself (v. 3)—not that he knows anything against himself (v. 4). He could say with Job, "My conscience gives me no cause to blush for my life" (Job 27:6, JB).

Having defined himself as living before God and acknowledging God as the source of all being (3:23), he defers all judgment to God: "It is the Lord who judges me" (v. 4). Because the sun neither rises nor sets with human beings, they cannot have the last word.

Second, he cautions against premature judgments (v. 5). His later remarks (4:8–13) suggest that some were claiming to have experienced Christian existence fully; they are already filled, rich, and reigning (4:8). Possibly, this attitude stemmed from their realized eschatology, leading them to think that the future was now. If this were the case, then Paul's remarks here are apposite, for they warn against presuming on the future. His advice is to let the future remain the future and not arrogate to ourselves the prerogative that belongs exclusively to the Lord at the final judgment (2 Cor. 5:10).

Rather, we are urged to understand truly what the Lord's judgment will ultimately mean—full disclosure of who we are and what we have done (Luke 8:17; Rom. 2:16). The darkened corners of our lives will be lit up with God's knowledge. The hidden will be revealed. God's light will eventually shine so that every deed is seen and assessed as if it were committed in the noonday sun.

Commendation may be in order, but in God's good time (v. 5).

Matthew 6:24–34

Today's Gospel reading moves us from Matthew 5, where we have been for four Sundays, into Matthew 6; but the subject is essentially the same—the higher righteousness, the life-style of those who belong to God's realm. Having considered what this theme meant in terms of human relationships, we turn now to think about the relation of God's people to material things.

Verses 24–34 belong to a larger unit beginning at verse 19. In verses 19–21, Jesus warns against amassing wealth and urges a life rich toward God. In verses 22–23, disciples are reminded that only the eye that is clearly focused can see and therefore bless one's whole life with light. Apparently, this is a call to singlemindedness away from a life of dark confusion created by double vision; that is to say, a life of split affections or loyalties. This image easily introduces verse 24, which says the same thing but less subtly and more rigorously: no slave can serve two masters. One cannot be a servant of both God and wealth. This image, in turn, introduces the subject of verses 25–33, anxiety about material goods. The word "worry" or "anxiety" translates a Greek term having the base meaning "split attention" or "divided concern." Hence, beginning at verse 22 the fundamental problem of double vision, two masters, or divided concern has remained at the center of Jesus' teaching.

Our lection proper consists of three parts: warning about trying to serve two masters (v. 24), injunctions against anxiety over material goods (vv. 25–33), and a call to a life in the present rather than borrowing tomorrow's woes (v. 34). By including verses 24 and 34 as part of the sermon text, the injunction "Do not worry," which governs the central body of the passage, is already being interpreted by Matthew's context. By opening with the image of serving a master, worrying about things already means making materials or wealth one's master or ruler. This is important to note because it moves the instructions about worry over food, drink, and clothing out of the normal place it occupies in a healthy life that bears responsibility for providing life's essentials for oneself and one's dependents. The teaching, then, is not a call to carelessness or irresponsibility or indifference to human need. In view of verse 24, the warning is against a slavish, anxious, worried service to wealth as though money were one's owner or master. This is the distortion that splits or divides a life between God and things, between persons and wealth, between love of others and greed. This is the distortion that dries up the springs of gratitude (no one can at the same time be grateful and greedy), closes the door of hospitality to strangers, refuses to open the purse before human need, trusts money rather than God with one's future, and learns too late the destructive force of greed's demand on marriage, family, and community.

The cure for such a diminished life is not to regard material things as evil. On the contrary, the text states that God knows we need these things and God will supply them (vv. 32–33). No, the cure is trust in the providence of the Creator. As the ancient sage drew lessons from nature, so Jesus points us to the birds of the air and the flowers of the field. Arguing from the lesser to the greater, Jesus simply asks, "Are you not of more value than they?" (v. 26). If one believes in a knowing and caring God, how absurd to think that there is a certain level of income that will add to the length of one's life (v. 27). The Creator is the Creator, and created things are created things. If we accept the value, but only relative value, of all creation and see ourselves, too, as part of creation, then the Creator becomes primary again, and God's concerns for the world become our concerns. Vision clears, we stand before only one master, and all these things are ours as well.

As stated above, just as verse 24 provides a contextual interpretation of verses 25–33, so also does verse 34. The introductory verse 24 interpreted worry as a slave trying to serve two masters; the concluding verse 34 interprets worry as a preoccupation with the future. Concern about what diseases, tragedies, pains, and privations tomorrow may bring can be totally debilitating. As a result, the gift of today is lost, and so will the gift of tomorrow be when it becomes today. In this saying, Jesus is surely prompting his audience to remember the daily feedings of manna in the wilderness. Or perhaps he is recalling a petition from the prayer he has just taught his followers: "Give us this day our daily bread" (6:11).

Ninth Sunday After the Epiphany

Deuteronomy 11:18–21, 26–28;
Psalm 31:1–5, 19–24;
Romans 1:16–17; 3:22b–28 (29–31);
Matthew 7:21–29

The threads that tie these texts together are the themes of the law and God's response to obedience and disobedience. The Old Testament lesson urges that the commandments be taught in every possible way; it proclaims that those who obey will be blessed and those who disobey will be cursed. Psalm 31, an individual complaint psalm, expresses confidence in God's mercy and concludes with reflections on the blessing and the curse. The texts from Romans present Paul's reflections on the relationship between faith, grace, and the law, concluding that the "law of faith" does not overthrow but upholds the law. The Gospel lection urges actions as well as words and distinguishes between those who will and those who will not enter the kingdom of heaven.

Deuteronomy 11:18–21, 26–28

The Book of Deuteronomy (from the title of the Greek translation, "second law") is so called because it includes the report of Moses' second presentation of the law to the people of Israel. The first was at Mt. Sinai, as reported in Exodus 19–Numbers 10:10. It is concerned throughout with the faithful obedience of the law, but the book is hardly a law code. In its structure as a whole, there is a narrative framework setting the scene on the plains of Moab, in the wilderness, before Israel's entrance into Canaan. Viewed as a whole, the book is an account of the last words and deeds of Moses, followed by the concluding narrative of his death. Virtually everything is framed in the form of direct address, with Moses speaking to the people. Both in style and contents, the great majority of the individual units are sermons. Where law or individual laws appear, they are preached; that is, explained, interpreted, reinterpreted, and laid upon the hearts of the hearers. The goal is to make the law effective, to evoke obedience. When the book contains references to the history of God's actions in behalf of the people, these too are preached, with the awareness of addressing a congregation of hearers who stand generations after those saving events. The people are reminded of what the Lord has done and are urged to remember and respond accordingly.

The Book of Deuteronomy contains many summary statements of its central theme, including the text assigned for this day. In two distinct paragraphs, the Israelites are addressed directly and are urged not only to be obedient to the instructions being conveyed but also to teach them in every possible way to future generations. The section between these two paragraphs (vv. 22–25) concerns the history of salvation, particularly the Lord's promise to give Israel the land if they are obedient to "this entire commandment," that is, to the laws in the Book of Deuteronomy.

Verses 18–21 emphasize the importance of daily attention to the laws revealed by God to Moses and give a number of specific and practical guidelines for remaining faithful. That the words of God are to be in the "heart and soul" (v. 18) means that they are to become a part of each person's very being. These words are to be written on the doorposts where they will be seen, and symbols of the law are to be worn (v. 19). But the words of the law are to be heard as well as seen, for the Israelites are admonished to teach them to their children and to talk about them daily (v. 19). Thus the home becomes a center for religious learning.

Behind this concern for daily attention to the revealed will of God stands the major transformation in Israelite worship sponsored by the authors of Deuteronomy. In order to deal with the threat of Canaanite religion and syncretistic religious practices, worship was centralized in Jerusalem, and all other sanctuaries were to be destroyed (Deut. 12:2–8; 2 Kings 22–23). Required worship at the one temple became three major pilgrimage festivals each year. The effect was thus less daily or weekly contact with religious observances. Deuteronomy responds to this situation in part by urging the integration of reflection upon and study of the law and the story of Israel into the daily lives of all Israelites.

Verses 26–28 give a brief summary of the blessings of obedience and the curses of disobedience that will be spelled out in minute detail in Deuteronomy 27–28. Here we encounter that doctrine of retribution persistent in the deuteronomic theology. That theology has its limitations, especially when applied to individuals. Experience teaches us what the Book of Job argues, that the righteous also suffer. However, in Deuteronomy the view is a corporate rather than an individualistic one. It is the people, the nation, who will live long in the land if they are faithful, and who will suffer if they are not. So we are led to ask if and in what ways does this view apply to groups, churches, or to nations. Above all, we will want to remember that at the heart of that view is the conviction that people are invested with control of their own destinies; they are urged repeatedly to choose one way or the other.

But this passage mainly concerns the law and the laws. Consequently, especially on a day when Paul's words on the subject also are read, this text provides the occasion for reflecting on the place of the Old Testament law in the Christian faith. The laws in view in our reading are those given in the covenant between God and people, and therefore define what it is to be the people of God. In no case is the law seen in Deuteronomy as oppressive or impossible to follow; rather, it is a gift that leads to life.

Psalm 31:1–5, 19–24

This psalm is a lament, interspersed with thanksgiving, composed to be prayed by one in trouble or distress. The following is an outline of the psalm: opening address and appeal (vv. 1–2), a statement of confidence in God by the worshiper (vv. 3–6), an anticipatory thanksgiving based on confidence in a favorable response from God (vv. 7–8), a description of personal distress and trouble (vv. 9–13), a plea for help interspersed with statements of confidence and trust (vv. 14–18), a further statement of confidence (vv. 19–20), a proclamation blessing God addressed to a human audience (v. 21), thanksgiving addressed to God (v. 22), and a sermonette admonishing the human audience to love and trust Yahweh (v. 23–24).

In spite of the misery and suffering of the worshiper, the psalm nonetheless expresses a sense of security and a strong faith in the outcome of an appeal to God. Luke (23:46) has Jesus quote verse 5 as his last words from the cross.

In the opening appeal and statement of confidence (vv. 1–5), images used to express the distress of the complainant draw from warfare ("fortress," "refuge"), trapping ("net hidden"), and personal self-evaluation and public judgment ("shame"). The troubles suffered, articulated in verses 9–13, suggest that the person suffered from social isolation and personality disturbances. Perhaps the problem was some illness such as "leprous" disease (see Lev. 13), which required living apart from society and under social ostracism and condemnation (see Lev. 13:45–46).

The worshiper prays for divine protection, that God would offer consolation and prove to be a hiding place. The willingness to commit oneself to the Divine (v. 5) would indicate not only a piety toward the Deity, but also a sense of the person's own innocence and confidence.

Perhaps in a service of worship focused on the individual or after spending the night in the temple, the worshiper, through priestly word or personal dream, became convinced that a good outcome was granted by the Deity. In verse 22, the psalm describes the earlier panic and plight but is confident that salvation awaits because God has heard the plea.

Verses 23–24 may have been spoken as words of encouragement to the complainant by the priest or to friends and family by the sufferer. It affirms the two attitudes that one may take—that of faithfulness or that of acting haughtily.

Romans 1:16–17, 3:22b–28 (29–31)

Today's epistolary reading consists of two parts, the first (1:16–17), a thematic summary of the Epistle to the Romans, the second (3:22b–28), a fuller elaboration of this summary. The second part of the lection does not correspond to the more commonly accepted paragraph division: 3:21–26 and 3:27–31 (NRSV, NJB, NIV). The decision to demarcate verses 29–31 is somewhat closer to REB: 3:21–26, 27–28, 29–31. As it stands, 3:22b–28 begins by emphasizing the universality of sin: "For there is no distinction [between Jew and Greek]." It concludes by emphasizing the motif of justification by faith apart from the law. A preferable option would be to read verses 21–26 as a single unit, or even verses 21–28.

In 1:16–17, Paul introduces key themes that will be developed in the letter: the gospel as God's saving power (cf. 1:1); the breaking of ethnic barriers between Jew and Greek; the revelation of God's righteousness through the gospel; salvation by faith.

Especially prominent in this introductory summary is the appropriation of Habbakuk 2:4, "The one who is righteous will live by faith," a passage that, in many senses, captures the essence of Paul's argument (cf. Gal. 3:11; Phil. 3:9; also Heb. 10:38). Throughout the letter, Paul insists that historically faith has been the means through which (sinful) people become people of God. Those who are "rectified by God" are those who have demonstrated the capacity for faith. Yet he also insists that this is now possible in a new way because of God's action in Christ. The gospel is both event and story. As event, it showed God at work in the death and resurrection of Christ. As story, it tells of this dramatic work in a manner that reveals the essence of who God is—one who reaches out to rescue wayward humanity.

The more expanded statement in 3:21–26 elaborates these basic themes, and in doing so delineates some of the major features of Pauline theology:

First, *God's righteousness manifested apart from the law*. A key word here, of course, is "righteousness" (*dikaiosune*), rendered by NJB as "saving justice." A major debate is whether "righteousness of God" refers to an aspect of God's character or to God's saving work. At stake is whether the phrase refers to a passive quality or an active work, to an attribute of God or an activity of God. It is probably more the latter than the former, because the term is fairly consistently used in the Greek Old Testament in contexts that speak of God's work of deliverance and salvation (Pss. 18:24; 71:2, 15–16; Isa. 46:13; 51:5–6). This dynamic dimension is captured effectively by NEB: "It is God's way of righting wrong" (v. 22).

But perhaps the crucial point for Paul is that "God's way of righting wrong" now occurs "quite independently of law" (v. 21, REB). The "now" is emphatic, referring to the eschatological turn of the ages. It suggests that a new era in God's dealings with humanity has begun, or at least, that God's age-old way of dealing with humanity is now seen in a new light: "The righteousness of God has been disclosed" (v. 21). The Christ-event has placed God's actions in the public domain, where they are now universally visible.

These actions, Paul insists, are "apart from the law." This suggests that at one time he saw the law as the singular statement of how God acts to reconcile humanity, but that this is no longer the case. He could no longer view Torah as the only window through which one could see God's justice at work. A repository of divine revelation it might have been, but it could no longer lay claim to exclusive revelatory status. Through Christ, a new way of conceiving and experiencing God's "saving justice" had been opened up, and it no longer had a "legal" texture.

Even though this new way of conceiving the divine-human relationship was radically new, it was not unforeseen. Instead, Paul insists that "it is attested by the law and the prophets." It conforms to scriptural expectations. As noted earlier, Scripture had already spoken profoundly of God's "righteousness." The psalmist envisioned God as providing deliverance and rescue "justly" or "righteously" (Ps. 71:2). God's work was seen as "righteous acts" (Ps. 71:15–16). As the epistle unfolds, Paul further expounds his theology of justification, defending it as compatible with the "law and prophets." In Romans 4, for example, he presents Abraham as the supreme paradigm of someone whose faith commended him to God and cites Old Testament chapter and verse to substantiate his argument.

But the point is clear: God's new way of "righting wrong," though foreshadowed in Scripture, now occurs "quite independently of law." Something has happened that has now superseded, and thus relativized, Torah.

Second, *faith in Christ as the new way of experiencing God's righteousness* (v. 22). The phrase might be rendered literally as "righteousness of God through the faith *of Jesus Christ*" (NRSV note; cf. Gal. 3:26). Some scholars have pressed the significance of the genitive to mean that we are able to appropriate God's righteousness because of the faith displayed *by* Jesus Christ (subjective genitive), that is, Christ's own fidelity or faithfulness demonstrated in the face of the temptation to disobedience. This is a clear alternative to the more traditional rendering, "faith in Jesus Christ" (objective genitive), which is followed by NRSV, NJB, REB, and NIV.

Whether Christ is regarded as agent or locus of "God's way of righting wrong," what is clear is the new texture of this relationship. God's reordering of human existence is no longer construed apart from the Christ-event. Neither can we participate in this reordering apart from Christ. This is the act of Christian faith: to believe that now God "rights wrong," both *our* wrong and *all* wrong, in a new way—no longer through Torah but through Christ. Christ thus becomes the new point of entry into God's reconciling love as well as the lens through which it is focused. When refracted through the Christ-event, God's righteousness is newly exposed to us.

Third, *the universal applicability of God's new way of righting wrong*. The picture sketched here is not one that is narrowly applicable to one segment of humanity or to one geographical region. Its effects reach across the board of all humanity. Entering God's righteousness is now available for "all who believe" (v. 22). Faith is no longer genetically construed. Being faithful is no longer a matter of ancestry. Jews are no longer privileged because of God's election of Israel and their role in salvation history, as distinguished as this history might have been. The way of faith is now a way "without distinction" between Jew and Gentile. It is literally a gift available to every single person on earth.

And why is this the case? Why is God's grace universally available? Because sin is a universal experience (vv. 23–24). Here Paul insists that every one of us, regardless of our presumed status before God or our presumed exclusion from the presence of God, is flawed by sin. We are "deprived of the divine glory" (v. 23, REB). The "glory" or "splendor" with which Adam was originally clothed (Gen. 1:26–3:24) was lost in the Fall. We have continued to exchange God's glory for a flash in the pan (Rom. 1:23).

The universality of human guilt is the basis for the universality of divine grace (cf. 1:16–17).

Fourth, *the death of Christ as the effective event of redemption* (vv. 24–25). Two metaphors are introduced here: redemption and expiation. The first signifies liberation from bondage and may recall the practice of manumitting slaves or even God's deliverance of Israel in the Exodus (cf. Mark 10:45). The other is cultic and regards death as a sacrifice in which blood is shed and through which ritual purification occurs (cf. Lev. 16). One exegetical question here is whether expiation (*hilasterion*) is to be understood as an act aimed at placating an offended, angry God, or as an act of purification in which God is the actor rather than the object being placated. It is probably the latter.

In either case, the death of Christ is seen as the pivotal event in God's act of righting wrong (cf. Rom. 5:6; 8:3).

Fifth, *justification by faith* (vv. 27–28). The way of salvation is through faith, not by our "success in keeping the law" (v. 28, NEB). The crucial question here is whether salvation is construed as gift or achievement. If the latter, we have reason to boast. It is ours because we earned it. If the former, "boasting . . . is excluded." To receive a gift is to participate in an act of generosity in which the only proper response is to say, "Thank you."

To be justified by faith is to see God's righteousness no longer as a quid pro quo, something God does to reward our efforts, as something we earn. Rather, it is rather God's generous response to our sinfulness, an act of grace that sets right our wrongs by canceling their effects. And how do we appropriate this righteousness? The short answer is, "in faith." Indeed, the gospel reveals God's righteousness from faith to faith (1:17). Our entry into this sphere of divine grace is an act of faith through and through. Faith is being responsive to an unwarranted favor, receptive to an undeserved gift. "Faith is the opposite of any kind of earning or achievement. It is the correlative of sheer grace—utter receptiveness, bringing absolutely nothing in your hand, simply making room for God and his action, acknowledging there is nothing you can do or contribute" (J. A. T. Robinson). Since faith is response to something unearned, it is "basically human receptivity, as actively as it may express itself in obedience" (Käsemann).

Sixth, *one God and one way of being saved* (vv. 29–31). Paul here insists that biblical monotheism implies something fundamentally important about soteriology. Belief in one God means that there must be one way of being saved. Implicit, of course, is the assumption that the one God is consistent in the way human beings are dealt with. But what's at stake is Paul's insistence that God does not have two ways of saving humanity—one for Jews, another for Gentiles. Paul's logic is this: one God, one way of salvation. And this way of salvation is "on the ground of faith." Moreover, he argues that this has been the case historically, which he proceeds to demonstrate in his treatment of Abraham in chapter 4.

Any one of these themes deserves extended thought and careful homiletical treatment. Perhaps a few words of caution are in order. We should distinguish between the underlying theological principles at stake here and the concrete religious issues through which they come to expression. Paul's immediate task is to address the Jew-Gentile question, but the issues are of much wider import. He in fact addresses questions that lie at the heart of every religious system: How do we construe our relationship with God? How is this relationship properly initiated? How is it sustained? These are questions that are part of every genuine religious quest, and Paul's answers are unequivocal: faith, not works; grace, not law; all humanity, not just some.

Matthew 7:21–29

This lesson for a ninth Sunday after the Epiphany, when that may occur, is offered for those traditions do not observe the Last Sunday After the Epiphany as Transfiguration Sunday. Those who do observe Transfiguration Sunday will find those texts immediately following.

Matthew 7:21–29 consists of three units: the first two (vv. 21–23, 24–27) conclude the Sermon proper with a double emphasis on obedience to what has been taught, and the third (vv. 28–29) is Matthew's conclusion to the Sermon in which he remarks upon the nature of Jesus' teaching and the response of the crowds.

The twofold conclusion to the Sermon on the Mount addresses two audiences: those who might deceive themselves into thinking that extraordinary religious activity is an acceptable substitute for obedience to the will of God (vv. 21–23) and those who might deceive themselves into thinking that there is saving merit in having heard Jesus preach (vv. 24–27). The former group is characterized as saying, "Lord, Lord," but without accompanying obedience. It is clear that Matthew intends by the title "Lord" in both verses 21 and 22 to refer to Jesus as exalted Lord of the final judgment, "that day" (Joel 2:1; Amos 5:18, 20; Luke 17:24; 1 Cor. 3:13; Heb. 10:25). Inasmuch as "Lord" can also mean "Sir" in the sense of addressing one's teacher, Luke's form of Matthew 7:21 (6:46) may be more nearly the original, set in the context of the ministry of the historical Jesus. But Matthew's perspective is that Christ is enthroned and calling his followers to account, and the issue is, Did you obey what I taught you during my ministry among you? If any in the church assumed that "every one who calls upon the name of the Lord will be saved" (Joel 2:32; Rom. 10:13) did not involve obedience, then verses 21–23 shatter that assumption. And if anyone assumed that an impressive ministry of prophesying, exorcising demons, and performing miracles would dazzle the Lord and effect a suspension of the demand for moral and ethical obedience, then verses 21–23 shatter that assumption. These are addressed as "evildoers" (NRSV) or persons whose "deed are evil" (REB), the words of the Lord's judgment being drawn from Psalm 6:8. Literally the word means "lawless," a translation that might better capture the emphasis of Matthew on doing what Christ instructed. Prophecy, exorcism, and miracle working are not evil in themselves; the evil is the disobedience, the lawlessness.

The second group addressed in our text (vv. 24–27) is a more familiar one: those who have heard great preaching, even that of Jesus himself, but whose lives exhibit no evidence of obedience. To these there need be no direct word of judgment as upon the first group; life itself will in time reveal the folly of hearing without doing. When the storms hit, the difference between the life of obedience and the life of listening alone will be dramatically evident. (The preacher may want to look at Luke 6:47–49 to see the different imagery that makes the same point. Luke's builders place their houses by a river that rises.) Verses 24–27 are reminiscent of James 1:22–25 in which, by means of a different image, doing and not hearing only is heavily underscored.

Matthew concludes the Sermon (vv. 28–29) with the phrase "When Jesus had finished this discourse," which is the formulaic conclusion to all five of the major bodies of teaching in Matthew (7:28; 11:1; 13:53; 19:1; 26:1). The crowds of 5:1 are reintroduced, and the description of Jesus as an authoritative teacher is taken directly from Mark 1:22, although in Mark the content of his teaching is not given. Jesus does not teach by passing along the interpretations of generations of rabbis but by providing a direct, unmediated interpretation of God's will for human behavior and relationships. Obedient attention to his teaching, says Matthew, is the key to life in the kingdom.

Last Sunday After the Epiphany
(Transfiguration Sunday)

Exodus 24:12–18;
Psalm 2 or Psalm 99;
2 Peter 1:16–21;
Matthew 17:1–9

A s Epiphany began with a proclamation of Christ to the nations, so the Last Sunday After the Epiphany is the occasion for an even more dramatic presentation of God's glory, this time from the mountaintop. Exodus 24 describes Moses' experience of God on the holy mountain. This text provides immediate background for Matthew's record of the Transfiguration of Jesus. By the time Second Peter was written, the Transfiguration had been enshrined in the tradition and used as proof that Jesus was God's son. Psalm 2, a psalm of coronation, proclaims the king to be a son of God, and Psalm 99 celebrates the coronation of the Lord as king. The Christian movement was early drawn to Psalm 2 in particular for proclaiming Christ as King and Son of God, quoting it both at Jesus' baptism and transfiguration.

Exodus 24:12–18

T he two paragraphs that comprise this reading on the one hand conclude the account of the ratification of the covenant on Mt. Sinai (Exod. 19–24) and on the other hand introduce the Priestly Writer's instructions for the building of the tabernacle (Exod. 25–31). The context, especially chapters 19 and 24, breathes an air of mystery because of the awesome presence of Yahweh. This account of the dramatic theophany of the Lord and the ascension of Moses as the mediator of the law and the covenant informs the Gospel accounts of the Transfiguration of Jesus.

It is not easy to sort out the sequence of events in Exodus 24. Consequently, commentators have long recognized that the chapter combines a number of different sources and traditions. In verse 1, the Lord calls Moses, Aaron, Nadab, Abihu, and the seventy elders to "worship at a distance." Then, after a covenant ceremony involving the people (vv. 3–8), those same parties "beheld God, and they ate and drank" (vv. 9–10). Later (v. 14), the elders are instructed to remain below while Moses—now another party, Joshua, appears (v. 13)— goes up on the mountain. Only some of the difficulties can be resolved by the traditional distribution of materials among the pentateuchal sources. At least verses 15*b*–18 come from the Priestly Document. Moreover, chapter 24 seems to duplicate some of the events reported in chapter 19. This diversity attests to the importance of Sinai, the covenant, and Moses in Israelite tradition.

Verses 12–14, the first paragraph of our reading, report Yahweh's command to Moses to come up on the mountain to receive the tablets of the law. Tradition follows Exodus 34:28 in concluding that the tablets contained the Decalogue; but the contents are not defined here, and the Hebrew of verse 12 is problematic, leaving it uncertain what the narrator meant. This reference is a foreshadowing of the story of the broken tablets in Exodus 32. Exodus 31:18 is even more explicit about the form of the writing, stating that the tablets were "written with the finger of God." When Moses ascends the mountain, he has the elders wait, leaving Aaron and Hur responsible for resolving any disputes that arise.

The second paragraph (vv. 15–18) gives an account of the theophany on the mountain. Significantly (cf. Gen. 1), Moses waits for six days, and on the seventh the voice of God calls to him. Attending the appearance of God are terrifying natural phenomena, the cloud (vv. 15, 18) and the "devouring fire" (v. 17). This contrasts with the description of the presence of God in verses 9–11, which seems to picture the floor of the divine throne room. More important, whereas verse 10 reports that Moses and Aaron, Nadab, and Abihu, and seventy of the elders "saw the God of Israel," here it is not God himself who appears, but "the glory of the Lord" (vv. 16, 17). Similarly, Ezekiel characterizes his vision of the presence of God as "the appearance of the likeness of the glory of the Lord" (Ezek. 1:28). God's "glory" is his visible manifestation. The purpose of this appearance of God is to communicate further instructions for the people.

Such texts as this one stress the holiness of God, the radical difference between the Divine and the human. But the passage also reflects on how that gulf between Divine and human is bridged. God is known in a covenant in which his will is communicated. God is known as an awesome presence at particular places, such as Sinai, and, later, Jerusalem. God is known not directly but through his "glory." Finally, God is known through a mediator of the covenant, Moses.

Psalm 2

The association of this psalm with Christian interpretations of Jesus was early and widespread in the early church. The Gospel accounts of the baptism of Jesus and the Epistle to the Hebrews are heavily dependent on this psalm in their christological formulations. In many ways, the New Testament writers were justified in their use of this text because it is messianic through and through. By "messianic" we mean that it reflects aspects of the ancient Israelite understanding of the reigning king (their messiah). In Matthew 17:5, Jesus is declared the Son of God; in like fashion, Psalm 2 speaks of the ancient Judean monarch as son of God.

Two features of the royal theology (messianic theology) are paramount in this psalm: the king's relationship to Yahweh and his place in the world of other nations. One form of interpretation sees this psalm as part of the spoken components of the royal coronation ceremony. It was thus used when a new king was crowned in Jerusalem. If this is the case, then the twofold relationship of the king—to God and to the other nations—focused on in this psalm is clearly understandable.

The first six verses may be seen as two stanzas in which the lines of the second are responses to those of the first. The opening stanza describes the planning and plotting of the nations (these represent historical chaos) against Yahweh and his messiah, the Jerusalem king (God and the king represent divine order and divine institutions). Placing the lines of the two stanzas in tandem gives the following parallels between the lament, or description of distress, in verses 1–3 and the description and responses of God in verses 4–6: The nations conspire and plot grandiose plans to deal with the problems of the Judeans—God in heaven chuckles; the kings busy themselves with implementation of their plans (building arms and raising armies)—God will speak to them in wrath and fury; and they desire to free themselves from God and his anointed, to proclaim their independence from divinely ordained orders—God reaffirms the role of the Davidic messiah and the holy city of Jerusalem in the world of the nations. In these stanzas, the Davidic rule is depicted as God's special agent, the anointed/the messiah, whose role in history sets bounds upon the nations of the world.

In verses 7–9, the messiah-God relationship is more fully spelled out. The king speaks, describing the conditions of his rule granted by God at the time of the coronation—the "today" of verse 7c. The king is declared to be the son of Yahweh, a son of the God. The Hebrews probably understood such sonship in terms of adoption rather than in terms of God's having sired the new monarch. (This may also be the perspective of the earliest Christology in Mark; Jesus was adopted as the Son of God at his baptism, which was understood as his anointment and coronation.)

According to verses 8–9, the king was promised that he would rule over the nations of the earth and smash them in pieces like a person breaking pottery with an iron rod. Such imagery of a universal rule no doubt draws upon the monarchical braggadocio fostered in ancient Near Eastern royal palaces and courts. That this is the case can be seen from the following assertions that an Assyrian king made about himself:

> I, Ashur-nasir-apli, strong king, king of the universe, unrivalled king, king of all the four quarters, sungod of all people, chosen of the gods, beloved of the gods, the pious who rules all people, strong male, who treads upon the necks of his foes, tramples on all enemies, the one who breaks up the forces of the rebellious. . . .

This claim to a universal rule, however, laid the foundations for the belief that the Messiah in God's kingdom would rule over the whole cosmos.

The final stanza of this psalm (vv. 10–12), probably with the new king speaking, calls upon the nations of the world to recognize God's act in establishing the new king in Jerusalem and to offer obeisance to the Judean monarch. Part of the call is a warning that failure to heed could bring divine retribution. Even in the ancient world, the issue of how one related to God's messiah on the throne in Jerusalem was of ultimate significance.

Psalm 99

The choice of this psalm for Transfiguration Sunday is based upon parallels in terminology and imagery between the psalm and the Gospel accounts of the Transfiguration: reference to past Israelite heroes (only Moses is shared in common by psalm and Gospel), a cloud out of which God speaks, and reference to a high/holy mountain.

In terms of who is speaking and who is being addressed, the psalm may be outlined as follows: a hymn extolling Yahweh as king but not addressed directly to the Deity (vv. 1–2), an address to the Deity (v. 3), a hymnic description of God as concerned with justice (v. 4), a call to the community to praise Yahweh in worship (v. 5), a description of God's response to three mediators (vv. 6–7), an address spoken to the Deity (v. 8), and a repeated call to worship God (v. 9). A number of elements are worthy of note in the psalm.

1. The three references to divine holiness (vv. 3, 5, and 9) remind one of the doxology of Isaiah 6:3 with its song of the seraphim.

2. The role of the great mediators in Israel's history is emphasized: Moses (Exod. 17:11–15; 32:11–14), Aaron (Exod. 28:29–30; Num. 17:11–15), and Samuel (1 Sam. 7:7–12; 12:19). If Moses is here called a priest, it is the only place he is so designated in the Bible. Verse 6, however, could be translated, "Moses, and Aaron among his priests, Samuel also. . . ." The three mediators who intervene and stand near God might be compared with Peter, James, and John in the transfiguration story.

3. The psalm stresses the present role of worship in the life of the people. Note the references to God "enthroned upon the cherubim" that stood in the holy of holies of the temple (1 Kings 8:6), "worshiping at the footstool of God" (before the ark; see Ps. 132:7), and at the "holy mountain" (Jerusalem or Mt. Zion; see Jer. 3:15–19). Worship now substitutes for those past events of holy history.

2 Peter 1:16–21

This text is chosen as the epistolary lection because of its explicit reference to the Transfiguration of Jesus in verses 17–18. It is a remarkable text because it appears to be the only New Testament text outside the Gospels that refers to the Transfiguration. It clearly presupposes knowledge of the Synoptic account (Matt. 17:1–13; Mark 9:2–13; Luke 9:28–36), though it is briefer and exhibits a different tone.

Mention of the Transfiguration is introduced in the context of a discussion of the "power and coming of our Lord Jesus Christ" (v. 16). There is some dispute as to whether the "coming" (*parousia*) referred to here is the Lord's first coming in the Incarnation or his Second Coming at the end of time. The word *parousia* is typically used for his Second Coming (Matt. 24:3; 1 Cor. 15:23; 1 Thess. 2:19; 3:13; 4:15; 5:23; 2 Thess. 2:1, 8–9; James 5:7–8; 1 John 2:28). It is similarly used later in the Epistle of Second Peter (3:4, 12). In fact, this epistle is written in response to those who were in some sense denying the Second Coming. Because the Lord had not yet appeared, they concluded that he would never appear (3:4). They argued that things were pretty much as they had always been and that they were unlikely to change.

Thus, if we take seriously the overall context of the epistle, it looks as if our text has in mind the Lord's Second Coming. The exegetical difficulty here is why the author introduces the Transfiguration to make this more plausible. Presumably, if he had in mind the first coming, it would make sense to mention the Transfiguration as an instance in which he served as an eyewitness. But it may be that he introduces it to establish credibility in the Second Coming by showing that Christ had already exhibited honor and glory as the Son of God. If such a graphic demonstration of his sonship could occur during his ministry, why not at the end of time? If his majesty had been seen once by eyewitnesses in the Transfiguration, why would it not be seen again at his Second Coming?

This helps explain the author's opening statement that the apostolic tradition did not consist of "cleverly devised myths" (v. 16; cf. 1 Tim. 4:7; 6:20; 2 Tim. 2:16). The opponents, or "scoffers" (cf. 2:1–3; 3:3–4), had apparently classified certain parts of the apostolic testimony with other incredible tales. Our text insists that this could not be the case because such events as the Transfiguration were verified by "eyewitnesses of his majesty" (v. 16). The letter, of course, is attributed to the apostle Peter (1:1), although it is now widely recognized as being pseudonymous. In any case, the claim here is that Peter, the author, had witnessed this event as one of those who had been with Christ on the "holy mountain" (v. 18).

The second part of today's lection (vv. 19–21) moves to another topic—the reliability of the prophetic witness. First there is the reminder that prophecy is not a matter of private interpretation (v. 20). This seems directed at the heretics who would often appeal to novel interpretations to support their position. It suggests that interpretation of Scripture must somehow be answerable to a wider public. The apostolic tradition serves as one norm against which Scripture interpretation is to be judged (1:12–15).

Second, there is a reminder that Scripture itself is not the product of individual initiative. Rather than being self-motivated, the prophets were impelled by the Holy Spirit to speak for God (cf. 2 Tim. 3:16; also Acts 2:1–6; 28:25).

Even though this passage presents several exegetical difficulties, it provides useful images for preaching on the Transfiguration. We should note the vivid images in verse 19: the lamp shining in darkness, the dawning of the day (Luke 1:78), and the rising of the morning star (cf. Rev. 2:28). Each of these extend the image of Majestic Glory (v. 17). The full significance of the Transfiguration could only be stated symbolically: dazzling light signified the presence of God and the divine confirmation of Jesus as God's Son. In the same way that God's radiance broke through in the ministry of Jesus, a similarly dazzling display may be expected at the Lord's Second Coming.

Matthew 17:1–9

Just as the Gospel for the First Sunday After the Epiphany always recalls the baptism of Jesus, so the reading for the last Sunday recalls the Transfiguration. The two records have many parallels: in both Jesus is passive, being acted upon; in both God reveals who Jesus really is. Both experiences immediately follow occasions that point up the humble obedience of Jesus. The Transfiguration follows after Jesus announces his coming death (16:21). Both the baptism and the Transfiguration are epiphanies, or more precisely, Christophanies.

The story in 17:1–9 is that of a Christophany by means of a metamorphosis ("transfiguration" is derived from the Latin translation). The word occurs in 2 Corinthians 3:18 and Romans 12:2. Jesus' whole being is transformed, including his clothing. There is no reason to argue that this is a misplaced resurrection story or Parousia story. That which someday "every eye will see" (Rev. 1:7) is here revealed to Peter, James, and John, the inner circle (Mark 5:37; 14:33), and through them to the reader; that is, the glory of the eternal status of the divine Son. That which flesh, blood, and human observation could not perceive, but which God revealed to Simon Peter at Caesarea Philippi (16:17), here shines through the face and frame of Jesus of Nazareth. Jesus is the Son of God.

In telling the story, Matthew follows closely Mark 9:2–8, as does Luke (9:28–36), although with more variations. Many of the details are drawn from Old Testament accounts of theophanies: after six days (Exod. 24:16), the shining of the face (Exod. 34:29–35), and being overshadowed (Exod. 40:35). Bright light is, of course, everywhere mentioned as a symbol of the divine presence (Rev. 3:4; 7:9; Col. 1:12; Heb. 1:1–3). The presence of Moses and Elijah confirm the witness of the law and the prophets to Jesus Christ, and Peter's suggestion of building booths recalls the Feast of Booths during which Israel commemorated very special times, such as being led of God in the wilderness by means of the cloud and the fire (Lev. 23:39–43). Whereas Mark introduces Simon Peter's fear at the appearance of the three figures, which fear prompts him to speak (9:5–6), Matthew says fear came upon all three at the voice from the cloud: "This is my Son, the Beloved; with him I am well pleased; listen to him" (vv. 5–6). These disciples did not hear this voice and the similar message at Jesus' baptism (3:17), but the reader recalls that account. At baptism, when Jesus submitted to the call of John to prepare for the kingdom, the voice from heaven announces who Jesus really is. At his prediction of death, when Jesus will submit to the experience common to us all (16:21), the divine voice again says who Jesus really is, and adds that he, not Moses or Elijah, is to be obeyed (v. 5). Given these two occasions brightened by heaven's attestation, one might anticipate that the confirming voice would come appropriately one more time, at the cross. But it did not, and the crowds were persuaded that Jesus, without heaven's voice or divine rescue, was not from God (27:39–43).

It is only at verse 7 that Jesus speaks or acts (this verse has no parallel in Mark). Jesus comes to them, a rare expression, given the fact that throughout the Gospel others come to Jesus. Here he approaches them, as he does in the post-resurrection scene in 28:16–20. The phrase could carry the force of a descent, of a kind of Parousia. Jesus' touch and his words bless and assure. It was enough to embolden them to open their eyes, and the vision was over. There is no reason to think they understood what had occurred, but in subsequent Christian history the event was enshrined as occurring on "the holy mountain" and was offered as proof of the truth of the apostolic witness to Jesus (2 Pet. 1:17–18).

Our lection closes with a post-Transfiguration note: "Tell no one about the vision until after the Son of Man has been raised from the dead" (v. 9). If the disciples understood who Jesus was only after the resurrection, there certainly was no reason to assume the crowds could. After all, if the baptism and prediction of passion seemed a contradiction of the terms "Messiah" and "Son of God," how much more would the cross? The people are not ready for the Transfiguration story because the disciples are not ready to tell it.

Ash Wednesday

Joel 2:1–2, 12–17 or Isaiah 58:1–12;
Psalm 51:1–17;
2 Corinthians 5:20b–6:10;
Matthew 6:1–6, 16–21

Providing guidance for Lent and setting the mood for the season are five texts concerning prayer and piety. The Old Testament reading from Joel is a prophetic and priestly summons to a community service of confession and repentance as the day of the Lord approaches; the alternative lection from Isaiah 58 calls for repentance and interprets fasting. The psalm is an actual prayer of confession and petition by an individual. In many such petitions, the psalmist asks for deliverance from illness or disaster, but here he prays for relief from sin and its effects. In the Gospel reading, the hearers of the Sermon on the Mount are warned that public piety—including prayer and fasting—for the sake of displaying one's faithfulness is false piety. The epistolary reading points to God's response to the confession of sin, for God "made him to be sin who knew no sin, so that in him we might become the righteousness of God" (2 Cor. 5:21).

Joel 2:1–2, 12–17

It is appropriate that verses from the Book of Joel lead the church on a solemn occasion that initiates a season of penitence, fasting, and self-examination, for the book developed and was used in similar liturgical contexts in ancient Israel. The book in general certainly is a prophetic one, and these verses in particular reflect that fact. But there are priestly and liturgical dimensions as well. In fact, many commentators rightly have called Joel a cultic prophet and the book a prophetic liturgy.

The verses before us today contain that merging of prophetic and priestly sensibilities and perspectives on the relationship between God and people. The prophetic dimension, although more detailed in chapter 1 and in 2:3–11, sets the tone at the outset. In Joel 1 and 2:3–11, it is present in the descriptions of the approaching judgment upon the land. In our reading, the prophetic perspective is apparent in the announcement that the day of the Lord is coming (v. 1). Thus, although the prophet's explicit message is a call to prayer, fasting, and repentance, that message assumes the announcement of impending divine judgment.

The expectation of the day of the Lord in Joel is almost, but not quite, an apocalyptic expectation. Joel 2:1–2, closely paralleled by Zephaniah 1:15, stands in a long prophetic tradition. One of the clearest articulations of that tradition is also one of its oldest:

> Alas for you who desire the day of the LORD!
> Why do you want the day of the LORD?
> It is darkness, not light. (Amos 5:18)

Clearly, Amos announces the reversal of a contemporary (eighth century BC) hope. The tradition behind the hope for the day of the Lord probably was the holy war, the time when Yahweh would act against his enemies. For Amos and other early prophets (cf. Isa. 2:9–11), the people of Israel had become Yahweh's enemies. That is no less true for Joel, who clearly indicates that Yahweh, marching at the head of his army, is indeed ready to destroy his enemies, the people of Israel (v. 11).

Thus the threat of the end, if not of history at least of the covenant people, provides the urgency for Joel's call. The cry is both an alarm—the trumpet (v. 1) announces the approach of the enemy, "a great and powerful army" (v. 2)—and a summons to assemble for a service of worship. What are the people to do in the shadow of the day of the Lord, before the threat of divine wrath? They must assemble to fast and pray.

The priestly-liturgical dimensions of Joel are present in the instructions for the service of worship. Speaking for Yahweh, the prophet calls for the people to "return" (vv. 12, 13) to the Lord, instructs them to fast, weep, and mourn, and then spells out the details of the assembly, including the duties of the priests (vv. 14–17). The religious ceremony in view here is one that is well-known from elsewhere in the Old Testament, especially from the psalms of lament or complaint. An individual who was ill or otherwise in trouble called for a priest, who would gather the person's primary group—family and neighbors—for a service of prayer. At the center of such services were the psalms of individual lament or complaint. Likewise, when the people were threatened by drought, famine, or enemy invasion, they gathered to plead with God. The prayers they offered (see Pss. 44, 74, 89; Lam. 5) included invocations of the divine name, confessions, affirmations of confidence in God, and, above all, petitions for divine favor. Other texts that reflect such services are Judges 20:26–28; 1 Kings 8:33–36, 44–45; Jonah 3:5–10, and Isaiah 63:7–64:11.

Joel, like the other texts, emphasizes the corporate, communal dimension of the prayer service. After all, it was the entire community that was in trouble. Thus everyone is to participate, men and women, from elders to nursing infants. Even the new bride and bridegroom are to join in (v. 16).

The people's public behavior is an important part of the time of prayer. Joel instructs them to fast, weep, and mourn. These actions are known elsewhere in the Old Testament as expressions of grief, as rituals of sorrow following death (1 Sam. 31:13; Jth. 16:24). Their purpose here is twofold: to convince God that the people know the seriousness of the threat and to demonstrate the sincerity of their repentance. Contemporary Christians, taking seriously New Testament texts such as our Gospel reading for today, often disparage such outward displays of piety, and rightly so. However, such rituals have their value, for habits of the body may even shape the habits of the heart. One's feelings may be trained by such rituals, even to experience genuine repentance. But lest the point should be missed, Joel enjoins his hearers, "Rend your hearts and not your clothing" (v. 13).

At the center of the text is the call for the people to return to the Lord their God. This "return" is the directing of their full devotion to the God of Israel, and it is also repentance. Remarkably, there is no mention of the sin or sins for which the community is to repent. The fundamental concern is with orientation in the right direction. On the one hand, the urgency comes from awareness of the impending day of the Lord, the possibility of a judgment that would end the community's life. But on the other hand, the call to repent is based on the conviction that God "is gracious and merciful, slow to anger, and abounding in steadfast love" (v. 13). Indeed, Joel urges all his hearers to repent, for God is one who "relents from punishing" (NRSV; better, "repents of evil," RSV, v. 13); that is, the Lord is both able and willing to be affected by the people.

Isaiah 58:1–12

This text is also the Old Testament reading for the Fifth Sunday After the Epiphany in this liturgical year. Refer to it for commentary on the background, literary context, and themes of the passage. In the period following the Epiphany, the emphasis was on the text's call for justice and kindness; on Ash Wednesday, the lection's definition of the true fast stands out. In both cases, true piety is linked with specific acts of social justice. It is a fundamental error of biblical interpretation to drive a wedge between concern for piety—individual or corporate—and concern for social justice. The psalms, as the fullest expression of piety, overflow with the same stress on justice and righteousness that one finds in the prophets.

Reflection on this text at the beginning of Lent certainly would call attention to physical acts, including fasting, as a means of confessing sin (see v. 2) and repenting. Such reflection will also recognize that "fasting" includes physical actions that are not so obviously "religious." The fast that the Lord chooses is not simply abstaining from eating, but sharing one's bread with the hungry, one's shelter with the homeless, and one's clothing with the naked (v. 7). In short, God's preferred fast is "to loose the bonds of injustice . . . to let the oppressed go free" (v. 6).

Psalm 51:1–17

This psalm, used on Ash Wednesday in all three years of the cycle, is the penitential psalm par excellence. When Jewish exegetes sought to associate the sentiments of this psalm with the realities of some historical event, they surmised that it must reflect the remorse, contrition, and yearning for forgiveness that David surely felt after being castigated by the prophet Nathan for David's order that led to the death of Uriah so he might possess Uriah's wife (see the superscription or heading of the psalm and 2 Sam. 12:1–23).

The psalm contains the typical structural features of a lament: an opening address to God (vv. 1–2); a description of the predicament, here in the form of a statement confessing sin and wrongdoing (vv. 3–5); a plea asking for help, in this case the forgiveness of sin and the rejuvenation of the self (vv. 6–12); and a vow committing the supplicant to acts expressive of thanksgiving, in this case, ministry in the form of evangelizing praise (vv. 13–17).

This psalm admirably fits with the other readings for today. The Old Testament text from Joel calls for fasting and repentance; the Epistle reading points to Christ as the means of forgiveness from sin; and the Gospel reading offers Jesus' word on the sentiments proper to the practice of piety (or "works of righteousness"), prayer, and fasting.

Psalm 51 may be viewed and preached as theological reflection on the human predicament. As such, the psalm touches on multiple aspects of human guilt and sin as well as the multiform character of human re-creation and the involvement of the Divine in both.

In preaching on this psalm, one entry into the text is to focus on what is said about the human predicament, about the human person as sinner.

1. Sin is experienced as a state of being, a condition of the total life. "I was brought forth in iniquity, and in sin did my mother conceive me" (v. 5). Such an assertion comes near not only to the Christian doctrine of original sin but also to the Freudian realization that the parenting generation stamps its image indelibly upon its custodial children. The concept of original sin sees each person sharing, in the act of being human itself, both the state of sin and the consequences of sin. Modern psychology similarly recognizes that children are inevitably, even it not totally, incarcerated in the personality prisons that their parents have inhabited; the scars and festers of the past always mark and contaminate the present.

2. Sin is willful action that ultimately means that human wrong is committed against God. "Against you, you only, have I sinned" (v. 4). Wrong and misconduct only become sin when viewed within a context that involves the Divine. To speak of sin is to move language beyond the realm of anthropology and into the arena of theology.

3. Sin contaminates, stains, pollutes, renders unclean. Much of this psalm is concerned with the discoloring and polluting quality of sin and speaks of salvation in "purifying" terminology—wash, cleanse, purge, blot out. The ancient rabbis recognized this dimension in the psalm and taught that "every man who commits a transgression is as unclean as though he had touched a dead body and must be purified." The idea that sin is a pollutant that permeates the whole person means that there is no such thing as an isolated event or action. A sinful act discolors, disrupts, and skews the entire personality like a fading cloth in a family wash.

Over against the psalm's intense sense of sin, presented confessionally, the composition also gives expression to components involved in forgiveness and the renewal of life, expressed in the form of pleas and petitions.

1. There are, first, the requests that God change the worshiper. In a series of pleas, the psalmist asks to be changed by divine action—teach me, purge me, wash me. There is no striving for divine favor, no effort to achieve divine approval; merely the cascading requests to be the passive recipient of divine action.

2. A second set of pleas focuses on requests for new or renewed experiences—joy, gladness, rejoicing. These may be viewed as concomitant with or the result of the changes in personal status requested.

3. Finally, the psalmist also requests an intimacy with the Divine (vv. 11–12).

The psalm reading also moves into the area of actions beyond and as a response to forgiveness and renewal. The worshiper vows to offer testimony that will instruct transgressors and lead sinners back to God (vv. 13–14). As the purest form of sacrifice, the worshiper will offer to God a broken and contrite heart and spirit (vv. 15–17).

2 Corinthians 5:20b–6:10

Parts of this text also occur elsewhere in the *Common Lectionary*: 5:16–21 in the Fourth Sunday of Lent in Year C and 6:1–13 in Proper 7 for Year B. Additional remarks may be found in connection with those readings.

What makes this text suitable for Ash Wednesday is its central emphasis on reconciliation. As Christians, we are called "to be reconciled to God" (v. 20*b*). Naturally, this requires a penitent spirit on our part. Being Christian means that we have been forgiven, but it also means that we stand in constant need of forgiveness. This text recognizes above all that our need to be reconciled to God is an ongoing need. We cannot presume that our status before God is ensured. It is rather a relationship that must constantly be nurtured and renewed, and this renewal begins when we acknowledge our need for God's reconciling love.

We should begin by seeing this text as directly confronting Christians—those already in Christ. Living together in community often finds us at odds with one another. This was certainly the context out of which our text emerges—Paul in serious conflict with other Christian teachers. The polemical tone of the Second Epistle to the Corinthians is well known, especially chapters 10–13, and the epistle as a whole unfolds the seriously strained relationship between Paul and the Corinthian church. The place where severe alienation had occurred was in the local congregation, which is often the place where alienation is most sharply felt and reconciliation is most difficult to achieve. What strikes us about today's text is that it rings so true to church life as most of us experience it. At one level, reconciliation is envisioned on a cosmic scale, as God and the entire world being reconciled to each other (v. 19). But at another, more familiar level, it is envisioned on a local scale, as something that must occur—and recur—among actual communities of believers.

Verse 21 reminds us that reconciliation is Christo-centric. It is "in him," that is, "in Christ" that we are enabled to become God's righteousness. Christ serves as the locus of reconciliation, the sphere in which our relationship to God and one another is renewed—not only the sphere but the catalyst. It was first the work of Christ, the one "who knew no sin" yet was made "to be sin" (v. 21*a*), that embodied the paradox of reversal: taking on a status that was not rightfully his—sin—so that we might acquire a character and existence that is not rightfully ours—God's righteousness. The text centers our thoughts on Christ as both agent and sphere of reconciliation—the meeting ground where enemies can become friends, the crucible where pride gives way to penitence.

Another theme presented by today's text is Paul's insistence that we are "God's fellow workers" (6:1, NIV). The one who has experienced reconciliation becomes a collaborator with God in extending reconciliation into the world. The experience of reconciliation translates into a ministry of reconciliation. The sense of forgiveness becomes expressed in a sense of mission. The God who reconciles us, who forgives us, also commissions us. Here we are reminded that our experience of God's grace, if it has any power at all, compels us to be instruments of that grace in the world. First there is the compelling encounter, then the compelling mission.

We should see clearly this connection between reconciliation and the ministry of reconciliation, between our experience of God and our ministry for God. In his inaugural sermon in the parish of Safenwil, Karl Barth told his congregation: "I am not speaking to you of God because I am a pastor. I am a pastor because I *must* speak to you of God, if I am to remain true to myself, my better self." The ministry of reconciliation derives from our profound experience of being reconciled.

In a similar vein, Martin Buber wrote: "Meeting with God does not come to man in order that he may concern himself with God, but in order that he may confirm that there is meaning in the world. All revelation is summons and sending. . . . God remains present to you when you have been sent forth; he who goes on a mission has always God before him: the truer the fulfillment the stronger and more constant the nearness."

If we have experienced God's reconciling love this directly, and if it has affected us this profoundly, we can understand the sense of urgency of today's text: "Now is the acceptable time; . . . now is the day of salvation!" (6:2). Our ministry can easily become a routine of postponement and accommodation. Ours can become a strategy of gradualism. We may work for change, but it may be glacial. There are times when slow change is better than rapid, radical change, but today's text sounds the latter note. It confronts us with God's *now*. God has responded decisively in our behalf (6:2). We are now called to respond as decisively on God's behalf.

Matthew 6:1–6, 16–21

Ash Wednesday begins Lent and the believer's journey to Holy Week and Easter. Over the entrance to that path of repentance and prayer are the words of Matthew 6:1: "Beware of practicing your piety before others in order to be seen by them; for then you have no reward from your Father in heaven." The words are not to frighten but to alert the pilgrim to the seductions that beset the practice of one's faith, seductions that can for the unwary rob piety of its power and appropriateness and turn the sanctuary of devotion into a theater. "Be careful" (REB, TEV). We will attend later to the dangers pointed out in our lection, but first a few words about the literary structure of Matthew 6:1–6, 16–21.

Today's reading consists of three parts:

First, there is a general warning against a public display of religion (6:1). Having stated at 5:20 that the righteousness of the disciples is to exceed that of the scribes and Pharisees, it is vital that Jesus warn against any distortions of righteousness that might be spawned by that demand. After all, "to exceed" or "to be greater than" could be taken by some as the language of competition that would, of course, disease at the outset the understanding of kingdom living.

Second, three acts of devotion: alms, prayer, and fasting (6:2–6, 16–18) serve as concrete cases in which the general alert of 6:1 is applied. Verses 7–15 are omitted for two reasons: first, they are of a different literary form, interrupting in a sense the trinity of "whenever you give alms," "whenever you pray," and "whenever you fast." This threefold formula bears all the marks of careful composition, apparently a portion of a catechism for new members. Second, verses 7–15 are omitted because it is clear Matthew used the introduction of the subject of prayer as the occasion to insert the Lord's Prayer. That Luke placed it elsewhere (11:1–4) indicates that the Lord's Prayer owes its specific context to the Gospel writer. Neither it nor verses 1–6, 16–21 are violated by its omission from our lesson here.

The third and final portion of today's reading consists of verses 19–21. Originally, verse 21, which is found almost word for word in Luke 12:34, may have existed separately. It is singular in its address (you, your) and in its reference to treasure or riches, whereas verses 19–20 are plural in both cases. The three verses address materialism and fit more easily with what follows than with what precedes. However, materialism is certainly not unrelated to the life of righteousness, especially to the first of the three acts of one's faith, giving alms. In fact, the injunction against laying up treasures on earth (v. 19) could without strain be related to verses 1–6, 16–18, in that piety for public display, which has its reward in human praise, could be a form of collecting earthly treasure.

Clearly, however, the heart of the text before us concerns the giving of alms, prayer, and fasting. These good works of Judaism are to be continued in the Christian community. After all, Jesus has already said that he did not come to abolish the law and the prophets (5:17). Any broad rejection of fundamental ethical behavior or acts of devotion toward God simply because the synagogue had embraced them was not and is not permitted the church. In fact, the interpreter must beware of easy dichotomies that falsely set an inner Christianity against an outer Judaism. And the warnings against hypocrisy are not given here in some triumphal attack on the synagogue but rather because the church suffers under the very same tendency.

What precisely is the danger about which the reader is being told to be careful? Are these acts of religion intrinsically flawed and hence to be avoided? Of course not. The text says *when you* do acts of charity, *when you* pray, *when you* fast. Who can imagine a life before God that offers no charity, lifts no prayer for self and others, never abstains from food so that those without can be fed? Is the warning, then, against doing these things by habit? Of course not. There is no better friend of the good and fruitful life than habit. Jesus went to the synagogue on the sabbath as was his habit (Luke 4:16). Not every Christian activity need be accompanied every time by emotional investment, nor does visceral authentication function as the criterion by which an act is called genuine or sincere. The danger is in turning the sanctuary of one's devotion to God into a theater, with alms, prayer, and fasting going on stage for applause. The text is laced with the language of a public show: trumpets, masked faces, acting (hypocrisy), and an applauding audience. Perhaps nothing is so attractive, so tempting, as public praise. It is meat and bread to the human ego, but it can erode the fundamental posture of the Christian life—before God.

First Sunday in Lent

Genesis 2:15–17; 3:1–7;
Psalm 32;
Romans 5:12–19;
Matthew 4:1–11

The leading concerns of the texts for the First Sunday in Lent are temptation, sin, and the effects of sin. The Old Testament reading consists of selections from the account of the creation and fall of the first human beings. The responsorial psalm is a thanksgiving song by an individual whose confession of sin has been followed by divine forgiveness and healing. In the epistolary text, Paul presents his interpretation of that Old Testament tradition in the light of the life, death, and resurrection of Jesus. Matthew's account of Jesus in the wilderness, a highly appropriate reading for a season of fasting and prayer, likewise focuses upon temptation.

Genesis 2:15–17; 3:1–7

In each of the years of the lectionary cycle, the Old Testament readings for the successive Sundays in Lent present summaries of the history of ancient Israel's relationship with God. For this year, the story begins with the Creation and the Fall (Gen. 2–3), moves on to the promise to Abraham (Gen. 12), leads us with the people of Israel out of Egypt and into the wilderness (Exod. 17), shows us the anointing of David as king (1 Sam. 16), and then, beyond the Babylonian Exile, leaves us with Ezekiel's vision of the valley of dry bones, bones that the Lord promises to revive.

These verses from Genesis 2 and 3 emphasize one part of the total story that begins with 2:4b and is concluded in 3:24. The two chapters are the Yahwistic Writer's account of the creation of human beings (2:4b–25), of the first couple's disobedience (3:1–13), and of the results of that disobedience (3:14–24). The Yahwistic source is generally considered to be the oldest written document of the Pentateuch, perhaps as early as the tenth century BC. In contrast to the creation story in Genesis 1:1–2:4a, this one refers to God with the proper name Yahweh ("Lord" in most translations), sees creation as presuming the existence of dry land (2:5–6), and concentrates on the establishment of the conditions of human existence rather than the creation of the cosmos as a whole.

The selections for the First Sunday in Lent emphasize the account of the initial sin by the first two human beings, their disobedience of the divine command, but these verses are best seen in their context. After an aside that gives the time and circumstances (2:4b–6), the writer presents—in almost systematic fashion—an account of the establishment of human life as God meant it to be. First, there is life itself, understood as a divine gift (2:7). The human being, according to this understanding, is not a two- or three-part creature, but the unity of physical matter—ordinary dust from the ground—and "the breath of life." This breath is no spirit with an existence apart from the physical stuff. Second, Yahweh gives the creature freedom and limits, leaving him with a choice to make: "You may freely eat of every tree of the garden; but of the tree of the knowledge of good and evil you shall not eat" (2:16–17). The initial sin must be seen against the background of this command. Third, Yahweh gives the man work to do, putting him "in the garden of Eden to till it and keep it" (2:15). Work itself is thus not a curse, but one of those factors that makes this creature human.

Another essential element is reported in the verses omitted from our reading for today, the creation of the first woman. One point of this episode is that community, even if only in the presence of the primary family unit, is necessary for this creature to be human. Another purpose is to affirm the goodness of sexuality: the two become "one flesh," that is, unite and produce children. Finally, in a narrative aside, the writer affirms that "they were both naked, and were not ashamed" (2:25). All these factors, however distorted, are seen to be present where full human life exists.

But the direction of the story changes dramatically in chapter 3 with the introduction of a new character, the "serpent." The writer is careful to point out that the serpent was "a wild creature that the Lord God had made" (3:1), but he is "more crafty" than any other. The snake is no divine or angelic force against God; he is part of creation. His role is simply to pose the tempting questions, to present to the woman the possibility of disobedience. Note that the serpent draws the woman into a conversation with a question that cannot be answered with a simple yes or no (v. 2), and that when the woman answers she actually makes the prohibition more restrictive than Yahweh had in the first place ("nor shall you touch it," v. 3). The snake's response denies Yahweh's threat of the death penalty and questions his motives: "You will not die; for God knows that when you eat of it your eyes will be opened, and you will be like God, knowing good and evil" (3:4–5).

The woman is convinced to taste the fruit because it was good to eat, was attractive, and—the serpent had told her—would "make one wise" (v. 6). She then offers it to her husband and he accepts. The traditional image of the woman as the temptress who led the man astray is an exaggeration of this account. To be sure, the man himself blames the woman, and in the same breath that he blames Yahweh: "The woman whom *you* gave to be with me." (3:12, italics added).

Following in the wake of the simple act of disobedience is a series of effects, none of them good. The man and woman do gain "knowledge," most of it amounting to the loss of innocence. First, they know that they are naked; that is, they experience shame (v. 7). Second, they know fear (3:8), hiding from Yahweh. Third, they experience estrangement, from one another, from the world—represented by the snake—and from God (3:12–13). Then Yahweh pronounces judgments upon each of the three in turn (3:14–19). The purpose of these poetic lines is to account for the pains and contradictions in the world and especially human life. Work is not a curse for the man—he had been a farmer from the beginning—but his work becomes harder and frustrating because the relationship between effort and results is unpredictable (3:17–19a). Moreover, death is not here the curse, for the creature had always been made of dust (here the apostle Paul goes beyond the Old Testament account). Rather, the man is to be reminded of his mortality every time he looks at the earth (3:19), and when God drives the first couple out of the garden, he prevents them from attaining immortality (3:22–24).

Taken as a whole, the purpose of Genesis 2:4b–3:24 is to account for—to explain and interpret—the present circumstances of human life, and in particular its brokenness. The first couple, and all their successors, carry with them the memory or vision of the way life could or should be, but they face the future with ambiguity and tension. A major purpose of the story, then, is to account for human evil and suffering, and it does so mainly in moral terms, by showing the effects of disobedience. It should not be difficult at all for contemporary readers and hearers to identify with the characters in the story, and thereby to understand better themselves, their world, and their God.

Psalm 32

One of the traditional seven penitential psalms, Psalm 32 is a prayer of thanksgiving offered by individuals after the forgiveness of sin and the experience of healing. Prayers of thanksgiving, like this psalm, were offered in ancient Israelite worship after the passage of trouble and the alleviation of distress. They reflect the people's tendency to look back upon the time of trouble and to celebrate the joy of salvation that had made the trouble a matter of the past (though certainly not something to be lost from memory). This helps explain two factors about thanksgiving psalms: (1) they have the character of a testimonial that bears witness to a prior condition that no longer exists but from which the worshiper has been delivered, and (2) much of the psalm is addressed to a human audience, inviting them to participate in the joy and new condition of the redeemed.

The following is the form-critical structure of the psalm: (a) pronouncements of blessedness spoken about or to the one offering thanksgiving, probably spoken by the priest to the worshiper or to the worshiper and the attending congregation (vv. 1–2); (b) the description, in the form of a thanksgiving prayer to the Deity, of the condition from which the worshiper was saved (vv. 3–5); (c) a prayer to the Deity formulated as an indirect call to prayer by those in attendance (v. 6); (d) the prayer response (v. 7); and (e) instruction by the one offering thanksgiving to those in attendance at the service (vv. 8–11).

The two opening verses proclaim the blessed condition or happy estate of the one whose sins have been forgiven. The psalm does not assume the existence of life without sin. It presupposes the existence of sinful persons and proclaims as blessed or happy those whose sin has become a matter of the past. The state of real happiness lies, for the psalmist, not prior to, but beyond, on the other side of, sin.

In verses 1–2, and elsewhere (see v. 5), the psalmist uses three different words for sin: (a) transgression (*pesha'*), or an act reflecting overt rebellion against God, (b) sin (*chattâth*), or an offense by which one deviates from the correct path or true course, and (c) iniquity (*'âwon*), or criminal distortion of life without regard for the Deity. The term "deceit," or "slackness," (*remiyah*) also appears in verse 2, and the claim of its absence can probably be seen as referring to the state of honesty that had to prevail when one confessed various sins. Note also that three descriptions are given with regard to the removal of sin: forgiven, covered, not imputed. Such terminological features can provide the bases for structuring a sermon on this psalm.

In the description of the earlier distress, in verses 3–5, the psalmist coordinates four factors: (a) lack of repentance followed by (b) sickness and strain, and (c) confession followed by (d) forgiveness. In ancient Israel, acknowledgement and confession of sin, as well as restitution to injured parties, were essential ingredients in the repentance process (see Num. 5:5–10). From a therapeutic or psychological point of view, one can say that the psalm writer was fully aware of the need for the sinner to tell his or her story as a form of self-identity and self-enlightenment and thus to claim responsibility for wrongdoing. In 2 Samuel 12:1–14, Nathan tells the "confessional" story with which David then identifies. In ancient Israelite theology, without confession there was no forgiveness of sin.

The association of sickness and unconfessed sin, noted in verses 3–4, illustrates the close psychosomatic connection between physical and mental health—a connection that is being recognized more and more in contemporary culture. Although the physical consequences are described as the result of unconfessed sins, they are also spoken of as the result of divine action as well ("thy hand was heavy upon me"). This suggests that the understanding of human sentiments and feelings and the understanding of divine actions are closely interrelated.

Verse 5 expresses something of the exuberance that comes after long-seething and secret sin is allowed to surface and be exposed to the light of day. The articulation, the coming to expression, of the nagging problem is the first step toward healing. Note that three expressions are used for this unveiling of the suppressed sin—acknowledged, did not hide, will confess. The close connection between confession and forgiveness is affirmed in the recognition that following confession "you forgave the guilt of my sin."

This section of the psalm (vv. 3–5) can be an ideal text for the minister to use in addressing the issues of human sinfulness, confession, and forgiveness. The sentiments and conditions described in the psalm are certainly appropriate for contemporary people. The latter, however, frequently assumes that what one does with wrongdoing is to "stuff" it or keep it under wraps—the exact sentiments seen as so destructive in the psalm.

Verses 6–11 are to be seen in the context of the thanksgiving ritual in which the worshiper calls upon those attending the service (friends, family, associates) to join in the celebration and to learn from the experience that the worshiper has gone through. The forgiven sinner pleads with the others not to be stupid and hardheaded like a mule or a horse that must be controlled with bit and bridle. That is, they are not to be like the worshiper was before the acknowledgment and confession of sin (see vv. 3–4).

Romans 5:12–19

It may be that Christ is the one through whom we are made righteous before God and come to have peace with God, as Paul declares in the preceding verses (5:1–11). But it is not at all obvious how this can be. How is it that one person can affect the destiny of all persons? It is one thing for one person to die for another person, for one life to be given in exchange for another life, perhaps even for several other lives. It is quite another thing to think of one person's destiny affecting and determining the destiny of every other person—for all time and in every place. How can one person have universal impact, either for good or evil?

These are the questions at the heart of today's passage. They trigger some of Paul's most original thinking about Christ; indeed, they help shape his Adam Christology. Today's text is one of two central texts in which he articulates his theological conviction that Christ should be seen as a new Adam (cf. 1 Cor. 15:20–22). His reflections on Christ as a second Adam should be seen in relation to this theology of the new creation (2 Cor. 4:6; 5:16–19).

As he saw it, the Christ-event could only be properly understood as a reenactment of Genesis 1. It was a moment of cosmic reordering, the results of which were as dramatically new as was God's original creation.

But the focus of today's text is not so much on the old creation as compared with the new creation, as it is on the *old* Adam and the *new* Adam. Paul's theological reflections are thoroughly influenced by Genesis 1–3 and its account of how sin and death entered the world through Adam's disobedience (cf. Gen. 2:17; 3:19). From the creation account Paul draws an inevitable conclusion: the effects of one person's actions can extend to many other persons. What Adam did had universal effects. Through his act of disobedience, and thus through him as a representative figure, sin and death entered the scene of world history (v. 12). The whole human race—the children of Adam—was affected by the life and deeds of a single figure, Adam. Thus, through a typological reading of Scripture, Paul came to see Adam and Christ as prototypical representatives of two essentially different aeons. Indeed, each inaugurated a new reign not only as the first figure of his respective era but as the one through whose work the reign came to be defined.

One of the first points Paul presses home is that one person's act can affect the destiny of many persons. This is obvious enough in one sense. Citizens are affected directly by the decisions and actions of their leader. But more than this is being said here, for Paul claims that Adam's actions had universal effect: "Sin came into the world through one [person] . . . so death spread to all" (v. 12). This should not be understood in the sense that sin is genetically transmitted from Adam to every succeeding generation, although this has been one way the passage has been interpreted historically. Rather, Paul insists that sin is a universal reality because all have sinned (v. 12). Rather than saying that each of us is born with the taint of sin, Paul is suggesting that sin is a universal disease that is endemic to the human condition. His basic point, however, at least at the outset (vv. 12–14), is that the nature and destiny of every human being have been affected, directly or indirectly, by the actions and deeds of the one man Adam. Through the actions of the one, the destiny of many has been affected.

The passage is not precisely clear as to how the action of Adam relates to the actions of every human being. Read one way, the passage suggests that all of humanity participated in the sin of Adam involuntarily. Read another way, this occurred "because everyone has sinned" (v. 12, NJB), that is, because of every individual's sins. In either case, the destiny of all humanity was affected by the work of Adam.

If one takes seriously the Genesis story, as Paul certainly did, it becomes clear that Adam was a representative figure. In him the destiny of the whole human race was prefigured. What he did radically affected what all others did after him.

By analogy, Paul insists that Christ too is a representative figure. Like Adam, his life and work had universal implications that affected the destiny of all humanity. If it is possible to think of one person's actions having universal significance, of the destiny of all humanity being linked with the destiny of the one man Adam, then it is fully conceivable how this can be possible with Christ.

But even though Adam "prefigured the One who was to come" (v. 14, NJB), there is a sharp contrast between the work of Adam and the work of Christ. The one was an instance of disobedience, the other obedience. In one case, what resulted was judgment and condemnation. In the other case, there occurred an "act of grace" and a "verdict of acquittal" (v. 16, REB). One introduced a reign of death into the world, the other a reign of life (v. 17). Both figures were representative, but they represented two radically different orders.

Our text, then, pushes us to see the similarity of Christ and Adam, but at the same time sharply contrasts them. We might note some of the points of contrast:

1. Just as Adam is identified with disobedience, so is Christ identified with obedience (v. 19). Adam comes to stand as a shorthand expression for "sin," "transgression," "trespass," "judgment," and "condemnation." Everything the disobedient Adam was not, the obedient Christ was. Accordingly, the work of Christ taken as a whole becomes the avenue through which the "grace of God" as "free gift" becomes manifested to the world (vv. 15–16). Adam and Christ thus come to represent not only two aeons, but two ways of living before God: the one resistance, the other obedient response. In this sense, Christ is "much more" than Adam.

2. The effects of the work of Adam and Christ may be similarly contrasted. If God's treatment of Adam demonstrated divine justice, God's treatment of Adam's successors through Christ displays divine generosity. In Adam's case, there is a single transgression, which resulted in condemnation (vv. 16–17). Thus, in Adam we see a display of divine justice; in Christ we see a display of divine love. What makes this remarkable is that the accumulation of sin over time might normally have prompted God to increase the punishment, to condemn in return for sin, indeed to give up on humanity. Yet the cumulative force of "many trespasses" (v. 16) was met with the most unexpected of responses: justification as a free gift (v. 16). Adam comes to symbolize condemnation, whereas Christ comes to symbolize acquittal and life (v. 18).

3. The era of Adam is an era of death; the era of Christ is an era of life. The one thing we all know is that death is inevitable for us. We are all terminal. Death, Paul insists, is the great universal (v. 12). If anything characterizes the entire period from Adam until Moses, it is death (v. 14). This was true even in those cases where persons did not flagrantly violate God's commands as Adam did (cf. Gen. 2:17; 3:19; also 2 Esd. 3:21–22, 26; 6:23).

It is important for Paul to stress that both sin and death are prior to the law, even to the principle of law (v. 13). If sin is understood as transgression of the Mosaic law, or of some universal law, what does it do to our understanding of sin if law is removed? Even though we recognize that putting a prohibition in words makes it concrete, we also know that the reality precedes the codification. This is Paul's point. The tendency and capacity for doing wrong exist even before we are able to formulate precisely what it is we have done wrong. Sin precedes law, even though law may serve as the way of articulating sin.

Just as this capacity for doing wrong afflicts all of us as human beings, so does it bring death. Human experience teaches us that wrongdoing is ultimately, if not immediately, destructive. Its effects are both personal and social, affecting us as individuals and others with whom we associate. According to the creation story in Genesis 1–3, the sin of Adam resulted in physical death, the expiration of life. Yet as the story is told, we clearly see that more is at stake than this. Ultimately, it meant separation from God's presence. This is the real meaning of death. The Genesis story depicts existential death.

But Paul insists that this is precisely what was reversed in Christ. Through this one man's "act of righteousness" occurs "acquittal and life for all" (v. 18). If the era of Adam was an era of separation, of alienation, the era of Christ is one of reconciliation (v. 11). If death is the ultimate separation from God, eternal life is the ultimate form of reunion with God that has been achieved through Christ (v. 21).

Homiletically, our text offers numerous possibilities. We should remember that as one of the classic statements of Adam Christology, it has had a profound influence on the history of doctrine and still informs the way many of us understand the nature of sin and humanity. In the context of Lent, the preacher's task may be to address some of these perceptions directly. In what sense, if any, are we basically inclined toward sin? Is it an inborn tendency or something acquired? To what extent is it a matter of our own human responsibility?

Matthew 4:1–11

The Gospel lesson for the First Sunday in Lent is always one of the Synoptic accounts of the temptation of Jesus. In fact, the forty days of Lent (excluding Sundays) as a period of struggle and preparation form a tradition based on the experience of Jesus and of Israel, Moses, and Elijah before him.

That Jesus was tempted or tested has New Testament attestation apart from the Gospels (Heb. 2:18; 4:15). To use the word *tempted* in relation to Jesus is not to state or imply weakness. On the contrary, temptation is a testimony to strength; the greater the strength, the greater the temptation. It is regrettable that temptation has become associated popularly with small morality games. It was not so with the first temptation, the desire to become as God is (Gen. 3:5), or with the testing of Jesus, as we will see.

Matthew, as does Luke (4:1–13), elaborates and diverges from the very brief account of the temptation of Jesus in Mark 1:12–13. Apart from a difference in the sequence of the three temptations, Matthew and Luke are sufficiently similar to suggest a common source. However, Matthew preserves Mark's order, keeping the temptation closely associated with Jesus' baptism. Luke separates the two with a genealogy (3:23–38). Paul, in warning the Corinthian church about the easy seductions of the world, recalled Israel's "baptism" in the Red Sea and the temptations that followed in the wilderness (1 Cor. 10:1–13).

A brief look at the world behind Matthew 4:1–11 will help in our understanding of the writer's portrayal of Jesus' experience in the wilderness. First, in later Judaism the figure of Satan came increasingly to replace God as the source of temptation. For example, compare 2 Samuel 24:1 and 1 Chronicles 21:1. However, there was never in later Judaism or in early Christianity the development of Satan into an independent and absolute power of evil over against God. Only God is absolute; all other powers are subordinate. God, therefore, continued to be associated even with events that tested human beings. Believing in only one absolute divine being makes the problem of sin and evil always a difficult one, but the Scriptures refuse to settle the difficulty by positing a good God and a bad God and putting on the bad God the blame for all that is dark and destructive in the world. Hence the Christian prays to the one God, "Lead us not into temptation" (Matt. 6:13, RSV; NRSV translates as "Do not bring us to the time of trial"), and Matthew can write of Jesus that he "was led up by the Spirit into the wilderness to be tempted by the devil" (4:1).

A second factor in the background of the text that helps our understanding is the experience of Israel in the wilderness for forty years. That period was described as a time of testing, a time of humbling Israel and letting the people hunger to learn that one does not live by bread alone (Deut. 8:2–3). Jesus is recapitulating the experience of Israel. Matthew even tells of the flight to Egypt when Jesus was a child and then the return so that Scripture might be fulfilled: "Out of Egypt I have called my son" (2:15; Hos. 11:1). But whereas Israel failed the tests in the wilderness, Jesus did not.

More important for understanding this text are the parallels between Jesus and Moses. Even as a child, Jesus was like Moses in that he was in Egypt, was with the rich and powerful, and was saved from the wicked king (Matt. 2:1–23). Here analogies continue: Moses was taken to a high mountain and shown all the land as far as the eye could see (Deut. 34:1–4); Moses was with the Lord for forty days (Exod. 34:28); and during those forty days Moses did not eat or drink. In Jesus, God has raised up one like Moses (Deut. 18:18) and at the same time one who would be a true son of God in complete obedience during the time of trial.

As for the three temptations spelled out by Matthew, the whole issue is the total seriousness with which Deuteronomy 6:4–5 is to be taken: "The Lord is our God, the Lord alone. You shall love the Lord your God with all your heart, and with all your soul, and with all your might." All Jesus' responses to temptation to waver from this single commitment of life toward political claims, or a ministry of bread to win over the masses, or the use of signs to coerce faith were quotations from Deuteronomy (6:13, 16; 8:3). The reader of Matthew is therefore given a nonmagician Jesus, one who later would speak sternly about those who would claim, "Did we not prophesy in your name, and cast out demons in your name, and do many deeds of power in your name?" (7:22). Later, on the mount of Transfiguration (17:5) and on the mount of Ascension (28:1–18), Jesus would have the authority and power he does not claim in the wilderness, but then that authority will have been given by God.

Matthew's account of Jesus' temptation is to say that the church encountered God in one who did not try to be God or as God (Gen. 3:5) and who did not try to use God to claim something for himself. The church, too fond of power, place, and claims, would do well to walk in his steps.

"Jesus vs. Satan"

Second Sunday in Lent

Genesis 12:1–4*a*;
Psalm 121;
Romans 4:1–5, 13–17;
John 3:1–17 or Matthew 17:1–9

With the texts for the Second Sunday in Lent, the church turns to consider human faith and divine faithfulness, God's promises and human responses. The Old Testament and the epistolary readings are linked directly by the figure of Abraham. The first is the account of God's call and promise to the patriarch and Abraham's faithful response. In Romans 4, Paul lifts up Abraham as one whose faith "was reckoned . . . as righteousness" and stresses that the promise came through grace and not the law. The responsorial psalm celebrates the faithfulness of God, who does not sleep but is the helper who watches over the faithful. Both Gospel readings concern the kingdom of God. The Johannine lesson, the account of Jesus' encounter with Nicodemus, calls for rebirth and emphasizes God's love in sending his only Son, whereas the passage from Matthew is the report of the Transfiguration.

Genesis 12:1–4*a*

This report of the call of Abraham is the key transition in the entire Book of Genesis. It marks a significant change both in the type of literature and in the theological direction of the story. Genesis 1–11 is the primeval history, the accounts of creation and the establishment of the circumstances of life for all peoples. The stories concern events that happened long ago and far away. Our passage begins the other major unit of the book, Genesis 12–50, the stories of the patriarchs—Abraham, Isaac, Jacob, and the sons of Jacob. Virtually all of these stories focus upon family matters, relationships between husbands and wives, parents and children, and conflicts among siblings.

As a theological transition, these verses in Genesis 12 are the pivot on which history turns. Up to this point, most of the stories—particularly those passed on by the Yahwistic Writer—add up to a history of human sin. It begins immediately after the creation stories with the disobedience of the first couple (Gen. 3), leads to fratricide (Gen. 4:1–16), reports the flood as divine judgment upon human corruption (Gen. 6–9), and then explains the dispersion of peoples into different nations with different languages as the result of an attempt to storm the heavens (Gen. 11:1–9).

With Genesis 12:1, the story becomes a history of salvation. First and above all, what makes the story a history of salvation is the divine initiative. Quite without explanation, Yahweh calls a particular individual, Abram, whose name will become Abraham (Gen. 17:5), and instructs him to leave his homeland and set out to a strange place. The Pauline interpretation is perfectly consistent with the Old Testament understanding: the election of Abraham is an act of grace, of God's freedom, and not in response to the patriarch's obedience to a law, for the law had not yet been given.

Second, this is a history of salvation because it begins with a promise. The promise, reiterated to each successive generation of the ancestors, includes several elements. The meaning of the first elements is clear: a "great" name, the land (implicit in v. 1 and explicit in 12:7), and progeny. Thus the descendants of Abraham will become a great nation with a territory of their own. But the last part of the promise presents problems of interpretation, as most modern translations indicate. One may read the particular verb form either as reflexive, "by you all the families of the earth shall bless themselves" (RSV, NRSV footnote; cf. NJPSV), or as passive, "in you all the families of the earth shall be blessed" (NRSV). The latter suggests that the purpose of the promise is the good of all peoples, whereas the former states that all peoples will use Abraham's name in pronouncing blessings. Throughout the Book of Genesis, the Priestly Writer speaks of covenant where the Yahwist reports a promise. Because the covenant comes at the initiation of God and includes a promissory oath, the two are not fundamentally different in the context of the patriarchal narratives.

Third, to speak of the accounts that follow this passage as a history of salvation means that history now has a direction, a salvific purpose. Our verses, then, are a foreshadowing of what is to come and point specifically to the events reported in the first six books of the Bible. In particular, they anticipate the exodus from Egypt, the covenant on Sinai, and the settlement of the land of Canaan in the generation after Moses. The promise to Abraham is reported from the perspective of those who have experienced its fulfillment, who are settled in the land in which he was only a sojourner, and who have become "a great nation." Only those who know the rest of the story will recognize just how momentous these words are. The good news actually applies to those descendants more than to the patriarch himself. Moreover, it is worth remembering that Abraham in the Book of Genesis is the ancestor not just of the people of Israel, but of others as well.

Note how little is stated explicitly here about the faith of Abraham. We do not hear him speak a word throughout the entire episode, although verse 8 notes that "he invoked the name of the Lord." But he is not passive. His faith stands out in understatement, in the simple note that when the Lord sent him, without telling him where he was to go, he went, as the Lord had told him (v. 4). The writer and those who read the text know more than Abraham did. They know that he sets out here on a journey that does not lead to a permanent home, that he and Sarah will live their lives as resident aliens in a land promised, not to them, but to those who come later.

The story does not moralize, although it points gently to Abraham as a model of the faithful servant of the Lord. Above all, it is good news, to be accepted with gratitude: God intends to work salvation in and through history, beginning with a particular individual who is willing to set out to a strange land.

Psalm 121

This psalm forms part of a collection of psalms put together for use by pilgrims as they made their way to Jerusalem to celebrate the various festivals (note the reference to ascents or pilgrimage in the heading). The psalm has a distinct note of departure about it and thus is fitting for use with the Old Testament reading about Abraham's journey to a new land.

The psalm is clearly human address, without any speech addressed to God. Thus the psalm is not a prayer. A particular feature of the psalm is the change of person between verses 2 and 3. The opening verses are spoken in the first person, whereas the remainder of the psalm is addressed to someone in the second person. The reason for this change of person will become clear in our subsequent discussion.

Before leaving on pilgrimage, the worshipers in a region assembled in a centrally located village in order to travel in a group to Jerusalem. After spending the night in the open air, to avoid any possible contact with uncleanness in the houses, the group moved out under the supervision of a director. The trip to Jerusalem, which might take several days, was not blessed with any special amenities (like constantly accessible toilet facilities) and, like all travel in antiquity, was beset with possible hazard and hardship.

Psalm 121 is best understood as a litany of departure recited antiphonally as the pilgrim group departed from the village where they had assembled. Verses 1–2 were sung by the pilgrims, and verses 3–8 were sung by those who remained behind or perhaps by the leader/director of the pilgrim group.

Verses 1–2 are to be understood as a confession (the second half of v. 1 should not be translated as a question but as a statement). The worshiper speaks of looking to the hills (of Jerusalem) from whence help comes. That is, one looks to the God of Jerusalem, who made heaven and earth.

The affirmation of God as creator of heaven and earth, that is, of everything, may seem so obvious to us and may even seem an innocuous statement. To appreciate fully the impact of such a perspective about the world, one has to realize that for most ancients the world was an arena of conflicting powers and beings. In a polytheistic religion, one god controlled one aspect of life or nature and another some other aspect. Often deities were considered in conflict with one another. Thus the world was neither a very hospitable nor a very predictable place. One constantly had to worry if the proper gods had been placated. On the other hand, the belief in one god as the creator of the heaven and the earth allowed one to see things as reflective of a single divine will. Such a worldview provided a sense of cohesion and security about life.

As the pilgrim faced the dangers of the forthcoming journey to Jerusalem, the confession that the creator God was the source of help was reassuring and confidence boosting.

Verses 3–8 are a response offering assurance to the individual pilgrim that God will constantly care for and preserve the worshiper. Note the number of statements with imagery concerning travel: the foot stumbling, the guardian constantly awake, a shade along the way, day and night as one was on the road constantly, going out (leaving) and coming in (returning). Both the moon and the sun, referred to in verse 6, were considered deities in the ancient world and could be objects of dread. Because pilgrims traveled by day and slept in the open at night, the sun and moon were constant features of their journey. Travelers feared sunstroke (see 2 Kings 4:19; Jon. 4:8), and many other disorders such as epilepsy, fever, and lunacy (related to the word *lunar*) were ascribed to the baneful influence of the moon.

A significant emphasis in this psalm is the constant presence and care of the Deity. God, unlike Baal or other deities (see 1 Kings 18:29), is described as one who does not sleep or slumber. That is, God is continuously on the job.

In developing sermonic ideas for using this psalm, the minister can easily move from the imagery of an actual pilgrimage reflected in the psalm to the understanding of life itself as pilgrimage.

Romans 4:1–5, 13–17

Parts of today's epistolary text also occur elsewhere in the *Common Lectionary*: 4:13–25 as the epistolary reading for Proper 5 in Year A and 4:13–25 as the epistolary reading for the Second Sunday in Lent, Year B. The reader may want to consult our remarks in those settings.

Several features of today's passage make it especially appropriate for the Second Sunday in Lent. At this time of the year, our thoughts focus on our relationship with God, the way our sins and transgressions obstruct that relationship, and penitence as a way of removing these obstructions. The concluding verse reassures us, reminding us that God "gives life to the dead and calls into existence the things that do not exist" (v. 17). With reference to Abraham, this recalls the God who was able to create life in a lifeless womb and bring into existence the son of promise, Isaac, and thus make good on the divine promise. With reference to the penitent, this offers hope in a God who creates and re-creates, who renews, who makes possible what we otherwise think impossible (cf. Isa. 48:13; 1 Cor. 1:28).

In a similar vein, we might note the words of Psalm 32:1–2, cited in verses 7–8, which are omitted from today's epistolary reading. These words also provide reassurance to the penitent as they offer blessings to those who experience genuine forgiveness from the Lord.

These are direct assurances to the penitent, but there is more. The central focus, of course, is on Abraham, the one Old Testament figure Paul regarded as the paradigm of faith. His main prooftext was Genesis 15:6: "Abraham put his faith in God and this was reckoned to him as uprightness" (v. 3, NJB; cf. Gal. 3:6; also James 2:23). The example of Abraham became crucial for Paul in his understanding of the way humans experience salvation.

Paul's theology of salvation is well known: we are saved by grace through faith in Christ, not by works of the law (vv. 4–5; cf. 3:28; 5:1; 11:6; Gal. 2:16; 3:2, 8, 24; Phil. 3:9; also Eph. 2:8–9). The essential question that he addresses in Romans 4 is how we are justified before God, how we experience salvation, how we come to participate in God's promise. For Paul, there were essentially two options: by works or by faith.

The way of works was most clearly embodied in the law of Moses, and circumcision was the most visible symbol. It was the initiation rite that sealed the relationship with God (4:9–12). In this way of construing the religious life, the way to God is through what we do. It is assumed that God rewards us for what we do. On this showing, God's acceptance of us is seen as a response to our good deeds. Salvation comes to be seen as a quid pro quo—something we receive from God in exchange for the good things we do. To paraphrase a modern commercial, we receive salvation the old-fashioned way—we earn it!

One of Paul's main difficulties with this approach is that it wrongly conceives the essential nature of God's saving act. Seen this way, salvation is a matter of earning wages, of being justly rewarded (v. 4). If we do good works, we may have reason to be rewarded, but not from God (v. 2). Salvation conceived this way is no longer a gift freely bestowed. It is a wage paid for work performed.

The other way is the way of faith. It is the polar opposite of the way of works because it construes God, and consequently our relationship with God, in a fundamentally different way. It is essentially a way of trust. But what makes it different is the nature of the God in whom our trust is placed. It is a God "who justifies the ungodly" (v. 5). This way requires us to see God not as one whose actions are calculated, who rewards good deeds with good wages, who responds in kind to our efforts. Rather, it is a God whose actions are uncalculated, a God who does the unexpected—forgives rather than condemns the sinner.

For Paul, the true paradigm of this second way—the way of faith—was Abraham. In the first place, Scripture itself asserts that God reckoned him as righteous because of his faith (v. 3; also cf. 4:9). It was his capacity to trust in God's promise, to believe in a God who could do the impossible, who could act out of character, as it were, and extend grace to a childless, aging couple with no hope of fulfilling God's promise on their own. In the second place, this display of implicit trust preceded circumcision (4:10–12). Abraham behaved this way before his formal initiation into the people of God.

The true children of Abraham, the legitimate heirs of the promise that God made through him (cf. Gen. 18:18; 22:17–18), are those who construe God, and their relationship with God, this way (v. 16). The God who extends righteousness to us is the God who "counts [us] as just, apart from any specific act of justice" (v. 6, NEB). It is God who, instead of responding in kind to sinners, forgives by extending grace. God is finally an uncalculating God who bestows salvation as free gift, not as wages earned.

John 3:1–17

The lectionary offers an alternative Gospel reading today, but the preacher is not to attempt to see any relationship between the two. The second lesson, Matthew 17:1–9, honors a long tradition in some churches to consider the Transfiguration of Jesus on the Second Sunday in Lent. If such a tradition seems unusual for Lent, it must be remembered that actually all Sundays in Lent are nonLenten in the sense that Sundays partake of Easter and are not fast days. In John 3:1–17, the church overhears Jesus tell a religious leader that the life abundant and eternal is a gift from above and is not attained by achievement, claim, or proof. Nothing could be more appropriate for Lent than a reminder that prayer and fasting do not earn anything.

John 3:1–7 consists of a conversation between two religious leaders, a conversation that gradually phases into a theological summary. Precisely at what point the conversation ends is uncertain (v. 12? 15? 16? 21?). For our discussion, verses 1–15 will be treated as the conversation and verses 16–17 as a portion of the theological summary ending at verse 21. Such summaries are common in John (3:31–36; 5:19–29). The conversation may be taken as set in the context of 2:23–25, that is, in Jerusalem at Passover, but time and place settings often appear more symbolic than historical. However, 3:1–17 does appear to be a particular instance of that which is generally stated in 2:23–25. Nicodemus represents a faith, unclear and seeking more proofs, that is based on signs, and to him and through him Jesus declares that God loves and gives life to the world.

The subject of the text from beginning to end is God. The issue is, How do God and human beings relate so as to please God and redeem the world? Jesus and Nicodemus meet "at night," an expression designating kind of time, not point in time. What follows, says the writer, will contain mystery and misunderstanding. By means of the Johannine device of double meanings (for example, bread, light, water, temple, and other terms carry two meanings in this Gospel), Jesus says life in the kingdom comes by birth "from above" (v. 3), but Nicodemus translates "from above" as "again," and is confused. How can an old man be born again (v. 4)? It is striking that the popularization of this expression has accepted Nicodemus' misunderstanding (born again) rather than Jesus' word.

At verse 7, the "you" of Jesus' address to Nicodemus becomes plural, indicating that we cease to have a private conversation and have a sermon to all. That this is a post-Easter sermon is further indicated by additional uses of plural "you" (vv. 11, 12), "we" (v. 11), references to baptism and the Holy Spirit, which in John is a post-Easter gift (7:39), and the reference to Christ's ascension as a past not future event (v. 13).

And so a conversation becomes a sermon to all who need to hear that life in God's realm is not achieved, calculated, or safely fixed on a faith that has been proven by signs. Rather, life is given of God, as free from our control as the whence and whither of the wind (v. 8). But this is not a truth about God that begins with Jesus. God has always offered life, as the serpent story in Numbers 21:49 (vv. 14–15) illustrates. There is no BC or AD on the love of God; John 3:16–17 announces what has always been true of God.

Matthew 17:1–9

The preacher may not wish to return so soon to the Transfiguration because the Last Sunday After the Epiphany (two weeks ago) always centers on this event and this year Matthew 17:1–9 was the text. If the Transfiguration is customarily treated today, the preacher may wish to review the comments on this text provided earlier. However, seasons affect interpretations of texts, and Matthew 17:1–9 does not say the same thing during Lent as it does following Epiphany. Therefore, the following comments on this lection are offered with Lent in mind.

Matthew 17:1–9 follows closely Mark 9:2–9, with Luke's account (9:28–37) departing more noticeably from the common source. All agree in placing the Transfiguration immediately after the confession of Peter, the first prediction of the passion, and Jesus' teaching on cross-bearing. The Transfiguration does not, however, rob those passages of their stern teaching and demand as though to say, "Do not take the cross seriously; Jesus is really the divine Son with eternal glory." On the contrary, the Transfiguration confirms the truth of the passion and the cross by assuring the disciples that the crucified one is not a victim of history but as Son of God is carrying out the divine will. The passion prediction is thus underscored, not erased, just as Easter interprets rather than removes Good Friday.

The background to this text is to be found in Exodus 24:16 and 34:29–35. Moses was six days on the mountain, God spoke out of a cloud, and afterward Moses' face shone. In the middle of a long and difficult wilderness experience, Moses and the people experienced God. If Lent is a journey to Easter involving prayer and fasting, then the people of God are blessed by the revelation of the Transfiguration. The unveiling of Jesus' eternal nature, the dramatic demonstration of his messianic glory, gives reason to go on when murmuring about turning back begins.

Moses and Elijah talk with Jesus (only Luke indicates the subject matter, 9:31), a clear indication of the unity of God's activity and purpose in the law, the prophets, and Jesus. Preachers want to avoid giving the impression that God tried with the law and failed, tried with prophets and failed, and so, finally, decided on a new plan in Jesus.

However, when the clouds lifted, Jesus stood alone and alone was to be heard. Jesus is not the abolition but the fulfillment of the law and the prophets (5:17–18). God's purposes have been long in unfolding, and God's servants have been many, but all have their center in Jesus Christ. It is no small matter to be a follower of Jesus (Heb. 1:1–3).

Luke says Peter, James, and John told no one about this in those days (9:36); Matthew and Mark say Jesus told them to be quiet until after the resurrection (Matt. 17:9; Mark 9:9). In either case, the silence was appropriate and perhaps necessary. Truth too soon is neither believable nor meaningful; both the speaker and the listener appear to be engaged in interesting rumors. But with Easter's help, both can say, "Now I see."

farce, melodrama or tragedy?

Third Sunday in Lent

Exodus 17:1–7;
Psalm 95;
Romans 5:1–11;
John 4:5–42

Water is the dominant motif of the texts for the Third Sunday in Lent, leading in various ways to reflection upon human need and divine grace. The Old Testament lesson is one of the many accounts of the people of Israel complaining in the wilderness, in this case because of thirst. The Lord's response is to tell Moses how to bring water from the rock. The psalm, a liturgy of praise, responds directly to Exodus 17, celebrating God's care for God's people and admonishing them with the example of the complainers in the wilderness. In Romans 5, Paul presents a picture of endurance in suffering that contrasts with that of Israel in the wilderness, and celebrates God's love in Jesus Christ as the foundation for rejoicing. The Gospel lesson is the account of Jesus at the well in Samaria, offering living water to the Samaritan woman.

Exodus 17:1–7

Exodus 17 finds the people of Israel on the way in the wilderness, between the exodus from Egypt and their entrance into the promised land. The wilderness stories frame a long account of the covenant and the giving of the law on Mt. Sinai (Exod. 19:1–Num. 10:10). In its immediate context, our passage is found between the story of the manna and quails in Exodus 16 and the account of the war with Amalek in Exodus 17:8–16. Exodus 18 then reports the visit of Jethro, priest of Midian and father-in-law of Moses, to the Israelite camp, and the establishment of institutions to resolve legal disputes among the people.

Although there are repetitions and tensions that suggest the presence of different sources or—more likely—a complex oral prehistory, most of our reading comes from the hand of the Yahwistic Writer. However, the location of the events had been established by the Priestly source, with its concern for geographical detail, as in the wilderness of Sin at a place called Rephidim (17:1), where there was no water.

What transpires is an all-too-familiar pattern throughout the period of the wandering in the wilderness. First, the people find themselves in need. In this case they are thirsty (vv. 1b–3a). Then they complain or murmur "against Moses." Their complaint becomes a standardized accusation: "Why did you bring us out of Egypt, to kill us?" (v. 3b). Second, Moses prays to the Lord. Often in such instances he intercedes for the people (cf. Num. 20:6), but here the petition itself contains a note of complaint, emphasizing Moses' concern with the seriousness of the situation: "What shall I do with this people? They are almost ready to stone me" (v. 4). Third, the Lord gives instructions for actions that will meet the people's need though miraculous means. Moses, with some of the elders as witnesses, is to take his staff and strike the rock on which the Lord stands (vv. 5–6). When he does so, water springs from the rock.

The conclusion of the episode gives an account of the place names Massah and Meribah. Remarkably, the names do not memorialize the miracle of the water, but the people's contentiousness and lack of faith. "Meribah" means contention or quarrel, and "Massah" means trial, test, or proof. Both names occur independently in the wilderness narratives (Deut. 6:16; 9:22; 32:51; Num. 20:13); their combination here is probably a relatively late stage of the tradition.

Noteworthy are the references to Moses' rod, to Horeb, and to Yahweh's standing on the rock. The writer reminds us that Moses' rod is the one he used to strike the Nile (v. 5), recalling the miraculous plagues against Egypt. The power for such actions resides not in the rod, but in the word of the Lord. It, like Moses, is an instrument of the divine power. The reference to "Horeb" (v. 6) is out of place, for the people are not at the sacred mountain. The allusion is one of those tensions that show a complex oral tradition behind the story. The reference to Yahweh's standing on the rock (v. 6) is difficult to understand, but most likely simply indicates the presence of the Lord as Moses carries out his instructions.

Two major themes predominate in the accounts of Israel in the wilderness, and both of them are present here. The first is the murmuring and rebellion of the people of God. Old Testament tradition is hard on the wilderness generation of Israelites. Having been rescued from slavery, and either on their way to or from Sinai, where God made them God's covenant people, they find every occasion to find fault or even to worship other gods. For these reasons they were not allowed to enter the promised land. Psalm 95 continues the criticism of these people, holding them up as bad examples. But are all their complaints illegitimate? After all, at Rephidim they found themselves without water. Small wonder that they should fear death by thirst and wish they were back in Egypt. However, the tradition takes their complaints as more than a prayer for water, for in complaining "against Moses" they are questioning the presence of the Lord among them (v. 7). Would not the one who chose them and rescued them also care for their physical needs? Such an understanding is conveyed in the typical divine response to the complaints: the Lord patiently gives them what they need.

The second leading theme of the wilderness traditions is thus the gracious care of the Lord for the people wandering in the desert. The promise first given to Abraham (Gen. 12:1–4) will be fulfilled; the people will be sustained so that their descendants can become a great nation and receive the land. Thus the story so full of contention is a tale of the grace of God, grace in the form of such a simple but essential gift as water to drink.

Psalm 95

This psalm may be divided into the following components: verses 1–2 are a communal call to offer praise to God. Verses 3–5 stipulate, in hymnic fashion, the reasons why God should be praised. Verse 6 reissues the call to praise, with verse 7a offering the reason for praise. Verse 7b calls on the people to listen to God's address, and verses 8–11 are an oracle delivered as a speech of God.

The opening call to praise (vv. 1–2) speaks of four sentiments or actions that manifest devotion to God: sing (or "shout for joy"), make a joyful noise (or perhaps "pay homage"), come into his divine presence with thanksgiving (or "greet him" or "approach his presence [enter the temple] with thanksgiving"), and acclaim him with songs. In these verses, only one metaphor is used to describe God—a rock of salvation, a rather common description in the Old Testament (see Pss. 18:2, 31, 46; 19:14; Isa. 44:8) that denotes God's reliability and stability.

The reasons offered for praising God focus on God's status as Lord over the world and the status of the world as divine creation (vv. 3–5). God is the great God (see Ps. 77:13) who rules as king over the other gods. Verse 3 thus clearly presupposes a polytheistic background. Yahweh is not the only god but the greatest of the gods. The whole of creation belongs to Yahweh. The concept of the totality of creation is expressed in the employment of opposites—the depths of the earth and the heights of the mountains and the sea and the dry land. The world is created by the Divine (v. 5), and thus as creator Yahweh controls it (v. 4).

The second call to praise (v. 6) is actually a call to worship, employing three synonymous expressions—worship, bow down, kneel. The image of God as creator is carried over in the expression "the Lord, our Maker" in verse 6. In verse 7, the emphasis is not so much on God as creator as much as caretaker; God is the shepherd, and the people are the sheep.

The divine oracle (vv. 8–11), similar to a prophetic address, is introduced by the last line of verse 7. In the oracle, the people are admonished not to repeat the disobedience and obstinacy of the past.

In their midrash on this psalm, the ancient rabbis understood the disobedience at Meribah and Massah as one of the ten rebellions in the wilderness.

> You will find that the children of Israel put the Holy One, blessed be He, to proof ten times, as is said *All those men that have seen My glory, and My miracles which I wrought in Egypt and in the wilderness . . . have put Me to proof these ten times* (Num. 14:22): twice at the Red Sea, as is said *Our fathers understood not the wonder in Egypt; they remembered not the multitude of Thy mercies; but provoked Him at the sea, even at the Red Sea* (Ps. 106:7); twice with the quail (Exod. 16:13; Num. 11:31–32); once with the manna (Exod. 16:20); once with the golden calf (Exod. 32); once at Paran (Num. 13:26) this one being the most provoking. You say ten proofs, but you instance only seven. What are the other three? The other three are mentioned in the verse *At Taberah, and at Massah, and at Kibroth-hattaavah, ye provoked the Lord to wrath* (Deut. 9:22). And why does not Scripture instance these with the others? Because these three were more provoking than the seven preceding ones.

Romans 5:1–11

Parts of this passage are employed elsewhere in the *Common Lectionary*: 5:1–5 as the epistolary lection for Trinity Sunday in Year C and 5:1–8 as the epistolary lection for Proper 6 in Year A. The reader may want to consult our remarks in these other settings.

In the context of Lent, this passage both challenges and reassures us. It speaks straight, without flinching, as it exposes our humanness for what it is and reveals what we know ourselves to be: "weak" (v. 6), "ungodly" (v. 6), "sinners" (v. 8). It also squarely confronts us with the reality of suffering (v. 3). Rather than blinking at this reality of life, it acknowledges what we all know and experience: suffering is part and parcel of the human condition, and being Christian does not exempt us. In fact, suffering may be the price we pay for being Christian. At one level, then, our text is coldly honest with us, leaving us with no illusions about ourselves and the life we are called to lead. It is a level of honesty that commends itself in periods of penitence and thoughtful examination. It sees life as we know it and live it.

At another level, however, the text reassures us, for with its honest assessment of the human condition there is the bold declaration of God's saving act. It begins with the premise that "we are justified by faith" (v. 1), the principle Paul has argued and established in the preceding chapters. Like Abraham, we are justified by God on the basis of our willingness to trust. But the locus of our trust is in Christ, the one through whom our new relationship is made possible. The work of Christ has resulted in several benefits:

First, *peace with God* (v. 1). In a sense, we find here the fulfillment of Isaiah's hope that "the effect of righteousness will be peace" (Isa. 32:17). Elsewhere, Christ is seen to be the locus of God's peace (John 16:33), the one enabling us to have confidence before God (1 John 3:21).

Second, *access to divine grace* (v. 2). Christ becomes, as it were, a sphere of divine grace, the space in which "we stand" (cf. 1 Pet. 5:12). Finding our footing in Christ grants us proximity to God that provides genuine access that otherwise does not exist (Eph. 3:12; Heb. 4:16).

Third, *hope in sharing God's glory* (v. 2). The emphasis here is eschatological. Paul looks to the future when God's glory will finally and fully be revealed (Rom. 8:18, 30; cf. Titus 2:13). But it cannot be thought of apart from Christ (cf. Col. 1:27).

Fourth, *the capacity to transcend suffering* (vv. 3–4). What is envisioned here is not a stoic endurance of suffering, a steeling of the will against pain. It is rather the capacity to experience suffering but at the same time be transformed by it into something different and better. There is first the recognition that it is real. It should neither be denied nor avoided (cf. James 1:2–4; 1 Pet. 1:6–7; 2 Cor. 12:9; also 2 Cor. 4:17). Yet properly experienced and interpreted, it can be transforming; it can teach us endurance and in doing so refine our character as it directs us to God's future, to which we look in hope.

Fifth, *the Holy Spirit as God's gift* (v. 5). The sure sign that God's love has been poured out among us is the Spirit (cf. Acts 2:17, 33; 10:45; Titus 3:6; 1 John 4:13). It is a lavish inundation of God's own presence (cf. Sir. 18:11).

Sixth, *God's love manifested in Christ* (vv. 5–8). As Paul states in the preceding chapter, our faith is in a God who "justifies the ungodly" (4:5). It is precisely in our helplessness as sinners that God responds in love (cf. John 3:16; 1 John 4:10; 1 Pet. 3:18). Specifically, the act of Christ was in our behalf (v. 8; 3:25; Eph. 1:7; cf. 1 Cor. 11:25).

Seventh, *salvation from God's wrath* (v. 9). One of the stark realities of salvation is that God's wrath is unleashed on all forms of human iniquity (Rom. 1:18; 4:5; cf. Matt. 3:7; 1 Thess. 1:10; 2:16).

Eighth, *reconciliation* (vv. 10–11). Formerly, we were enemies of God (v. 10), with a mind-set hostile to the nature of God (Rom. 8:7; James 4:4). But through Christ, reconciliation enables us to participate in his saving life (cf. 2 Cor. 4:10–11; 5:18; Col. 1:21–22). In this sense, Christ himself is our reconciliation (cf. 1 Cor. 1:31; 2 Cor. 10:17; Gal. 6:14; Phil. 3:3).

Today's epistolary reading thus presents us with reality and possibility: an honest assessment of who we are without God and apart from Christ, but also of what life with God can entail. But at the same time, it speaks of God's saving work through Christ that creates new realities, and with them new possibilities as we face both present and future.

John 4:5–42

John 4:5–42 is a story of unusual dramatic force as well as theological insight. The writer offers us the story in several clear movements. First, Jesus and the Samaritan woman are alone on stage, the disciples being removed by a trip into town for food (v. 8). Following the conversation between Jesus and the woman, the longest recorded in the New Testament between Jesus and anyone, the disciples return (v. 27) and the woman leaves (v. 28). Following the conversation between Jesus and his disciples, the Samaritan villagers come to Jesus because of the woman (v. 39). Jesus abides (a key word in John indicating the strongest and deepest level of faith) two days at their request (v. 40), and the Samaritans arrive at profound faith: "We know that this is truly the Savior of the world" (v. 42).

A second way to view the text is in terms of geographical movement. John 4 is in many ways a missionary text. In Acts 1:8, it is reported that the gospel was to move from Jerusalem to Judea to Samaria, and to the world. In John 4, Jesus moves from Jerusalem into Judea and then into Samaria. At the close of John 4, Jesus is declared "the Savior of the world" (v. 42). Whether there is any literary or historical connection between this text and the Samaritan mission of Acts 8:5–25 is unclear, but John 4 certainly gives Jesus' authorization to the proclamation of the gospel in Samaria.

A third perspective on this text available to the preacher is that of noting the stages in the movement of the woman's faith. At first the conversation seems to hold no promise, the two being distanced by race, gender, and religion. Again the Johannine double meanings appear: Jesus says "water" and she says "water," but the subjects are not the same. However, the conversation moves to a deeper level as this man is compared to Jacob, who had drawn water from this well without having to draw. According to legend, living or bubbling water rose to the surface for Jacob. Now the woman is asking Jesus for the water he can give (v. 15). The conversation deepens further as the woman recognizes Jesus as a prophet (v. 19). Her faith in him as prophet is based on his having supernatural knowledge, as in the case of Nathaniel (1:47–49). But in the Johannine church, believing Jesus has special powers is not sufficient, for she has not yet "seen his glory"; that is, seen him as the revelation of God. At this point, the woman, apparently uncomfortable, tries to be evasive by introducing the tensions between Jewish and Samaritan religions (vv. 20–24). It is an old ploy: when on the spot, begin an argument. The maneuver failed, the woman expresses a hope in a coming Messiah, and Jesus responds, "I am" (vv. 25–26).

It is a question whether Jesus' response "I am" should be translated, "I am he"; that is, "I am the Messiah you have been looking for." After all, in this Gospel Jesus is not simply the Messiah; he is that and more. Jesus is God's presence among people looking for a Messiah. The messianic expectation had become so corrupted and distorted by social, cultural, and political definitions of Messiah that to say Jesus was the Messiah was true but also in a measure false. At any rate, there is no clear indication of the degree or shape of the woman's faith. She witnessed to others with a question, "He cannot be the Messiah, can he?" (v. 29), and her characterization of Jesus was of a man "who told me everything I have ever done" (vv. 29, 39). However, a word needs to be said about her as a witness. She may not have arrived at a full faith in Jesus as son of God, but she witnessed to the extent of her faith. Others were invited to affirm what for her remained an uncertainty: "He cannot be the Messiah, can he?" And the point is, her word about Jesus initiated a relationship between others and Jesus, the fruit of which was a faith beyond her own. They said, "We know that this is truly the Savior of the world" (v. 42). Had she waited until her own faith was full grown, that remarkable conclusion to this story would have been aborted.

In this Gospel, there are various kinds and qualities of faith. Growth is possible if the believers "abide," but no faith is so new, so partial, so unclear that witnessing to Jesus Christ out of that faith is inappropriate.

Fourth Sunday in Lent

1 Samuel 16:1–13;
Psalm 23;
Ephesians 5:8–14;
John 9:1–41

The Old Testament reading continues the Lenten recital of ancient Israel's history. With the report of the election and anointing of David to be king, 1 Samuel 16 takes us from the wandering in the wilderness, beyond the settlement in the land, and to the next decisive turning point—the establishment of the monarchy. Psalm 23 expresses the deepest possible trust in the Lord. Both New Testament readings contrast light and darkness. Ephesians 5 is a call for the faithful to forsake the "unfruitful works of darkness," for they are now "children of light" (v. 8). John 9 contains the account of Jesus' healing of the man born blind, including the debate with the Pharisees over the blind man's guilt and the authority of Jesus.

1 Samuel 16:1–13

In ancient Israel's memory, the establishment of the monarchy ranks in importance with the exodus from Egypt, the Exile, and the return from Babylon. In Israel's understanding, the promise to Abraham (Gen. 12:1–3) set into motion a history of salvation that reached its fulfillment with the settlement of the people in the land. But the Lord's care for Israel does not end there. New problems and needs arise, and God responds, not only with the fulfillment of old promises but with new promises as well.

One of Israel's major problems in the promised land led to theological controversy. What would be the form of government for the people of God? Specifically, would they have a king or not? After all, Yahweh was their king. Samuel presided over that debate, which seemed to have been resolved with the anointing of Saul as king. Yes, as long as the people of God are in the world, they will need a human government. However, the kingship of Saul failed. That failure is reported in the chapter that immediately precedes the reading for today. Although Saul will continue to rule for many years, the matter has already been settled, for "the Lord was sorry ["repented," RSV] that he had made Saul king over Israel" (1 Sam. 15:34). After David was anointed, "the Spirit of the Lord departed from Saul" (1 Sam. 16:14).

The text before us is the first of the stories of David, and it marks the final public appearance of Samuel. David will go on to become king, to establish an empire, and to leave the throne to his son Solomon. The climax of the David stories is found in 2 Samuel 7, the account of the Lord's promise that one of David's descendants would always sit on the throne in Jerusalem. That promise subsequently became the basis for messianic expectations and for the early Christian emphasis on Jesus as a son of David. The foundation for it was already laid in the chapter before us with the anointing of David. From the Hebrew word for "anoint" (*mashah*) comes the designation "Messiah."

On the surface, the central character in 1 Samuel 16:1–13 is the old prophet Samuel, serving as a bridge between the period of the judges and that of the monarchy. The contrast between the old and the new is heightened in the contrast between the aged prophet, who has seen so much, and the youngest son of Jesse. Samuel, however, is only the instrument of the word of Yahweh. Except for his initial objection to the Lord's command, he does nothing except as instructed. David, too, is a passive participant in the drama, speaking not a word. Thus the central actor is Yahweh, who is setting his will into motion through Samuel and David.

The episode has both priestly and prophetic dimensions, but the latter predominate. The setting is a liturgical one, and Samuel performs several liturgical acts including the sacrifice of the heifer and the consecration of the participants (v. 5). Also, it seems that the sequence of events suggests ritual designation by lot. When Yahweh instructs Samuel to go to Bethlehem and anoint one of the sons of Jesse—note that his name is not revealed until the end—the prophet objects, fearing that Saul will get word of the plan and kill him (v. 2). Yahweh instructs Samuel to take an animal and perform a sacrifice. Such a ruse would not be effective if Samuel were not known to do such things, that is, to perform priestly functions.

One may even take the anointing of David to be a more or less priestly act. There are many reports of anointing in the Old Testament. Some have to do with sacred objects connected with places of worship (Gen. 28:18; Exod. 29:36; 30:26; Lev. 8:12; Ezek. 28:14), but frequently the reports concern the designation of a king (Judg. 9:8, 15; 1 Sam. 10:1; 15:1; 2 Sam. 5:3, 17; 1 Kings 1:39; 2 Kings 9:3, 6, 12). Often the king is described as "the Lord's anointed" (1 Sam. 24:6, 10; 26:11, 16, 23). Anointing was a simple but solemn ritual involving the pouring or smearing of oil. The ritual sanctified the object or person (Exod. 29:36; Lev. 8:12) by transferring the sacredness of the Deity. One who was anointed thus was holy, set apart from the profane or ordinary, and given divine authority.

However, the Samuel of this story is mainly a prophetic figure who receives his instructions at each step through the word of Yahweh. Even his objection (v. 2) is similar to that of prophets at their call (Jer. 1:6; Isa. 6:5; cf. Exod. 3:13–4:17). Above all, the prophetic perspective concerns the "Spirit of the Lord" (v. 13). Once the youngest son has been brought out and Yahweh reveals to Samuel that this is the one, Samuel anoints him, and "the spirit of the Lord came mightily upon David from that day forward" (v. 13). This sentence is the heading for the entire story of David that is to follow. He is the divinely designated ruler of Israel.

At this stage of the narrative as a whole, the Lord's choice is quite unexpected. The one chosen is the youngest son of Jesse, who belongs to the smallest clan of the smallest tribe of Israel. David was not even allowed to come to the sacrifice, but was left to keep his father's sheep (v. 11). The oldest son, Eliab, obviously because of his size, seemed to be the right one, but although human beings look on the outward appearances, "the Lord looks on the heart" (v. 7). Despite this observation, the narrator cannot avoid commenting on the physical beauty of David when he appears (v. 12).

After this episode, the story of Saul will continue, and David will appear on the public scene. There are two quite different accounts of that appearance, one in which David is recommended to Saul as an attractive and skilled musician and soldier (1 Sam. 16:14–23), and another in which the unknown but courageous shepherd boy turns up on the battlefield to defeat the Philistine giant (1 Sam. 17:1–58). But in both of them we are to understand David's remarkable abilities as manifestations of his divine designation, the presence of the Spirit of the Lord.

Psalm 23

This, the best known of all the psalms, has been selected to accompany the reading of the account of David's anointment in 1 Samuel 16:1–13. The imagery of sheep and shepherd is common to both.

If we analyze Psalm 23 in terms of speaker and addressee, we find the following pattern: the worshiper, confessing confidence in God, is apparently speaking to some human audience (vv. 1–3); the worshiper, addressing the Deity, stresses what God has done (vv. 4–5); and finally, the worshiper, again addressing the audience, summarizes the person's assurance of divine favor (v. 6).

It is possible to understand the images of God in this psalm in two different ways. In one, God is the skillful and compassionate shepherd who leads the worshiper like a good shepherd who cares for the sheep, a widespread view of both gods and kings in the Near East (vv. 1–3). If the shepherd imagery in verses 2–4 is applied to verse 5, it can be said that the shepherd looks after the feeding and care of the sheep. Shepherds in the Middle East (Lebanon and Syria) used the expression "to set the table" when referring to preparing fields for grazing. Such activities included uprooting poisonous weeds and thorns and clearing the area of the sheep's enemies, such as snakes and scorpion's nests. In the evening, as the sheep were corralled, the injured or sickly ones were separated from the others and treated with oil and a curative drink made of fermented material and herbs sweetened with honey. If one follows this line of interpretation, then the imagery of the shepherd runs throughout the psalm.

It is also possible to look at the psalm as presenting a double image of God, that of shepherd for the sheep (vv. 1–3) and that of a human host for a guest (vv. 4–5). (Note that this breaks the text between the section spoken to a human audience, vv. 1–3, and that spoken to God directly, vv. 4–5.) The image of God as host emphasizes not only the sufficiency of the Divine to feed but also the care that God takes to meet the other needs of the guest—anointing oil for the head and soothing cup for the psyche.

To decide between these two alternative interpretations is almost a matter of taste, although the latter is certainly found more widely in literature on the psalms.

If the psalm compares the experience of God and his care to that of a shepherd and/or a human host, then what does the imagery of the person's distresses refer to? That is, what has happened to the worshiper? From what straits has he or she been saved? Some possibilities are these: (1) one could see the imagery to be that of sheep changing or entering new pastures; thus the psalmist could be describing one of life's points of transition; (2) another view is to see the prayer as one offered by a wandering traveler who has safely returned to Jerusalem; (3) the entire imagery may be simply that of a worshiper who eats a sacrificial meal in the sanctuary; (4) a further alternative is to see all the imagery as merely verbal images without any exact frames of reference; and (5) a final interpretation suggests that this psalm may have been used by a fugitive guilty of manslaughter or accidental killing who took refuge and sought asylum in the temple and who thus lives beyond the reach of the family of the deceased. (See Exod. 21:12–14; Deut. 19:1–13; 1 Kings 1:49–53; 2:28–35 for this practice.) Dwelling in the temple or house of God would thus be taken literally. There the fugitive could eat in the temple in the presence of his or her enemies but without fear that vengeance would be taken.

Regardless of how one interprets the psalm, the general picture of what is stresed is quite clear. One who has known trouble or experienced life-threatening situations has also experienced the protection of the Divine. The psalm exudes confidence that God protects, so that whatever life brings to his people, they will not be overwhelmed.

Preaching on this text, one could focus on the diverse expressions of human experience found in the psalm. One set emphasizes the troubles that threaten to overwhelm human life: valley of the shadow of death (or darkness or total darkness), evil, and enemies. Another set stresses the positive instruments and acts of God's care: green pastures, still waters, reviving of the soul, reliable paths, rod and staff, table, oil, and cup. Human life, of course, experiences both the negative and the positive. At times, even the Shepherd must use the rod and staff against his own sheep for their best interests.

This closing verse affirms that goodness and mercy, not tribulation or ravenous enemies, shall be a constant companion. To dwell (or to return) to the house of Yahweh in this verse did not refer to immortality but to either residence in the temple (by a priest or a fugitive) or, if read as return, to a visit to the temple.

Ephesians 5:8–14

From earliest times, Lent served as the time when catechumenates prepared intensively for their baptism at the Easter Vigil. Over the centuries, the explicit connection with baptism diminished as Lent came to be viewed as a time of preparation generally for all Christians who moved toward the celebration of Easter. Vatican II served to reemphasize the baptismal features of the Lenten liturgy.

These baptismal allusions are dominant in today's epistolary text. The opening contrast "once you were . . . but now you are" is widely regarded as formulaic instruction for Christian initiates to set their former way of life in contrast to the new way they have embarked on. It is easy to see how this could have provided a basic form of early Christian teaching, perhaps connected with the "two ways" scheme (cf. Eph. 2:11, 13).

The contrast between light and darkness is also emphasized. In fact, these two themes are interwoven throughout today's passage. So universal are these images that they are frequently found in a variety of ancient religions and are used to typify two contrasting ways of life. The common assumption is that light is identified with the good and true, whereas darkness betokens what is sinister and evil (cf. 1 Thess. 5:5; also Luke 16:8; John 12:36). Accordingly, conversion is typically viewed as the transition from darkness to light (1 Pet. 2:9).

One striking feature of today's passage is that the readers are actually identified with darkness and light. It is not the usual "you were living *in* darkness, but are now living *in* the light." It is, rather, "once you *were* darkness, but now . . . you *are* light" (v. 8). Such direct identification reminds us of Jesus' injunction "you are the light of the world" (Matt. 5:14). It was thoroughly in character with this emphasis when early Christian initiates were referred to as "the enlightened ones."

It is at this point that today's epistolary text converges with the Gospel reading, the story of the man born blind (John 9). This highly ironical account, which is typical of the

Johannine narrative, unfolds for us the story of a blind man who becomes enlightened, and as such provides a counterpoint to those around him who presumably have 20/20 vision but who fail to "see." It is John's way of portraying faith in Christ as an illumination, an enlightenment, a coming to the light.

Along with the transition of status comes the appropriate behavior. We are thus enjoined to "live as children of light" (v. 8; cf. 1 John 1:7). Positively, this means learning what "is pleasing to the Lord" (v. 10; cf. Rom. 12:2; 14:18; 2 Cor. 5:9; Heb. 13:21). Negatively, it means casting off the unfruitful "works of darkness" (v. 11; cf. Rom. 13:12), indeed turning against them in order to expose them. We now become aggressive foes of darkness, bent on exposing evil in all its forms. This is a hard saying, but there are numerous sharp-edged injunctions that call us to be active in censure and rebuke (1 Tim. 5:20; 2 Tim. 4:2; Titus 1:9, 13; also Gal. 2:14).

What is called for here is a form of life that is out in the open, transparent, as it were, before God. There is a hint in verse 12 at things done in secret too shameful to be mentioned. We are reminded elsewhere that the gospel has no truck with secret, underhanded methods (2 Cor. 4:2).

The final verse appears to be a fragment of an early Christian hymn, sung perhaps in a baptismal liturgy. As such, it would have been addressed to the initiate, who is invited to awake to the new life in Christ and be enlightened by Christ himself (v. 14; cf. Rom. 13:11; 1 Thess. 5:6).

All of these motifs are fitting reminders during the Lenten Season that our baptism marks a transition from an old way of life to a new, enlightened existence. They also serve as ethical imperatives, enjoining us to conform our lives to the nature of true existence in Christ.

John 9:1–41

The Gospel lesson for today is one lengthy narrative, and the preacher would do well not only to study the text as a whole but to try to preserve the dramatic narrative quality of the text in the sermon itself. Above all, it is important to keep in mind that this is not simply a story of Jesus healing a blind man but Jesus healing a blind man *according to John's Gospel.* In Mark 8:22–26, Jesus heals the blind, but one has only to read the two stories to see the difference.

John 9:1–41 and John 5:1–17 are healing stories that resemble each other and bear the marks of Johannine theology. Both are healings on the Sabbath, both are signs revealing God and are not presented as acts in response to need, both portray Jesus taking the initiative rather than healing persons who come to him in faith, both involve persons who suffer hardship because Jesus healed them, and both accounts are followed by theological discourses. The two most unusual features of both stories are that two lives are changed by divine initiative and not because of anything said or done by the one in need, and much of the action of both stories occurs in Jesus' absence. In John 9, Jesus comes and heals and then is gone. He returns at the end of the story to encourage and vindicate the one healed. In other words, our text records what life is like for those whom Jesus has blessed but who are living in the world between the first and second appearances of Jesus. John's church was suffering a great deal (15:20–16:4) and most likely identified closely with the healed man who received abuse from family, neighbors, and religious leaders.

If we may think of John 9:1–41 as a drama, then the action can be followed most easily by focusing on the six scenes presented by the story. Scene one (vv. 1–7) is introductory. Jesus and his disciples see a man blind from birth. The disciples want to discuss the man's malady theologically, but Jesus will have none of it. Rather, Jesus sees the occasion as one in which the works of God can be revealed. With a procedure very much the same as used by other healers in that day, Jesus restores the man's sight. In scene one, Jesus disappears from the story. In scene two (vv. 8–12), we find the healed man back in his old neighborhood, but not comfortable. Friends and neighbors are disturbed that he is no longer blind. They bombard him with questions: Who did it? How? Where is the healer now? Arguments break out among those who believe the man is healed and those who do not; there is no joy, no praise, no thanking God, no encouragement, only quarreling.

In scene three (vv. 13–17), the poor fellow is hauled before the religious authorities. After all, this healing was perpetrated on the Sabbath, and therefore, the healer, if there was one, is a criminal to be punished. The clergy are divided, and so the healed man is asked to testify. He calls Jesus a prophet of God, his testimony is rejected, and further evidence is sought. In scene four (vv. 18–23), the authorities quiz the parents. Intimidated and afraid of punishment by reason of association or consent, they ask not to be involved. A house has been divided over Jesus and his power to help the needy, and the healed man is feeling very much alone.

Scene five (vv. 24–34) returns to scene three: the authorities again interrogate the healed man. Pressure builds and tempers flare. The man answers with personal testimony ("I was blind, now I see") and with reason (Jesus must be of God to have the power to heal). The authorities are in a bind; they must accept the man as healed and accept the healer as a person of God, or they must hold to their view of the law concerning the Sabbath and reject the healed and the healer. The healed man is excommunicated. And he never asked to be healed in the first place! Those who are blessed by Jesus soon run into trouble in the world because good news has enemies.

In the final scene (vv. 35–41), Jesus returns. The healed man meets and confesses faith in Jesus, whereas the oppressors come under the judgment of the revelation of who they really are. And this is the judgment, that "the light has come into the world, and people loved darkness rather than light" (3:19). The healing has made it clear: light comes to those who recognize that life is blindness without Christ; darkness comes to those who without Christ claim to see.

Fifth Sunday in Lent

Ezekiel 37:1–14;
Psalm 130;
Romans 8:6–11;
John 11:1–45

In their contrasts between life and death, the texts for today anticipate Easter. However, all of them focus more upon the life of the people of God this side of the grave than upon the resurrection as such. Ezekiel's vision of the valley of dry bones is a prophecy that the people of Israel, dead in exile, will live again on their land. The responsorial psalm is an individual complaint song, a prayer that the Lord, who redeems Israel and is motivated by his "steadfast love," will save the person in trouble. In the epistolary reading, Paul compares the spirit with life and the flesh with death, for "to set the mind on the Spirit is life and peace" (Rom. 8:6). John 11 is the account of Jesus' raising of Lazarus from the dead.

Ezekiel 37:1–14

With this season's summary of Israel's history from the Old Testament, we are left to supply a major event between last Sunday's reading and the one for today. The anointing of David introduced the period of the monarchy, and Ezekiel 37 announces the revival of Israel. What occurs between these two is the Exile. The end of Israel's history through military defeat and exile had been anticipated in prophetic announcements as early as the eighth century BC, as judgment upon the sinful people. First the Northern Kingdom was defeated by the Assyrians and the population dispersed throughout the empire (722/21 BC). Then the Babylonian king Nebuchadnezzar captured Judah, destroyed Jerusalem with its temple, and carried off the population to Babylon (597, 587 BC).

The prophet Ezekiel must have been one of the leading citizens of Jerusalem, for he was taken with the first wave of captives in 597. Although the captives had some autonomy, were allowed to gather, and could continue some of their religious practices, it is difficult to exaggerate the seriousness of the Exile as a national disaster and a crisis of faith. The Judeans had lost the land promised to their ancestors and granted in the time of Joshua. The last of the Davidic kings was a captive, first in prison and then at the court of the Babylonian monarch (2 Kings 25:27–30). The temple, where the Lord made his name to dwell and where his glory was known, lay in ruins. Ezekiel envisioned defeat as the departure of the glory of the Lord from the temple (Ezek. 10–11). Small wonder that the exiles asked if the history of Yahweh with his people had come to an end.

Ezekiel 37:1–14, the vision of the valley of dry bones, is the prophetic answer to that question. It presents one of the most memorable scenes of the Bible. The prophet reports that he was taken by the Spirit of the Lord and set down in the middle of a great plain covered with bones, dry bones—human bones. As is so often the case in prophetic vision reports, a dialogue transpires within the vision itself between the prophet and Yahweh. This stresses an important fact: what is heard is essential, for it is the word of the Lord, a message for the people. Thus the vision report moves from a description of what was seen to an interpretation of its meaning.

The dialogue within this vision concerns life and death, opening with Yahweh's question to Ezekiel, "Can these bones live?" The prophet's answer is not an evasion, but an acknowledgment of the source of life, "O Lord God, you know" (v. 3). The Lord then makes it clear how he intends to work his will, for he commands Ezekiel to prophecy to the bones. He does as commanded, and, with a rattling, the bones come together and are covered with sinews, flesh, and skin. But still they do not live. So through the prophet, Yahweh calls for the breath from the four winds, and when it breathes upon the bones they live (vv. 9–10).

The interpretation of the vision follows (vv. 11–14). The vision is an announcement, a promise of life, not of a general resurrection, but of the revival of the people beyond the Exile. The vision stresses that this revival is corporate; it is the restoration of the people of God. It is accomplished by word and spirit, the word of God through the prophet and the life-giving spirit as a divine gift.

Ezekiel is not, of course, to keep this vision to himself, but to report it to the people. It then becomes unqualified good news to those who consider themselves dead. It is the good news that people can live and can be enlivened by the Spirit of God, even on this side of the grave. It is a promise of release to exiles who have been oppressed by military powers, by the overwhelming political forces that control their existence. It is good news to the oppressed exiles who have been beaten down by their own sins and are suffering under the weight of the sins of their ancestors. To all those, the Spirit of God can and will give life. To such people this vision brings hope, beginning with release from bondage to the hopelessness of the situation. The history of God's work with his people is not yet done.

Psalm 130

An initial word about the structure and content of the psalm is in order. Although the psalm may be read as rather straightforward and continuous in content, it is actually rather complex. This can be seen from the different addresses in the psalm. In verses 1–4, God is addressed in a petitioning, supplicating tone by an individual worshiper. In verses 5–6, some human audience is addressed in very confessional tones. Finally, in verses 7–8 the community (Israel) is addressed in an admonishing and directive tone.

The address to the Deity (vv. 1–4) is fundamentally a description of the human condition, although verse 2 appeals to and makes requests for help from God. The human condition is described as "the depths," or at least this is the condition from which prayer is offered. The term "depths" is frequently used to refer to the depths of the seas (see Isa. 51:10; Ezek. 27:34). As such, the expression could be used to symbolize remoteness from God and to characterize the distress of the human predicament (see Jon. 2:2–3). The "depths" may be another way of speaking about Sheol, the world of the dead, the world isolated and estranged from God. At any rate, the "depths" give expression to that experience of life when everything seems askew and out of harmony. It is that point that lies at the outer edge of human control.

A second description of the human condition is found in verse 3. Humans experience life and know themselves as sinners. If God kept a full record, a complete tab on human sin, then no one would warrant being spared (see 1 Kings 8:46; Ps. 143:2; Prov. 20:9). Other texts, for example Psalms 15 and 24, assume that human beings can measure up to divinely set standards. Here, however, we have a very pessimistic, or realistic, reading of the human situation.

Over against the human experience of being overwhelmed by life (the depths of v. 1) and the realization of the complete misalignment of our existence (the iniquities of v. 3), there stands a theological affirmation about God, an affirmation that relativizes the human predicament—with God there is forgiveness (v. 4). Such an affirmation of forgiveness in spite of the human condition led Martin Luther to speak of the Pauline quality of this psalm.

The second section of the psalm, verses 5–6, is a confessional statement to a human audience. In addressing God, the worshiper in verses 1–4 assumed a position of subordination, perhaps to elicit a favorable response from the Divine. In addressing the human audience, the worshiper is allowed to exude confidence and to affirm a hopeful expectation. The speaker describes the waiting as being as intense as that of a watchman—a military sentry— watching for the dawn, when he would be relieved of duty and allowed to relax without the strain and responsibility of staying constantly alert. Perhaps the worshiper has been charged with some crime or has been accused of some wrong. If so, then "to wait for God" was to wait for a verdict on the worshiper's case.

The final stanza, a call for the nation to trust in Yahweh (vv. 7–8), sounds a bit odd in the context. Does some individual worshiper suddenly address the nation? Or the community assembled in the temple? Or is this perhaps the king speaking? Or maybe a priest addressing worshipers assembled in the sanctuary? Under whatever circumstances, the psalm affirms that with God there is constancy of love and a plenitude of redemption. Ultimately, the power behind all life is benevolent and beneficent.

Romans 8:6–11

The part of today's epistolary reading that resonates with the readings from the Old Testament and the Gospel is the final verse, with its emphasis on resurrection. Here we are told that God's Spirit, who raised Jesus from the dead, lives within us, and by virtue of this indwelling our mortal existence will eventually be enlivened (v. 11).

A cardinal element of early Christian faith was the conviction that God raised Christ from the dead (Rom. 4:24; 1 Cor. 15:15, 20; Gal. 1:1; cf. 2 Cor. 13:4). Equally central was the conviction that God would raise those "in Christ" (1 Cor. 6:14; 2 Cor. 4:14). In the Christ-event, God unleashed the dynamic force that Paul calls "resurrection life." To be incorporated into Christ is to be introduced to this new force, to share in the resurrection. Even though resurrection existence begins now, it is not fully realized or consummated until the eschaton.

What is striking about today's text is the role of the Spirit in this process. The Spirit becomes the mediating locus of this force. The Spirit who dwells within us is the carrier of God's resurrection power. Indeed, the Spirit is so closely identified with this power that the two are indistinguishable. The means, the energizing force, through which God brings about resurrection life within us is the Spirit.

Here we can see how the Christ-event inaugurates a new era that is defined by the Spirit. Because the Spirit is the earmark of the new aeon, the sign that God has bestowed marking the beginning of the new age, hence the eschatological gift (Rom. 1:4; 2 Cor. 1:22; 3:3, 6, 7–18; cf. Acts 2), it becomes the defining norm for existence. Accordingly, Paul envisions two realms, or two spheres, of existence: that of the flesh and that of the spirit (8:4–5). The two are antithetical. They represent two ways of construing reality that are fundamentally opposed. They form reference points for our minds (v. 5), or as the REB suggests, they constitute two essentially different "outlooks"—"the spiritual outlook" and the "outlook of the unspiritual nature" (vv. 6–7; cf. John 3:6).

These two opposing outlooks bring fundamentally opposite results. They bring us to radically different destinations. The "outlook of the flesh" eventually leads to death, whereas the "outlook of the spirit" eventuates in "life and peace" (v. 6; cf. Rom. 6:21; Gal. 6:8). "As the kingdom of Christ the community stands in conflict with the flesh as the sphere of subjection to the world" (Käsemann). What distinguishes them is their orientation toward God. The one is essentially "hostile to God" (v. 7; cf. 5:10; John 4:4), and for this reason does not, because it cannot, yield itself to the divine will, spoken of here as "God's law" (v. 7; cf. John 5:44; 6:60; 8:43; 12:39). For certain, it brings about God's displeasure (v. 8).

The other outlook, the "outlook of the spirit," is so dynamically intertwined with God's own Spirit that the relationship is reciprocal. We dwell "in the Spirit" as the domain of our existence (v. 9), but the Spirit also dwells within us as the concrete form in which God's presence exists within the world (v. 11). It is in this sense that the Spirit serves as the sign of possession. The true mark of Christian identity is whether we possess the Spirit. Nor is this a possession of spiritual enthusiasts alone, those who claim special, visible measures of the Spirit that distinguish them from the ordinary believer. Rather, it is the characteristic feature of existence "in Christ" (*en Christo*) and as such marks off Christian existence from other forms of existence. It comes to expression within ordinary forms of life and service.

The presence of the indwelling Christ acknowledges, on the one hand, the existence of our mortal bodies, which are "dead because of sin" (v. 10). They reflect the old order that is on the way out, even though they provide the form in which we experience the world. Yet, on the other hand, our inner selves, our "spirits," have already begun to feel the impact of acquired righteousness and hence are "alive" (v. 10). As difficult as this verse is, it points to the inner transformation at work within us as the result of God's indwelling Spirit. It is a process that will eventually be finished in the final resurrection.

In many senses, today's text, with its strong emphasis on the Spirit, takes us ahead to Pentecost. It certainly points us toward Easter as we are directed to think of both Christ's resurrection as well as our own. Yet within the context of Lent, it speaks a direct message, urging us to see clearly the contours of two fundamentally opposed ways of living that continue to pose options for us, even though we have taken up the "outlook of the Spirit." The moral tension reflected in the text especially rings true. This is what Lent forces us to confront before we celebrate Easter.

John 11:1–45

Next Sunday is Passion/Palm Sunday. It is appropriate that we come to it with a Gospel text that prompts in the reader the thought of Jesus' approaching death. John 11 does just that, for the raising of Lazarus recorded in this chapter is the event in this Gospel that precipitates the plot against Jesus' life (11:45–53). In fact, as we will see, the story seems to be about the death and raising of Lazarus, but just beneath the surface the careful reader discerns the deeper subject—the death and resurrection of Jesus. But first a word of warning to the preacher: John 11 is filled with one-liners, phrases and sentences that easily seduce the reader into focusing on them for catchy messages rather than for the whole story.

The raising of Lazarus is a sign story. This is to say two things: first, Jesus will act on his own, or more precisely "from above," rather than responding to the urging of others or the contingencies of the situation. Hence, he does not go running to Bethany upon news of his friend's illness; he stays two days longer where he is (v. 6). Second, as a sign story, the primary function of the event is to reveal God. What is about to occur, says Jesus, "is for God's glory" (v. 4). However, this sign has another purpose: "that the Son of God may be glorified through it" (v. 4). The purpose of what Jesus does for Lazarus is to glorify the Son, which, in this Gospel, refers to the Son's return to God (12:23). The means of this return to God would be the cross. "When I am lifted up from the earth" (12:32) carried a double meaning: the cross and the ascension. The reader is told at the outset, then, that the story to follow is not about a family crisis in Bethany so much as it is about the crisis of the world caught in death and sin, not so much about resuscitating a corpse as it is about giving life to the world. So understood, the text is relieved of having to answer nagging questions such as: Why did Jesus not rush to Bethany when he heard of Lazarus' illness? Or, does being a friend of Jesus mean that private miracles will give back your deceased loved ones? Or, does the raising of Lazarus mean Martha and Mary will now have to experience two bereavements and pay for two funerals?

Of course, problems remain because we want always to know historical facts. But the story of Lazarus becomes unclear on one level because bleeding through the page from beneath is the deeper truth of which the death and resurrection of Lazarus is but a sign: apart from trust in God, the world is a cemetery, but into that world God sends Jesus Christ as the offer of resurrection. "I am the resurrection and the life" (v. 25). In chapter 6, the crowds wanted bread, and Jesus gave them that but offered also the bread of life; here the sisters want a brother, and Jesus gives them that but offers also life to the world through his own death and resurrection.

To see the many clues that point to Jesus' own death and resurrection, one has but to read the story carefully. At verse 4, we are told that the end of this story will be the glorifying (death) of the Son. At verse 16, Thomas says, "Let us also go, that we may die with him." And verses 28–44 can best be understood in the light of Jesus' having said that his own death would be effected by what takes place. So much here is reminiscent of Gethsemane, Golgotha, and Easter. Notice: Jesus is deeply moved and troubled (vv. 33, 38); Jesus weeps (v. 35); the tomb is near Jerusalem; the tomb is a cave with a large stone covering it; the stone is rolled away; Jesus cries with a loud voice; the grave cloths are removed from the one dead but now alive. One can hardly read the account and continue to think of Lazarus; one thinks of Jesus.

Lazarus left the tomb, but the price was that Jesus had to enter it (vv. 45–53). Jesus himself said it: one cannot give life unless one dies (12:24). Jesus made no exception in his own case. "Now my soul is troubled. And what should I say? 'Father, save me from this hour'? No, it is for this reason that I have come to this hour." This willingness to submit to the giving of life, which he had asked of his disciples, is dramatically stated in verse 34. When Jesus asked where Lazarus had been laid, they said to him, "Come and see." This expression, "come and see," is in this Gospel as an invitation to discipleship (1:39, 46; 4:29). Here the word is turned upon Jesus himself. The hour has come for the Son of Man to be glorified. Perhaps this realization interprets the next verse: "Jesus began to weep."

Sixth Sunday in Lent
(Passion/Palm Sunday)

Matthew 21:1–11;
Psalm 118:1–2, 19–29;
Isaiah 50:4–9*a*;
Psalm 31:9–16;
Philippians 2:5–11;
Matthew 26:14–27:66 or Matthew 27:11–54

The final Sunday in Lent is either Palm Sunday, Passion Sunday, or both. The Palm Sunday Gospel reading is Matthew's account of Jesus' triumphal entry into Jerusalem. The response for the Palm Sunday celebration from Psalm 118 is part of a liturgy for entrance into the temple, including the blessing pronounced on the one who enters in the name of the Lord. The same Old Testament and epistolary readings serve for both Palm and Passion Sunday. The Old Testament lesson stresses the latter, emphasizing the suffering of the Lord's servant. The Epistle takes us through the suffering to the exaltation of Jesus. The long form of the Passion Sunday Gospel is Matthew's full account of the passion and death of Jesus, from before the Last Supper to the sealing of the tomb. The shorter version recounts the trial and crucifixion of Jesus, concluding with the centurion's affirmation of faith.

Matthew 21:1–11

To observe this Sunday as Palm Sunday is to create an experience of praise and shouts of hosanna, an entirely different mood from that of Passion Sunday. It is to recall Jesus' entry into Jerusalem. Only John's account mentions palm branches (12:13), but all report an occasion of great acclamation. Matthew and Luke (19:28–38) follow Mark (11:1–10), but Matthew cites explicitly what lies only implicitly in Mark, the oracle in Zechariah 9:9. Matthew prefaces it with a line from Isaiah 62:11, "Tell the daughter of Zion." In quoting the Greek translation (Septuagint) of Zechariah 9:9, which gives the impression of two animals, a donkey and a colt, Matthew builds his story around two animals (vv. 2, 5, 7). By so doing he creates a circus effect: "They put their cloaks on *them* and he sat thereon" (literally, "on *them*," v. 7). But even with this unusual element in the story, Matthew's account makes a declaration important to the church's understanding of Jesus.

179

First, the story itself. Following the expression "While Jesus was going up to Jerusalem" (20:17), Matthew records three events prior to our lection: the third prediction of the passion (20:17–19), the incident involving the request by the mother of the sons of Zebedee for chief places for James and John (20:20–28), and the healing of two blind men as Jesus was leaving Jericho (20:29–34). This route would mean that Jesus and those with him now travel the steep fifteen-mile road up from Jericho to Jerusalem. Any trip up to Jerusalem revived national hopes fanned by good memories of grand days, but for Jesus it was clearly a move to his death. Near Jerusalem Jesus sends two disciples for the animals (21:1–2). That the owner released them probably is not intended to indicate prearranged plans, but the divine foreknowledge and authority of Jesus (v. 3). Thus the messianic king approached the city "humble, and mounted on a donkey" (v. 5), the garments of his disciples serving as a saddle and the garments of the pilgrims, along with tree branches, serving as a carpet along the road (vv. 7–8).

According to Matthew, great crowds followed Jesus as he entered Judea (19:2; 20:29) and as he made his way toward Jerusalem. Here a great crowd both preceded and followed him (v. 9). Luke identifies the participants in the event as "the whole multitude of the disciples" (19:37), whereas for John they are persons already in Jerusalem for the feast who come out to meet Jesus (12:12–13). The shouts of the crowd: "Hosanna" ("save us") and "Blessed is the one who comes in the name of the Lord" (v. 9) are lines from Psalm 118: 25–26, a processional psalm. "The Son of David," meaning not only one of David's line but one like David, indicates the nature of the expectation of some of the people. The other Evangelists have other titles on the lips of the shouting crowds.

Mark closes the story with Jesus entering the city, making a quiet visit to the temple, and then going out to Bethany (11:11). However, in Matthew, Jesus entering the city creates quite a stir (turmoil, a form of the word translated "earthquake"), with all the city asking, "Who is this?" (v. 10). The answer is not "Son of David," as one would expect from verse 9, but "the prophet Jesus from Nazareth in Galilee" (v. 11). Whether this is a specific reference to the prophet like Moses whom God would raise up (Deut. 18:18) is not clear. What is clear is that all Jerusalem is affected by the presence of Jesus. Matthew had said this earlier (2:3) when the Magi came seeking the king of the Jews. That disturbance of the city initiated a plot on the life of Jesus while he was yet a child. Now he comes again, and again he is childlike. He is humble, riding a donkey (21:5); he is "gentle and humble in heart" (11:29); he is the suffering servant of Isaiah 42:1–4 who "will not wrangle or cry aloud, nor will anyone hear his voice in the streets. He will not break a bruised reed or quench a smoldering wick" (12:19–20).

We know, of course, what happened to him in the city. But let us not pick on Jerusalem. What city is there today with its values, its centers of power, its established institutions, that would not resist strongly the radical realignment of values and relationships, of priorities and commitments, that Jesus teaches and models in his own life?

Psalm 118:1–2, 19–29

Psalm 118 is appropriate for Palm Sunday reading for three reasons: (1) it is a psalm originally used by a leader (probably a king) entering the city and sanctuary triumphantly; (2) it is a psalm deeply rooted in the Jewish celebration of Passover, a festival around which much of the Christian passion narrative revolves; and (3) according to the Gospel tradition (Mark 11:9–10; Matt. 21:1–10; Luke 19:37–38), the psalm was sung by pilgrims accompanying Jesus as they entered Jerusalem on Palm Sunday. Before looking at verses 19–29, let us note some factors associated with the first two points just mentioned.

1. The depiction of the distress undergone by the worshiper indicates a major battle as the background to the psalm. Nations surrounded and assailed the person (v. 10). Songs of victory were sung in soldiers' tents on the field of battle (v. 15). All Israel is called upon to participate in the services of thanksgiving (vv. 2–4).

2. Psalms 113–118, called the Egyptian-Hallel psalms, were sung in Passover celebrations. On the afternoon of Passover, when the lambs were being slaughtered in the temple, these psalms were sung by the Levites in the temple precincts as part of the worship services. Again, in the evening, when the Passover meal was being eaten in the homes, the diners sang Psalms 113–118 as part of the Passover Seder. The ending of Psalm 118, from verse 22 on, could be understood as a messianic text anticipating the coming of one who had been rejected by men but who would be God's chosen. Thus the Passover celebration, which always commemorated the national birth of Israel, also looked forward to coming redemption.

With verse 19, the psalm becomes complicated in terms of the speakers and addressees. The following represents one possible way of looking at the psalm in terms of an entry ritual:

verse 19	the victorious king requests entry to the temple
verse 20	priests or others respond to the request
verses 21–22	the king offers thanksgiving addressed directly to God
verses 23–24	worshipers or a choir proclaim the celebration as a consequence of God's intervention
verse 25	people, choir, or priests offer a prayer to God
verses 26–27	the king is blessed as he enters the sacred precincts of the temple, and reference is made to part of the festal celebrations
verse 28	the king offers thanksgiving
verse 29	a general summons to offer thanks

Several aspects of Psalm 118:19–29 are worthy of special note: (1) the celebration that is reflected in the psalm is one of triumph, success, and victory; (2) the royal features of the ritual, that is, their connection with a ruler or king, seem clearly evident; (3) the celebration is one in which a key emphasis is God's action and intervention on behalf of the triumphal figure; and (4) the triumphal figure describes himself as one who has been rejected but who has now become victorious. In verse 22, we have what was apparently a common proverb: "The stone that the builders rejected has become the chief cornerstone." Such a saying implies that someone or something has moved from a state of rejection to a position of prominence, in fact, to a position that is irreplaceable. "The chief cornerstone" would suggest either a cornerstone, a foundation stone, or perhaps the keystone in an arch. The first part of the psalm refers to how the figure was threatened, challenged, and nearly defeated on the field of battle before God granted triumph.

The numerous parallels between this psalm and Jesus' career and triumphal entry into Jerusalem, the Holy City, should be obvious, although Psalm 118 should not be read as a prophetic prediction of Jesus. The analogy between the psalm and Jesus' activity is to be found in the fact that in both God worked to elevate and exalt the lowly to a place of prominence. Though in each case the lowly had to move through oppression and opposition, they were not overtaken by death, literal or otherwise (see v. 18).

Isaiah 50:4–9a

With the exception of Holy Thursday, the Servant Songs of Second Isaiah provide all of the Old Testament readings for Palm/Passion Sunday through Good Friday. Commentators have long recognized that these four poems (Isa. 42:1–4; 49:1–6; 50:4–11; 52:13–53:12) are distinctive units both in terms of form and contents. In fact, they stand out so much that some have attributed them to a different author. However, we concur with the majority of modern commentators in attributing them to the same prophetic poet responsible for all of Isaiah 40–55, Second Isaiah.

Although we know virtually nothing about Second Isaiah, it is not difficult to identify his date and historical circumstances. His work contains allusions to historical circumstances that can be dated with precision on the basis of external evidence. More than once (Isa. 44:28; 45:1–7), he mentions the campaigns of Cyrus the Mede, who is on the march toward his eventual capture of the city of Babylon and then the establishment of the Persian Empire. The new king is on the scene, but he has not yet arrived in Babylon. Because Cyrus took Babylon in 538 BC, the work of Second Isaiah is widely and confidently dated ca. 539 BC. The prophet speaks so strongly of Cyrus as the Lord's "anointed," the one chosen by God to accomplish his will, that some commentators have argued that the one who was about to conquer Babylon and set Israel free is the servant of the songs.

Second Isaiah lived and worked in Babylon among the Israelite captives who had been taken there some fifty or sixty years earlier. One of his favorite themes is to ridicule the religious practices he must have observed there, including the worship of idols and the Babylonian liturgies. But his leading message is the announcement of release from exile and return to Judah. Like most of his prophetic predecessors, his message comes with divine authority, and it is contrary to the expectations of his audience. When the people of Israel expected peace and prosperity, earlier prophets such as Amos and Hosea announced judgment in the form of military defeat and exile. Now, to a people who have lost hope, Second Isaiah announces unqualified—and unmerited—salvation. Basing his proclamation on the ancient traditions of Israel's election, of God's creation of the world, and the promises to the ancestors, the prophet announces a "new thing," but one like the old salvation event, an exodus out of Babylon, a glorious return through the wilderness, and reestablishment of Jerusalem. The Servant Songs must be read in the context of that message as a whole.

Opinions differ considerably on the question of the identity of the servant. Most of the evidence, especially in the context that surrounds the songs, argues for a collective interpretation, in which case the servant is the people of Israel. But much of the language of the songs themselves is highly personal and individualistic. Some interpreters have identified the servant with specific individuals, such as the prophet himself (because some of the language is autobiographical), earlier figures such as Jeremiah, or even Cyrus. However, it is not even clear what traditional role the servant filled. Was he a royal, messianic figure or a prophetic figure? It is even possible that the concept of the servant is fluid and that the different passages have different figures or roles in view. In the second of the songs, the passage before us today, form and style are autobiographical—that is, the servant himself is presented as the speaker—and the emphasis is upon the servant's prophetic functions.

Both the structure and contents of the passage suggest three themes for our consideration on this occasion. The first, expressed in verse 4, concerns the prophetic word. The servant affirms that the Lord God has given him the power of speech and the knowledge of what to say. This is consistent with the deep prophetic tradition in Israel in which prophets understood themselves to be called by God and given specific messages to deliver, messages concerning the future. The servant has listened to God's voice as a student listens to a teacher. Moreover, like all true prophetic words, the message of the servant has been powerful and effective. He does not tell us what that word was, but because its purpose was "to sustain the weary with a word" we may conclude that it was a message of encouragement and salvation, good news to those—such as the Babylonian exiles—who were discouraged.

The second theme is the servant's obedience to the divine call in spite of serious opposition (vv. 5–6). He suffered because of his particular message, and that suffering included physical abuse, ridicule, and shame. We are not told who handed out such harsh treatment. It could even have been those same ones whom he sought to sustain with a word. He was not the first bearer of God's word to receive such treatment—consider Jeremiah 15:10–21; 26; 36:11–21—nor was he the last. The servant's reaction was courageous and persistent obedience to the God who called him to speak, and it was nonviolent. He turned the other cheek.

Third, the servant was able to endure opposition because of his trust in God's support and confirmation (vv. 7–9). Acts of personal courage were possible for the servant not because of his own strength of character but because of his confidence in the justice of God. The confession of confidence, common in individual lament or complaint psalms, includes a general affirmation of God as helper (vv. 7a, 9a) and a more specific assertion that God vindicates (v. 8a) the servant. Such vindication calls up images of both the law court and the practice of worship. Metaphorically, God is like the judge or jury that determines a charge and declares one party to be not guilty (cf. v. 9a). Likewise, the priest, either before a worshiper was allowed to enter the sanctuary or with the offering of a sacrifice, could declare the one before him to be innocent.

Heard in its original context, this passage was the self-defense of the servant of God and the argument for the validity of his message of good news. Its goal was to evoke a response of affirmation from an audience of Judean exiles. Heard in Christian worship in this season, the lines interpret for the church the life and death of Jesus. Certainly, Christians will hear in the obedience of the servant parallels to the life of Jesus. In addition, one of the specific contributions this text can make is to call attention to the prophetic dimensions of the life and death of Jesus.

Psalm 31:9–16

This lament, perhaps written for use by persons suffering some form of illness, contains all the features of this particular genre. Most of the psalm is speech directly addressed to the Deity. Verse 21, a bit of praise and proclamation, and verses 23–24, admonition in the form of a sermonette, are addressed by the worshiper to a human audience.

The overall structure of the psalm is as follows: (1) a general opening address to God, which already contains the initial plea for help (vv. 1–2); (2) a statement of confidence and trust in God (vv. 3–6); (3) a future-oriented statement of confidence (vv. 7–8); (4) a description of the trouble and distress (vv. 9–13); (5) a third statement of confidence (vv. 14–15a); (6) a second plea for help (vv. 15b–18); (7) a third assertion of confidence (vv. 19–20); (8) proclamation (v. 21); (9) thanksgiving (v. 22); and (10) admonition (vv. 23–24).

The imagery of verses 6–19 clearly suggests the employment of this psalm by one suffering from some form of illness. The author of Ecclesiasticus (or Sirach) in the Apocrypha outlines four steps to be taken when sick:

> My child, when you are ill, do not delay,
>   but [1] pray to the Lord, and he will heal you.
> [2] Give up your faults and direct your hands aright,
>   and cleanse your heart from all sin.
> [3] Offer a sweet-smelling sacrifice,
>   and a memorial portion of choice flour,
>   and pour oil on your offering,
>   as much as you can afford.
> [4] Then give the physician his place,
>   for the Lord created him;
>   do not let him leave you, for you need him. (Sirach 38:9–12)

The four steps therefore were (1) prayer (perhaps the recitation of a psalm such as Ps. 31), (2) repentance, (3) the offering of a sacrifice (perhaps in conjunction with step 1), and (4) a visit to the physician. (This, by the way, is the first "biblical" text that has a good word to say about doctors.)

The description of the distressful situation in verses 9–13 presents the person as one decimated by physical suffering (vv. 9–10) and as a social outcast forced to endure life at the periphery of society without the benefit of friends or close acquaintances (vv. 11–13).

Few psalms use as graphic descriptions to depict human misery and affliction as does Psalm 31. The descriptions are very graphic although reasonably nonspecific. Thus, when persons used this psalm in worship to describe their state of being, they could vent true feelings yet do so in highly stylized terms. Praying this psalm allowed persons to verbalize and express the deep-seated sense of alienation and hurt that they were feeling. The language appears to be highly metaphorical, probably using stereotypical and formulaic expressions that were highly graphic in content and emotional in nature. The labeling of one's troubles in such graphic fashion was probably therapeutic in and of itself, for it allowed one to express sorrow and grief.

The expressions drawn from the arena of illness, in verses 9–10, if taken literally, suggest that the person was near death and had suffered miserably for years. The common words of suffering and affliction appear throughout these verses: distress, grief, sorrow, sighing, misery, wasting away.

In verses 11–13, the depiction of the distress uses the language of social ostracism. The descriptions here seek to present the worshiper's distress in the severest form possible. Adversaries, neighbors, acquaintances, and even the persons encountered in casual street meetings are all depicted as standing in terror and expressing disdain at the person's appearance (v. 11). Perhaps the supplicant was a person with some physical malady that rendered him or her unclean and required special isolation from general society (see Lev. 13:45–46). Job's description of his predicament, in Job 19:13–22, sounds very much like the cries of the outcast in verse 11.

The psalmist declares that he or she is like one already dead: passed out of life and even out of memory, cast aside like the shattered pieces of a broken pot—unwanted, useless, fit only for the garbage heap of the city dump (v. 12).

In fact, the psalmist describes the many out there who not only dislike him or her but who even scheme and plot to take his or her life (v. 13). Such language as this may sound like the ravings of a paranoid but should be seen as therapeutic language that allowed distressed persons to objectify their suffering to its most graphic, even exaggerated, level.

This psalm is not simply a recitation or a vale of sorrows. Throughout the text, there are frequent statements of a calm confidence in the Deity. Such is to be found in verses 14–15 in which the worshiper confesses trust in God and affirms that come what may the times of one's life are in the hand of God, who can deliver one from the hand of enemies and persecutors.

Confidence in the Deity fades naturally into plea and petition for salvation (vv. 15b–16). In spite of the description of the supplicant's condition in such sorrow-drawn and affliction-etched contours, confidence and calm flow through the psalm like a soothing stream. In this way, it may parallel the composure of Jesus as he rode into Jerusalem—the man of sorrows but one confident of being in the hands of God.

Philippians 2:5–11

This passage also serves as one of the options for the epistolary reading in all three years for the day celebrating the Holy Name of Jesus: Solemnity of Mary, Mother of God. The reader may want to consult our remarks on this text earlier in this volume. The larger literary unit (2:1–13) serves as the epistolary reading for Proper 21, which is treated later in this volume.

Today's text consists of an opening exhortation (v. 5) followed by a pre-Pauline Christian hymn rehearsing the drama of Christ's descent to the earth and exaltation to heaven. How the opening exhortation and the hymn that follows relate to each other is disputed. The fundamental exegetical question is whether the Christ-hymn is quoted in order to provide the readers an example of humility and self-abnegation, or whether it rehearses the Christ-story to establish the basis of the moral exhortation in the preceding verses. The Greek wording of verse 5 is obscure and may be rendered in at least two ways: "Let the same mind be in you *that was in* Christ Jesus" (NRSV, italics added) or "Let the same mind be in you *that you have in* Christ Jesus" (NRSV, note, italics added). In the former interpretation, the Christ-hymn unfolds the example of Christ to be followed. In the latter, the story of Christ's incarnation and exaltation serves as the authorizing warrant for the ethical injunction; it sketches the "indicative" that underlies the Christian "imperative."

These two interpretive options are reflected in the various modern translations. The first option is reflected in NJB ("Make your own the mind of Christ Jesus"), REB ("Take to heart among yourselves what you find in Christ Jesus"), and the NEB note ("Have that bearing towards one another which was also found in Christ Jesus"). The second option is rendered well in the NEB text ("Let your bearing towards one another arise out of your life in Christ Jesus").

Although these differences may appear slight, the preacher will need to be attentive to the wording of the text being used, because the various translations might point in different homiletical directions.

At issue is a serious theological difficulty. Although the Christ-hymn in verses 6–11 has traditionally been understood as an *imitatio Christi* passage, and in this regard has exercised great influence on Christian piety, the question is whether the actions of Christ unfolded in the hymn can, in the strictest sense, be imitated. The Savior's descending from heaven, accepting a human form, and becoming obedient to death, although an exemplary drama, is clearly the story of a divine figure. In what sense, realistically, can mere mortals expect to imitate this cosmic drama of descent and ascent? It is one thing to be asked to imitate the actions of the earthly Jesus, yet this seems reasonable enough because we readily identify with his humanity. But it is another thing to identify with a heavenly figure whose world and experience are so far removed from life as we know it. The grander the story, the less likely it will seriously challenge us.

And yet, the suggestion that the drama of Christ's incarnation and exaltation is unfolded to show how and why the Christian exhortation in verses 1–5 is possible has not convinced everyone. The exhortation seems to call for an example, yet the example offered is not one we can easily identify with.

However one resolves this exegetical difficulty, there is broad agreement that verses 6–11 contain an early Christian hymn and that it predated Paul. He appears to have quoted this early hymn at this juncture even though he makes certain editorial changes. Precisely how the hymn should be arranged into strophes and stanzas is not clear. Generally, it is arranged in two strophes consisting respectively of verses 6–8 and verses 9–11. Each of these strophes can then be subdivided into three stanzas.

The drama, of course, begins with the preexistent position of Christ (v. 6), and the language is reminiscent of wisdom traditions (cf. John 1:1–16). Christ voluntarily relinquishes his heavenly status, choosing to take the form of a slave. This language probably recalls the Suffering Servant imagery from Deutero-Isaiah (cf. Isa. 53:3, 11). His humanity is further stressed (v. 7; cf. Rom. 8:3), and the "descent" stage culminates in his obedience unto death. The phrase "even death on a cross" (v. 8) appears to be Paul's editorial addition to the hymn. The theme of obedience echoes that of texts treated earlier in the Lenten Season (cf. Heb. 5:7–10; 12:2).

With verse 9, there is an abrupt change ("therefore"). At this point, God becomes the subject of the action: "God also highly exalted him." This phrase includes both his resurrection and ascension. In other New Testament passages, these two stages of Christ's exaltation are kept separate (cf. Acts 2:33; 5:31). The name "above every name" (v. 9) anticipates the final acclamation in verse 11: "Jesus Christ is Lord." The submission of the whole universe to the exalted Lord is an expansion of Isaiah 45:23 (cf. also Rom. 14:11).

In one sense, the Christ-hymn might appear inappropriate as a reading for Palm Sunday because Good Friday is so thoroughly overcome by Easter and Christ's exaltation to heavenly preeminence. Even Paul seems to sense the danger of an exclusively triumphalist reading of this hymn, for he inserts "even death on a cross" in verse 8 as a salutary reminder of the centrality of the crucifixion. Philippians 3 suggests that some readers might well have begun to think that "resurrection life" was the *summum bonum* of the Christian life.

There is ample time in the Christian year to celebrate the triumph of Christ in the resurrection and ascension, and the minister's task here may be to see that the passion of Christ is not passed over too quickly.

Matthew 26:14–27:66 *or* Matthew 27:11–54

The lectionary respects the two traditions about this Sunday, offering readings for its observance both as Passion and as Palm Sunday. For Passion Sunday, the reading is the passion narrative of the appropriate Gospel or an alternate, briefer reading from within the longer narrative, usually focusing on the crucifixion itself. As we will see in the next lesson, the Palm Sunday reading is the record of Jesus entering Jerusalem.

First, a few words about the passion narrative itself (in Matt. 26:1–27:66). The apparently disproportionate amount of space given to this material by all the Evangelists testifies to its central place in the church's recollection of Jesus and in its preaching. And the fact that all four Gospels present basically the same sequence of events indicates that this tradition became fixed quite early and writers did not deal with it in the same freedom as with the remainder of the sources about Jesus' life. Matthew follows Mark closely, perhaps more closely than elsewhere. Except for variations in wording here and there, Matthew alters Mark primarily with four insertions: the death of Judas (27:3–8); the disturbing dream of Pilate's wife (27:19); Pilate washes his hands and all the people accept the guilt of Jesus' blood (27:24–25); and the placing of the guard at Jesus' tomb (27:62–66). One notices in this material the disappearance of the Pharisees as Jesus' opposition and the emergence of the chief priests and elders of the people as the primary force in effecting Jesus' death (26:3, 14, 47; 27:1). As a final introductory comment, notice how few are the sayings of Jesus in the passion narrative. Except at the table during the Last Supper, Jesus is relatively silent and is more the recipient of the actions of others than the one acting.

But how will the preacher handle this extensive body of material in the sermon? Of course, the alternate reading is much briefer, and the message could confine itself to that. In fact, the preacher could restrict the sermon's focus even further, leaving the remainder of the narrative to be carried by the liturgy. In some traditions, the entire passion narrative is read with appropriate songs and prayers. It is here urged that whether through readings without comment, or with running comments interspersed, or with summary comments at noticeable breaks in the story, the entire passion narrative be shared in the service. This is the foundational tradition of the Christian community, providing its identity, its basic definition, and its message to the world. So seldom does the congregation get a continuous story, a sense of historical movement of cause and effect in its exposure to Scripture, that opportunities such as this should not be sacrificed in favor of a smaller and more manageable sermon text.

One way to divide the text for reading and comment is as follows:

The treachery of Judas (26:14–16)

The Last Supper (26:17–29), involving
> preparation for the Passover (vv. 17–20),
> Jesus foretelling his betrayal (vv. 21–25), and
> the institution of the eucharist (vv. 26–29).

The arrest in the garden (26:30–56), involving
> Jesus' prediction of Peter's denial (vv. 30–35),
> the hours of prayer (vv. 36–46),
> betrayal and arrest (vv. 47–55), and
> the disciples abandoning Jesus (v. 56).

The trials of Jesus (26:57–27:26), involving
> his appearance before the Sanhedrin (vv. 57–68),
> Peter's denials in the courtyard (vv. 69–75),
> the appearance before Pilate (27:1–23), and
> Pilate washing his hands of the affair (vv. 24–26).

The crucifixion, death, and burial (27:27–66), involving
> the mockery of Jesus (vv. 27–31),
> the crucifixion (vv. 32–44),
> the death (vv. 45–56), and
> the burial (vv. 57–66).

On this particular Sunday, the minister will want to resist the temptation to moralize, to exhort, or to grow sentimental. The text will create its own world in the minds and hearts of the listeners.

Monday in Holy Week

Isaiah 42:1–9;
Psalm 36:5–11;
Hebrews 9:11–15;
John 12:1–11

A ll of the texts for the day evoke christological reflection and are more in the mood of Palm Sunday than Passion Sunday. Their tone is hopeful, pointing beyond the crucifixion and even the resurrection of Jesus to the meaning of these events not only for the faithful but also for all peoples. Thus both the Old Testament and the epistolary lections look to a covenant for the peoples. The responsorial psalm is a hymn of praise to God for his steadfast love. One hears in the Gospel reading foreshadowings of all that will take place in Holy Week, from meals together with friends, to betrayal, to death, and even to resurrection.

Isaiah 42:1–9

T his passage consists of the first of the Servant Songs (vv. 1–4) plus the beginning (vv. 5–9) of a unit (42:5–17) announcing and praising God's triumph in nature and history. During Holy Week, this text will serve to call attention to the obedience of Jesus as God's chosen servant and to set the events of the week in an eschatological context, for verses 5–9 announce and characterize the ultimate reign of God. The same verses from Second Isaiah provide the Old Testament lesson for the Baptism of the Lord (the First Sunday After the Epiphany); refer to our remarks in that setting for a fuller commentary. For a general introduction to the Servant Songs and their literary and historical context, see the commentary on Isaiah 50:4–9a for Palm/Passion Sunday in this volume.

Three points are of particular importance in the song, any one of which call for proclamation in Christian worship. First, the servant has been chosen—and therefore authorized and empowered—by God (v. 1a). Forms of the Hebrew word translated here "chosen" express the divine election of the people of Israel (Deut. 7:7; Isa. 14:1), of individuals such as Abraham (Neh. 9:7), of groups such as the Levites (Deut. 18:5; 1 Chron. 15:2), of David as king (1 Sam. 10:24), and of the city of Jerusalem (2 Chron. 6:6). Here the Lord expresses his warmth and pleasure in choosing this one ("in whom my soul delights") and confirms that election with the gift of the divine spirit.

Second, in terms of demeanor and behavior, the servant is gentle, strong, and persistent. At this point we encounter some of the more difficult exegetical problems of the passage.

189

Verse 2 probably means that he will speak quietly, not shouting in the street. It is the metaphors in verse 3*a* that are not clear. The "bruised reed" and "dimly burning wick" probably refer to the weak and downtrodden, those who have virtually lost hope if not life, whose fire is about to die. That would be consistent with the prophetic concern for the weak and oppressed.

Third, the role of the servant is to establish justice, and in the entire earth. This is the same justice that Amos (Amos 5:24) and Isaiah of Jerusalem (Isa. 1:17; 5:7) called for. It includes fair and equitable procedures, especially in the law courts, and equitable distribution of resources, particularly in its concern for the weak. Above all, its substance is based upon divine justice. Here that is expressed in the parallel between justice and "teaching" (v. 4; "law" in RSV). The teaching in view here probably is not the Torah or the law of Moses itself, but the servant's instructions and his application of the divine will in particular circumstances. The prophet envisages a world in which justice prevails because all live under the same law, the divine will.

The other part of today's reading (vv. 5–9) gives a summary of the message of Second Isaiah as a whole, and in this context suggests a particular interpretation of the servant. First, in a series of subordinate clauses, the prophet states his understanding of God. God is the one who created the world and gave life to all its inhabitants (v. 5); God is not to be compared with any other, especially with "graven images" (v. 8). Second, this same God has called and chosen his people Israel, and kept them as his own (v. 6*a*). Third, Israel has been called for a particular purpose, quite consistent with the role of the servant to establish justice in the earth. Israel is "a covenant to the people, a light to the nations" (v. 6*b*). It is their role to set prisoners free and to open the eyes of the blind. Doubtless this language is both literal and metaphorical. It includes actual release from prison or captivity and the enlightenment of those who do not see that God is doing "new things" (v. 9).

Thus verses 5–9 suggest a national but not a nationalistic interpretation of the servant as the people of Israel. They are the ones to bring justice to the nations, through the law of the Lord. If the church understands itself to be the chosen people of God, then it will assume that role as its own. But the passage contains more good news than law, more announcement of the saving will of God than obligation. It is, after all, God who intends to establish justice in the earth, both through his servant as an individual and his servant as the people.

Psalm 36:5–11

These verses of hymnic praise appear almost as a counter to verses 1–4 of the psalm. The latter describe the self-sufficiency, the self-flattery, the deceitful action, and the mischief plotting of the wicked. One would anticipate such a depiction to be followed by a similar, contrasting portrait of the righteous (as in Ps. 1). This, however, is not the case because with verse 5 the focus shifts to affirmations about God, to descriptions of divine righteousness and qualities. Humans again enter the horizon of the psalm with verse 7*b*, but here the focus is on the benefits humanity derives from God. Verses 7*b*–9 may thus be seen as the contrast to verses 1–4. The description of the wicked (vv. 1–4) in speaking of such people presents a picture of isolated individuals, living without any sense of fear before God, taking actions based on their own plans, constantly plotting and continuously being obsessed with their doings. On the other hand, the benefits described in verses 7*b*–9 speak of humans as a class sharing unstrivingly in what the Divine gives. In speaking of evil, the psalm speaks of the lone, isolated, self-occupied individual; in speaking of the good, it speaks first of God and then of the people enjoying the blessings under the divine umbrella.

The ancient rabbis exegeted this text (at least v. 6) in terms of punishment for the wicked and reward for the righteous. In the midrash on the psalm, one rabbi put it this way: "Even as there can be no numbering of the mountains, so there can be no numbering of the rewards for the righteous. Like the deep which has no bounds, so the punishment for the wicked has no bounds. Like the mountains which are high and lofty, so the rewards for the righteous are high and lofty. And just as the waters of the deep are not all alike, some salty, some bitter, and some sweet, so the punishment for the wicked is not all alike."

In verses 5–6, God's love and faithfulness are extolled in terms of their immeasurable quality. In height, they extend to the heavens and up to the clouds. In constancy, they are like the mountains and the great deep beneath the earth. In breadth, God's concern to save is not limited by the boundaries of human existence but extends even to the beasts of the earth.

In verses 7–9, the poet focuses attention on the human benefits that accrue from the Divine or on what might be called the delights of enjoying God and his love. In verse 7, the neutral inclusive term "all people" is used instead of the more customary "children of Israel." One could suppose that the psalmist here made a deliberate choice so as to universalize those included under divine favor. The image for protection in the verse—"in the shadow of your wings"—may draw upon the protective role of the parent fowl in caring for its young. Such imagery, however, could be based on the fact that the ark, the representative symbol of God, rested in the Holy of Holies beneath the outstretched wings of the cherubim (see 1 Kings 8:7).

Just as verse 7 emphasizes the nature of protection offered by the Divine, so verse 8 emphasizes the divine provision of food and drink. Some uncertainty exists about what "your house" refers to. Is it a reference to the earth or the world as a whole? (See Ps. 93:5, where this appears to be the case.) Or is it a reference to the temple as the house of God? In the former, "feast on the abundance of your house" would refer to eating the fruits and products of the earth. In the latter case, the expression would refer to the sacrificial meals consumed in the temple precincts, where eating and drinking were common (see 1 Sam. 1:3–8). In any case, the psalm emphasizes the value and worth of the more sensual aspects of life—eating and drinking—that are to be viewed and enjoyed in relationship to the Divine.

Two images characterize the statement in verse 9—life and light; God is seen as the source of all life, and divine light as the source of human light.

Lest the blessings of God prove to be temporary, the psalmist prays that God will continue divine love and salvation (v. 10). Here the request is hemmed in somewhat when compared with verse 7b. In verse 10, those who know God and the upright of heart are the expected recipients of God's favor. The negative pole of the redemptive process is requested in verse 11. The worshiper asked to be saved from the arrogant and the wicked.

The association of this psalm with Holy Week can be made through its emphasis on God's loving-kindness and on the divine blessings bestowed upon humanity.

Hebrews 9:11–15

Some of the exegetical difficulties presented by this epistolary text, as well as its place and function within the Epistle to the Hebrews as a whole, are treated in our remarks on the text in Years B and C. Today's remarks will be more broadly focused.

One of the real difficulties for modern readers of this text, clergy and laity alike, is its foreignness. It speaks of priests, animal sacrifices, and sanctuaries. We find this language drawn from the Israelite cult both ancient and mystifying. To complicate things further, our text envisions the cult at two levels—earthly and heavenly. Most of us find it difficult enough to understand the complexities and nuances of primitive religious cultic practices as they were actually practiced, or described, in historical settings, much less how they might have been envisioned as taking place in some supraterrestrial universe. To break through this barrier of unfamiliarity, the minister is well advised to consult commentaries on the Epistle to the Hebrews as well as relevant dictionary or encyclopedia articles on topics such as "worship," "cult," and "sacrifice." In short, to understand this text and the conceptual framework it presupposes will require homework.

Having said this, however, we can make several observations. First, this text, like the Epistle to the Hebrews in general, is a critique of the cult. We are told earlier that the Levitical "offerings and sacrifices cannot give the worshipper a clear conscience and so bring him to perfection" (v. 9, REB). The Levitical sacrificial system is repeatedly criticized as being deficient: it consists of "external ordinances" (v. 10, REB).

As sharp and unqualified as this critique is, it is by no means the first or final polemic against the cult. The Old Testament consistently recognized the way in which the cult could sidetrack religious devotion. Offering sacrifices and being truly obedient need not be the same. In fact, the one may be done as a poor substitute for the other. Samuel chides Saul for divorcing the two, reminding him that at the heart of meaningful sacrifice there must be obedient service (1 Sam. 15:22–23). It is a theme that the prophets hammer home: "For I require loyalty, not sacrifice, acknowledgement of God rather than whole-offerings" (Hos. 6:6, REB; Amos 4:4–5; 5:21–24; Mic. 6:6–8).

As long as sacrificial forms of religion have existed, the limitations of the cult have been recognized. Perceptive observers have always seen the inadequacy of religious rites and the ease with which worshipers substitute form for meaning. We properly view today's text when we see it as a critique of the cult standing within a long critical tradition.

Second, we should observe that the critique is distinctively christological. What was deficient about the Levitical system is now remedied by Christ. At the heart of our text is the conviction that Christ's death was sacrificial. It is compared with animal sacrifices and found to be eminently superior. For one thing, it was a *human*, as opposed to an *animal*, sacrifice. For another, it was no ordinary human, but the Son of God whose life was one of unblemished perfection (vv. 14; 4:15; 5:9). Moreover, it was a death that ushered Christ into the very presence of God, the "heavenly sanctuary." What is implicit here, of course, is the conviction that Christ's resurrection elevated him to God's eternal presence (4:14; 8:1). Christ's role is thus seen as that of an extraordinary high priest, one who has gained access to the heavenly "Holy of Holies" in the most paradoxical fashion imaginable—by offering himself as a sacrifice.

What we find here is a critique thoroughly informed by Christian confession—Christ the perfect, unblemished high priest offering himself for the sins of the people.

Third, we should note the central emphasis on inward transformation. The sacrificial death of Christ somehow broke through a barrier and enabled a form of inner purification, a cleansing of the human conscience, that was not possible previously (v. 14). It enabled a form of genuine "service of the living God" (NEB).

We do well to ask how this was done, for it is a remarkable claim and one not altogether obvious from the text. There appear to be two aspects to the answer, both of which are functions of the work of Christ: (1) Christ as the paradigm of obedience, and (2) Christ's death as effecting moral purification.

At one level, the death of Christ is seen as an act of quintessential obedience in which the Son yields to the will of the Father (5:8–9). In this respect, he proves obedient and confirms Samuel's insistence that loyalty to God's will surpasses sacrificial offerings. What Christ offers us is a clear example of the superiority of obedience to sacrifice.

At another level, the death of Christ is seen as the event in which the effect of human sin is canceled. It is not simply a matter of sacrificial transfer, as if the moral purity of Christ is somehow transferred to those on behalf of whom he died. It is rather that the shedding of his blood actually serves as the effective cleansing of human impurity. It becomes a rite of purification in which the blood of Christ shed on the cross serves as a sacrificial offering through which God forgives those on behalf of whom the offering was made—in this case, those in Christ.

John 12:1–11

We have had many occasions to observe how a Gospel writer's location of a particular story within the narrative affects the meaning of the story. It is also true that the lectionary's location of a particular text in the Christian year affects the interpretation of that text. John 12:1–11 is a case in point. In John's Gospel, the anointing of Jesus precedes his entry into Jerusalem (12:12–19), and in this same order the lectionary placed this text for the Sunday preceding Passion/Palm Sunday for Year C. Here, however, this lesson follows Passion/Palm Sunday, alerting the preacher that the text is to move the listeners even closer to Good Friday and the cross. By placing this story between Palm Sunday and Good Friday, the lectionary is using the chronology of Matthew (26:6–13) and Mark (14:3–9). However, even though John has the anointing precede Passion/Palm Sunday, the story is most certainly a Holy Week event theologically, for this Evangelist fills the story with many pointers to Jesus' death.

First, let us separate the account from those of Matthew and Mark. (Luke has, at 7:36–50, the record of an anointing of Jesus by an unnamed sinful woman, in Galilee, in the house of Simon a Pharisee, and the message of the event is unrelated to Jesus' death.) For both Matthew and Mark, the anointing occurs in Bethany near Jerusalem, in the house of Simon the leper, is performed by "a woman," and is interpreted by Jesus as an anointing for his burial. John also locates the event in Bethany, and Jesus says of the anointing, "She bought it so that she might keep it for the day of my burial" (v. 7). However, it occurs in the house of Lazarus, and it is Lazarus' sister Mary who performs it. All the accounts have enough common elements to suggest they are derived from one occurrence, but the text before us has its own special accents.

The anointing in Bethany, like the event of the raising of Lazarus (11:1–44), which precedes it, has as its primary focus the prophecy of Jesus' death. This is stated explicitly in verses 9–11, which elaborate on 11:45–53 to the effect that the raising of Lazarus not only precipitated the plot to kill Jesus but also tied the fate of Lazarus to that of Jesus. However, prophecies of Jesus' death also fill the small drama of verses 1–8. The scene is Bethany, where a cave tomb waits for a new occupant; the time is six days before Passover, the festival that in this Gospel prompts death talk as easily as 2:13–22 and 6:4–59; the house is that of Lazarus, whose life will cost Jesus his (11:4); the anointing itself points to Jesus' burial (v. 7); and at the table is Judas, who will betray Jesus (v. 4).

It will be important for the preacher of this text to distinguish between what the reader knows and what those present knew. The gloom and sorrow of Golgotha should not hang over that table. Out of love and gratitude for a brother restored, Martha and Mary provide a supper for Jesus. Mary enlarges that act of hospitality into a drama of devotion, submission, and beauty. It is the reader and not Mary who knows that the raising of Lazarus will effect Jesus' death, that Passover will be death time, that Judas will be a chief accessory in Jesus' death, that the sweet aroma of the room prophesies the odor of burial spices. This is, or will soon be, a time of both grief and joy for Mary: grief that within a few days of preparing her brother's corpse she now anoints her friend's body for burial; joy that she was permitted to have a small role in the drama of Christ's redeeming passion. Mark adds to the story these words of Jesus: "Truly I tell you, wherever the good news is proclaimed in the whole world, what she has done will be told in remembrance of her" (14:9; Matt. 26:13).

That Mary anointed Jesus for burial unwittingly does not rob the event of its meaning. In fact, that she did so unwittingly may even deepen the significance of her act. It is God's gift added to our simple acts that often elevates them to a place in the grander purposes that God has in mind. What we do and say is not limited in scope or effect to what we intended at the time.

Tuesday in Holy Week

Isaiah 49:1–7;
Psalm 71:1–14;
1 Corinthians 1:18–31;
John 12:20–36

The Gospel lections for Holy Week take the church at worship through the last days of Jesus and provide the framework for the other readings. John 12:20–36 gives us scenes of Jesus teaching the disciples and the crowd concerning the nature and meaning of his death. Isaiah 49:1–7 recounts the life, suffering, and exaltation of the servant of God. The psalm is a prayer for deliverance from enemies, the kind of petition that Jesus considered but decided not to make (John 12:27). The epistolary reading is Paul's meditation on the meaning of the cross as folly and the power of God.

Isaiah 49:1–7

Today's reading includes the second Servant Song in Deutero-Isaiah (vv. 1–6), plus one additional verse. For information on the songs in general and on their historical and literary setting, see the commentary on Isaiah 50:4–9a for Passion/Palm Sunday in this volume. The text is also the reading for the Second Sunday After the Epiphany. The reader may want to consult our remarks on this text earlier in this volume.

In the first of the Servant Songs (Isa. 42:1–4; see the commentary for Monday in Holy Week), the Lord introduced the servant to the people of Israel. In this poem, the servant himself is the speaker, addressing the peoples of the world as a whole: "You peoples from afar" (v. 1). The prophetic aspects of the servant's role, mentioned in the first song, are central in our passage. He speaks in a prophetic tone and style, opening the address with a typical call to attention (cf. Isa. 1:10; Amos 3:1; 4:1; 5:1) and speaking in the name of the Lord. Like many other prophets, the servant reports that he was called by God. His call before he was born, in his "mother's womb" (vv. 1b, 5a) is a direct parallel to Jeremiah 1:5. Moreover, his frustration with his mission (v. 4a) is similar to that of other prophetic figures, especially Jeremiah. But just as in the first song, the Lord insisted that he had called the servant, in this one the servant himself confirms and accepts that call (vv. 5b, 6a), despite the difficulties he has encountered.

The passage is rich in themes and issues for reflection. Among these are the stress on the power of the divine word, the naming of the servant, and the role of the servant to the nations.

1. Because the prophetic dimensions of the servant's role are central, it is not surprising that his preparations for his task concern speaking. As in prophetic vocation accounts (Isa. 6; Jer. 1:10–17; Ezek. 1–3), attention is called to the mouth of the prophet (v. 2). Strong metaphors ("sharp sword," "polished arrow") emphasize the power and effectiveness of the servant's mouth. Assumed as well is the fact that the authority of the servant's words—like that of a true prophet—stems from the fact that they are not his own but the Lord's. It is clear that in ancient Israel the word of God was creative (Gen. 1:3, 6) and that such creative power was unleashed through the speeches of prophets:

> "See, today I appoint you over nations and over kingdoms,
> to pluck up and to pull down,
> to destroy and to overthrow,
> to build and to plant." (Jeremiah 1:10; cf. Amos 1:2)

It is clear, then, that the servant is to accomplish his call (bringing Israel back, restoring Israel, and extending God's salvation, vv. 5–6) by means of the word that God gives him to speak.

2. The servant knows who he is because the Lord has told him so: "You are my servant" (v. 3). Notice how much is said about the identity of the servant of God. God, he says, "named [him]" (v. 1) and gave him as "a light to the nations" (v. 6), and he is confident that his "cause" and "reward" are with God. Such words convey far more than information. Such designations identify, but they also establish identity. The servant knows who he is because God has declared him to be that one.

3. That the servant has a role toward Israel is clear: he is to bring the people back and to restore them. That return and restoration are not simply "spiritual," for example, to revive their morale, but are concrete and political; that is, the servant will be an agent in Yahweh's plan to return the people to their land. But the servant also has a task to the whole world. The meaning of that task is not so obvious, especially in view of the numerous passages in Second Isaiah that condemn, criticize, or even ridicule foreigners and their religious practices in particular (41:11–13; 43:3–4; 49:7, 22–23). But here, God says, the servant is a "light to the nations, that my salvation may reach to the end of the earth" (v. 6). It seems unlikely that the prophet anticipates explicit missionary activities to bring all peoples to acknowledge that Yahweh is God, and he certainly considers Israel to be a special, chosen people. However, because he knows that there is but one true God, whose will is justice, the prophet's vision finally cannot be contained. God will establish "salvation" to the ends of the earth, and that salvation will include justice and peace.

Psalm 71:1–14

This psalm, sharing features and wording with Psalm 31, is a lament, as are all the psalms in Holy Week except for Psalm 116 used on Holy Thursday. Psalm 71 begins with a statement of trouble and a plea for help, that is, with a lamenting situation, but concludes with a strong sense of confidence and assurance that matters will be rectified. A sense of trust and a feeling of comfort and encouragement run throughout the psalm.

The following elements go to make up the psalm's content: description of trouble (vv. 7–11), appeals for help (vv. 2–4, 12–13, 17–18), statements of trust and confidence (vv. 1, 16, 19–21), and vows to perform certain actions in the future (vv. 14–15, 22–24).

We can examine the salient features of this psalm in terms of (1) the nature of the distress, (2) the worshiper's statements of confidence, and (3) the nature of the help requested from God.

1. The troubles undergone by the worshiper are related primarily to enemies. The gallery of opponents are described as "the wicked," "the unjust and cruel man," and "enemies" who seek the worshiper's life. (Reference is made to "accusers" in v. 13.) The bitterest opponents appear to be those enemies who consider the person forsaken by God and thus without help and support (vv. 10–11). One might assume that the malady or problem the person had was taken as a sign that God has forsaken or is no longer supporting the one praying.

2. This psalm is permeated by a strong sense of trust and confidence. As the person looks back to the past, he or she affirms that God has been his or her trust from youth. God is even seen as the one who like a midwife took him or her from the mother's womb (v. 6). Looking to the future, the psalmist prays that the trust in and association with God, which was begun as a child, will continue into "old age and gray hairs" (vv. 9, 18). A common theme throughout the psalm is that God is a refuge. The worshiper confesses that God is a refuge and at the same time prays that God will be a refuge (compare vv. 1 and 7 with v. 3). The concept of a refuge is further explicated with reference to God as a strong fortress and a rock—all expressive of both stability and protection.

An interesting feature of the psalm's statement of confidence is the reference to the special role the person has for making known or proclaiming God not only to the contemporaries of the day but also to generations yet to come (vv. 7–8, 18). This would suggest that the psalm was not originally composed for an ordinary Israelite but was probably written for the king who had a special responsibility for proclaiming the nation's God.

3. The petitions and appeals made to God for help focus primarily on the requests that God not forsake the worshiper (vv. 9–10) or let the person be put to shame (v. 1). Shame plays both a positive and a negative function in the psalm. The worshiper asks to be preserved from shame (v. 1) and at the same time prays that the accusers be put to shame and consumed (v. 13). Shame, of course, meant being put in a humiliating situation and at the same time having to accept the identity that the situation imposed.

This psalm can be exegeted and preached in the context of Holy Week, for it expresses many of the factors that we think of in terms of Jesus' suffering: the opposition of enemies who do not believe God is his supporter, the trust and confidence of the worshiper, and a message to be proclaimed and made known to generations yet to come.

1 Corinthians 1:18–31

Today's epistolary text also serves as the second reading for the Fourth Sunday after the Epiphany in Year A and has been treated earlier in this volume. Part of this text (1:18–24) provides the epistolary reading for Holy Cross (September 14). Another portion (1:18–25) serves as the epistolary text for the Third Sunday in Lent in Year B. The reader may want to consult our remarks in these other settings.

Naturally, a text so popular and so historically influential within the church has many facets and can be explored in numerous directions.

First, we should note the polarizing effects of the "message about the cross" (v. 18). It forces options among those it addresses, dividing "those who are perishing" from those "who are being saved" (v. 18). This is a common distinction in Paul, who insists that his gospel of the cross is veiled to outsiders (cf. vv. 23–24; 2 Cor. 2:15; 4:3; also 2 Thess. 2:10). They fail to see because their eyes are blinded by "the god of this world" (2 Cor. 4:4). To see the cross as a display of God's power, as a moment of illumination, requires special discernment (1 Cor. 2:14).

Seen one way, the cross represents a tragedy played out as a human drama—political forces at work against an unfortunate messianic pretender. But to see it this way, Paul insists, is to see it with blinded eyes. Much more is at work: in this event, cosmic forces struggle against the divine will (1 Cor. 2:8–10). It is not a moment of human darkness but an event through which God's light shines (2 Cor. 4:4). In brief, it is a revelatory event. In it we learn something fundamental about God and the way God works in the world.

Paul knows full well that seeing the cross in this way is more than a matter of objective perception: it requires us to stand inside the cross and experience it as transforming event. Getting inside this event involves a special calling (v. 24). Some look at the cross and feel repelled, others are summoned. Seeing and experiencing the cross this way becomes a saving event that creates a community of believers, those "who are on the way to salvation" (v. 18, REB; cf. Acts 2:47; Luke 13:23).

This transformed vision of the cross sees in it a unique display of divine power (v. 18). If the crucified death of Jesus was a moment of weakness, his resurrection became a display of divine power (2 Cor. 13:4). This is the same gospel through which God's saving power is mediated to the believer (Rom. 1:16). What happened in the Christ-event also becomes normative for Christian existence. Human weakness, or human existence in all its limitations, serves as the focal center through which God's power is experienced (2 Cor. 12:9). Christ is "the power of God" (v. 24) because he serves as the focal event through which divine power transformed human weakness.

Second, the cross highlights the difference between divine and human wisdom. In this text, human ways are sharply contrasted with God's ways. Here Paul launches a sustained critique of human wisdom and its limitations. In doing so, he is informed by a long and rich set of Old Testament traditions. There are passages he quotes explicitly (v. 19; Isa. 29:14; Ps. 33:10), but there are also various other echoes. The threefold: "Where is the wise . . . ? Where is the scribe? Where is the debater?" (v. 20) recalls prophetic critiques that question the limits and capacity of human wisdom (Isa. 19:11–12; 33:18; 44:25). We hear similar echoes in the wisdom tradition (Job 12:13, 17). Just as Israel was reminded that God has no need of human consultants, so we are reminded in today's text that God's way of confronting us through the cross need not conform to our expectations, much less require our approval.

There is an ironic thread woven throughout our text: what appears wise to us is foolish to God. Human systems of thought at their best are inadequate to contain or express God's wisdom. If we try to build intellectual towers of Babel to God's presence, they are bound to collapse (Rom. 1:21). Consequently, God takes the drastic action of reversing "the wisdom of the world" (v. 20). God turns our wisdom on its head. The mysteries of God become hidden to the "wise and intelligent" and are revealed instead to infants (Matt. 11:25; cf. Rom. 11:33).

The prime example of human misguidedness is our fixation on the wrong indicators of God's divine presence: signs and wisdom. One way to look for evidence of God's power in the world is to look for signs and wonders, graphic displays of divine intervention (Matt. 12:38; Luke 11:16, 29–32; Matt. 16:1–4; Luke 23:8; John 2:18; 4:48; 6:30; 9:16; 11:47). For Paul, this way will surely misguide us. The paradox of the cross is that it appears to be a sign of divine impotence, of God's absence, when it is precisely the opposite. We turn our heads away from the cross because it does not square with our expectations of divine presence, nor does it present us with grand, visible displays of the divine.

As such, the cross becomes a scandal, a stumbling block, something on which the mind trips (cf. Matt. 16:23; also Isa. 8:14; 1 Pet. 2:8; Rom. 9:32–33). It does not conform to the way Paul's Jewish predecessors historically experienced God's presence. They were more inclined to "demand signs" (v. 22).

The other way of authenticating God's presence and power is through human wisdom: "Greeks desire wisdom" (v. 22; cf. Acts 17:18). This is the way of the intellect where God stands at the end of a syllogism. But one cannot look at the cross and see reasonableness. Instead we find ourselves scratching our heads, unable to see its logic. When we measure the cross by the canons of human reason, we conclude that it is "foolishness" (v. 23). Because this is the inevitable assessment, the cross calls our rational faculties into question. It seriously challenges our categories of reason and requires us to reconsider our universe of meaning.

For Paul the cross represents a third option, another way of "getting at" God. It breaks the horns of the dilemma posed by signs and wisdom. It provides us an altogether different lens through which to see God. As such, it becomes a testimony to God's power and wisdom (v. 24; cf. Rom. 1:16; Col. 2:3; Wisd. of Sol. 7:24–25; Hab. 3:19; Job 12:13).

What Paul is calling for in today's text is an epistemological transformation. We are being asked to reconfigure the way we construe reality, but especially the way we see and know God. For Paul, the cross calls us to look for God's presence in unexpected places: in suffering, weakness, and abandonment rather than in signs, wonders, and reason. But it also does something else: it challenges the way we see ourselves. It undercuts our own tendency to make God in our image and thereby makes it impossible for "any human being to boast in the presence of God" (v. 29; cf. Jer. 9:22–23; 2 Cor. 10:17; Rom. 5:11; Gal. 6:14; Phil. 3:3). It teaches us that God is "the source of our life in Christ Jesus" (v. 30; 2 Cor. 5:18, 21; Phil. 3:9). The cross is the constant reminder that we stand before God and that God does not stand before us, that we live subject to God, under and not over God. It is a reminder of the transcendent God.

John 12:20–36

We continue throughout Holy Week with texts from the fourth Gospel. Today's lesson follows John's account of Jesus' entry into Jerusalem (vv. 12–19), a unit replaced this year with Matthew's record of the same event (21:1–11), the Gospel lection for last Sunday. The preacher may want to reread John 11:4–12:19, not only to locate our text in Jerusalem at Passover time but also to capture the atmosphere of death and betrayal that surrounds the festivities of the high sabbath of Passover. The reader will also be reminded that in the midst of the celebrating and plotting, Jesus stands clear and firm as to "the hour" of God's purpose for his life.

"The hour has come for the Son of Man to be glorified" (v. 23). This statement of Jesus was prompted by the coming of Greeks to see Jesus (v. 20), which in turn was prompted by a statement of the Pharisees, "Look, the world has gone after him" (v. 19). In other words, the unwitting comment by some Pharisees that the whole world was drawn to Jesus is a prophecy fulfilled in preview by the coming of Greeks. Who these Greeks are, what their origin is, and what happens to them are not primary concerns of the Evangelist. One would guess them to be Greeks who practice Judaism. Some commentators understand them symbolically as representing through Philip and Andrew (v. 22) a subsequent mission to Gentiles. For the writer, they serve to prompt from Jesus a series of statements about his death, his return to God, and the meaning of that glorification (John's word for Jesus' death and exaltation) for the life of the world. Once Jesus' comments begin, the Greeks vanish from the story.

Apparently, the line of thought prompted by the request of the Greeks to see Jesus is as follows: in order to be available to the Greeks, that is, to the world, Jesus must die and be exalted to God's presence. The earthly career of the historical Jesus must now continue in the ministry of the dead and risen Christ, who will be present and available to the church everywhere. The presence and availability of the living Christ will be the primary subject matter of the farewell discourses of chapters 14–16. The extensive and repeated treatment of this theme testifies to its importance for the Johannine church, and for us. Whether stated in terms of the living Christ or the Holy Spirit, the divine presence is essential for the life of the church.

The line of thought continues. Jesus reflects upon death in a threefold soliloquy: (1) there is a law of nature that death is a necessary precondition for the increase of more life (v. 24); (2) there is a law of discipleship that demands hating, or releasing, or giving one's life in order to have life (v. 25); and (3) the question arises immediately, But is the lord of nature and the master of disciples exempt from the law of death as essential for life? (v. 27). The answer is clearly a no. Instead of the Synoptics' "remove this cup," Jesus says, "Father, save me from this hour? No; it is for this reason that I have come to this hour" (v. 27). Instead of the cry of dereliction from the cross (Mark 15:34), Jesus here receives heaven's confirmation (v. 28). Even though Jesus' soul is troubled (v. 27), very little of Gethsemane's painful struggle appears in John's Gospel. In fact, Jesus did not actually need the confirming voice of heaven; it was, he said, for the benefit of those nearby (v. 30). Not all heard the voice, of course (v. 29); Scripture and experience teach us that events that are for some people occasions of God's self-disclosure are for others natural occurrences.

The time has come; Jesus will be lifted up, both in the sense of being put on a cross and of being elevated to God (v. 32). From this point through verse 36, Jesus speaks of his death in two ways. His death is judgment in that light is judgment upon those who prefer darkness and in that life is judgment upon those who prefer death. And Jesus' death is victory over the ruler of this world (v. 31), for in Christ's presence in word and in the Holy Spirit persons of all nations and of all times will be drawn again to God (v. 32).

But even the clear word of judgment is softened a bit. "The light is with you for a little longer" (v. 35). For the sake of those of Jesus' time, of John's time, and of ours, the grace of God has stayed the end of all things.

Wednesday in Holy Week

Isaiah 50:4–9*a*;
Psalm 70;
Hebrews 12:1–3;
John 13:21–32

The Old Testament lesson contains an address of the servant of Yahweh to a human audience. In this speech, the servant confesses a serene confidence in God, in the instruction given by the Divine, and in an ultimately successful vindication against charges hurled against and oppression carried out against the servant. The psalm is a prayer replete with pleas for help in a time of trouble. The Epistle text calls upon the Christian to endure suffering and hostility as did the Christ and a host of earlier Christians who in their trials bear witness to the faith. In the Gospel passage, the future course of suffering is set for Jesus by his dialogue with the disciples over the betrayal and the departure of Judas into the night to perform his act of darkness.

Isaiah 50:4–9*a*

This is the same Old Testament reading that began Holy Week as the lection for Passion/Palm Sunday. For a commentary, see our remarks in that setting.

Psalm 70

An almost identical doublet of Psalm 40:13–17, Psalm 70 is composed totally of speech directed to God (prayer). Except for verse 5, the psalm is all pleas and requests for God to act in behalf of the supplicant. Verse 5*a* may be said to describe the condition of distress ("poor and needy"), whereas 5*c* is a statement of faith and trust in God ("You are my help and my deliverer").

The psalm could be interpreted in terms of four persons or groups spoken about in the psalm.

1. There is first of all the supplicant who is speaking. This supplicant says two things in self-description. (a) "My life is lived under threat and persecution." Various expressions give vent to this sense of living under the gun—others seek my life, desire my hurt, and already say, "Aha, Aha," as if my guilt and humiliation were already evident and clearly

201

deserved. (b) In the self-description, the supplicant is said to be poor and needy. Such a depiction may be taken as mercy seeking through pathetic appeal, as enticement to get God to act, or as a human response to anxiety. Perhaps all three factors underlie the expression.

2. A second group consists of the enemies/opponents of the supplicant. They are characterized in two fashions. (a) On the one hand, they are vicious, destructive, and eager to witness the downfall of the worshiper. Remembering that such descriptions may be stereotypical and stylized rather than actual and historical, we are unable to produce a composite drawing of culprits. Was the worshiper a king? Thus the enemies may have been conceived as foreigners. If the worshiper were an average Israelite, then the enemies may have been fellow citizens or the imaginative product of the worshiper, and thus only symbolically real. (b) Other comments on the enemies are pleas for their embarrassment and failure. Note the strong terms expressive of harsh emotions—shame, confusion, turned back, brought to dishonor, appalled.

3. A third group spoken about are those "who seek you" and "those who love your salvation." This group, among which the supplicant would have been counted, could be called the faithful or righteous. The supplicant intercedes on their behalf asking that they be made to rejoice and be glad and allowed to affirm continuously that "God is great."

4. The final figure in the psalm is God. Two nouns describe the Deity (help and deliverer); two verbs ask for divine intervention (help and deliver); and one adjective characterizes God (great).

These four were also part of the scenario of the last week of Jesus' ministry, and thus this psalm manifests and reflects frequently encountered universal human situations.

Hebrews 12:1–3

What makes this an especially fitting text for Holy Week is its singular focus on Jesus as the one who "leads us in our faith and brings it to perfection" (v. 2, NJB). We are reminded of his willingness to "endure the cross" while "disregarding the shame of it" (v. 2, NJB). This is an illuminating remark concerning Jesus' own inner perspective. It suggests that he was fully aware of the scandal of the cross. Its curse he knew as he faced and experienced it, even as Christians recognized it in retrospect (Gal. 3:13–14).

We are told not only that he "endured the cross," but did so "for the sake of the joy that was set before him" (v. 2). The preacher will do well to pause at this phrase, because it jars us. If we read it too glibly, it looks as if Jesus headed to the cross with a sadomasochistic smile, as if the endurance of such pain could be motivated by some twisted desire for joy and blessedness. The Greek is not altogether clear, and the NEB provides an alternative rendering, "who, in place of the joy that was open to him" (similarly, NRSV note reads "who instead of" as an alternative to "who for the sake of"). This would be in keeping with the sentiment of the Christ-hymn in Philippians 2:5–11, where Christ lays aside his elevated status in order to become flesh (cf. 2 Cor. 8:9). To read it this way, the pain of the cross is a clear alternative to the joy of staying alive. If, however, we retain a reading that sees the joy as something lying in the future (as do NRSV, NJB, REB, NIV), we should see it as the *future* joy that would be his eventually in his exalted position as God's Son (cf. Acts 2:33; Ps. 110:1).

In either case, we should note that Jesus' endurance is not mitigated by his eventual exaltation. His was still a decision made in faith. In this respect, he was not unlike the host of faithful witnesses described in Hebrews 11. He looked to the future in hope and endured the cross. He did not endure the cross because the future was somehow already his. It is in this sense that he is "pioneer and perfecter of our faith" (v. 2). In faith he forged his way ahead, committing himself fully to the God of promise. Even though looking back we know that humiliation gave way to exaltation, our text insists that Jesus had no clue of this as he looked ahead. His joy still lay *in the future* (so v. 2, NJB), and the future lay beyond the cross, not before it.

Now Jesus has been fully exalted (v. 2), and for this reason he is the "perfecter of our faith." The witnesses mentioned earlier "did not receive what was promised" (11:39). Their faith, like ours, is still to be vindicated. But unlike everyone else, Jesus has already been vindicated by God. His example is singular.

The point of this exposition is clear: it is to keep us from losing heart and growing weary (v. 3; cf. Gal. 6:9). The author is genuinely concerned that his readers might lapse into unbelief. In fact, we are told that some have already turned back (6:1–8). What is desperately needed is a strong, compelling incentive for the readers.

This is how the athletic metaphor is intended to function. The Christian is envisioned as the runner who lays aside every encumbrance and prepares to join the race that others have run (cf. 1 Cor. 9:24–27; Phil. 3:14). Surrounding us is the "cloud of witnesses," those who have run before us. This gallery is populated by those mentioned in chapter 11, and they are to serve as reminders and examples. The author realizes how powerful an incentive is provided by those who have gone before us in faith. The deeds of our predecessors are well worth rehearsing even though we tend to idealize them. In retrospect, their flaws tend to fade. They should not for that reason be forgotten.

The preacher may wish to compare today's text with the extended list of Israel's notable predecessors in Sirach 44–50. It is much longer than Hebrews 11, with the list of figures running from Enoch to Simon, son of Onias; that is, from the patriarchal to the Maccabean period. Unlike Hebrews 11, the various figures are not portrayed in Sirach in terms of a single virtue such as faith, but they are praised nevertheless.

In this connection, we do well to note the way in which figures from the past provide both examples and incentives: Abraham (Rom. 4; James 2:21–24), Rahab (James 2:25–26), Job (James 5:11), Elijah (James 5:17–18). But like Sirach, we can extend the list into our own time, so that our immediate ancestors are placed in the great succession of God's witnesses. This is precisely the move the author of the Epistle to the Hebrews makes: the list that begins with Abel ends with Jesus. It is brought from the remote past into the recent past, and the readers are expected to link themselves with this story of faithful witness that has preceded them for centuries.

In the midst of Holy Week, our text provides us with a powerful incentive to be faithful. In one sense, the example of Jesus is singular and stands out from all the rest. He is, after all, the center of faith in a way no one else is. And yet we stand surrounded with a gallery of witnesses who, like us, committed themselves to the future of God's promise and leaned into it in hope. Theirs is an example of expectant faith even as Jesus is an example of realized faith.

John 13:21–32

The Gospel lessons for today and tomorrow are drawn from John 13. We begin today at verse 21 so that the earlier verses, which provide the account of the last meal itself, may direct our thoughts for tomorrow, Holy Thursday. Chapters 13–17 of John's Gospel are devoted to Jesus' preparation of his disciples for his farewell. Luke is the only other Evangelist to deal extensively with Jesus' departure, and he does so in two ways: (1) the risen Christ remains with his disciples forty days, teaching and preparing (Acts 1:1–5); and (2) Luke follows his Gospel with a second volume (Acts), which narrates how the disciples continue Christ's work in the world. John has no forty days or a second volume. Rather, he compresses into what seems to be one night prior to Jesus' arrest Jesus' preparation of the Twelve through exemplary act, discourse, and prayer.

In John 13, the crowds are not present and neither are the opponents; only Jesus and his followers are in view. Clearly, the message here is for the church and not for outsiders. And the message is a strong one, warning the church against arrogance and triumphalism. As we will see in tomorrow's lection, the warning is first given in Christ's example of washing the disciples' feet, but it also occurs in the fact of treachery in the inner circle: "The one who ate my bread has lifted his heel against me" (v. 18; Ps. 41:9). The act of Judas served as a painful reminder to the church of the ever-present possibility of disloyalty and betrayal within the community of faith. But Judas was a problem for the church, not only as a reminder that believers should never cease asking, "Lord, is it I?" but also as a burden upon the church's efforts to understand the death of Jesus. How else would one explain the fact that next to Jesus it is Judas whose presence is most determinative in the conversation and action of 13:1–32?

In verses 21–30, the action unfolds quite simply: Jesus predicts his betrayal, the disciples seek to learn who it is, Jesus reveals the betrayer by giving to Judas the morsel of bread, Jesus commands Judas to move quickly to his ugly deed, the disciples do not understand what Jesus meant, and Judas leaves. For the preacher to paint Judas in the obvious colors of a villain would be to miss the point of the text. Were he clearly the epitome of undisguised evil, then Jesus would not have had to point him out and the disciples would not have missed the meaning of the interchange between Jesus and Judas (vv. 28–29). In fact, were Judas the very picture of evil, then his act would not have been so ugly. The stabbing truth is, Judas was chosen by Jesus to be a disciple, he had participated in all the benefits of working with Jesus and belonging to the inner circle, and he had been selected as treasurer of the group. Verses 21–30 give absolutely no indication that Judas had created in the other disciples any cause for suspicion. They simply do not see or hear betrayal in Jesus' words to Judas or Judas' early departure from the table. Of course, the Evangelist has been alerting us to Judas' treason since 6:71, but those are statements of hindsight and retrospection, and they are addressed to the readers. John is not alone in the New Testament or in subsequent church history in the effort to understand the motives for Judas' behavior. Perhaps the quest has continued so long because the church has known that to understand Judas is to understand a darker side of itself.

Two details in verses 21–30 deserve brief attention. The first is the reference to "one of his disciples—the one whom Jesus loved" (v. 23). This unnamed disciple appears in six scenes in chapters 13–21, and except for the one at the cross with Jesus' mother (19:25–27), all will be in the company of Simon Peter (13:21–26; 18:15–18; 20:1–9; 21:4–7; 21:20–24). Commentaries will provide all the speculation about this disciple's identity. Suffice it here to say that this disciple was especially close to Jesus and gave to the Johannine church its authoritative continuity with Jesus. And because this disciple is presented as always preceding Peter in knowledge, faith, and relation to Jesus, we can assume that the Johannine circle of Christianity regarded itself as closer than the Petrine circle to the heart and truth of the Jesus tradition.

The second detail drawing our attention is the expression "and it was night" (v. 30). One suspects that the Evangelist is here, as in 3:2, using night symbolically to convey the nature of the activity being described. However, it is not without its literal reference to the time of betrayal. The earliest known tradition related to the Last Supper preserves the time of that supper by referring to Judas' act: "The Lord Jesus on the night when he was betrayed took a loaf of bread" (1 Cor. 11:23).

Verses 31–32, vital to the service tomorrow (Maundy Thursday), are here joined to the consideration of Judas' act in order to set the betrayal in larger context. What Judas did was offensive even to nonbelievers, but we are here reminded that in the purposes of God even such a deed can be used for good. By this act of betrayal, Jesus will be handed over to the authorities and crucified. However, in this Gospel crucifixion is "glorifying the Son"; that is, returning the Son to the presence of God (11:4; 12:23). And as Jesus has already said, "And I, when I am lifted up from the earth, will draw all people to myself" (12:32).

Holy Thursday

Exodus 12:1–4 (5–10) 11–14;
Psalm 116:1–2, 12–19;
1 Corinthians 11:23–26;
John 13:1–17, 31b–35

The remembrance of Holy Thursday is awash in rich and multifaceted imagery. The visions ignited by the sparks of that imagery bring to mind the holy eating, drinking, and storytelling that memorialized the Passover celebration of the Exodus from Egypt (recalled in the Old Testament reading). Psalm 116 was one of the traditional psalms sung in conjunction with Passover, first in the temple as the paschal lambs were being slaughtered and then in the evening when the Passover meal was eaten in the homes. Christian celebrations bring to memory not only the imagery of the Passover but also, as in the Epistle lesson, they recall Jesus' last meal with the disciples and his words instituting the Eucharist celebration. Foot washing (the Pedilavium) has long been a component in celebration of Maundy (Holy) Thursday recalling the episode reported in the Gospel reading.

Exodus 12:1–4 (5–10) 11–14

The account of the institution of the Passover, the most appropriate Old Testament lesson for Holy Thursday, stands very close to the heart of the Old Testament story and ancient Israel's faith. Nothing was more central to that faith than the confession that Yahweh brought Israel out of Egypt. The Passover, believed to have been instituted on the very night that Israel was set free from Egypt, takes its meaning from the connection with the Exodus. Thus each time the Passover was celebrated, including in the time of Jesus, the people of God remembered that they were slaves set free by their God.

Although the section before us is relatively straightforward, it is part of a very complex section in the Book of Exodus. Because it is the climax of the Exodus traditions, it has attracted a great many diverse elements. The unit, which reports the events immediately surrounding the departure from Egypt, begins in Exodus 11:1 and does not end until Exodus 13:16. One can identify four distinct motifs within this section. The most important is, of course, the departure from Egypt itself. Although this is noted quite briefly (12:37–39), it is the focal point of all other motifs. Second is the report of the final plague, the killing of the firstborn children of the Egyptians. This plague is quite distinct from those that preceded it, both in the fact that it was effective and in the extensive preparations for it. The third and fourth motifs are the religious ceremonies connected with the Exodus, the celebration of Passover and the Feast of Unleavened Bread. Passover is linked to the final plague because it entailed a procedure for ensuring that the Israelite firstborn would not be killed, and it is connected in very direct ways with the immediate departure from Egypt. The final plague is what motivated the pharaoh to release Israel, and the Passover was to have taken place just before they left.

Within this section of the Book of Exodus there are duplicates, repetitions, and inconsistencies that reveal the presence of at least two sources, the Priestly Writer and the Yahwist. The style and technical terminology of Exodus 12:1–13 reveal that it comes from the Priestly Writer and thus would date from the postexilic period, ca. 500 BC. Exodus 12:14 begins a section that probably comes from the J source, perhaps as early as 900 BC.

It is important to keep in mind that this passage is part of a narrative, a story more of divine actions than human events. Its setting is the history of salvation, the account of Yahweh's intervention to set his people free. In that context, Exodus 12:1–14 is a report of divine instructions to Moses and Aaron concerning the celebration of the Passover. Thus everything except verse 1 is in the form of a speech of Yahweh, a direct address to Moses and Aaron. These instructions have the tone and contents of rules established for perpetuity and thus reflect the perspective of Israelites centuries after the events.

The instructions are precise and detailed with regard to both time and actions. The month in which the Exodus takes place is to become the first month of the year, and the preparations for the Passover begin on the tenth day of the month (vv. 2–3a). It is a family ceremony, with a lamb chosen for each household—that is, unless the household is too small for a lamb, in which case neighboring families are to join together to make up the right number to consume the lamb (vv. 3b–4). A lamb without blemish is to be selected and then killed on the fourteenth day of the month (vv. 5–6). Blood is to be smeared on the lintels and doorposts of the houses, and the meat is to be roasted and eaten with unleavened bread and bitter herbs (vv. 7–9). The meal is to be eaten in haste, and anything not consumed by morning is to be burned (vv. 10–11).

After the instructions follows an explanation of the meaning of the meal and of the practices associated with it. The Lord will pass through the land of Egypt to destroy the firstborn, but will see the blood and "pass over" the Israelites (vv. 12–13). Verse 14, which comes from another writer, stresses that the day is a "day of remembrance," and forever. In its celebration, later generations will remember the Exodus.

In both the present text and later practice, Passover was combined with the Feast of Unleavened Bread. The former was a one-night communal meal, and the latter was a seven-day festival. The combination was quite ancient, but the two originally were distinct. It seems likely that the Feast of Unleavened Bread was a pre-Israelite festival related to the agricultural year in Canaan. Passover, on the other hand, probably originated among semi-nomadic groups such as the Israelites as a festival related to the movement of their flocks from winter to summer pasture. The feast certainly was a family ceremony during the early history of Israel. In later generations, Passover was one of the three major annual pilgrimage festivals for which the people were to come to Jerusalem (Deut. 16:2–7).

The word "passover" (Hebrew *pesach*) is explained in this passage by connecting it with a verb for "to skip" or "hop over," but the actual etymology of the word is uncertain. Throughout the Old Testament it refers either to the festival described here or to the animal that is killed and eaten. Many passages use the word in both senses (e.g., 2 Chron. 35:1–19). The ceremony had both sacrificial and communal dimensions in that the animal was ceremonially slaughtered but then consumed as a family meal.

No ceremony was more important in ancient Israel or early Judaism than Passover. It was the festival in which the people acknowledged and celebrated who they were and who their God was. In remembering the day as the memorial day for the Exodus (Exod. 12:14), they acknowledged that God is the one who sets people free and makes them his own. They knew thereby that they were God's people. Moreover, in the gathering of family and friends for a communal meal in which the story of release from slavery was told, they bound themselves together and to that God who acted to make them who they were.

Psalm 116:1–2, 12–19

John Hayes

This particular reading for Holy Thursday has been selected on the basis of the reference to the cup in verse 13 and thus its connection with the imagery of the Last Supper.

Psalm 116 was composed as a thanksgiving psalm to be offered by someone who had escaped the clutches of death, who had stood at the doors of Sheol, but who had recovered from sickness and could again worship and celebrate in thanksgiving at the temple.

In early Judaism, at the time of Jesus, this psalm, along with Psalms 113–115 and 117–118, was sung in the temple by the Levites at the time of the slaughter of the Passover lambs and again at dinner when the Passover meal was eaten in a family celebration.

Verses 1–2 introduce the psalm with a statement reflecting good relationship with the Deity, who has responded to a plea and granted redemption. On the basis of this, the promise is made to worship God faithfully as long as one lives.

Verses 12–19 of this psalm are concerned with the fulfillment of vows made earlier, probably at the time when the worshiper petitioned God for deliverance from trouble, most likely during a debilitating illness. In rendering the vows, which would certainly have included offering sacrifice, the worshiper addresses a human audience (vv. 12–15, 18–19) as well as the Deity (vv. 16–17). We should think of such thanksgiving rituals as times of great happiness and jubilant celebration. A person whose life had been threatened, disoriented, and removed from the normal course of activity had been restored to wholeness. The life that had fallen into the grip of hell itself and had been invaded by the power of death was now free of both the illness and the anguished turmoil that the sickness brought. Now the worshiper can look back and speak of the sorrowful plight of the past, which now is only a life-transforming memory. There certainly must be "scars" from such a past, but they are the marks of past triumphs and the residues of God's grace, to be cherished and celebrated, not embarrassingly hidden. At such a celebration, friends and family of the formerly ill person would have attended worship with the redeemed. Such worship would have included not only thanksgiving in word but also feasting, drinking, and dancing. These festive symbols marked the end of a former state and the beginning of a new state of living. They were enjoyed as the sacramental signs of God's concern and care.

In verses 12–15, the worshiper addresses a human audience of friends and family. The elements of the thanksgiving spoken of included the offering of a cup of salvation, the worship of God, and the fulfillment of vows. The cup mentioned is best understood as the drink offering made as part of the thanksgiving sacrificial ritual (see Num. 28:7) or perhaps the cup of wine drunk in the thanksgiving meal (Ps. 23:5). Such a cup symbolized God's deliverance, the opposite of the cup of God's wrath (see Isa. 51:17; Jer. 25:15). The worshiper reminds the listeners that God does not wish the death of one of his faithful worshipers, because for God such a death is a serious, weighty matter (v. 15; not precious, as in the NRSV).

The place of the thanksgiving celebration was the temple in Jerusalem, where sacrifices would be made (vv. 18–19). In such thanksgiving services, most of the animals sacrificed would have reverted to the worshiper to be cooked and eaten in the temple precincts before the next day had passed (see Lev. 6:11–18). Thus the sacrifice of thanksgiving imposed lavish and extravagant eating and communal sharing.

Verses 16–17 would have been prayed directly to God in conjunction with offering the thanksgiving sacrifice. The worshiper thus declared his or her status before God, "I am your servant," a status dependent upon the redemptive work of God, "You have loosed my bonds."

1 Corinthians 11:23–26

Here we have Paul's account of the institution of the Lord's Supper (cf. Matt. 26:26–28; Mark 14:22–24; Luke 22:14–23). It is especially remarkable in being the earliest Christian account of the institution of the Eucharist. Because Paul's First Epistle to the Corinthians was written in the early 50s, this account precedes the written Gospel accounts by some fifteen to twenty years at least.

It is, of course, even earlier than this. When Paul speaks of "receiving" and "handing on" this tradition (v. 23a), he is using the technical language used in both Jewish and non-Jewish traditions to describe the transmission of sacred teachings or tradition. He uses similar language to introduce summaries of early Christian preaching (1 Cor. 15:3). What we have here, then, is a tradition that is older than Paul, one that he had received "from the Lord" (v. 23). This is his way of underscoring its divine authority (cf. 1 Cor. 7:10, 12, 25, 40; 9:14; 14:37; 15:3; 1 Thess. 4:5). Rather than signifying that he had received it in a moment of inspired ecstasy, the language suggests that this tradition is ultimately traceable to the Lord (cf. Gal. 1:12). It was a tradition begun by Jesus and transmitted through successive witnesses who faithfully preserved it intact. Paul stands in this succession as a faithful tradent.

The tradition is cited here in response to certain abuses within the Corinthian church (11:17–22). Their celebration of the sacred meal had become an occasion for accentuating the social differences within the church. The rich were being distinguished from the poor (v. 22). Rather than serving as an occasion for reinforcing a sense of community, the sacred meal was becoming a divisive force (v. 18). In addition, it had become an occasion for overindulgence (v. 21). In a word, it had ceased to be the "Lord's Supper" (v. 21). It had lost its sacred function as it served their own ends.

This helps explain some of the distinctive features of the Pauline version of the eucharistic tradition. We notice first that the bread is celebrated as the "body that is for you" (v. 24). The stress is on an act performed in behalf of others. In the Matthean and Markan accounts, we find a similar interpretation of the cup that is "poured out for many" (Matt. 26:28; Mark 14:24; cf. Luke 22:20). In one version of the Lukan account, the bread is similarly interpreted. But in the context of 1 Corinthians 11, where Christians are observing the sacred meal with "robust individualism" (Bornkamm), Paul's words serve as an important corrective. The bread serves as a reminder that the death of Christ should solidify the church as a community of believers—all believers, poor and rich alike. It is not the sole possession of any one person, much less an event observed by indulging the self.

Another remarkable feature, which is shared with the Lukan account (Luke 22:19), is the injunction "Do this in memory of me" (v. 24, REB). The Greek word for "memory" (*anamnesis*) has a long and rich history and seems to imply both recollection and reenactment. If so, it invites us to recall the event as a past event, but in doing so to appropriate the event to our own present by making that historical moment part of our own history. The text clearly envisions that the meal would be celebrated subsequently as Christians gathered for worship. Thus, "as often as" Christians ate the bread and drank the cup (v. 26), they would celebrate the death of Christ in expectation of his return.

We should also note the stress on the cup as the "new covenant" (v. 25), another feature the Pauline account has in common with the Lukan account (22:20). What was envisioned by Jeremiah (Jer. 31:31; 32:40; cf. Zech. 24:8) is now seen to be fulfilled in the death of Christ. The fuller implications are explored by Paul in the Second Epistle to the Corinthians (2 Cor. 3:6; cf. Heb. 7:22).

The preacher will do well to note these distinctive features of the Pauline tradition of the Eucharist. Its similarities with the Lukan version may suggest dependence or common origin. But the Synoptic accounts are one with Paul in their insistence that the Eucharist celebrates a sacred moment in the Christ story. It serves as a reminder that the breaking of Christ's body and the shedding of his blood are central elements of Christian belief and practice.

John 13:1–17, 31b–35

N ow before the festival of the Passover" (13:1), says this Evangelist, alerting the reader that the account that follows will be different from the Synoptic records of the last meal. In the Synoptics, Jesus eats the Passover meal with the Twelve (Matt. 26:17–19; Mark 14:12–16; Luke 22:7–13, and esp. Luke 22:15) and, following the meal, institutes the Lord's Supper (Matt. 26:26–29; Mark 14:22–25; Luke 22:15–20). In John, the last meal is before Passover, and there is no account here of the institution of the Eucharist. For this Evangelist, Jesus does not *eat* the Passover; he *is* the Passover, bleeding and dying as the Passover lamb (19:31–37). In chapter 6, John presents the feeding of the five thousand as a Passover meal with a eucharistic interpretation. The commentaries will discuss whether John is to be taken as a correction of the Synoptics, as exhibiting evidence of a different source, or as the writer's willingness to sacrifice chronology for theology.

For this Evangelist, therefore, the last meal is the occasion, the setting for particular words and acts of Jesus. The central act of Jesus in this text is the washing of the disciples' feet (vv. 2–5). The act is not understood (v. 7), even though it is followed by two interpretations (vv. 6–11, 12–20). It is very important, however, for the reader to understand that Jesus knows exactly what he is doing and what it means. Notice: "Jesus, knowing that the Father had given all things into his hands" (v. 3); "for he knew who was to betray him" (v. 11); and, "I know whom I have chosen" (v. 18). This portrayal of Jesus is consistent with the way John presents him from the prologue through the entire Gospel. Whatever clashes with other portraits of Jesus this may create for the reader, it should be appreciated that John is giving confidence and engendering faith (v. 19) in Christians who might otherwise look upon the events of betrayal, arrest, and death as defeat. After all, John's readers were experiencing betrayal, arrest, and death (15:20–16:3), and to understand these events in Jesus' life as part of a divine plan of redemption would help them interpret their own experiences as having purpose. In other words, Jesus was not really a victim, and, even in death, neither are they victims.

The scene, then, is a powerful and moving one. Jesus is fully aware of his origin in glory; he is fully aware that he is soon to return to that glory; he is further aware that while on earth, all authority from God is his (vv. 1–3). The stage is set by verses 1–3 for Jesus to act in a dazzling way. Will he be transfigured before their eyes? Will he command the disciples to bow in adoration? No; instead he rose from the table, replaced his robe with a towel, poured water in a basin, washed the disciples' feet, and dried them with the towel (vv. 4–5).

Following the foot washing, two interpretations of the act are offered. Whether the fact that there are two represents two traditions about the meaning of Jesus' act or whether both were from the beginning associated with the event is a matter debated in the commentaries. As we will see, the two interpretations are not unrelated. The first (vv. 6–11) insists that the church is in the posture of recipient, having its identity and character in the self-giving act of the servant Jesus. The church exists by the cleansing act of Jesus. (Some ecclesiastical traditions therefore associate the washing with baptism.) It is this understanding that Simon Peter resists (vv. 6–9). The church in the person of Simon Peter does not want its Lord and Savior to wash its feet.

The second interpretation (vv. 12–17, but it actually extends through v. 20) understands Jesus' act as a model of humility and service that the church is to emulate. The servant is not greater than the master, and the posture of washing feet, whether understood literally or figuratively, vividly holds that truth before the church's eyes. This has been the more widely embraced interpretation, both by the few churches that have accorded foot washing sacramental status and the many that have not. The lesson is not lost even among those who do not continue the practice of foot washing. Perhaps one reason this second interpretation is more widely embraced than the first is that giving service is easier for the ego than receiving it. However, the two interpretations are not necessarily independent of each other. In fact, the church in a state of spiritual health and with a clear sense of its own nature and calling would practice the second because it had embraced the first.

In verses 31b–35, the writer turns up the lights to their brightest, and the dark of Judas' betrayal is scattered by the declaration of God's purpose. (See the comments at the end of the previous lesson). Jesus' prediction of his passion is almost gentle: "Little children, I am with you only a little longer" (v. 33). But whether soft or harsh (as in Mark), the disciples must deal with the absence of Jesus, and they will be able to do so if their relationship with each other is informed and determined by his relationship to them. "As I have loved you" (v. 34) is the key. In fact, this is probably the sense in which the command to love is new. If referring to love as a command is a problem, it most likely is due to thinking of love as a feeling. However, if love is the way God acts toward the world and the way Jesus acts toward his disciples, then love means telling the truth, being faithful in one's witness, and caring for others, even to the point of death.

This commandment, joined to the instructions about foot washing (in this Gospel) and to the Eucharist (in the others and in 1 Cor. 11), gives to Holy Thursday the ancient designation "Maundy," a form of the word "mandate."

Good Friday

Isaiah 52:13–53:12;
Psalm 22;
Hebrews 10:16–25 or Hebrews 4:14–16; 5:7–9;
John 18:1–19:42

Good Friday services tend to focus on the suffering of Jesus as the servant of God. This is a correct and proper theme for the day. Good Friday also, however, looks forward, beyond itself, beyond suffering and humiliation, to exaltation, triumph, and Easter. Suffering is a theme in all of today's texts, but the readings also point beyond suffering. The so-called fourth Servant Song in Isaiah ends on a note of triumph, as does the psalm reading. Both selections from Hebrews exhort Christians to meditate on the sufferings of Christ, sufferings that reflect his identity with humans but sufferings over which he was triumphant. The text from chapter 10 draws the moral implications for Christians of the suffering and death of Jesus; the other epistolary reading urges the hearers to have confidence in their salvation. The Gospel lesson speaks of the suffering and death of God's elect, but the narrative it tells is not the final word of the gospel.

Isaiah 52:13–53:12

Second Isaiah's fourth Servant Song is the obvious Old Testament reading for Good Friday. As early as the first century, Christians have seen in these lines a prophecy of the suffering and death of Jesus (cf. Acts 8:34), but clearly the passage served as far more than proof that Jesus was the one sent by God. It helped the earliest church both to understand the meaning of the death of Jesus and to communicate that understanding to others. Furthermore, in addition to seeing Jesus through these verses, Christians through the centuries have recognized themselves here as well, letting many of the words spoken by the crowd about the servant express their own responses to the death of Jesus.

Such inclinations to hear a Christian meaning in this text certainly are strengthened on Good Friday, one of the most important days in the church year, and in the last analysis they should not be resisted. However, if the Old Testament reading is to make its particular contribution to worship and understanding on this occasion, it is important to remind ourselves that it comes from a different religion than the Christian faith and from an age distant not only from ours but from the early church as well. The poem was originally written about 539 BC, and its audience was the Judean exiles in Babylon. (For a general introduction to the Servant Songs of Second Isaiah in their literary and historical context, see the commentary on Isa. 50:4–9a for Passion/Palm Sunday in this volume.)

The poem evokes theological reflection on matters essential to faith, including vicarious suffering, redemption from sin, and the will of God. Certainly this text lends support to a Christology that sees the power of God revealed in weakness. Far more important than deriving dogma from the text, however, is allowing its narrative and dramatic features to be heard, seen, and felt.

The dramatic aspects include the shifts in speakers. At the beginning (52:12–15) and the end (53:11b–12), the Lord is the speaker. The addressees are not indicated but probably are the people of Israel. Nevertheless, the content of the divine speeches concerns the whole world. God presents the servant as his chosen one and indicates that he intends to exalt him through and beyond his suffering, because he has faithfully fulfilled his vocation (52:13, 15; 53:12). In the central part of the poem (52:1–11a), the words are spoken by a corporate body, doubtless the members of the servant's community. They speak to and among themselves, recounting the life and suffering of the servant as well as their own reaction to him and meditating on the meaning of his life and death. It amounts to dramatic understatement that the servant himself speaks not a word in the poem. His life and death are the subject of the entire passage, but, as in his trial (53:7), he is silent. Everything here concerns the reaction of others—both divine and human—to the servant's faithfulness.

Dramatic also are the numerous reversals of roles and expectations. God exalts the lowly one (52:13–15), so that those who were astonished at his horrible appearance will be amazed at his elevation. The one who was considered guilty is the one who carries away the guilt of others (53:11–12). Those who rejected him as guilty and repulsive (53:2–3, 7–9) reverse themselves, confessing their own guilt and the servant's innocence (53:5–6, 9–10). Nothing, it seems, is as it first appears.

The narrative dimensions consist primarily in the people's recital of the story of the servant's life. The report begins with an expression of astonishment at what they have seen, indeed, at the power of God that has been revealed to them (53:1) through the life and suffering of the servant. Then they report how he grew up among them, suffered, and was despised (53:2–3). They describe in some detail, but also through the use of metaphorical language, a trial and the subsequent death of the Lord's servant (53:7–9). Legal language and images dominate. He was hauled into court, tried, condemned as guilty, and executed.

In addition to its dramatic and narrative aspects, the passage includes reflection upon and interpretation of the meaning of the servant's life and death. Two points in particular must be noted. First and above all, there is the astonishing realization that the death of this one who was despised and rejected is vicarious, on behalf of those very ones who had considered him guilty. His suffering is for others, and it is salvific: "He was wounded for our transgressions, crushed for our iniquities . . . and by his bruises we are healed" (53:5). Second, the suffering of the servant is seen to bring about a dramatic transformation in those who have seen it. The community had considered him repulsive and guilty of some crime. But when they see his trial and death, they realize that this one has suffered on their behalf. They recognize that he was innocent and they were guilty. It is not simply that they realize that they were wrong, that they made a mistake in condemning him. It was a legal fact that they were the guilty ones. So in one sense the Servant Song becomes a confession of sin by and on behalf of those who have seen God's suffering servant. That makes it possible to take the next step, to accept the servant's suffering on their behalf, that he "bore the sin of many" (53:12) and that his pain has made them whole (53:5–6). And all of this—the suffering of the servant in order to redeem those who considered him the guilty one—is the will of God. Thus confession of sin leads to hearing the good news that God has chosen this way to make sinners whole.

Psalm 22

Like Psalm 51, this psalm has become traditional for use during Holy Week. The reasons for the association of this psalm with Good Friday are threefold: (1) its content bears striking resemblance to the events of Jesus' trial and crucifixion (so much so that the psalm may be seen as one of the "sources" used by the church in describing the events surrounding the crucifixion); (2) according to Mark 15:34, Jesus quoted at least the opening lines of this psalm while hanging upon the cross; and (3) John 19:24 quotes from this psalm to illustrate the belief that actions and events in the life and career of Jesus were to fulfill scripture, in this case Psalm 22:18.

In this psalm, we find an opening address infused with a strong complaint against God for divine inactivity (vv. 1–2), a statement of confidence (vv. 3–5), a description of distress (vv. 6–8), a second statement of confidence (vv. 9–10), a plea for help (v. 11), a second description of distress (vv. 12–18), a second plea for salvation (vv. 19–21a), a vow to God to offer testimony (vv. 21b–22), a little sermonette to the human audience calling upon the people to offer God praise (vv. 23–24), a short prayer of thanks to God (v. 25a), and proclamation to the human audience of the consequences of the salvation that has been experienced (vv. 25b–31).

In the Gospel reading, John places the crucifixion of Jesus prior to Passover (see John 18:28) at about the time the paschal lambs would have been slaughtered in the temple (see John 19:14). The early Christians certainly seem to have combined this psalm, Jesus' death, and the Passover celebration. Given John's Gospel with its particular chronology, it is not out of place to see themes from Passover as providing some perspectives through which to interpret Psalm 22.

The Mishnah, in describing the Passover celebration, noted that in telling the story of the Exodus, the "father" of the household "begins with the disgrace and ends with the glory," that is, begins with the slavery, the servitude, and the suffering, and moves to the escape, the freedom, and the joy of the redemption. The Mishnah continues:

> In every generation a man must so regard himself as if he came forth himself out of Egypt, for it is written, *And thou shalt tell thy son in that day saying, It is because of that which the Lord did for me when I came forth out of Egypt* (Exod. 13:8). Therefore are we bound to give thanks, to praise, to glorify, to honour, to exalt, to extol, and to bless him who wrought all these wonders for our fathers and for us. He brought us out from bondage to freedom, from sorrow to gladness, and from mourning to a Festival-day, and from darkness to great light, and from servitude to redemption.

In Psalm 22, two themes run through the statements about the person's distress: a sense of alienation from the Deity and hostile opposition from opponents.

The theme of God's distance and correspondingly the person's sense of alienation are sounded in the opening lines. A sense of divine forsakenness pervades the words—God is too far away to hear the sufferer's groanings; day and night move through their ceaseless revolutions, but for the worshiper there is neither answer nor rest from God but only dismay at the divine silence and the loneliness of feeling forsaken.

The theme of human opposition parallels that of divine alienation. If God is too far distant, humans are too near. Human opposition and enmity are described in various ways. People mock, wagging their heads and making faces, ridiculing the person's dependence and seemingly futile reliance on God (vv. 7–8). Powers described as bulls, lions, dogs, and a company of evildoers assail the worshiper (vv. 12–13, 16). The depiction might suggest that the speaker was a king and the enemies were foreign powers. In any case, the opponents are portrayed as menacing, life threatening, and life destroying. They seize the person's abandonment by God as the occasion for attack.

The consequences of the worshiper's status are described in terms suggesting low self-esteem, complete despair and disorganization, and overall desperation. The image of a person's self-designation as a worm implies a feeling of utter hopelessness and helplessness, a state of feeling horribly subhuman (v. 6). Fright and incapacitation run through the imagery of verses 14–15 and 17–18, which are extremely graphic. Life seems no longer to have legitimate boundaries and normal structures ("poured out like water"); things do not function as they should ("bones are out of joint"); fear pervades everything ("heart is like wax . . . melted"); strength has ebbed away ("dried up like a potsherd"); speech fails ("tongue sticks to my jaws"); death seems to be the only foreseeable certainty; and emaciation exposes the body's boney structure ("count all my bones"). The enemies are pictured as already going through the postmortem ritual of dividing up the belongings of the deceased as if death had already occurred. The psalmist speaks of his or her own demise and the distribution of his or her goods in a game of fortune and luck. Although not greatly emphasized in the psalm, it appears that God is the real enemy of the worshiper. The last line of verse 15 declares that it is God who has already laid the supplicant in the dust of death. Behind the opposition and oppression of the enemy lies the activity of God, so God becomes the real opponent.

In spite of the dismal picture that the descriptions of distress paint, the psalm is shot through with the statements and confessions of great confidence in the Deity. Verses 3–5 affirm that God is holy and that in the past the faith and trust of the fathers were rewarded with divine favor. Such confidence in the worshiper was based on both the nature of God and the experience of the past; that is, the paradigm of the past functions as a source of hope for the future. The confidence in God, expressed in verses 9–10, stresses the prior intimacy that existed between the one praying and God. The psalmist seems to be implying that previously God had been his or her "father," his or her caretaker from the days of birth and youth.

The confidence in God displayed throughout the psalm moves in verses 22–31 to pride of place and suggests that the worshiper received from God some oracle or sign affirming that a reversal of fate was in store, that tears and pains would be replaced by songs and celebration. Good Friday ends with the pain and tribulation but like the psalm looks forward to Easter with its victory and triumph.

Hebrews 10:16–25

Today's epistolary lection opens with a quotation from Jeremiah 31:33–34, the well-known prophetic promise of a new covenant that figures prominently earlier in the epistle (8:8–13).

Actually, these Old Testament verses bring to a conclusion the extended argument that encompasses 9:11–10:18, which is a full exposition of the sacrifice of Christ. We have already been told that the death of Christ is a sacrifice and that its cleansing effect extends to all. It is his sacrificial death that has made possible the fulfillment of the prophetic promise "I will remember their sins and their lawless deeds no more" (v. 17). Through his death, true and lasting forgiveness has been achieved, and for this reason sin offerings are no longer needed. They were necessary only as long as forgiveness was partial.

What, then, are the consequences of the shedding of Jesus' blood as the final, ultimate sacrifice for sin? First, it provides a basis for genuine confidence (4:16; 10:35; Eph. 3:12; 1 John 3:21), because it opens up a way of access to God that was previously impossible (7:19, 25; 10:1; Rom. 5:2; Eph. 1:4; Col. 1:22).

In our text today, this is visualized as our being able to enter the sanctuary, the sacred area of the tabernacle that was off-limits to the ordinary worshiper. But through the once for all sacrifice of his life, Christ has become the supreme high priest over the house of God (2:17; 3:1; 4:14; 5:5, 10; 6:20; 7:26; 8:1; 9:11; 10:21; cf. Zech. 6:11–12). In this supreme role, his resurrected body provides an opening in the curtain separating the Holy Place from the Most Holy Place (6:19; 9:13).

As high priest over the house of God and as one who has opened the way of access to the very presence of God, Christ becomes a "new and living way" of access (v. 20; 7:25; cf. John 14:6). Not only has he entered the sanctuary (9:11–12), he has also made it possible for us to follow him in. Through him, we are able to enter the sanctuary, draw near to God, and have unprecedented access to God's very presence.

But such access is never casual. It rather requires proper preparation and calls for at least three exhortations, introduced with the familiar words "Let us . . ."

First, *an exhortation to moral purity* (v. 22). We are able to approach God fully assured in our hearts (4:16; Isa. 38:3), but it is a prerequisite that we do so with purified hearts and bodies. The former refers to our having a clean conscience, free of the guilt of sin (9:14; 10:2; 13:18; cf. 1 Tim. 1:5, 19; 3:9; 2 Tim. 1:3; Acts 23:1). The latter recalls the custom of ritual purification through washing the body with water before entering the sanctuary, and here probably refers to Christian baptism (cf. Exod. 29:4; Lev. 16:4; Ezek. 36:25; 1 Cor. 6:11; Eph. 5:26; Titus 3:5; 2 Pet. 1:9).

Second, *an exhortation to fidelity* (v. 23). Here we are urged to hold fast to the confession (3:1; 4:14). This is to be done hopefully (Rom. 5:2; Col. 1:23), because our God is not only a God who promises but a God who is faithful in keeping those promises (1 Cor. 1:9; 10:13; 2 Cor. 1:18; 1 Thess. 5:24; 2 Thess. 3:3; 2 Tim. 2:13; Heb. 11:11; Rev. 1:5).

Third, *an exhortation to fellowship* (vv. 24–25). Personal purity and fidelity are not enough. We are also encouraged to stir up within one another a deeper level of love for the community of believers as well as urge one another to do good deeds (cf. Titus 2:14; 3:8, 14; 1 Pet. 3:13). Essential to this are times of meaningful corporate worship, when we "meet together." Such times, our text reminds us, are not to be neglected, even though it had already become the habit of some to prefer privacy to church attendance. But these times together become meaningful only insofar as they are occasions for encouraging one another (3:13; 13:22). Even more important than mutual upbuilding, they serve as occasions to prepare for the coming of the Lord, the approaching Day (v. 25; cf. 1 Cor. 1:8).

Hebrews 4:14–16; 5:7–9

This set of texts serves as the alternate epistolary reading for Good Friday in all three years. The first part of this set of texts overlaps with the epistolary reading (Heb. 4:12–16) for Proper 23 in Year B. The second part overlaps with the epistolary lesson (Heb. 5:5–10) for the Fifth Sunday in Lent in Year B. The reader may wish to consult our remarks in these other settings.

The dominant christological image of these texts is Christ, the great high priest. It is the major christological theme elaborated in the Epistle to the Hebrews (2:17; 3:1; 5:5, 10; 6:20; 7:26; 8:1; 9:11; 10:21). Great emphasis is placed on the uniqueness of this role, so much so that Jesus is likened to the enigmatic Old Testament priest Melchizedek (5:10; 7:1–28; cf. Gen. 14:17–20). The metaphor of Jesus as high priest is employed as a way of comparing the work of Jesus with that of Levitical priests. One of its values is that it provides an image with which the readers can identify—the priest as a human figure known in everyday life. It thus serves as an effective image for underscoring the humanity of Jesus. But at the same time, the comparison serves to highlight the differences between Jesus and his priestly counterparts. What emerges is a figure who is incomparably superior.

The context in which today's epistolary text is read is Good Friday. Although it is important for the preacher to understand the Levitical priesthood and the elaborate, intricate christological argument unfolded in the Epistle to the Hebrews, we must not get lost in this sacerdotal labyrinth. We must grapple with the essential message of our text within this liturgical setting.

Above all, we should note the way in which our text encapsulates the essential paradox of the Christ-event that we celebrate. There are two strands woven together in our passage. On the one hand, our text speaks of *the* Son of God, the exalted Christ, the great high priest. Unlike the Levitical high priest, who annually passed through the outer sanctuary and entered the Most Holy Place, Christ has "passed through" in a more dramatic fashion: he has "passed through the heavens" (v. 14). No longer does this high priest enter the Holy of Holies, where God dwells *in absentia*. Instead, he presides at the heavenly throne of God. Here we have the heavenly exalted Christ.

But another strand is also woven through today's text. Alongside this image of the exalted Son of God is the high priest who knows human existence as we know it. We are told that "in the course of his earthly life" (5:7, REB) he begged God to deliver him from death. Here we detect a note of urgency, if not desperation. We are told of "prayers and supplications" uttered "with loud cries and tears" (v. 7). This is not the mood of quiet resignation, of stoic resolve. It is rather the imploring cry of a desperate human being facing death, looking for a way out. This may be a reference to the tradition of Jesus in Gethsemane (cf. Luke 22:32, 39–46; also John 17), or the author may have some other tradition or reminiscence in mind. The particular historical referent is immaterial. What is important is for us to see that it is the kind of fear with which we can all identify.

Our text also insists that Jesus "has been put to the test in exactly the same way as ourselves" (4:15, NJB). This is a claim against which the church has traditionally recoiled. It asserts a level of humanity that we find it hard to grant. Naturally, this was the central mystery with which the church dealt in the early christological controversies—how the divine Son of God could have been fully human, even to the point of experiencing every kind of testing that we undergo. Even so, we are told that he did, yet was "without sin" (4:15).

As much as Christian faith is anchored in the exalted Christ, so is it tied to the human figure Jesus. Thus we are reminded that "although he was a Son, he learned obedience through what he suffered" (5:8). It is a remarkable claim, because we all know that status and privilege often mean exemption from certain experiences. Not so here. Full participation in the human order of things was required for the Son of God to complete his work, that is, to be perfected (5:9). Consequently, he becomes the "source of eternal salvation for all who obey him" (5:9).

Another feature of today's text is that christological reflection is most fully realized in Christian behavior. We are invited to perceive truly who Christ was, but at the same time we are enjoined to "hold fast to our confession" (4:14). We are also urged to "approach the throne of grace and to do so "with boldness" (4:16). Christian belief must translate into Christian praxis. Christ's full identification with humanity gave us full access to God, and we are assured that it is possible to "receive mercy and find grace to help in time of need" (4:16).

Our great high priest may be lofty and exalted, but he has succeeded in bridging the gap between us and God. Like the true priest, he lives to assist us in finding God—even more, in being bold in this pursuit.

John 18:1–19:42

The reader will recall that on the Sixth Sunday of Lent, when observed as Passion rather than Palm Sunday, the lectionary offered the preacher two avenues in the Gospel texts. One possibility was to read, with or without comments, the Matthean narrative from the conspiracy of Judas (26:14) to the placing of guards at Jesus' tomb (27:66). The other was to develop a message on the crucifixion itself (27:11–54). Today, however, there is no alternative reading, and the text is John's, recording the story from the events in the garden (18:1) to the burial of Jesus (19:42). Of course, one has the choice to speak only of the crucifixion (19:17–30). Notice that whereas the Synoptics present Jesus' moving from the Last Supper to the garden, John separates the two scenes with Jesus' farewell discourses (chaps. 14–16) and his farewell prayer (chap. 17). John's time frame, however, seems to be the same as that of the Synoptics.

If it is the tradition of the congregation or choice of the minister to attend specifically to the crucifixion, two matters will be very important. One, let the descriptive element of the message be provided by the text rather than being a composite from all the Gospels. Hence there will be no crowds at the cross, no taunting passersby, no mocking, no conversation between Jesus and the others being crucified, no earthquake, and no splitting of the temple veil. The account of the crucifixion is very brief, briefer even than Mark's. Jesus is totally in charge. Jesus himself rather than Simon of Cyrene carries the cross. Jesus speaks and acts not out of need or desperation but to fulfill Scripture. There is no crying out to God as one forsaken. Rather, he commits his mother into the care of the disciple whom he loved (neither of whose names are ever mentioned in this Gospel), says that all is now complete or finished, and gives up his spirit. Unwitting contributions to the event are made by the soldiers, who fulfill Scripture (Ps. 22:18), and by Pilate, who proclaims in three languages that all may understand, "Jesus of Nazareth, the King of the Jews" (vv. 19–20).

The second matter of importance in developing a message on the crucifixion is giving attention to Johannine theology of Jesus' death. In verses 31–37, the Passover lamb interpretation is developed, but in verses 17–30, the image of king is very strong. Earlier, self-serving crowds had tried to make Jesus king (6:15), but Jesus' kingship is not by popular election. Curious crowds had hailed him king (12:13), but they had no idea what the title would mean for Jesus or for themselves. Pilate tossed about the title "king" in his interrogation of Jesus and in talking with the crowds outside the praetorium (18:28–19:16). But in his sarcastic baiting of the religious authorities into confessing "We have no king but the emperor" (19:15), Pilate has no understanding of Jesus' kingship. He, therefore, says more than he realizes when he proclaims Jesus "King of the Jews" (19:19). And so Jesus is lifted up on the cross, but also lifted up to God, enthroned by his executioners and glorified by those who think they have the power of life and death over Jesus. And through it all Jesus is in charge; even Pilate would have no authority were it not given to him from above (19:11). The final irony is complete: the violence of an unbelieving world is used of God for the world's salvation.

Long tradition, however, urges that the entirety of John 18:1–19:42 be used, perhaps in a three-hour Good Friday service. In this case, first priority should be given to the public reading of the text. This reading would create its own world in its own way and, therefore, need not be accompanied by comments, especially exhortations. The readings could well be divided into the following units, with music and prayers intervening. If brief comments attend each reading, these would properly precede rather than follow in each case and be descriptive, with only such explanations as would serve clarity.

The arrest (18:1–12)

Interrogation by religious leaders (18:13–27)

Interrogation by Pontius Pilate (18:28–19:16)

The crucifixion (19:17–30)

The burial (19:31–42)

Holy Saturday

Job 14:1–14 or Lamentations 3:1–9, 19–24;
Psalm 31:1–4, 15–16;
1 Peter 4:1–8;
Matthew 27:57–66 or John 19:38–42

These are somber texts for a somber day, but the church that confesses the resurrection of Jesus also confesses his death and burial. The Old Testament lections can be heard as stating the problems to which Easter is the response. Job raises but rejects the possibility of human rebirth or resurrection. The reading from Lamentations is a plea for God's help, a plea that ends on a note of confidence. Likewise, the responsorial psalm, a prayer for deliverance from trouble, includes expressions of trust in God. The epistle is appropriate on this day because of its allusion to the preaching of the gospel to the dead and also because it acknowledges human suffering and draws moral implications from the suffering of Christ. Both Gospel readings give accounts of the events between the crucifixion and the resurrection of Jesus. Matthew reports the burial of the body of Jesus and the sealing and guarding of the tomb. John tells how Joseph of Arimathea, with the help of Nicodemus, prepared the body of Jesus and placed it in a new tomb.

Job 14:1–14

Both the mood and the contents of this reading from the Book of Job provide important—one could argue, essential—preparation for Easter morning. Those who look forward to the proclamation of the resurrection of Jesus may dwell just one more day with the dark background for the light of the good news.

The passionate arguments of Job can be understood in part as challenges to a popular ideology in Israel, prominent in the wisdom literature and among the sages, an ideology that equated suffering and trouble with sin and guilt. The author of the book, through the main character's speeches, has no patience with simple answers to real problems. He rejects the arguments of his friends—who stand for the sages—that all suffering is the result of sin because God is just. To be sure, often it could and can be observed that it is the case that evil or unwise actions lead to baleful consequences. But not always. Consequently, Job even throws down the gauntlet to God, whom he accuses of being unfair.

In the text before us, Job goes beyond the problem of the suffering of the righteous to complain about the human condition as a whole. Our reading is part of the second cycle of speeches in the book, in which Job, responding in sequence to his interlocutors, speaks both to them and directly to God. In 14:1–14, he continues the address to God begun in chapter 13. The section, like other material in Job, has some of the features of a legal argument:

> "I have indeed prepared my case;
> I know that I shall be vindicated" (Job 13:18)

Job intends to prove to God that he is innocent and thus suffers unjustly (13:23–27). He pleads that God withdraw his hand and not terrify him (13:21).

In 14:1–14, the poet has Job argue his case in four movements. First, Job makes a general statement about the human condition (vv. 1–3). His complaint encompasses every human being. Every mortal is "few of days and full of trouble" (v. 1). Life is not only short, as ephemeral as a flower or a shadow, but it is filled with pain. Thus the argument concerns both life and death—life because it is full of trouble, and death because it comes too soon. He uses these observations—to him "facts"—as a basis for his argument with God, whom he addresses directly with rhetorical questions: Why would you bother to pay any attention to such a creature, or "bring him into court before you?" (v. 3, REB).

The second movement in the argument (vv. 4–6) leads to a plea that God simply leave human beings alone to count their days like laborers count their hours. The plea is driven by Job's protest that human days are determined. God knows the length of those days, and God has "appointed the bounds that they cannot pass" (v. 5). This probably does not refer to a specific length set by God in advance for every individual, but to death—that final boundary for all mortals.

The third movement (vv. 7–12) continues the train of the argument concerning human mortality, vigorously but unhappily affirming that "mortals die . . . humans expire" (v. 10). Job emphasizes the unfairness of that sad fact by comparing humanity with the tree. Even a tree has "hope," for if it is cut down it will live again; all it needs is water. The poet explicitly denies that mortals can rise again when they lie down; when they die they cannot "live again" (v. 12, REB). When he says that the dead remain so "until the sky splits open" (REB) or "until the heavens are no more" (NRSV), he is not speaking of an apocalyptic transformation of the world but is using hyperbole: There is as much chance of the dead living again as there is that the sky will split open.

In the final movement (vv. 13–14), Job almost wistfully expresses the hope for the impossible. He wonders if God could hide him away in the underworld (sheol) until God's wrath is past and then release him. The same Job who vehemently asserted that death is the end has his doubts, or possibly moments of denial. In the verse that follows our reading, Job expresses the wish that God would then long for the work of his hands, that is, his servant Job. Throughout the passage, Job alternatively wishes that God would let him alone in his sad lot and yet hopes to be with God, a God who will accept him. He bemoans both the presence and the absence of God.

An argument that begins with the sadness of life is driven by the acknowledgment of death. The rejection of immortality or resurrection is so vehement that it might be polemic against such beliefs, for example, as found in Egyptian religion from the earliest times. But Job's view is typical of ancient Israel and widely assumed in the Old Testament. With the exception of two texts that speak of resurrection (Dan. 12:1–3, Isa. 26:19), the Old Testament takes it for granted that death is the final boundary. Although that view can lead to Job's frustration with God or Qohelet's disillusionment, it is remarkable that the people of

Israel—and individual Israelites—could throughout the centuries live the life of faith within the boundaries set by birth and death. Above all, on the day before Easter, the day before Jesus was raised from the dead, Christians could well ponder the fact that the resurrection of Jesus and the Easter faith mean little without death as a reality.

Lamentations 3:1–9, 19–24

Framed in the Book of Lamentations by four complaints of the community, chapter 3 is the complaint of an individual, the unnamed "one" (NRSV, "man" REB) of verse 1. The identity of the community in the other poems in the book is clear: it is the people of Israel. But for whom does the complainant of chapter 3 stand? In the liturgical context of the Christian church on Holy Saturday, the words of the sufferer will be heard as the voice of Jesus, very much in the sense of the words of Psalm 22 (another individual complaint) uttered from the cross: "My God, my God, why have you forsaken me?" But because Jesus in his suffering and death stands with all who suffer and die, these words may express their feelings as well.

The background and the theme of the Book of Lamentations is the destruction of the city of Jerusalem by the Babylonians in 587 BC. During and after the Exile, these poems functioned in liturgical settings—quite possibly on fast days—to help the survivors and their descendants come to terms with that national disaster and the crisis of faith it produced. The laments are similar in mood, tone, and function to dirges or funeral songs. By recounting and bewailing the destruction and even acknowledging that God had become the enemy, the people expressed and hoped to come to terms with their sense of loss, their grief, and their anger. Moreover, by understanding the destruction as punishment for sin, those people confessed their corporate sins.

Like the four other poems in the book, chapter 3 is an alphabetic acrostic; that is, successive lines begin with successive letters of the Hebrew alphabet. But chapter 3 stands out from the others as the voice of an individual. It would not have been surprising if this individual were a woman, because the other complaints often personify the destroyed city of Jerusalem as a woman. But the individual clearly is male, and that fact has led to many attempts to identify the speaker. Because the prophet Jeremiah often uttered similar complaints, he has been proposed as this individual. Others have argued that the speaker is the servant in Isaiah 40–55, at times an individual but also identified as Israel. But within the literary and liturgical context of the book, chapter 3 most likely views the national disaster and disgrace from the perspective of an individual who experienced it.

Our reading encompasses two parts of the fuller lament. In the first section (vv. 1–9, 19–20), the unidentified individual utters his complaints against God. The leading image is darkness (vv. 2, 6), contrasting with living in the light of God's presence. The tone of the complaint is similar to that of the Book of Job, seen in the other Old Testament reading for Holy Saturday. But although Job objected to unfair or unmerited suffering, in this prayer the sufferer is struggling for a way to live with suffering that is justified, that is punishment for sins. God has turned his hand against this person and even refuses to answer his prayers (v. 8); God has put him in chains and boxed him in (vv. 7, 9). The particulars of the suffering are not detailed and could fit any number of circumstances, including physical illness. But the petitioner makes it abundantly clear just how much he has suffered. This account of suffering continues through verse 20.

The second part of our reading (vv. 21–24) begins a longer unit in which the mood, tone, and contents are dramatically different. Now the petitioner expresses his hope (vv. 21, 24) and confesses his confidence in the Lord. He knows that the "steadfast love" and the "mercies" of the Lord never cease, that God is faithful; therefore, the one in trouble can turn to him.

This poem, including the shift of mood and contents, is parallel in many ways to the individual complaint songs of the Book of Psalms. The central element of these songs is a petition, a request that God help the one in trouble. They also contain complaints about the suffering and about God's failure to help or God's absence, as well as confessions of sin or of innocence. There will be expressions of confidence in God's capacity and willingness to help. Parallel to verses 21–24 are the affirmations that God has heard and will act (e.g., Ps. 6:8–10). It is very likely that in the liturgical use of such songs another voice, that of a priest, would have been heard just before these affirmations. The priest would have pronounced a salvation oracle, a message from God to the petitioner, for example, "Fear not, the Lord has heard your prayer."

Songs such as this one, and the liturgical patterns they reflect, may provide guidance for our meditations, our words, and our actions. This poem moves toward the affirmation of faith in the gracious and merciful God who hears prayers, but it begins with vigorous complaints against God. Ancient Israel clearly believed that all feelings could be brought before God. Can prayers—even those that confess the experience of divine punishment or the absence of God—be answered unless they are expressed?

Psalm 31:1–4, 15–16

Few psalms use such graphic descriptions to depict human misery and affliction as does Psalm 31. The descriptions are very graphic although reasonably nonspecific. Thus, when persons used this psalm in worship to describe their state of being, they could vent true feelings yet do so in highly stylized terms. Praying this psalm allowed persons to verbalize and express the deep-seated sense of alienation and hurt that they were feeling. The language appears to be highly metaphorical, probably using stereotypical and formulaic expressions that were highly graphic in content and emotional in nature. The labeling of one's troubles in such graphic fashion was probably therapeutic in and of itself because it allowed one to express sorrow and grief.

The overall structure of the psalm is as follows: (1) a general opening address to God, which already contains an initial plea for help (vv. 1–2); (2) a statement of confidence and trust in God (vv. 3–6); (3) a future-oriented statement of confidence (vv. 7–8); (4) a description of the trouble and distress (vv. 9–13); (5) a third statement of confidence (vv. 14–15a); (6) a second plea for help (vv. 15b–18); (7) a fourth assertion of confidence (vv. 19–20); (8) proclamation (v. 21); (9) thanksgiving (v. 22); and (10) admonition (vv. 23–24).

The relevance of this psalm for Holy Saturday lies in its usage of the imagery of death to describe a human situation. The psalmist declares that he or she is like one already dead—passed out of life and even out of memory, cast aside like the shattered pieces of a broken pot; unwanted, useless, fit only for the garbage heap of the city dump (v. 12).

In fact, the psalmist describes the many out there who not only dislike him or her but who even scheme and plot to take life (v. 13). Such language as this may sound like the ravings of a paranoid but should be seen as therapeutic language that allowed distressed persons to objectify their suffering to its most graphic, even exaggerated, level.

This psalm is not simply a recitation of a vale of sorrows. Throughout the text there are frequent statements of a calm confidence in the Deity. Such is to be found in verses 14–15, in which the worshiper confesses trust in God and affirms that come what may the times of one's life are in the hand of God, who can deliver one from the hand of enemies and persecutors.

Confidence in the Deity fades naturally into plea and petition for salvation (vv. 15b–16). In spite of the description of the supplicant's condition in such sorrow-drawn and affliction-etched contours, confidence and calm flow through the psalm like a soothing stream. The crucified, dead, and buried awaits the resurrection, life in the morning.

1 Peter 4:1–8

In the context of Holy Saturday, we think especially of Christ's suffering in the flesh, the note on which today's epistolary lection opens (v. 1). This opening verse recalls 1 Peter 3:18, where the atoning effects of Christ's death are highlighted.

Another element in our passage that makes it appropriate to this liturgical setting is the cryptic reference in verse 6, where the gospel is said to have been "proclaimed even to the dead." This was done, we are told, "so that, though in their bodies they had undergone the judgement that faces all humanity, in their spirit they might enjoy the life of God" (v. 6b, NJB).

It is possible that the "dead" referred to here are the spiritually dead (cf. Eph. 2:5), in which case verse 6 would be a general statement explaining the purpose of the Christian mission. Possibly in view are Christians who have died, in which case the reassurance is similar to that given by Paul in 1 Thessalonians 4:13–18. More likely, however, our text recalls the Christian tradition mentioned earlier (1 Pet. 3:19–20) that while Jesus was entombed he proclaimed salvation to those who had already died ("the spirits in prison," 3:19). According to this tradition, during Christ's descent into Hades, the realm of the dead, in the interval between his death and resurrection he preached to those who had preceded him, either faithful Jews whose deeds were recorded in the Old Testament, or those disobedient in the days of Noah, or all of humanity. Regardless of the specific identity of the addressees, the point is to emphasize that Christ extended the message of God's saving grace to those who are ostensibly excluded, those who lived prior to his time. Because those who had lived before the time of Christ had heard the gospel, God's judgment is appropriately universal (v. 5).

We should note especially the connection made in today's text between Christ's suffering (death) and the moral life. In fact, our text consists largely of moral exhortation, whose general theme is a summons "to live . . . no longer by human desires but by the will of God" (v. 2). The pagan life-style recently abandoned by these newly converted Christian readers is vividly sketched (v. 3), and they are now warned to be prepared to pay the price of nonconformity (v. 4). They are reminded that society will be "surprised" at their newly acquired life-style and that they will have to endure verbal abuse from their detractors (v. 4). But assured that their "cultured despisers" will have to give their own accounting (vv. 5–6), the readers are reminded of the nearness of the end (v. 7a) and asked to conduct themselves accordingly. They are to be serious about life, disciplined in their spiritual pursuits (v. 7), and are asked to commit themselves to "constant love for one another" (v. 8).

What is called for here is a form of community where forgiving love is the preeminent reality—love that "covers a multitude of sins."

An especially intriguing exegetical question and one well worth pursuing occurs in verse 1: "For whoever has suffered in the flesh has finished with sin." The remark is treated parenthetically by the NRSV, but not by NJB, REB, and NIV. Some commentators observe that this may be a variation of a current proverb "Death pays all debts" and thus should be construed as a comment about the finality of death. Because of the emphasis throughout 1 Peter on suffering (1:6; 2:20; 3:14; 4:1, 12–13, 16; 5:9–10), some have taken it to mean that a martyr's death has an atoning effect. Because of its similarity with the proverbial expression in Romans 6:7, "For whoever has died is freed from sin," it perhaps should be understood in a similar sense: the one who has undergone the ritual death of baptism experiences liberation from the bondage of sin. This latter interpretation seems supported by verse 2.

Regardless of the interpretation we adopt, it is important to do justice to the explicit connection made in the passage between suffering and sin. The sense seems to be that suffering itself, especially that which results from being treated unjustly for a just cause, throws sin into a fresh perspective—not only the sin of those who cause others to suffer but the sin of the sufferer. In the one instance, it exposes the inanity of sin; in the other, the insanity of sin. If we suffer unjustly at the hands of others, we experience the senselessness of such wrong. Yet even while experiencing such injustice, we rethink our own wrongs, wishing we had never done them, resolving never to do them again. It is this preemptive role of suffering that seems to be in view here. Christ's suffering simultaneously exposed humanity's sin and the need to live by the will of God. So should our own suffering and death, both our ritual enactment of Christ's death in baptism as well as the suffering that we experience as humans, either as part of our own human experience or as a direct result of our faithful witness, cause us to abandon the impulse to live by our "human desires" and compel us to live "by the will of God" (v. 2).

Matthew 27:57–66 or John 19:38–42

For those churches providing Holy Saturday services, alternate readings are available. Both are accounts of the burial of Jesus. The preacher will notice that both lections were part of extended readings earlier: Matthew 27:57–66 on Palm/Passion Sunday and John 19:38–42 on Good Friday. Most likely the reappearance of these texts on Holy Saturday restrained the preacher from making comments earlier about the burial itself. On Palm/Passion Sunday and Good Friday the lectionary suggested a wide-angle lens; here, a close up.

Three reminders may be in order here. First, these are alternate readings and are not to be conflated or harmonized. Matthew and John do have a number of common elements (Joseph of Arimathea, request for the body from Pilate, Friday evening, new tomb, etc.), but one needs to respect the different purposes and audiences of the Evangelists. Second, the burial of Jesus is not an insignificant item in Christian theology. Perhaps proof of the resurrection of the body is involved here. Or the writers may be addressing those Christians found in some early churches who had no place for the physical in their views of Jesus Christ. Persons who denied that Jesus Christ had come in the flesh were certainly known in the Johannine community (1 John 4:2–3). But whatever the reasons, the burial of Jesus came to be stated explicitly in Christian confessions, as early as 1 Corinthians 15:4 and as officially as the Apostles Creed. And finally, restraint on the part of both preacher and liturgist is essential for the worship to be truly a Holy Saturday service. It is, of course, tempting and easy to steal from tomorrow, to break the seal on the tomb, and to have a pre-Easter Easter service. Admittedly, it is difficult for the church to say, even for two days, "Jesus is dead."

Matthew devotes two paragraphs to the burial of Jesus (vv. 57–61, 62–66). There needs to be a conclusion to the crucifixion story. After all, closure demands answers to basic questions: What happened to the body? Who prepared it? Where was it entombed? But Matthew has more in mind; he is concerned to argue for, to provide proofs for, the resurrection of Jesus. Therefore, he tells the reader that the body was released to Joseph by Pilate's order; Joseph placed the body in a new tomb hewn out of a rock; a huge stone was placed over the opening to the tomb; two women witnessed all this; religious authorities secured the support of Pilate to prevent a theft of the body and a claim of resurrection; the tomb was governmentally sealed (a stronger safeguard than a police cordon today); Roman guards kept sentinel watch. Matthew is not simply witnessing to the resurrection, as was the case with early Christian preaching (Acts 2:32; 3:15; 4:33), but he is already involved in what later became quite common, attempts to *prove* that Jesus was raised from the dead. Such an approach to the resurrection, and to other doctrines, assumes that faith is the response of the mind to the evidence presented. Such faith is not without merit, but it is *belief that,* not *trust in.*

John also devotes two paragraphs to the corpse of Jesus (vv. 31–37, 38–42), but only the second is our concern here. The former is an extraordinary theological treatise relating the body of Jesus to fulfilled prophecy, the Jewish Passover, the Eucharist and baptism. In verses 38–42, it seems important to this Evangelist to point out that two disciples who had been private, secretive, and fearful in their relation to Jesus now act openly, with courage and at great expense. Some readers of this account are quite critical of Joseph and Nicodemus, observing that the two come out of hiding now that the battle is over. Jesus needed disciples, they say, not caretakers. Other readers are more positive, finding in this burial scene the consistency of John's theology. Even in his death, they say, Jesus continues to draw the hesitant and unbelieving. Jesus had said as much: in death I will draw all people to myself (12:32).

Easter Vigil

Genesis 1:1–2:4a
    Psalm 136:1–9, 23–26
Genesis 7:1–5, 11–18;
    8:6–18; 9:8–13
    Psalm 46
Genesis 22:1–18
    Psalm 16
Exodus 14:10–31; 15:20–21
    Exodus 15:1b–13, 17–18
Isaiah 55:1–11
    Isaiah 12:2–6
Baruch 3:9–15, 32–4:4 or

Proverbs 8:1–8, 19–21; 9:4b
    Psalm 19
Ezekiel 36:24–28
    Psalm 42 and 43
Ezekiel 37:1–14
    Psalm 143
Zephaniah 3:14–20
    Psalm 98
Romans 6:3–11
    Psalm 114
Matthew 28:1–10

In the ancient church, the tradition of the Easter Vigil played an important role. Catechumens, after remaining awake and watchful throughout Saturday night, were baptized early on Easter morning and then joined the Christian community in Holy Communion. Although this tradition was lost in the later Western church, it has been somewhat restored in churches that hold midnight services. The readings for the Easter Vigil provide a compendium of the sacred past of Israel and of texts seen to foretell and foreshadow the messianic age.

Genesis 1:1–2:4a

For further commentary on this text, which contains the Priestly Writer's account of creation, see the commentary for Trinity Sunday in this volume.

In contrast to the Yahwist's account that follows in chapter 2, the mood of the story is solemn and measured; the repetition of phrases lends a liturgical dignity to the recital. If the account was not actually put into this form for worship, it certainly was shaped by persons with a deep interest in liturgy. In terms of structure, the report consists of two uneven parts, Genesis 1:1–31 and Genesis 2:1–3, that is, the six days of creation and the seventh day of rest. One of the purposes of the story in its present form is to account for the sabbath rest. It was divinely ordained from the very first, and thus is taken by our writer as the most universal of laws.

Creation is not *ex nihilo*, out of nothing, but out of chaos. Before creation there were the primeval waters, within which God established the world. Moreover, as the Priestly account of the Flood indicates (Gen. 7:11), the waters of chaos stand as the alternative to creation. If God withdraws his hand, the waters can return. In that sense, then, this chapter actually understands God as both creator and sustainer of the world.

In sharp contrast to the other account of creation that begins in Genesis 2:4b, God is transcendent and distant. The only actor or speaker in this chapter is God, by whose word or act all things that are come into being. Human beings certainly occupy an important place. They are created last of all and then are given stewardship over the creation. If this moving and majestic account can be said to have a major point, it is in the divine pronouncement that recurs throughout: "And God saw that it was good." The natural order is good not only because God created it, but also because God determined that it was so.

Psalm 136:1–9, 23–26

Psalm 136 is a communal psalm of thanksgiving recalling the great activities of God in the past. In its structure it parallels much of the first six books of the Bible—the Hexateuch, Genesis to Joshua. The following is the structure of the psalm: (1) the community is called to offer thanksgiving (vv. 1–3); (2) God is praised as creator (vv. 4–9); (3) as the one who brought Israel out of Egypt (vv. 10–15); (4) as the one who led them in the wilderness (v. 16); (5) as the one who granted the people the land of promise (vv. 17–22); and (6) as the one who continues the divine action of providing for the people (vv. 23–26). The constantly repeated refrain "for his steadfast love [or mercy] endures forever" indicates that this psalm was sung or chanted antiphonally.

The verses selected for the Easter Vigil are those concerned with God's acts in creation (vv. 4–9), the personal affirmation of divine care (vv. 23–25), and the call upon all to give thanks (vv. 1–3, 26).

Genesis 7:1–5, 11–18; 8:6–18; 9:8–13

Like Genesis 1, the account of the Flood is part of the primeval history, the story not just of Israel but of the entire human race. Between that initial chapter and Genesis 7, a great deal has transpired. There was the second account of creation coupled with story of the Fall, ending with the expulsion of the original pair from the garden. Next came the story of Cain and Abel, when a brother kills a brother. Then follow genealogies along with short reports of events in the lives of the earliest generations. The immediate background of the flood story is the little account in Genesis 6:1–4 of how the "sons of God" took the "daughters of humans" and gave birth to a race of giants. From the accounts of creation to the time of Noah, the story is basically one of human sin and disorder, culminating in God's decision to put an end to the race, with the exception of Noah and his family.

The Flood marks an important turning point in biblical history, but as the Book of Genesis is organized, it is not the most decisive one. Following the Flood, the history of human sinfulness continues with the story of the Tower of Babel. The critical event is reported in Genesis 12:1ff., the call of Abraham. To be sure, sin continues, but now, with the promise of Abraham, the direction of history is known. It becomes a history of salvation.

The verses for this reading comprise a rather full account of the Flood, with the exception of the report of God's decision and his instructions to Noah (for further commentary, see below, Proper 4). The assigned text comes mainly from the Priestly Writer, but some of it is from the Yahwist, whose name for God in most translations is LORD. It is also the Yahwist who reports that seven pairs of clean and one pair of unclean animals went into the ark; P has one pair of every kind. Moreover, in P the water comes when the floodgates of heaven are opened; the Yahwist speaks of rain. But according to both writers, God put an end to all human beings except that one family, and afterward vowed not to do it again. The reading appropriately ends with the good news that the natural order will abide and the rainbow will be a sign of God's promise.

Psalm 46

This psalm praises God for the divine care of the people and especially for Jerusalem, the City of God. With its emphasis on security in the midst of great turmoil and disruptions in the earth, it provides a proper response to the narrative of the Flood. The worshipers confess, as Noah and his family may have, that they have nothing to fear should the mountains quake and the whole of the cosmos become chaos again.

Genesis 22:1–18

One must keep in mind the framework in which this reading is placed—both in the Book of Genesis and in the Old Testament—or important aspects of it will be missed. The context is the narrative of the patriarchs, Abraham, Isaac, Jacob, and the sons of Jacob, the leading theme of which is the promise that their descendants will become a great nation, will own their land, and will be a blessing to all the peoples of the earth (Gen. 12:1–3). The fulfillment of those promises comes first with the Exodus and then with the occupation of the land of Canaan as reported in the Book of Joshua. (For further commentary on this text, see below, Proper 8.)

The immediate prelude to this story is the report in Genesis 22:1–7 of the birth of Isaac. The promise of descendants had been repeated to Abraham and Sarah over and over. Just when it appeared that all hope was lost, they are given a son in their old age. Isaac is not simply symbolic testimony that the divine promise is trustworthy; he is also actually the first step in the fulfillment of that promise.

And then comes the account in Genesis 22:1–18 of God testing Abraham by means of a command that threatened to take away the child of the promise. It is certainly one of the most poignant and moving stories in the Bible, and all the more so because of its restraint. Emotions are not described or analyzed, but the reader or hearer can sense the fear and grief. Even though we know how the story comes out, each time we read it we can experience the rising tension, feeling that the results may still be in doubt. Will Abraham go through with the sacrifice of Isaac? Will the angel speak up before it is too late?

The story is so meaningful and fruitful and has been told in so many ways over the centuries that it would be a serious mistake to reduce it to a single point. At one level, in the old oral tradition, it probably dealt with the question of child sacrifice. Being among cultures where child sacrifice was a genuine possibility, some early Israelites could well have asked, "Does our God require that we sacrifice our children?" The answer, through this account, is a resounding no. Our ancestor was willing, but God did not require it. The sacrifice of a ram was sufficient. In the framework of the Easter Vigil, one is reminded that God gave his Son.

The leading theme of the story, as recognized through centuries of interpretation, is faith. It is, as the initial verse says, the test of Abraham's faith. What is faith? The biblical tradition answers not with a theological statement, or with a set of propositions, or with admonitions to be faithful, but with a story. It is the story of Abraham, who trusted in God even when God appeared to be acting against his promise. Faith is like that. Faith in this sense is commitment, the directing of one's trust toward God. And it entails great risk, not in the sense of accepting a set of beliefs, but by acting in trust. Did Abraham know that the God he worshiped would not require the life of Isaac? We cannot know. We are told only how the patriarch acted and how God acted.

Psalm 16

This psalm, probably originally used as a lament by an individual during a time of sickness, contains a strong statement of devotion of God and thus can be read as a theological counterpart to the narrative of Abraham, whose faithfulness led him to the point of sacrificing his son, Isaac. Like Abraham, the psalmist shows confidence in whatever fate or lot God might assign. This psalm came to be understood in the early church as a prediction of the resurrection, especially Christ's resurrection, and was quoted in this regard by Peter in his sermon at Pentecost (see Acts 2:22–28).

Exodus 14:10–31; 15:20–21

With this reading, we come close to the heart of the Old Testament story and the Old Testament faith. In ancient Israel's faith, no affirmation is more central than the confession that the Lord is the one who brought them out of Egypt. Traditions concerning the Exodus provide the fundamental language through which Israel understood both herself and her God. The basic focus of most of those traditions is upon the saving activity of the Lord; this history is a story of salvation.

The account in Exodus 14 actually follows the Exodus itself. The departure from Egypt had been reported in Exodus 12 and 13; the rescue of the people at the sea happens when they are already in the wilderness. The two themes that mark the stories of the wandering in the wilderness are already present in this chapter, namely, Israel's complaints against Moses and the Lord (14:10–13) and the Lord's miraculous care (14:13–18, 30–31). The report does mark, however, Israel's final escape from the Egyptian danger, and this relates directly to the theme of the Exodus itself.

This reading, like the flood story, is the combination of at least two of the sources of the Pentateuch, those of the Priestly Writer and of the Yahwist. Two virtually complete accounts have been combined. The writers tell the story differently, with P reporting a dramatic crossing of the sea between walls of water (v. 22) and J speaking of a "strong east wind" (v. 21) and the chariots clogged in the mud as the water returns (v. 25). But a more important implication of the source division for our use of the text in the context of worship is the recognition that the sources place very different theological interpretations upon what happened. For the Priestly Writer, the emphasis is on revelation. The Lord "hardened the heart of Pharaoh" (vv. 8, 17) to pursue the Israelites in order to "gain glory for myself over Pharaoh and all his army" (v. 17). That is, the Lord's purpose is for the Egyptians to "know that I am the Lord" (v. 18). For the Yahwist, the purpose is the salvation of the people (v. 13) and their consequent faith, not only in the Lord, but also in Moses (vv. 30–31). In the combined report, both themes are important. God acts in order to reveal who God is and also to save the chosen people. And the people, led by Miriam and "all the women," are called to respond with a song of praise.

Exodus 15:1b–13, 17–18

The psalm text overlaps with the Old Testament reading and continues it. Moses, having led the Israelites in their escape from the Egyptians at the sea, now leads them in worship. The expression of praise is generally identified as the Song of Moses, and much of it is in the first person singular, "I will sing to the Lord." But the introduction points out that it was sung by Moses and the people, and its communal, congregational character is evident throughout. Although the song is not in the Psalter, it is a psalm nonetheless and probably was used in worship by faithful Israelites through the centuries. The initial lines are placed in the mouth of Miriam in Exodus 15:21, except that they are in the second person instead of the first; she calls for the people to sing to the Lord.

The song is a hymn of praise, specifically praise of the Lord for saving the people at the sea. The hymn is, for the most part, narrative in form; that is, it praises God by recounting the story of God's mighty deeds. In one sense, what emerges is another interpretation of the rescue at the sea, different in some respects from the accounts in Exodus 14. But the language is at points highly metaphorical and rich in imagery that goes beyond the immediate events.

Recollection of the Lord's saving activity at the sea evokes two leading themes in the hymn. The first concerns God's awesome power over events and nature. The specific form of that theme here emphasizes the image of the Lord as a warrior who triumphs over his enemies. But it also asserts that the God praised here is incomparable; there is none like this one (vv. 11, 18). The second theme of the hymn concerns God's love and care for the people whom he has redeemed. God is strength, song, salvation (v. 2), the one who cares for these people out of steadfast love (v. 13). Moreover, God's past care for the people gives rise to the hope that he will continue to act in their behalf in the future (v. 17) and will reign forever (v. 18).

Isaiah 55:1–11

Again, as is so often the case in the lectionary as a whole, the words of Second Isaiah come before us. This text from the end of the Babylonian Exile was a call for hope and trust and a promise of salvation to the hearers; it reiterates that same call and promise during the Easter Vigil.

The passage has two distinct parts, verses 1–5 and 6–11, which are similar in both form and content. In the first section, God is the speaker throughout, addressing the people of Israel as a whole. The speaker begins with a series of imperatives (vv. 1–3a) that resemble on the one hand Lady Wisdom's invitation to a banquet (Prov. 9:5) and on the other hand the calls of street vendors. The invitations to come for what the Lord has to offer are both literal and metaphorical: God offers actual food, and "food" that enables one to live the abundant life ("that you may live," v. 3*a*). What the people are invited to "come, buy and eat" is the proclamation of salvation that follows in verses 3*b*–5. God announces that the ancient covenant with David (2 Sam. 7) now applies to the people as a whole. Again, Israel has in no sense earned this new covenant; it is a free act of God's grace. Moreover, as the Lord made David a witness to the nations, now all nations will come to the people of Israel. The proclamation of salvation, then, is ultimately directed toward all peoples.

The second section (vv. 6–11) also begins with imperatives, calls to "seek the Lord" and to "call upon him." The "wicked" and "unrighteous" are invited to change their ways and "return to the Lord." These invitations, although addressed to the human heart, are quite concrete. To "seek" and "call upon" the Lord refer to acts of prayer and worship. For the wicked to "forsake their way" is to change behavior. The foundation for the imperatives is stated at the end of verse 7, "for he will abundantly pardon." The remainder of the section (vv. 8–11) gives the basis for responding to God's call. God's plan for the world ("ways," "thoughts") is in sharp contrast to human designs. That plan is the announcement of salvation that the prophet has presented throughout the book, the redemption and renewal of the people. The will of God is effected by the word of God, another theme found throughout Isaiah 40–55. That word is the one uttered at creation (Gen. 1:3ff.), and it is the divine announcement of the future through the prophets. In its emphasis on the word of God and its contrast between human and divine wisdom, this concluding section of Second Isaiah alludes to the beginning of the work (Isa. 40:1–11).

Isaiah 12:2–6

Not all Old Testament psalms are found in the Psalter. Isaiah 12 actually includes two, along with traces of the liturgical instructions (vv. 1*a*, 4*a*). The songs conclude the first section of the Book of Isaiah and suggest that the prophetic book was used in worship even before an official canon of scripture was established. Both psalms are songs of thanksgiving. The first (vv. 1–3) celebrates and gives thanks for deliverance from trouble. In verse 2 is echoed the vocabulary of the Song of Moses (Exod. 15:2), moving from thanks for a specific divine act to generalizations about the nature of God as the one who saves and who is the strength, song, and salvation of the worshiper. The second psalm (vv. 4–6) consists almost entirely of calls to give thanks and praise (v. 4). God is praised especially for mighty deeds. Because God, the Holy One of Israel, is great, all the earth should know this, and those who live in the shadow of the temple in Zion should sing for joy.

Baruch 3:9–15, 32–4:4

This passage, often characterized as a hymn to wisdom, is not actually a song of praise such as those in the Book of Psalms. Although it does characterize and praise wisdom, it is basically an admonition to the people of Israel to listen to and learn from wisdom.

The Book of Baruch is attributed to Jeremiah's scribe and placed in the Babylonian Exile, but it actually originated in a later time. The section from which this reading comes is like other late wisdom literature such as the Wisdom of Solomon. It identifies wisdom with the law of Moses, "the commandments of life" (3:9), and "the way of God" (3:13; see also 4:1). Behind that answer stands a question that became prominent in the so-called intertestamental period: Is there a conflict between the truth that can be discerned by human reflection and that which is revealed in the law?

Our text alludes to the Babylonian Exile (3:10–13), but the Exile is characterized as a spiritual situation of separation from God rather than the actual captivity. The verses not included in the reading (3:16–31) also contain somewhat spiritualized allusions to the history of Israel. The reading finds its place in the Easter Vigil, first because of the references to death and its alternative. Israel, growing old in a foreign land, is as good as dead (3:10–11) because the people have forsaken "the fountain of wisdom" (3:12). If they will attend to wisdom, they will gain strength, understanding, life, and peace (3:14). All who hold fast to wisdom will live, and those who forsake her will die (4:1). The second reason for the use of this passage in the Easter Vigil is its theme of wisdom as the gift of God that reveals the divine will to human beings. This is quite explicit in 3:37, which is echoed in John 1:14 and has been taken as a reference to the coming of Jesus.

Proverbs 8:1–8, 19–21; 9:4b

The reading from Proverbs 8 is part of a unit that is among a series of twelve extended addresses in Proverbs 1–9. These are instructions concerning wisdom or speeches by wisdom herself. All are reflections upon the nature of wisdom as well as admonitions and exhortations to follow wisdom. Each is a carefully crafted composition that probably arose among Israel's sages for the purpose of teaching their students.

Chapter 8 is the eleventh address. Following an introduction of the speaker in verses 1–3, the remainder is an address by wisdom herself. Beginning with rhetorical questions (v. 1), the writer sets the stage for the speech by wisdom, personified as a female figure. As in the NJPSV, one could appropriately capitalize her names: Wisdom and Understanding. Her speech will be in all kinds of public places: "On the heights," "beside the way," "at the crossroads," "the gates," "the entrance to the portals." These lines indicate that wisdom is easy to find and eager to be heard by all.

In verses 4–8, Wisdom speaks in the first person, urging all to pay attention, but she particularly urges "the simple ones" to listen to her. Then she gives the reasons why people should attend to her words: she speaks only "noble things," "what is right," "truth," and straight words that are "righteous."

Verses 19–21 continue to present reasons for following the words of Wisdom. First, the fruit of wisdom is better than gold and silver (8:19). Second, Wisdom walks in and therefore leads her followers in the paths of justice and righteousness (8:20). Here we see that the sages were concerned with the same values as were the prophets. Third, it is prudent to follow Wisdom because the one who does so prospers (8:21).

Wisdom, understood as present in the world, describes herself as the first of God's creations, the principle that guided God's formation of all that is (8:22–31). Certainly those who wrote and those who read wisdom literature were concerned about the relationship between wisdom and the revealed law, between knowledge gained by experience and piety. They concluded that, in the final analysis, there was no conflict between the two: "The fear of the Lord [genuine piety] is the beginning of wisdom, and the knowledge of the Holy One is insight" (9:10).

Psalm 19

This psalm of hymnic praise of God declares that God has communicated the divine will and knowledge of the Divine through nature—verses 1–6—and through the law, or Torah—verses 7–13. Without speech, God's voice is heard in the world of nature, and divine communication, like the light of the sun, falls everywhere and nothing can hide from it. In the Torah, God's will is embodied in commandment and precept, and offers its blessings to those whose ways it directs and guards.

Ezekiel 36:24–28

This reading is the central section of a passage in which Ezekiel presents the divine announcement of a new Israel. God, through the prophet (see vv. 22, 32) is the speaker. This dramatic announcement of good news presupposes that the people of God are in trouble. The description of that trouble is given in the context (vv. 16–21) and alluded to in our reading. Israel is in exile, away from the sacred land, but the trouble is even deeper. Separation from the land corresponds to separation from their God. They are in exile because of their sin, their disobedience that led to uncleanness. Now God is about to act, not because Israel deserves it, but for the sake of "my holy name" (v. 22).

There are two aspects to the coming work of salvation, one external and one internal, corresponding to Israel's present plight. First, the Lord will gather up the people and return them to their land (v. 24). But if they are to remain there (v. 26), a major transformation must occur. That is the second aspect of the good news, the establishment of a new covenant (see Isa. 54:10; 55:3) with a new Israel. This transformation is spelled out in terms of three distinct steps: (1) the Lord will sprinkle (cf. Exod. 24:6) the people with water, purifying them from their uncleanness; (2) God will give them a new heart and a new spirit, replacing their heart of stone with one of flesh (cf. Jer. 31:31); and (3) God will put his own "spirit" within them. "Spirit" here represents both the willingness and the ability to act in obedience. The promise is summarized by the reiteration of the ancient covenant formula "You shall be my people, and I will be your God" (v. 28). The radical difference between this new covenant and the old one is that the Lord himself will enable the people to be faithful.

Psalm 42 and 43

Although divided into two psalms in the course of transmission, Psalms 42 and 43 were probably originally one psalm. This is indicated by the repeated refrain in 42:5, 11 and 43:5.

This psalm can be closely associated with the sentiments of Ezekiel 36:24–28, the Old Testament lesson to which it is a response. Ezekiel predicts the coming rescue of God's people from exile and the transformation of the human personality and will. The psalm, originally used as an individual lament, early became associated with the Easter Vigil because it expressed the people's longing for redemption and their lamenting over being absent from the sanctuary. The psalm presupposes that the speaker is living away from the Sacred City. The psalmist's thought about former days when the worshiper went on a pilgrimage to Jerusalem only intensifies the depression and despair that accompany living in a foreign and hostile land and heightens the desire to be at home again in the temple.

Ezekiel 37:1–14

This text is also the Old Testament reading for the Fifth Sunday in Lent. See that setting for further commentary.

Ezekiel's vision of the valley of dry bones, like so many other Old Testament readings for this season, stems from the era of the Babylonian Exile. That it is a vision report is indicated by the introductory formula "The hand of the Lord came upon me," which the prophet uses elsewhere to begin reports of ecstatic experiences (Ezek. 3:22). The report is in the first person and, like most prophetic vision reports, consists of two parts, the description of what was revealed (vv. 1–10) and the interpretation (vv. 11–14). Throughout there is a dialogue between Yahweh and Ezekiel.

The message from the Lord communicated through the report is the response to the problem stated in verse 11. The people of Israel are saying, "Our bones are dried up, and our hope is lost; we are cut off completely." Ezekiel sees himself carried by the spirit of Yahweh to a valley full of bones, like the scene of an ancient battle. When the Lord asks if the bones can live again, Ezekiel gives the only possible answer, "O Lord God, you know" (v. 3). Although the nuance of the response is not immediately plain, it becomes clear in the context; the God of Israel can indeed bring life in the midst of death. When the prophet obeys the command to prophesy to the bones, a distinct sequence of events transpires: bones to bones, sinews to bones, flesh on the bones, and then skin covering them. The importance of the next step is emphasized by a further divine instruction. The prophet calls for breath to come into the corpses, and they live. The view of human life as physical matter animated by the breath that comes from God is found throughout the Old Testament (cf. Gen. 2:7).

The interpretation (vv. 11–14) emphasizes that the vision is a promise of national resurrection addressed to the hopeless exiles. In no sense is the seriousness of their plight denied. They are as good as dead, and death in all possible forms is acknowledged as a reality. But the word of God in the face of and in the midst of death brings to the people of God a new reality, life. It is a free, unconditional, and unmerited gift. When read on the eve of Easter, this text is a strong reminder that God is the Lord of all realms, including that of death. Moreover, the promise of life is addressed to the people of God, and resurrection is a symbol not only for a life beyond the grave but also for the abundant life of the community of faith this side of physical death.

Psalm 143

Originally used as an individual lament by worshipers suffering from illness, this psalm prays for God's intervention and rescue. The condition of the worshiper's distress is described in terms of death, of going down to the pit. Such depictions fit well with the description in Ezekiel 37 of the Exile as a graveyard. Like those awaiting Easter morning, the psalmist asks to "hear in the morning of [God's] steadfast love" (v. 8).

Zephaniah 3:14–20

The last of the Old Testament readings for the Easter Vigil is a shout of joy and an announcement of salvation to Jerusalem. The passage begins with a series of imperatives addressed to the Holy City, calling for celebration (v. 14). The remainder of the unit in effect gives the reasons for celebration. These reasons include the announcement that the Lord has acted in behalf of the city and is now in its midst as king (v. 15), and a series of promises concerning the renewal of the city and the return of its people (vv. 16–20). Both the mood and contents of the text anticipate the celebration of Easter.

Our unit is the fourth and last section in the Book of Zephaniah and stands in sharp contrast to the remainder of the book. The section that immediately precedes this one (Zeph. 3:1–13) had announced a purging punishment upon the city and its people. But now darkness has become light; fear and terror have become hope and celebration.

The prophet Zephaniah was active in the seventh century, not long before 621 BC. He was concerned with the coming judgment upon his people, particularly because of their pagan religious practices. It is possible that this concluding section of the book was added in a later age, perhaps during the Babylonian Exile (cf. 3:19–20), by those who had actually been through the fires of destruction and who looked forward to celebrating God's forgiveness, which the return from exile represented. But in any case, the theological interpretation presented by the structure of the book in its final form is quite clear. The celebration of God's salvation follows the dark night of judgment and suffering.

Psalm 98

Like Zephaniah 3:14–20, this psalm is an exuberant affirmation of divine triumph and success. This affirmation is noted by the word "victory" in each of the first three verses. The psalm proclaims the victory of God and calls upon the whole world to break forth into song with the sound of musical instruments. As part of the Easter Vigil, this psalm contributes its call for a celebration of salvation and for the recognition of God as king.

Romans 6:3–11

This epistolary text is also included in the second reading (Romans 6:1b–11) for Proper 7 in Year A. The reader may want to consult our remarks in that setting later in this volume.

What makes this an appropriate text for the Easter Vigil service is its central emphasis on the death, burial, and resurrection of Christ. Dual themes run through the passage: death and life, old and new, sin and righteousness.

We should note the context in which Paul rehearses these stages of the Christ-event. Unlike the Gospel readings used in each of the three years (Matt. 28:1–10; Mark 16:1–8; Luke 24:1–12), this is not a narrative rehearsal of the Easter story. It is rather intertwined with the initiation rite of baptism. In fact, what we have in this passage is a fairly extensive account of Paul's theology of baptism. It makes sense only if we remember that the early Christian practice was for initiates to be immersed in water. It was only natural to interpret this as a "burial," an act of being submerged underneath the water. Obviously, one did not remain under water, but "arose" from the water to live again. To undergo baptism in this fashion was seen as a reenactment of the death and resurrection of Christ. Indeed, Paul speaks of being baptized *into* Christ (v. 3). Through this act one is actually said to enter Christ.

Although this way of understanding baptism may seem logical to us, it was not the only way of understanding this rite. The Fourth Gospel uses an entirely different metaphor: it is a new birth (John 3). Thus baptism is understood as being "born of water and the Spirit" (John 3:5).

But at least from the viewpoint of today's text, baptism is inextricably linked with the death and resurrection of Christ. But how? Merely as a reenactment of a past event? No. If this were the case, the Christ-event and the believer's baptism would be chronologically separated. In one sense, this is true, of course. But our text envisions the fusion of these two moments. We see this by the pervasive use of the language of participation. The believer dies *with* Christ, is buried *with* Christ, is raised *with* Christ, and lives *with* Christ. This level of full participation is rendered especially well in REB: "For if we have become identified with him in his death, we shall also be identified with him in his resurrection" (v. 5). Similarly, we are said to be "in union with Christ Jesus" (REB, v. 11).

Such language presupposes that the Christ-event is not bound by time. The Christ with whom we are united is the living Christ. To put it another way: each time a baptism occurs, the Christ-event, in a sense, recurs. We actually become coparticipants with Christ in his death, burial, and resurrection. It is not so much that we reenact the event that happened *back there*. It is rather that God's act *back there* becomes unbounded by time. It occurs *up here*, now, within us. "In baptism the new world initiated by Christ seizes the life of the individual Christian too, in such a way that the earthly path of the exalted Lord is to be traversed again in this life and Christ thus becomes the destiny of our life. Baptism is projection of the change of aeons into our personal existence, which for its part becomes a constant return to baptism to the extent that here dying with Christ establishes life with him and the dialectic of the two constitutes the signature of being in Christ" (Käsemann).

Our entry into the corporate Christ results in moral transformation (vv. 6, 11). What occurred in the death and resurrection of Christ was more than the expiration or the resuscitation of life. In his death, he "died to sin, once for all" (v. 10)—not just to any sin, but to Sin as a universal power. With sin also went death: Christ is no longer "under the dominion of death" (v. 9, REB). Instead, he "lives to God" (v. 10). What was achieved by God in the Christ-event is appropriated by the believer, who is incorporated into Christ. We then are urged to recognize this transformation in our own identity: we must regard ourselves as "dead to sin and alive to God" (v. 11).

Psalm 114

This psalm, read as a response to Paul's discussion of the association of Christian baptism with the death of Jesus, is a celebration of the Exodus from Egyptian bondage and of the entry into the promised land. Typologically, one might say that the Exodus, like Christ's death, symbolizes the end of an old state of life and the dawning of a new state. The entry into the promised land, like Christian baptism, was a time when the benefits of redemption became real. In this psalm, exodus from Egypt and entrance into the promised land are closely joined, so that parallel events are seen as characteristic of the two episodes. At the Exodus, the sea fled and the "mountains skipped like rams"; at the Jordan, the river rolled back and the hills skipped like lambs (vv. 3–4). The address to the sea and river, the mountains and hills in verses 5–6, which is continued in the address to the earth in verses 7–8, serves as the means for making contemporary the Exodus and entrance events. Thus the users of the psalm, which was always read at the celebration of Passover, "became" participants in the past events of salvation as the Christian in baptism becomes contemporary with the death of Jesus.

Matthew 28:1–10

Easter Vigil is primarily a service of readings marked by anticipation of the full Easter service. The preacher will therefore use restraint in sharing the biblical texts because some of them, such as Matthew 28:1–10, offer Easter itself and not the waiting for Easter. In fact, today's reading is the alternate text for the Easter service. If the preacher chooses to comment on Matthew 28:1–10 at the Vigil, then it might be best to use the other Gospel reading (John 20:1–18) for the service of Easter.

Matthew's resurrection narrative consists of four units: the empty tomb and the appearance of the angel (vv. 1–8); the appearance of Jesus to the women (vv. 9–10); the bribing of the guards (vv. 11–15); the reunion of Jesus and the disciples in Galilee and the commission to preach to the nations (vv. 16–20). This narrative is a revision and an elaboration of Mark 16:1–8. Mark is not, of course, our earliest record of the resurrection tradition. That is to be found in 1 Corinthians 15:3–8, a summary that makes no reference to an empty tomb or to appearances of the risen Christ to women. Mark tells of the empty tomb, the appearance of a "young man" inside the tomb who tells the women to tell the disciples and Peter that Jesus will meet them in Galilee, and the hasty departure of the women in fear and silence. Matthew omits Mark's third woman, Salome, and simply says the two women who had been at the burial (27:61) now go "to see the tomb" (v. 1). Matthew omits conversation between them about getting the stone rolled away, adds the earthquake, and describes the descent of the angel and the removal of the stone. The bribing of the guards (vv. 11–15) is also Matthew's, because only this Evangelist has guards at the tomb (27:65–66; 28:4).

The portion of Matthew's resurrection narrative for this Vigil reading (vv. 1–10) underscores two messages. The first consists of the multiple attestations to the resurrection. The earthquake, the descent of an angel who rolls away the stone, the message of the angel to the women, and the appearance of Jesus to the women testify to Matthew's concern to establish the truth of the gospel: Jesus Christ is risen. The two episodes that follow (vv. 11–15, 16–20) argue the point even further. Mark's abrupt ending will hardly satisfy Matthew's church.

The second message in verses 1–10 is the promise that Jesus will meet his disciples in Galilee. That this promise repeats a statement of Jesus before his death (26:32) serves to join firmly the risen Christ to the historical Jesus. The one raised is the one crucified; Easter cannot be separated from Good Friday. That the promised reunion in Galilee is stated three times (26:32; 28:7; 28:10) indicates the importance of Galilee for Matthew's church. Jesus' ministry was primarily in Galilee, and for both Matthew and Mark (16:7), Galilee was the point of continuing that ministry through the apostles. Luke alters the tradition to say, "Remember how he told you, while he was still in Galilee" (24:6), for in Luke the disciples are to remain in Jerusalem, waiting for the Holy Spirit (24:44–53).

One further note: in Matthew, Jesus is worshiped. The women (v. 9) and the disciples (v. 17) worship him, as did the Magi at the beginning of this Gospel (2:2, 11). Apart from Matthew, only at John 9:38 is it said in the Gospels that persons worshiped Jesus. The major impression is that God was worshiped and Jesus was followed as the one who reveals God and speaks of God's kingdom. To speak of Jesus' being worshiped reflects the central and elevated place of Jesus in Matthew's church. Such a Christology most likely was hammered out in debate with those who denied the authority (28:18) of Jesus in the community of faith.

Easter Day

Acts 10:34–43 or Jeremiah 31:1–6;
Psalm 118:1–2, 14–24;
Colossians 3:1–4 or Acts 10:34–43;
John 20:1–18 or Matthew 28:1–10

*(If the first lesson is from the Old Testament, the
reading from Acts should be the second lesson.)*

The Old Testament selection given for this Sunday is provided for the use of those congregations that wish to retain an Old Testament reading and/or that may not have celebrated an Easter Vigil with its heavy orientation to the Old Testament. The reading from Acts inaugurates the sequential reading of this book throughout the fifty days of Easter.

The Jeremiah text anticipates the coming time when the disruptions and disappointments of Israel's life will be reversed and in their place Israel will experience the redemption of God, which will return life to normalcy with its patterns of rest and rejoicing, dancing and adorning, planting and pilgrimages. Psalm 118 is a song of thanksgiving celebrating victory over the enemy and the exaltation of the rejected. Both Epistle readings celebrate the redemption that has come in Christ and through his resurrection. Both Gospel readings retell the story of the first Easter morning and report on the visits to the tomb.

Acts 10:34–43

Besides serving as the first (or second) reading for Easter Sunday in all three years, this passage also serves as the second reading for the Baptism of the Lord (First Sunday After the Epiphany) in Year A. The reader may want to consult our remarks on the text in this setting earlier in this volume.

What makes this an appropriate text for the principal Easter service is the compact way in which it summarizes the essential points of the gospel story. This brief, but surprisingly comprehensive, résumé has long been regarded as a kerygmatic summary that occurs on the lips of Peter as he addresses the household of Cornelius. It begins with Jesus' baptism by John (v. 37) and moves through his ministry in Galilee to his final days in Judea and Jerusalem. There is explicit mention of his "death by hanging [him] on a gibbet" (v. 39, REB), his resurrection on the third day (v. 40), and his being made manifest to a select group of witnesses (v. 41). Yet this is no new, unanticipated story, but one that continues the prophetic story (v. 43).

It is, of course, a Lukan summary and probably tells us more about Luke's theology and literary purpose than it does about what Peter is likely to have said on the occasion. The preacher might do well to examine each of these motifs in the sermon summary in light of Luke's Gospel. There are some striking parallels: for example, the stress on Jesus' anointing with the Spirit (v. 38; cf. Luke 3:22; 4:1, 14, 18), his works of healing (v. 38; cf. Luke 4:31–41), and the dawning of Easter faith in the context of a sacred meal with the risen Lord (v. 41; Luke 24:30–35).

As useful as it might be to examine each of the details of this compact summary and explore the way they are elaborated in the larger work of Luke-Acts, the preacher must finally remember that this text will be read on Easter Day. We should ask, then, what themes are especially heard in this liturgical setting.

First, *the Easter faith*. Perhaps above all, we will hear the proclamation that "God raised him to life on the third day, and allowed him to be clearly seen" (v. 40, REB). But even if we hear this note above the rest and read it as the climax of the story, we do well to remember that it is part of a larger, and longer, story whose roots lie in the Old Testament (v. 43) and was heard first by Israel (v. 36). As climactic as the moment of Easter is, it is not a moment suspended from history but part of a larger drama interwoven with history. The story occurs in places such as Galilee, the country of the Jews, and Jerusalem. It involves human actors such as John the Baptist and those with whom Jesus worked and ministered. It was in ordinary places and among ordinary persons that the Extraordinary was manifested.

Also worth noticing is our text's insistence that the Easter faith was acknowledged by a select group of "witnesses whom God had chosen in advance" (REB, v. 41). We should also note that the Easter faith was experienced as the disciples ate and drank with the risen Lord (v. 41). This doubtless reflects early Christian reminiscence and practice that the presence of the risen Lord was celebrated and experienced in the Eucharist.

A second theme woven throughout today's text is actually a set of twin themes: *the impartiality of God and the universality of salvation*. The sermon opens on the note that "God has no favourites" (v. 34, NJB, REB). It is an axiom of Jewish thought that God was impartial, which meant that God could not be bought or bribed (Deut. 10:17; cf. Job 34:19; 2 Chron. 19:7). Among other things, this meant that God was not deaf to the cries of the poor and the disadvantaged, most notably widows and orphans (Sir. 35:12–13). What was axiomatic in Jewish thought also became normative in Christian thought (Rom. 2:11; Gal. 2:6; Eph. 6:9; Col. 3:25; 1 Pet. 1:17; James 2:19).

The natural corollary to God's impartiality is God's universal concern for all humanity—a recurrent theme of today's text. Even in the form of the Christian confession given in the sermon, this note of universality is emphasized: "Jesus Christ—he is the Lord of *all*" (v. 36, NJB, italics added). Similar concern was shown in his earthly ministry: Jesus went about doing good and healing *all* who were demonically possessed (v. 38). We are also assured in the sermon that "*everyone* who believes in him receives forgiveness" (v. 43, italics added). In this context in which the gospel is being proclaimed to the Gentile Cornelius, the particular force of these claims is to insist that God's salvation no longer rests exclusively with Israel. It now reaches beyond Israel to all nations. To be sure, it includes Israel, but not Israel exclusively. In fact, the reference to God as "judge of the living and the dead" (v. 42) may mean the God who finally judges both Jews, those to whom God extended life, and Gentiles, those whom Jews could regard as dead (cf. Eph. 2:1, 12).

What is striking about today's text is the way in which Peter himself comes to believe in God's impartiality and universality. Note the opening line: "I now really understand . . ."

(v. 34, NJB). In fact, one of the unusual features of this sermon is that it is evangelistic in an odd way. It addresses Peter as much as it does Cornelius. It is not so much proclamation as self-confession. What is rehearsed is familiar. The main points of the gospel story are well known. But it seriously challenges Peter's familiar world.

Perhaps this suggests a possible way for the text to be developed homiletically. It rehearses the main outline of a very familiar story. For many who hear it on Easter Sunday, it is a table of contents of a well-known book. Nothing new is being introduced—at least not ostensibly. But a closer look may suggest that some of our most cherished religious convictions are being called into question. Hearing this text may mean that we open ourselves to a gospel in which God does not play favorites—to one race over the other, one sex over the other, even one religion over the other.

Jeremiah 31:1–6

As an alternative first reading for churches that do not celebrate the Easter Vigil, Jeremiah 31:1–6 provides something of a brief summary of the history of salvation given in greater detail in the Old Testament lections for the Vigil. The text does not deal directly with the Easter event, but on the one hand leads up to it with allusions to Israel's history, and on the other hand celebrates God's love manifest in saving actions in behalf of the people of God.

In terms of literary context, this passage is part of a collection of prophetic materials in Jeremiah 30–31, generally called "the Book of Consolation" because most of it is good news. Note, however, that the verses that immediately precede our reading announce the almost apocalyptic judgment by Yahweh because of his "fierce anger" (30:24). The effect of this juxtaposition is to heighten the good news in 30:1ff. The Book of Consolation itself is quite late, coming from the exilic period, but most of the individual addresses come from Jeremiah. It is generally accepted that Jeremiah 31:2–6 comes from the prophet; but some commentators place it early in his career, during the time of Josiah, and others place it late, during the time of Gedaliah (after 597 BC), when Jerusalem had been captured and the capital moved north to Mizpah.

Our passage consists of two distinct parts, verse 1 and verses 2–6, the former in prose and the latter in poetry. Verse 1 is an introduction, not just to verses 2–6, but to the entire chapter that follows, and probably comes from the editor who organized the section. It is a comprehensive statement of the good news of the chapter as a whole, that Yahweh will establish a new covenant with his people (31:31–34). "At that time" is a general reference to an unspecified time in the future. Yahweh's twofold promise is a version of the most basic Old Testament covenantal formula "I will be your God and you shall be my people" (cf. Jer. 30:22; Amos 3:1; Hos. 1:9, 10). The distinctive feature of the announcement here is the reference to "all the families of Israel." That signals a particular concern of the unit before us, and of much of chapter 31, namely, the reunification of the Northern and the Southern Kingdoms, of Israel and Judah.

What follows the introduction, after an appropriate messenger formula, is a prophecy of salvation (vv. 2–6). The prophecy has two parts: the affirmation of God's love for his people (vv. 2–3) and the promise that this love will be manifest in new saving events (vv. 4–6). This word is addressed in a particular context to a people who had been in trouble and are seeking "rest." It also assumes some need for renewal and rebuilding (cf. the allusions in

vv. 4–6). Verses 2b–3a contain allusions to the early history of salvation. "Survived the sword" appears to be an allusion to the escape from Egypt (Exod. 5:21; 15:9; 18:4), and "grace in the wilderness" refers either to the gifts that sustained life (e.g., Exod. 16–17) or to the covenant on Mount Sinai. The first line of verse 3 contains textual and translation problems (read with NRSV but cf. its footnotes), but certainly refers to the theophany at Sinai. The "rest" that Israel sought included having a place to call one's own, that is, an end to wandering and freedom from threats (Deut. 28:65).

At the center of the prophecy stands God's love. That Israel "found grace" (*hēn*) in the wilderness indicates that God regarded the people with favor and affection. Verse 3b could be read "I have loved you with an everlasting love" (NRSV) or "I have dearly loved you from of old" (REB). In either case, it stresses the continuity and stability of Yahweh's commitment to Israel. The final line of verse 3 makes the same point. The word used here, *hesed* (NRSV "faithfulness," REB "unfailing care"), is common to covenantal relationships and often is translated "steadfast love." At this point, Jeremiah clearly is indebted to Hosea (cf. Hos. 11:4).

Just as the Lord's love had been manifest in saving actions, so it will again. The specific good news is the announcement of the rebuilding of Israel (v. 4a), the revival of northern Israel's vineyards (v. 5), and the reunification of the tribes at Mount Zion (v. 6). Thus it includes the reestablishment of physical culture, the renewal of nature, and the proper integration into worship of all the people of God. The announcement seems to contain a definite allusion to Jeremiah's commission at the time of his call, "to build and to plant" (Jer. 1:10). The prophecy assumes that Israel and Judah are separated from one another, that the Northern Kingdom is in trouble, and that it is God's will to bring all the families together again, to worship in the temple in Jerusalem.

What response is called for to this prophecy of divine love and its manifestation in concrete historical events? The passage gives no instructions, no laws, and does not even call for the people to renew the covenant. It limits itself to promises. But two of those promises characterize the response of the people of God to the love of God. First, there is the most unbounded celebration of this good news, even with dancing and making merry (v. 4b). Second, there is the summons to come to Zion to "the Lord our God" (v. 6b), presented not as an order but as a promise, a promise that the invitation will be issued. It is an invitation one can only accept.

Psalm 118:1–2, 14–24

A portion of Psalm 118 is the reading for the Liturgy of the Palms on Passion/Palm Sunday, for it is already associated with this occasion in the Gospels. Because the psalm text for today overlaps that of Palm Sunday, the discussion at the latter should be consulted.

Verses 1–2 (along with vv. 3–4) set the following material of the psalm into a context, namely, that of community worship. The refrains in verses 1–4 suggest antiphonal singing. The refrain parallels that used in Psalm 136.

Verses 14–24 unfortunately contain only certain elements of the larger thanksgiving composition that is Psalm 118. Specifically, these verses contain (1) a confession by the person previously endangered (v. 14, which form critically and otherwise belongs with the preceding verses); (2) a description of the victory celebrations in the camp following victory that also concludes with confessional assertions (vv. 15–18); (3) the spoken elements of a gate liturgy used as the triumphant figure enters the sacred temple precincts (v. 19 spoken by the one entering and v. 20 the response given by the priests or the assembled audience); (4) the worshiper's short prayer of thanksgiving to God; and (although this is not completely clear) (5) antiphonal acclamation and praise by the triumphant worshiper and/or the priests/assembled worshipers (vv. 22–24).

Characteristic of this psalm is its celebrative tone, which, of course, makes it so appropriate for reading on Easter. Further, the pattern displayed in the psalm is strikingly parallel to the passion-resurrection of Jesus. The worshiper in Psalm 118 had been placed in a position of danger, apparently a military campaign (see vv. 10–13). This danger is depicted in terms of a struggle against death itself (vv. 17–18), a struggle in which God protected the threatened and refused to allow a servant to be overcome by death.

In the psalm, of course, the fundamental celebration is carried on and praise offered by the one who has been redeemed. This would be somewhat analogous to hearing the resurrected Christ offer up thanksgiving for the resurrection. In the New Testament, it is, of course, the Christians who offer testimony and thanksgiving. Yet even in the psalm, the congregation (which may be seen as the ancient counterpart to the early church) joins in the celebration and praise, and affirms the corporate benefits of the divine redemption (see vv. 23–24 with their plural pronouns).

The litany of entering the temple gates (vv. 19–20) can be compared with similar entry liturgies in Psalms 15 and 24. Inside the temple precincts, the monarch offers thanks (v. 21). Verse 22 may be seen either as part of the king's thanksgiving and thus a continuation of verse 21 or else as part of the community's response and proclamation and thus a link with verses 23–24. At any rate, the theme of verse 22, like the Easter theme, emphasizes the movement from humiliation/rejection to exaltation/glorification. A stone (=the king= Jesus) that has been rejected by the builders (=the nations=the Jews/Romans) as unworthy and a possible structural defect has been elevated to a place of prominence (=the corner of the building=the king's victory in battle=Jesus' resurrection).

The congregation responds to the new reality as "marvelous" and "the Lord's doing" in verses 23–24. Thus the psalm lection closes out with a confessional affirmation.

Colossians 3:1–4

A longer form of today's epistolary reading (3:1–11) also serves as the second reading for Proper 13 in Year C. The reader may wish to consult our remarks on the text in that setting.

It is one thing to believe and confess that Christ has been raised, quite another to be told that *we* have been raised. Yet this is the dramatic step taken in today's second reading. Whichever Gospel lesson is chosen, the focus is the same—the risen Lord on Easter morning. A similar perspective is seen in the kerygmatic summary in Acts 10:34–43: Christ the risen Lord is proclaimed as Lord of all. But the focus shifts in the epistolary reading from Christ's resurrection to our own resurrection.

The text begins with a conditional clause, "So if you have been raised with Christ . . ." (v. 1, NRSV), but the form of the sentence in Greek indicates that it is a present reality, not a future possibility. This is captured especially well in NJB: "Since you have been raised up to be with Christ." REB renders it as a rhetorical question: "Were you not raised to life with Christ?" We may find this claim somewhat jolting, especially if we recall that Paul ordinarily reserves to the future this level of participation with the risen Lord (cf. Rom. 6:5, 8). It is a form of present realization typical of the post-Pauline letters (cf. Eph. 2:6). Clearly, what is in view here is a form of full sacramental union in which the believer has both died and come to life again. In both instances, this has been achieved *with* Christ (2:20; 3:1). In some definitive sense, we are being told that what Christ experienced on Good Friday and Easter we have already experienced: we are coparticipants with him in his death and resurrection.

The effect of such union is to conform our own destiny to that of the exalted Christ, who is "seated at the right hand of God" (v. 1; cf. Ps. 110:1). It is transforming in that our perspective is shifted from things below to things above. This well-known spatial distinction between earth and heaven now comes to signify moral choices. The earthly outlook is detailed in the list of vices that follow (vv. 5–8), just as the heavenly outlook is profiled with a list of virtues (vv. 12–15). We are thus urged to direct our thoughts to the heavenly realm where Christ dwells (cf. Phil. 3:19–20).

This is possible because we have undergone a death: "I repeat, you died" (v. 3, NEB). As a result, our "life lies hidden with Christ in God." We are no longer who we once were. Our identity is explainable only in terms of the risen Christ, with whom we have become united (cf. Phil. 1:21). There is a part of us that resides with the risen Lord in the very presence of God.

So close is this union between us and Christ that Christ can be said to be "our life" (v. 4). This is probably true in several senses. Christ is the one through whom the life-giving Spirit is mediated to us and indwells us (1 Cor. 15:45; Rom. 8:10–11). He is also the defining norm of our existence (Phil. 1:21). Similar claims are made in the Johannine tradition (1 John 5:11–12; John 14:6).

In spite of these claims that we have already been raised with Christ, our text still envisions a future "when Christ is revealed" (v. 4, NJB; cf. Luke 17:30). Not everything is experienced yet. Thus, at the coming of Christ the fullness of this union will be manifested (cf. 1 Cor. 15:43; 1 John 3:2; 1 Pet. 5:1).

The word of today's epistolary text, then, is that Easter involves not only celebration but moral renewal. It calls for reflection that is bifocal: Christ's being brought back to life and our own resurrection to "true life with Christ" (v. 1, JB). So celebrated, Easter becomes a fusion of two stories—our own story with the story of Christ. If the two narratives remain separate and fail to intersect and intertwine, Easter may remain as a beautiful story, but we are none the better for the telling.

John 20:1–18 *or* Matthew 28:1–10

Because Matthew 28:1–10 was the Gospel of Easter Vigil and commentary was offered there, attention here will be solely on John 20:1–18.

In the Gospels, resurrection narratives are of two kinds: reports about finding the tomb empty and reports of appearances of the risen Christ. The differences in the Gospel records indicate uses of different sources as well as particular emphases by the Evangelists themselves.

In the Gospel of John, the resurrection narrative consists of two stories (20:1–18, 19–29). Each containing two parts, the two stories bear striking similarities. Both are Sunday stories (20:1, 19), perhaps once having existed separately and used in the worship of the church. Each story involves members of the original circle of disciples, then focuses on the faith experience of one individual (Mary Magdalene in the first, Thomas in the second), and concludes with a witness to all believers. In neither story does the writer speak of the resurrection so as to shock or to coerce faith. Some later Christian documents speak of the risen Christ appearing in public places, astounding unbelievers with a faith-overwhelming wonder. In the New Testament, disciples relate the resurrection of Jesus as that of which "all of *us* are witnesses" (Acts 2:32, italics added).

As stated earlier, John 20:1–18 is actually the interweaving of two episodes, one involving Mary Magdalene and the other Simon Peter and the beloved disciple. (See comments on John 13:21–30 for Wednesday in Holy Week for a summary statement about this disciple.) As in all their appearances together (for example, see 13:22–25; 18:15–16), the beloved disciple takes the favored position over Simon Peter. Peter comes in second in the race to the tomb (v. 4), and although Peter actually enters the tomb first, there is no evidence that what he saw and did not see generated in him any faith. The beloved disciple, although hesitant to enter at first, did believe once he went into the tomb and saw what Peter saw (v. 8). However, because neither as yet understood the Scriptures that Jesus must rise from the dead, they left the tomb and went home (vv. 9–10). Miracles and faith that understands are not as closely joined as some might suppose. What is striking, however, is that the beloved disciple became the first believer in the resurrection, and on the slightest evidence—an empty tomb containing grave cloths.

The major portion of John 20:1–18 focuses on Mary Magdalene. Unlike the Synoptic accounts (see comments on Matt. 28:1–10 for Easter Vigil), John has Mary Magdalene alone at the tomb (v. 1). The empty tomb does not move her to faith; she thinks the body has been removed to another place (v. 13). The appearance of two angels (v. 12; a young man in Mark 16:5; an angel in Matt. 28:2; two men in Luke 24:4) neither allays her grief nor prompts faith in the resurrection. In fact, when Jesus appears she does not recognize him (v. 14). Only when he speaks her name does she believe (v. 16). This fulfills what had been said earlier of Jesus as the shepherd: he knows his own, he calls them by name, and they recognize his voice (10:3–4).

Unlike the beloved disciple, Mary Magdalene comes to faith not by the evidence of an empty tomb and grave cloths, not by the revelation from angels, and not even by the sight of the risen Christ. She came to faith by his word, a word that prompted the memory of a relationship that had already been formed and that, by the resurrection, was vindicated and sealed as an abiding one. Easter alone is a marvel; Easter for those who have followed all the way, even to Golgotha, is a confirmation of trust, a promise kept.

But even for disciples like Mary, Easter does not return her and Jesus to the past; Easter opens up a new future. The earthly ministry is over; now the ministry of the exalted, glorified, ever-abiding Christ begins. "Nevertheless I tell you the truth: it is to your advantage that I go away, for if I do not go away, the Advocate will not come to you" (16:7). In fact, the one who believes will do even greater works than Jesus did, "because I am going to the Father" (14:12). Therefore, Jesus says to Mary Magdalene, "Do not hold on to me" (v. 17). Rather, she is to go and announce his resurrection and his ascension to the presence of God, from whose presence the Holy Spirit will come to lead, comfort, and empower the church.

Easter Evening

Isaiah 25:6–9;
Psalm 114;
1 Corinthians 5:6b–8;
Luke 24:13–49

These readings are for occasions when the main (eucharistic) Easter service must be late in the day, not for Vespers on Easter Evening. The Old Testament lesson is an almost apocalyptic vision of the celebration on Mount Zion of the time when God "will swallow up death forever." Psalm 114 is a hymn of praise celebrating God's acts of salvation. The note of celebration also continues in the epistolary reading, where Paul urges his readers to celebrate the Christian Passover. The Gospel reading combines both themes of resurrection and celebration: the risen Lord encounters the two men en route to Emmaus and is revealed to them in the breaking of bread.

Isaiah 25:6–9

The date and authorship of these magnificent verses are unknown. They are part of a section of the Book of Isaiah (chaps. 24–27) often identified as the "little Isaiah apocalypse" because some of its themes are common in later apocalyptic literature. These include resurrection of the dead (Isa. 26:19), universal judgment, God's imprisonment of some of the heavenly host, as well as the eschatological banquet and God's triumph over death mentioned here. But because the chapters lack so many of the specific features of apocalyptic texts, such as are present in Daniel 7–12 and Revelation, the section is better identified as a collection of eschatological prophecies. They are visions of the future restoration that provided grist for the mill of apocalyptic eschatology. The section also includes a great deal of liturgical material, especially prayers and songs of praise. Isaiah 24–27 as a whole cannot be earlier than the postexilic period.

Isaiah 25:6–9 is framed by negative words about the enemies of the people of God. Our reading is preceded (25:1–5) by a song of praise for the God who destroys the city of an unnamed enemy. But this same hymn praises God as a refuge for the poor and the needy. The verses that follow the lection (vv. 10–12) announce judgment against Moab.

Given these harsh words about enemy nations, it is remarkable that the good news announced in our text is "for all peoples" (v. 6). The vision of a time when God would "swallow up death forever" is universal in its scope, without losing the particular concern for God's elect (v. 8). In that respect, as well as the view that God's reign would have its center on Mount Zion, the passage is similar to Isaiah 2:2–4.

Our reading is not a prophetic oracle in which the words of God concerning the future are cited, but a promise of what God will do. It has two main parts, verses 6–8 and verse 9. In the first section the time is indefinite, referring to some future day. But the place is clear: God's dramatic action will take place "on this mountain" (vv. 6, 7), that is, Mt. Zion in Jerusalem. Verse 6 announces the banquet that the Lord will prepare for all peoples. This celebration has its background in texts such as Exodus 24:9–11, which reports that Moses and the elders ate in the presence of God on Mount Sinai. Such celebrations have their roots in ritual meals such as the Passover (cf. also 1 Sam. 9:13). And the banquet has its future in the eschatological meal, as in Revelation 19:7, 17. Read in the context set by Luke 24:13–49, one can see the Christian Eucharist as such a meal.

The reason for the celebration is stated in verse 7: The Lord will "swallow up death forever." All peoples will come to Mount Zion to participate in the celebration of God's ultimate triumph on behalf of all peoples. The "shroud" probably refers to a mourning garment. Particularly since the publication of the Ugaritic texts from Ras Shamra, many commentators have recognized in these lines, as well as the reference to the great banquet, parallels to the victory over death in Canaanite religion. But there is no doubt that this expectation becomes a part of apocalyptic eschatology, and the lines are cited in Revelation 21:4.

Verse 8 characterizes the effects of God's destruction of death and continues the theme of the end of mourning. Without death there will be no need for tears.

The second part of the unit, verse 9, is a hymn that gives the words the peoples will sing in celebration. The verse parallels the words of Psalm 9. In the song, the people affirm that God is theirs, that they have waited in the expectation that he would save them. So they rejoice in that salvation. Full homage and honor are accorded to God alone.

The main theme for the day is, of course, the one stated in verse 7: death is swallowed up. Life is utterly transformed, and the only possible response is the one described here— celebration and praise of God.

Psalm 114

In Jewish worship, Psalms 113–118 came to be associated closely with the festival of Passover. This collection of six psalms was then called the "Egyptian Hallel" because they were seen as praise for the redemption from Egypt. How early this use of these psalms developed cannot be determined, but it was certainly already a custom at the time of Jesus.

The lambs designated for Passover were slaughtered and dressed in the temple in the afternoon to be cooked for the Passover dinner eaten in the evening. (Additional lambs were often cooked if the size of the Passover party required it. But at least one lamb, from which all observers ate a portion, had to be so designated and slaughtered and cleaned in the temple.) The people with their lambs were admitted to the temple in three different shifts. As the lambs were slaughtered on each of the shifts, the Levites sang Psalms 113–118 in the main courtyard of the temple. These psalms were again sung as part of the Passover meal. Psalms 113–114 were sung at the beginning of the meal and Psalms 115–118 at the conclusion.

Psalm 114 was clearly written for the celebration of Passover. Some of these psalms were originally composed for other celebrations and secondarily adopted for Passover usage.

The psalm opens with general summarizing statements about the Exodus from Egypt and the occupation of the land of Canaan (vv. 1–2). Egypt is described as a people of strange language. Egyptian belongs to a completely different language family (Hamitic) from Hebrew (Semitic) and was written, of course, in a strange, nonalphabetic, hieroglyphic form. In verse 1, Israel and house of Jacob refer to the larger inclusive Hebrew people (both "Israel" and Judah). In verse 2, Israel and Judah denote the Northern and Southern Kingdoms after the death of Solomon. That Judah is claimed to be his (God's) sanctuary suggests that Judah is considered more special than Israel, which is spoken of as his (God's) dominion. It also suggests that this psalm originated in Judah. The reference to sanctuary is no doubt an allusion to Jerusalem and the temple.

In verses 3–6, four entities are noted—the sea, the Jordan River, the mountains, and the hills. The references to the (Red) sea and the Jordan River hark back to the stories of the crossing of the sea in the Exodus from Egypt (see Exod. 14) and the crossing of the Jordan River to move into the promised land (see Josh. 3, especially vv. 14–17). In both cases, the water parted, fled, or turned back to allow the Hebrews to cross. It is interesting to note, and certainly appropriate for the setting of this psalm in the Passover observance, that the Passover preceded the Exodus from Egypt (see Exod. 12) and was the first celebration of the Hebrews in the land of Canaan (see Josh. 5:10–12). The Passover was thus celebrated as the last taste of Egypt and as the first taste of the promised land. The Passover recalls not only the scars of Egypt but also the first fruits of the land of promise.

The mountains and hills that skipped like rams and lambs (vv. 4 and 6) are not mentioned in the Exodus and Joshua stories. That they are mentioned as skipping around suggests that the language is metaphorical. The same might be said for the action of the sea and the Jordan River, although the final editors of the Hexateuch took both crossings as miraculous but actual events. Verses 5–6 are a taunt so formulated to heighten the action described. The one responsible for such actions does not get mentioned until verse 7, which refers to the presence of Yahweh.

The psalm concludes (vv. 7–8) with a call to the earth to "dance" (probably a better translation than the NRSV's "tremble"). Whether one should read "earth" (=the world) or "land" (=the promised land) remains unknown, although the latter seems more likely. The land is called on to break out in celebration at the presence of God, who worked wonders in the wilderness.

1 Corinthians 5:6b–8

This text is appropriate for the second reading on Easter Evening because it speaks of the sacrifice of Christ, "our paschal lamb" (v. 7, NRSV; "our Passover," NJB), and urges us to "celebrate the festival" (v. 8). It creates a mood of festivity that befits the Easter celebration. By connecting the death of Christ with a continuing season of celebration, it serves to remind us that Easter is not merely a day, but a season that extends for seven weeks until Pentecost.

We should note the context in which this graphic image of Christ as the sacrificial Passover lamb occurs. We may be surprised to find that it occurs not in a set of liturgical instructions but as part of moral instruction. At issue is a case of sexual misconduct that Paul had heard about: one of the Corinthian church members was "living with his father's wife" (5:1). Apparently, a man was married to his stepmother, a practice forbidden by Jewish law (Lev. 18:8; 20:11; Deut. 22:30; 27:20) and also unacceptable among Greeks and Romans (cf. Euripides, *Hippolytus*; Cicero, *Pro Cluentio* 14).

What Paul finds shocking is not only that a Christian is engaged in such a practice but that the church blithely accepts it, in fact regards it as something worth boasting about (vv. 2 and 6). It is interesting to note that Paul's following remarks are not directed to the parties involved but to the church because of its surprisingly smug attitude about the matter. The arrogant attitude displayed here is reflected elsewhere in First Corinthians (cf. 3:18; 4:6–8, 19). Somehow, their newfound freedom in Christ had led to an unhealthy level of self-confidence that blinded them to the conspicuously huge sin in their own midst. Thus our text is preceded with a word of censure: "your boasting is not a good thing" (v. 6a) or "your self-satisfaction is ill founded" (NJB). To penetrate this barrier of smugness, Paul employs familiar Jewish images and reinterprets them for this situation.

Before doing so, however, he cites a piece of popular wisdom, introduced with the phrase "Do you not know . . . ?" This formula is commonly employed to confront readers with the familiar—what they already know or should know (cf. 3:16). It is an argument from common sense. Our own experience tells us that "only a little yeast leavens the whole batch of dough" (v. 6, NJB; cf. Gal. 5:9). Graeco-Roman popular wisdom knows a similar saying: "Yeast is itself also the product of corruption, and produces corruption in the dough with which it is mixed; for the dough becomes flabby and inert, and altogether the process of leavening seems to be one of putrefaction; at any rate, if it goes too far, it completely sours and spoils the flour" (Plutarch, *Quaestiones Romanae* 289F).

This negative connotation attached to leaven is also reflected in the teachings of Jesus (cf. Matt. 16:6–12; Mark 8:14–21; Luke 12:1; cf. Matt. 13:33; Luke 13:21; also Gospel of Thomas, par. 96).

The point is clear: give sin an inch and it will take a mile. The only proper response is to expunge evil at its first appearance. To make his point, Paul employs imagery drawn from the Jewish practice of observing the Passover and the Feast of Unleavened Bread. According to one biblical tradition (Exod. 12), Passover was celebrated in the spring, in the month of Nisan, as an occasion for remembering God's deliverance of Israel from Egypt. It began on the tenth day of the month, when the head of the household selected an unblemished year-old lamb. On the fourteenth of Nisan, the lamb was slaughtered for the celebration of Passover that evening. The Passover evening meal began a seven-day festival during which unleavened bread was eaten, hence its name the Feast of Unleavened Bread (cf. Exod. 23:15; 34:18; Deut. 16:3–4). In preparation for this week, every scrap of leaven had to be removed from the house. Leaven was regarded as ritually unclean because it involved ferment and corruption (cf. Lev. 2:11).

We should note the sequence: first the Passover lamb is slaughtered and the celebration of the Feast of Unleavened Bread immediately follows. It is a time of ritual purification, when all visible signs of evil are removed from sight. Accordingly, it requires moral cleanliness on the part of the participants.

Against this background, Paul insists that Christ is the Passover lamb who has already been slaughtered (v. 7). It is an unusual metaphor for Paul (though cf. Rom. 3:24–26), but one developed elsewhere in the New Testament (cf. 1 Pet. 1:19; John 1:29, 36; 19:36; Rev. 5:6, 9, 12; 12:11). If Christ is so understood, his death may be seen as the event that begins the celebration of the Feast of Unleavened Bread. By extension, then, we who are in Christ are expected to make ourselves ready for the festival celebration, and this above all requires moral purification (cf. Exod. 12:19; 13:7; Deut. 16:3–4). It means getting rid of "the old yeast, the yeast of malice and evil," and feeding on the "unleavened bread of sincerity and truth" (v. 8).

In the setting of Easter evening, today's epistolary text serves to link festal celebration with community behavior. What was done in Christ has rippling effects within the community that celebrates his death and resurrection. Above all, the celebrants are expected to adopt a life-style that befits the One whom they worship as the risen Lord. This produces a community of faith where arrogance, pride, and self-satisfaction are alien, but where sincerity and truth are the native virtues.

Luke 24:13–49

One could hardly imagine a more appropriate text for an Easter evening service than Luke 24:13–49. This passage involves an experience with the risen Christ "toward evening" of the first Easter (v. 29), reflects upon the meaning of the day's events, includes a eucharistic meal, ties the meaning of the resurrection to the ministry of the historical Jesus and to the Hebrew Scriptures, offers the promise of the Holy Spirit, and commissions the disciples to witness to the nations. Easter morning announces; Easter evening interprets.

Luke's resurrection narrative consists of five parts: (1) verses 1–12, the women at the tomb; (2) verses 13–35, the appearance of the risen Christ on the road to Emmaus; (3) verses 36–43, Jesus' appearance to the eleven and to others with them; (4) verses 44–49, instruction and commission; and (5) verses 50–53, the departure of Jesus. Our lection for today consists of parts 2, 3, and 4.

Verses 13–35, the appearance of the risen Christ to two disciples on the road to Emmaus, is a narrative unit bearing the marks of artistry that we have come to associate with Lukan stories. The preacher may want to treat this passage as a unit, even though there certainly are distinct accents within it that the sermon can well emphasize. Three will be treated here.

First, verses 13–15 record a resurrection appearance without parallel in the other Gospels and absent from the list in 1 Corinthians 15:3–8. There are evidences, however, that by the time of Luke's writing, resurrection accounts had begun to influence one another. For example, verse 12 (not in many of the best manuscripts, omitted in the RSV, and restored in the NRSV) reflects John 20:6–10; verse 34 agrees with 1 Corinthians 15:5; verse 40 (not in many of the best manuscripts, omitted in the RSV, and restored in the NRSV) seems to borrow from John 20:20; and the phrase "and was carried up into heaven" in verse 51 (not in many of the best manuscripts, omitted in the RSV, and restored in the NRSV) is probably a line from Acts 1:9–10. This is not to say that the witness to the resurrection is offered with uncertainty either by Luke or by his translators. Rather, it is to register the fact that in the early church the different accounts of the resurrection began to blend into one. It is likely that Genesis 18:1–15 is also influencing Luke, for it is his frequent practice to tell his stories so as to echo Old Testament stories. Consistent with the remainder of Luke 24 and with the other Gospels, the resurrection appearance here does not coerce or overwhelm faith. Matthew says some doubted (28:17); Luke has already said the disciples regarded the report of the women at the tomb as an idle tale that they did not believe (24:12); and John records the hesitant faith of both Mary Magdalene (20:11–18) and Thomas (20:24–29). In fact, Luke says of the two disciples on the road, "But their eyes were kept from recognizing him" (v. 16) until they had received the witness of Scripture (vv. 25–27) and sacrament (vv. 30–35).

The second distinct accent in verses 13–35 is the role of Scripture in generating faith in the disciples (v. 32). Scripture, that is, the Old Testament, is not only central in Luke's portrayal of the life and ministry of Jesus (2:21–39; 4:16–30) but also in Luke's understanding of the formation of faith in the disciples of Jesus (16:31; 24:44–47; Acts 2:14–36). According to Luke, the death and resurrection of Jesus and the preaching of the gospel to the nations is continuous with a proper understanding of the law, the prophets, and the psalms (vv. 27, 44–47).

The third distinctive element in verses 13–35 is Christ's self-revelation in the breaking of bread (vv. 31, 35). That the meal was a eucharistic meal is evident in the language used to describe it (v. 30). Although a guest, Jesus is host because it is the Lord's Supper. The generation of faith by word (Scripture) and sacrament and the experience of the living Christ in the eucharistic meal not only reflect the theology and practice of the Lukan church but offer to the reader the possibility of faith and the promise of Christ's presence.

The next unit of our lection is verses 36–43. This records the appearance of Jesus to the eleven and to those with them (v. 30) in a scene marked by fear, wonder, and "[disbelieving] in their joy" (v. 41). This unit, though much briefer than verses 13–35, is framed on the same pattern: the risen Christ appears, the disciples do not recognize him, they are scolded for doubting, food is shared, Jesus enables them to understand the Scriptures, and they respond in wonder and joy. In this unit, the point is stressed that the risen Christ is not a spirit or phantom; he is the one crucified. The one they followed, believed, and obeyed is the one vindicated by God's raising him from the dead. To be a disciple of one is to be a disciple of the other, for they are one and the same.

The final unit of our lection, verses 44–49, repeats one theme and introduces two others. The theme repeated is that of the continuity of the words of the risen Christ with the words of the historical Jesus and with the words of the Old Testament (vv. 44–47). The two new themes are the commission to preach the gospel (for Luke, repentance and forgiveness of sins) to all nations beginning from Jerusalem (vv. 47–48; Acts 1:8) and the promise of the power of God (v. 49). This promise of the gift of the Holy Spirit, for which the disciples wait, is fulfilled at Pentecost (Acts 1:4, 8; 2:1–18).

Second Sunday of Easter

Acts 2:14*a*, 22–32;
Psalm 16;
1 Peter 1:3–9;
John 20:19–31

I t is important to note that Easter begins a seven-week period of sustained reflection and celebration. As such, it is the first Sunday of the Easter Season. Accordingly, the following Sundays are designated Sundays *of* Easter and not Sundays *after* Easter. At the end of the fifty-day season stands Pentecost, the Eighth Sunday of Easter.

Several themes are prominent during this period. We naturally continue to celebrate the paschal mystery of the suffering, death, and resurrection of Christ. But other themes also emerge: Christ's ascension and the coming of the Spirit. It is quite fitting, then, that the first reading for each of these Sundays is taken from the Acts of the Apostles, which provides a narrative sequel to the death and resurrection of Christ. Prominent among the events it records are Christ's ascension (Acts 1), the coming of the Spirit on Pentecost to mark the beginning of the church (Acts 2), and a succession of events in which the apostles, most notably Peter and Paul, witness to the gospel.

The second reading during the Easter Season is taken from First Peter, First John, and Revelation for Years A, B, and C respectively, because "these texts seem most appropriate to the spirit of the Easter Season, a spirit of joyful faith and confident hope" (Introduction to the *Lectionary for Mass* [Collegeville, 1970], chapter II, section IV.1, page xxxv).

The Gospel readings for this season focus on the appearances of the risen Lord (Second and Third Sundays) and the farewell discourses and prayers of Jesus from the Gospel of John (Fourth through Seventh Sundays).

Today's texts include a portion of Peter's Pentecost sermon (Acts 2) that focuses on Christ's resurrection (the first main section after the Old Testament quotation from Joel). Quite appropriately, the psalm encompasses the portion quoted in Peter's sermon (16:8–11). The epistolary reading from First Peter, an opening prayer of blessing that begins with a firm declaration of the resurrection hope, continues the theme of the first lesson. The reading from the Fourth Gospel records the famous episode where Jesus appears first to the disciples, then to Thomas, and concludes with a summary stating the purpose of this Gospel (20:30–31).

Acts 2:14a, 22–32

This is the first of several summaries of early Christian preaching found in Acts (cf. 3:12–26; 4:8–12; 5:29–32; 10:34–43; 13:16–41). It occurs here on the lips of Peter as he addresses the crowd of Jews gathered in Jerusalem to celebrate the Feast of Pentecost (2:1; cf. Exod. 23:14–17; Lev. 23:15–21). Today's text consists of the middle portion of this speech. In the preceding section (2:16–21), Peter asserts that the outpouring of the Spirit signifies the arrival of the last days, of which Joel had prophesied (Joel 3:1–5).

In this section, Peter turns to the topic at hand—Jesus of Nazareth (v. 22; cf. 3:6; 4:10; 6:14; 22:8; 26:9; also Luke 18:37; 24:19; John 18:5, 7; 19:19). What follows is a brief rehearsal of the main points of the kerygma: (1) Jesus' messianic ministry authenticated by displays of divine power (v. 22); (2) his crucifixion (v. 23); and (3) his resurrection (v. 24). Clearly, the accent falls on the last item, for it is expounded most thoroughly in the following verses (vv. 25–32). Indeed, today's text moves toward this proclamation of Christ's resurrection as its grand climax (v. 32). We can consider each of these items in turn.

1. *Jesus the messianic prophet* (v. 22). Peter begins with what the crowds cannot deny—that a Nazarene named Jesus had recently traveled among them performing signs and wonders. The capsule summary of the Gospel of Luke further connects these authenticating works with his prophetic role (Luke 24:19; cf. Acts 10:38). It was commonly assumed that such displays of power were signs of divine legitimacy (cf. John 2:18; 3:2). They indicated that God was working through him (v. 22; cf. John 5:36). Nor did the work of God end with Jesus. What began with Jesus continued in the early church (Acts 2:43; 4:30; 5:12; 6:8; 7:36; 8:13; 14:3; 15:12; cf. 2 Cor. 12:12).

2. *Jesus crucified through divine necessity and human conspiracy* (v. 23). Responsibility for the death of Jesus is dual. The Jews whom Peter addresses are charged with crucifying and killing him (Acts 3:13–17; 4:10; 5:30–31; 7:52; 10:39–40; 13:27–30), but they did not act alone. The actual execution was carried out "by the hands of those outside the law," or "by men outside the Law" (v. 23, NJB), that is, the Romans. At one level, then, his death was the result of human complicity.

But at another level, his death occurred "according to the definite plan and foreknowledge of God" (v. 23). Early Christians could hardly bring themselves to believe that Christ's death had been a historical accident. As tragic as it was, it could be fitted into God's divine plan. How? It was seen to have unfolded "according to Scripture," which meant in keeping with the divine plan (Luke 24:26–27, 44–47; Acts 3:18; 4:28; 13:29; cf. Luke 22:22). Ultimately, Christ's destiny was seen to have been set "before the foundation of the world" (1 Pet. 1:20).

3. *Jesus whom God raised from the dead* (vv. 24–32). This is the crux of the matter, the burden on Peter's heart. His main task is to show that the crucified Messiah has been vindicated by God, that human misdeeds have been reversed by divine power.

This Peter proceeds to do from Scripture, specifically Psalm 16:8–11. We read this psalm as an expression of trust on the part of the psalmist, who is confident of being delivered by God from peril—nothing more. But early Christians read it differently. They naturally assumed that it was written by David. But if so, it posed a problem. How could David say that God would not abandon his soul to Hades or let his faithful one see the Pit, or grave

(v. 27 = Ps. 16:10)? The problem was even more sharply focused in the Septuagint, which spoke of God's faithful one seeing "corruption," which seemed to imply more than mere death. Christian readers of this psalm well knew that David was "dead and buried" (v. 29, NJB; cf. 1 Kings 2:10; cf. Acts 13:36). They logically concluded that it must speak of someone else.

Combined with this was their reading of another psalm that spoke of a scion of David being raised up as his successor sometime in the future (Ps. 132:11–12; also Ps. 89:4). This could only be seen as a prophetic vision on David's part.

Their logic of Scripture interpretation enabled them to see Christ as the one being spoken of in Psalm 16. His resurrection was seen as God's rescuing him from the snares of death (cf. Ps. 18:4–5; 116:3; 2 Sam. 22:6). Death was unable to "keep him in its grip" (v. 24, REB).

In addition to this scriptural proof, the apostles claimed to be witnesses to the risen Lord (v. 32; cf. 1:22; 3:15; 4:33; 5:32; 10:41; 13:31; also 1 Cor. 15:15). What they had seen and experienced in their encounter with the risen Lord enabled them to make sense of otherwise inexplicable Scriptures. And what they read in Scripture enabled them to make sense of their Easter experience. It was a mutually reinforcing set of interpretations. Scripture illuminated their experience, and their experience illuminated Scripture.

Psalm 16

In his Pentecost sermon, Peter uses Psalm 16 to argue that David had spoken of the resurrection of Jesus (Acts 2:25–28). This example of Christian utilization of the Jewish Scriptures is somewhat typical. Certain allusions and particular terminology in the Hebrew Scriptures were exegeted by the early Christians in terms of beliefs and positions already held by the church.

The ancient rabbis understood this psalm as David writing about himself. In addition, they understood the text as speaking about actual death, at least in verse 3a. This text, read as "the holy that are in the earth" (and therefore dead), was said to speak about the deceased because "the Holy One (God) does not call the righteous man holy until he is laid away in the earth. Why not? Because the Inclination-to-evil [the evil *yetzer* of the human personality] keeps pressing him. And so God does not put His trust in him in this world till the day of his death. . . . That the Lord will not call a righteous man holy until he is laid away in the earth is what is meant."

In spite of the translation difficulties found in verses 2–4, where the worshiper appears to refer to the worship of other gods ("the holy ones" and "the noble" may denote the holy and mighty god mentioned in v. 4), the remainder of the text makes reasonably good sense. (In addition to the NRSV, one should consult the New Jewish Publication Society Version.)

Verses 5–11 open with a short confessional statement addressed to a human audience (v. 5a) and is immediately followed by a confessional statement of trust addressed to God (v. 5b). The terminology of this verse, as well as verse 6, speaks of what one has inherited or been given in life—portion, cup, lot, lines, and heritage. The NJPSV translates as:

> The Lord is my allotted share and portion;
>   You control my fate.
> Delightful country has fallen to my lot;
>   lovely indeed is my estate.

Instead of being guilty of worshiping false gods, the psalmist is depicted as one who constantly thinks of God (vv. 7–8). The counsel God gives (v. 7a) is matched by that of the person's own conscience (NRSV: "heart," although literally "the kidneys," denoting the inner self). The term translated "night" in verse 7b is actually the Hebrew plural "nights" (="watches of the night," "every night," or "the dark night"). The human activity and consistency (v. 8a) are matched by God's consistent preservation, with the consequence that the psalmist can confess, "I shall not be moved," that is, threatened or overcome.

The last section (vv. 9–11) returns to direct address to God, confessing assurance that the request made in verse 1 will be granted, that is, the person will live and not die. It was this section that led to the psalm's usage in early Christian preaching and confession. Again, the NJPSV conveys the meaning better than the NRSV:

> So my heart rejoices,
>   my whole being exults,
>   and my body rests secure.
> For You will not abandon me to Sheol,
>   or let Your faithful one see the Pit.

Sheol and Pit refer to the realm of the dead. Probably the psalm was used originally by persons near death as a result of some sickness. Of course, they do not want to die but want to remain alive to enjoy their heritage (vv. 5–6, 11b).

1 Peter 1:3–9

Today's epistolary text occurs in the form of an opening prayer of blessing addressed to "the God and Father of our Lord Jesus Christ" (v. 3). It conforms to a well-known form of Jewish prayer that opens by addressing God as blessed (Berakah). Along with prayers of thanksgiving, these prayers of praise serve as opening sections of New Testament letters (cf. 2 Cor. 1:3; Eph. 1:3).

It may be useful to discuss the limits and division of the pericope. The suggested division (vv. 3–9) conforms to the NRSV and NIV. NJB divides the section at verse 6. Another outline is followed in REB, with paragraph divisions occurring at verses 3, 6, and 8. This latter arrangement is similar to that adopted in Nestle 26th ed., in which the prayer includes verses 3–12, with divisions occurring at verses 3, 6, 8, and 12. There is general agreement that a new major section begins with verse 13, as the language shifts to the imperative mood, which is typical of the way moral exhortation begins.

If we adopt the framework of Nestle 26th ed. and REB, today's text may be divided into three sections.

1. *New birth and living hope* (vv. 3–5). In language reminiscent of the Fourth Gospel (1:13; 3:3–5; cf. 1 John 2:29; 3:9), we are said to have been given a "new birth" (v. 3, NJB) as God's children. It is a theme continued in the letter (1:23). Because of this strong baptismal imagery, some scholars have suggested that the Epistle of First Peter at an earlier stage of redaction functioned as a baptismal liturgy. It is a plausible suggestion, because it is easy to imagine how the opening section (vv. 3–12) might have been used as a prayer in a

baptismal setting and how the following material (1:13–2:10) might have served as a baptismal sermon in which the newly baptized were exhorted to holy living.

The basis of the new birth is God's "resurrection of Jesus Christ from the dead" (v. 3). Here we have a mixing of the Johannine notion of the baptism as a new birth (John 3:3–5) and the Pauline understanding of baptism as a dying and rising with Christ (Rom. 6:3–4). The new birth imagery is crucial in linking our new status as God's children with the inheritance that is ours (v. 4). Bestowal of this new status as God's children is seen as an act of "great mercy" (v. 3; cf. Eph. 2:4; also Sir. 16:12).

The inheritance is no ordinary legacy, such as land, prosperity, or political security (cf. Gen. 17:1–8). It is rather a heavenly inheritance that "nothing can destroy or spoil or wither" (v. 4, REB; cf. Eph. 1:18; Col. 1:5, 12; 3:24; Heb. 9:15; also Matt. 6:19–20). Even though it lies in the future as a "salvation ready to be revealed in the last time" (v. 5; cf. 1:20), it is protected by divine power (cf. 1 Cor. 2:5). It is reserved for those who live "in faith."

2. *Suffering and the refinement of faith* (vv. 6–7). As the prayer unfolds, there is a shift from the lofty language of future salvation and the divine inheritance to the harsher realities of life below: "For a little while you have had to suffer various trials" (v. 6). Later in the letter, the references to suffering become even more explicit (4:12–13, 19; 5:10).

Suffering is not without value, however. It is like a refining fire (James 1:2; Prov. 17:3; Mal. 3:2–3; 1 Cor. 3:13; Wisd. of Sol. 3:6; Sir. 2:5). But what emerges from Christian suffering is even more valuable than gold. Though refined, gold is perishable, whereas Christian faith is not. For this reason, suffering properly experienced can become an occasion for rejoicing (v. 6; cf. Rom. 5:3; 1 Pet. 5:10).

3. *Loving and believing without seeing* (vv. 8–9). As the prayer moves toward its conclusion, it sounds more Johannine in its insistence that we can believe without having actually seen (John 17:20; 20:29; 2 Cor. 5:7). This becomes reassuring especially for those who were not privy to the words and deeds of the historical Jesus, but who are not for that reason disadvantaged in the life of faith. Historical and geographical proximity do not ensure faith in the New Testament sense, which involves loving One whom we have not seen with our eyes (cf. Eph. 6:24; 2 Tim. 4:8).

John 20:19–31

It remains the case experientially if not cognitively that for most congregations Easter is a day and not a season. The lectionary has as one of its benefits as well as its tasks the weekly reminder that today and every Sunday until Pentecost are Sundays *of* Easter and not *after* Easter. Of course, every Sunday, even those during Lent, is an Easter Festival, but human nature being what it is, matters of great importance lose their impact when given only generalized attention. Therefore, for seven Sundays we will be attending to texts that spell out implications of the resurrection of Jesus Christ.

Today's lesson consists of two parts: 20:19–29 and 20:30–31. Verses 19–29 provide the second half of John's resurrection narrative, the first (vv. 1–18) having been considered for the Easter Day service. Verses 30–31 constitute a concluding statement by the Evangelist. Chapter 21 is an epilogue and may have been added by the Evangelist or one of his disciples after the Gospel had been formally concluded.

In the comments on John 20:1–18, it was pointed out that both 1–18 and 19–29 involve double stories. In verses 1–18, the resurrection of Jesus touches Mary Magdalene and two of the Twelve, Simon Peter and the beloved disciple. As was stated, faith was generated in the beloved disciple by the sight of an empty tomb and grave cloths, and in Mary Magdalene by the word of Jesus. Again now, in verses 19–29 two stories are interwoven, with faith being generated in different ways. On Sunday evening of the same day as the events of verses 1–18 (v. 19), Jesus appears to his disciples (except Thomas, v. 24). He bestows on them his peace (vv. 19, 21), commissions them to continue the work that God had given him (v. 21), breathes on them, giving the Holy Spirit (v. 22), and grants to them apostolic authority for retaining or forgiving sins (v. 23). Verses 19–23 contain, therefore, not solely an appearance of the risen Christ, the sight of whom generated in the disciples faith and joy (v. 20).

In this brief digest are two additional elements. One is the Johannine Pentecost. Luke, the other recorder of Pentecost, makes the experience a historical narrative consisting of Jesus' forty days of appearances as the risen Christ, his promise of the outpouring of the Holy Spirit, the Ascension, ten days of prayer and waiting, and the coming of the Spirit at Pentecost (Acts 1:1–2:42). John has no such chronology or drama, but the promise of the giving of the Spirit as discussed in chapters 14–16 is here fulfilled. A rereading of those chapters will impress again upon the church the life-giving necessity of the Spirit for the life and work of the community.

The other significant event in verses 19–23 is the granting of apostolic authority (v. 23; Matt. 16:19; 18:18). Through the apostles, the continuity between Christ and the church is established, and through them the benefits and the work of Christ remain in the world after his ascension. Through the Holy Spirit, the departed Christ abides to grant comfort, instruction, and power in the life of the church.

This brings us to Thomas, whose absence and hesitation in believing (vv. 24–26) has brought upon him the name "Doubting Thomas" and negative attention, which forgets his earlier courage (11:16) and theological probing (14:5). However, after his experience with the risen Christ the next Sunday (v. 26), Thomas makes a confession of faith as strong as any in the Gospel: "My Lord and my God!" (v. 28). Whether Thomas actually touched Jesus is not clear (vv. 26–27); Jesus simply refers to his having believed because he had seen (v. 29). At this point, Jesus pronounces a blessing upon all who have not seen and yet who believe (v. 29); that is, upon all who come to faith through the word of Christ through the apostles and the church (17:20). Nothing could be more encouraging to the Johannine church or to us than the assurance that faith is available to all persons in all places regardless of distance in time or place from Jesus of Nazareth.

The Evangelist's concluding statement (vv. 30–31) says three things: (1) the events recorded here are but a selection from many signs that Jesus performed, (2) but these have been related in order to generate faith in Jesus as Christ and Son of God, and (3) the purpose of generating faith is to give life. Saying that these stories are to help the reader believe does not clearly identify the reader. Because the Gospel assumes some familiarity with Jesus and his work, very likely the book is addressing those of weak faith, or misguided faith, or faith that depends too much on signs, or new faith that needs to grow. After all, in this Gospel there is faith seeking, faith confessing, faith faltering, faith questioning, faith praising, and faith deepening. All of us are addressed in these "signs which he did."

Third Sunday of Easter

Acts 2:14*a*, 36–41;
Psalm 116:1–4, 12–19;
1 Peter 1:17–23;
Luke 24:13–35

The first lesson from Acts consists of the final section of Peter's Pentecost sermon, in which he urges his hearers to repent, be baptized, and receive the gift of God's Spirit. If the first lesson sees salvation as a gift extended, the second lesson looks at salvation in retrospect, as something already experienced. It reminds us of what is already ours in Christ and how we should behave accordingly. The Gospel lesson records the familiar episode of Jesus' encounter with the two men en route to Emmaus. Here we see faith in the risen Lord arising from nothing: they first encounter Jesus as one unknown, but eventually their hearts are opened to the true reality of his New Being. The reading from the psalm is the final section of a psalm of thanksgiving in which the psalmist reflects on an experience of divine deliverance and offers himself in thankful praise to the God who delivered him. In one way or another, all four readings today develop the theme of salvation—as something offered, experienced, discovered, and that elicits a response of thanksgiving.

Acts 2:14*a*, 36–41

In today's first lesson, we have the concluding portion of Peter's Pentecost sermon and a description of its impact on the crowd. A few verses intervene between this week's lesson and last week's lesson, but they provide a crucial link in the argument from Scripture and should be read in preparation for this text.

The sermon ends on a note of finality: "Let the entire house of Israel know with certainty that God has made him both Lord and Messiah, this Jesus whom you crucified" (v. 36). These two christological titles are intended to encapsulate the arguments from Scripture that were referred to earlier. Psalm 110:1 has just been cited to show that David envisioned a heavenly Lord other than himself to whom God promised a position of exalted dominion (vv. 34–35). Psalm 16:8–11 had been cited to show that God's Holy One, the Messiah, would triumph over the pangs of death. By his resurrection, Jesus was seen to have qualified on both scores. He was unable to be bound by death; thus he qualified as the Christ. Having been vindicated by God, he now reigned as heavenly Lord.

A critically important claim was that the *crucified Jesus* now bore these titles. More than that, the hearers, some of them at least, had participated in his death. The logic was

259

compelling enough for the hearers to be "cut to the heart" (cf. Ps. 109:16, "the broken-hearted"), and they issued the cry of salvation, "What shall we do?" (v. 37). It is the earnest cry of those multitudes who had earlier heard John the Baptist preaching repentance (Luke 3:10). It is echoed later as others are confronted with the challenge of the gospel (Acts 16:30; 22:16).

Peter's response is a call to repentance and baptism. In this instance, repentance involves both the recognition of their mistake in misconstruing the true identity of Jesus and remorse for their misdeeds in putting him to death. Naturally, as it did in the preaching of John the Baptist, repentance required reorientation of life that was visibly displayed in merciful and just behavior (Luke 3:8, 10–14; cf. Acts 3:19).

Baptism "in the name of Jesus Christ" probably meant baptism in which the name of Jesus was spoken over the initiate (cf. Acts 8:16; 10:48; 19:5). Like John's baptism, it bestowed forgiveness of sins (Luke 3:3; 24:47; cf. Acts 5:31; 10:43; 13:38). But unlike John's baptism, it was accompanied by a bestowal of the Spirit (cf. Acts 19:1–7; also 8:15; 10:47). What is implied here, of course, is that the prophecy of Joel that spoke of an outpouring of the Spirit on all flesh (2:17–21) now becomes a fulfilled promise among these believers. As participants in the events of the "last days," they are now recipients of God's Spirit.

They are assured that God's promise extends to them, their children, and those near and far away. Whether this is to be understood geographically, that is, Jews present in Jerusalem as well as those living in remote regions, or ethnically, that is, Jews (those near) and Gentiles (those afar off), is not certain. Given the prominence of the Gentile mission in the Book of Acts, it is likely the latter. Also, similar language is used elsewhere in the New Testament to distinguish Jews and Gentiles (cf. Eph. 2:12–13; also Acts 22:21; Isa. 57:19; Sir. 24:32). In either case, the gospel is understood as a summons by God. The promise is extended to those "whom the Lord our God calls to him" (v. 39; cf. Joel 2:32 = Acts 2:21).

The hearers are urged to deliver themselves from "this crooked age" (v. 40, REB). The language is supplied by Deuteronomy 32:5 and Psalm 78:8 (cf. Phil. 2:15).

The response was overwhelming. The word reached home, and the hearers responded by submitting to baptism (cf. 8:12, 16; 18:8; cf. Matt. 28:19). In one day, three thousand persons joined the messianic community, the first of several staggering responses recorded in the Book of Acts (cf. 2:47; 5:14; 6:7; 9:31; 11:21, 24). This is Luke's way of showing that the movement was far from negligible. It eventually reaches Rome and en route convinces many that "these things were not done in a corner" (26:26, NJB).

The intent of today's text is clear. It seeks to show the impact of the resurrection faith on Jewish hearers. More specifically, it intends to present the crucified Jesus as the most compelling candidate for messiahship and lordship, as the one who most convincingly makes sense of Scriptures such as Psalm 16 and Psalm 110. As such, he is presented as the bringer of the new age of the Spirit in which salvation and forgiveness of sins are extended to the penitent and obedient. What's more, our text wants us to see that proclamation of Jesus as Lord worked its effects on multitudes who were looking for an alternative to a generation of crookedness and an age of brokenness.

Psalm 116:1–4, 12–19

This psalm, portions of which are a lection for Holy Thursday, like Ezekiel 37 gives expression to the theme of "escape from death." Although frequently interpreted as expressing a belief in the resurrection (so similarly Ps. 16; see Acts 2:25–31), the psalm was originally composed to be used in a thanksgiving ritual following recovery from sickness.

Thanksgiving rituals, in ancient Israel as in most cultures, were intent on two goals: (1) celebration of the new or renewed status of the person/group/community and (2) offering testimony to the one who had granted the status being celebrated. Both of these goals focus more on the human situation than on gaining the attention of the Divine. (This is unlike the lamenting situation, where exactly the opposite is the case.)

Thus, in this psalm the addressee is fundamentally the human audience. (God is addressed only in vv. 16–17 and possibly in v. 8. In v. 7, the worshiper engages in self-address and self-assurance.)

The condition of trouble or the state of distress from which the worshiper has been saved is depicted in various ways throughout the psalm: snares of death, pangs of Sheol, distress and anguish, brought low, death, tears, stumbling. All of these illustrate the marginal state of existence into which sickness had thrown the person.

The worshiper's actions in taking to God the predicament of illness is noted in verse 4 as calling "on the name of the Lord" or simply praying for help. The recovered or assured worshiper even provides a summary of the prayer spoken on that earlier occasion (see v. 4b).

Verses 12–19 are the closing portions of the thanksgiving psalm and are concerned with the fulfillment of vows made earlier, probably at the time when the worshiper petitioned God for deliverance from trouble, most likely a debilitating illness.

In rendering the vows, which would certainly have included the offering of sacrifice, the worshiper addresses a human audience (vv. 12–15, 18–19) as well as the Deity (vv. 16–17). We should think of such thanksgiving rituals as times of great happiness and jubilant celebration. A person whose life had been threatened, disoriented, and removed from the normal course of activity had been restored to wholeness. The life that had fallen into the grip of hell itself and had been invaded by the power of death was now free of both the illness and the anguished turmoil that the sickness brought. Now the worshiper can look back and speak of the sorrowful plight of the past, which now is only a life-transforming memory. There certainly must be "scars" from such a past, but they are signs of past triumphs and the residues of God's grace, to be cherished and celebrated, not embarrassingly hidden. At such a celebration, friends and family of the formerly ill person would have attended worship with the redeemed. Such worship would have included not only thanksgiving in word but also feasting, drinking, and dancing. These festive symbols marked the end of a former state and the beginning of a new state of living. They were enjoyed as the sacramental signs of God's concern and care.

In verses 12–15, the worshiper addresses a human audience of friends and family. The elements of the thanksgiving spoken of included the offering of a cup of salvation, the worship of God, and the fulfillment of vows. The cup mentioned is best understood as the drink offering made as part of the thanksgiving sacrificial ritual (see Num. 28:7) or perhaps the cup of wine drunk in the thanksgiving meal (Ps. 23:5). Such a cup symbolized God's deliverance, the opposite of the cup of God's wrath (see Isa. 51:17; Jer. 25:15). The worshiper reminds the listeners that God does not wish the death of one of his faithful worshipers, because for God such a death is a serious, weighty matter (v. 15).

The place of the thanksgiving celebration was the temple in Jerusalem, where sacrifices could be made (v. 18–19). In such thanksgiving services, most of the animals sacrificed would have reverted to the worshiper to be cooked and eaten in the temple precincts before the next day had passed (see Lev. 6:11–18). Thus the sacrifice of thanksgiving imposed lavish and extravagant eating and communal sharing.

Verses 16–17 would have been prayed directly to God in conjunction with offering the thanksgiving sacrifice. The worshiper thus declared his or her status before God: "I am your servant," a status dependent upon the redemptive work of God, "You have loosed my bonds."

1 Peter 1:17–23

Today's epistolary lesson sounds like instructions given to new converts. In an earlier form, it could have been part of a baptismal homily or catechetical instructions for those recently baptized.

The language suggests that the readers are Gentile Christians who have turned from pagan ways. They are reminded of the "desires you cherished in your days of ignorance" (v. 14, REB) and the "futile way of life handed down from your ancestors" (v. 18, NJB; cf. 2:10; 4:3). To characterize pagan life as "ignorant" and "futile" ("empty," NIV) reflects the attitude of moral superiority that Jews, and in this case Jewish Christians, presumed toward Gentiles (cf. Matt. 5:47; 1 Thess. 4:5). It is, of course, a caricature, because there existed a strong moral tradition in Greek and Roman thought, exemplified in the likes of Epictetus and Plutarch, as well as among numerous ordinary citizens. But cases of pagan immorality are well attested too, and there is no reason to deny that some Gentiles who became Christians had left behind a profligate way of life (cf. 4:3–4).

Newly converted Gentiles would find themselves living in a hostile environment, feeling quite alien as "strangers in the world" (1:1, NIV). Their time on earth could well be conceived as a time of exile (v. 17). In this respect, there was a long Jewish legacy of living in the world as sojourners and foreigners (cf. Gen. 23:4; 24:37; Ps. 39:12; cf. Heb. 11:13). For Gentile readers, this could have been true in several senses. They may have been living away from their homeland literally—in scattered regions of Asia Minor (1:1–2). But in another sense, Christians saw themselves as exiles on earth whose real hometown was in heaven (cf. Phil. 3:20; Col. 3:1–4; Heb. 13:14). In yet a third sense, our readers may have felt like foreigners. They were now part of a new religion, and its frame of reference, rituals, and moral expectations were equally new and unfamiliar.

And what is appropriate instruction for persons in this situation? To define the contours of responsibility in light of the change they have recently experienced. This is precisely the move that is made in today's text. It occurs as part of a much larger section of moral instruction (1:13–2:10).

The text contains two familiar types of material: imperatives that give specific instructions about how to behave and indicatives that describe the basis for such behavior. Thus the readers are charged to be holy in their conduct (vv. 15–16), to be "scrupulously careful" in their living (v. 17, JB), and to love one another deeply and sincerely (v. 22). But these moral instructions are grounded in a particular theological understanding, and thus the readers are reminded of certain things about God, the nature of their conversion, and the work of Christ. Let us consider each of these briefly.

1. *The nature of God* (vv. 17, 21, 23). In the verses immediately preceding today's text, the readers are reminded of God's holiness (v. 16; Lev. 11:44–45) and the way their own character is expected to participate in and reflect the character of God. But in addition to this, they are reminded of what it means to address God as Father (v. 17). This was a long-standing tradition in Jewish thought, as when David (Ps. 89:26), Isaiah (Isa. 63:16; 64:8), and the Jewish sage (Sir. 23:1–6) address God in this manner or when Yahweh expects to be

addressed in this way (Jer. 3:19). It is a tradition that Jesus appropriates and seems to sharpen even further (Matt. 6:9; cf. 7:11; 23:9). Accordingly, it becomes an appropriate form of address for Christians (Rom. 8:15).

The understanding of God is rendered more specifically, however, as we are told that God renders judgment impartially, which means that God judges "without favouritism" (v. 17, NJB; cf. Acts 10:34; Rom. 2:11; Gal. 2:6; Eph. 6:9; Col. 3:25; James 2:9; also 2 Chron. 19:7; Sir. 35:14–15). The basis of God's judgment lies in what we do: we are judged according to our works (Ps. 62:12; Matt. 16:27; 2 Cor. 11:15; 2 Tim. 4:14; Rev. 2:23).

2. *The nature of conversion* (vv. 18, 22–23). One basis for the moral life is to recall the nature of one's conversion. In this instance, the readers are reminded that they were "ransomed." This metaphor of buying freedom from slavery has Old Testament roots (Isa. 52:3) and becomes a standard way for understanding the Christian experience of deliverance from sin (1 Cor. 6:20; 7:23; Gal. 4:5; Titus 2:14). What makes Christian redemption especially valuable, however, is the purchase price—"the precious blood of Christ . . . a lamb without defect or blemish" (v. 19). The image here is Christ seen as the lamb sacrificed for the sins of the people (Heb. 9:12, 14; Rev. 5:9; also John 1:29).

Conversion is also seen as a purification of the soul (v. 22) that occurs as the result of "obedience to the truth" (cf. Acts 6:7; Rom. 1:5; 15:18; 16:26; Gal. 3:2–5; 2 Cor. 10:5). In addition, it is a new birth (v. 23), a metaphor familiar in the Johannine tradition (John 1:13; 3:3–5). The image is taken further here, as we are told that the creative seed responsible for the new birth is the imperishable word of God (cf. Luke 8:11; James 1:18). Unlike grass and flowers, it never fades but abides forever (vv. 24–25 = Isa. 40:6–9). Presupposed here is a dynamic understanding of God's creative word (cf. Heb. 4:12; Eph. 6:17; Rev. 1:16; 2:12; also Wisd. of Sol. 7:22–30; Isa. 49:2).

3. *The work of Christ* (vv. 19–21). We have already mentioned Christ as the sacrificial lamb whose blood purchases our redemption. New converts need to be reminded that Christ's work is part of an age-old plan that reaches back to the time "before the foundation of the world" (v. 20; cf. Acts 2:23; Eph. 1:4; John 17:24). They are now living in the "end of the ages" (v. 20) when God's revelation has been manifested (Rom. 16:25–27; 2 Tim. 1:9–10). The decisive act was God's raising Christ from the dead (v. 21; cf. Rom. 4:24; 8:11; 10:9; Eph. 1:20), and this provides the basis for Christian confidence and hope (cf. Col. 1:27).

The true test of such theological reflection, however, is the form of life that it produces, what might be called its social implications. Today's text insists that this way of understanding God, Christ, and one's conversion results in a form of community in which love is deep and genuine (v. 22; cf. 1 Thess. 4:9; Rom. 12:10; Heb. 13:1; 2 Pet. 1:7). This is a variation of the Johannine new commandment that was to serve as the guiding principle for Christian community (also 4:8; cf. John 13:34; 15:12–13, 17; 1 John 2:7–11; 2 John 5; also cf. Gal. 6:2).

Luke 24:13–35

The reader is referred to the commentary on the Gospel lection for Easter Evening. The discussion of Luke 24:13–49 at that point was devoted primarily to verses 13–35.

Fourth Sunday of Easter

Acts 2:42–47;
Psalm 23;
1 Peter 2:19–25;
John 10:1–10

Today's first lesson is the first of several Lukan summaries in the narrative of Acts designed to typify life in the earliest Christian community. It reflects the exuberant mood of a new movement pulsating with the life of the Spirit. The other three texts, the second lesson, the Gospel lesson, and the psalm, all reflect the common theme of shepherd and shepherding. The famous Twenty-third Psalm depicts Yahweh as the Shepherd of Israel, and the Gospel reading from John applies the shepherd image to Jesus, the "good shepherd [who] lays down his life for the sheep" (John 10:11). The epistolary reading further extends the shepherd imagery to Christ, drawing on Isaiah 53:5–12, and reminds us of our former status as straying sheep who have been rescued by the "shepherd and guardian" of our souls (1 Pet. 2:25).

Acts 2:42–47

With these remarks at the conclusion of Peter's inaugural sermon on Pentecost, Luke intends to provide us with a sketch of life within the newly formed messianic community, the church. It is clearly an ideal portrait, typical of the way primordial beginnings are often sketched. In retrospect, we tend to look at the beginning of a movement, a group, or a nation in romantic, highly idealized terms. This is what Luke does here as he looks back on the beginning of the church perhaps a half-century or so after it began. We are shown a community of believers solid in their commitment to the apostolic faith that brought them into existence, but equally solid in their commitment to one another in their common life. It bears all the earmarks of a vital religious community.

First, they are *absorbed in religious teachings* to which they are committed (cf. 4:2, 18; 5:21, 25, 28, 42). In this case, they adhered to the "apostles' teaching," which probably refers to instruction designed to fill out the original proclamation (*kerygma*) and explore its implications for Christian living (cf. Heb. 6:1–2). We might regard 1 Corinthians 7–16 as typical of such instruction. It consists of Paul's detailed instructions on various topics about which Christians at Corinth have written him. In several instances, he cites earlier, foundational preaching and teaching (e.g., 1 Cor. 11:23–26; 15:3–11), but expands it and explores it more fully as he relates it to actual Christian practice.

Second, they have *regular fellowship in both social and religious settings*. They are portrayed as seeing each other daily and meeting together to worship and eat the sacred meal (Acts 20:7; 27:35). The word for fellowship is *koinonia* and is best rendered in a dynamic, participial form—"sharing." Not surprisingly, it can be used in the New Testament as a synonym for financial contributions (cf. 2 Cor. 8:4), the act of sharing one's material possessions with others.

In this summary, Luke places great emphasis on this aspect of their common life as he describes their activity of selling "their possessions and goods" and making appropriate distribution to all who had need. Fellowship in this setting means *active care for one another*. The particular form that it took here was a community of goods where the members "had all things in common" (v. 44). By mentioning this, Luke manages to portray the church as the embodiment of a common Hellenistic proverb, "for friends all things are common." That this was a sought after ideal is clear from the writings of Plato and Aristotle, among others, who presented the ideal community as one in which the needs of the citizens were cared for by the common efforts of everyone.

Combined with this generous spirit was the *spirit of oneness*: "all who believed were together" (v. 44). We are later told that they were "of one heart and soul" (4:32). This too is reminiscent of a Hellenistic proverb, "friends are one soul." Generosity and unity are seen as two sides of the same coin. Willingness to share possessions grows out of a sense of solidarity with one another as well as nourishing and reinforcing it. At this early stage, the church is experiencing unity and harmony (Acts 1:14; 4:24).

Third, they *continue steadfastly in prayer*. This becomes a hallmark of the early Christian community (cf. Acts 1:14; 6:4; Rom. 12:12; Eph. 6:18; Phil. 4:6; Col. 4:2; 1 Thess. 5:17; 1 Tim. 2:1). We can surmise that these were prayers of thanksgiving for their experience of divine grace (v. 47; cf. 1 Pet. 1:3–9), for deliverance from tight circumstances (cf. Acts 4:23–31), as well as petitions on behalf of their own members (cf. Acts 9:36–43). We should also note the correlation between prayer and the spirit of unity (Acts 1:14).

Fourth, they exhibited a *proper sense of awe before God* (v. 43). This was directly related to the "many wonders and signs" that continued to be done in their midst by the apostles (v. 43). Thus, as JB puts it, "The many miracles and signs worked through the apostles made a deep impression on everyone" (v. 43). What Luke wants to stress here is that the same power of the Spirit that manifested itself in Jesus' signs and wonders (cf. Luke 4:31–41) continues into the life of the church (cf. 4:30; 6:8; 8:13; 14:3; 15:12; also 7:36). The church thus embodies the eschatological vision sketched by Joel (2:28–32; cf. Acts 2:17–21). This respect before the power of the Divine continues to characterize the community (cf. 5:5, 11; Acts 19:17).

Fifth, they *grew and flourished* (v. 47). To the original three thousand (v. 41) the Lord adds members daily. As Luke unfolds the story of the church, it is a story punctuated by numerical growth (cf. 6:7; 9:31; 11:21; 12:24; 14:1; 16:5; 19:20). This is Luke's way of showing that the movement has God's approval. It also attests the power of the word to convict.

How should this text inform preaching? As a blueprint against which to measure performance? As an ideal toward which we should aspire? As a primitive vision to which the church should be recalled? Perhaps all, perhaps none. We all know that churches at every level—local congregations, denominations, and the church universal—are more fractured than this portrait allows. Nor should we assume that community of goods is the only, or even the best, form of responsible sharing—certainly not in every time, place, or situation. Even

Luke-Acts allows for the possibility of other forms of fellowship, such as almsgiving and showing hospitality. We also know that fidelity may not necessarily produce numerical growth. For whatever reason, churches may teach, pray, worship, and share, and still not grow numerically. Should we use this text to flail them? Perhaps. But neither should we bow before the idol of numerical growth and assume that if the numbers are there, we are therefore faithful. They may be high for the wrong reasons.

So we best use this text as Luke intended it—as a broad stroke sketch of the church at its beginning: faithful in teaching; active in sharing; devoted to eating, praying, and worshiping together; fearful before the Divine; exuberant in its praise of God. It is a picture of the church on its best behavior.

Psalm 23

This psalm was discussed for the Fourth Sunday in Lent.

1 Peter 2:19–25

The immediate context for today's epistolary reading is provided by the verse preceding: "Slaves, accept the authority of your masters with all deference, not only those who are kind and gentle but also those who are harsh" (v. 18). What follows in our passage, then, are instructions specifically addressed to Christians who served as slaves in their master's household. To modern ears, verse 18 sounds anachronistic if not offensive in its call for slaves to be docile in their obedience. Accordingly, the compilers of the *Common Lectionary* have decided to begin the pericope at verse 19.

This set of instructions to slaves (vv. 18–25) occurs as part of a comprehensive set of exhortations on how to behave in various social and personal relationships. It is an abbreviated "household code," a form of Greco-Roman moral instruction adopted by Christian writers for enumerating the duties of various members of a household: masters and slaves, husbands and wives, parents and children (cf. Col. 3:18–4:1; Eph. 5:22–6:9). In the Epistle of First Peter, the author intends to instruct his readers in their political (2:13–17), social (2:18–25), domestic (3:1–7), and ecclesiastical (3:8–12) responsibilities.

The specific problem dealt with in today's text is how to behave when treated unjustly. For the original addressees, the question was what a slave should do when mistreated by a cruel master. We can well imagine the abuses that must have occurred in that social situation. Our knowledge of a more recent era when slavery was an accepted practice in American life may supply ample illustrations. In particular, our text may be addressing the tension created within a household where a slave had become a Christian. Old allegiances were perhaps being threatened by newly formed allegiances to another Lord and Master, Jesus Christ.

In any case, our text instructs slaves to be obedient and respectful to masters of every stripe, whether kind and gentle or overbearing (v. 18). We are told that suffering pain unjustly has "some merit . . . if it is done for the sake of God" (v. 19, JB). If slaves were beaten because they had done wrong, they were arguably getting what they deserved. Thus there was no particular credit in that kind of suffering. But what if they were beaten when they had done nothing wrong and were simply doing their duty? If they could keep from retaliating and find within themselves the capacity to endure such wrong patiently, they are assured that they have "God's approval" (v. 19). A slightly different slant is provided by REB: "It is a sign of grace if, because God is in his thoughts, someone endures the pain of undeserved suffering."

As an incentive to bear up under unjust suffering, the readers are presented with the example of Christ (vv. 21–25). He is presented as the one who suffered for us, and in doing so set an example that all who suffer unjustly could follow (cf. Matt. 16:24). Various echoes from Isaiah 53 suggest that Christ is understood here as the Suffering Servant: he did not perjure himself (v. 22=Isa. 53:9); "he . . . bore our sins" (v. 24=Isa. 53:12); "by his wounds you have been healed" (v. 24, JB=Isa. 53:5).

One of the distinctive features of this passage is how Jesus' conduct at his trial is presented as exemplary for Christians. Elsewhere in the New Testament, other aspects of his life and teaching serve as examples, but rarely events from his trial. We are assured that "he committed no sin" (v. 22), which may be rendered in a softer form as "he had done nothing wrong" (NJB). Legally, this may have meant that he was not guilty as charged, but in Christian teaching his innocence came to mean his sinlessness in the broadest sense (3:18; cf. John 8:46; 2 Cor. 5:21; Heb. 4:15; 7:26; 1 John 3:5; also John 7:18).

One of the elements preserved in the story of the trial was his nonretaliation: he did not return insult for injury, threats for torture (v. 23; cf. Matt. 27:14, 26, and parallels). This was in keeping with his teaching of nonretaliation (cf. Matt. 5:39), which became a standard element of Christian teaching (Rom. 12:19, 21; 1 Thess. 5:15).

What was especially exemplary was the level and quality of trust Jesus displayed in the trial: he committed his cause to the One who judges justly (cf. Jer. 11:20). God is finally the one who vindicates the cause of the elect (Rom. 12:19; Deut. 32:35).

Not only is the death of Christ exemplary; it is redemptive as well. His sacrificial death is seen as the act through which our own cause is vindicated before God (cf. Col. 1:22; Heb. 10:10; also John 1:29; Rev. 5:6, 12). In language strikingly Pauline in tone, we are reminded that Christ's death makes it possible for us to "cease to live for sin and begin to live for righteousness" (v. 24, REB; cf. Rom. 6:11, 18).

At this point, another christological image is introduced—Christ the shepherd (v. 25). This is, of course, also suggested by Isaiah 53, where the Suffering Servant is pictured as a lamb led to the slaughter (53:7), as is the reference to us as those who have "gone astray like sheep" (53:6; cf. Matt. 9:36; also Ezek. 34:5, 16). It is an image more fully expanded in the Gospel reading for today (John 10) and also resonant with the image of Yahweh as shepherd in today's psalm (Ps. 23). The image of the "guardian" (*episkopos*) is a natural extension of the same image.

The preacher may want to connect this christological image of Jesus as shepherd with the Gospel reading and the psalm and explore the ways in which Christ serves as our example. The first part of the text will be more problematic homiletically because it rubs against the grain of the modern conscience, which is less willing to yield in docile submission to oppressive forces and masters. The issue remains perennially current, for in every age there are instances when people suffer unjustly. The difficult task is to frame a response that is appropriate to our calling (v. 21) and that is properly "aware of God" (v. 19).

John 10:1–10

The language and imagery of John 10:1–10 are so stirring and homiletically suggestive the preacher may prefer not to wrestle with the literary problems related to this text. However the problems are there, and knowing what they are, even when not satisfactorily resolved, is a requirement of honest study and undergirds preaching with confidence.

The problems are three. The first has to do with ascertaining the context for 10:1–10. These verses are a portion of the larger unit, 10:1–21, but does 10:1–21 continue chapter 9, or does it belong with what follows, 10:22–42? In subject matter, 10:1 seems to continue 9:35–41, which deals with leadership of the people of God. If this is the position taken, then the preacher may locate the teaching of Jesus in 10:1–10 in Jerusalem at the Feast of Tabernacles, because the last time reference (7:2) was to that feast. On the other hand, 10:22 states, "At that time the festival of the Dedication took place in Jerusalem." Does that reference apply only to what follows or to the entirety of chapter 10? The preacher may decide that the uncertainties are greater than any value to be gained by indicating when and where John 10:1–10 can be placed. Historical curiosity may have to give way to the conclusion that our text has its own integrity and does not depend for its meaning on geographical or chronological context.

The second problem has to do with the writer's introduction at 10:6 of the word "figure," sometimes translated image, analogy, or even parable. This Gospel contains no parables of the kinds we meet in the Synoptics, but Jesus does speak "in figures" (16:25, 29), which refers to language that is not plain. Note two statements that make this clear: "I have said these things to you in figures of speech. The hour is coming when I will no longer speak to you in figures, but will tell you plainly of the Father" (16:25). And: "His disciples said, 'Yes, now you are speaking plainly, not in any figure of speech'" (16:29). As with the parables in Mark (4:10–11), Jesus' language in this Gospel is not such as to make the truth of the kingdom immediately obvious to any and all within earshot, whether they are committed or not. Understanding Jesus is more a matter of faith and character than it is of intellectual ability. As stated in 7:17, whoever wills to do God's will shall know whether the teaching is of God.

The third problem related to our lesson has to do with its internal unity. This is not simply an academic problem. Within 10:1–10 and extending to verse 16 there are so many rich images that no one sermon can clearly embrace all of them. Even a casual reading raises questions prompted by confusion, Is Jesus the shepherd who enters the door while others steal their way in, or is Jesus the door by which all must enter? Perhaps clarity will be served by regarding verses 1–6 as one unit and verses 7–10 another (some commentators further divide 1–6 into 1–3a and 3bc, and 7–10 into 7–8 and 9–10). Verses 7–10 seem to offer commentary on verses 1–5.

The governing thought in verses 1–6 deals with leadership of God's people, the shepherd being one type, thieves and robbers the other. The shepherd comes naturally to the flock, acting in trust and loving care. The relationship between the shepherd and the sheep was a familiar one and of such special favor as to provide both Old and New Testaments with images of divine caring (Isa. 40:11; Ps. 23; Mark 6:34; Luke 15:3–7). But who were the thieves and bandits? It seems insufficient to identify them totally with uncaring leaders among the Jews; throughout the New Testament, warnings about false church leaders make it evident that from the beginning the Christian communities were plagued by those whose concerns were pride, power, and purse (Matt. 7:15–23; Acts 20:29–35; Phil. 3:18–19; 1 Pet. 5:1–5). Despite twenty centuries of warning, the church continues to have difficulty discerning a thief in the sheepfold.

In verses 7–10, the governing image is that of Christ as the door. This is to say, Christ, both doctrinally and pastorally, both in word and in example, is the canon by which to measure and evaluate Christian leadership. The Shepherd is the door to shepherding; the flock that knows the Shepherd can recognize his voice in the teaching, preaching, and pastoring of those who are his shepherds. And not only to the leaders but also to the whole membership, Christ as door is the promise of both security ("will be saved") and freedom ("will come in and go out and find pasture," v. 9). In the background of these statements is the description of Joshua as shepherd of Israel (Num. 27:15–17). In the foreground lie those guarantees of the continued relationship between Christ and the church: the word of Christ, the apostles, and the Holy Spirit.

Fifth Sunday of Easter

Acts 7:55–60;
Psalm 31:1–5, 15–16;
1 Peter 2:2–10;
John 14:1–14

The first lesson from Acts reports the final scene of the death of Stephen. It comes at the end of his highly provocative sermon in which he rehearses Israel's history from Abraham forward. The reading from the Psalter is a lament in which the psalmist prays for deliverance from his enemies. It provides one of the most well-known last sayings of Jesus: "Into your hand I commit my spirit" (Ps. 31:5=Luke 23:46). The second lesson provides another selection from First Peter with a clear christological focus on Christ as the rejected stone. Like other passages from First Peter, christological reflection is combined with moral exhortation. The Gospel lesson is taken from John 14, the well-known passage in which Jesus declares himself to be the way, truth, and life, and thus the only true access to God.

Acts 7:55–60

In this passage is recorded the death of Stephen. It comes at the end of a sermon in which he rehearses Israel's history from the call of Abraham down to the time of Solomon's temple, but treating mainly the lives of Joseph and Moses. It is a highly provocative sermon, to say the least, especially in its concluding remarks, when Stephen launches a penetrating criticism of the Jerusalem temple. He regards Solomon's decision to build a temple for God as a major step backward, siding instead with the prophetic sentiment that God's presence cannot be confined to sacred buildings (vv. 47–50; cf. Isa. 66:1–2). The language becomes ever sharper as he accuses his audience of hardhearted resistance to the will of God and a consistent history of destroying those messengers whom God sent, the last of whom was Christ (vv. 51–53).

Apart from these concluding sentiments, which were bound to be received unfavorably before an audience of Jewish temple loyalists gathered in Jerusalem, other themes in the sermon could be read as direct challenges to the established order. One common theme that links his treatment of Abraham, Joseph, and Moses is locating the primary sphere of their dealing with God in Egypt, and thus outside Palestine. Read one way, this would be seen as a direct affront, for it could imply that God has had some of the most decisive encounters with the patriarchs *outside* the land. The Gospel will pose a similar challenge to the entrenched values of Jews bent on resisting the mission to the Gentiles.

In any event, the audience is enraged to the point of gritting their teeth against Stephen (v. 54; cf. Ps. 35:16; 37:12; 112:10; Job 16:9; Lam. 2:16). Their anger forces them to cast him out of the city (v. 58), a move reminiscent of Jesus' eviction from Nazareth after his inaugural sermon (Luke 4:29). The form of death was stoning, which was prescribed in the Old Testament for certain serious offenses (cf. Lev. 24:14; Num. 15:35–36; Deut. 17:7).

Here we see a man die, but from the way his death is recorded, it is clearly a triumphant death—the death of a martyr vindicated by God. We are assured that it is the death of another of God's prophets who is "full of the Holy Spirit" (v. 55). Earlier, Stephen's character is attested in this way (Acts 6:3, 5), and he belongs with others so designated in the narrative of Acts, including Barnabas (11:24) and the disciples (13:52). But most notably, he stands in the succession of Jesus himself (Luke 4:1, 14, 18, 21). Because Stephen is described in this way, the actions of the crowds against him are fully in character: another of God's prophets has fallen in Jerusalem (cf. Luke 13:33).

Not only does Stephen die as a prophet, but as a prophet vindicated by God. The heavens are opened, as they were at the baptism and confirmation of Jesus (cf. Luke 3:21 and parallels), which is typical of revelatory moments (cf. Acts 10:11; John 1:51; Rev. 19:11). As he gazes into the heavens, like the psalmist (Ps. 63:2) and Isaiah (6:1; cf. John 12:41), he beholds "the glory of God" (v. 55). He also sees the exalted "Son of man standing at the right hand of God," as Jesus had promised (v. 56; cf. Luke 22:69; also Matt. 26:64 and parallels).

But above all, Luke wants us to see the death of Stephen in terms reminiscent of the death of Jesus. Thus his last words recall the last words of Jesus. There is first the prayer "Lord Jesus, receive my spirit" (v. 59; cf. Luke 23:46) and finally the prayer of forgiveness, "Lord, do not hold this sin against them" (v. 60; cf. Luke 23:34). His death is one of confident expectation that his cause has been vindicated. It is a death experienced in a mood of forgiveness. Like God's own Son, Stephen is vindicated by God even in death.

This text portrays the death of a martyr. It is in no sense tragic, but triumphant. Stephen's cause is clearly aligned with the cause of God and the exalted Son of Man. A host of similar martyrdoms will be described in subsequent Christian history, such as those of Polycarp, Ignatius, and many others.

There are several homiletical possibilities here. The preacher may want to play out the similarity between the death of Stephen and that of Christ, and explore the ways in which Luke depicts God's messengers, such as Peter, Stephen, and Paul, carrying out the work of Christ in word, deed, and life. There is also the triumphant tone of the episode that fits well with the overall tone of Luke-Acts. The persistent danger, however, is that triumph can easily shade off into triumphalism and its bedfellow, imperialism. The preacher needs to be cautious in this respect. But there are many appropriate ways to expound the Easter faith as it leads to forms of daring, prophetic witness. One such way may be to interpret the death of Stephen as the result of posing a serious challenge to the established religious order.

Psalm 31:1–5, 15–16

This psalm has been discussed for the Sixth Sunday in Lent and Holy Saturday.

1 Peter 2:2–10

Like the other readings from First Peter on the previous Sundays, today's text resembles baptismal catechesis. It appears to give instructions to recent converts. In doing so, today's text employs a series of images with which new Christians could define themselves. Seen in another sense, today's text provides us several images for the church.

First, *newborn infants* (vv. 2–3). It was natural enough to liken the beginning of the religious life to the birth and growth of an infant. Thinking of baptism as a new birth (1:3; John 1:13; 3:3–5) was the logical launching point for this metaphor. Consequently, Christian instruction comes to distinguish between elementary and more advanced instruction in terms of milk and meat (Heb. 5:12–14; 1 Cor. 3:1–3). It could even affect liturgical practice, as was the case in the second century AD, when Christian initiates were fed milk and honey after their baptism.

It was also a truism that for milk to be truly nourishing, it should be pure (v. 2). Informing the author at this point is Psalm 34:8: "O taste and see that the Lord is good!"

Second, a *living temple* (v. 5). For Christians to be likened to "living stones" grows out of their christological understanding in which Christ is seen as the rejected stone who has become the cornerstone of the building. Certain Old Testament passages were crucial in this development. Psalm 118:22 is cited in verse 7: "The stone that the builders rejected has become the very head of the corner." Early Christians used this to interpret the death and resurrection of Jesus. On the one hand he was rejected, but through his resurrection he has been exalted to a position of prominence, like the capstone in an arch or the cornerstone in a building.

Two other passages also employed the stone imagery: Isaiah 28:16 and 8:14. The former envisions God's "laying in Zion a stone, a cornerstone chosen and precious" (v. 6), whereas the latter speaks of a "stone that makes them stumble, and a rock that makes them fall" (v. 8). In the one instance, those who believe in God's promise are pictured as resting their faith on a solid rock foundation. In the other instance, the stone becomes a stumbling block for those who disbelieve and disobey.

With Christ viewed as the stone that God lays in Zion, the readers are urged to come to "that living stone" that was rejected by humans but regarded as precious by God (v. 4). By extension, followers of Christ are said to be "living stones." This is logical enough, considering that believers were understood to be incorporated with Christ in a close, even mystical, union. They partook of the nature of the one with and to whom they were joined. Accordingly, they are pictured as a "spiritual house," or temple. This same image can be used as a way of visualizing the Christian body or the Christian church as the dwelling place of the Spirit, much as the temple was the place where the Shekinah was located (1 Cor. 3:16–17; 6:19–20).

Third, *holy priesthood* (vv. 5, 9). If Christians are understood as a temple, it is not a long step to extend the metaphor and compare them with the priests who officiate in the temple. It is common for Christians to be compared with priests who offer sacrifices, either their own lives as spiritual sacrifices (Rom. 12:1) or appropriate forms of worship as fitting sacrifice (Heb. 13:15–16). Paul can think of his apostolic service in similar terms (Rom. 15:16). The usage is also informed by the Old Testament notion of Israel as a "holy priesthood" (Exod. 19:6; cf. Rev. 1:6).

Fourth, the *elect people of God* (vv. 9–10). Election actually encompasses several images: "chosen race . . . holy nation, God's own people" (v. 9). As Israel had been regarded as

God's Elect, the chosen people (Isa. 43:21), so does the church come to be understood in similar terms (Col. 3:12). The relationship is one of close identity, even possession, so much so that Yahweh lays claim to Israel as "the people whom I formed for myself" (Isa. 43:21; cf. Mal. 3:17).

As the elect people of God, Israel lives to give glory to God (Isa. 43:21). Similarly, the church sees itself as basking in God's glory and hence as having moved from darkness into light (v. 9; cf. Acts 26:18; 2 Cor. 4:6; Eph. 5:8; 1 Thess. 5:4–5).

The transition can be stated even more sharply, drawing on language from the prophet Hosea. It will be remembered that two of the children born to Hosea and Gomer were given names to symbolize the status of Israel's broken covenant with Yahweh: a daughter "Not pitied" (Lo-ruhamah) and a son "Not my people" (Lo-ammi). Today's text seizes on these two names to signify the status of Gentiles prior to their conversion, but asserts that those who were "no people" have now become "God's people," and those who "were without mercy" have now "received mercy" (v. 10; Eph. 2:4).

The preacher will find here numerous suggestive images for defining the nature of the church and our commitment as those who have embarked on the life of faith. If nothing else, the text sharply etches the contours of life as it "once was" over against life as it "now is." This contrast, if properly drawn, can provide powerful incentive to those who have committed themselves to that living stone.

John 14:1–14

The Gospel reading for today falls within a larger body of material extending from 13:31 to 17:26. This large section, usually referred to as the farewell discourse and prayer of Jesus, is set in Jerusalem, following Jesus' last meal with his disciples (13:1–30) and ending with the group's movement to the garden where Jesus was arrested (18:1). The Synoptics have nothing comparable. The entire section consists of Jesus' words to his disciples (except for the prayer in 17:1–26), broken only now and then by a question or a comment by one of the disciples (14:5, 8, 22). The material is marked by a great deal of repetition that quite possibly could be the result of drawing from several sources. Embedded within the discourses are smaller units that have their own integrity and that may have existed previously in other contexts, similar to sayings in the Synoptics that occur in various literary settings with almost no change in form. Notice, for example, 14:1–3 or 14:6. On the whole, however, natural breaks such as change of time or place or audience are missing, and the preacher will be hard pressed to determine where a unit begins and ends.

The themes developed in the farewell materials are not for the public but for the disciples, that is, for the church. The primary concern is not what events will soon befall Christ, but rather what will happen to his disciples after he is gone. The reader will, therefore, find here an interweaving of promises and commands. Although the textures of these two kinds of statements from Jesus may seem at first very different, it gradually becomes clear that Jesus' promises carry a commission and his commissions imply a promise. He who sends also goes with those whom he sends, and he who commands to love empowers to love. And the reverse is equally true; he who loves expects the loved to love others, and he who abides with his followers expects them to go just as the Father sent him.

Because 14:1–14 comes early in the farewell material, it is not surprising that the primary thrust of this unit is to soften with assurance the blow of Jesus' announcement of his departure. It requires only minimal reflection to realize that the departure of Jesus, leaving behind a group of followers to continue faithfully in an indifferent and sometimes hostile world, was the first major crisis of the church. The assurance to the church takes the form of three promises.

First, there is the promise of an abiding place with God. The image here is of the future, even though the principal eschatological accent of this Gospel is on the present, that is, on a realized eschatology (3:36; 5:24; 11:25–26). The word translated "dwelling-places" (NRSV, REB) or "mansions" (KJV) is the noun form of the verb "to abide." This is a key term throughout this Gospel (see 15:1–11, for example) and represents a relationship characterized by trusting and knowing, such as exists between Christ and God. Christ's death and departure will not sever but will rather fulfill that relationship between the disciples and Christ.

The second promise is that of a sure and clear way to God (vv. 5–7). For this Evangelist, the way to the God whom no one has ever seen is Jesus Christ, for "it is God the only Son, who is close to the Father's heart, who has made him known" (1:18). Although this is clear to the Johannine church, what is not clear to the reader is whether "no one comes to the Father except through me" (v. 6) is a polemic and, if so, against whom. The writer is very much aware of the John the Baptist sect and the Jewish synagogue. However, given the strong and repeated words about the Holy Spirit (14:1–16:15), the statement could be addressed to pneumatics who discounted the historical Jesus in favor of new experiences in the Spirit.

The third promise in 14:1–14 is that of a power not only to sustain the believing community in the world but also to enable it to do even greater works than Jesus did (v. 12). Next Sunday, the lesson will deal with the promise of the Holy Spirit (vv. 15–21). However, here it is important to notice that the promise is to those who believe in Christ and pray in his name (vv. 13–14). Two comments are in order: (1) the "you" in verses 13–14 is plural, implying a promise to the community and not a private one; and (2) praying in Jesus' name is not simply a formula for closing a prayer. To use Jesus' name as authorization for one's petitions to God implies that those who do so know Christ, abide in Christ, and make their requests from that relationship rather than making selfish requests imported from another value system. To pray in Christ's name means, among other things, to be thoughtful about one's prayers, and to pray about what to pray.

Sixth Sunday of Easter

Acts 17:22–31;
Psalm 66:8–20;
1 Peter 3:13–22;
John 14:15–21

The readings for today announce the meaning of the resurrection of Jesus Christ to persons who live in a variety of difficult circumstances. In John 14:15–21, Jesus says farewell to his disciples, soon to feel alone and abandoned in a hostile world. He charges them to continue in obedient love and promises the comfort of the Spirit. Similarly, 1 Peter 3:13–22 speaks to suffering Christians, recalling Christ's suffering, death, and triumph in which they participate. In Acts 17:22–31, Paul announces the resurrection as God's call to those trapped in idolatry, with its attendant ignorance and sin. Even Psalm 66 calls the suffering to worship and praise the God who sustains life and answers prayer.

Acts 17:22–31

The Book of Acts is distinguished by the amount of space (approximately 20 percent) it devotes to speeches. Today's text consists of one of these speeches, Paul's sermon at Athens. Unlike some of the readings from Acts during the previous Sundays, which gave only portions of lengthy sermons, today we have the complete sermon. When we say "sermon," naturally we mean sermon summary, because it is generally understood that Luke, at best, gives us in Acts abstracts rather than verbatim accounts of early Christian sermons. What we have today, then, is a résumé of early Christian preaching as it is likely to have sounded when addressed to a sophisticated pagan audience. It should be compared with the rather brief summary in Acts 14:15–17, which gives an idea of the Christian kerygma addressed to a less sophisticated, popular audience.

The sermon is set in Athens during Paul's mission in the Aegean area. Previously, Luke has given rather extended treatment to Paul's stay in Philippi (Acts 16:11–40) and shown us a typical "day" in the life of Paul, the missionary to the Gentiles. In Philippi, the gospel effectively reaches every social stratum. After rehearsing Paul's movements through Thessalonica and Beroea (Acts 17:1–15), Luke pauses to give a more detailed account of his stay in Athens. The audience he addresses is populated with Epicurean and Stoic philosophers, representatives of Greco-Roman popular philosophy (v. 18). The situation is described as one in which intellectual inquiry and debate are the norm, and thus Paul is portrayed standing "in front of the Areopagus" (v. 22), that is, positioned as a Greek orator, and addressing this learned audience.

The tone and substance of the sermon are unlike every other extended kerygmatic summary in Acts. It is, of course, missionary preaching, as many of the other sermons are, but most of them occur in synagogue settings. Consequently, they often rehearse Israel's history and link Christ with that history. In this sermon, however, we have no such rehearsal of Israelite history, although there are numerous echoes from the Old Testament. Rather, the sermon attempts to establish common ground between Paul and his non-Jewish hearers.

Paul begins by acknowledging that the Athenians are "extremely religious" (v. 22); as the REB says, "I see that in everything that concerns religion you are uncommonly scrupulous." This observation is reinforced by Luke's graphic description of the numerous idols that decorated the city (v. 16), one of which had the inscription "To an unknown god" (v. 23). Luke intends this as an indication of their genuine religious thirst for knowledge of the Divine. Accordingly, it serves as an invitation for Paul to "make known" his God (v. 23).

Fundamentally, Paul's sermon is about God, although at the end he finally gets around to mentioning Christ (v. 31). The Christian understanding of God is presented in stark opposition to the pagan understanding of God. For one thing, it was a difference between polytheism and monotheism, and thus this episode serves as a critique of pagan polytheism. In this respect, Christian preaching was heavily indebted to the Jewish critique of pagan religion begun in the Old Testament and continued in the Hellenistic-Roman period (cf. Isa. 40:18–20; 42:17; 44:9–20; 45:16–20; 46:1–7; Jer. 10:1–5; Wisd. of Sol. 13:1–15:17). But what is absent in Paul's sermon at Athens is the supercilious, satirical tone that characterizes much of the earlier Jewish, and even pagan, critique of idolatry. He gives his hearers the benefit of the doubt, pictures them as earnest seekers of God, and sees their previous, misguided attempts as forgivable instances of ignorance (v. 30; cf. 3:17; 13:27).

Positively, we have God presented in two ways: as Creator and Preserver of life.

1. *God as Creator* (vv. 24, 26). In language reminiscent of the Old Testament, the Lukan Paul proclaims, "The God who made the world and everything in it" (v. 24; cf. Exod. 20:11; 2 Kings 19:15 [= Isa. 38:16]; Neh. 9:6; Ps. 146:6; Isa. 42:5; Wisd. of Sol. 9:1, 9; also Acts 4:24; 14:15; Rev. 10:6; 14:7). The corollary is that God is consequently "Lord of heaven and earth" (Tob. 7:16; Matt. 11:25).

Not only has God created the whole universe as we know it, heavenly and earthly, inanimate and animate, but human life as well: "From one single principle [God] . . . created the whole human race" (v. 26, NJB; "from one stock," REB). This reflects the theology of the Genesis creation story (Gen. 1:26) as well as the later narrative that sees God scattering the various nations throughout the earth (Gen. 10). Not that it was random scattering; instead, God "determined their eras in history and the limits of their territory" (v. 26, REB; cf. Ps. 74:17; Deut. 32:8).

In proclaiming God as Creator, Paul would have been on common ground with much Greco-Roman philosophy. In the well-known Stoic hymn of Cleanthes, Zeus is praised above all other gods with the opening declaration: "The beginning of the world was from thee."

2. *God as Preserver* (vv. 25, 28). God not only creates, but sustains life. It is God "who gives everything—including life and breath—to everyone" (v. 25, NJB; cf. Isa. 42:5; 57:15–16; Wisd. of Sol. 9:1). Earlier, in the sermon at Lystra, Paul provides a variation on this theme as he proclaims God as the one who gives "rains from heaven and fruitful seasons" (Acts 14:17; cf. Jer. 5:24; Ps. 147:8; Lev. 26:4).

But God is more than provider in the active sense of giving us what we need. As the Greek poet Epimenides observed, God is the one "in whom we live and move and have our being" (v. 28). It was common Stoic theology to say that God lives in us, indeed in everything. It was less common, if not unusual, to claim the reverse—that we live *in God*. This may be a way of saying that *through God* we are sustained, or it may suggest that God is the sphere of life in which our own life is sustained. A modern way of putting it would be to say that God is the oxygen tent in whom we live. To live, move, and have being suggests life in its most comprehensive sense; every fabric of our being is sustained by our life in God.

If life as we know and experience it is traceable to God, who creates and sustains it, two things follow:

First, as the Greek poet Aratus observed in his *Phaenomena*, we are God's "offspring" (v. 28; also Gen. 1:27). In our very being we are like God because we owe our existence to God.

Second, we should acknowledge our dependence on God in appropriate forms of worship. As aesthetically pleasing as portraits and images of God might be, they can only be inadequate representations of God, because they by definition impose limits on the Unlimited. They also lead to misplaced emphasis—on the house in which God lives rather than on the God who lives there (v. 24), on the service that worshipers can render to God rather than on God's sovereignty (v. 25), on human imagination rather than on divine nearness (v. 29). What Paul calls for is a form of worship that captures the essence of God as Creator and Preserver of life. The worship of idols fails essentially in this respect: it neither reveals to us who God is nor does it reveal to God who we are.

Toward the end of the sermon, Paul moves the readers' attention into the future, to a time when God the Creator and Preserver becomes Judge (v. 31; cf. 10:42; Rom. 2:16; 14:9–10; 2 Tim. 4:1; 1 Pet. 4:5). We are assured that God does not judge capriciously (as many of the pagan gods were observed to do), but righteously (v. 31; cf. Pss. 9:8; 96:13; 98:9). Testimony to this is provided by his raising Jesus from the dead (v. 31; cf. Acts 2:24, 32; 4:10; 5:30; 10:40; 13:36–37; also 1 Thess. 1:10).

At this point, the sermon stops rather abruptly. The response was mockery combined with delay (v. 32). Converts were few (vv. 33–34). The gospel does not win every time, even when dressed in sophisticated clothing. But Luke remains convinced that the God presented here is the One whom we all seek, indeed grope for (v. 27; cf. Deut. 4:29; Isa. 55:6; Wisd. of Sol. 13:6), and the irony is that this God is not that far away (v. 27; cf. Ps. 145:18; Jer. 23:23).

Psalm 66:8–20

Few psalms fall into the category of community or communal thanksgiving. As a rule, ancient Jewish worship probably used general hymns of praise to express thanks on behalf of the whole community rather than psalms of thanksgiving that focused specifically on the particular reason for thanksgiving. (At least, this is one explanation for the almost total absence of psalms of community thanksgiving.) Even in Psalm 66, one of the best candidates for a community thanksgiving, the focus shifts in verses 13–20 to individual speech (note the "I" throughout this section), perhaps suggesting that a community leader or the king representing the community is the speaker.

The psalm appeals to the people (the nations, the earth) to participate in the praise and to behold the works of God (vv. 1, 5, 8, and 16; the opening verbs in these verses are all plural imperatives). The reasons for praise and observance are given in verses 3–4, 5b–7, 9, and 17–19. These include God's awesome deeds (v. 3), mighty works (v. 5), sustenance of life (v. 9), and response to prayerful requests (v. 18).

Different audiences are addressed in the psalm: verses 1–9 call upon the peoples of the world; verses 10–11 are communal speech to God (note the plural pronouns); verses 13–15 are addressed to God (note the singular first person pronouns); and verses 16–20 are individual speech addressed to a plural human audience.

Although not included in this particular lection, verses 1–7 emphasize Yahweh's triumph over enemies and the parting of the Red Sea and the Jordan River (see Exod. 14; Josh. 3; Ps. 114:5–6).

Verses 8–9 praise God for having kept the people alive and for protecting their way, suggesting that this psalm may have been employed in some annual thanksgiving ritual.

God as the tester and protector appears in verses 10–12. The NJPSV translates these verses as follows:

> You have tried us, O God,
>   refining us, as one refines silver.
> You have caught us in a net,
>   caught us in trammels.
> You have let men ride over us;
>   we have endured fire and water,
>   and You have brought us through to prosperity.

Neither the nature of the trouble, in spite of the various images (being refined, being caught like a bird or wild animal, being overrun by horsemen, and being forced to endure extremes), nor the goal of such calamities is discussed. The troubles are there as divinely sent phenomena but as phenomena through which divine guidance has carried the community, carried it to prosperity (the harvests of another year?).

Verses 13–15 have a worshiper (the king?) speak of fulfilling the vows made earlier in a time of trouble. Note the extravagance as a token of thanksgiving.

Finally, the psalmist invites people to hear the testimony, the witness offered about what God has done (vv. 16–20).

1 Peter 3:13–22

The latter portion of today's text (3:18–22) serves as the epistolary lesson for the First Sunday in Lent in Year B. The reader may want to consult our remarks in that setting.

This passage, like the rest of First Peter, confronts the reality of Christian suffering (cf. 1:6; 2:20–21; 4:12–19; 5:9–10). It envisions just people being dealt with unjustly. It echoes the sentiments of the Matthean beatitude that followers of Jesus would be persecuted for righteousness' sake (v. 14; Matt. 5:10). In the words of a recent popular book, our text recognizes that bad things happen to good people.

What should be the Christian's response in this situation? Several suggestions are offered in today's text.

First, we should be assured that ours is a just cause and that we are in the right (vv. 13–14, 17). Earlier, we are cautioned against doing wrong (2:20). The New Testament is consistent in urging good, responsible conduct as the norm (Rom. 13:3; Titus 2:14). It is this that enables us to live with a good conscience (v. 16). Luke draws a consistent image of Paul as one who pursued his work with a clear conscience (Acts 23:1; 24:16; cf. 2 Cor. 1:12). A clear conscience is also important enough to become a prerequisite for service as a deacon (1 Tim. 3:9). Later in today's text, we are assured that the central motivation for Christian baptism is "an appeal to God for a good conscience" (v. 21).

Suffering is made more bearable, then, when our minds are cleared of the cobwebs of evil, mixed motives, and injustice. If we are "eager to do what is good" (v. 13), we have already eliminated a number of false adversaries (cf. Isa. 50:9; Rom. 8:34).

Second, we are not to be fearful (v. 14). It is advice drawn from Isaiah, who urges his hearers not to be intimidated by leaders who act out of fear: "You must neither fear nor stand in awe of what they fear" (Isa. 8:12, REB). Rather, be committed to the Lord of hosts: "Let him be your fear, and let him be your dread" (Isa. 8:13). In our text, Christ now replaces Yahweh as the ground of our confidence: in our hearts we are to "sanctify Christ as Lord" (v. 15). If early readers were being threatened because of their fidelity to Christ as opposed to state rulers, this injunction would remind them of their sole allegiance to Christ. In a later setting, the Johannine apocalypse calls Christians to face suffering without being fearful (Rev. 2:10).

Third, we should stand ready to make our defense (v. 15). The word for defense is *apologia,* which by the second century AD had become a technical term to describe the case Christians made for themselves against their detractors. Today's text may not envision such protracted apologies as those of Justin Martyr, Athenagoras, and other early Christian apologists, but it does call for the ability to articulate our faith in ways that are both intelligible and responsible to the faith. The New Testament, in various ways, speaks of giving responsible account. At the final judgment, we will be held accountable for what we have said (Matt. 12:36; cf. Rom. 14:12). Christian leaders will have to give account for the quality of their leadership (Heb. 13:17; cf. 4:13).

There is the suggestion here that such occasions may take us by surprise and that we will be called on to state the case for our belief on the spot. We are thus urged to "always be prepared." Along with this constant readiness, we are instructed to do so in the proper spirit—"with gentleness and reverence" (v. 15; cf. Col. 4:6).

Fourth, we are to relate our suffering to that of Christ (vv. 18–19). Somehow, the suffering of Christ is intended to be definitive for us, especially when we suffer unjustly. It is likely that at this point in our text, the author quotes an early Christian hymn. It is printed strophically in Nestle, 26th ed., although not in NRSV, REB, NJB, and NIV. In any case, these verses direct our attention to Christ's suffering, especially because it was a case of the "righteous [dying] for the unrighteous" (v. 18). His was a clear case of a just person suffering unjustly (cf. Acts 3:14; 7:52; 22:14; Matt. 27:14; Luke 23:47).

In addition, the death of Christ served a purpose beyond himself. It was a death for sins, thus a vicarious death (v. 18; cf. 2:21–24; Heb. 9:26–28; 10:12, 14). His death is instructive in showing us how suffering can become an occasion for transcending our own self-interest and acting in behalf of others.

At this point, our text moves in another direction. The end of the Christ hymn referred to Christ's enigmatic preaching mission to the "spirits in prison" (v. 19). These mysterious figures are said to have been disobedient in the days of Noah, and this prompts the author to compare the salvation of Noah and his household with Christian salvation. Both were achieved through water, although in one instance water destroyed, whereas in the other instance it saves. This baptism theme reflects a recurrent concern of the letter.

The text concludes with a reference to the ascension of Christ, which foreshadows our next liturgical event, Ascension Day.

John 14:15–21

The introductory comments on verses 1–14 for last Sunday set the context for today's lection and need not be repeated here. A word does need to be said about the parameters of the text before us. Very likely, verses 15–24 would be a more natural unit than verses 15–21. Although the question of Judas in verse 22 seems to provide a break, in fact that question simply calls for an elaboration of verse 21. Actually, verse 24 ends the unit as it began in verse 15, with the statement about love that keeps God's commands. A literary unit that ends as it begins is called an inclusion, a way of framing a body of material. Knowing this, the preacher may want to treat the whole unit (vv. 15–24). However, because verses 22–24 elaborate on verse 21 at the request of Judas, we can safely assume that the central thought had already been stated in verses 15–21, even if not fully comprehended by the disciples.

In order to understand this and other passages in this Gospel that join love and obedience, the reader must think of love as other than feeling. Feelings are not commanded, but love can be, for to love is to be for another person, to act for another's good, to do that which brings benefit to the other. This is much more than liking a person or having a particular set of feelings that may be contingent on a variety of factors. To love obediently is to submit to God's own precedent (3:16) and call, even if loving costs dearly, as God's love did. By placing love and obedience at the beginning (v. 15), middle (v. 21), and end (v. 24) of this unit, it is clear that the promises offered are not for any and all who may be passing by, but for those who love obediently.

The promises in our text are two, one a Johannine form of Pentecost and the other a Johannine form of the Parousia (the coming of Christ). In the sense that Pentecost has come to represent the giving of the Holy Spirit to the disciples (Acts 2:1–13), verses 16–17 may be called the promise of Pentecost. This is the first of five passages in the farewell discourses that present the Holy Spirit's work in the church (14:15–16, 26; 15:26; 16:7–11, 12–14), all of which make it clear that Easter is completed in the coming of the Spirit. The meaning of the Holy Spirit for the church, according to verses 16–17, is as follows: (1) the Spirit will come from God at the request of Jesus; (2) the Spirit will replace Jesus as "another Advocate," being to the church the helper, comforter, companion that Jesus had been; (3) the Spirit, unlike Jesus, will never go away but will be with the church forever; (4) the Spirit will be with and in the church forever; (5) the Spirit will be with and in the church in ways distinct from any functioning of the Spirit in the world; and (6) the Spirit will be for the church a source and a confirmation of truth.

The second promise of verses 15–21 is a Johannine form of Parousia; that is, of the coming of Christ (vv. 18–21). "I will not leave you orphaned; I am coming to you" (v. 18). One should not attempt to make in this Gospel too sharp a distinction between the coming of the Spirit and the coming of Christ. The presence of the Spirit and the presence of the Christ in the church are not clearly differentiated. In fact, verse 23 includes also the promise of the presence of God: "We [Father and Son] will come to them and make our home with them." Whatever the distinctions that must be honored by one's theology, the fact remains that experientially "God with us," "Christ with us," or "the Spirit with us" are for the church one promise of power, guidance, and comfort without which the church cannot live faithfully.

Ascension of the Lord

Acts 1:1–11;
Psalm 47;
Ephesians 1:15–23;
Luke 24:44–53

The Ascension Day service is set by Luke's calendar; forty days after Easter and ten days before Pentecost. While Luke in Acts 1:1–11 provides the basic narrative, the Gospel reading offers an appearance of the risen Christ to his followers to answer them, to promise his continued presence, and to commission them to a worldwide mission. Ephesians 1:15–23 grounds that mission in the universal lordship of Christ risen and seated at God's right hand. Psalm 47 likewise praises God as sovereign over all nations of the earth.

Acts 1:1–11

Today's text overlaps with the first lesson (Acts 1:6–14) for the Seventh Sunday of Easter in Year A, which is treated next in this volume.

Today's first lesson is Luke's account of the Ascension of Christ forty days after his resurrection (v. 3). To be more accurate, we should say that one portion of today's text describes the Ascension (vv. 6–11). This first part of the passage consists of a preface to Acts (vv. 1–2) and a brief summary of the tradition relating to the appearances of the risen Lord to his disciples (vv. 3–5).

We may fail to appreciate this Lukan account of Christ's ascension unless we realize how unusual it is in the New Testament. It is by far the most detailed narrative account of this event in the New Testament. We might say that Luke is the only New Testament writer for whom the event has appreciable significance, at least as a separate event in the life of the Lord. To understand this better, let us examine some of the other traditions in the New Testament relating to Christ's ascension.

Among the Synoptic Gospels, Matthew knows of no ascension tradition in its original form, nor does Mark. In the much disputed "longer ending" of Mark, it is reported that "the Lord Jesus, after he had spoken to them, was taken up into heaven and sat down at the right hand of God" (Mark 16:19). This is rightly regarded as a later tradition and is probably dependent on Luke's account of this event.

The Gospel of Luke concludes with Jesus' leading the disciples out to Bethany, where he lifts his hands and blesses them. Then we are told, "While he was blessing them, he withdrew from them and was carried up into heaven" (24:51). One ancient textual tradition omits the second phrase in verse 51, "and was carried up into heaven." If the longer version of verse 51 was the original part of the Gospel of Luke, it stands in tension with Luke's account in Acts 1. The Gospel account implies that Christ's ascension occurred on Easter Day (as do all the other events recorded in Luke 24), whereas Acts 1 places it forty days later (Acts 1:3). Some have also noted a discrepancy in the location: in Luke, it occurs in Bethany, whereas Acts 1:12 implies that it occurred on Mt. Olivet, "a sabbath day's journey away."

In the Gospel of John, the risen Lord forbids Mary to touch him, claiming, "I have not yet ascended to the Father" (John 20:17). She is instructed to tell the brothers that he is ascending to the Father (v. 17). There are other allusions to the Son of Man's ascending to the Father (John 6:62; cf. 3:13). It is more usual for John to speak of "going to the Father" or "returning to the Father" (cf. 7:33; 14:12, 28; 16:5, 10, 28). For John, Christ's ascension is to be understood as part of the glorification that occurs after his resurrection. It signifies the return of Jesus to the presence of the Father, his original and natural abode. It does not function as an explanation of how various post-Easter appearances came to an end.

In the Pauline tradition, there is no real place for Christ's ascension as an event separable from his resurrection. Paul seems to regard Christ's resurrection as equivalent to his exaltation (Rom. 8:34; cf. Eph. 1:20). In the well-known Christ hymn in Philippians 2:5–11, which is probably pre-Pauline, the work of Christ unfolds in a "V-shaped" fashion, descent to the earth to take on human form (vv. 7–8), and ascent, or exaltation by God, to heavenly status (vv. 9–11). Other references are more cryptic (cf. Rom. 10:6). At a later stage in the Pauline tradition, we find a more fully elaborated notion of ascension, but not distinguishable from resurrection (cf. especially Eph. 4:8–10). What appears to be an early christological creedal statement is preserved in 1 Timothy 3:16, which concludes with the phrase "[he was] taken up in glory." This too sounds like ascension language, but there is no separate mention of Christ's resurrection.

The Epistle to the Hebrews ordinarily speaks of Christ's exaltation, not his resurrection per se. Thus we find that Christ "has passed through the heavens" (4:14), is "exalted above the heavens" (7:26), has entered the heavenly sanctuary (9:24).

In 1 Peter 3:21–22, mention of "the resurrection of Jesus Christ" prompts the description of Christ as one who "has gone into heaven and is at the right hand of God." This may very well be an allusion to a tradition that approximates Luke's account: resurrection, ascension, and exaltation.

Against this background of various New Testament witnesses, which reflect a variety of understandings of Christ's return to God, Luke's narrative account in Acts 1:6–11 is set in sharper relief. Its literary function appears to be a way of terminating the post-Easter appearances of Christ, Luke's way of saying that thereafter Christ's presence would be experienced by the church in a different way. Moreover, because Luke stresses that the risen Lord had instructed the disciples concerning the kingdom of God during this forty-day interval (Acts 1:3), the Ascension marks the transition to the period when the apostles, as Christ's witnesses, function as preachers and teachers on his behalf. It has a legitimating function. After Christ is gone, the apostles serve as the legitimating link between Christ and the church. Their task is to wait for the outpouring of the Spirit (v. 8), after which they will serve as harbingers of the new age.

Luke, then, has sensed the theological problem posed by the physical absence of Christ. With Christ gone, how does the church function? It listens to the apostolic witness, assured that in and through it Christ is speaking. It also waits in expectation for the return of

Christ (v. 11). But it does so with a new realization that the focus of the kingdom of God is not on liberating Israel from Roman rule but on witnessing to the presence of the Spirit in the world.

Psalm 47

Like a number of other psalms (Pss. 93, 95–100), Psalm 47 seems to have been employed in ancient Israel during the annual celebration of God's kingship. According to such an interpretation, the kingship of God was celebrated in the cult just as was the kingship of the ruling earthly monarch. The emphasis on the kingship of God can be seen in Isaiah's temple vision (Isa. 6), in which he says he saw Yahweh the king sitting upon a throne, high and lifted up.

The center of this psalm is verse 5, which proclaims that "God has gone up with a shout, Yahweh with the sound of a trumpet." (The NJPSV translates this verse: "God ascends amidst acclamation; the Lord, to the blasts of the horn.") Parallels to this can be seen in the accounts of the anointment and acclamation of Solomon and David's successor: "Zadok the priest took the horn of oil from the tent, and anointed Solomon. Then they blew the trumpet; and all the people said, 'Long live King Solomon!' And all the people went up after him, playing on pipes, and rejoicing with great joy, so that the earth was split by their noise" (1 Kings 1:39–40; see also 2 Kings 11:12–14). The texts from Kings reflect several features in the king's coronation that are also found in Psalm 47: (1) the king (God) goes up to the place of enthronement; (2) the people engage in vocal and joyous celebration; and (3) the sound of the trumpets plays an important role.

Ephesians 1:15–23

A longer form of today's epistolary lesson (1:11–23) provides the second lesson for All Saints Day in Year C. Additional comments on this text are provided in this setting. This text also serves as the epistolary reading for Proper 29, Christ the King or Reign of Christ Sunday, in Year A, which occurs later in the year.

The setting for today is the celebration of Christ's ascension into heaven. The practice of remembering this event in the life of Christ as a special day dates to the late fourth century.

In celebrating Christ's ascension, we do more than ponder the historical question, What actually occurred when Christ finally departed from the disciples? Luke's narrative account in today's first lesson supplies one answer. The epistolary lection offers a different perspective. It is not concerned with any particular moment when the risen Lord took leave of the disciples. It rather views Christ's exaltation to the presence of God in much broader, grander terms.

Two Old Testament texts are formative influences on today's text. Psalm 110:1 underlies the statement in verse 20: "[God] seated him at his right hand in the heavenly places." Psalm 8:6 supplies the image in verse 22: God "has put all things under his feet." In both instances, we see a clear formulation of the early Christian conviction that Christ embodies the messianic hope as no one else had done. He had died, but more than that, God had "raised him from the dead" (v. 20).

Early Christians well knew what a staggering claim this was. They could conceive of it in no other terms than as an event in which God demonstrated, and unleashed, incredible power. Indeed, it was seen as an instance of "the immeasurable greatness of his power" (v. 19). But power in what sense? In the sense that God had reversed the course of nature by bringing Christ through death to a form of life that was unprecedented and therefore new. This resurrectional life was thus called "new life."

In today's text, there is the recognition that the vistas of our thinking will have to be stretched to grasp the full implication of this faith in Christ's resurrection. Our tendency will be to think of Christ's departure from the earth in terms too small, too restricted, too limited for the event as it was. At work may have been a form of gnostic thinking comparable to what we find combatted in Colossians, in which Christ is viewed as a heavenly figure to be sure, but as one among many figures in the angelic hierarchy. He could be seen as high and exalted in this hierarchy, but not necessarily at the pinnacle of the heavenly order.

Whether our text is directed against such a Christology that is too low, too tentative, it nevertheless succeeds in pulling out all stops as it depicts the heavenly status of Christ. The claims are unqualified: "far above *all* rule and authority and power and dominion, and above *every* name that is named" (v. 21, italics added). Christ breaks every spatial barrier that we can imagine and every temporal barrier as well: "not only in this age but also in the age to come" (v. 21). The boundaries of time are unable to contain Christ, for he has transcended "this age" in a way that qualifies him to dominate "the age to come." Like the victor in battle, he can stand with one foot on the vanquished enemy. The enemy may be death (cf. 1 Cor. 15:51–57), but now he is seen as having subjected "all things."

Even though Christ may be seen as having cosmic dominion, his exalted Lordship is most properly defined and experienced with reference to the church, here conceived as "his body" (v. 23). Once again, our minds are being stretched to think of the "body of Christ" in terms greater than his physical body, his crucified body, even his resurrected body. He now is seen to have a corporate existence large enough, expansive enough, to incorporate the existence and identity of hosts of others, those "in Christ." Obviously, the church is being conceived here in terms larger than the congregation, but also larger than the "church universal" in the sense that the latter represents the sum of all living communities of faith on earth. It is rather a reality that extends into "the heavenly places" (v. 20), where Christ is.

We are being summoned to think of Christ in the most comprehensive sense possible, as the One who encompasses all reality as we know it, as the One who brooks no rivals, as the One who has transcended both space and time and in doing so has redefined both.

We begin to see that Ascension Day challenges our limited views of Christ. It recognizes, to paraphrase J. B. Phillips, that our Christ may be too small. It is for this reason that these exalted reflections on Christ's heavenly status are prefaced with the prayer of enlightenment (vv. 17–18). To grasp the full significance of Christ will require an uncommon measure of wisdom, revelation, and knowledge (v. 17). It will require an increase in wattage within our own hearts so that we can see our hope more brightly. It will require a fuller appraisal of the true value of our inheritance, which may entail using a different currency (v. 18). But above all, we must understand that achieving this level of understanding is a gift of God (v. 17). Our text speaks of enlightenment, to be sure, but not in the ordinary sense. It is rather receiving light from above, where Christ is, "at the right hand of God."

Luke 24:44–53

That Jesus Christ is Lord, seated at the right hand of God, is an affirmation found frequently in the New Testament, often framed on the declaration of Psalm 110:1: "The LORD says to my lord: 'Sit at my right hand until I make your enemies your footstool.'" Less frequent, however, is the expression of the lordship of Christ in the form of an ascension story. The narrative in Acts 1:1–11 is the most complete, but in the Gospel lection for today reference to Christ's ascension is made.

Luke 24:44–53 continues the Lukan resurrection narrative (24:1–53). A review of the comments on Luke 24:13–49 for Easter evening will set our verses for today in context. The two parts to verses 44–53 are instruction, commission, and promise (vv. 44–49), and blessing, departure, and waiting (vv. 50–53). In verses 44–49, several Lukan themes are stated and are central to the entire Luke-Acts presentation of Christ and the church. One such theme is the continuity of Jesus' mission with that of Israel. What the risen Jesus is saying is what the pre-resurrection Jesus said, and these teachings are totally congruous with the Old Testament (v. 44). Luke has repeatedly stressed this point (2:21–40; 4:16–30; 24:25–27; 24:44–45). The death and resurrection of Jesus and the proclamation of the gospel to all peoples were in the plan of God revealed in the Hebrew Scriptures and do not constitute a new departure following the failure of previous efforts. However, it is the risen Christ who enables this understanding of Scripture (v. 45; see also at vv. 25–27). Given this perspective, Luke insists that the Scriptures are sufficient to generate and to sustain faith (16: 27–31). A second theme is the universality of God's offer of repentance and forgiveness of sins (v. 47). Luke made this point as early as the presentation of the infant Jesus in the temple (2:29–32), and Jesus placed it on his agenda at the opening of his ministry in Nazareth (4:16–30). Of course, both the commission (Acts 1:8) and its fulfillment in the proclamation to the nations (Acts 2:1–36) are central to Luke's second volume. And just as justification by grace through faith is the gospel for Paul, for Luke it is repentance and forgiveness of sins.

A fourth and fifth theme in verses 44–49 lie in the command to the disciples to stay in Jerusalem until they receive "power from on high" (v. 49). Jerusalem is the center from which the word of the Lord is to go to the nations (Isa. 2:3), whereas Mark 16:1–18 and Matthew 28:10, 16–20 focus upon Galilee as the place of the risen Christ's reunion with the disciples. For Luke here and throughout Acts, Jerusalem is the center of Christian mission. However, that activity has to wait on the outpouring of the Holy Spirit (v. 49; Acts 1:48). Without the Holy Spirit, they would not be able to take the gospel beyond the comfort zone of Israel to all the nations of the world.

The second portion of our lection, verses 50–53, relates very briefly the departure of Jesus from the disciples on whom he has pronounced his blessing. The manuscript evidence for the phrase "and was carried up into heaven" (v. 51) is mixed and debated, but if it is absent here, the account appears quite fully in Acts 1:9–11. The disciples return to Jerusalem and to the temple in particular. For Luke's story both of Jesus and of the church, the temple in Jerusalem is important (Luke 2:22–38, 41–51; Acts 2:46–3:1; 22:17). The disciples' waiting for the Holy Spirit was in joy, praise (vv. 52–53), and constant prayer (Acts 1:14). The reader of Luke is now ready for volume two, Acts.

Seventh Sunday of Easter

Acts 1:6–14;
Psalm 68:1–10, 32–35;
1 Peter 4:12–14; 5:6–11;
John 17:1–11

All the biblical texts for today, although quite different from one another in many ways, have in common two emphases: the world contains much evil and violence, some of it directed against the faithful; and those who trust in God recall the former deliverance by the Lord who rides upon the clouds and comes in the mysterious power of wind and fire. Acts 1:6–14; Psalm 68:1–10, 32–35; and 1 Peter 4:12–14 employ such imagery to encourage the believers to be strong (1 Pet. 5:6–11) and to be in prayer (Acts 1:6–14). In John 17: 1–11, it is Christ who prays that his followers will remain true and faithful in an unfaithful world.

Acts 1:6–14

Because the first part of Acts 1 (vv. 1–11) has been treated under Ascension Day, we will concentrate our remarks here on the second section of the chapter (vv. 12–14). After Christ's ascension into heaven, the disciples return to Jerusalem from Mt. Olivet (v. 12). Luke notes that it was only "a sabbath's day journey away," a half mile or so. This incidental note about distance serves to keep events located in close proximity to Jerusalem. A similar preoccupation is seen in Luke 24, where all the events recorded occur within close range of Jerusalem. For Luke, Jerusalem is more than a geographical location. It has great theological significance as the place where God's prophet was destined to meet his death (Luke 13:33). Jerusalem was also to be the gathering place for the newly established messianic community. The disciples are thus urged by the risen Lord to stay close by and await the promise of the Spirit (1:4). From here, the kingdom of God would emanate to the ends of the earth (Acts 1:8).

Luke takes time to record the names of the eleven apostles. They are to form the nucleus of the messianic community, but not before the Eleven are restored to the original Twelve. The replacement of Judas by Matthias serves to reconstitute the full apostolic circle (Acts 1:15–26). The number is important for Luke, for the Twelve serve to represent the tribes of Israel, and they are now to function as God's representatives in the newly established kingdom of God (cf. Luke 22:29–30).

287

This list takes its place alongside other such lists of the apostles (Matt. 10:2–4; Mark 3:16–19; Luke 6:13–16; cf. John 1:40–49). It is remarkable in several respects. For instance, it is unusual in naming Peter and John first, instead of the usual grouping together of brothers. This is probably because they emerge in the later narrative as apostolic colleagues (cf. 3:1, 3, 4, 11; 4:13, 19; 8:14). James is in the prominent third position, likely because his death is recorded later in the narrative (Acts 12:1–2). The others fade from the story, except in those various references to the apostles as a group (cf. 2:14, 37, 42, 43; 4:35; 5:12; *passim*).

Luke stresses the solidarity among the group: "All these were constantly devoting themselves to prayer" (v. 14). As the apostolic circle expands to include other members of the messianic community, a similar spirit of unity and harmony prevails (2:43–47; 4:24; 5:12).

In addition to the apostles, the nucleus of the faithful include "certain women, including Mary the mother of Jesus, as well as his brothers" (v. 14). Earlier in the Gospel of Luke, women played a prominent role as close associates of Jesus in his ministry (Luke 8:2) and were among those who witnessed his crucifixion (Luke 23:49). Members of his family as well were counted among his close followers (Luke 8:19–21; cf. Mark 3:31–35; Matt. 12:46–50; cf. Matt. 13:55; John 2:1, 12; 6:42; 7:3; 19:25).

With this description, we are pointed toward Pentecost. By this time, the company of believers numbered some one hundred twenty (1:15). After the selection of Judas' successor, the stage is set for the dramatic outpouring of the Spirit (2:1–4).

Psalm 68:1–10, 32–35

Like Psalm 47, this psalm is built around the imagery of a grand procession. The procession is, on the one hand, that of God's worshipers (v. 27) and, on the other hand, that of God himself (v. 24). Again, we should probably think of this psalm as used originally in an annual celebration that commemorated the kingship of God and a divine victory over God's and the nation's enemies.

Some general features of the psalm should be noted as backdrop for verses 1–10 and 32–35.

1. Military imagery—battles, victories, the gore of battle, the distribution of war spoils—abounds throughout the psalm. This would suggest the psalm's usage in victory celebrations following warfare or that the psalm was used in the fall New Year festival when God's triumph over all enemies was celebrated.

2. The procession of God depicts the divine coming from Mt. Sinai to take up residence in Zion or on the sacred mountain (vv. 7–8, 15–17). The procession is pictured as a journey through the wilderness accompanied by rainstorms and earthquakes.

3. The description of the procession of the people blends into the description of the procession of God (see vv. 24–27). The people accompanying God (see Ps. 24:7–10) participate in music making, dancing, and singing (see 2 Sam. 6:12–15).

The first ten verses of this psalm are comprised of human to human address (vv. 1–6) and human to divine address (vv. 7–10). Verses 1–3 are what might be called an indirect request; it asks that God do something but does not ask God directly. The request takes the form of a double wish: destroy the enemies (vv. 1–2) and bless the righteous (v. 3). Obviously, the righteous are those singing the psalm.

In the call to praise God, in verse 4, we find probably an ancient but infrequently used designation for the Divine—"him who rides upon the clouds." Even this translation is somewhat uncertain, as the NRSV marginal note indicates. The imagery elsewhere in the psalm, however, suggests a close association between God and storms and thus the correctness of this translation.

The description of God in verses 5–6 emphasizes divine support, care, and responsibility for the powerless and dispossessed in Israel: the fatherless (perhaps illegitimate and abandoned children rather than orphans), the widows (who had no male to defend them in a patriarchal culture), the desolate (perhaps those without either social support in the form of families or clans or the economically uprooted), and the captives. The final line of verse 6 provides a summarizing statement on the wicked in general. God's work is not just positive and protective; it is also negative and destructive.

An epiphany of God is the subject of verses 7–10. Perhaps the description of God's appearance here has a thunderstorm as the background for the imagery. Several features of this description are noteworthy: (1) God marches at the head of the people, probably as they process to the sanctuary; (2) God comes from, or at least is associated with, Mt. Sinai, the old traditional mountain of God; (3) thunderstorm and rainfall accompany God's appearance; such imagery and interests would have been right at home in the fall festival, which celebrated the close of the old year and the beginning of the rainy season inaugurating a new agricultural year; and (4) God's coming restores and rejuvenates the people and offers them new hope for the time ahead.

In the concluding verses 32–35, a call goes out to the kingdoms of the earth to rejoice and sing praise because God is now enthroned in the heavens and reigns over Israel in majesty.

1 Peter 4:12–14; 5:6–11

With this reading from First Peter, we come to the end of selections from this epistle that began on the Second Sunday of Easter. The passage actually has two parts, but they are linked by the common theme of suffering, which, as we have seen, is a constant concern addressed in First Peter. The second part of today's passage is especially appropriate for this day because it provides a powerful ending to the season of Easter celebration. We are confronted with the God who calls us, who also restores, establishes, and strengthens us (5:10). To this God belongs everlasting dominion (5:11).

Once again, suffering is spoken of in stark, realistic terms, here as "the fiery ordeal that is taking place among you to test you" (4:12). The image of fire recalls the earlier reference to gold that is tested and refined by fire (1:7). This may be an allusion to the celebrated burning of Rome in AD 64 and Nero's blaming the Roman Christians for arson.

The text also speaks of suffering reproach "for the name of Christ" (4:14), and the possibility is later allowed that one may "suffer as a Christian" (4:16). This is an unusual reference because it is one of the rare instances in the New Testament where the word "Christian" occurs (cf. Acts 11:26; 26:28). It suggests a time when followers of Christ were already distinguishable as a separate religious group in the Roman world. It may suggest that they had no legitimate legal status and that simply bearing the name "Christian" was a criminal offense.

That this was the case in the second century is clear. Justin Martyr wrote his *Second Apology* protesting the execution of three persons merely because they bore the name

Christian rather than because of any illegal or immoral conduct. In the late second century, Athenagoras wrote an apology addressed to Marcus Aurelius in which he asked, "Why is a mere name odious to you? Names are not deserving of hatred; it is the unjust act that calls for penalty and punishment." Tertullian made a similar protest in his typically memorable fashion, "No name of a crime stands against us, but only the crime of a name." He went on to ask, "What crime, what offense, what fault is there in a name?"

Several responses to suffering are suggested in today's text.

First, suffering should not take us by surprise (4:12). When Christians are forced to endure pain for the sake of Christ, we should not act as if "something strange were happening" (4:12). Suffering is part and parcel of the Christian experience. It should not be considered exceptional. Yet it is not as if this were a uniquely Christian approach. Traditionally, it is expected that the righteous will be tested through suffering (cf. Wisd. of Sol. 3:4–5; Sir. 2:1).

Second, suffering should be an occasion for rejoicing (4:13). This is not an unqualified remark, however. It is not as if we should find some perverse delight in having to undergo pain. It is rather that, given the choice between grinning and grimacing in the face of suffering, somehow we should find within ourselves the capacity to view it positively. Meeting various trials should be done in a way that produces steadfastness and a refined will (James 1:2; Matt. 5:11–12). There are, however, occasions when it should be a source of pride to endure rather than cave in under pressure (cf. Acts 5:41; 2 Thess. 1:4). Some things are more important even than life itself.

There is also a future dimension. How we respond to suffering now helps shape the way we respond in the future and finally how we participate with Christ when he is revealed in glory (4:13; cf. 1 Cor. 1:7; Phil. 3:20; 2 Thess. 1:7; also Rom. 8:17).

Third, our suffering should link us to the suffering of Christ (4:13). The condition for being joyful in suffering is that we "share Christ's sufferings" (4:13). The word for share is *koinoneo*, which suggests full participation. In another context, Paul speaks of completing "what is lacking in Christ's afflictions" (Col. 1:24). Both passages suggest that we should not think of Christ's suffering merely in terms of the historical event of the cross, as if when he finally died his suffering ended. It is rather that his suffering on the cross symbolized a much larger, more enduring part of his experience that continues on into the life of the church.

Fourth, we should view our suffering in solidarity with others who suffer (5:9). We all know the relief and strength we gain when we find others who have experienced pain in ways that we have. We discover that our form of suffering is not unique to us. We also learn from one another ways of coping effectively. We also come to realize that suffering is larger than any one of us and that we stand linked with the rest of humanity in our frailty and limitations.

Fifth, instead of detaching us from God, suffering connects us with God (4:14; 5:10–11). We are assured that the "spirit of glory, which is the Spirit of God," will rest on us (4:14; cf. Isa. 11:2). Also, we are promised that the God who has called us (1 Thess. 2:12; 5:24; 2 Pet. 1:3) will also "restore, support, strengthen, and establish" us (5:10; 2 Thess. 3:3). This is a worthwhile reminder, because the common assumption is that where pain and suffering are present, God is absent. Our text assures us that God is present with us precisely when we hurt.

It is in this overall context that we should read the general exhortations in 5:6–8. We are called on properly to define ourselves before God in humility (5:6; cf. James 4:10).

Anxieties are bound to come, but they should be entrusted to the God who cares (5:7; cf. Ps. 55:22; also Matt. 6:25–34; Luke 12:22–32; Phil. 4:6; also Wisd. of Sol. 12:13). We are to be alert in the presence of evil: "Be self-controlled and alert" (v. 8, NIV; Mark 13:37; Matt. 24:42; Acts 20:31; 1 Cor. 16:13; 1 Thess. 5:6, 8, 10; 2 Tim. 4:5). We should not face the world naively, as if good can overcome evil without a struggle (5:8; James 4:7; Eph. 6:11–13, 16).

John 17:1–11

The Gospel for today is a portion of Jesus' farewell prayer for his disciples. This prayer follows the discourses of chapters 14–16 and immediately precedes the arrest in the garden (18:1–12). Although the prayer is set within the ministry of the historical Jesus, the perspective of the prayer is also that of the glorified Christ looking pastorally on his church in the world. Notice: "And now I am no longer in the world" (v. 11); "While I was with them" (v. 12); and "But now I am coming to you" (v. 13). The prayer seems, then, to hang between heaven and earth, between the historical and the glorified Christ. But this characteristic is not confined to this prayer; this Evangelist unites the two, often indistinguishably, throughout the Gospel.

Those who speak of John 17 as more a sermon than a prayer properly identify the homiletical quality of Jesus' prayers in this Gospel (11:42; 12:30). However, two comments are in order: First, in the Bible words addressed to the people and words addressed to God are often interwoven. Psalm 23 and Moses' farewell speech (Deut. 32–33) are two examples. Sermons are prayerful, and prayers are sermonic. Second, the reader can best experience John 17 as a parishioner listening to a pastoral prayer. Such a listener overhears, is involved, and is represented in the prayer but not, of course, addressed by it.

The prayer in John 17 consists of three movements: Jesus' own return to glory (vv. 1–5); intercession for the disciples (vv. 6–19); and intercession for the readers who are disciples at least once removed (vv. 20–26). Our lection includes the first movement and part of the second. The first movement (vv. 1–5) gathers up in summary fashion several major themes of this Gospel. One has to do with Jesus' "hour." Jesus' ministry unfolded according to his hour (2:4; 7:6), and his death likewise (7:30; 12:23; 13:1). This Evangelist is persistent in his view that the life and death of Jesus were not contingent on circumstances, family, friends, or enemies, but on the will of God. The Christ of this Gospel came from God, knows God, and returns to God (13:3). This perspective provides a second major theme: God's purpose extends beyond Jesus to the church as those whom God has given to Jesus (6:36–40, 65; 17:2). This "all things are from God" viewpoint does not rob us of responsibility, but it gives encouragement to those so overwhelmed as a minority group in a hostile world that they can easily nurse a victim mentality. To say God's will prevails not only supports the believers but also reminds them of the radical grace that has taken initiative in Christ for our salvation. That initiative cannot be finally countered by any force that seeks to destroy. This thought introduces a third theme; God's offer is eternal life (v. 3; 3:16, 36; 5:24; 11:25–26). And finally, this life eternal is a relationship with God, here called "knowing God," which is possible through faith in Jesus Christ. This, says John, was the purpose of Christ's coming, to reveal the God whom no one has ever seen (1:18).

The second movement of the prayer (vv. 6–19; our lection ends at v. 11) concerns the apostles, the original band of disciples. One might wonder why include intercessions for a group who were probably deceased at the time of the writing of this Gospel. One answer lies within the petitions themselves: the apostles were given of God to Jesus (v. 6); Jesus gave to them the word of God (vv. 6–8); they had received, believed, and kept that word (vv. 6–8); they had not been corrupted by the unbelieving world in which they had to live and work (vv. 9–11). All of this is to assure the church of the clear and authoritative continuity between Jesus and the church. In chapters 14–16, the tie between Jesus and the church was presented in terms of the Holy Spirit; here that tie is the apostles. The Evangelist leaves no one in doubt: the church is not an orphan in the world, an accident of history, a thing dislodged, the frightened child of huddled rumors and superstitions. The pedigree of truth is established and unbroken: from God, to Christ, to the apostles, to the church.

Pentecost

Acts 2:1–21 or Numbers 11:24–30;
Psalm 104:24–34, 35*b*;
1 Corinthians 12:3*b*–13 or Acts 2:1–21;
John 20:19–23 or John 7:37–39

Pentecost concludes the Easter Season because the resurrection of Christ has its promise fulfilled in the giving of the Holy Spirit to the church. The name of the day itself and the powerful image of the coming of the Holy Spirit like the sound of rushing wind and the appearance of tongues like fire are given to us in the account of Acts 2:1–21 (which may function either as the first lesson or the Epistle). However, the other readings provide rich and meaningful expressions of the giving of the Spirit of God: "rested on them" (Num. 11:25, 26); "send forth" (Ps. 104:30); "varieties of gifts, but the same Spirit" (1 Cor. 12:4); "breathed on" (John 20:22); and "rivers of living water" (John 7:38).

Acts 2:1–21

The celebration of Pentecost as a Christian feast day is linked directly with this first lesson from Acts, in which Luke gives his account of the church's beginning. The place is Jerusalem within the temple precincts, and the time is the day of Pentecost.
This is only one of three references in the New Testament to the Jewish feast of Pentecost (cf. Acts 20:16; 1 Cor. 16:8). It was one of the three most important Jewish festivals, along with Passover (the Feast of Unleavened Bread) and the Feast of Tabernacles (the Feast of Booths). It was also known as the Feast of Weeks (Exod. 23:16; 34:22; Num. 28:26–31) because it was observed seven weeks after Passover (Lev. 23:15–21). Accordingly, it came to be designated Pentecost ("fiftieth") because it was celebrated on the fiftieth day after the sabbath on which Passover began.
In Christian practice, Pentecost occurred fifty days after Easter, although the entire season from Easter to Whitsunday, or Pentecost, was observed as a time of festivity and joy. No fasts were observed during this period, and it was the practice to pray in a standing position to symbolize the resurrection of Christ.
In today's text, we have the first portion of Acts 2, which includes an opening description of the day's events (vv. 1–4), a detailed roster of those in attendance (vv. 5–11), their response to these events (vv. 12–13), and the first section of Peter's sermon (vv. 15–21), the major part of which is a quotation from the prophet Joel (vv. 17–21). Let us consider the text in the following three sections.

293

1. *The coming of the Spirit* (vv. 1–4). As the band of faithful followers of Jesus, who are described earlier (1:12–14), are gathered in one place, they experience a shattering noise that is accompanied by a spectacular vision. It should be noted that by this time in Jewish history, Pentecost had come to be observed as the anniversary of the giving of the law on Sinai (cf. Jubilees 1:1; 6:17). The Old Testament describes this event as accompanied by deafening sounds and dazzling sights (Exod. 19:16–24). Such imagery is typically used to dramatize moments of divine revelation (cf. Judg. 5:4–5; Pss. 18:7–15; 29:3–9; 1 Kings 19:11–13).

It is against this background that we should understand Luke's account. It is an equally dramatic moment in that God is now being manifested through the Spirit. Something as significant as, indeed more significant than, the giving of the law is occurring.

2. *The universal audience* (vv. 5–11). Luke takes the trouble to itemize all the nations represented at this event. The "devout [Jews] from every nation under heaven" (v. 5) possibly refers to pilgrims attending the feast, but more likely refers to Diaspora Jews resident in Jerusalem. In either case, the nations are doubtless mentioned because of the common conception that the final messianic ingathering would be a time when Jews from every part of the earth would stream to Jerusalem to participate in God's restoration of Israel (Isa. 2:2–4; Mic. 4:1–4). This vision became translated into eschatological hopes and thus described what the New Age would be. Against this background, Peter claims these to be the events of "the last days" (v. 17).

3. *The response of the audience and Peter's sermon* (vv. 12–21). The effect of various people's speaking in other tongues was dumbfounding and perplexing. The apostles are accused of being drunk, which Peter denies (v. 15). Instead, these marvelous signs point to this event as the fulfillment of Joel's eschatological vision (Joel 2:28–32a).

The quotation from Joel has several prominent features: (1) God's Spirit would be poured out on all flesh, Jews and Gentiles alike; (2) a variety of persons, male and female, young and old, would become spokespersons for the Spirit and would prophesy; (3) the inbreaking of the New Age would be accompanied by a host of signs, both visible and audible; and (4) the universal quest for salvation would be answered.

This quotation becomes programmatic for the rest of Acts. We see the people of God come to include Gentiles as well as Jews. Various prophetic figures emerge through whom God's message is spoken. At every turn, as the Spirit impels the church to new action, there is a visible display of signs and wonders to attest the presence of God. In case after case, individuals and groups of individuals are confronted with the Word of God, they ask what they must do, and they are extended God's invitation to call on the name of the Lord.

The mood of today's text fits the spirit of Pentecost. Festive it is, even rollicking. Luke wants us to see that a New Age had broken in, that the people of God are being reconstituted. The work of Christ begun at Easter is coming to fruition as the people of Christ become empowered with the Spirit.

Numbers 11:24–30

Highly appropriate for the day of Pentecost is this account of the distribution of the divine Spirit among the Israelite elders and the outbreak of prophecy among the people. The setting of this report concerning the Spirit of God is the wilderness wandering of Israel. It is intertwined with yet another story of the rebellion of the people against the leadership of Moses, and thereby against the God who had called Moses to lead the people out of Egypt.

Two themes recur repeatedly throughout the account of the wandering in the wilderness: God's gracious care for the people and their rebellion or murmuring against God and Moses. Our text reports how the Lord cared for the people in a particular way. The larger story of this particular rebellion begins in 11:3 and concludes in 11:35. As is often the case, the complaint concerns food. The people are tired of the regular diet of manna and ask for meat (11:4); not only that, they long for the diverse and well-flavored menu they had in Egypt. In response to the complaining of the people, Moses protests to God (11:10–15), whose response in turn concerns both the problem of the people's desire for meat and Moses' grievance about the burdens of leadership. The answer to the people's complaint is the divine vow to give them so much meat that they will become sick of it. Our text concerning the distribution of the Spirit is the reaction to Moses' struggle with his burdens.

The reading for the day (11:24–30) is the final part of a story begun in verses 11–12 and continued in verses 14–17. When Moses complains that he cannot bear the burden of this people alone, God commands him to select seventy from the twelve tribes (v. 16) who are elders and officers and bring them to the tent, where God will take some of the Spirit that is on Moses and put it on them "so that they shall bear the burden of the people" along with Moses (v. 17). Our text reports how these instructions and promises were carried out. In its concern for the allocation of authority and responsibility, the text is similar to Exodus 18.

There is no new appearance of the divine Spirit when Moses brings the seventy to the tent, but the distribution of God's Spirit already given to Moses. Note also that the gift of the Spirit entails both responsibility and authority. The elders are to share Moses' authority and to help him bear the burdens. The structure is hierarchical; that is, the seventy do not communicate directly with Yahweh, and their authority is derived from that of Moses. Still, the Spirit is spread more widely among the people.

Already in the account of the giving of the Spirit to the elders there is a hint of controversies to follow. When the Spirit rested upon them, the elders prophesied, but only once. That they "did not do so again" (v. 25) indicates some uneasiness in the tradition either with the dilution of Moses' authority or with widespread prophecy.

The latter concern comes to the fore in the report of the outbreak of prophecy, not before the tent, but back in the camp by Eldad and Medad (v. 26). The flow of the narrative suggests that these two were numbered among the seventy ("registered") but stayed in the camp. Joshua, concerned about any challenge to the authority of Moses, reports this irregular behavior and asks Moses to put an end to it (v. 28). But Moses rebukes him with the famous words "Would that all the Lord's people were prophets, and that the Lord would put his spirit on them!" (v. 29).

As the story began, the distribution of the Spirit meant the distribution of authority and responsibility, but as it concludes, the gift of the Spirit leads to prophecy. Prophecy in this case will have referred to some kind of ecstatic behavior that could have been observed by others, including Joshua. More fundamentally, prophecy meant the capacity to mediate between God and the people, to understand and interpret the will of God. But can anyone besides Moses do such a thing? In that respect, the story touches on the issue posed in Deuteronomy 18:15–22, the question of prophets whom God will raise up after the death of Moses. Certainly, the biblical tradition knows, such figures will be needed. But can they be trusted? How will one test the spirits?

The appearance of the Spirit is controversial, and that is because it will not be confined to the "authorized" or the familiar structures. It is powerful and often perceived as dangerous. In Numbers 11, the controversy is related to the concern that these prophetic figures have usurped the authority of Moses. Joshua knew that the spirit of prophecy threatened established authority. Moses, on the other hand, is reported to have welcomed and encouraged such an outbreak of the Spirit. So the text encourages its readers not to fear the appearance of the Spirit of God.

This is one of the many Old Testament accounts of the divine Spirit. It is the Spirit as the breath of life that makes the human being a living being (Gen. 2:7). Frequently, the Spirit of the Lord "falls upon" someone to empower them to accomplish God's will, as in the case of Saul (1 Sam. 11:6) and David (1 Sam. 16:13). The Spirit empowers leaders, and it inspires prophetic activity (1 Sam. 10:10). The Hebrew term for it is *ruach*, which means both "spirit" and "wind," as well as other things. This dual meaning ties the account of the distribution of the Spirit in our chapter with the story of the rebellion, for in 11:31 it is the "wind" (*ruach*) sent by God that brings flocks of quails that land outside the camp. Like the wind, the Spirit of God cannot be seen, it is powerful, its effects can be perceived, and its coming and going cannot be predicted.

Although the appearance of the Spirit is awesome and even frightening, the last word is that of Moses. It is a prayer that God's Spirit would fall on all of God's people, just as the Book of Acts reports that it did on Pentecost.

Psalm 104:24–34, 35b

An ancient Egyptian pharaoh, Akhenaton (ca. 1380–1363 BC), composed or had composed a hymn to the sun god Aten, which praised Aten as the only god (other than the pharaoh, who claimed divinity). This ancient hymn has many parallels to Psalm 104. Whether the Hebrews copied this text from the Egyptians or not cannot be known. Perhaps the contemplation of aspects of creation in both cultures led to similar perspectives and parallel descriptions.

The selection of this lection for Pentecost Sunday is based on its emphasis on the role of God's Spirit in creation (see v. 30) and the psalm's universal perspectives. Verses 24–34, however, should be seen within the overall structure of the psalm.

The various stanzas in the psalm, excluding the summarizing depiction and the conclusion in verses 27–35, focus on the various wonders of creation: the sky (vv. 2–4), the earth (vv. 5–9), the water (vv. 10–13), the vegetation (vv. 14–18), the moon and sun (vv. 19–23), and the sea (vv. 24–26). (It is instructive to compare these with the structure and characterization of the six days of creation in Gen. 1.)

The selection for the lectionary picks up with the depiction of the sixth wonder. Verses 24–34 may be divided into three units: verses 24–26 center on the sea in the world of creation; verses 27–30 offer a reflection on creation's dependence upon God; and verses 31–35 (which are no longer addressed to the Deity) marvel at the grandeur and awesomeness of the Lord of creation.

For the psalmist, the sea (vv. 24–26) is God's pond, not some murky, mysterious, monster-laden source of chaos. From the ships and Leviathans (see Ps. 74:14; Job 41:1; Isa. 27:1) that ply its waves to the innumerable creatures small and great that scurry through its waters, they all have been made in the wisdom of God.

Verses 27–30 speak of what might be called "vertical universality." All living things are seen as dependent upon God—for food that fuels and sustains the living and for the breath of life that creates new being. That is, every part of life from top to bottom is the gift of God, not the possessor of that life. When God turns away, the creatures (including humans; note v. 23) become dismayed; when God withdraws his life spirit, the creatures succumb and return to dust. For all the world's greatness, for all its wonder and amazement, for the psalmist the world is no independent entity. Without divine sustenance it would not survive. Creation is depicted so that, in the words of the Heidelberg Catechism, God "rules in such a way that waves and grass, rain and drought, fruitful and unfruitful years, food and drink, death and sickness, riches and poverty and everything else come to us not by chance, but by his fatherly hand."

The psalm concludes with a confessional statement addressed to a human audience (vv. 31–35). These verses affirm gratitude and praise for the grandeur of the cosmos and its creatures, and above all for the God who creates and cares.

1 Corinthians 12:3b–13

Carl Holliday Prof of N.T.
Candler
ST
Emory U.

This text overlaps with the epistolary lection (12:1–11) for the Second Sunday After the Epiphany in Year C. It also overlaps slightly with the epistolary lection (12:12–30) for the Third Sunday After the Epiphany in Year C. The reader may want to consult our remarks in these other liturgical settings.

It is somewhat awkward to begin the lection with the second half of verse 3, which claims that no one can confess Jesus as Lord except when motivated by the Spirit. Because the first half of the verse speaks of cursing Jesus, it is understandable why it might be thought an offensive opening for a public reading. In any case, the lection has been defined as beginning with verse 3b to highlight the role of the Spirit in the Christian confession.

The context in which today's lection occurs is Paul's discussion of spiritual gifts in 1 Corinthians 12–14. His remarks are given in response to a question sent him by the Corinthian church (cf. 12:1). The question had to do with either "spiritual gifts" or "spiritual persons," depending on how one renders *pneumatikon* in 12:1. The overall issue being dealt with is Christian enthusiasm that manifests itself chiefly through glossolalia, the gift of speaking in tongues. In chapter 14, Paul provides an extensive comparison of tongues and prophecy, arguing for the superiority of the latter over the former, at least in this particular situation. As often happens, those who specialized in speaking in tongues apparently came to assume that their gift was of paramount importance and that every member should aspire to this as the highest manifestation of spirituality. For them, it would be better for everyone to have the same gift (assuming that it is the chief gift) than for there to be a plurality of gifts.

It is in response to this theology of uniformity that Paul crafts his remarks in today's text. Throughout his remarks, he underscores the preeminent importance of the Spirit, and perhaps this is what we should see especially in the context of Pentecost. Several observations are worth making.

First, the Spirit provides the primary impulse for making the Christian confession (v. 3b). The New Testament recognizes that there are various ways in which people can say "Lord." But the mere utterance of the word is not self-authenticating. Confession must be embodied in appropriate forms of obedience (Matt. 7:21; Luke 6:46). The name that is confessed should correspond appropriately to the One confessed (John 13:13). The heart of the Christian confession is that "*Jesus* is Lord" (italics added; Rom. 10:9; 2 Cor. 4:5; Phil. 2:11; Col. 2:6; 1 John 5:1), and this, Paul contends, can only be done "in the Spirit," or "under the influence of the Holy Spirit" (REB).

Second, the Spirit is the source of the various gifts in the church (vv. 4–11). Paul insists that diversity is axiomatic in the life of the church. In the church there are "varieties of gifts . . . varieties of service . . . varieties of working" (vv. 4–5). Whether one thinks in terms of personal gifts, ministerial functions, or forms of activity, diversity is the norm, not the exception.

It is perhaps with a slight bit of irony that Paul makes this point in trinitarian terms: the same Spirit, the same Lord, the same God. Even God can be spoken of in terms of diversity! But even with this division of labor, the accent lies on the Spirit, which is singled out as the common source of his exposition of the various gifts. The sheer repetition of the phrase "the same Spirit" (vv. 4, 8, 9, 11) would have a hammering effect. He intends his readers to see that the Spirit cannot be straitjacketed, but rather distributes gifts "to each individual at will" (v. 11, REB, NJB; cf. Rom. 12:6; Heb. 2:4).

Third, the Spirit is the unifying force within the body of Christ (vv. 12–13). Paul reminds us that Christ himself is multimembered (v. 12). We should note the line of his argument: just as the human body is one yet has many parts, *so it is with Christ.* Apparently this was not self-evident to some of the Corinthians. There is one Christ, Paul insists, but our participation in the one Christ must be conceived in diverse terms.

Naturally, the danger in a theology of pluriformity is that the church will lose its organizing center and be flung apart. But the cohesive force within the church, Paul insists, is the Spirit. The Spirit is both the agent and medium in which we were baptized. In one sense, it is the Spirit who baptized us, and it is also the Spirit who is the sphere in which we have our existence in Christ. Regardless of our ethnic or social status, we all drank from the common source of the Spirit (v. 13; cf. Gal. 3:28).

Fourth, the Spirit works for the common good (v. 7). A theology of pluriformity works as long as the various gifts are deployed for the common purpose—the upbuilding of the whole church. One of the consistent tests that Paul applies in his churches is to ask whether a certain attitude or activity "edifies" (1 Cor. 6:12; 10:23; 14:26). Similarly, here he insists that diversity becomes productive only when we each exercise our gift(s) in the interest of others (cf. 10:33).

In the context of Pentecost, Paul's words in today's text point the way toward a vital theology of the Spirit that energizes rather than enervates the church.

John 20:19–23

Pentecost completes Easter. Without Pentecost, Easter must carry all the pathos of saying farewell to a Christ who rises to return to glory. Without Pentecost, Easter reminds the church that Jesus has now gone to be with God and his followers are left alone in the world. Without Pentecost, Easter offers us a risen Christ whose return to glory leaves the church to face the world armed with nothing but fond memories of how it once was when Jesus was here. But with Pentecost, Easter's Christ promises to return and has returned in the Holy Spirit as comforter, guide, teacher, reminder, and power. With

Pentecost, the church does not simply celebrate but participates in Easter. With Pentecost, the risen Christ says hello and not good-bye to the church.

Because Luke has elaborated on Pentecost in a dramatic and powerful narrative, his account (Acts 2:1–21) has tended to govern the thoughts and images spawned by the firm and central Christian belief that the Holy Spirit was and is a gift of God to the church. However, the Gospel of John makes the same affirmation. It is concise to be sure, but it contains the basic elements of the conviction: the Holy Spirit is from God through the crucified and risen Christ; the Holy Spirit is associated with the commission of Christ to the church to continue his mission in the world; and the Holy Spirit empowers the apostles to give authoritative leadership to the church. This, in essence, is the content of John 20: 19–23. This text received our attention as the Gospel lesson for the Second Sunday of Easter and further comments on it can be found there. We will here devote the remainder of our commentary to the alternate Gospel lection.

John 7:37–39

The major portion of the discussion of the Holy Spirit in the Fourth Gospel is confined to the farewell section; that is, to chapters 14–20. That location of the discussion is appropriate because the coming of the Holy Spirit is consistently presented as subsequent to the resurrection and exaltation of Jesus. "If I do not go away, the Advocate will not come to you; but if I go, I will send him to you" (16:7). The brief account of the giving of the Spirit to the disciples (20:19–23) involves the postresurrection Christ. Given this scheme—Jesus is raised, receives the Spirit from God, and gives it to the disciples—any mention of the Holy Spirit earlier in the Gospel would have to be anticipatory; that is, in the framework of Jesus' earthly ministry, an offer of the Holy Spirit would be a future promise.

This is precisely the case in 7:37–39. Earlier, in the conversation between Jesus and Nicodemus (3:1–15), the Holy Spirit is referred to as essential to the birth from above, and that birth is of both water and Spirit. Close examination of that conversation, however, reveals that its perspective is postresurrection, but set within the framework of Jesus' earthly ministry. For example, verse 13 states, "No one has ascended into heaven except the one who descended from heaven, the Son of Man." Statements about the Spirit are offered by Jesus who, from the writer's angle of vision, "has ascended into heaven." Likewise, in 7: 37–39 the Spirit is associated with water (v. 38) and is promised subsequent to Jesus' ascension in glory (v. 39). The promise of living water is reminiscent of the conversation between Jesus and the Samaritan woman (4:4–26) and of Isaiah 44:1–5. Apparently, the association of the Spirit with water in baptism was rather widespread in the early church (Mark 1:9–11 and parallels; Acts 2:38; 1 Cor. 12:13). The union of the Spirit with the image of drinking (v. 37) may be an association of the gift of the Spirit with the Eucharist. This seems to be the case in 1 Corinthians 12:13: "and we were all made to drink of one Spirit."

But regardless of whether the gift of the Spirit was and is joined to baptism or the Eucharist or both, the promise itself is repeatedly and consistently made. Jesus crucified, dead, and buried, who sits in glory at the right hand of God, sent and sends the Holy Spirit to sustain and to nourish the church in its life together and in its mission to the world.

Trinity Sunday

Genesis 1:1–2:4*a*;
Psalm 8;
2 Corinthians 13:11–13;
Matthew 28:16–20

T rinity Sunday was introduced into the liturgical cycle of the church as the celebration of a doctrine. The texts for the day enable the church at worship to reflect upon
that doctrine, but, more than that, they direct attention to the reality that called
forth the doctrine in the first place. In the biblical tradition, the one God is experienced as
transcendent Creator, as incarnate, and as present in and among the lives of believers. The
Old Testament reading, the classic account of creation by the Priestly Writer, portrays God
as the Creator of a magnificent, orderly universe. Psalm 8 continues this emphasis on God's
creative work, giving special attention to the exalted status of human beings within the
created order. Both the Gospel and epistolary lections, the concluding sections of their respective books, contain pronouncements in the name of the triune God.

Genesis 1:1–2:4*a*

T his lection begins the semicontinuous reading from the Old Testament for this
season of study and reflection, the first of as many as twenty-six readings (depending
upon the particular year) from the Pentateuch, Joshua, and Judges. These lessons
take us through the major events in the biblical account of history from the creation of
the world to the period immediately following Israel's settlement in the land promised to the
ancestors. In hearing these texts read and preached, the church may better understand and
identify with its roots in ancient Israel's faith.

Our reading is the first, but also the younger, of two distinct accounts of creation in the
Book of Genesis. The other begins where this one ends, continues through the remainder of
Genesis 2, and is followed by the account of the story of the first sins of the first human pair
in Genesis 3. It has long been recognized that these very different accounts stem from distinct sources, separated from one another by centuries. Genesis 1:1–2:4*a* comes from the
Priestly Writer in the time of the Babylonian Exile or, more likely, from the postexilic period
(538 BCff.). The other comes from the Yahwist writing in the time of the Israelite monarchy,
perhaps as early as 900 BC.

It is appropriate that the first chapter of the Bible begin our semicontinuous readings for
the season. It is especially appropriate that the Priestly Writer's words initiate that summary of

our reflection on the history of salvation, because that writer's document as a whole presents a carefully organized account of that history. The last sentence of the reading ("These are the generations of the heavens and earth . . . ") is a formulaic genealogical expression that recurs throughout the Book of Genesis indicating the successive "chapters" in the work (Adam, 5:1; Noah, 6:9; sons of Noah, 10:1; etc.). The Priestly Document is organized genealogically, chronologically, and also in terms of a series of covenants (Noah, 9:8–17; Abraham and Sarah, 17; Jacob, 35:9–13) leading up to the covenant at Mt. Sinai (Exod. 19ff.).

Both in its tone and contents, Genesis 1 is a highly liturgical account of the beginning of the world. There is a powerful structure set out with more than one refrain repeated throughout: "God said, 'Let there be light'; and there was light" (1:3). "And there was evening and there was morning, the first day" (1:5). The tone is majestic, characterized by "sober monotony" (von Rad). The refrains in particular lend a cadence if not rhythm to the account that could easily be chanted. Although the contents concern God's creation of all that is, there is a particular liturgical focus on sacred time, for God works according to a weekly pattern and completes creation by the establishment of the sabbath.

Because of the weekly pattern and the clear refrains, it is not difficult to outline the story. It has an introduction (1:1–2) followed by seven parts, the acts of creation for each successive day. But those seven actually amount to two sections, the six days of work and the one day of rest. So one of the aims of the account is to show that the most ancient of ordinances was the sabbath day. Once God had "finished the work that he had done . . . he rested on the seventh day. . . . So God blessed the seventh day and hallowed it" (2:2–3). The understanding here is mirrored in the sabbath commandment in Exodus 20:8–11. Deuteronomy 5:12–16, on the other hand, gives humanitarian reasons rather than the creation of a sacred day as the explanation for the sabbath. But in virtually all Old Testament traditions, the sabbath is fundamentally a day of rest rather than a day for formal worship. By refraining from work on that day, human beings participate in the very rhythm of the creation, the pattern of God's activity.

As most modern translations such as the NRSV suggest, the first two verses of the account provide an introduction, a statement of the circumstances at the time of creation. Verse 1 is not a heading for the chapter but a temporal clause, best read "When God began to create . . ." (NRSV footnote; see also NJPSV). There is no human analogy for God's activity; in the Old Testament God is the only subject of the verb *bara'*, "create." The second verse describes what "existed" before creation: "The earth was a formless void and darkness covered the face of the deep." Consequently, in the Old Testament view, creation was not *ex nihilo*, but out of chaos. The dominant image is that of the dark, wind-tossed primeval waters. As the story of the Flood (Gen. 6–9) will show, this chaos is the persistent alternative to creation. Considerable debate continues about the correct translation of the second half of verse 2 (see NRSV footnotes), but in no case could it be taken as a reference to the Holy Spirit.

There is a recognizable pattern in the six days of creation, the second three paralleling the first three. In the first three days God created light (1:3–5), the dome separating the waters (1:6–8), then land and vegetation (1:9–13). The acts of the last three days correspond in order to those of the first three: lights (1:14–19), fish and birds (1:20–23), then animals and human beings (1:24–31). The cosmology presumed by the writer is one widely known in the ancient Near East. The earth is flat, floating on the primeval waters below, covered by a dome that protects it from the waters above. The sun, moon, stars—indeed, all the created order—is within that space bounded by earth and dome.

There are more riches in this wonderful chapter than could possibly be mined in a week of Sundays. There is, first of all, its meditation on the nature of the world. It is remarkable that ancient Israelites saw no need to argue with the "science"—even the foreign science—of the day, but assumed the same basic worldview as their neighbors. There is, however, engagement with alternative religious understandings to the point of polemic. Where Babylon saw creation as the result of a struggle among the gods, Israel saw everything coming from the act or the word of God. Specifically, where other Near Eastern religions saw all the heavenly bodies as deities, this text quite explicitly indicates that they were created by God and given limited functions. They are to mark the times—day and night and the calendar (1:14–18).

Then there is the question of the place of human beings in this created order. Unlike the Yahwistic account in 2:4b–25, the origin of human life is not the dominant concern. God, the sole actor in the account, creates human beings on the sixth day, along with other animals. Also unlike the Yahwistic story, this one reports that human beings were created plural, male and female, from the beginning (1:26–27). God blesses them with the command to procreate (1:28) and gives specific instructions for their role in relation to the rest of creation. Misunderstanding of these instructions has led to considerable mischief. But the command to "subdue" and "have dominion" over the earth is in no sense a license for the rape of creation. That the human beings are in the "image" and "likeness" (1:26) of God indicates that they are destined to be royal stewards of this beautiful world. Their special place, in the biblical view, is the incarnation of the divine will in the world, to act as God's representatives.

Finally, the dominant theme of the account is the moral and aesthetic evaluation of the world. From beginning to end, the writer insists that the world is God's creation. And every day God pronounces that same benediction over the results of God's work: "God saw that it was good." The Hebrew *tob*, like the English "good," has a wide range of connotations, and most of them seem to apply here: morally right, appropriate, beautiful. At the end of the sixth day there is that comprehensive pronouncement filled with joy: "God saw everything that he had made, and indeed, it was very good" (1:31). Perhaps this human representative of God should follow God's example, to admire and enjoy this good creation.

Psalm 8

This psalm has been treated earlier, as a reading for January 1.

2 Corinthians 13:11–13

What makes this epistolary lesson especially appropriate as a text for Trinity Sunday is the final verse, "the most explicitly Trinitarian formula in the entire Pauline corpus" (Spicq). It reflects Paul's triadic understanding of Deity (cf. 1 Cor. 12:4–6), which he shared with other early Christian traditions (cf. Matt. 28:18–20). It is remarkable because it is formulaic, occurring as the prayer of benediction concluding this letter.

At the outset, we might note the differences in versification employed in the translations: verse 12 in NRSV and NJB is treated as two verses in REB and NIV, and the latter accordingly render NRSV and NJB's verse 13 as verse 14. Here, our remarks follow NRSV.

The unusual order of the benediction is worth noting: "Grace of the Lord Jesus Christ . . . the love of God . . . the communion of the Holy Spirit." This in itself sets it apart from later Trinitarian formulations in which God occupies the prominent first position (cf. Matt. 28:19). God is not further defined as Father, nor is Christ identified as Son. There seems to be less emphasis on identifying personal or relational aspects between each of the members of the Godhead. Rather, the emphasis falls on certain attributes, or active aspects, typical of them, or to state it more dynamically, acts done by them in our behalf, "grace . . . love . . . communion."

One exegetical question is whether each phrase is to be understood as an objective or a subjective genitive. The former would be rendered "grace whose object or goal is Christ . . . our love toward or for God . . . communion that exists, or reaches fruition, in the Holy Spirit." The latter would be rendered "grace displayed by, or bestowed in, Christ . . . God's love for us . . . communion created, enabled, sustained by the Holy Spirit." The question is left unresolved in NRSV, NJB, NIV, and REB.

We may comment briefly on each of the three items.

First, *the grace of the Lord Jesus Christ*. This is a form of benediction typically, and frequently, used by Paul (cf. Rom. 16:20; 1 Cor. 16:23; Gal. 6:18; Phil. 4:23; 1 Thess. 5:28; Philem. 25). Because the death of Christ is to be understood as an act of uncalculated generosity by Christ, where he exchanged wealth for poverty (2 Cor. 8:9), this most certainly is to be understood as grace displayed by the Lord Jesus Christ (in our behalf). It is thus understood as "the free gift in the grace of the one man, Jesus Christ" (Rom. 5:15–16).

Second, *love of God*. This should be understood in light of the most unusual reference earlier to "the God of love" (v. 11), which occurs only here in the New Testament and never in the Greek or Hebrew Old Testament. By contrast, "God of peace" is more frequent in the New Testament (Rom. 15:33; 16:20; Phil. 4:9; 1 Thess. 5:23; cf. 1 Cor. 14:33), although infrequent in Jewish writings. The assurance in verse 11 is that a loving and peaceful God will be with us. Paul's stress here on the "love of God" is best understood in close connection with the grace of Christ. Christ's life and death become the supreme demonstration of God's love for us (cf. Rom. 5:5, 8; cf. John 3:16). Indeed, God's love has its focus in Christ (Rom. 8:39). Through the work of Christ and in the person of Christ, God's love reaches its most intensely brilliant radiance as a dazzling shaft of light. The direct result of God's love is our election (1 Thess. 1:4).

Third, *communion of the Holy Spirit*. "Communion" translates *koinonia*, which NJB, REB, and NIV render "fellowship." The term may be rendered more dynamically as "sharing" or "participation" (Furnish). It suggests an active relationship where there is dynamic, mutual interplay among the participants. Those who participate both give and receive, and what results is a relationship of sharing. The idea of partnership is central (cf. 2 Cor. 1:7; 6:14; 8:4, 23; 9:13). For this reason, Paul aptly uses *koinonia* to designate financial contributions made as free-will offerings (2 Cor. 8:4). In urging the Philippians to be one, Paul speaks of the possibility of "sharing in the Spirit" (Phil. 2:1). The Spirit they share as a common possession serves as the basis for their solidarity. Most likely, then, this third phrase is to be taken as an objective genitive—the communion, fellowship, or participation that we have in the Holy Spirit. This not only suggests that the Spirit is what we possess in common, but also the common sphere in which our life together is sustained. The Spirit is, after all, living proof that God's love has been bestowed on us (Rom. 5:5).

Scholars have noted the eucharistic overtones of today's passage. The exhortation toward self-examination in the preceding section (v. 5) recalls Paul's earlier instructions about appropriate behavior at the Eucharist (1 Cor. 11:23–34). The charge to greet one another (v. 12; Rom. 16:3–16; 1 Cor. 16:20; Phil. 4:21; 1 Thess. 5:26) fits well within a eucharistic setting. In later Christian worship following the prayer, the saints greeted one another with a holy kiss before presenting the elements for consecration (Justin, *Apology* 1.65; cf. 1 Cor. 16:20; also Rom. 16:16; 1 Thess. 5:26; 1 Pet. 5:14).

As for homiletical possibilities, the preacher should note that the Trinitarian benediction occurs at the end of a series of moral exhortations. Paul commends a life of self-examination and mutual edification within the church (vv. 5–10). The readers are charged with responsibility for developing a form of life together that is coherent, harmonious, peaceful, and upbuilding (vv. 11–12). They are responsible for repairing broken relationships within their midst and for adjusting their course. It is a reminder that Christian conduct should be self-correcting, responding to the demands of life as well as to the demands of the gospel. Trinity may be a doctrine, but in this text it relates to practice.

Second, one may wish to explore the relationship between the three Persons in verse 13. To what extent, in Christian experience, does Christ become the primary Way, or One through whom we are led to, and experience, God, and in whom we experience participation in God's Spirit?

Matthew 28:16–20

I t is understandable that the Sunday following Pentecost suffers by comparison. However, to say that is not to accept a place of lesser importance for this day designated Trinity Sunday. In fact, it is vital for the experience and the theology of the church that the historic faith in one God, creator, redeemer, and sustainer, be reaffirmed. This is especially important after a season of centering our attention on Jesus and a day of focusing on the Holy Spirit. It is, after all, God who sent Jesus Christ and God who sends the Holy Spirit. Today's Gospel statement of the Trinity is Matthew 28:16–20. These verses conclude not only the resurrection narrative of Matthew but also the entire Gospel. We may assume, therefore, that this lection will gather up central themes both of the resurrection story and of the Gospel as a whole.

Matthew 28:16–20 falls naturally into two parts: verses 16–17, which describe the disciples, and verses 18–20, which present the appearance and words of the risen and exalted Christ. Verse 16 assumes that Jesus had appointed (commanded) a specific mountain as the place of rendezvous with his disciples. The reader is not told of that instruction nor is the place specified, if, indeed, a mountain in the geographical sense is intended. Mountains are frequently referred to in the Bible as the scenes of theophanies and Christophanies. What we do know is that the passage affirms Matthew's and Mark's designation of Galilee as the center of post-Easter experiences with Christ, a noticeable difference from Luke's insistence that Jesus would have his disciples stay in Jerusalem (24:47–53). The meeting in Galilee between the risen Christ and his disciples was, according to Matthew, in keeping with the word of the pre-Easter Jesus (26:32), the angel at the tomb (28:7), and the risen Christ (28:10; see Mark 14:28; 16:7).

According to verse 17, seeing the risen Christ produced both worship and doubt. Because none other than the Eleven are mentioned, we must assume they are the worshipers and the doubters. Worshiping Christ is a response found elsewhere in Matthew (2:11;

8:2;14:33), and the doubt is in keeping not only with reason but also with the accounts of the other Evangelists (Mark 16:8; Luke 24:11, 36–41; John 20:4–10; 24–29).

The second part of the reading, verses 18–20, begins rather unusually. Why would the writer, after saying that the disciples saw and worshiped Jesus, say, "And Jesus came and said to them"? Was he not already there? It could be that verses 18–20 were not a part of the original text, and the fact that verse 18 has its own narrative beginning testifies to its being a separate unit added by Matthew or a later edition. Or it could be that the expression "Jesus came" simply refers to his drawing nearer, approaching the disciples who thus far had only seen, worshiped, and doubted. It may be important that in only two stories in Matthew does Jesus draw near or come to anyone; in all others it is the people who come to Jesus. Those two are in the text before us (v. 18) and in the account of the Transfiguration (17:7), both of which are stories of the appearance of the glorified Christ.

But even if the reference to Jesus coming to his disciples does not persuade the reader that Matthew is here presenting the exalted and enthroned Christ who has come and will come, the claim of Jesus does: "All authority in heaven and on earth has been given to me" (v. 18). Although stated differently, Matthew has here offered the readers (the church) the enthroned Christ and Lord no less than in the more familiar enthronement passages (Phil. 2:9–11; 1 Tim. 3:16), which draw more directly on Psalm 110:1 and Daniel 7:14. This text expresses one of the earliest, if not the earliest meaning of Easter—the exaltation of Jesus as Lord. And to that universal lordship is tied the natural corollary—the universal mission of the church (v. 19) to which Matthew had referred earlier in anticipation of Jesus' exaltation (8:11; 12:21; 25:31–32).

The accents in Jesus' commission are clearly Matthean, touching upon central themes of the Gospel: "make disciples" and "obey everything that I have commanded you." Going, baptizing, and teaching are participles in the service of the command to make disciples. The Trinitarian formula is attached to baptism, which, however obscure its origins, was the common practice of the early churches. Except at this point, baptism is in the New Testament associated with the name of Jesus (Acts 2:38; 8:16; 10:48; Rom. 6:3; 1 Cor. 1:13, 15; 6:11). Perhaps by the time of Matthew the church felt the need to set baptism and, in fact, Jesus and the Holy Spirit into the larger context of its understanding of the one God who creates, redeems, and sustains.

The expression "to the end of the age" (v. 20) very likely involves the triumphal return of Christ, but the accent of the passage is not there in the sense of Christ rescuing his disciples who have been very much alone in the world. The end of the age is rather a finale, a consummation of Christ's work through the church, which has labored all the while in the assurance that the enthroned Christ is also present in and with his church.

Proper 4 [9]
(Sunday between May 29 and June 4 inclusive (if after Trinity Sunday))

Genesis 6:9–22; 7:24; 8:14–19;
Psalm 46; or
Deuteronomy 11:18–21, 26–28;
Psalm 31:1–5, 19–24;
Romans 1:16–17, 3:22b–28 (29–31);
Matthew 7:21–29

The season after Pentecost is a time for serious, focused study of Scripture. In the *Common Lectionary*, the Old Testament lessons, beginning with Trinity Sunday, provide a series of twenty-three readings from the Pentateuch, from the creation to the death of Moses, and conclude the season with texts from the Books of Joshua and Judges that take the story through the conquest and into the period of the judges. In the other lectionaries, the Old Testament lessons make no attempt to present a continuous sequence of readings, but are taken instead from various parts of the Bible. In both lectionary traditions, specific psalms are chosen for each Sunday, with no attempt made to cover the Psalter continuously. In both lectionary traditions, however, the epistolary readings are semicontinuous. In Year A, all of the epistolary lections are from three Pauline letters, sixteen from Romans and the remainder from Philippians and 1 Thessalonians. Similarly, for both traditions Matthew is the Gospel for continuous study this year. The advantage of such semicontinuous selections is that the church can hear and reflect upon single books or other units of the Bible in some depth. The disadvantage, of course, is that often on given Sundays the themes of the texts do not converge.

In the *Common Lectionary* for today, the story of Noah serves as the Old Testament reading. Following naturally on last week's creation account, this text provides an opportunity to reflect on the consequences of human actions on the created order. In a similar vein, the responsorial psalm, Psalm 46, proclaims God's rule over chaos. In the other lectionaries, the Old Testament reading is supplied by Deuteronomy 11, which rehearses the blessing and curse offered by Moses. The responsorial psalm, Psalm 31, is a prayer of lament asking deliverance from personal adversaries.

From the epistolary reading we hear Paul's classical statement concerning righteousness, grace, and redemption. The sequence of readings from Matthew begins with sayings of Jesus concerning those who profess to follow him.

306

Genesis 6:9–22; 7:24; 8:14–19

In the semicontinuous readings from the Old Testament, the story turns from good news to bad, from the divine creation of the world to human actions that lead to the great Flood, ending with a reordering of human life.

The full account of the Flood includes Genesis 6:5–9:28. That composition is the result of the editorial combination of material from the two major documents of the Pentateuch, the Priestly Document and the Yahwist (J). There are numerous indications of the presence of the two sources, including duplicates and contradictions, as well as the different divine names, Yahweh (Lord) and Elohim (God). In one case (6:19–20), one pair of every animal went into the ark, and in another (7:1–4) there were seven pairs of clean animals and one pair of the unclean. It is the Yahwist who makes the distinction between clean and unclean; the Priestly Writer scrupulously avoids the anachronism of such a distinction, which he reports was not given until Mt. Sinai (Lev. 11:1–30). For the same reason, unlike J, he does not report that Noah performed a sacrifice when the Flood was ended. The nature of the Flood, the reasons for it, and the length of time involved also are different in the two sources.

When the sources are separated, we have before us two full accounts, the combination of which makes a third version. Our reading for the day consists entirely of sections of the Priestly Writer's account. One way to understand the point of view of this writer is to contrast it with that of the Yahwist. In both instances, the Flood is divine judgment upon the world, but the two writers describe the reasons and the reaction of the Deity quite differently. The J writer focuses typically upon the evil of the human heart and quite freely characterizes the emotions of Yahweh in anthropomorphic terms (6:5–7). God suffers and is sorry. The Priestly Writer, on the other hand, speaks in more cosmic terms—"the earth was corrupt in God's sight and the earth was filled with violence" (6:11), and simply reports God's decision to put an end to "all flesh," without reference to any divine emotions. The character of Noah is different in the two accounts as well. In J, Noah "found favor in the sight of the Lord" (6:8), and in P he "was a righteous man, blameless in his generation" (6:9). In the story as a whole, J's Noah is wise and P's Noah is pious. When the Flood comes, in J it simply rains for forty days and forty nights (7:4, 12, 17), but in P "all the fountains of the great deep burst forth, and the windows of heaven were opened" (7:11). This is the same cosmic perspective and worldview seen in the Priestly account of creation (Gen. 1:1–2:4a). In both cases, of course, all life except that in the ark was wiped out, setting the stage for a new beginning. In our reading, P is quite specific about the length of time involved. The waters began in the six hundredth year of Noah's life, in the second month (7:11), and were dried up in the first day of the first month of the next year (8:13). Here we see reflected the Priestly Writer's persistent concern with chronology.

Our reading concludes with the Priestly Writer's report of Noah's departure from the ark (8:18). Following that, J reports Noah's sacrifice and the divine promise (8:19–22), and P reports God's blessing and the covenant with Noah's descendants (9:1–17), promised at the outset (6:18). God gives Noah the same command he had given the original couple—be fruitful and multiply (9:7)—and a sign of the covenant. Note especially that the sign of the rainbow is not a reminder to human beings but to God: "I will remember my covenant that is between me and you and every living creature." (9:15).

This account of the Flood provides the occasion for reflection on the relationship between the fate of the created order and human actions. The Priestly Writer specifically correlates the corruption of that order to violence. He does not specifically locate the problem in the human heart, as does J, but our text persistently stresses how human life is part of the whole of the cosmos. Indeed, God's covenant is not simply with Noah and his descendants, but also with "every living creature" (9:15). In the biblical understanding, the best name for the world is not "cosmos" but "creation," because all that is exists because of the divine will. Moreover, although this story certainly is the occasion to reflect upon divine wrath and judgment, it is also the occasion to meditate on God's covenant—God's bound relationship—with the creation. The last word is God's assurance that God will be faithful to that covenant.

Psalm 46

This psalm affirms God's rule over chaos and gives expression to some of the beliefs held about the city of Jerusalem (or Zion) by the ancient Judeans. This psalm, like Psalms 48 and 76, celebrates Zion as the city of God and proclaims divine protection for the city. The earth and existence may be threatened, but Zion is declared steadfast and divinely protected.

Originally, Psalm 46 was probably used in the great autumn festival, the Feast of Tabernacles, which celebrated the end of the old year and the beginning of the new year. One of the functions of the fall festival was to put the old year behind and to greet the new year. One way in which this was done was through the celebration of God's power to overcome chaos and the forces of disorder. (Note how this is a theme of our political campaigns and part of the promises of each new administration.) As part of the ritual celebration, the world was described as temporarily returning to chaotic conditions (the Good Friday motif). In reaffirming divine rule over the universe, God reenacted the original creation. Thus every new year or autumnal celebration was, as our new year's days are, a new beginning.

Psalm 46 shares in this thinking about chaos and order but presents the city of Zion as so divinely protected that, whatever the chaotic conditions are, Zion will remain an unshaken refuge.

In verses 1–3, the text speaks of chaos in the world of nature. The NJPSV translates verses 2–3 as:

> God is our refuge and stronghold,
> a help in trouble, very near.
> Therefore we are not afraid
> though the earth reels,
> though mountains topple into the sea—
> its waters rage and foam;
> in its swell mountains quake.

The second stanza speaks of chaos and uncertainty in the historical realm—"nations rage, the kingdoms totter"—but the people of Yahweh have no need to fear (v. 6). Verse 4 refers to a river whose streams make glad the city of God. Jerusalem, of course, had no major stream nearby. What then does this refer to? Three options suggest themselves:

1. The ancient high gods, such as El in Canaanite thought, were assumed to live on a sacred mountain (like Olympus in Greek mythology). This sacred mountain was also considered the source of one or more rivers. Thus it is possible that language that was originally used to speak of some other deity and some other sacred site has been transferred to Yahweh and to Zion.

2. The Garden of Eden was assumed to be located on a mountaintop in some texts (see Ezek. 28). Because streams flowed from the garden (see Gen. 2:10–14) and if Zion was identified with the Garden of Eden, then one could expect talk about streams in regard to the site.

3. Maybe the stream referred to was the spring Gihon, which supplied Jerusalem with its source of water. It is interesting to note that one of the streams flowing from the Garden of Eden was called Gihon (Gen. 2:13).

At any rate, water, the source of life and such a precious commodity in Palestine, is here associated with Jerusalem. The prophet Ezekiel later built on this imagery of water and Zion, and predicted a time to come when a stream would flow from under the temple and water the land of Palestine, transforming it into a paradisaical state (Ezek. 47:1–12).

Verses 8–9 invite people to behold the works of Yahweh, namely, how God works desolation in the earth, brings wars to an end, and destroys the weapons of war—the bow, the spear, and the chariot. Thus we have in the schematic framework of the Zion theology the idea of chaos followed by divine intervention, followed by universal peace or at least the destruction of the weapons of war (see Isa. 2:2–4). War dances, war games, and the symbolic destruction of the enemy may have been a part of the ritual of the fall festival.

In verse 10, a divine oracle occurs, probably spoken in worship by a cultic official. The NRSV translates the opening word as "be still." This assumes that the divine word is addressed to the people of Yahweh. The term basically means "leave off," "abandon," or "stop." Perhaps the oracle is here assumed to be addressed to the enemies, the nations of verse 6. If so, it demands that they recognize Yahweh and halt their aggressive actions, probably against Zion.

Throughout this psalm, the emphasis falls not only on the inviolability of Zion, where to live was considered a special privilege (see Isa. 4:3), but also on God as the protector of the city. The refrain in verses 7 and 11, as well as verse 1, praises God as the source of the city's security. Zion was a secure fortress because Yahweh was a sure refuge.

Deuteronomy 11:18–21, 26–28

This is the same Old Testament reading assigned for the Ninth Sunday After the Epiphany in Year A. For commentary, see our remarks in that setting.

Psalm 31:1–5, 19–24

This psalm has been discussed under the Ninth Sunday After the Epiphany and Holy Saturday in this volume.

Romans 1:16–17, 3:22b–28 (29–31)

With today's epistolary reading, we begin the semicontinuous reading of the Epistle to the Romans that runs for sixteen weeks through Proper 19 [24]. This is an appropriate combination of texts, for they state, in a shorter and longer form, the thesis of the epistle. In these passages, Paul introduces themes that will be explained and developed throughout the rest of the letter.

Because this same couplet of texts serves as the epistolary reading for the Ninth Sunday After the Epiphany in Year A, we have provided commentary in this setting earlier in this volume.

Matthew 7:21–29

Now that the liturgical year has ended, the lectionary offers during this "ordinary time" semicontinuous readings in the biblical texts. This means that, except for the few special days, we will be reading through Matthew until Advent. The benefits to the listeners and the preacher are many. Among them are (1) getting a sense of the narrative of Jesus' life and work, (2) attaining some understanding of the theological perspective and literary skills of a single writer, (3) building a series of messages on themes too large for single sermons, and (4) experiencing the cumulative effect of proclamation with continuity. We begin with the conclusion to the Sermon on the Mount, earlier portions of Matthew having been read during the Christmas, Epiphany, and Lenten seasons.

Matthew 7:21–29 consists of three units: the first two (vv. 21–23, 24–27) conclude the Sermon proper with a double emphasis on obedience to what has been taught, and the third (vv. 28–29) is Matthew's conclusion to the Sermon in which he remarks upon the nature of Jesus' teaching and the response of the crowds.

The twofold conclusion to the Sermon on the Mount addresses two audiences: those who might deceive themselves into thinking that extraordinary religious activity is an acceptable substitute for obedience to the will of God (vv. 21–23) and those who might deceive themselves into thinking that there is saving merit in having heard Jesus preach (vv. 24–27). The former group is characterized as saying, "Lord, Lord," but without accompanying obedience. It is clear that Matthew intends by the title "Lord" in both verses 21 and 22 to refer to Jesus as exalted Lord of the final judgment, "that day" (Joel 2:1; Amos 5:18, 20; Luke 17:24; 1 Cor. 3:13; Heb. 10:25). Inasmuch as "Lord" can also mean "Sir" in the sense of addressing one's teacher, Luke's form of Matthew 7:21 (6:46) may be more nearly the original, set in the context of the ministry of the historical Jesus. But Matthew's perspective is that Christ is enthroned and calling his followers to account, and the issue is, Did you obey what I taught you during my ministry among you? If any in the church assumed that "every one who calls upon the name of the Lord will be saved" (Joel 2:32; Rom. 10:13) did not involve obedience, then verses 21–23 shatter that assumption. And if anyone assumed that an impressive ministry of prophesying, exorcising demons, and performing miracles would dazzle the Lord and effect a suspension of the demand for moral and ethical obedience, then verses 21–23 shatter that assumption. These are addressed as "evildoers" (NRSV) or persons whose "deeds are evil" (REB), the words of the Lord's judgment being drawn from Psalm 6:8. Literally, the word means "lawless," a translation that might better capture the emphasis of Matthew on doing what

Christ instructed. Prophecy, exorcism, and miracle working are not evil in themselves; the evil is the disobedience, the lawlessness.

The second group addressed in our text (vv. 24–27) is a more familiar one—those who have heard great preaching, even that of Jesus himself, but whose lives exhibit no evidence of obedience. To these there need be no direct word of judgment as upon the first group; life itself will in time reveal the folly of hearing without doing. When the storms hit, the difference between the life of obedience and the life of listening alone will be dramatically evident. (The preacher may want to look at Luke 6:47–49 to see the different imagery that makes the same point. Luke's builders place their houses by a river that rises.) Verses 24–27 are reminiscent of James 1:22–25 in which, by means of a different image, doing and not hearing only is heavily underscored.

Matthew concludes the Sermon (vv. 28–29) with the phrase "When Jesus had finished this discourse," which is the formulaic conclusion to all five of the major bodies of teaching in Matthew (7:28; 11:1; 13:53; 19:1; 26:1). The crowds of 5:1 are reintroduced, and the description of Jesus as an authoritative teacher is taken directly from Mark 1:22, although in Mark the content of his teaching is not given. Jesus does not teach by passing along the interpretations of generations of rabbis but by providing a direct, unmediated interpretation of God's will for human behavior and relationships. Obedient attention to his teaching, says Matthew, is the key to life in the kingdom.

Proper 5 [10]

(Sunday between June 5 and 11 inclusive (if after Trinity Sunday))

Genesis 12:1–9;
Psalm 33:1–12; or
Hosea 5:15–6:6;
Psalm 50:7–15;
Romans 4:13–25;
Matthew 9:9–13, 18–26

In the *Common Lectionary*, the Old Testament reading is the call of Abraham and his response, initiating the history of salvation that will find its center in the exodus from Egypt. The responsorial psalm celebrates and expresses trust in the might and mercy of the God of salvation. In the other lectionaries, the Old Testament lesson is the well-known text from Hosea sounding the theme of Yahweh's willingness to extend mercy to repentant Israel. The emphasis in Psalm 50 on God's desire for obedient hearts more than sacrificial offerings echoes the concluding portion of the Old Testament reading, Hosea 6:6.

The epistolary reading, which focuses on God's promise to Abraham and his descendants, has explicit thematic connections with the Old Testament reading in the *Common Lectionary*, which focuses on the call of Abraham. Its emphasis on faith as obedience to the will of God also resonates with the Hosea text. The Gospel lection has two parts: the account of Jesus' controversy with the Pharisees because tax collectors and sinners followed him and ate with him (which, it should be noted, concludes with an explicit quotation from Hosea 6:6) and Jesus' healing of the synagogue leader's daughter.

Genesis 12:1–9

Part of this lesson is the Old Testament reading for the Second Sunday in Lent. See our remarks in that setting for further commentary.

These verses that introduce the story of Abraham may also be said to introduce the patriarchal narrative as a whole. Moreover, according to the Yahwist, who is responsible for all but verses 4*b*–5 (the Priestly Writer), the events recounted here are the pivot upon which history turns. That history concerns not just Israel but, ultimately, all of humankind, and it is a history of salvation.

Chapter 12 marks a change in both the subject matter of the Book of Genesis and in literary genre. Genesis 1–11 is the primeval history, the account of beginnings, long ago and far away. Genesis 12–50 contains the stories of the patriarchs of Israel, narratives that focus upon family life. Genesis 12:1–3 in particular is the turning point in history, for up to this point the Yahwist has written a history of sin. After the creation of the first pair (Gen. 2), there was the initial disobedience in the garden followed by its dire effects. Then follows a case of fratricide (Gen. 4:1–16), the disruption of the order of creation by the intermarriage of divine and human beings (Gen. 6:1–3), and eventually the corruption of the race leading to the Flood (Gen. 6–9). Even after that new beginning, human hubris leads to the dispersion and division of people into different races and tongues, as the story of the Tower of Babel indicates (Gen. 11:1–11).

But a new history begins with the call of Abraham, identified as salvation history by the promises that accompany the call. We can recognize at the outset what becomes more and more clear as the story unfolds, namely, that God now has set history on a course that leads to blessing. The promise, reiterated to each succeeding patriarch, unfolds in three movements.

The first is directed to Abram himself: "I will make of you a great nation, and I will bless you, and make your name great, so that you will be a blessing" (v. 2). Although addressed to the patriarch himself, the blessing is a promise for the future, that one day his descendants would be a mighty and renowned nation. Implicit here and explicit elsewhere in the patriarchal traditions is the promise of progeny and land (v. 7), the main prerequisites for nationhood. The reader familiar with the preceding report—Genesis 11:27–32 is a transition into the Abraham story—will find the promise of a future for Abram's progeny all the more remarkable, for Sarah was barren (Gen. 11:30).

The second movement concerns God's solidarity with Abraham in his relations with others: "I will bless those who bless you and the one who curses you I will curse" (v. 3a).

The final development goes even further to include all peoples in the divine blessing expressed to this individual: "And in you all the families of the earth shall be blessed" (v. 3b). As the NRSV footnote indicates, there are no clear grammatical grounds for deciding whether the final verb should be read as reflexive ("shall bless themselves") or passive ("shall be blessed"). In either case, however, the universal goal of the divine blessing through the descendants of Abraham is clear.

We should bear in mind that this text was originally heard by a people who, in the monarchical period, experienced their national life as the fulfillment of this blessing. The Yahwist believed that the "great nation" of which he was a part was the result of the divine blessing uttered by Yahweh and set into motion in antiquity. Built into this promise are two factors to temper any nationalistic pride that might arise. On the one hand, according to the genealogical scheme, Abraham had other descendants besides Israel. On the other hand, the purpose of the blessing of Israel is the blessing of all human families.

If verses 1–3 are the turning point for a history that reaches from creation to the settlement of the land and even beyond into the monarchy, verses 4–9 introduce both Abraham himself and the patriarchal stories as a whole. They report how the ancestor responded to the divine instructions. The word of the Lord in verse 1 is less a call than a command. There is no drama in the patriarch's response, no question of his obedience to the command. We hear simply that Abraham set out on his journey in response to the Lord's instructions. Then verses 6–9 present an itinerary, the list of the places where Abraham stopped, along with a few important notes, mainly concerning altars he built. His movement is from north to south through the land of Canaan.

Abraham, like his parents before him (Gen. 11:31–32), was a migrant. Thus the Lord's command to leave his country and kindred, although involving both separation and adventure, is not a call to abandon a settled existence for that of a nomad. Note also that he is not alone. With his wife Sarah, his nephew Lot, all their property—doubtless including livestock—and "all the persons whom they had acquired in Haran" (v. 5) he sets out. Along with the narrator, we know more than Abraham and Sarah knew—that they would never find a place they could call home, but would travel as resident aliens in a foreign land. In the end, when Sarah dies, Abraham has to buy a burial place from one of the present legal owners of the land promised to his heirs (Gen. 23).

Abraham's obedient and courageous response to set out on such an adventure, especially in view of his advanced age (v. 4), is an important dimension of the passage. However, it is not so decisive as the promise of blessing. We are given here a picture of God's salvific purpose, and it finally is global in its direction and scope. In that context, Abraham's response in faith is a gift to the generations that follow.

Psalm 33:1–12

The following is an outline of the entire psalm: communal calls to praise (vv. 1–3), hymnic praise of the Deity (vv. 4–19), communal response expressing confidence in God (vv. 20–21), and a communal appeal addressed to the Deity (v. 22).

The psalm opens with calls to the community to join in celebration. Five imperative verbs are employed: "rejoice" (a better translation is "shout out"), "praise," "make melody," "sing," and "play skillfully." All are terms denoting making music or singing loudly.

Israelite worship differed drastically from that of most modern church services. Nothing comparable to our sitting and listening to a sermon expounding Scripture actually existed, or if so, it was the unusual rather than the normal. (The structure of worship centering on Scripture reading and preaching was borrowed by Christians from the later synagogue.) Cultic celebrations in the Jerusalem temple were characterized by throngs of pilgrims, processions, chanting, singing, dancing, and so forth. Even acrobatic and simulated games were performed. (See the activities noted in 2 Sam. 6:2–19.) Theological affirmations were carried by the rituals and the singing.

In such worship, the congregation that assembled for worship often joined in the singing/chanting of hymns. These hymns performed two functions for the participants. On the one hand, they allowed the congregation to give expression to their feelings. On the other hand, they served to indoctrinate the community in proper theology. (The hymns, probably like all the psalms, were written by religious professionals associated with or members of the temple staff.)

Hymns generally offer reasons stating why God should be praised, or they give the motivations for praise. These warrants for praise generally speak about the qualities or acts of Yahweh that evoke doxology and commendation. Two groups of these reasons are found in today's lection.

The first following the introductory "for" (*ki* in Hebrew) occurs in verses 4–7. Verses 4–5 comprise what reads like a small confession of faith (for similar texts, see Exod. 34:6–7; Ps. 145:8–9). The five imperatives in verses 1–3 are matched by five terms describing Yahweh or divine characteristics: "upright," "faithfulness," "righteousness," "justice," and "steadfast love" (or "mercy"). Two parallels are drawn between the worshipers in verse 1 and the statements about the Divine in verse 4. Both are upright and righteous.

The description of the Divine and the world in verses 4–5 assumes a well-ordered universe, stability and consistence in the world, and an optimistic attitude toward the status quo.

If verses 4–5 depict present realities, then verses 6–7 look back to creation, to the past. The word that manifests itself in the present is the word through whom God created the heavens and their host (the angelic beings). Just as there is the identification of Christ with the word incarnate and with the creative word at the beginning, so here the identification emphasizes the unity and consistency of divine purpose and action.

Verse 7 stresses both the greatness of Yahweh and the dependency of the world (see Isa. 40:12–17). God collects the waters of the oceans like a water-fetcher filling a bottle. Even the deeps God keeps in storage.

Verse 8 may be taken as a second call to "praise," although it does not open with an imperative verb form. As verses 1–3 called on the Israelites to manifest certain attitudes of celebrative praise, so verse 8 calls on all the earth and its inhabitants to fear Yahweh and be in awe. Perhaps fear of Yahweh is here seen as a universal attitude before the Deity rather than just an attitude demanded of non-Yahwistic worshipers.

The call to "fear" in verse 8 is followed by a description of the reasons in verses 9–11. Again, creation by word and command is noted (v. 9). Such an emphasis on creation by the word stresses two factors: (1) God is distinct from the world of creation and yet Lord over creation; and (2) just as the spoken word makes sense and communicates, so also the world makes sense, and its structures and orders communicate the divine will.

In verses 10–11, contrast is drawn between the plans and counsels of the nations and the counsel and thoughts of God. God can frustrate the plans of nations and empires, whether they be ancient like Assyria and Babylon or modern like the world powers of today.

The particularism of the psalm shines through in verse 12, with its emphasis on Israel as the one nation that worships Yahweh and as the one nation out of all others that has been divinely chosen.

Hosea 5:15–6:6

This lesson from the Book of Hosea takes us back to the eighth century BC and evokes reflection on the meaning of worship itself. It allows the prophet to confront us with issues central to his message, and to that of the other early prophets as well.

The historical circumstances of the prophet and of this particular text are surprisingly well known, given its great antiquity. Hosea is the only prophet of the Northern Kingdom of Israel whose words have come down to us in a prophetic book. On the basis of historical allusions in that book, we are confident that he was active in the final decades of Israel, from about 750 BC until the fall of its capital city, Samaria, to the Assyrian army in 721 BC. Politically, the times were particularly troubled, both internally and internationally. On the international front there was the rising threat of the Assyrian Empire as well as conflicts with immediate neighbors, including Judah to the south. Internally, there were numerous conflicts over the throne. Although always interpreting these political dynamics in terms of Yahweh's judgment or salvation, Hosea focused more on the specifically religious problems of his day. For him the most dangerous threats to the people came from failure to give exclusive allegiance to Yahweh. Given the strength of Canaanite religious symbols and practices, the threats were real.

The historical setting of today's lesson is revealed in its immediate context as part of the unit that begins in Hosea 5:8 and concludes with 6:6. The passage alludes to border conflicts between Israel and Judah and alliances with Assyria, indicating that it probably stems from the time of the so-called Syro-Ephramitic war of 734 BC (cf. Isa. 7:1–2; 2 Kings 15:27–30). When the Assyrians under Tiglath Pileser III began to move into the region, Israel and some other states formed an alliance against them, but Judah refused to join them. Israel then moved against Judah, who responded by appealing to the Assyrians for help. In the verses that precede our reading, the prophet pronounces judgment on both Israel and Judah, the latter for appropriating Israelite territory (5:10a) and the former for consorting with Assyria (5:13).

Hosea 5:15–6:6 has three distinct parts, distinguishable on the basis of the speaker. The first is 5:15, in which the speaker is Yahweh, continuing the address begun in 5:10. But now instead of announcing punishment, Yahweh declares that he will withdraw and wait for the people to turn to him in penitence, "acknowledge their guilt and seek my face . . . beg my favor." The second part (6:1–3) is a penitential song of the people, set up as their response to Yahweh's demand. It echoes the images of judgment in 5:11–14 and sounds genuine. The language is liturgical; formally, it is a call to repent and is in the first person plural. It expresses the confidence that Yahweh has punished only in order to heal, and that within a short time ("after two days . . . on the third day," v. 2) he would revive the stricken people. Language characteristic of Hosea is the call to "know" the Lord, that is, to acknowledge Yahweh and maintain an intimate relationship with him. The penitential liturgy concludes with the affirmation of confidence in the Lord's positive response: Yahweh is as trustworthy as the dawn and as refreshing as the rain (v. 3). Is the repentance real and sincere or superficial? Although the lines do not include a confession of sin, taken out of context there would be no reason to doubt their sincerity. But if one allows verses 4–6, the final part of the unit, to interpret the song of the people, it is clear that the act of penitence is inadequate.

In verses 4–6, Yahweh speaks again, in response to the words of the people. Typically, one would expect an expression of contrition to be followed by a priestly oracle of salvation or an assurance that the worshipers have been heard by God. Here, however, Yahweh is exasperated: "What shall I do with you, O Ephraim?" He criticizes their devotion directly: "Your love is like a morning cloud, like the dew that goes away early" (v. 4). He then affirms that this ephemeral devotion is the reason he has punished them in the past. The climax of the passage and the answer to the question of true repentance is verse 6. Echoing a motif found in other early prophetic books (Amos 5:21–24; Isa. 1:10–17; Mic. 6:6–8), Hosea has the Lord state the characteristics of true devotion. True faith is recognized not in acts of worship, even sacrifices and burnt offerings, but in "steadfast love" (hesed) and "the knowledge of God" (da'at 'elohim). These terms frequently are juxtaposed when Hosea states what is most fundamental (see 4:1–3). The first of these refers to covenant loyalty, fidelity to the Lord alone. The second is a rich expression that may include cognition (knowing the meaning of faithfulness [see Hosea 4:6]), acknowledgment of Yahweh as God, and intimate knowledge for which even human sexual relationships (Hos. 1; 3) or the relationship between parents and children (Hos. 11:1–4) may serve as metaphors. Any worship—explicitly, sacrifices and burnt offerings, and implicitly, acts of contrition—that is not based on covenant loyalty and such knowledge of God is corrupt.

Psalm 50:7–15

The opening verses of this psalm (vv. 1–6) form an extended call to worship. They affirm Yahweh's coming to judge the people. The reference to "the rising of the sun to its setting" (v. 1) may not refer to the geographical extent of judgment (that is, from east to west) but rather to the fact that one day, from sunrise to sunset, would be a special day of calling Israel to accountability and judgment. If so, this would be most likely one of the days of the fall festival.

The remainder of the psalm consists of two divine addresses. The first, in verses 7–15, is addressed apparently to the faithful members of the community. These would be the faithful ones (the *hasidim*) mentioned in verse 5. The second speech, in verses 16–23, addresses the wicked (note v. 16a).

Undoubtedly, in the context of worship it would have been left for the individual persons to place themselves in one camp or the other. The terms "faithful ones" and "the wicked" are thus more rhetorical than specific. Verses 5b and 16bc would suggest that the special day being celebrated was a time of covenant renewal. Verse 5b can be translated "the ones making a covenant with me by sacrifice." The statements in verse 16 about reciting the divine statutes and taking the covenant on the lips could refer to the ceremony of covenant renewal. According to Deuteronomy 31:10–13, all the people were to be assembled every seventh year at the Feast of Booths (the fall festival). At this convocation, the law (the Book of Deuteronomy) was to be read.

The lection for today is comprised of only the speech to the faithful ones. Because the NJPSV provides a better translation than the NRSV, the lection is given here in its entirety.

> "Pay heed, My people, and I will speak,
> > O Israel, and I will arraign you.
> I am God, your God.
> I censure you not for your sacrifices,
> > and your burnt offerings, made to Me daily;
> > I claim no bull from your estate,
> > no he-goats from your pens.
> For Mine is every animal of the forest,
> > the beasts on a thousand mountains.
> > I know every bird of the mountains,
> > the creatures of the field are subject to Me.
> Were I hungry, I would not tell you,
> > for Mine is the world and all it holds.
> Do I eat the flesh of bulls,
> > or drink the blood of he-goats?
> Sacrifice a thank offering to God,
> > and pay your vows to the Most High.
> Call upon Me in time of trouble;
> > I will rescue you, and you shall honor Me."

Three elements in the speech are noteworthy. (1) Yahweh declares that as ruler and governor of the universe, he is not dependent on the sacrifices of humans for survival. The text, however, does not condemn the offering of sacrifices and should not be seen as condemnation of cultic worship. (2) Worshipers are requested to offer a sacrifice of thanksgiving or to offer thanksgiving to God (v. 14). The term for "thanksgiving" can refer to both the attitude and the sacrifice, so the issue is not completely clear (see the marginal note in the NRSV to the verse). Thanksgiving is the attitude requested. Thanksgiving services required conspicuous consumption and sharing, for all the sacrifice had to be eaten on the day it was offered (see Lev. 7:11–15). (3) Yahweh appeals to the people to call upon God in time of trouble (an authentication of foxhole religion!) with the promise that the Divine would respond and grant deliverance. The human response for such deliverance was to glorify Yahweh through testimony and thanksgiving sacrifice (v. 15).

Romans 4:13–25

In Romans 4, we have Paul's extended treatment of Abraham, whom he regarded as the classic Old Testament example of someone who was justified by faith. Indeed, of all the Old Testament figures who informed Paul's understanding of faith, Abraham was the most formative and influential. In him, Paul saw foreshadowed what life before God means—implicit trust in a God who promises the impossible and does it!

Today's epistolary text is the latter half of this extended exposition. It should be read and studied as part of the entire chapter.

Even before Paul's time, the case of Abraham had presented a problem for Jewish exegetes who saw the law of Moses as the sum and substance of God's revelation. If God's will were embodied in Torah and if obedience to God meant being obedient to Torah, how could one explain those prominent figures in Jewish history whose lives were regarded by God as praiseworthy but who had lived prior to the giving of the law at Sinai? This would include such persons as Enoch and Noah, and most especially Abraham, for to him God had made the well-known promise of people and land (cf. Gen. 12:1–3; 15:5–6; 17:7–8).

Various explanations were offered. One suggestion was that even though Abraham antedated the giving of the law, he actually embodied the Torah in advance. He was, as it were, an instance of "en-souled law," even before it was actually revealed to Moses and written down. Other interpreters, apparently without sensing any anachronism, actually asserted that Abraham kept the law: "He kept the law of the Most High, and entered into a covenant with him" (Sir. 44:20a).

Paul opted for still a third line of interpretation. As he read the Hebrew Scriptures, he saw that God's promise to Abraham (Gen. 12) and God's "reckoning" Abraham as righteous (Gen. 15:6) actually *preceded* the covenant of circumcision (Gen. 17:1–27). For Paul, the implication to be drawn from this scriptural order of events was all too clear: Scripture itself attested that God's righteousness had been extended to Abraham *prior to* the covenant of circumcision. Thus, Abraham had been justified before God apart from circumcision, the primary mark of admission to the people of God. Whatever else this signified, it meant that Abraham was "father," or "ancestor," in a redefined sense: he should be understood as "father of the faithful," not as "father of the circumcised" (Rom. 4:11–12). The true heirs of Abraham, Paul insists, are not those who have undergone a similar initiation rite, but those who have exhibited a similar faith.

From this, Paul concluded that Genesis 17:5 ("I have made you the father of many nations," v. 17) must have wider import than normally understood. Abraham was not to be regarded merely as the father of the Jewish nation, but of *many* nations, which could only include Gentiles as well. *His real progeny are the faithful, not the circumcised* (v. 16).

This way of reading the Abraham story in Genesis enabled Paul to set "law" over against "faith" as two fundamentally opposed ways of appropriating God's righteousness. Granting the sharp wedge he drove between Abraham and the law, we can understand his insistence that "the promise that he would inherit the world did not come to Abraham or to his descendants through the law but through the righteousness of faith" (v. 13). The way of law, where one breaks a clearly understood commandment and thereby incurs God's wrath (v. 15; cf. Rom. 1:18; 5:9; also 3:20; 5:13, 20; 7:8, 10–11, 13; Gal. 3:19), all came later. According to Paul's way of reading Genesis 12–18, the "way of law" was not how God's relationship to Abraham was initially defined.

But Abraham also illustrated something else: faith in a particular kind of God—the Creator God. Abraham placed his faith in One "who brings the dead to life and calls into existence what does not yet exist" (v. 17, NJB). This, of course, is a reference to God's enabling Sarah to conceive even when she was well beyond the age of childbearing. At their ages, they were "as good as dead" (v. 19). For Abraham to accept God's promise that Sarah would have a child, he had to believe that God could create life where there was none. This was the essence of Abraham's faith: he received a promise from God that was palpably absurd—that he would become the "father of many nations" (v. 18)—yet he acted *in faith*, as absurd as this action seemed. And in doing so, he captured the essence of biblical faith, as Paul saw it—implicit trust in God's promise. "No distrust made him waver" (v. 20). However irrational or ephemeral the promise seemed, Abraham leaned into it with the full weight of his life so that his trust became God-oriented action.

In Abraham, Paul saw foreshadowed the essence of Christian existence and faith. To believe in Christ, after all, is to entrust ourselves to a God who, in raising Christ from the dead, created life where there was none, and who can do so again (Rom. 4:24–25). So it is that Abraham serves as the true paradigm of *Christian* faith.

Matthew 9:9–13, 18–26

Although today's Gospel reading does not follow immediately the text for last Sunday, the central theme is the same—doing the will of God in both word and act. In Matthew 9:9–13, the will of God has to do specifically with human relationships; that is, does the will of God call for separation from sinners or association with sinners? Jesus expresses God's will in words. In verses 18–26, the will of God has to do with human suffering, and Jesus responds with actions.

In a rather lengthy section consisting primarily of miracle stories, Matthew inserts two conflict stories, one with Pharisees (9:9–13) and one with the disciples of John the Baptist (9:14–17). Only the controversy with the Pharisees is our concern today. The story is found also in Mark 2:13–17 and Luke 5:27–32, but with noticeable differences in the identification of Jesus' critics and the name of the tax collector. In addition, Matthew alone includes Jesus' use of Hosea 6:6 in his response to the critics.

According to Matthew, the tax collector who follows Jesus is named Matthew. Mark calls him Levi, the son of Alphaeus (2:14), and in Luke he is simply Levi (5:27). The reason for the different names is unclear: different sources, different events (very unlikely), and a change of name after becoming a disciple are all possibilities. In all the lists of the Twelve (Matt. 10:2–4; Mark 3:16–19; Luke 6:14–16; Acts 1:13), a Matthew is named, but there is no Levi. When Jesus called him, Matthew was sitting at the booth or table near the city gate or in the marketplace. He was collecting taxes for the Romans and for their puppet tetrarch, Herod Antipas. Taxes on the people were many and burdensome: road taxes, bridge taxes, tax on trade goods passing by caravan, and at times personal or household tax. The taxes alone were enough to alienate the collector; the fact that the taxes went to a foreign government multiplied the hostility toward the collector.

The conflict with the Pharisees was prompted by the presence of Jesus and his disciples at a dinner in Matthew's house (Luke 5:29 makes clear what is implied in Matthew, that the meal was in the tax collector's house). Matthew's other guests are tax collectors and sinners; that is, tax collectors and others who had been labeled "sinners" and put out of the synagogue. Mark says they were followers of Jesus (2:15), but Matthew leaves us with the assumption that they were friends and business associates of Matthew. The occasion and the nature of the group caught the attention of the Pharisees. (By the time of Matthew, Pharisees are treated as a group in conflict with the church. A more careful distinction, such as "some Pharisees," has now been lost.) The issue is clear: Jesus is having table fellowship with persons morally and ritually unclean (v. 11).

The response of Jesus consists of two parts. First, Jesus recites a well-known maxim about the physician: his place is with the sick, not with the well. Second, Jesus uses a rabbinic formula, "Go and learn" (v. 13), to send his critics back to their Scriptures and to Hosea 6:6 in particular. Matthew quotes from the Greek translation of Hosea 6:6: "I desire mercy." The Hebrew word translated "mercy" is *hesed*, an extraordinarily rich and significant term meaning steadfast love, righteousness, loyalty. The Old Testament uses the word to describe God, God's relation to Israel, and the quality of life expected of Israel. Hosea 6:6 became a favorite verse for Israel in exile and away from the sacrificial system of the temple. It continued to be important for the synagogue and its leaders, the Pharisees, especially after the fall of the temple.

Jesus, then, cites a central text to his critics (used again at 12:7 in response to the charge of sabbath breaking) and sends them back to learn what it means. And what does it mean? Do the character of God and the will of God call for a response of distancing oneself from all whose lives are tainted with sin and compromise, or does it call for a response of drawing near in love and forgiveness? The issue is not solely between the synagogue and the church of Matthew's day, but within the church, then and now.

Verses 18–26 return to the central content of chapters 8–9, that is, miracle stories. Two of ten miracles are narrated here. Matthew used Mark's form of a story within a story, but so condenses the accounts (twenty-three verses in Mark 5:21–43; seventeen in Luke 8:40–56) that they are rather colorless. Matthew prefers to chronicle Jesus' extensive ministry of miracles rather than focus the camera on the real human drama within the stories.

In the outside story (vv. 18–19; 23–26), "a leader" (of what?—the NRSV adds "of the synagogue") whose daughter has died wants Jesus to raise her from the dead. In Matthew the man asks for a resurrection, expressing a faith much stronger than that which asks for healing. And Jesus raises her, carrying out God's will in the face of the laughter, mocking, and unbelief of the funeral musicians and mourners. The inside story (vv. 20–22) is an interruption of Jesus' journey to the leader's home, but even so, it too is an appeal of faith. Jesus responds to faith's request with healing. Both are stories of faith's petition for Jesus' care and his power, and neither are disappointed. If we understand Jesus to be demonstrating the will of God, bringing life as it is within the reign of God, then the lesson is clear: the messiahship of Jesus consists in declaring and enacting God's opposition to suffering and death. God, through the activity of Jesus, is *for* health and life and moves to end sorrow and mourning. Let all those who work in whatever ways small or great, for the life and health of human lives, be encouraged by the thought that they care about what God cares about and that they do what God does.

It should not be overlooked, however, that both of these stories are about people alienated by disease and death. The woman's bleeding separates her by ritual law from family and friends. Likewise, death isolates the family and all who attend the corpse from ritual participation in the very religion to which they look for support. But in both cases, by being touched and by touching, Jesus breaks through the barriers. The gift of his healing is also the gift of relationships restored. The healing in each case is a double one, and who is to say which is the greater blessing?

Proper 6 [11]
(Sunday between June 12 and 18 inclusive (if after Trinity Sunday))

Genesis 18:1–15 (21:1–7);
Psalm 116:1–2, 12–19; or
Exodus 19:2–8a;
Psalm 100;
Romans 5:1–8;
Matthew 9:35–10:8 (9–23)

The *Common Lectionary* Old Testament reading, the promise and birth of Isaac to Abraham and Sarah, follows as a natural sequel to last week's lesson. Today's lesson shows how God's promise to Abraham is fulfilled. Although Psalm 116 is a prayer of thanksgiving offered for physical healing, the omission of verses 3–11 gives it broader applicability. Consequently, the congregation will hear it as a more general prayer thanking God for being responsive to human requests for help. Juxtaposed with Genesis 18 (and 21), the psalm virtually echoes the gracious sentiments of Abraham and Sarah, but also those of every faithful person whose prayers have been answered by God.

In the other lectionaries, the Old Testament reading is the account of God's appearance to Moses at Sinai; the account concludes with Israel's expressed willingness to follow God's commands. Psalm 100 heralds the goodness and faithfulness of Yahweh.

Today's epistolary lection exudes confidence and trust in the God who has justified us through Jesus Christ, enabling us to be at peace with God and to have access to God's sustaining grace. The Gospel lection reports how Jesus taught and preached the good news of the kingdom and how he began to commission the Twelve. The additional verses highlight the cost of discipleship.

Genesis 18:1–15 (21:1–7)

The main theme of this reading is the fulfillment of the promise to Abraham reported in Genesis 12:1–4; thus it continues the semicontinuous reading from the previous Sunday. If Abraham's descendants are to become a great nation, he and Sarah must have a son. But a great deal has transpired between Genesis 12 and 18. Abraham and Sarah had set out in response to the Lord's command and begun their sojourn in the land promised to their descendants. The Priestly Writer reports in chapter 17 the covenant of God with Abraham and Sarah. According to Genesis 13:18, Abraham had arrived at Mamre, the location of the events of chapter 18, where he built an altar. The setting for the events reported in our text is Mamre, a traditional holy place just north of Hebron.

The story is similar to many other biblical accounts of remarkable, even "miraculous," births (Samson, Judg. 13; Samuel, 1 Sam. 1–2). Typically, such stories concern the birth of individuals destined to be great, but this one concerns the parents and the promise more than the child. The birth of Isaac to the aged parents is a family story that contains more than a little humor, but it is also designed to emphasize God's faithfulness toward the people descended from those ancestors and that child.

This reading has three distinct parts, two of which concern the promise of progeny. Genesis 18:1–8 is the account of the arrival of three guests and of the patriarch's hospitality to them. Genesis 18:9–15 reports the Lord's promise that Sarah would bear a son to Abraham in their old age and the matriarch's incredulous reaction. Genesis 21:1–7 narrates the birth of that promised son, Isaac.

The main characters in the first scene (18:1–8) are Abraham and the three "men" whom he welcomes and entertains. Verse 1 ("The Lord appeared to Abraham") is a heading that informs the reader of the real identity of the guests. In the narrative itself, beginning in verse 2, Abraham knows only that three "men" have arrived. He greets them with traditional and generous hospitality (see also Gen. 23:7). He offers them water to wash their feet and shade to rest their bodies, and then instructs Sarah to make bread for them while he chooses a calf "tender and good" for his servant to prepare for the meal. The three strangers, Abraham learns later, turn out to be Yahweh and two attendants or angels. It is reported in 18:22 that the two continue their journey to Sodom (19:1) while Yahweh remains with Abraham, who wants to negotiate over the fate of Sodom. So if our story concerns God's gracious care and faithfulness, it has divine judgment in the background.

In the second scene (18:9–15), the central characters are Yahweh and Sarah. It is a subtle literary touch that Yahweh need not ask, for he already knows the name of Abraham's wife (v. 9). This should evoke the interest of the hearer or reader, who already knows the identity of the characters. But there is no indication that Abraham picked up on this. Then Yahweh reveals that the arrival of the guests at Mamre is not accidental but in order to promise the birth of a son (v. 10). In case the reader had forgotten just how old Abraham and Sarah were, the narrator reminds them in an aside: both were very old, and Sarah was long past menopause (v. 11). Sarah, eavesdropping at the entrance to the tent, is incredulous. Although her laughter and her comments (v. 12) are not out loud but to herself, Yahweh hears. First he responds to her indirectly, to Abraham (vv. 13–14), affirming with a rhetorical question that nothing is impossible for the Lord and reiterating that Sarah will indeed have a son at a specified time. The references to "the set time" and the "due season" are no new promise but are stated to emphasize that the birth is the result of divine intervention and not some normal situation or a human accident. When Sarah fearfully denies that she had laughed, Yahweh for the first time addresses her directly, correcting and reprimanding her (v. 15).

Genesis 21:1–7 is the account of the fulfillment of the promise. The sequence concerning the birth of Isaac had been interrupted by the story of Sodom and Gomorrah (18:16–19:29), the narrative of Lot and his daughters (19:30–38), and the account of Abraham, Sarah, and Abimelech (v. 20). Verses 1–2 pick up directly where 18:9–15 had left off, indicating that Yahweh fulfilled the promise made to Abraham and Sarah at "the time" indicated. Here, however, the emphasis is upon the blessing to Sarah. Verses 3–4 report the important rituals following the birth—first the naming of the child and then his circumcision when he was eight days old (see Gen. 17:9–14). The name Isaac is a play on the word for "laugh," a pun reminding us of Sarah's reaction in 18:12. So the story of Sarah's laughter is in effect a popular etymology for the name of the patriarch. Laughter characterizes the mood of this paragraph, but it is quite unlike the laughter of 18:9–15. Here it is the laughter of joy at the birth of a son, the rejoicing of the mother and of all those who will hear of her blessing. Whereas earlier she had laughed at Yahweh's ridiculous idea, now she expresses her pleasure and her pride. In the background stands God's plan to fulfill the promise to Abraham that his descendants would become a great nation, but in the foreground stands the happy mother with her baby boy.

Psalm 116:1–2, 12–19

This psalm has been discussed above for Holy Thursday and the Third Sunday of Easter.

Exodus 19:2–8a

This reading is part of the account of the theophany on Mt. Sinai. Exodus 19 begins the lengthy report of the establishment of the covenant and the revelation of the law by reporting the appearance of Yahweh and his initial instructions to the people through Moses. The Sinai pericope is the longest single unit in the Pentateuch, beginning at Exodus 19:1, including the remainder of the Book of Exodus, the entire Book of Leviticus, and concluding only in Numbers 10:10, which is followed by the report of the departure from the sacred mountain.

It is easy for the contemporary reader to pass quickly over the first two verses of the chapter, the notes concerning the chronology and the itinerary, if not ignore them entirely. These matters were, however, of great significance, especially to the Priestly Writer, and for theological and liturgical rather than historical reasons. Precise dates are important for ritual calendars. Moreover, the writer was eager to show an unbroken genealogy and chronology from creation to Sinai and beyond. He saw history organized according to a divine scheme of covenants that gave both structure and meaning to the past and therefore the present. There were covenants with Noah, Abraham, and the other ancestors, but at Sinai God has reached the goal of all the others. For the Priestly Writer, and for earlier sources and traditions as well, what happened at Sinai was of central importance for all future history, for there the law was revealed to a particular people.

Following the introductory report that the people arrived at Sinai, the passage is organized in terms of the travels of Moses up and down the mountain, and the speeches of the parties. Moses went up "to God" on the mountain (v. 3), and God told him what to say to the people (vv. 4–6). Moses went down, convened the elders, and reported the words of God to the people (v. 7). The people responded, and Moses—presumably after going up the mountain—reported the words of the people to God (v. 8). Then the Lord spoke again to Moses, who reported again to the people (v. 9).

This pattern of ascent and descent, speech and report, continues through the chapter. What this pattern makes clear is the role of Moses as the mediator between God and people, between people and God. His role as spokesman for God is parallel to that of a prophet. As speaker for the people, he is more like a priest, especially when one realizes that he is mediating a service of commitment, the establishment of the covenant.

The theological content of the passage is carried in the speeches, both of God and of the people. A great deal is conveyed in God's first speech (vv. 4–6). God identifies himself in terms of his deeds, reminding the people of his mighty acts in Egypt and his preservation of them in the wilderness (cf. Josh. 24:7; Deut. 32:11; 7:6; 14:2). Then he states first the conditions and then the effects of the covenant about to be established. The conditions are obedience to the stipulations of the covenant ("covenant" in verse 5 is a virtual synonym for law). The effects are to make Israel God's people. It is tempting to take verse 6*a* as part of the conditions, but syntactically it states some of the effects, the promise of the covenant. The "if" clause, or protasis, is "if you obey my voice and keep my covenant." The apodosis, or conclusion, includes both "you shall be my treasured possession out of all the peoples . . . and you shall be for me a priestly kingdom and a holy nation."

The Lord's second speech (v. 9) announces a theophany, God's appearance "in a dense cloud," and states the purpose of the encounter. This actually begins the theme that will become central in the remainder of the chapter. The purpose of the encounter is quite different from that indicated in the first speech. No longer is there reference to the establishment of the covenant, the election of a particular people, but the purpose is revelation and belief. This form of appearance is in order for the people to hear God when he speaks to Moses in order to confirm the authority of Moses.

Only once do the people speak, and they do so very briefly: "Everything that the Lord has spoken we will do" (v. 8). That such a response is part of a cultic ceremony of covenant renewal is shown by the pattern of events and speeches here as well as by the use of similar language in Joshua 24:16–18, 21. Yahweh has pledged himself to the people in deed and word, and now the people corporately accept the conditions of obedience and solemnly pledge themselves to the Lord.

This passage is rich in possibilities for exploration in the context of Christian worship. (1) *Making and renewing covenants.* Notice that God takes the initiative; thus the first word of biblical covenants is grace. Then obedience to the divine will is expected. Furthermore, biblical covenants are corporate, between God and the people of God. (2) *The meaning of election.* God makes a covenant with a particular people in history. Having already chosen and delivered Israel, God invites them to affirm and confirm their election through the covenant. Notice that election is put into a worldwide context: "Indeed, the whole earth is mine" (v. 5), says the Lord. (3) *The identity of the people of God.* Covenant and election above all serve to make it clear to these people who they are: they are God's. More specifically, through obedience they will be a "priestly kingdom and a holy nation" (v. 6; cf. Exod. 15:17ff.; Deut. 33:2–5; 1 Pet. 2:9). Their kingship and their holiness in all of life are defined by the rule of the sacred God. (4) *The role of mediator.* In this passage, Moses, the only individual human being mentioned, says not a word of his own but is the conduit of revelation and response. That role, of course, does not define his full responsibilities as a leader of the people of God, but it is an essential dimension of any ministry, whether lay or ordained.

Psalm 100

This psalm is one of only a few in which its use is noted in the superscription (see Pss. 30, 102). The occasion for its usage is said to be the presentation of a "thank offering," a sacrifice offered when an individual or the community wished to express its appreciation to the Divine (see Lev. 7:11–18). Such sacrifices were consumed—that is, the entire slaughtered animal except for gift portions paid to the priests was cooked and eaten—by the worshipers in a great "religious barbecue" in the temple courtyard. According to the law in Leviticus, the thanksgiving sacrifice had to be consumed completely on the day it was presented (7:15). This meant that extravagance, even gluttony, for the day was a requirement. Thanksgiving was a joyful celebration.

Psalm 100 is a communal psalm. All the imperative verbs are in the plural in the Hebrew, a fact that is not apparent in English translation. The psalm does not contain the full features of a thanksgiving psalm; in fact, it is an extended summons or call to praise and to thank God. Those called upon to make a joyful noise to God were probably only the Israelites in the psalm's ancient usage.

The elements in thanksgiving are noted as "joyful noise," "gladness," "singing," "thanksgiving," "praise." When we think of thanksgiving only as verbal expressions or as cognitive communication, we restrict too greatly its range of meaning and its forms of expression.

Two motivations are given for the praise and thanksgiving. The first stresses God as creator and preserver of human life (v. 3). Thus thanksgiving flows from the dependent humans to the Divine. Here thanksgiving is anchored in a theology of creation, although the creation spoken of may refer to the creation of Israel, its origination in the past (see Isa. 29:23; 41:1, 21). The second, although not as clearly drawn, offers as the reason God's fidelity in history (v. 5). Here the idea is the continuing, recurring love and fidelity of God. Thanksgiving throughout the psalm is associated with public worship; in the temple "come into his presence," "enter his gates . . . and his courts."

Romans 5:1–8

Romans 5:1–11 has already been treated earlier in this volume as the epistolary reading for the Third Sunday in Lent. Here we will focus on other aspects of the text. The reader might also want to consult our remarks on Romans 5:1–5, which serves as the second lesson for Trinity Sunday in Year C.

We are so accustomed to thinking of God as one who generously acts in our behalf that we sometimes overlook the radical paradox of Christ's death. In today's text, Paul probes this paradox, trying to expose the interior of this central mystery of our faith. Death and dying are prominent motifs, occurring four times in verses 6–8.

We speak so glibly of "the death of Christ" that it comes to have a certain obviousness. No scandal here. Part of God's eternal plan. Foreordained. Inevitable, given the circumstances. Not so, according to Paul. In fact, the enigma of God's Messiah dying in behalf of helpless, ungodly sinners is perhaps reflected in Paul's broken, somewhat tortured syntax. It is not something he can write about with absolute clarity. We find him struggling, in verse 7, to get at the heart of the matter—introducing one thought, stopping in mid-sentence to replace it with a more fitting example. Even with this start-and-stop syntax, the flow of his argument is clear—there is something inexplicable, even inconceivable about the death of Christ.

Paul insists that it is one thing for someone to die in behalf of a "righteous person" (v. 7a; "a just man," REB; "someone upright," NJB). There is a certain logic about it, even though it is a rarity. It "hardly" occurs (NJB, REB; "very rarely," NIV). But what if you raise the ante? What about dying in behalf of "a good person"—not someone who is "just," or hard-nosed, but someone "good," or fair-minded and generous? The logic here is much more compelling. Someone so good is arguably worth dying for. We can even think of cases where this might "perhaps" occur.

In either case, dying for someone "just" or "good" can be defended. Such a death would have redeeming value. One life is given up so that another worthwhile life is spared or extended. Society benefits when the life of a "really good person" (NJB), or even "someone upright" (NJB), is preserved and extended.

But there is no such social defense to explain the death of Christ. Those who benefited are "weak . . . ungodly . . . sinners" (vv. 6–8). Why should Christ have acted in behalf of such persons? What benefit is there in extending the life of people like this? Why help the helpless? Even more to the point, why extend the life of the morally bankrupt?

Surely this is the force of verse 6: not "at just the right time" (NIV), or "at the right time" (NRSV), or "at the appointed time" (NJB, REB; cf. Gal. 4:4), but "at the very time when we were still powerless" (NEB). Paul's point is not so much that the death of Christ was good timing on God's part, but rather that it was morally inexplicable. "The point is that Christ did his saving work at an unexpected and, morally considered, even inappropriate moment. Unworthy, genuinely ungodly people benefited from it" (Käsemann following Furnish).

God's action through Christ is logic-shattering. It can only be seen as a visible, forthright expression of divine love: "God's proof of his love towards us" (v. 8, REB; cf. John 3:16; 15:13; 1 John 4:10; also Rom. 8:32). To die for a morally upright or a "really good person" may be an act of bravery; to die for a morally bankrupt person can only be an act of love.

To be sure, Paul does not treat the matter at a safe, objective distance. Note how pervasive the first person plural is. Clearly, he is existentially involved: the death of Christ is in *our* behalf.

This becomes especially clear in the verses that follow. On the one hand, there is the objective reality of justification: "We have been justified by his blood" (v. 9), or "at the cost of his blood" (Barrett). Here Christ's death is regarded as sacrificial: his blood brings about purification like that of a sacrificial animal (cf. 3:25; Lev. 16:11–28; 1 John 2:2).

This is reinforced when Paul introduces the language of reconciliation (vv. 10–11). It is, of course, a different metaphor—enemies being brought together again and reconciled to each other (cf. 11:15; 2 Cor. 5:18–20; Eph. 2:16; Col. 1:20–22; also 1 Cor. 7:11). It is a process through which hostile forces, notably flesh and spirit, are neutralized (Rom. 8:7; cf. James 4:4).

In both cases, the death of Christ is the common meeting ground between us and God. In the one instance, God "makes things right" through Christ's death. The shedding of Christ's blood becomes the basis for our acquittal before the righteous Judge. In the other instance, God "makes peace" through Christ's death. It becomes a peace-treaty event, where two sides, formerly at odds, are reconciled to each other.

The effects are both present and future. Justification and reconciliation are objective realities of the present, but their thrust is future: we will "be saved . . . from the wrath of

God" (v. 9); we will "be saved by his life" (v. 10). We can now be delivered from God's eschatological wrath that was unfurled in the New Age (Rom. 1:18–32; 4:15; also Matt. 3:7; 1 Thess. 2:16), and Christ is the agent of deliverance (1 Thess. 1:10; 5:9). The resurrection life that he now enjoys will be ours eventually (v. 10; cf. 2 Cor. 4:10; Phil. 1:20).

The focus of our rejoicing, literally our "boasting" (v. 11), is God, who acted through Christ in bringing about our reconciliation (cf. 1 Cor. 1:31; 2 Cor. 10:17; Gal. 6:14; Phil. 3:3; also Jer. 9:23–24).

Homiletically, we might note how closely Paul identifies with the death of Christ, as seen by Paul's frequent use of "we" and "us" in our passage. Paul is not discussing the death of Christ from a safe, objective distance. Rather, he is standing in the eye of the storm, looking at justification and reconciliation from the inside, as one who is himself a "weak . . . ungodly . . . sinner," yet the inexplicable object of God's love.

Also, the preacher's task with today's text may be to break through the barrier of the obvious to expose the radical paradox of Christ's death. Paul himself will be instructive here. As we examine the text closely, we see the apostle struggling to articulate this essential mystery of the faith.

Matthew 9:35–10:8 (9–23)

In the Gospel reading for last Sunday we saw that the followers of Jesus found in his word and example their authority for inclusive table fellowship. Today our lesson reveals that the church understood its own mission in and through both the command of Jesus and the model of his own ministry. The summary description of Jesus as teacher, preacher, and healer is offered by Matthew as foundational for his description of the mission of the Twelve.

Matthew 9:35 virtually repeats Matthew 4:23, forming what is termed in literature an inclusion. By concluding a section of material with the words of its introduction, a writer gives unity to the whole. In other words, between 4:23 and 9:35 Matthew has given teachings and miracles of healing, the whole of which not only characterizes Jesus' ministry but will now characterize that of his disciples as well.

Verse 36 provides us with the motivation for Jesus' ministry, again implying that his followers will be likewise motivated. Jesus had compassion on the people in their state of oppression, confusion, fear, and frustration, much like sheep without a shepherd (Num. 27:17; 1 Kings 22:17; Ezek. 34:5). So great was the need that Jesus could not, even with the help of his disciples, meet it. He calls upon his followers to pray that God will send more laborers (v. 37; see also John 4:35). The analogy of harvest, used elsewhere in Matthew to refer to the last judgment (3:12; 13:8, 39–40), here includes the present and urgent work that will, of course, have its final consummation and revelation on the last day.

Matthew has now laid the foundation for the call and commissioning of the Twelve. The structure of 10:1–8 is quite clear: Jesus calls the Twelve, he gives them power to exorcise demons and to heal, the Twelve are named, and then Jesus gives specific instructions for their work. Slight variations occur in the four lists found in the New Testament (Matt. 10:2–4; Mark 3:16–19; Luke 6:14–16; Acts 1:13), but all begin with Simon Peter and end with Judas. The only time Matthew calls them apostles is here at 10:2. Most of them are known only by their names; the church looks to tradition for any word about their subsequent work.

Jesus' instructions to the Twelve define the arena of their work and the work they are to do. That they are to restrict themselves to Israel, going neither to Gentiles nor Samaritans

(10:5–6), is without parallel in the other Gospels and difficult to reconcile with other passages in Matthew, such as 8:11 and 28:18–20. Some take the statement to refer to the chronology of the Christian mission: to the Jew first, then to the Gentile. Others see the passage as the reflection of a very conservative Jewish Christian community, which confined itself to the circumcised. We know from Acts 15 and Galatians 2 that such groups existed in the early church. As to the work the Twelve were to do, the list fits the contours of Jesus' own ministry as recorded by Matthew: preaching, healing the sick, raising the dead, cleansing lepers, and casting out demons. In Luke's account of the ministry of the church (Acts), all but cleansing lepers are recorded. Jesus' word that they were to give without pay just as they had received without pay (v. 8) is without parallel in the other Gospels but found its most conscientious practitioner in the Apostle Paul (1 Cor. 9:3–18; 2 Cor. 11:7).

This final word to the effect that the church freely received and should freely give returns the instruction to the description of Jesus' own tireless ministry: "When he saw the crowds, he had compassion for them" (9:36).

If the preacher chooses to read through verse 23, then the lection concludes not with the missionary assignment itself but with an internal description of the nature of the mission. The service will be undertaken in total dependence on God (vv. 9–10a), which in practical terms will be dependence on the hospitality of others (vv. 10b–13). The entire mission will be conducted with eschatological urgency (vv. 14–15, 23). The hostility, both religious and civil, that will be aroused must be faced wisely; one must be fully aware of the cost of discipleship (vv. 16–18). When such faithfulness prevails, God's Spirit will convert courtroom defenses into Christian witnessing (vv. 19–20). But opposition will not come from strangers alone; families will divide on the issue of loyalty to Christ (v. 21). Many will fall away, but those who endure will be saved (v. 22).

Matthew's church lived and witnessed under extreme circumstances, but persecution was not confined to that area, as Acts, Paul's letters, and subsequent church history amply testify. And in many parts of the world today, these words of Christ are heard not only as a commission with high costs but also as a comfort to those already paying the price. Those not facing hostility remain alert to the subtle and seductive forces that no less effectively silence Christian witness.

Proper 7 [12]
(Sunday between June 19 and 25 inclusive (if after Trinity Sunday))

Genesis 21:8–21;
Psalm 86:1–10, 16–17; or
Jeremiah 20:7–13;
Psalm 69:7–10 (11–15) 16–18;
Romans 6:1*b*–11;
Matthew 10:24–39

The Old Testament reading in the *Common Lectionary* relates the moving story of the rejection of Hagar and Ishmael and their eventual rescue by God. Following on last week's account of God's fulfillment of the promise to Abraham and Sarah through the birth of Isaac, today's text provides an important statement about the extension of God's gracious care beyond a single hereditary line. Psalm 86, in which the psalmist prays for rescue and deliverance, echoes the sentiments of those who, like Hagar, reach out to God for help when mistreated and rejected by their adversaries, and do so confident that God's favor will be extended to them.

In the other lectionaries, the Old Testament reading is provided by Jeremiah's fifth lament, in which he strongly protests God's actions against him, yet concludes affirming his faith in God's care for the needy. In a similar vein, Psalm 69 expresses the psalmist's irritation with his enemies and his earnest request for God's mercy and comfort to be extended to him.

The epistolary reading, which consists of the first part of Paul's response to the question whether his theology of salvation by grace through faith leads to moral relativism, emphasizes the believer's union with Christ and the moral implications of this union. In Matthew 10:24–39, Jesus instructs the disciples about how they should relate to their master, reassures them by distinguishing between their seeming adversaries and their true Adversary, clarifies the nature of true and false confession, and honestly confronts them with the critical choices disciples have to make.

Genesis 21:8–21

Genesis 21:1–7, which brought the story of the birth of Isaac to a conclusion, sets the stage for the self-contained episode reported in this reading. The account of the expulsion of Hagar and her son is a troubling yet powerful text. It is a carefully crafted story that begins in human jealousy and ambivalence and ends with divine grace. As is so often the case with the stories in Genesis, individual and family conflicts and actions are seen in the light of the divine purpose concerning history and nations.

Although the story doubtless stems from an ancient oral tradition, the unit has the distinctive marks of the Elohist, who identifies the Deity as *elohim*, "God," who has God communicating with human beings through angels, and who has a high level of moral sensitivity. Moreover, there is a parallel to this story in the Yahwistic narrative (Gen. 16).

The plot of the story is unmistakable, moving from a peaceful situation to conflict to the elevation of tension to its resolution. Verse 8 provides the background to the events: Sarah's child grows up and Abraham holds a "great feast" on the day he is weaned, a happy scene of family celebration. The conflict is set into motion (v. 9) by Sarah's glance at another pleasant scene, that of her young son, Isaac, playing with his half-brother. This other boy is left unnamed throughout the entire episode. Here, in an allusion to the events of Genesis 16, he is identified from Sarah's perspective as "the son of Hagar the Egyptian." According to that earlier account, Hagar was Sarah's "slave-girl," whom Sarah, because of her infertility, had taken to Abraham so she could bear him a son. But here she is Abraham's concubine. The conflict comes to the surface when Sarah insists that Abraham "cast out" the woman and her son. Her jealousy is obvious: "The son of this slave woman shall not inherit along with my son Isaac" (v. 10). The rivalry runs deep, however. According both to ancient Near Eastern customs and the sense of the Abraham story, this unnamed son is a legitimate heir. Moreover, in the culture where the tradition arose, the mother's security lay first with her husband and then with her son (cf. Gen. 38). So there is a conflict over the rights of inheritance, and at two levels. The obvious level concerns property, but the deeper level concerns the inheritance of the promise to Abraham. Through whom will that line run that leads from Abraham to the great nation that will inherit the land?

The tension of the plot is elevated by Abraham's uncharacteristically ambivalent reaction to Sarah's proposal. We are informed only about his distress because of "his son," that is, the son of Hagar (v. 11). But even without being asked, God intervenes to resolve the dilemma, instructing Abraham to do as Sarah asks. Moreover, lest the reader's concern for Abraham's inhumane act be transferred to God, the narrator has God reassure the patriarch about the fate of Hagar and her son (vv. 12–13). God resolves one conflict by emphasizing that the old promise to Abraham (cf. Gen. 12:1–3) will go through Isaac, and makes a new promise that the other son will be the ancestor of a nation.

Although it would seem that these divine words would assure the story of a happy outcome, the tension continues to arise, now focusing on the immediate fate of Hagar and her son. First there is the touching scene of the farewell (v. 14), with the patriarch sending Hagar away, burdened down with bread, water, and the boy, setting off to the south to wander in the wilderness of Beer Sheba. The climax comes in the poignant picture of the outcast mother and her son, on the verge of death by thirst (vv. 15–19). Unable to face the suffering of the boy, Hagar puts him in the shade of a bush and moves off to await his death, weeping. The readers are invited to identify with Hagar rather than judge her. Remarkably, God's intervention comes in response to the baby's cries rather than those of the mother. The angel assures Hagar that God has heard the voice of the child, promises that God "will make a great nation of him," and only then turns to the immediate crisis, opening Hagar's eyes to see the well of water. The subsequent fate of the two outcasts is summarized in verses 20–21: the boy grew up, lived in the wilderness, became an expert with the bow, and his mother got him a wife from the land of Egypt.

The story that arises in family conflicts, jealousy, and ambivalence becomes the vehicle for addressing far-reaching concerns. What is the relationship between the chosen people of God and other peoples? The line that leads to Israel goes through Isaac, the son of the promise. But Ishmael, that other son of Abraham, also receives a promise and is viewed as the ancestor of those bedouin peoples of the south whom Israel knew as neighbors. Although the promise to Abraham is not compromised, the Israelite narrator—and those who passed this story on through the generations—viewed Hagar and Ishmael with genuine affection. So the story is a gentle criticism of a national and exclusivistic theology. It is also a reminder that the God who watches over history also watches over outcasts.

Psalm 86:1–10, 16–17

This psalm intermingles elements of a lament, hymnic praise, and thanksgiving. These can be seen in an outline of the psalm's contents: (1) a plea addressed to God asking for help but also describing the petitioner as one who is a loyal servant and devotee to Yahweh (vv. 1–7); (2) a hymnic section praising God in direct address but concluding with a request that Yahweh would teach the worshiper the divine way so that the penitent could walk in God's truth and revere Yahweh's name with complete devotion (vv. 8–11); (3) thanksgiving joined with a vow (vv. 12–13); (4) a short description of the distress (v. 14); (5) an affirmation of the character of God as that of a merciful Deity (v. 15); and (6) a final appeal for help (vv. 16–17).

The description of the person's trouble is noted in very general terms, but in words suggesting some form of external enemy: "the insolent," "a band of ruffians," and "those who hate me" (vv. 14, 17). The hoped-for redemption involves some sign of divine favor, which the enemies will see and be put to shame (v. 17). Likewise, the consequences of divine action will impact the nations, which implies that the original speaker was the Hebrew king (v. 9). Only very general terms are used to denote the sufferer: "poor and needy," "your servant," and "the child of your serving girl" (maidservant).

Jeremiah 20:7–13

Even though the prophetic tradition remains far more interested in the words of the Lord through the prophets than in the individuals themselves, the Book of Jeremiah presents us with a great deal of information about this particular prophet, some of it quite personal. This information comes mainly in the form of reports of Jeremiah's activities, either by himself or by third parties. The text before us today gives us an instance of another kind of material—found almost exclusively in Jeremiah among the prophetic books—the prophet's complaints about his life and experience with the word of God. These personal prayers—often called the Confessions of Jeremiah (see Jer. 11:18–23; 12:1–6;

15:10–21; 17:14–18; 18:18–23; 20:7–13, 14–18)—provide insight not only into Jeremiah's thoughts and feelings but also into the institution of prophecy in Israel.

For all its highly personal tone and language, this passage is indebted to a prayer tradition in Israel. This confession, like most others in Jeremiah, closely resembles the individual lament or complaint psalms. Like most prayers, they begin with an invocation of the name of God ("O Lord," v. 7). They contain complaints that describe the person's suffering (vv. 8–10), and they reproach Yahweh for the trouble (v. 7). The one who prays wants God to understand the situation and take responsibility for it. Often there is a confession of sin (Ps. 7:3–5) or of innocence (Ps. 17:1–5), all in order to give God every reason for responding favorably. That element is not present here, but Jeremiah does affirm that he has done his best (vv. 8–9). The heart of such prayers often is a petition for divine help, giving reasons for God to respond. In this case, as in many others, the petition is a plea for vengeance on those who oppose the prophet (v. 12). Frequently we hear an affirmation of confidence in the Lord (as in v. 11) and sometimes at the end of the prayer an expression of assurance that the prayer has been heard and God will act (v. 13). This last element is directly related to the priestly salvation oracle pronounced in a prayer ritual, not unlike words of absolution or assurance following confession in Christian worship.

Jeremiah's cry of anguish is distinctive in both its passion and its cause. His suffering is a direct result of his vocation. His complaints concern his call to proclaim the word of Yahweh. He confesses to inner anxiety and compulsion. Because proclamation of Yahweh's word has led to ridicule and persecution, he tries to hold the word in, but cannot. It burns in his heart and exhausts him (v. 9).

Jeremiah's complaint does not exaggerate the trouble he has experienced; it was real and continuing. His words of judgment hardly were calculated to make him popular, and he was ridiculed when the judgment was slow in coming. Often his life was in danger. The passage immediately before this prayer (20:1–6) reports how Jeremiah was beaten and thrown into the stocks. He was also hauled before court with the charge of blasphemy (Jer. 26) and on another occasion was beaten and put into prison (Jer. 37:11–21). Small wonder that he complains!

We must keep in mind that he complains to God. That he addresses God with such strong accusations ("you have enticed me") is an embarrassment to many readers, and some commentators speak of his language as almost blasphemous. But this is not blasphemy. Jeremiah, like other Israelite faithful, knew that no thought or emotion was forbidden in prayer. To the contrary, one may speak honestly and directly to God. Note that although Jeremiah prays for relief, he knows that he cannot escape his calling, and he does not.

Prophets reacted differently to the experience of the word of Yahweh. When Ezekiel was handed a scroll filled with "words of lamentation and mourning and woe," he ate it, and it was "as sweet as honey" (Ezek. 2:10–3:3). Jeremiah is horrified at the judgment he has to proclaim. But all prophets agree that they have been grasped by Yahweh (cf. Amos 7:15) and that their words are no longer their own.

Some human anguish stems from the experience of the absence of God. Not so in Jeremiah's case. It is the very presence of God—specifically, the word of God—that troubles him so deeply, so he prays to be let alone. Some anguish stems from the hiddenness of God's purpose. Not so in Jeremiah's case. He knows God's purpose all too well. Some anguish stems from lack of vocational clarity. Not so in Jeremiah's case. It is his very vocation, unavoidable despite all his efforts, that places such a burden on him.

Psalm 69:7–10 (11–15) 16–18

Psalm 69 is an individual lament composed to be used in worship during a time of personal crisis. The structure of the entire psalm should be noticed so that this lection can be seen in its context. The following elements make up the psalm: (1) an opening address to the Deity, which already makes an appeal and speaks of the worshiper's trouble (vv. 1–3); (2) a short description of the distress (v. 4); (3) a plea incorporating an acknowledgment of wrongdoing (vv. 5–6); (4) a further description of the distress (vv. 7–12); (5) a further appeal to God for assistance (vv. 13–18); (6) a fourth description of the distressful trouble (vv. 19–21); (7) a fourth appeal to the Deity, this time asking for the destruction of the enemy (vv. 22–28); (8) a final short description of the distress and an appeal (v. 29); (9) a vow to praise God addressed to a human audience (vv. 30–31); (10) an admonition addressed to a human audience (vv. 32–33); and (11) a statement of confidence (vv. 34–36).

This psalm has been selected to be read in conjunction with the Old Testament text because it presumably describes a person's plight that is analogous to that described by Jeremiah in his lament.

In verses 7–12, the psalm again picks up on the description of distress already noted in verse 4. Two factors are the central motifs in this section. On the one hand, references are made to religious actions performed by the worshiper as signs of service "for your sake" (v. 7). On the other hand, there is noted the alienation and ridicule that these acts of religious devotion produced. Verse 7 may be seen as a summarizing statement about both of these. The worshiper claims that it is devotion to God or some act undertaken for God that has resulted in personal dishonor and shame, which, as verse 6 notes, threatens to spill over onto others. The religious acts and pious devotion noted are zeal for the temple (v. 9), weeping and fasting (v. 10), and the wearing of sackcloth (v. 11). The last two of these refer to actions one would take while in grief, suffering, and repentance. (For a case of wearing sackcloth, see Isaiah 20, where the prophet is lamenting over the participation of his people in plans for revolt. Isaiah's subsequent removal of his clothes was a more drastic demonstration!) What zeal for the house of God means is uncertain. There are a number of options: a desire to have a case heard by God in the temple (note that the end of v. 3 suggests that a charge of theft may have been involved), a desire to worship, general concern for the temple, and so on. The shame and reproach are reflected in a number of statements: becoming a stranger to friends, being alienated from family (v. 8), suffering insults and reproach (vv. 9–10), becoming the butt of jokes and gossip (v. 11), and even the subject of barroom songs (v. 12). Obviously, the descriptions here are intent on making matters seem as bad as possible. Nonetheless, they are at least honest expressions of a feeling of alienation, a sentiment better expressed than suppressed.

In verses 13–18, the worshiper expresses complete reliance on God. In this appeal, one again finds the terminology of anarchy and of being overwhelmed: sinking in the mire, my enemies, deep waters, flood, deep, and the pit. Appeal is made, not in the name of just deserts, but to Yahweh's love and faithful help. For solace and salvation, the soul turns to God with an appeal for the personal presence of the Divine.

Romans 6:1b–11

A portion of this text (6:3–11) serves as the epistolary lection for the Easter Vigil in all three years. The reader may want to look at our remarks on the text in that setting.

Having articulated his theology of salvation by grace in chapter 5, Paul now responds to the charge that his soteriology would result in moral relativism. Consequently, his discussion here begins with the rhetorical question "Should we continue in sin in order that grace may abound?" (v. 1b). If God's grace is extensive enough to encompass our sin, presumably (his imaginary opponent argues) more sin on our part would prompt more grace on God's part.

"By no means!" Paul rejoins (v. 2a), insisting that moral renewal is a consequence of the believer's union with Christ. This correspondence between these two transformative events—Christ's death and resurrection and the believer's baptism—prompts Paul to provide an extended discussion of his baptismal theology.

We should remember that this act of Christian initiation is variously understood in the New Testament. In the Johannine church, it was understood as a new birth (John 3:1–15), a metaphor that allowed it to be seen as the beginning of a new life of organic growth. The metaphor of circumcision (Col. 2:11–15) suggests the image of stripping away "fleshly" desires and actions, a way of emphasizing that baptism marks a shift in behavior—away from the life of the flesh toward the life of the Spirit (cf. Rom. 8:1–8). It could also be interpreted in light of the story of Noah and the Flood, with emphasis placed on the salvific effects of water (1 Pet. 3:18–22).

But in today's text, baptism is interpreted by Paul in light of the Christ-event—as a death and resurrection. To make sense of Paul's remarks here, we must remember that early Christian baptism, so far as we can gather, was an act in which adult believers were immersed in water—"buried" under water and "raised" out of the water (cf. Acts 8:36–39). Similar initiation rites were known in certain ancient Greco-Roman religions, where the initiate's immersion in water was seen as a reenactment of the dying and rising of the pagan deity. How much Paul's thinking here is indebted to these contemporary practices has long been debated. But for our purposes, the source of his thinking is less important than its contours and significance.

Our text speaks of being "baptized into Christ Jesus" (v. 3). This is probably traditional language arising from early Christian worship and teaching (cf. Gal. 3:26). It suggests that Christians are *incorporated* into Christ through baptism. Such language makes sense in light of Paul's understanding of the Body of Christ (1 Cor. 12). In the resurrection, the corpse of the crucified Jesus took on new form. Rather than being confined to a human frame, the resurrected and exalted body came to be understood as cosmic in scope, something in which others could share and into which they could be incorporated. Accordingly, Paul insists that the church is the Body of Christ—not a body of Christians. The former suggests a corporate union with a living figure, the latter a collection of persons with common interests. In our text, baptism is seen as that moment of entry, that act of incorporation, when the person and identity of the believer are welded to that of Christ.

One way of seeing this is to note the "with" language throughout our passage (vv. 4, 5, 6, 8). By stressing that the believer in baptism actually dies *with* Christ, is buried *with* Christ, and rises *with* Christ, Paul underscores the union of the believer with Christ (v. 5). What is being claimed here is union and participation, not mere reenactment and imitation. In the one, the believer and Christ are actually coparticipants in an event that can only be described as a death and coming again to new life. In the other, the believer goes through a ritual action *like* that of Christ. It is a difference between lines that converge and lines that remain parallel.

Obviously, in one sense when we "die and rise" in baptism, we do so in a way that is unlike Christ's own death and resurrection. On the cross, Christ expired physically, which is obviously not the case when we are baptized; but Paul is really not thinking of Christ's death in this physical sense. True, Christ *died* on the cross, but it was a double death: expiration of physical life, but, more important, a death to sin: "The death he died, he died to sin, once for all" (v. 10). He died "to sin" in the sense that his death culminated a life resistant to sin and victorious over it. He also died as a result of others' sin against him. Indeed, he died "for sin." The cross must be seen, Paul insists, as more than Christ's last breath. It was also sin's last breath. In the cross, Christ died, but sin died as well, and in this sense both Christ's death on the cross and our death in baptism are alike: they signal the death of sin—for him, in a cosmic sense; for us, in a personal sense. This seems to be the force of his claim that "our old self was crucified with him so that the body of sin might be destroyed" (v. 6).

But if something died, something also came to life—resurrection life. For Christ, the resurrection meant entering a new plane of existence, one where "death no longer has dominion" (v. 9). It also launched a new level of life before God, what our text calls "living to God" (v. 10). This dimension of our existence, though begun in baptism, still lies in the future. Eventually, "we will certainly be united with him in a resurrection like his" (v. 5; also vv. 4, 8, and 11). This is the "not yet" part of Christian existence. Even so, to the degree that we put sin behind us, no longer yielding to its dominion, to that degree we are participating in resurrection life. These ethical implications Paul spells out further in the following verses (vv. 12–23), which constitute next week's epistolary reading.

All of this may seem obvious and all too familiar to us, and yet Paul introduces his remarks by asking, "Have you forgotten . . . ?" (v. 3, REB). The preacher's task is often that of unfolding the implications of the familiar as much as it is introducing the new and unfamiliar. Especially is this the case when the clue to our true identity lies as close to us as our own experience of baptism.

Matthew 10:24–39

We continue today the instructions of Jesus to his disciples prior to sending them on a mission. This instruction began in last Sunday's reading and will continue through next Sunday. In fact, the formulaic ending at 11:1, "now when Jesus had finished instructing his twelve disciples," identifies this section as one of the five major bodies of teaching in Matthew, all of which are concluded in this way (7:28; 11:1; 13:53; 19:1; 26:1).

If one takes the view that Matthew is here giving to his church, which is living under social, economic, and political as well as religious pressure, the word of Jesus for their situation, then two benefits follow. First, we are better able to understand how the words of Jesus functioned for the early Christians. Here in 10:24–39 we have sayings of Jesus found in partial and modified parallels in the other Gospels, but which are now gathered into a single body of instructions for the mission. Collecting and editing these sayings for a church in a particular situation is Matthew's gift to his church and to us. Second, having seen how the church appropriated Jesus' teachings for a given time and place, we are not only permitted but also obligated to hear those teachings afresh and anew in our own situation. To read Matthew and come away with an appreciation for the trials, difficulties, and faith of early Christians is laudable, but not enough. To call Matthew Scripture is to be addressed by it.

Even though Matthew 10:24–39 is a body of collected sayings that probably existed originally in other contexts, thematic unity is not absent, and the preacher need not despair. Jesus both charges and encourages the church to face opposition without being paralyzed by fear. That overall theme unfolds in the following units: verses 24–25, verses 26–27, verse 28, verses 29–31, verses 32–33, and verses 34–39.

In verses 24–25, Jesus tells his followers that they surely can expect opposition because he, their leader, faced it, and the servant is not greater than the master. Expect no exemptions. John 13:14–16 and 15:18, 20, elaborate on this theme. As an example of abuse to himself, Jesus refers to his being called Beelzebul, an Aramaic word and one of many names for the devil. Matthew will relate the Beelzebul controversy in chapter 12. Here the point is simply that Jesus' followers should expect to be called names and to be misrepresented. To be called a servant of Satan when one is seeking to share the love of God is not casually dismissed with "Sticks and stones may break my bones, but words will never harm me."

Verses 26–27, unlike the partial parallels in Mark 4:22 and Luke 12:2–3, carry the force of the imperative. What Jesus has told his disciples privately, and therefore safely, must now be proclaimed publicly, and therefore, dangerously.

Verse 28 is difficult to understand because of the reference to destroying both body and soul in hell. Luke 12:4 radically alters the saying to make it clearer. Surely the point is not to offer a new theory about hell, to the effect that in hell the wicked are totally annihilated. The point seems rather to be in the contrast: you will stand before judges who can execute you, but you also stand before a God whose power is not physical only or confined to the world only. In view of the difference, which will most affect your behavior?

Verses 29–31 do not convey warning but encouragement. God will never, in all that you endure, abandon you. God knows and is concerned about the fall of a sparrow, worth only a half-penny. God is so attentive to your life that even the number of hairs on your head is known to God. Can anyone doubt, then, the attention and care of God for those who love and serve faithfully?

Verses 32–33 lift the theme to the final and ultimate level. Before earthly tribunals, pressure to be silent, to deny Christ, will be very strong; but remember, those who acknowledge the lordship of Christ will have their names spoken in advocacy before the throne of God. Conversely, silence or denial of faith under duress will have its recompense in the removal of one's name when Christ presents his own to God. And confession/denial crises have not ceased among the followers of Christ.

Verses 34–39 picture scenes of domestic strife created by loyalty to Christ but claim that separation from family is not to be compared with the possibility of separation from Christ. In the background of the passage is Micah 7:6. The statements are stern, to be sure, but the reader may be aided in understanding by three observations. First, verses 34–36 are presented in the Semitic perspective that views result as purpose. That is to say, the result of an action is then stated as having been the purpose of the action. For example, the result of Isaiah's preaching was the hardening of hearts, and so Isaiah 6 says that Isaiah preached *in order to* harden hearts. So here in our text, commitments to Christ divided some persons from their families, and so the writer says that the purpose of Christ's call to faith was to divide families. Those in Matthew's church who have experienced such domestic strife can be encouraged to know that such pain was and is no surprise to God. Strangely enough, the words of verses 34–36 are words of encouragement to those already divided rather than a call to alienation from one's family. Second, these words were addressed to cultures, Jew and Gentile, that possessed strong family connections. Whatever religion the head of a household held, all the family and servants embraced the same. For one in the family to become a disciple of Jesus had serious personal, domestic, social, political, and economic consequences.

And finally, the call to love Christ more than one's family is an indirect way of paying honor to the family. Jesus gave his call for loyalty over against the strongest, not the weakest, claim a person otherwise knew, the claim of family love. Jesus never offered himself as an alternative to the worst but to the best in society. As Paul would put it, when one counts life's good, life's gain, as loss, then the real test of discipleship has been passed.

Verses 38–39 change the imagery to cross bearing and losing one's life, but do not really alter the accent of the preceding verses. Bearing a cross and losing/finding life are sayings joined in the tradition here, at 16:24–25, and at Mark 8:34–35.

Proper 8 [13]
(Sunday between June 26 and July 2 inclusive)

Genesis 22:1–18;
Psalm 13; or
Jeremiah 28:5–9;
Psalm 89:1–4, 15–18;
Romans 6:12–23;
Matthew 10:40–42

In the Old Testament reading of the *Common Lectionary*, the story of Abraham continues with the account of the near sacrifice of Isaac. Psalm 13 is a prayer for help from enemies that becomes a prayer of rejoicing because God heard the prayer of the trustful supplicant. In the other lectionaries, the Old Testament reading is supplied, like last week, from Jeremiah. It relates Jeremiah's words to the prophet Hananiah concerning Israel's return from Babylonian exile. The selections from Psalm 89 emphasize God's fidelity in keeping the covenant and the resultant peace experienced by Israel, God's covenant partners.

The epistolary reading, the continuation of last's week's epistolary text, spells out in greater detail the ethical implications of union with Christ. The Gospel reading stresses the identity between disciple and master, emphasizing that hospitality and acts of mercy extended to a disciple are, in effect, extended to Christ himself.

Genesis 22:1–18

Our assigned reading contains two closely related but quite distinct units. The first, verses 1–14, is doubtless one of the most intense but also dismaying passages in the Old Testament, the story of Abraham's near sacrifice of his son Isaac. The second, verses 15–18, is the reiteration of the promise of blessing to Abraham, heard already in the reading from Genesis 12 for Proper 5. Although at the time of his call the promise was given to Abraham as an act of grace and without qualification, here it is repeated and strengthened precisely because the patriarch has demonstrated his faith in God.

The story of Abraham and Isaac, momentous in itself, takes on particular theological meaning when viewed in its context as a whole. Abraham and Sarah had set out to a strange land with the promise that their descendants would become a great and powerful nation, possessing the land in which the patriarchs would only be resident aliens. The report of the fulfillment of the promise begins in the Book of Exodus and is not concluded until the Books of Joshua and Judges. Thus this pithy narrative is a chapter in the history of salvation, including the Exodus, the covenant on Sinai, the wilderness wandering, and the settlement of Israel in Canaan. Awareness of this larger story heightens the drama—as if there were not drama enough already—for it is not only the life of a single child that is in jeopardy, but the life of the future people of God as well.

More directly, the immediate prelude to this chapter is the story of the birth of Isaac (Gen. 21:1–7, see the commentary for Proper 6). Long after the aged pair had given up hope for a son, and therefore for the fulfillment of the promise of descendants, Isaac is born to Sarah. His birth is a blessing in itself, especially for Sarah, but also the necessary first step in the fulfillment of the promise.

The story begins with an explanation of what it is about: "God tested Abraham" (v. 1). As is so often the case in biblical narrative, the readers and hearers know more than the characters do. Abraham, not having been told that he is being tested, hears only the horrifying command to take Isaac to the land of Moriah and offer him as a burnt offering. The narrator, who knows everything, gives us virtually no description but only action and dialogue, and even that with great restraint. There is no speculation on the emotions or feelings of the characters, but the language and pace lead us on. The repetition in the command "Take your son, your only son Isaac, whom you love . . . " (v. 2) stresses the deep affection and strong ties between father and son, as does the image of the two headed off on foot to the mountain with the instruments of death in their hands (v. 6).

Although we have heard the story many times and know how it turns out, to hear it again is to become engaged in its poignancy and power. Will the angel of the Lord arrive in time? We know that it is a "test," but quickly we also realize that it is a matter of life and death. The question "Will Abraham pass the test?" soon becomes less significant than the other one, "Will Isaac live?" At the climax, both questions are answered at the same time. Abraham, who had never hesitated, is willing to obey, but God will not require the life of Isaac (vv. 10–12).

The story has evoked much serious reflection in the history of the church and the synagogue both because of the seriousness of the issues it considers and because of all that is left unsaid. When the boy asked the obvious question "Where is the lamb for the burnt offering?" (v. 7), Abraham's answer (v. 8) was a foreshadowing of what would happen. But did he know, did he hope, or was the response a ruse to keep Isaac quiet, to end the conversation with a religious platitude? Why, we may ask but find no satisfying answer, did God need to test Abraham in the first place?

It would be a serious mistake to reduce this rich narrative to a single point or meaning, for it has many points and more than one meaning. In one sense, the story is an etiology of a place and its name (v. 14). At some stage in the oral tradition, the story probably dealt with the question of child sacrifice, which was not unheard of in the surrounding cultures. Early Israelites could well have asked, "Does our God require that we sacrifice our children?" Failure to do so does not mean lack of faith, for our ancestor was willing but God did not— and will not—require it. The sacrifice of a ram will be sufficient.

Central to the story is the issue of faith. It is Abraham's faith that is tested and in the process the biblical tradition leaves us with a profound understanding of what faith is. It is not defined by means of a theological treatise or a set of propositions, nor are we left with admonitions to be faithful. Rather, the question is answered by means of example, with a story. It is the story of Abraham, who trusted in God even when God appeared to be acting against his promise. Faith is like that. Faith is commitment, the directing of one's trust toward God. It entails the courage and risk of action. Whether Abraham believed that the God he worshiped would not require the life of his son we cannot know. However, as we reflect upon this passage in teaching and preaching, and consider the difference between faith and fanaticism, it is well for us to remember how the story ended; the biblical God does not require such sacrifices.

Abraham's obedience becomes the occasion for the repetition and elaboration of the original promise (vv. 15–18). There is an almost ironic note: Because you have not withheld your son, I will "make your offspring as numerous as the stars of heaven and as the sand that is on the seashore" (v. 17). As in Genesis 12:1–3, this is a promise of blessing for the future, including the great and powerful nation, and the blessing will extend to "all the nations of the earth" (v. 18).

Psalm 13

This is a psalm of individual lament. The following is the structure of the composition: (1) complaints addressed to the Deity (vv. 1–2), (2) an appeal addressed to God for help (vv. 3–4), (3) an affirmation of faith and confidence as the motivation for divine help (v. 5), and (4) a statement of optimistic confidence about the future (v. 6). Except for verse 6, all the material in the psalm is addressed to Yahweh. The final and exceptional verse was perhaps addressed by the worshiper to some human audience, perhaps the cultic leader who officiated at the ritual in which the psalm was employed.

Generally, the psalms of lament contain a section describing the plight and distress from which the worshiper wished to be saved or redeemed. This lament contains no clear statement of such distress but intermingles this with the complaints and appeal. Presumably, the person who used this psalm was one suffering severe pain and facing potential death.

The opening verses of the psalm are clearly complaints lodged against the Deity. These consist of four questions beginning with "how long." The NJPSV provides a better translation than the NRSV:

> How long, O Lord; will You ignore me forever?
> How long will You hide Your face from me?
> How long will I have cares on my mind,
>   grief in my heart all day?
> How long will my enemy have the upper hand?

The form of these questions indicates that the worshiper is willing to lay the blame for the condition of distress at the feet of Yahweh. At least, God is the one assumed to know the answers to the questions and to be able to rectify matters.

The distress of the worshiper is spoken of in terms of a set of three relationships.

1. The human-divine relationship is described as one in which the worshiper feels forgotten by God, whose face is hidden (v. 1). In ancient court etiquette, a person was not allowed to look directly at the face of the king until the king indicated this was all right. Such a procedure was followed to show respect and also to protect the king from evil

influences. If the monarch wished to show displeasure, he would simply never have face-to-face contact with a supplicant. Thus, to hide one's face was to show displeasure. The worshiper in this text depicts the Divine as not only unresponsive but also hostile. As we will note from time to time in this lectionary series, worshipers were encouraged or even forced in the cult to give vent to their anger toward the Deity.

2. The person-to-self relationship is noted in verse 2*ab*. Here the situation is one of constant cares (the Hebrew term is "counsels") on the mind or in the soul and sorrow in the heart. The worshiper acknowledges the deep problems and troubles that upset and burden the health of the personality.

3. Finally, the relationship to the outside world is one of alienation and enmity (v. 2*c*). The sense of alienation and trouble is not merely experienced as an enemy out there but as an enemy who has the upper hand, an enemy to whom one is subservient. Who the enemy is is never clarified and it does not need to be, for it could be either the problem itself or whatever is causing the problem.

The appeal in verses 3–4 is introduced by three imperatives: "consider, answer, give light to my eyes" (or "restore my strength"; see 1 Sam. 14:27–30; Ps. 38:11; Ezra 9:8). These three requested actions include a plea that God subject the worshiper's life to an examination, hear the worshiper's case, and then give aid to the petitioner that will result in the restoration of health.

If God does not aid, then two consequences could result: (1) the worshiper could die (v. 3*b*) and (2) the enemy would be able to rejoice in having triumphed over Yahweh's servant (v. 4).

In verse 5, the worshiper expresses to the Deity a confidence in being heard and responded to affirmatively. The basis of the confidence is having trusted in Yahweh's love or faithfulness (v. 5*a*). Although the psalmist never admits sin or any wrongdoing as the cause of the distress, there is no appeal to innocence as a motivation for divine help. In the last analysis, the hope for grace and help rests on divine favor.

In verse 6, we encounter a confident worshiper who vows to sing praise to Yahweh for the help God has granted. This verse is no longer addressed directly to God but rather to a human audience, for God is spoken of in the third person. Perhaps in worship the temple official in charge of the ritual proclaimed a positive word of assurance to the worshiper, who then responded with confidence and hope, with a new perspective on life. No mention is made of the enemy's destruction; there is just a statement that the worshiper can now rejoice on the basis of God's bountiful dealings. The reassertion of faith (v. 5) itself may have been sufficient to alter the outlook of the worshiper.

Jeremiah 28:5–9

Historical considerations are important in understanding this story about two prophets. The fourth year of the reign of Zedekiah (28:1) would have been 594/3 BC, that is, between the first sack of Jerusalem by the Babylonians in 597 and the second—and more complete—destruction of the city by the same army in 587. In the period between the two disasters, there seems to have been a continuing debate in Jerusalem about how Judah should respond to the Babylonian control. Those in power favored rebellion, but Jeremiah advocated nonresistance. This debate over international politics stands in the background of Jeremiah 27–28.

As the expression "in that same year" in verse 1 reminds us, Jeremiah 28 is a direct continuation of the events reported in the previous chapter. Chapter 27 tells how Jeremiah had performed a symbolic action, wearing a yoke on his neck and proclaiming that Judah should submit to the yoke of Babylon, for Yahweh himself had given nations into the hand of Nebuchadnezzar (27:6). This symbolic action and its interpretation provided the occasion for a public debate (28:1–9), Hananiah's symbolic action of breaking the yoke (28:10–11), and Jeremiah's prophecy against the other prophet (28:12–17).

Hananiah, the narrative is careful to point out, was a prophet, and he confronted Jeremiah with a prophetic announcement in the name of Yahweh: "I have broken the yoke of the king of Babylon" (v. 2). He goes on to announce that the Exile will end within two years, the looted treasures of the temple will be returned, and king Jehoiakim will be set free (vv. 3–4).

Here, then, is the issue. Two prophets, both speaking and acting in the same manner, announce the word of the Lord, but they contradict one another directly. How can the hearers—the priests and all the people standing there—know which is the true prophet? Moreover, there are immediate political and military implications of what each prophet says is the will of God. The one calls for submission to the Babylonian yoke and the other calls for rebellion.

Jeremiah's response to Hananiah's announcement of good news is surprising: "Amen! May the Lord do so . . . " (v. 6). It is possible that these words are sarcastic, but more likely, Jeremiah genuinely holds out the possibility that he is wrong and Hananiah is right. Surely he has never taken pleasure in crying doom and destruction. The prophets of Israel expected surprises from their Lord. For the moment, he does not react with a word of Yahweh but appeals to a rational argument based on a pragmatic principle. The pragmatic principle had been stated in Deuteronomy 18:21–22: You will know the true prophet when what he says comes to pass. Pragmatic, yes, but hardly helpful in the moment when one has to decide. Jeremiah then points out the evidence of history as he reads it, namely, that prophets who prophesied war, famine, and pestilence turned out to be right. So to the first principle—fulfillment of the word—Jeremiah adds a second—true prophecy announces judgment. Those who announce salvation prophesy lies (see also Jer. 14:11–16). Elsewhere Jeremiah suggests that false prophets are those who "speak visions of their own minds" (23:16–17).

The Book of Deuteronomy indicates another, more theological, criterion by which to test the veracity of prophets. If a prophet gives a sign or a wonder, and what he says does indeed come to pass, and then he calls for the people to serve other gods, he is a false prophet and should be put to death (Deut. 13:1–5). This, finally, is the best the Old Testament can offer on the problem: Test what all prophets say against the heart of the faith, the faith that calls for singleness of devotion to the one Lord. Any word that leads away from that devotion is false.

Our account of the confrontation between Jeremiah and Hananiah would have been put into its final form by the Deuteronomistic editors of the book. They worked not long after that second destruction of Jerusalem, which Hananiah said would not come, and wrote for the exiles in Babylon, whom the false prophet said would return within two years. One of their concerns here was to show that the fault for the Exile lies with false prophets whose optimistic nationalism led people astray. By pointing out the causes, they sought to avoid a repetition of the disaster.

Psalm 89:1–4, 15–18

This psalm offers the fullest exposition of the divine covenant with David and the promises it involved that can be found anywhere in the Old Testament (see vv. 19–37). In some respects, 2 Samuel 7 may be seen as merely a narrative adaptation of the Davidic promises celebrated in this poetic form in the royal cult of the Jerusalem court.

Psalm 89 is in reality a lament that speaks of the divine promises to David after they have all been called into question. The conclusion of the psalm, verses 38–51, bemoans the humiliation of the Davidic ruler, who is the object of divine wrath, whose covenant is renounced, whose strongholds are in ruin, and for whom all the promises of God seem to have failed. The description of the king's condition simply piles up one disappointing condition upon another. The psalm ends with a complaint about the loss of God's love and faithfulness, and a prayer for God to note how the king bears in his bosom the insults of the nations roundabout and how the enemies mock the footsteps of the anointed (the Messiah).

If one takes this material as reflective of some actual historical situation, then the king must have suffered a severe humiliation in battle. In fact, the psalm sounds as if it is a description of the consequences that resulted from the destruction of Jerusalem by the Babylonians.

But this week's psalm lection does not focus on the humiliation aspects of the psalm; it focuses on the positive. Verses 1–4 both remind and praise God for divine faithfulness and steadfast love, which are always the basis for confidence. Note that God is reminded that steadfast love is forever and divine faithfulness as sure as the heaven. (Although the minister may not wish to highlight the point, these are exactly the divine qualities called into question in v. 49. Perhaps few psalms so stress the twofold quality of the Deity—the divine care and the divine forsakenness—as does this psalm.) God is made to recall that he swore to David that his descendants would rule forever and his throne endure for generations. The ancient Hebrews were not bashful when it came to reminding God of the divine commitments and to reiterating the promises on which they banked their hopes. (One should remember that when this psalm was read or used in public worship, the person who spoke the first four verses with their calm serenity and secure promises was aware of the trauma yet to be expressed before the Psalter scroll was rolled together and neatly tied and tucked away again.)

Verses 15–18 declare blessed those who participate in the festival observance in which the community joined in celebrating the divine election of David and the Davidic king's rule over the people.

Romans 6:12–23

As we noted in discussing last week's epistolary text, in chapter 6 Paul answers the charge that his view of salvation by grace lacked any compelling moral imperative. Presumably, his detractors insisted that if one stopped living "under law" and began living "under grace" (v. 14), this would mean not only that clearly established guidelines for ethical conduct would disappear but that the fundamental motive for ethical behavior would be removed as well. At stake was not only the "how" but the "why" of religious ethics.

In today's text, Paul responds directly to this fear by employing the metaphor of slavery. Using this metaphor allows him to speak of ethics in terms of fundamental loyalties. In a broad sense, Paul thinks it possible to conceive of the religious life in one of two ways: as living "under law" or "under grace" (v. 14). For him, the former meant specifically living under the Mosaic law, but it included more than this. "Life under [the] law" signified for Paul a way of ordering our lives by certain (divinely given) principles. This way of construing the religious life also implied a certain view of God and a corresponding view of our relationship with God. In a word, it saw God as the giver of laws and human beings as the keepers of law. But Paul insisted that this way of viewing the religious life not only misconstrues the nature of God, but also results in a distorted understanding of how we relate to God. Because we are never able to please God fully, neither can we please ourselves. It has the effect of turning us into religious overachievers. This way of construing the religious life, Paul insists, must be abandoned and exchanged for an alternative view that better represents God and better understands the relationship between us and God.

Living "under grace," by contrast, conceives God not so much as one who legislates but as one who makes promises and bestows gifts. Accordingly, we are seen as gracious recipients of God's promises. As such, we respond to God in gratitude. We live before God not so much as those who keep God's laws but rather as those who have been offered—and have accepted—God's promises.

But does this way of construing the religious life necessarily mean that our behavior is any less well directed or that it is less highly motivated? Not so, according to Paul. "Living under grace" still recognizes "sin" and "righteousness" as competing dominions. It also recognizes full well the addictive power of sin: it can "exercise dominion in [our] mortal bodies" and "make [us] obey their passions" (v. 12). It understands the reality we all know: we are "slaves of the one whom [we] obey" (v. 16). What we habitually submit to is what rules us. Ethics, then, is not a matter of choosing whether we will be ruled, but rather choosing what (or who) will rule us. The ultimate choice is whether we will become "slaves of sin" or "slaves of righteousness" (vv. 17–18).

This way of conceiving the ethical life may strike us as overly dualistic and, thereby, too simplistic. Yet there are elements that ring true. When Paul speaks of "sin," he is thinking not so much of individual sins or even "sin" as a force that constantly threatens us as individuals. He understands it more as a larger reality, a cosmic force, as it were, a term that deserves to be written with a capital S. But he also conceives of "righteousness" this way— "Righteousness," an equally cosmic force that stands over against "Sin." Those who have experienced addictions well understand Paul's insights. Individual addiction is part of a much larger reality; it has both individual and social dimensions. Its effects are incremental, but eventually become compounding. Caught in this life-style, "slaves to impurity" are led to "greater and greater iniquity" (v. 19). So caught, we become inured to righteous impulses: we are "free in regard to righteousness" (v. 20). We may desire to "be good," but such desire has little effect. Once released from this bondage, we look back and find ourselves "ashamed" (v. 21). Above all, we see bondage to sin as an ultimately destructive life-style: its end is "death" (v. 21).

What emerges, then, are two contrasting life-styles that Paul calls "slavery to sin" and "slavery to righteousness." The shift from one to the other occurs as the result of divine action—God's bringing us "from death to life" (v. 13). Our "obedience to the form of teaching to which [we] have been entrusted" (v. 17) marks a transfer of loyalties that results in an ironic shift. Formerly, we were enslaved to sin with no obligations to righteousness; now we have been liberated from sin and find ourselves enslaved to God (v. 22). In one sense, nothing has changed. We are slaves all the same. But in another sense, everything has changed. We have radically different loyalties. And because the religious life is now construed relationally as a response to the One who rescued us, the obediential impulse is as compelling, if not more so, than it was "under law." Thus salvation by grace, Paul insists, does provide a satisfactory answer to the question "Why be good?"

Matthew 10:40–42

With this brief unit, Matthew concludes the second major section of Jesus' teachings in this Gospel (9:35–10:42; the Sermon on the Mount was the first). These teachings are not to the crowds but to the followers of Jesus (11:1). Even though Matthew has gathered these sayings of Jesus under the rubric "instructions prior to a mission," there is no report in Matthew of the disciples actually going on or returning from such a mission. Both Mark (6:12–13) and Luke (9:6; 10:17) report the mission and its successful completion. Apparently, Matthew has subordinated any historical interest in a mission journey of the Twelve to a larger concern with what Jesus says to the church for its life and ministry in a context of hostility and suffering. In fact, the mention of cross bearing in verse 38, coming as it does prior to Jesus' introduction of the subject at Caesarea Philippi (16:13–26), indicates clearly that the text before us is Matthew's reflection on the demands of discipleship after the fact of the crucifixion and resurrection. We may so hear it and appropriate it for ourselves.

These closing verses 40–42 now shift the focus to speak of those who are hospitable to Christ's disciples. The reward of discipleship goes not only to those followers who have lost their family ties but also to those who welcome such disciples, knowing who they are and what their loyalties are. It is, of course, clearly implied that although receiving Christ's disciples brings a disciple's reward, it also brings upon one the threat and hostility that the disciples themselves bear. Verses 41–42 are structured on three parallel expressions: receiving a prophet, receiving a righteous person, and receiving a little one. All three may be taken as referring to the extension of hospitality to Christians. This text gives one an increased appreciation for the significance of the frequent biblical injunctions to practice hospitality. However, the point to be underscored is that in this text Christians are not being urged to welcome prophets or righteous persons or little ones. On the contrary, Christians are the ones receiving hospitality, being welcomed, being guests of others. Being in such a position may make some of us feel a bit awkward, but so does being recipients of God's grace. It is difficult to acknowledge dependence on God or on other persons. But the fact is, it is we who are sometimes the stranger at the door.

Proper 9 [14]
(Sunday between July 3 and 9 inclusive)

Genesis 24:34–38, 42–49, 58–67;
Psalm 45:10–17 or
Song of Solomon 2:8–13; or
Zechariah 9:9–12;
Psalm 145:8–14;
Romans 7:15–25*a*;
Matthew 11:16–19, 25–30

The Old Testament reading for the *Common Lectionary* relates the story of Rebekah and her marriage to Isaac; Psalm 45, appropriately enough, is a love song written for a royal wedding. In the portion of the psalm selected for today (vv. 10–17), the queen is urged to transfer her loyalty from her ancestral family to her husband, and the king is promised sons and fame. The alternate responsorial reading from the Song of Solomon in a similar manner echoes romantic themes.

In the other pair of opening readings, the Old Testament text presents a portion of the prophetic oracle that introduces Deutero-Zechariah. Envisioned is a coming king who will usher in an era of peace. The accompanying psalm reading (Ps. 145:8–14) praises Yahweh as a compassionate God and heralds the glorious majesty of Yahweh's kingdom. In tone and substance, the psalm provides a fitting complement to the Old Testament reading.

The epistolary reading contains perhaps the most well-known portion of Romans 7, where the inward struggle between good and evil receives its classic Pauline statement. The Gospel reading includes, along with Jesus' invitation for the weary of heart to take up the yoke of discipleship (11:25–30), a text exposing the fickleness of humans as they respond to God's duly appointed messengers.

Genesis 24:34–38, 42–49, 58–67

In the biblical account of Abraham's family, the events narrated here transpire between the death of Sarah (Gen. 23 reports the purchase of the place where the ancestors will be buried) and the death of Abraham (25:1–12). In order for the family line to continue, the patriarch must see that his son Isaac is properly married.

In its tone and contents, Genesis 24 stands in sharp contrast to the previous reading from Genesis 22. The account of the awesome events leading to the binding of Isaac was

347

fraught with danger, gripping the reader with the threat to both the child and the history of salvation. The reading for today is a captivating account of the matchmaking of the patriarch and of the wisdom and piety of his faithful servant. It includes a delightful account of the patriarch's relatives in Haran and even a touch of romance in what could be a straightforward legal transaction. There is a plot with dramatic tension, but the story holds the reader's attention with its delightful description of scenes and the portrayal of character through well-crafted speeches.

In the background of this engaging tale stands the central theological theme of the patriarchal stories—the promise of land, progeny, and blessing to all the world—and the constant threat to its fulfillment. Would the line of Abraham be mixed with the Canaanite inhabitants of the promised land? Would Abraham's descendants—specifically, the very next generation—continue to live, like Abraham and Sarah, as sojourners in that promised land? Would obedience as well as the promise be passed on to the next generations? Such threats move the story forward, but in this episode they are never allowed to become serious.

Because the story itself contains so many repetitions—instructions, reports of how they were carried out, summaries of events in long speeches—the verses assigned for today give a rather complete version of the story. In the chapter as a whole, the initial scene in verses 1–8 provides the introduction. The ancient and prosperous patriarch called in his servant and had him swear to find a proper wife for Isaac, not among the Canaanites but in "my country" and from "my kindred" (vv. 2–4). We are not informed of the reason for this concern, for example, whether it relates to purity of genealogy or of religion. But the servant anticipates a problem. "Perhaps the woman will not want to come. Do I move your son back there?" (see v. 5). If that turns out to be the case, Abraham absolves the servant of the oath. Here we have a reminder of the promise of this land and of the call to leave that old homeland. It is clear that human action makes possible the fulfillment of the promise, just as Abraham and Sarah had set out in Genesis 12.

The name of the servant who sets out on the journey in obedience to his master is never given (but cf. Gen. 15:2). This servant is no butler but the chief steward of Abraham's household; he is entrusted with the authority to act on his master's behalf in the most important of decisions concerning the family. He is one of two central characters in this narrative; the other is Rebekah.

The next scene (vv. 10–27) takes place at a well in the region of Haran, in upper Mesopotamia, the locality where Abraham heard the promise and the call in Genesis 12. (For similar stories of encounters at a well leading to marriage, see Gen. 29 and Exod. 2.) Much of what transpires in this scene takes place in the mind and heart of the servant. He prays to Yahweh, God of his master Abraham, to make known the right woman to him, and patiently waits as Rebekah arrives and then meets the request expressed in his prayer.

Most of the assigned verses for the day come from the third and largest scene (vv. 32–60) in which the main characters are the servant and Laban, Rebekah's brother. Verses 34–39 repeat information that we already know, but is now in the long speech to Laban. The purpose of the speech is persuasion. The servant makes it clear to Rebekah's family that this match is indeed made in heaven, that he had prayed, and that Yahweh had revealed the right woman to him. Laban could hardly stand in the way of the will of the Lord. The actual climax of the story is in material omitted from the reading, verses 50–57, where Laban agrees to the proposal. When the family requests that Rebekah be allowed to remain a while, the servant insists on the urgency of his mission, and the bride is allowed to decide. She agrees to leave immediately (v. 58). The family sees her off with a blessing (v. 60; see also Ruth 4:11).

The final scene (vv. 62–67) describes the arrival of the caravan back in Canaan and the marriage. Here is where the story goes beyond the legal negotiations concerning marriage to suggest that Rebekah found Isaac attractive when she first saw him and that he loved her.

There are a number of suggestions if not direct comments on Rebekah's character. She generously responds to the servant's request for water and thus passes the test he has set. She immediately accepts the request to go with the servant to a strange land and become the wife of a man she never met—in itself not at all unusual in that culture. But she is prepared to accept the risk of leaving her homeland. Moreover, she is described as beautiful (v. 16).

All the references to the Deity notwithstanding, it is a relatively secular story when compared with most others of the Pentateuch. Yahweh is not one of the characters who acts in the story. The intervention of Yahweh is hardly dramatic. Prayer and ordinary events take place and then are interpreted as revealing God's intentions. But God does not speak or act directly at all. Nevertheless, one of the themes of the story is the way God cares for people in the ordinary events of life: birth, marriage, and death. Over and over there is the concern that the Lord will make the servant's journey a successful one (vv. 21, 40, 42, 56). So this text can provide the occasion for reflecting on the question of God's guidance in personal and every-day events. Moreover, the piety of the characters is stressed, particularly in the prayers of Abraham's servant. So this unnamed leading character is presented as an example to the reader of piety combined with the wise and competent accomplishment of his commission.

Psalm 45:10–17

This psalm was composed for the marriage of a king in ancient Israel. As such a genre, it is unique in the Old Testament. Wedding ceremonies as religious occasions held at a sanctuary or place of worship, as we know them today, were not present in ancient Israel. Although there were religious dimensions to marriages and celebrations associated with weddings, the events themselves were primarily nonreligious. Marriages tended to be arranged and to constitute "business" agreements between families. In spite of this, marriages were considered as covenants between the spouses over which God acted as a protector or guardian.

This psalm has been interpreted by Christians in such a way as to identify the husband with Christ and the bride with the church. This of course represents an extreme allegorization of the material.

The opening verse indicates that the psalm was a composition by a "poet" at the royal court in praise of the wedding couple. Verses 2–9 praise the king, who in verse 6 is addressed as God (Elohim).

The verses in today's lection focus on the bride. This is clearly the case with verses 10–15. Verses 16–17, however, appear to address again the king, but the text is not overly clear. (Note that the NRSV inserts "O King" in v. 16.)

That the bride is associated with the Phoenician city of Tyre (v. 12) has led to the conclusion that this psalm was written for Ahab's marriage to Jezebel, the Phoenician princess, daughter of Ethbaal, king of Tyre and Sidon (1 Kings 16:31). This is certainly possible, but it should also be noted that marriage between the royal houses of different nations was quite common in antiquity, and thus an Israelite or Judean monarch may have frequently married a Tyrian princess (see 1 Kings 11:1–2). Such marriages were part of treaty arrangements that fostered economic and political cooperation. (Such marriages also allowed one monarch to place an "ear" or informant in the foreign king's court.)

The following admonition to the new bride (vv. 10–11, NJPSV) may strike many as an expression of patriarchal machoism:

> Take heed, lass, and note,
>> incline your ear:
>> forget your people and your father's house,
>> and let the king be aroused by your beauty;
>> since he is your lord, bow to him.

In preaching on this text, one should inform the audience of the material's origins in a highly patriarchal culture.

Song of Solomon 2:8–13

The Song of Solomon, or Canticles/Song of Songs, celebrates the erotic and sensual love between two humans. This is now the common opinion that holds sway in practically all scholarly treatments of the book. Such a view was not always the case. Until modern times, most interpreters read the book allegorically. Early Jewish commentators understood the work as expressing love between God and Israel, a factor reflected in using the book liturgically in conjunction with Passover. Christians have read the book as an allegory of Christ and the church, of the soul's devotion to God and truth, or of the Virgin Mary.

In this lection, the female imagines hearing the voice of her beloved, whose coming to her is described as a gazelle or a young stag bouncing among the mountains. Arriving at her home, she imagines him inviting her into the fields, where the signs of spring give evidence that winter is now passed.

Zechariah 9:9–12

The themes of the nature and reign of God are emphasized in the reading from Psalm 145. This passage from Zechariah depicts the nature and rule of an earthly monarch. The Zechariah text is quoted in the New Testament description of Jesus' entry into Jerusalem (Matt. 21:1–6; John 12:14–15). Traditionally, it has been taken as a depiction of the prince of peace arriving in triumph.

The four verses in this lection contain (1) a call to the city of Jerusalem to greet an arriving king (v. 9); (2) a description of the consequences to result from the actions of the king (v. 10; although in the Hebrew text the opening word of v. 10 is first person—"I [God] will cut off"); (3) a statement to Zion about the release of her prisoners (v. 11), and (4) a call to the prisoners to be restored or to return (v. 12).

The configuration of the material and its imagery are strikingly arresting. The sacred city is called upon to break out in celebration at the arrival of the triumphant king who enters riding on a donkey. The arrival of this humble monarch will have significance far and wide and will inaugurate new forms of existence in the world.

Rather than moving quickly to the New Testament and taking Zechariah 9:9–12 as a prediction about Jesus, perhaps we should reflect for a moment about the origin and content of this text's imagery. Several factors come to mind.

Today most scholars assume, with legitimate reasons, that the Book of Zechariah is a composite work subdividable at least into chapters 1–8, 9–11, and 12–14. Chapters 1–8 are dated to the years 520–518 BC or to the time just after the Jewish return from Babylon to rebuild the Jerusalem temple after the decree of the Persian king granting them this right in 538 BC (see Ezra 1:1–4). The material in these chapters is highly symbolic and visionary, speaking about the events of the day in imagery that is at times almost cryptic. Chapters 9–14 are more restrained in imagery but are shot through with the motifs of battle, slaughter, divine victory, and a final peaceful existence for Jerusalem. When this material originated and what relationship it has to historical events and circumstances remain uncertain. The reference to Greece in 9:13 has led many to see the texts as belonging to the time when Alexander the Great marched down the Syrian-Palestinian coast in 333–332 BC. However, Greeks marauding along this coast are already noted in Assyrian texts four centuries earlier, and Greek settlements in Syria date from the ninth century. Thus historical circumstances don't appear to help very much.

The imagery of 9:9–12 can probably be understood against the background of actions and ideas associated with the celebration of the Davidic king's (the messiah's) rule in Jerusalem. Verse 9 describes a procession to Jerusalem in which the king humbly but triumphantly reenters the city. In some ancient cultures, and probably in Judah, the king was annually and ritually "dethroned," forced to give up the signs of royalty and even subjected to humiliation. This was done to emphasize the king's humanity, his reliance on the Deity, and his responsibility to rule justly. The departure of David from Jerusalem in 2 Samuel 15:30 may reflect some aspects of this humiliation—weeping, head covered with dust, and barefoot. The animal ridden on such occasions may have been reflective of the king's humble or humiliated status. In 1 Kings 1:33, 38, Solomon rides a mule during the coronation procession. The king's ritual humiliation would have been reversed when the king was reenthroned amidst the cheers of the citizens.

Verse 10 contains two motifs of the royal-messianic theology: (1) the rule of the righteous king will bring wars to an end, even to the disarming of the people (see Isa. 11:1–9) and (2) the Davidic messiah will rule over the entire earth (see Ps. 72). The NJPSV expresses the sense of verse 10:

> He shall banish chariots from Ephraim
> And horses from Jerusalem;
> The warrior's bow shall be banished.
> He shall call on the nations to surrender
>   [see Deut. 20:10–12],
> And his rule shall extend from sea to sea
> And from ocean to land's end.

The prisoners or those bound will be set free and restored to their proper status (vv. 11–12). Again, this may reflect elements of the royal administration. Probably in Judah and Israel, as in other ancient cultures, a king at his coronation or at some anniversary celebration would issue decrees that sought to "establish justice" in society by righting wrongs and creating more equitable conditions. This might include such things as canceling debts and freeing prisoners. For society, it could signal a new beginning.

The reference to the "blood of my covenant" remains obscure. The phrase occurs elsewhere only in Exodus 24:8. Does it refer to the Jerusalem sacrifices or some special sacrifice? One way of understanding the text is to see it as reflecting God's marriage relationship to the city of Jerusalem. In the ancient world, a capital city was considered to be the "wife" of the national god. Here there may be an allusion to Jerusalem as the wife of Yahweh and to the marriage blood that accompanied the wedding, with marriage understood as a covenant relationship (see Ezek. 16:8–14 for the imagery).

Clearly, this text came to be understood with a futuristic orientation as describing that time in the future when the symbolized would become reality. And so the church felt free, even compelled, to apply this text to Jesus and his entry into Jerusalem on Palm Sunday.

Psalm 145:8–14

An alphabetic psalm, Psalm 145 consists of a series of short affirmations that extol the reign and kingship of God. The text oscillates between words addressed to the Deity (vv. 1–2, 4–7, 10–13a) and words spoken about the Deity but addressed to a human audience (vv. 3, 8–9, 13b–21). The lection for this Sunday consists of both types of material: speech about God (vv. 8–9, 13b), speech to God (vv. 10–13a), and speech about God (vv. 13b–14).

Verses 8–9, which speak about God, offer a formulaic definition or description of God or what classical theology calls the attributes of God. The same description, in almost exact terminology, appears in Exodus 34:6; Joel 2:13; Jonah 4:2; and Psalms 86:15 and 103:8. Six characteristics of the Deity are emphasized, all of which stress the benevolent aspects of the Divine: gracious (or perhaps "dutiful," as in the appropriate relationship between master and servant), merciful (or "compassionate"), slow to anger (or "patient, long-suffering"), abounding in steadfast love (or "extremely loyal"), good to all (or "universally concerned"), and compassionate to all the Divine has made (or "tenderly caring for all God's creatures"). Such a text as this is the nearest one finds in the Old Testament to a descriptive definition of the Divine. Although the emphasis is placed on the benevolence of God, verse 20 indicates that moral considerations—the issue of justice and injustice—that receive so much emphasis elsewhere in the Hebrew Scriptures are not ignored in the theology of this psalm.

The central topic in the praise of God in verses 10–13a is the kingdom of God. The kingdom of God is here understood, as in most places in the Bible, as the dominion or rule of God. In verse 13a, "kingdom" and "dominion" are parallel to each other and thus can be seen as synonyms. Thus the focus of this text is concerned with the present manifestation of God's kingdom—God's rule as king at the moment—rather than an eschatological emphasis that comes to dominate in the New Testament. Nonetheless, the futuristic elements do appear in verses 10–11, where the verbs can be translated, as in the NRSV, in a future tense.

Both the deeds and the devotees of God—that is, the world of creation at large and the world of God's special people—offer their testimony regarding the rule of God (vv. 10–11). Both offer witness to all people. Thus both creation and the covenant community point to the reign of God, a reign that is eternal and forever enduring (v. 13a).

Verses 13b–14, which is human-to-human address—perhaps the priest addressing the worshiper—reiterate the emphasis on the eternal and continuing reign of God, who keeps promises ("is faithful in all his words") and is unchanging in all that God does ("gracious in all his deeds"). Thus one can trust God and rely on his word.

The preaching on this text should stress the eternal, consistent, abiding character of God's reign. As creator, God is king, and the world and all that is in it are divine subjects.

Romans 7:15–25a

There are two questions interpreters of this passage have consistently debated: (1) whether these remarks are primarily autobiographical and thus primarily depict Paul's own moral struggle, and (2) whether what is in view is the struggle *before* becoming a Christian or *while* living as a Christian.

The answer to the first question will turn on how we understand the "I" that is repeatedly used in the passage. Is Paul the fundamental referent, or is "I" used in a generic sense, as the equivalent of "one" or "everyone"? Or is it the "I" of the religious person or, more specifically, of the Jew striving to be faithful to Torah? The preacher will need to consult other passages where Paul uses "I" in an ambiguous sense (cf. 1 Cor. 8:13; 9:15–27; 13:1–3, 8–13).

To answer the second question, we must look carefully at the tenses of the verbs used in the chapter. We should note especially that the past tense dominates the first part of the chapter (7:1–13), whereas the present tense dominates the latter part (7:14–25). What is striking about today's text is the way the moral struggle is envisioned as a present reality, as something ongoing.

Obviously, how one answers these questions will affect how the text can be appropriated homiletically. If, for example, we read the text as the agonized struggle of the religious person, indeed of a mature Christian, it may address the perennial Christian questions: If I am already a Christian, why do I continue to sin? Does not being Christian mean that I should be able to do what I know is right and avoid doing what I know is wrong? Pursued this way, the text can be explored as a set of profound, and chillingly honest, insights directed to those who are already religious but who nevertheless continue to know and experience the tension between is and ought.

If, however, the text is taken to describe pre-Christian existence, it will lend itself to a different form of homiletical interpretation. Among other things, it will be read as depicting a life that was left behind and transformed through our union with Christ (vv. 24–25).

Even so, several observations are in order. First, these remarks are made in the context of Paul's defending the law, in this case, the law of Moses (v. 14; also cf. 7:12). A sharp distinction is made here between sin as an overarching, cosmic principle, and the law as the articulated commandment of God. Devout Pharisee that he was, Paul found it difficult to concede that Torah, as God's revelation, was somehow deficient. Indeed, it had positive value in giving expression to wrongful acts, such as coveting (7:7–12). It should be regarded as "spiritual" (v. 14), because it comes from God. The real culprit is something else, a force far more sinister—Sin. It takes on personified form and can be conceived as a force lurking within the self that distorts our best intentions and keeps the law from achieving its desired purpose.

The force of Paul's remarks here is clear: we cannot explain our moral dilemma by harping on the deficiencies of the law. The place to begin is with honest introspection, with a true understanding of the human self. He places the locus of moral responsibility within the human heart, "in my inmost self" (v. 22), not somewhere else—not with God, nor with the law. For him, contrition is the beginning of morality, and in this respect he echoes the sentiments of the Qumran *Community Rule* 11:7–8: "As for me, I belong to wicked mankind, to the company of ungodly flesh. My iniquities, rebellions, and sins, together with the perversity of my heart, belong to the company of worms and to those who walk in darkness" (cf. Ps. 51:5).

Second, our text, in a most unforgettable fashion, sketches the tension between willing and doing: "I do not understand my own behaviour; I do not act as I mean to, but I do things that I hate" (v. 15, NJB). Naturally, others besides Paul knew, and wrote about, this conflict between knowing and doing. The Roman poet Ovid, an earlier contemporary of Paul (d. AD 17), wrote: "Desire persuades me one way, reason another. I see the better and approve it, but I follow the worse" (*Metamorphoses* 7.19–20).

But we miss an important Pauline insight if we read these words as the soliloquy of the quintessential negative thinker, of one who simply has not thought positively long enough and hard enough. It is more than an inward human struggle. It is rather a war between the cosmic powers being carried on within the self—the "law of God" pitted against the "law of sin" (vv. 22–23; cf. Gal. 5:17; James 4:1, 5; 1 Pet. 2:11). The struggle depicted here is not merely the failure of the individual to realize her or his human potential; it is rather the hopeless struggle of the person who is "sold into slavery under sin" (v. 14). What is being described here is a form of savage enslavement (v. 23) from which we must be rescued.

It is on this note of spontaneous thanksgiving at the thought of being rescued that our passage concludes (v. 25; Rom. 6:17; 1 Cor. 15:57; 2 Cor. 2:14; 8:16; 9:15).

As we think about preaching from this text, we are reminded that it is one of those texts where our own human experience may be as illuminating as reading commentaries. To be sure, we must understand the contours of Paul's thoughts, but equally important, we must know the contours of our own hearts. Doing so will allow our own "I" to identify with the "I" of the text, both in its moments of desperation and in its moments of hope.

Matthew 11:16–19, 25–30

The listener and perhaps the preacher will welcome this lection as a break from a series of statements about the very heavy demands of discipleship. Matthew 11:16–19, 25–30 puts discipleship into the context of revelation and grace.

This is not to say that the passage is easy to understand. On the contrary, it is difficult, and primarily for two very different reasons. First, the text is unique in the Synoptics, being based on wisdom Christology and, as we will see, is more at home in Johannine thought. Second, this passage is very popular, being claimed by every reader who feels burdened and heavy-laden. That the original audience very likely were Israelites burdened under the yoke of the law is for many readers no longer a pertinent historical item: Jesus' promise of rest and a light burden is heard and appropriated by all whose lives are pressed down, for whatever reason. Once a text is owned by all who hear it, it is the historical interpreter who seems the intruder.

Clearly, the heart of today's lesson is verses 25–30. However, this unusual announcement of divine revelation and offer of grace in Jesus Christ can best be heard when set in its sharply contrasting context. The two preceding stories are of rejection and unbelief: in verses 16–19, Jesus rebukes those who reject both John and himself; in verses 20–24, he reproaches the cities in which he had ministered and which still refused to receive him. Only the first story provides the context here for verses 25–30.

Jesus has been extolling the importance of the ministry of John the Baptist, now in prison (v. 2). John is, says Jesus, at the end of a line of prophets looking forward to the reign of God that now is here. John is the Elijah who was to come prior to the Messiah (vv. 10–15). But both John and Jesus suffer rejection by a generation acting like spoiled children who refuse to be satisfied. They refuse to play wedding or funeral (vv. 16–17). Likewise, they refuse John as too austere and nonsociable; they refuse Jesus as too sociable. John has table fellowship with no one; he is a desert preacher. Jesus has table fellowship with anyone, even tax collectors and sinners (vv. 18–19). In a society in a measure defined by what, when, and with whom one eats, both John and Jesus are unacceptable.

"Yet wisdom is vindicated by her deeds" (v. 19). In a practical way, this proverb is similar to "By their fruits you will know them," but it is important here that the figure of Wisdom is introduced, and in a personified form. In the remainder of our text, Jesus will be described in the image of divine wisdom.

Matthew 11:25–30 consists of three parts: a thanksgiving (vv. 25–26), a proclamation (v. 27), and an invitation (vv. 28–30). The first two parts are found in Luke 10:21–22 in a different context but seem already to have been joined in the tradition common to Matthew and Luke. Some commentators speculate that these two parts were joined because they are both sayings about revelation or sayings about "the Father." More likely, however, they are joined not only to each other but also to the third, verses 28–30 (found only in Matthew), because all three draw upon the wisdom tradition of Judaism.

One meets the desirable but elusive figure of Wisdom (Sophia) in many places in the Old Testament, most noticeably in Job 28:12–28: "But where shall wisdom be found?"; Proverbs 8:22–36: "The Lord created me at the beginning of his work . . . then I was beside him, like a master worker"; Ecclesiasticus 24:1–24: "My Creator chose the place for my tent. He said, 'Make your dwelling in Jacob'"; and Wisdom of Solomon 7:22–30: "For she [Wisdom] is a reflection of eternal light, a spotless mirror of the working of God, and an image of his goodness."

Even a casual reader of these passages can see how some early Christians saw in Jesus Christ the incarnation of God's eternal wisdom, or in its masculine form, eternal Logos. One finds in 1 Corinthians 1:20, 26–29, Paul's way of saying Matthew 11:25–26. And Matthew 11:27 is so much like John 1:18; 6:35–59; 7:25–30, and many other such passages, that the German scholar von Hase called the verse "a meteorite from the Johannine heaven."

And finally, verses 28–30, Christ's invitation to the weary and burdened, clearly echo Ecclesiasticus 51:25–27, in which Wisdom calls out to an Israel bent low beneath the heavy yoke of the law. Wisdom says, "Come, take my yoke, and find for yourselves rest." In our text, Jesus is God's eternal wisdom making that offer of refreshment and release.

In summary, then, two statements need to be made. First, in the immediate context, Jesus has just finished upbraiding certain Galilean cities in which his mission failed (vv. 20–24). Jesus, however, understands their rejection in terms of the concealed/revealed wisdom of God. In their own vaunted pride and wisdom, they have missed the revelation God grants to the humble and receptive. Second, in the larger context of Jesus' moral and ethical demands on all who would follow him, these verses come as a clear reminder: apart from the twin gifts of God's revelation and God's grace, we would all be bent low beneath the burden of those very demands. However, Christ's offer is not permissiveness but that of a shared yoke, of love, and of forgiveness.

Proper 10 [15]
(Sunday between July 10 and 16 inclusive)

Genesis 25:19–34;
Psalm 119:105–112; or
Isaiah 55:10–13;
Psalm 65:(1–8) 9–13;
Romans 8:1–11;
Matthew 13:1–9, 18–23

Today's *Common Lectionary* reading from the Old Testament tells the story of Esau's selling of his birthright to Jacob, and in doing so poignantly sketches contrasting profiles of these twin brothers and the family conflict they represent. The psalm is a portion of the lengthy Psalm 119 that consists of a prayer expressing confidence in God's word and the need for divine assistance in life's struggles.

For the Old Testament reading, some confessions will use the richly poetic selection from the celebratory hymn of Isaiah 55 that compares the fruitful fidelity of God's word with the regularity of seasonal rain. Psalm 65, a thanksgiving hymn studded with rich images, praises God's creative work (vv. 5–8) and acknowledges God as the source of nature's sustaining care (vv. 9–13).

The epistolary reading, the introductory section of the climactic eighth chapter of Romans, strikes a note of confidence and strength, reassuring us that our existence in Christ eliminates the fear of condemnation. The Gospel reading is the parable of the sower and its interpretation, a lesson concerning the response of those who hear the word of the kingdom of God.

Genesis 25:19–34

The patriarchal stories extend over four generations, those of Abraham, Isaac, Jacob, and the children of Jacob. For reasons that are not obvious, the four generations do not receive equal attention. Abraham, through whom the history of salvation was initiated, is the model of faith; Jacob, who becomes Israel, is the ancestor of the chosen people; and the twelve sons of Jacob are the patronymic ancestors of the tribes. There is remarkably little material in which Isaac is the central character (Gen. 26). He appears, of course, in the Abraham story and figures in important incidents in the life of Jacob. Although the events reported in today's reading transpire in Isaac's household, Genesis 25:19 actually marks the beginning of the Jacob story.

Genesis 25:19–34 contains three relatively distinct parts, verses 19–26, 27–28, and 29–34. There is evidence that various elements of the material once circulated independently in the oral tradition, but in the final written form, the first two sections provide the background and setting for the third. The first two of these parts are not stories at all, but basically reports of events; that is, they do not attempt to create interest by developing the tension of a plot, but simply list what happened. In the context, however, they prepare us for the anecdote in verses 29–34. The theme shared by the entire passage is that of conflict between the two brothers, a theme that will continue to recur in the rest of the Jacob narrative.

Verses 19–26 are framed by the genealogical and chronological notices common to the Priestly Writer (vv. 19–20, 26b), by which the connections are drawn, eventually from creation to the establishment of Israel as a nation in the land. The lengthy report of Isaac's marriage to Rebekah in the more ancient document (Gen. 24) here becomes a brief notice (v. 20). There follows the observation that Isaac prayed to God because his wife was barren, and thus she conceived. She is troubled by the struggle within her womb, so she inquires of the Lord. The oracle in response takes us far beyond the family situation to a prophecy of struggle between two nations, the descendants of the yet unborn twins (v. 23). The account of the birth of the boys is full of humor, made of plays on words, puns and ridicule. The hand of the narrator is heaviest on Esau. The firstborn is red (the Hebrew is a play on the name Edom) and hairy (a play on "Seir," where the Edomites lived). The narrator and his audience were laughing at the Edomites by ridiculing their ancestor, but they did not leave their own patriarch unscathed, for he came out of the womb grasping the heel of his brother. There is a pun on his name as well, for "Jacob" is here explained as "heel," perhaps a double entendre. (Actually, the name means "God protects" or "may God protect.")

Verses 27–28 provide the transition from the birth of the twins to the story in verses 29–34, setting the scene by characterizing the sharp differences between the two brothers. One is a hunter, living out in the open; the other is more civilized, living in the tents of the shepherd. One is loved by his father and the other by his mother.

The humor of caricature and ridicule continues in the story of Esau's sale of his birthright to Jacob (vv. 29–34). The former is drawn as a rough, impetuous man, more concerned about his stomach than his future. "Give me some of that red stuff to gulp down, for I am famished" (v. 30, NJPSV), he says. In the end, he impolitely "ate and drank, and rose and went his way" (v. 34). Jacob is shrewd, calculating, and mistrustful, demanding an oath before handing over the food. The plot turns on the transfer of the birthright from the older to the younger, but the story is silent on the meaning of this right. Deuteronomy 21:17 specifies that the firstborn is to receive a double share of the inheritance, but it seems unlikely that our story has such a specific meaning in view. Beyond the story, in the wider patriarchal narrative, we must think of the promise of blessing that has been passed down from Abraham to Isaac and will now pass through Jacob.

Except for this last feature, which, after all, belongs not to our passage but to its context, theological concerns are almost completely missing from this passage. There are, of course, the religious matters of prayer (v. 21) and inquiry of the Lord (vv. 22–23), but these are hardly developed at all. The anecdote about the brothers does have a "moral," explicit in the narrator's criticism of Esau, "Thus Esau despised his birthright" (v. 34). The strangeness of the biblical world is patently obvious here, and we must resist the temptation to moralize. Nevertheless, two issues emerge for serious reflection:

1. There is the theme of the reversal of expectations in general—the last shall be first—and of the triumph of the "lesser," or younger, brother in particular. Whatever the specific inheritance rights, in patriarchal societies the firstborn son had the advantage. However, the stories of Israel's ancestors, like most of the Bible, are told from the perspective of those who did not have the advantage, but still were chosen. Thus the oracle announces what will begin to be fulfilled in the story: "The one shall be stronger than the other, the elder shall serve the younger" (v. 23).

2. The leading motif of these paragraphs, present in each of them and persistent in the entire Jacob narrative, is conflict. Conflict and competition are seen to exist at every level of human society. Conflict is in the family, for the brothers struggle with one another even before they are born, and even the affection of parents is divided (v. 28). Its existence on the cultural or socioeconomic level is reflected in the ridicule of the hunter by the bearers of the tradition, who identify with the shepherd. Finally, it is present on the political, national, and international level, for the two brothers are ancestors of the states of Israel and Edom. Immediate neighbors, their rivalry persisted from earliest times until the end of the Old Testament era, and frequently broke out into violence. Ancient Israel was neither sentimental nor sanguine about "brotherhood," but knew that conflicts at all levels are as old as the race and as persistent as time. Thus, for all its exaggeration and caricature, the story presents a realistic view of human life and calls our attention to realities that we ignore only at our peril. It offers no solution except to poke a little fun at human frailties and foibles.

Psalm 119:105–112

Portions of this psalm have been discussed for the Sixth and Seventh Sundays After the Epiphany. As noted there, the 176 verses of this psalm divide into twenty-two stanzas of eight lines each. In each individual stanza, all eight lines begin with the same Hebrew letter, working through the alphabet in order. In each of the stanzas there is a play on a series of synonyms for the law or the will of the Deity. Generally, there are eight such synonyms per stanza, and generally the same eight are used throughout the entire psalm.

The reading for this Sunday constitutes the fourteenth stanza or strophe. The eight terms used to refer to the will of Yahweh are word (repeated), ordinances (repeated), law, precepts, testimonies, and statutes. God's will is described as a light illuminating life's pathways (v. 105), as a heritage, and as a joy (v. 112). The worshiper rehearses the commitment made to observe and live by the commandments (vv. 106, 109, 112) in spite of the distractions and hostilities that come to divert one from the way (vv. 107, 109, 110).

Isaiah 55:10–13

This text concludes the section of the Book of Isaiah (40–55) attributed to Second Isaiah, the prophet of the end of the Babylonian Exile. In some respects, the passage parallels the beginning of the work (40:1–11). Both passages stress the power of the word of God, and both proclaim the good news that God will bring the people out of exile and return them to their land. The words would have been spoken originally in 539 BC, the year before the end of the Babylonian Empire. The first audience was the community in exile.

Our assigned reading is part of the longer discourse that includes all of chapter 55. (Isaiah 55:1–11 is one of the texts assigned for reading during the Easter Vigil.) In language resembling that of a hymn, the chapter consists of admonitions to listen to and believe in the word of God and celebrations of the Lord's word and works. God's grace to the exiles includes food that will satisfy both physical and spiritual needs. The one who seeks the Lord finds life.

Isaiah 55:10–13 consists of two parts, closely related but distinct in terms both of form and content. In the first part (vv. 10–11), Yahweh is the speaker, continuing the previous discourse. In the second part (vv. 12–13), the prophet is the speaker.

Verses 10–11 give reasons for following the exhortations of verses 6–7: "Seek the Lord. . . ." The "For" of verse 10 parallels those of verses 8 and 9. This third reason is in the form of an extended comparison between water from heaven—rain and snow—with its effects (v. 10) and the word of the Lord (v. 11). Just as the rain and snow bring about growth, seeds, and bread, so the word of the Lord is effective, accomplishing what the Lord intends. God accomplishes his will through the word, as in Genesis 1 and as in the announcements of the Lord's prophets.

Verses 12–13 begin with another "For," which may give yet another set of reasons for seeking the Lord. The verses contain proclamations of salvation concerning the exiles and their future. When they go out—from Babylon—in joy and are led in peace, nature itself will join in the celebration. Second Isaiah's poetry is rich in the imagery of creation because of his sense of the cosmic scope of God's work. The thornbush and the brier will be replaced by the cypress and the myrtle. The only point not clear in the concluding verse is the antecedent of the "it" that will be the memorial and sign. It could refer to the people or to the saving event itself, the going out in joy and peace. Salvation, or those saved, will be a perpetual sign, calling to mind the Lord of Israel.

The purpose of this passage is the proclamation of good news. It means to evoke in the hearers and readers confidence in God's word and the joyful celebration of hope.

Psalm 65:(1–8) 9–13

Very few psalms of community thanksgiving are found in the Psalter (see Pss. 67, 92, 107). A hymn may have served as the community's response to specific acts of divine providence, and thus no great need existed for writing special thanksgiving psalms. Psalm 65 is probably one of the exceptional psalms of communal thanksgiving.

All of the psalm is direct address to the Deity, although some scholars see a radical change of tone between verses 1–4 and verse 5 following. Some even argue for three psalms (1–4, 5–8, 9–13). The composition appears, however, to be a unity, and the elements of sin, creation, and divine blessing of the crops/harvests noted in the text are not so unrelated.

Verses 1–4 focus on the human admission and divine forgiveness of sin. Difficulties in translating verses 1–2 make the exact meaning uncertain. For example, in the Hebrew, the opening line says, "To thee praise is silent" or "is waiting." Note the KJV, which reads, "Praise waiteth for thee." Verses 2b and 3a can be translated, "Unto you all flesh shall bring the requirements of iniquity." At any rate, certain factors seem clear.

1. The occasion for the celebration and the praise of God is the fulfillment of vows. These may have been vows made to be carried out if certain conditions were met by God,

such as providing a good crop year or forgiving sins, probably the latter. Moderns look judg-mentally on vows or deals with God, or at least we publicly express ourselves that way. An-cient Israel was unashamed of such arrangements.

2. A public, communal acknowledgment of sin is made. A basic feature of Israelite reli-gion was a routine day of national repentance (Yom Kippur). Other days of repentance were held when deemed necessary. The minister who preaches on this psalm should imaginatively think about what such days of national repentance might do in contemporary culture, where admitting wrong and guilt is itself considered to be a national sin.

3. Worship in the temple is viewed as an exhilarating source of joy and blessedness. The goodness of the temple (v. 4c) probably refers to the sacrificial feasts eaten in the temple in conjunction with thanksgiving. (The covered dish dinner has a long genealogy and a most sumptuous ancestry!)

In verses 5–8, the psalm shifts to focus on the divine creation of the cosmos and the establishment of order in the world. Chaos is represented by the seas, the waves, the people (and the roaring and tumult). Over against these, God establishes, stills, and pacifies so that the regularity of nature in which the mornings and evenings follow each other provides successive shouts for joy.

The verses in the psalm most reflective of the theme of thanksgiving as an agricultural festival are verses 9–13. The entire cycle of the harvest year is reflected in these verses. There is reference, first, to the autumn rains (called the early rains) that water the ground and make plowing and sowing possible. In Palestine, the summer, from about mid-May until late September or early October, is completely rainless. During this period, the land dries up and vegetation dies. The early fall rains, from "the river of God" in the heavenly world, soften the land and seeding follows. The winter rains make possible the growth of grain. Then in the late spring, harvest occurs. The harvest in verses 11–13 speaks of the bounty of the spring season; God's wagon drips fatness upon the land. Pastures, hills, meadows, and valleys give forth their crops and newborn animals, all considered the blessings of God.

Romans 8:1–11

A portion of today's text (8:6–11) serves as the epistolary reading for the Fifth Sunday in Lent in Year A. The reader may want to consult our remarks on this text earlier in this volume.

One thing that distinguishes today's text from its earlier use during Lent is that it oc-curs as part of the semicontinuous reading of the Epistle to the Romans that began with Proper 4 [9]. The first move, then, is to place it in its literary context and to see it as arising from Paul's discussion of the law in chapter 7.

If Paul, in chapter 7, succeeds in underscoring the tension and despair experienced by everyone who tries to live morally, in chapter 8 he strikes a much more confident note. His spontaneous prayer thanking God for being rescued through Christ (7:25) now gives way to the bold declaration that "there is therefore now no condemnation for those who are in Christ Jesus" (8:1). Any ambivalence that was previously experienced is now replaced by the believer's firm confidence that God's decisive action in Christ has dramatically changed things.

Here he contrasts two "laws," or two principles, by which religious existence can be ordered: "the law of the Spirit of life in Christ Jesus" and "the law of sin and of death" (v. 2). The former is said to have liberated us from the latter. Here Paul sees God's action in Christ—"sending his own Son in the likeness of sinful flesh, and to deal with sin" (v. 3)—as achieving what had not and could not be achieved through the Mosaic law. A central feature of Paul's argument is his understanding of the death of Christ as a sacrificial act, understood in terms of Levitical sacrifice. To be sure, his death was not completely analogous to the sacrificial offering of an animal, and Paul was well aware of this. And yet Paul regarded Christ's death as sacrificial in the sense that his life was being given up, "sacrificed," on behalf of others, in particular on behalf of others' sins. Moreover, his form of death bore its own stigma, and in this sense acquired the stigma of sin. Because his form of death technically violated the law, Christ thereby became "sinful flesh." Accordingly, the strict requirement of the law was met, namely, that a sacrifice was offered for the sin of others, and thereby we became the recipients of his sacrificial death.

But what was at work in this process, according to Paul, was a higher principle, one in which God's life-giving Spirit became focused in Christ Jesus (v. 2). Because Christ represented the locus of this energizing force, his beneficiaries, those "in Christ," are thereby defined by this newly expressed principle. The resulting life-style is thus described as "walking according to the Spirit," which is sharply contrasted with its antithesis, "walking according to the flesh" (vv. 4–5). Each of these modes of life is typified by "outlooks," here described as "setting one's mind" toward these respective domains.

The contours of these two "worlds" are described in verses 9–11. When Paul speaks of "in the flesh" and "in the Spirit" as two mutually hostile realms of existence where we might live, he envisions two spheres of influence that pose options for establishing our identity. Here his thought is thoroughly dualistic: flesh and Spirit represent two antithetical forces (8:5).

But Paul recognizes that deciding on the world in which we live is part of a reciprocal process. Where we live is actually determined by another, perhaps even prior, decision: who or what we allow to live within us. What we inhabit is determined by what inhabits us. The way we shape our world results from what we allow to shape us. Living "in the Spirit" is predicated on the Spirit "living within us" (vv. 9, 11). Moral transformation may occur within us so that our existence may be said to be "in Christ Jesus" (8:1, 2), but the vital complement to our being in Christ is God's presence within us (v. 10).

This close association between our being in God's presence and God's presence within us is reflected in the psalmist's prayer: "Do not cast me away from your presence, and do not take your holy spirit from me" (Ps. 51:11). For the psalmist, to be "in God" is to be indwelt by God's divine Spirit. To have God's Spirit taken away is to be banished from the divine presence. Not to have God's Spirit within is to be evicted from life and before God.

To be sure, divine presence in our text is understood christologically. "Spirit of God" and "Spirit of Christ" are all but indistinguishable, and yet the presence of Christ within us is a clear sign of identity, possession, and ownership (vv. 9–10). Moreover, our own resurrection hinges on Christ's resurrection (v. 11; cf. 1 Thess. 4:14; 1 Cor. 6:14; 15:20-21; 2 Cor. 4:14; 13:4; Rom. 6:5; Eph. 2:6; Col. 1:18; 2:12–13; 2 Tim. 2:11). It is the Spirit of God who demonstrated the capacity to bring life from death in the resurrection of Christ that now provides the energizing, life-giving force to Christian existence—but not *in absentia*, not remotely, but by its indwelling presence "within us" (v. 11).

For Christ to be "in us" does not ignore the reality of our moral struggle (v. 10). We still experience the presence of Christ within our mortal existence, within our bodies that are "dead because of sin." When Christ comes into the house, it is not as if all the inhabitants immediately evacuate (cf. Mark 3:27). Sin still occurs. When we sin, we still place ourselves on a collision course with death. But while our "bodies," our "selves," still work under normal, human constraints and weaknesses, our "spirits" begin to experience a new life. The Christ-event of death and resurrection begins to play itself out within us. We go through the cycle of death, and in doing so, experience the effects of sin; yet we also go through the cycle of resurrection, and in doing so taste God's righteousness as we experience God's "righting" action. Death in us still? Yes! But Life emerging too? Yes! Death in conflict with Life, but gradually giving way to Life and Righteousness—eventually realized fully when God bestows on us resurrection life (v. 11).

Matthew 13:1–9, 18–23

We have today the first of three lections drawn from Matthew 13, a collection of parables with some explanations. This constitutes the third major body of Jesus' teachings in Matthew (ending at 13:53), the Sermon on the Mount and the Mission Charge being the first two. Because three Sundays will focus on parables, the preacher will probably want to study verses 10–17, omitted from our lection, and read one or two commentaries on the nature of parables and methods of interpretation. Verse 9, "Let anyone with ears listen," certainly implies a weight of importance and a burden on the listener beyond that which would accompany simple stories or illustrations, as some have supposed parables to be.

The entirety of Matthew 13:1–23 consists of four parts: (1) the parable of the sower (vv. 1–9); (2) Jesus' explanation of why he speaks in parables (vv. 10–15); (3) Jesus' blessing on the disciples (vv. 16–17); and (4) the interpretation of the parable of the sower (vv. 18–23). Our present concern is only with the parable and its interpretation.

All three Synoptics have the parable of the sower and its interpretation (Mark 4:1–9, 13–20; Luke 8:4–8, 11–15). Both Mark and Matthew locate the parable teachings beside the sea. Matthew has Jesus going out of the house (13:1), perhaps vaguely referring to the house in Capernaum, but Capernaum has not been mentioned since 9:28. Perhaps it is more helpful to take the sea as the public side of Jesus' teaching in parables, and the house (13:1, 36) as the private, because the parables both reveal and conceal. Efforts by Joachim Jeremias and others to recover the original locations and audiences of the parables have never been very successful.

On the face of it, the parable of the sower is a simple story drawn from ordinary life. A sower scatters seed in a field prior to plowing, as was the custom in Palestinian farming. Naturally, the seed fell indiscriminately among weeds, on rocks, on the path worn by passersby, as well as in the good soil. And again quite naturally, the yield at harvesttime was largely determined by the differences in the soil. Verse 9 implies that the story is very important, but not everyone will understand it. Verses 10–17 give the clear impression that the crowds are confused by this and other parables, whereas the disciples discern the meanings. However, such was not the case apparently, for the parable had to be explained to them.

The interpretation of the parable of the sower (vv. 18–23) presents a number of problems for the reader. In the first place, it is doubtful that Jesus explained his own parables. The explanation seems to lie in the Christian tradition between Jesus and the Gospel writers. Second, the interpretation is allegorical; that is, each item of the story (sower, seed, weeds, rocks, good soil) is said to represent something else. To allegorize is to say something other than what one is saying. Once a popular method of biblical interpretation, allegorizing is today viewed with suspicion; it allows meanings to run rampant. Third, the wording of the interpretation is confusing. Matthew improves upon Mark, but the phrasing leaves it unclear whether the various hearers are what is sown (although the seed is the word of the kingdom, v. 19) or the soil or both.

Even so, the preacher can safely assume that the parable deals with the variety of ways listeners respond to the word. For different reasons, different hearers fail to become fruitful Christians, whereas others respond so positively as to make the enterprise of witnessing and teaching worthwhile. We cannot know for sure whether Jesus' intent was to explain why there is some failure in the mission or to encourage his disciples by pointing to the good soil and the abundant yield. Both perspectives are valid, for they are two sides of the same coin. Certainly in Matthew's context, and in the context of many communities since that time, doubt, criticism, rejection, and disappointment make the parable a welcome word not simply of explanation, but of assurance to Jesus' followers.

Proper 11 [16]
(Sunday between July 17 and 23 inclusive)

Genesis 28:10–19a;
Psalm 139:1–12, 23–24; or
Wisdom of Solomon 12:13, 16–19 or
Isaiah 44:6–8;
Psalm 86:11–17;
Romans 8:12–25;
Matthew 13:24–30, 36–43

The Old Testament lection in the *Common Lectionary* is the report of Jacob's dream at Bethel in which he receives the promise that his descendants would become a nation through whom all peoples would be blessed. Even though Psalm 139 is a lament, the opening and closing verses that constitute today's psalm, in familiar words and memorable images, reassuringly acknowledge God's universal presence and power.

A choice of Old Testament readings is provided for those not using the *Common Lectionary*. The text from the Wisdom of Solomon highlights the theme of God's leniency, whereas the selection from Isaiah 44 affirms God's uniqueness. The concluding portion of Psalm 86, which is a direct request for God's instructive help, stems from confidence in God's love and compassion.

Following directly on last week's epistolary lesson, today's Epistle reading testifies to the Spirit's presence in enabling filial obedience, but also graphically envisions the cosmic transformation that will eventually result in the liberation of the created order. The Gospel reading, the Matthean version of the parable of the weeds in the field, speaks about salvation, redemption, and judgment.

Genesis 28:10–19a

In the story of his dream at Bethel, Jacob will experience divine revelation and receive the promise originally given to Abraham. It is one of the two high points in the Jacob tradition; the other is in the Old Testament reading for Proper 13 [18], Genesis 32:22–32. Given our usual expectations about those whom God calls and blesses, this story is all the more remarkable when we consider the character of Jacob as presented in the rest of the tradition. From his very birth he was a grasper (Gen. 25:26), and in his early manhood he took advantage of his hungry and less civilized brother, buying Esau's birthright for a bowl of soup (Gen. 25:29–34). Then when Isaac, his father, was dying, and with the assistance of his mother, Jacob deceived his father to gain the blessing that he had bartered from Esau. In that process he played upon his father's weaknesses. Although he was initially tricked by his father-in-law, Laban, eventually he outwitted Laban on two occasions, once to obtain wealth (Gen. 30:37–43) and once to flee from Laban's homeland (Gen. 31:17–42). When he returns to meet his brother, Jacob is afraid of Esau in spite of God's promise of protection, so he hides behind the women and children (Gen. 32:6–8). He is nowhere presented, like Abraham, as a hero of faith. He is the shrewd and successful shepherd who can get the best of anyone he encounters.

Jacob's experience at Bethel comes at a critical point in the story. The patriarch is leaving the land of Canaan, in which his father, Isaac, and his grandfather, Abraham, had lived as resident aliens, to return for a while to the territory of their ancestors in northwest Mesopotamia, where he will eventually acquire wives and children before returning. The encounter with God takes place during his trip from the one land for the other. It is not a simple journey, however, but an escape. Jacob is a fugitive fleeing for his life from the wrath of his brother, on the advice of his mother. He is at great risk from the known behind him and the unknown before him.

Genesis 28:10–17, although a coherent unit, includes only the first part of the story of Jacob's dream at Bethel; the complete account includes verses 18–22 as well. Our reading is the interweaving of material from the two older pentateuchal sources, the Yahwist and the Elohist. Different divine names, Yahweh ("Lord") and Elohim ("God"), appear in consecutive verses (vv. 12–13 and vv. 16–17), and verses 16 and 17 are repetitions. In verse 12 the revelation is a dream of angels (E), whereas in verse 13 (J) Yahweh himself addresses Jacob. Characteristic theological interests of the different writers have been merged into a single story. The Elohist (vv. 10–12, 17–18, 20–22) understands revelation in terms of dreams and angels, whereas the Yahwist (vv. 13–16, 19) never loses sight of the promise to the patriarchs.

Skillfully, the narrator reports that Jacob stopped to spend the night at an unnamed "certain place" (v. 11). The designation of the name, of course, is reserved for the conclusion, and there is already a distinct sense of the site as a place of destiny. The ancestor did not plan to spend the night there, but stopped where he was when the sun went down. Thus the events that follow take place at night.

The remainder of the narrative consists of the account of the revelation (vv. 12–15) and of Jacob's reaction to it (vv. 16–22). The revelation occurs in a dream of a ladder—"stairway" (NRSV footnote and NJPSV) is a more accurate reading—connecting earth and heaven, and "the angels of God were ascending and descending on it" (v. 12). Commentators since the late nineteenth century have recognized here connections with the Mesopotamian ziggurats, temple towers where the Divine and human met. Then Yahweh, identifying himself as the God of Abraham and Isaac, spoke to Jacob and proclaimed the by-now familiar promise. Jacob's reaction upon awakening is awe, acknowledgment of the meaning of the revelation, and acts of piety.

The passage is concerned with explaining the origin of a sacred place and rituals associated with it, and on more than one level. The story explains the name Bethel ("house of God") in terms of Jacob's exclamation when he awoke (vv. 17, 19). In fact, this is not the first time the place name has been encountered in the patriarchal stories. Abraham had built an altar there (Gen. 12:8) and returned to it later (Gen. 13:4). Bethel was well known during the era of the Israelite monarchy. More important than the origin of the name is the story's understanding of holy places. One does not simply choose a place and make it holy, for example, by building a sanctuary or an altar. Its sacredness must be either discovered or disclosed, and then recognized.

Theologically, the heart of the story is the Lord's promise to Jacob. It begins with only a slightly modified form of the promise initially given to Abraham (Gen. 12:1–3) that the patriarch's descendants would possess the land (v. 13). They would become a great nation both numerically and geographically (v. 14a) through whom all nations would be blessed (v. 14b; see the comments on Gen. 12:1–9 for Proper 5 [10] in this volume). In addition, there is a special promise appropriate for the specific occasion. Jacob is leaving the land, and Yahweh promises to be with him and bring him back (v. 15). Behind this pledge is the uncertainty that stems from the ancient idea that gods were attached to particular lands. Yahweh, however, will be where he chooses to be and with whom he chooses to be.

The biblical text does not make specific connections between the patriarch's character and the promise. We cannot help but note, however, that the grace of God comes to the fugitive fleeing for his life, the one who is no model of faith. What is manifest here is the Lord's will, not human design. The Lord wills to bless a particular people and through them all families of the earth.

Psalm 139:1–12, 23–24

This psalm appears to be a composition produced for use in legal procedures in the temple when an individual was charged, perhaps falsely, with some particular wrong or crime. In Psalm 139, the wrong appears to be some form of idolatry or turning away from Yahweh, the God of Israel. This is suggested by three factors: (1) there is no indication in the psalm of charges about injury or wrong done to humans; (2) the "wicked way" (v. 24), or, in some readings of the Hebrew text, "idolatrous way," suggests apostasy or false worship as the problem; and (3) the plea for action by God in verses 19–24, especially verses 19–22, focuses attention on those who defy God, lift themselves up against him, and hate him, which demonstrates the concern for the proper relationship to the Deity as the focus of the psalm.

The psalm is best understood as the lament of one who feels unduly and falsely accused of infidelity to God. Verses 1–18 speak about the Deity's knowledge of the worshiper, whereas verses 19–24 are a call for God to judge and slay the wicked. Thus the latter verses would have functioned as one's self-curse if the person praying them fit the category of those upon whom the judgment is requested. At the same time, verses 21–22 are also an affirmation of the worshiper's innocence. The worshiper can claim to hate, with a perfect (or utter) hatred, those who hate God. Although such an expression may shock our sophisticated sensibilities, it was a way of expressing devotion to God, championing the divine cause, and placing oneself squarely in God's camp. Under these circumstances, such extravagance in terminology would have been expected in ancient cultures.

Verses 1–8 all speak or confess the knowledge that God has of the human/individual situation. (Note that the entire psalm is human speech to the Divine; that is, prayer.) Verses 1–6 describe the *insight* God has into the life of the individual. Verses 7–12 describe the divine *oversight* that God has of the individual life. Verses 13–18 speak of the divine *foresight* that

God has over the person from conception to death. In a way, all these sections seek to say the same thing by approaching the matter from different perspectives or slightly different angles. The reason for such extensive coverage of the topic of God's knowledge of the individual is the fact that the supplicant in the legal case was claiming innocence, and one way to do this was to point to the omniscience of God. Had anything been amiss, were there any infidelity, then the Deity would surely have known and taken action.

The insight that God is said to have into the person in verses 1–5 is expressed in a number of ways, mostly in the form of opposites: sitting down—rising up (inactive—active); inward thoughts—from afar; my path (where I go, my walking)—my lying down (where I rest, my reclining); behind—before. All these are ways of saying that persons in the totality of their behavior are known to God. Even the thought, before it finds expression on the tongue in words, is known (v. 4). The knowledge of God, the psalmist confesses, is a fathomless mystery (v. 6).

Verses 7–12 affirm that there is no escaping the Deity, whose presence (=Spirit) knows no limit and who is not subject to the normal conditions of existence. A number of geographical metaphors, again in opposites, are employed to illustrate the point: heaven—Sheol; winds of the morning (to the east)—uttermost parts of the sea (to the western horizon). In all these places, the psalmist says he or she would find God (see Amos 9:2) or be found by God. The psalm, however, not only affirms the all-pervasive knowledge and oversight of God, but also the universal sustaining quality of the Divine—"Thy hand shall lead me, and thy right hand shall hold me."

For the Divine, according to the psalmist, normal conditions do not prevail. Verse 11 makes this point, a point best expressed in the new NJPSV which, following medieval Jewish exegetes, translates: "If I say, 'Surely darkness will conceal me, night will provide me with cover,'" then darkness does not conceal, because for God light and darkness do not determine or set limits regarding knowledge.

Wisdom of Solomon 12:13, 16–19

This alternate Old Testament lesson occurs in a section that praises the sovereignty of God. In the preceding verses, God is said to have shown leniency even to the Canaanites, even though their practices were inimical to Israelite ways. This theme is continued into the section from which today's passage is taken.

The (implied) author of our text first comes to God's defense, asking a series of rhetorical questions that relate to God's ways of dealing with the nations. Yet quite emphatically are we told that God's care is universal in scope. Moreover, because God has acted equitably toward all people, no accusations can be made against God that really stick. Thus God is not required to answer before a human court.

These themes are repeated in the second half of today's text. God's universal sovereignty is said to translate into universal leniency. Those who wonder about God's power can be expected to see demonstrations of this power. Yet God is able to combine sovereign strength with merciful forbearance in a way that commends respect in any court, earthly or heavenly.

Thus we have before us in this text a brief but powerful statement about God's benevolence and impartiality combined with an uncompromising belief in God's universal sovereignty.

Isaiah 44:6–8

The mood of enthusiastic and animated gladness in these verses is typical of the speeches of this prophet, Second Isaiah. His proclamations both express the joy of the good news he brings and mean to evoke happiness in his audience. That audience would have consisted of the Babylonian exiles from Judah, ca. 539 BC, just before the end of the Exile. Obviously, a great many of them had lost all hope of returning to their homeland, the land promised to the patriarchs and given to them in the time of Joshua. Their hopelessness was one of the impediments to the actualization of the good news that the prophet proclaimed. So one of the tasks that Second Isaiah faced was that of kindling the expectation that God would act to save them.

The three verses of today's reading are part of a fuller unit, Isaiah 44:1–8, and are best understood in that context. The unit is a prophetic address that begins with a traditional call to attention that identifies the addressees: "But now hear, O Jacob my servant, Israel whom I have chosen" (v. 1; cf. Amos 3:1; 4:1; 5:1; Isa. 1:2, 10). It contains messenger formulas ("Thus says the Lord," vv. 2, 6) indicating that the prophet is not speaking for himself, and the speaker clearly is God. In terms of both form and content, the passage contains two distinct units. The first, verses 1–5, is a proclamation, or announcement, of salvation concerning the immediate future. The second, verses 6–8, is a divine disputation in which God speaks to argue that there is no other god. The larger section of which our text is a part (Isa. 43:8–44:8) is a poetic imitation of a legal process in which the question of who is God is argued. Verses 6–8 conclude that all others are pretenders, beyond comparison with God, and insist that the people of Israel can testify as witnesses to this fact. They know that God announced events before they happened, and then they came to pass. What ties the two units together is a phrase they have in common, "Do not fear" (vv. 2, 8). The expression is a salvation oracle, long known in Israelite worship and prayer, a formula pronounced by priests or prophets to people in trouble who petitioned God. It means what it says—the people should no longer fear—but it also conveys the sense that God has heard the people's deepest prayers and means to act in their behalf.

These eight verses contain the basic message of Second Isaiah. Above all, Yahweh is about to intervene to save Israel, his chosen and beloved people (vv. 1–2), from their distress. Their problems are "spiritual," but they are also concrete and physical. Thus the Lord will bring them back to their land, giving them their freedom. Here that promise is stated somewhat metaphorically in the allusions to "water on the thirsty land" (v. 3a), suggesting the return to Israel through the desert (cf. Isa. 40:3, 17–20). The foundation for that message of good news is the affirmation that Israel's God is in fact God, the only one. This confession insists that God is both powerful ("King") and loving ("Redeemer," v. 6a).

The distinctive motif in this passage as a whole is the announcement of the gift of the Spirit of God and its effects (vv. 3–5). The pouring out of the Spirit upon the people of God is compared to pouring "water on the thirsty land" and is parallel to the granting of divine blessing. The Spirit of God is an extension of God's will, God active in and through human beings, and it brings dramatic transformations of the people to whom it is given. Two transformations are described, one metaphorically and the other quite directly. First, the people will grow and thrive "like a green tamarisk, like willows by flowing streams" (v. 4); they and their descendants will receive new life with the gift of the Spirit (cf. Ezek. 37:1–14). Second, they will know and affirm who they are, saying and writing on their hands that they belong to the Lord and calling themselves by the name of Jacob or Israel (v. 6). In view of the opening lines of the address (vv. 1–2), it appears that to identify with Jacob or Israel is to acknowledge that one is God's chosen servant. It is entirely possible that the gift of the Spirit is not limited to the people of Israel, but that others will now choose to identify themselves with the chosen people of God.

Thus the outpouring of the Spirit is a gift from the one who alone is God (vv. 6–8); it is given not fundamentally to individuals but to the people of God; it brings those people to life; and it enables them to know who and whose they are.

Psalm 86:11–17

A portion of this psalm was discussed earlier at Proper 7 [12]. Verse 11 may be taken as the plea or appeal for help, which in this case appeals, first, for God to instruct the worshiper so that divine truth may be known and, second, for a unified, committed heart or will that resolves to reverence the divine name, that is, to live in harmony with the knowledge of the Divine.

Verses 12–13 contain the vow of thanksgiving made by the worshiper, a vow in which promises are made to serve and praise God sincerely. The vow takes a very positive form as if the worshiper had already been granted a positive hearing by God. According to verse 13b, the person is thankful for having been rescued from Sheol, that is, from a life-threatening illness. Sheol was the realm of the deceased (see Deut. 32:22; Ps. 6:5) where existence continued but in a greatly diminished form. The "depths" of Sheol does not mean that levels of existence were characteristic of Sheol, although this view did develop in later apocalyptic thought.

In verses 14–17, lamentation is renewed, and the worshiper's distress is again described, but in very general terms. Verse 15 may be compared with Exodus 34:6. The description of the worshiper in verse 16 places the person in a state of need by claiming the status of a child born to a slave in the household. (NRSV's "serving girl" as a translation probably should be avoided. The older translation "maidservant" or "handmaiden" is less demeaning.) The usage is metaphorical; the psalm may actually have been spoken by the king (see v. 9 and the discussion at Proper 7 [12]).

Romans 8:12–25

I n last week's epistolary lection (8:1–11), we noted a distinction between "living in" and "living according to." Whereas the former stresses the sphere of existence in which we might live, the latter stresses the norms or standards by which we might live. In verses 1–11, there is a recurrent emphasis on the locative: where we live, our participation *in* the Spirit, ourselves as the residence of the Spirit. In the opening part of today's text (vv. 12–17), we note a shift from life "in" to life "according to," from *is* to *ought*, from indicative to imperative, where the concern is not so much on *where* we live but *how* we live.

In verses 12–17, we note an emphasis on moral obligation: "so then," that is, in light of how your existence is defined—by living in the "world" of God, Christ, and the Spirit, and by having all Three "live in" us—"we have an obligation" (v. 12, NIV). This is the language of ought, or ethical imperative.

We should first note the correlation between "living in" and "living according to." Where we live has norming effect on us. Context does affect behavior. Two norming possibilities are held out: flesh and Spirit. The one is associated with death, the other with life. Indeed, death and life not only set the contours of existence within each, but define the *teloi*, the ends toward which each inexorably takes us.

More is envisioned in life "with Christ" than divine presence. It is not simply that the Spirit indwells us; it actively directs us: we find ourselves being "guided by the Spirit of God" (v. 14, NJB). So powerful is this pull that its effect is transforming: slaves become transformed into children. To be a slave is to be without freedom, under oppression and tyranny from forces or persons over whom we have no power (8:2). The natural corollary of slavehood is fear (v. 15).

But being a child means becoming an heir (v. 17). As "children of God" we share in Christ's own cherished status as "child of God," thereby becoming coparticipants with Christ of God's blessing of resurrection life, and with it genuine freedom before God and the world.

But to be God's child in the sense that Christ was should not be idealized or romanticized; it entails suffering and scandal (v. 17). Yet God's Spirit bears witness to our true identity precisely in those moments when we not only question who we are, perhaps even forget who we are, but also when we may desert who we are. In those moments, we feel the tug of God's Spirit reminding us, "You are God's child. Now behave like one!"

The second part of today's text (vv. 18–25) follows naturally from the first, which concludes by mentioning "sharing [Christ's] suffering, so as to share his glory" (v. 17, NJB). If it was Christ's lot to suffer, so does it appear to be ours, who are co-heirs with him (cf. Mark 10:39–40; Luke 22:28–30; Rom. 5:3–5). How, then, can we cope with the reality of suffering and its inevitability?

The answer of today's text is: "live in hope." The thrust here is forward: suffering in this life is contrasted with "the glory, as yet unrevealed, which is in store for us" (v. 18, REB). Suffering and splendor, pain and glory—these are the two poles of the Christ-event. They correspond to death and resurrection. Christ suffered death, to be sure, but God raised him to new life, a life of splendid glory. His fate, his destiny, charts the course for everyone who enters his story, lives in it and by it, and thus is said to be "in Christ" (2 Cor. 4:10–11; Col. 3:3–4).

What keeps Paul's response here from being artificial and hollow is to recall that Christ himself suffered "in hope." Because we read the gospel story from this side of Easter, we tend to think that Christ knew in advance that glory would be his automatically and that this somehow diminished the impact of his suffering. Yet the Gospel accounts of Christ's passion and death suggest otherwise. They show him suffering and facing death in a way that tested his faith and refined his hope. To think otherwise is to suppose that Christ lived by sight rather than by faith. Experiencing the splendor of divine salvation is "something we are able to wait for with persevering confidence" (v. 25, NJB), even as Christ did (Heb. 5:7–10).

There is something else besides the example of Christ that makes it possible to cope. It is to realize that our own suffering is part of a much larger process. This is more than simply saying that other people suffer as we do, even though realizing that what we endure others have endured often helps us cope.

Rather, Paul envisions "the whole creation" (v. 19, NJB), or "the created universe" (REB), as having been launched on a course of suffering by the sin of Adam. Behind his remarks in verses 19–20 are clear allusions to the creation story, especially Genesis 3:17–19. We are told that the created order "was made subject to frustration, not of its own choice but by the will of him who subjected it" (v. 20, REB). The crucial exegetical question here is, Who is "him"—

God or Adam? Was it God who subjected the created order and set it on its course of pain and suffering, as punishment for Adam's sin? So suggests JB: "It was not for any fault on the part of creation that it was made unable to attain its purpose, it was made so by God" (v. 20). Or, if this sounds too vindictive and incompatible with our conception of God, we might prefer to fault Adam, the one whose sin was ultimately responsible for things going awry.

In spite of its predicament, however, the created order still lives "in hope" (v. 20). Here we face another exegetical choice—whether "in hope" concludes verse 20 or introduces verse 21. If the former, it would appear that God subjected the created order to an existence of frustration, yet did so "in hope" that such punishment would be redemptive. If the latter, the hope of creation is that it might someday be freed "from its slavery to corruption" (so NRSV, REB, NIV). This may even be a hope that is seen from our own vantage point—looking back, "yet with hope" (v. 20, REB).

In spite of this exegetical difficulty, the point is clear: the created order, taken in the most comprehensive sense, is viewed as living in hope. To be sure, it has been shackled with mortality, encumbered with all the pain and suffering that accompany earthly existence. Yet it looks for a better day and faces the future with hope rather than despair.

To make his point even more vividly, Paul uses the metaphor of childbirth. He envisions the created universe as "groaning in labor pains" (v. 22). In its attempt to usher fresh, innocent life into the world, the universe is afflicted with severe labor pains. Thus, to give birth to life inevitably entails pain and suffering. We are asked to imagine the whole cosmos crying out with groans and labor pains as it tries to bring forth new life. It is a vivid image and one we do well to ponder.

What happens in the cosmos also happens in the person. Macrocosmic pain and suffering have their counterpart in the microcosm of individual suffering. In Christ, we have experienced the "first fruits of the Spirit" (v. 23; cf. 2 Cor. 1:22; 5:5; Eph. 1:14); that is, God has given us the Spirit as payment in advance of the life to come. New life has entered us through the insemination of God's Spirit, and now we too "are groaning inside ourselves, waiting with eagerness for our bodies to be set free" (v. 23, NJB; cf. 2 Cor. 5:2, 4). The metaphor shifts slightly here, but the point is clear. Like the cosmos in general, we too experience the painful groaning that accompanies our mortal existence, and we await that moment of birth to a new existence where our salvation becomes complete.

Few of us are accustomed to thinking of the created order in terms as personalistic as this. For us, the created order consists of animate and inanimate existence. Humans and animals may squeal with pain, but not rocks, trees, and stars. Yet for Paul the whole created order is engaged in a painful process of cosmic transformation that will culminate in the Eschaton, when suffering gives way to splendor. To think this way might give us greater pause as we plunder the earth, and now space. It may help shatter the illusion that we can do as we please with the inanimate and lifeless, as if no pain can be inflicted on it. Yet we are gradually learning that the fate of the earth and of space is also our fate, that our destiny is indissolubly connected to the destiny of creation.

Matthew 13:24–30, 36–43

We continue today with the second of three lessons from Matthew 13, a chapter devoted to Jesus' parables and comments about them. A quick review of the statements introducing last Sunday's lection might be helpful. As was true of that lection, today's text consists of a parable and its interpretation.

The parable of the weeds growing in the wheat replaced the parable of the seed growing secretly, in Mark's sequence (4:26–29), a story with which Matthew's replacement has very little in common. In fact, Matthew's parable of the weeds is different from most of Jesus' parables in one important respect. Although its story line is based on a common fact of experience (weeds grew in wheat fields; weeds were gathered in bundles and burned for fuel while the wheat was preserved in "barns"; and some weeds resembled the wheat in early stages so that wheat was lost in the removal of weeds), still there are elements in the story that call unusual attention to themselves. These elements do not serve to make the story natural and normal but alert the reader to anticipate special meanings. In other words, the reader is "set up" by the story to receive an interpretation, almost as though Matthew began with the interpretation and worked back to the story. For example: the seeds are sown, not by the servants as one would expect, but by the owner, and the weeds by "his enemy." Who would assume common weeds were sown by anyone? A conflict situation is created. Or again, twice it is said the householder sowed "good seed." What other kind would he sow? The word "good" prepares us for its counterpart, evil. Or again, the servants are not to separate the weeds until the harvest when, in fact, farmers of that day more than once during a growing season would remove weeds from a grain field. We are prepared to antici-pate a day of reckoning.

This parable and its interpretation, found only in Matthew, is clearly Matthean in its perspective. The interpretation is again allegorical and needs little comment. However, a few elements call for attention. The parable presupposes a church situation in which Jesus' disci-ples are tempted to become involved in purging evil. Because "the field is the world" (v. 38), it is unclear whether the desire of Jesus' followers is to remove evil from the world or, as is more likely, from within the church. Matthew's church certainly contained undesirable ele-ments (7:21–23; 18:15–20), and in that church, as in many others, the desire to achieve purity and perfection was in tension with the obligation to accept, forgive, and restore.

The master's injunction against efforts to expunge evil had three reasons behind it. First, such attempts now are premature. Second, such attempts have as their usual result the disturbance and loss of the faithful in the process of seeking to eliminate the unfaithful. And third, the task of judging between good and evil belongs not to us but to Christ. We are not to judge (7:1) but rather to work at reconciliation (18:15–16) and to forgive without limitation (18:21–22). Christ will come in the end time as judge of all people (16:27; 25:31–46). Once the weeds (evildoers) have been separated forever, then the wheat (righteous) will be gathered into the kingdom of God (vv. 42–43; 1 Cor. 15:24–28).

However Matthew's frequent theme of a final judgment may sound to subsequent readers, to the church originally addressed it spoke two words clearly: first, do not fret over evildoers, for neither their present nor their future is your responsibility; and second, God will bring history to a close with justice, and the saints finally will be freed from abuse and oppression. The parable of the weeds in the wheat is therefore not a threatening but a comforting word.

Proper 12 [17]
(Sunday between July 24 and 30 inclusive)

Genesis 29:15–28;
Psalm 105:1–11, 45b or
Psalm 128; or
1 Kings 3:5–12;
Psalm 119:129–36;
Romans 8:26–39;
Matthew 13:31–33, 44–52

The story of Jacob's marriage to Leah and Rachel, occasioned by Laban's deception, provides the Old Testament reading for the *Common Lectionary*. The selection from Psalm 105 celebrates God's fidelity to the covenant made with Israel, whereas Psalm 128 speaks of the blessings of prosperity and family that come to those devoted to God.

Today's Old Testament reading for those who use other lectionaries is Solomon's prayer for wisdom, couched in pious sentiments not ordinarily associated with this colorful Israelite king. The portion of Psalm 119 that constitutes this responsorial reading, in tones reminiscent of Solomon's prayer, acknowledges God as the source of wisdom and shows the psalmist eagerly yielding before God for instruction and guidance.

In the Epistle lesson, Paul assures his audience of the divine help available in living the Christian life and in shaping the community of those chosen by God. The Gospel lesson contains six parables about the nature and life of the kingdom.

Genesis 29:15–28

Today's reading is among those texts that remind us just how strange the world of the Bible is. Genesis 29:15–28, with its allusions to polygamy and servitude for wives, sounds almost quaint to modern Western ears. Even in the narrator's day, many of these customs were antiquated. For the writer and the early readers, these were events of a time long ago and far away. The practice described here without any reprobation at all is expressly prohibited in Leviticus 18:18: To marry two sisters, either at the same time or successively, constitutes incest (from the later priestly legislation). Part of the attraction of the story, even for the ancient readers, lay in its strangeness.

373

Despite the alien features of the story, we can quickly find ourselves identifying with the characters, suspending our own sense of proper social and family relationships and living in the narrative's world for a while. Most of the information necessary to understand the cultural background of the story can be deduced from the narrative itself or from its context.

Although it can and should be seen as a self-contained story, it is useful to remember its broader context in the saga of Jacob. The events take place in Laban's land, the region in upper Mesopotamia where Abraham had originated and sent for Rebekah, Jacob's mother. Jacob was there because he had fled from the wrath of his brother. These events stand between the two key turning points of the Jacob story, the encounter at Bethel (Gen. 28:10–22) and at the ford of the Jabbok (Gen. 32:22–32). We may remember, although the narrator does not remind us, that Yahweh had vowed to be with Jacob (Gen. 28:15) during this period of absence from the promised land and eventually bring him back.

The story actually begins in 28:1–14, another meeting at a well that will lead to marriage that is similar in important respects to Genesis 25 and to Exodus 2, especially the latter account of Moses and the daughters of the priest of Midian. In Genesis 25, the future wife had given water to Abraham's servant; here Jacob helps Rachel water her father's flock. They meet and greet one another as relatives, and Rachel's father, Laban, welcomes the penniless relative into his household.

As our text begins, we are unaware of the conflict that will arise. Laban initiates a discussion with Jacob concerning his remuneration and his status, for he is neither a servant nor a hired man but a relative. The narrator pauses to point out that Laban had two daughters, Leah, whose eyes were "lovely" (or "weak," NJPSV—the meaning of the Hebrew is uncertain), and her younger sister, the beautiful Rachel whom Jacob had already met. Having followed the story to its conclusion, we will recognize that this note sets up the conflict to follow. Jacob very generously offers to work for seven years for the hand of the younger sister, whom he "loved" (v. 18). It is a subtle touch that Laban's response (v. 19), heard as agreement, leaves the door open for the future deception.

When Jacob has served his term, he asks for his reward, and Laban hosts the marriage feast. Only when it is time to bring the bride to the groom do we learn of Laban's deception, the substitution of Leah for Rachel (v. 23). We are not supposed to ask how Jacob could have been so blind. The bride was veiled and it was dark. By the time Jacob discovers the treachery it is too late, for he has consummated the marriage with the wrong sister.

Naturally, Jacob objects to this deception. The reader is invited to identify with his anger, but also to laugh at him and with Laban at the monstrous practical joke. Moreover, we are supposed to accept—as Jacob is—Laban's explanation: It would be contrary to our customs to give the younger daughter in marriage before the older (v. 26). Laban urges Jacob to "complete the week" of Leah (v. 27), that is, allow the week-long marriage feast (Judg. 14:12) to continue. The conclusion is anticlimactic: Jacob can have Rachel as well for another seven years of service. Presumably, Jacob did not have to wait but married her when the week was out. Laban has accomplished several things besides demonstrating his superior wit. He has secured a husband for not one but both of his daughters, and within the family, and he has gained another seven years of service from this naïve relative.

Our reading, this tale of two sisters, concludes before the story points out that Jacob loved Rachel more than he loved Leah (28:30). Behind this note is both the sibling conflict between the older and the younger, and the tribal conflict between those who traced their ancestry to the one mother and the other.

If we remember that Jacob had deceived his father by posing as his older brother, we may feel that Laban's deception—substituting the older sister for the younger—serves him right. In the Jacob story as a whole, this ironic twist is not to be missed. It is the story of the trickster who is tricked. And it will happen again, for in the end Jacob will outwit Laban (Gen. 30:25–31:18).

If the preacher is hard-pressed to find a moral in this text, it is because none is explicit. It is no idyllic picture of perfect family harmony. Nor is it fundamentally a story of the patriarch's dedication or even his deep love for the one he chooses—although those themes are present. If traits of character are held up as examples, they are shrewdness and wit. Moreover, there is no reference whatsoever to God or to divine guidance in this story. In the wider scheme, its significance is genealogical: How does it turn out that tribes trace their ancestry to the same patriarch and different matriarchs? The references to the two maids (vv. 24, 29) is parenthetical but crucial in the future story, reminding us of the importance of the matriarchs. With the two wives and the two maids, we are provided in this account with the parents necessary for the twelve tribal ancestors. Leah will be the mother of Reuben, Simeon, Levi, Judah, Issachar, Zebulun, as well as their sister Dinah. Rachel will be the mother of Joseph and Benjamin, Zilpah will give birth to Gad and Asher, and Bilhah will be the mother of Dan and Naphtali. But there is not even a comment in the story on this genealogical significance, to say nothing of the divine leading—which many readers, both ancient and modern, will discern hidden in these ordinary and even humorous events.

Although the narrator does not moralize on the issues at all, the story can be the occasion for reflection upon questions of status, poverty, and wealth. Jacob arrives alone and penniless and will eventually depart with a household and great property, having deceived his father-in-law out of his rightful inheritance. Jacob begins work in an ambiguous state, neither a slave nor a regular employee, and becomes an adopted son of Laban. Then there is the status of the sisters. They are viewed as property by father and husband alike, and are in conflict with one another because of their family status. The sisters, treated as property by father and husband alike, do not accept this situation in silence, although it was standard practice in their world. In 31:14–15, they encourage Jacob against their father who had "sold" them and now seems bent on depriving them of any inheritance. And along with their husband, they become the parents of the people of Israel.

Psalm 105:1–11, 45b

Only a few of the psalms focus on the history of Israel (see Pss. 78, 106, 135, 136) and employ this history in hymnic fashion. Psalm 105 does so in order to create a sense of thanksgiving among the people. The recital of the sacred events of salvation history (what the Germans call *Heilsgeschichte*) appears in numerous places in the Bible (see esp. Deut. 26:1–11).

In Psalm 105, reference is made to the patriarchs (vv. 7–15), Joseph in Egypt (vv. 16–22), the stay in and exodus from Egypt (vv. 23–43), and the settlement in the promised land (vv. 44–45).

This Sunday's reading has been selected to accompany the story of Jacob's marriages to Leah and Rachel, especially because of the appearance of verse 6b.

The two emphases of the lection are the call to be thankful, based on the memory of God's guidance in history (vv. 1–6), and the fidelity of God to the covenant throughout the three generations of Abraham, Isaac, and Jacob (vv. 7–11). In the marriage of Jacob, the covenant line is assured.

Psalm 128

This psalm, as an alternative reading to Psalm 105:1–11, 45*b*, is selected to accompany Genesis 29:15–28 because of its emphasis on offspring.

Psalm 128 belongs to a collection of psalms (Pss. 120–134) used as pilgrim songs in going to the festivals in Jerusalem (see the discussion of Ps. 122, the First Sunday of Advent). The hopes for a large family and numerous offspring were a part of the motifs at the fall festival, when blessings were requested for the coming year (see 1 Sam. 1 and Hannah's request).

The psalm opens with a blessing declaring that "happy" are those fearing and serving God. Verses 2 and 3 explain the content of what such a blessing means. First, the blessed person enjoys the fruits of one's labors (v. 2). This may sound like a trite blessing until we realize how much of our labor goes to others—paying interest on debts, rent, and so forth. In ancient Israel, crops were often owed to others, and foreign troops marching through the land often harvested the crops and collected what the locals had harvested. The second element of the blessing is a wife who produces numerous children who gather like olive shoots around the dinner table (v. 3). In these two factors we probably have outlined the basic hopes of most Israelites. Food to eat and a family not wasted by the ravages of death! How simple these appear when compared with our contemporary wish lists!

The psalm concludes with an additional set of blessings: to see Jerusalem prosper throughout one's life and to see one's children's children; that is, to live long enough to be a grandparent.

1 Kings 3:5–12

In the Bible (see 1 Kings 4:29–34) and in legend, Solomon has had a reputation for wisdom. In the biblical tradition, he was treated as the patron saint of wisdom, and the wisdom books (Proverbs, Ecclesiastes, Song of Songs, and The Wisdom of Solomon in the Apocrypha) were attributed to him. This Sunday's reading contains Solomon's prayer for wisdom and God's response.

In the narratives about Solomon's rule (1 Kings 3–11), only the statement about his marriage to pharaoh's daughter (3:1–2) precedes the narrative about his request for wisdom.

The association of special wisdom with the ruling monarch was a common motif in ancient near eastern cultures. Assyrian kings claimed to carry out their activities through special wisdom granted by the gods. A common form of Egyptian literature has the king passing along his wisdom to the next generation.

This text has Solomon worshiping at the revered high place at Gibeon, perhaps the old capital city during Saul's last years. The story is, of course, placed in a time before the building of the Jerusalem temple.

In a dream, Solomon is offered his choice of charisma. In several Egyptian texts, a deity appears to the future ruler in a dream to confirm the king's right to rule. Although Solomon is already king, this episode is placed at the beginning of his reign to authenticate his rule as having been filled with wisdom (see 1 Kings 3:16–28; 4:29–34; 5:22, 27; 10:1–10). Because Solomon built the temple to Yahweh, he needed an extra blessing of wisdom.

In his response to God, Solomon describes himself as "only a little child" not knowing "how to go out or come in" (v. 7). This is probably the language of hyperbole and self-deprecation claiming youthfulness and inexperience. Because Solomon is said to have ruled forty years (1 Kings 11:42) and his son Rehoboam was forty-one years old when he succeeded Solomon (1 Kings 14:21), Solomon was probably already a father when he became king. Youthfulness and inexperience simply form the antitheses to wisdom and express humility.

Solomon requests of God "a hearing heart" (v. 9; NRSV "an understanding mind"). Perhaps the meaning here is something like a feeling for the truth. The goal of Solomon's wish is to be given the ability to govern wisely, or the gift of leadership, and the ability to distinguish between what was good and what was bad for the people.

In the narrative, God praises Solomon for requesting a wise and discerning mind (v. 12; see Deut. 1:13; 4:6) rather than wealth, long life, or triumph over enemies.

Psalm 119:129–36

Portions of Psalm 119 have been used as lections for the Sixth and Seventh Sundays After the Epiphany and Proper 10 [15]. This Sunday's lection may be analyzed to stress three factors.

1. There is, first, the positive assessment of the "law" or God's revelation. It is wonderful or wondrous, that is, marvelous in what it contains (v. 129; see Ps. 119:18). When God's words become known or reveal themselves, they give light to illuminate the way. They are so enlightening that even the simpleminded or those with simple faith can find understanding (v. 130). Thus the law is not presented as a burden to be borne or an obligation to be fulfilled but as a wondrous gift that brings benefits in its wake.

2. The person's disposition toward the law is presented as one of expectant longing. "I pant" and "I long for" are strong expressions of expectation (v. 131). This sense of expectation may be illustrated by the statement of Job that in former times the people waited for God's counsel "as for the rain; and they opened their mouths as for the spring rain" (Job 29:23). The psalmist here suggests this "thirsty waiting" as his attitude before the commandments. The desire for the commandments is equivalent to desiring God's presence itself, "Turn to me and be gracious" (v. 132), or to experiencing the constant consoling support of the Divine, "Keep steady my steps" (v. 133).

3. The service of God and the goal of life are found in following the law. In this text, the person prays that certain conditions will not prevent observance of the law. (a) There is, first, the possibility that one's personal iniquity—moral worthlessness or antagonism toward God—will lead to an incapacity for obedience (v. 133). (b) Human oppression—bondage to another—is seen as something from which one needs to be redeemed in order to be obedient. Oppression here does not necessarily refer to enforced bondage but simply to commitments and obligations to another that hinder and stifle the opportunities for obedience (v. 134). (c) Finally, the blessing of God, which is reflected in the expression "your face shine upon your servant," makes possible the hearing and keeping of the law (v. 135). Negatively, the same idea can be expressed by saying that without God's blessing, that is, without the normal benefits of life, obedience becomes more difficult. If one's time is spent fighting

chaos in one's personal life or struggling to feed oneself and family, then little energy is left for the law and its contemplation.

The lection closes with a statement of the sorrow that comes from experiencing the world as a place where the law is not kept. The psalmist speaks of weeping streams or canals of tears—weeping brought on by the heartbreak of watching people live in a fashion incommensurate with their own best interest.

To preach from texts like Psalm 119 that extol and praise the law, the Christian minister needs to avoid one old pitfall—the (misunderstood) Pauline view of the law as serving only a negative function—and at the same time attempt to create one new perspective—that of appreciating, even loving, the law. To be avoided is the view that the law is a burdensome imposition of a deadening code that stifles freedom and life. Over against this, one can emphasize the values of seeing the world as an ordered place in which law serves as an ordering principle. At the same time, the listeners should be made aware of the pleasures of a good conscience and the legitimate satisfaction that can come from pleasing duty for duty's sake or, to put it psychologically, from doing what is ultimately for the doer's benefit. Living in a house built by law may be no less pleasurable or fulfilling than living in a house where freedom has torn down all walls.

Romans 8:26–39

There is a slight overlap between today's epistolary reading and the first option for the New Testament reading for Pentecost in Year B (8:22–27). The reader may want to consult our remarks in that setting for further comments.

Today's text, with its introductory word "likewise" (v. 26, NRSV; or "in the same way," REB), recalls verse 23, with its mention of the "groaning" that is experienced both by ourselves and by the created order. Yet creature and creation have been infused with God's Spirit, the "first fruits," an advance payment of God's presence. It is, after all, the God present among us who has launched creation toward ultimate redemption. But because this salvation is still unfolding and not fully realized, we experience it as suffering and pain mingled with patience and hope. The one is giving way to the other but not without the agony that accompanies every meaningful transformation.

But the Spirit is more than a mere representative of God's presence in the process of painful change. Today's text assures us of the Spirit's active role in relating us, as fellow participants in this transformation, to God: "The Spirit helps us in our weakness" (v. 26). We look about us and see forces at work that are truly cosmic. They are larger than life, hidden from our view, difficult even to identify. We are victims, and our utter weakness is exposed.

So overwhelmed are we that words escape us. Our loss of words leaves us feeling helpless. In spite of having Jesus' model prayer (Matt. 6:9–13), even an abundance of prayers in both the Old and New Testaments that reflect the whole spectrum of human experience, we nevertheless find ourselves speechless. We find ourselves not knowing *what* we ought to pray, or perhaps not knowing "*how* to pray as we ought" (v. 26; NRSV, REB). Awkward confusion abounds: what to say? how to say it? Such sighs may be reminiscent of Jesus' own experience (Mark 7:34; 8:12). In any case, anxious sighing characterizes existence of this aeon (2 Cor. 5:2, 4).

Because Christian prayer is prayer in the Spirit (1 Cor. 14:15; Eph. 6:18–19; Jude 20) and because the presence of the Spirit within us is an axiom of Christian existence (Rom. 5:5; 8:14–16), the Spirit comes to our rescue. It is the Spirit who acts as the intermediary between us and God to put our inarticulate thoughts into words. In Johannine terms, the Spirit is the Paraclete, who advocates our case before God (John 14:15–17, 26; 15:26; 16:7). This intercessory work the Spirit also shares with Christ himself (8:34; Heb. 7:25; 1 John 2:1).

One exegetical question that arises in verse 26 is whether the *Spirit's* intercessory prayer remains inarticulate, or whether the Spirit takes *our* inarticulate concerns and interprets them before God. NRSV opts for the former: "For that very Spirit intercedes with sighs too deep for words" (also NIV). REB opts for the latter: "Through our inarticulate groans the Spirit himself is pleading for us." JB represents a happy compromise: "The Spirit . . . expresses our plea in a way that could never be put into words."

In either case, we stand before God, "who searches our inmost being" (v. 27, REB). It is the sentiment of the psalmist, who acknowledges that the Creator has full, intimate knowledge of the creature (Ps. 139:1; cf. Jer. 11:20). Just as the Spirit knows the inner recesses of the mind of God (1 Cor. 2:10), so does God know "what is the mind of the Spirit" (v. 27). Theirs is a reciprocal relationship in which unobstructed communication occurs. Yet what commends the Spirit's appeal to God is that "the prayers that the Spirit makes for God's holy people are always in accordance with the mind of God" (v. 27, NJB).

If participating in God's cosmic transformation can leave us feeling helpless, it can also test our own sense of calling as well as the fidelity of the God who called us. To this concern the next section (vv. 28–30) is addressed.

Again we face a crucial exegetical question in verse 28. One manuscript tradition, which is followed by KJV and NRSV, reads, "All things work together for good." Another manuscript tradition reads, "And we know that in all things God works for the good of those who love him" (NIV; similarly, NJB, REB). The former implies a process of impersonal providence, whereas the latter more directly involves God in history. Indeed, our text posits God in a *cooperative* role with us: "In everything, as we know, [God] *co-operates* for good with those who love God" (v. 28, italics added, REB). One of the remarkable features of Paul's theology is the dramatic involvement of humans in the work of God (1 Cor. 3:9; 2 Cor. 6:1).

But here the stress lies on God's dramatic involvement with us. Again, we should note the context—suffering (8:18, 35). When we suffer, the lingering question is, Where is God? How can this possibly be for our good? The question becomes even more pressing when it is asked by those who love God.

Our text is quite explicit in locating God's cooperation among "those who love God" (v. 28). Only rarely does Paul speak of the Christian's relationship with God in this way (1 Cor. 2:9; 8:3), but when he does so it is significant. Quite clearly, loving God is the crucial complement of knowing God, in fact is the more primary of the two. Yet our love for God is axiomatic in Christian teaching (James 1:12; 2:5; Matt. 22:37).

To live in the love of God is to be responsive to the call of God (v. 28). Through the gospel, the call of God is issued, and there our election becomes formally initiated (1 Thess. 2:12; 4:7; 2 Thess. 1:11; 2:13–14; 1 Pet. 5:10). Yet we are assured that this is part of a much longer process that stems from the beginning of time (Eph. 1:4, 11: 3:11; 1 Pet. 1:2): foreknowlege, predestination, election, justification, and glorification (vv. 29–30).

These verses have obviously been formative in the history of doctrine, and questions still abound concerning divine foreknowledge and election. The emphasis here, however, is less on the particular "doctrine" suggested by each of these terms than it is on the overarching assurance of God's purposeful activity in the whole of history (cf. 2 Tim. 1:9). From start to finish, God's active concern has been shown for those who live in loving response to the divine call. Even when the purposes of God seemed hidden and when human forces were ostensibly at work thwarting the divine will, God was still actively at work. As in the case of Joseph, evil seemed to threaten the divine purpose, but what his conspirators meant for evil, God meant for good (Gen. 50:20).

This part of today's text begins with the recognition of human weakness. It may take the form of abject speechlessness or absolute despair in not being able to recognize the presence of God in the midst of our own pain. As to the one, Paul assures us that when we know neither what to say nor how to say it, when circumstances make us dumbstruck before God, the Spirit who knows us as well as God knows us, brings to appropriate expression what life has left us unable to say. As to the other, we are asked to believe in God's capacity to be present with and among us when our love has responded to the divine call—but not only to be present but to be *at work with us in everything,* even if human circumstance blinds us to the presence and work of our Collaborator.

The final section of today's text (vv. 31–39) flows directly out of the earlier section. The theme of human weakness has been a recurrent theme of chapter 8. It is expected that God's children will suffer (8:17–18), that God's creation will undergo cosmic strain as it moves toward the fulfillment of the divine purpose. Even with God present among us through the Spirit, we inevitably experience the inexplicable and unutterable (8:26–27). Confounded by life, we wonder about God's purpose and whether it will finally be achieved. We ask whether the evil we experience merely masks the good that God intends to achieve or whether it negates it altogether.

In response, Paul has assured us that the Spirit present within us can render our speechless groans in ways that God can hear. He also sketches the purposes of God broadly as extending over history from primordial foreknowledge to eschatological glorification.

But there is more, and the latter half of today's text supplies it. We should read these words "with all this in mind" (v. 31, REB), that is, in light of what has been said earlier in the chapter.

To say that "God is for us" (v. 31) is to recall the mighty acts of God (vv. 29–30). For God to call, justify, and glorify us is to have "God on our side" (REB). God with us constitutes a majority, and thus, "who is against us?" Such confidence is reminiscent of the psalmist who said, "With the Lord on my side I do not fear. What can mortals do to me?" (Ps. 118:6).

Yet another step is taken in today's text, however. Still more can be said, and Paul now says it: "Since God did not spare his own Son, but gave him up to benefit us all, we may be certain, after such a gift, that he will not refuse anything he can give" (v. 32, JB). The gift of Christ becomes the clue to God's solidarity with us. If we find ourselves speechless, wondering whether God can be present in the midst of evil, indeed within the evil we experience, we have only to reflect on the Christ-event.

The language of "not withholding his own Son" recalls the sacrifice of Isaac (Gen. 22:1–4). God praises Abraham, "You . . . have not withheld your son, your only son" (Gen. 22:16). In this case, Abraham's absolute fidelity was proved. So in the giving of Christ was God's integrity upheld. Abraham's act becomes a paradigm of divine fidelity (Heb. 11:17). The sending of Christ also became an unexcelled instance of divine love (cf. John 3:16, 18; Rom. 8:3; Gal. 4:4; 1 John 4:9).

The work of God in Christ becomes a clue to the work of God within us: "Will he not with him also give us everything else?" (v. 32). It may be important here to underscore *with him*. This may point to our complete solidarity with Christ as those who are "in Christ." If Christ is to be thought of essentially as gift, as that bestowed by God the generous Giver, by identifying with Christ, indeed by entering Christ, we fully participate in God's generous love. We may be unable to see evidence of this love in our own circumstances, but we can at least see it vividly in the Christ-event. In that moment, all the ambiguities of death and life converged, yet through them divine love became manifest.

To be sure, when we side with God and take our place among God's elect, we will have our detractors. We may even hear the detractor's cry in our own protests as we bring charges against God. We may charge God with being absent, unintelligible, or even negligent. What should we do when such voices of protest are raised?

At this point, our text becomes problematic. Depending on how we punctuate verses 33–34, the text yields different answers. The different options may be determined by careful comparison among the NRSV, NJB, REB, and NIV. The preacher will also want to consult commentaries in this regard. But the gist of Paul's line of argumentation seems to be this: any charges leveled against God's elect by detractors who wish to condemn come to grief on the Christ-event.

The Christ who died, was raised and exalted, illustrates how God vindicates the divine purpose. Christ now serves as intercessor on our behalf (v. 34; Heb. 7:25; 9:24). What cannot be denied is that the Christ who died was a Christ who loved (v. 35; 2 Cor. 5:14). What's more, the Christ-event was both instance and extension of God's own love. We can only speak of "the love of God *in* Christ Jesus our Lord" (v. 39, italics added; cf. Rom. 5:5). God's love was not sketched in broad, general terms but embodied in a single human figure, a definable, visible human event. It was located *in Christ* and thus locatable within time and history.

To be in Christ is to be located within the sphere of divine love. The result is that nothing "can cut us off from the love of Christ" (v. 35, NJB). Two kinds of realities threaten this relationship: distresses "down here" and those "up there." First are those everyday menaces: "being troubled or worried, or being persecuted, or lacking food or clothes, or being threatened or even attacked" (v. 35, JB). These are "life's tribulations" (Rom. 2:9; 5:3; 2 Cor. 11:23–27; 12:10) that even the psalmist knew as daily realities (Ps. 44:22; cf. 1 Cor. 4:9–13; 15:30–31).

But there are also those forces that are larger than life, bigger than any one of us: death, life, the realm of spirits, superhuman powers, the world as it is, the world as it will be, forces in the universe, heights, and depths (v. 38, REB). These are the forces that stretch time to its limits, that push the boundaries of space to their outer edge, that hover above us even as they conspire within us, that oppress and dominate. Yet these too come to grief in the Christ-event, for that is where they were vanquished by the "love of God made visible in Christ Jesus our Lord" (v. 39, JB).

This text bears witness to a sense of power and triumph as it is focused in the Christ-event. It should be noted that Paul nowhere denies the existence of these earthly and heavenly menaces that threaten our relationship with Christ, but he does deny that they are ultimately catastrophic.

Matthew 13:31–33, 44–52

This reading concludes this series of three Sundays on the parables of Jesus and is also our final lection from the third of the five major bodies of teaching in Matthew (the Sermon on the Mount and instructions for mission were the first two). Matthew 13:31–33, 44–52 consists of six parables, if indeed the sixth unit (vv. 51–52) can be called a parable. Each parable is brief, self-contained, without an informing context, and virtually unrelated to the other three. The preacher will be a bit pressed to find thematic unity for one message on these six units. Perhaps the fact that they are spoken to the disciples and not to the public (v. 36) will provide focus. Or possibly the phrase "kingdom of heaven," common to all four, will be sufficient to gather under one topic these six glimpses into the kingdom life that Jesus offers. One should keep in mind that "kingdom of heaven" in Matthew is synonymous with "kingdom of God" in the other Gospels. "Heaven" is a pious way of avoiding use of the holy name and is not intended to point the reader beyond here to the hereafter.

On second thought, perhaps the congregation will be better served if the preacher proposes no thematic center for these six parables. What is the kingdom of God like? It is many-splendored, but we catch glimpses of it. It is as though Jesus held it up to the light, turned it as one turns a prism in the sun, and in these stories told us what he saw. We listen, enjoy, ponder.

The mustard seed (vv. 31–32). At least one variety of mustard growing in Israel could reach the height of the eye of a rider on horseback. The seed was small and was for Jewish rabbis a commonly used image for describing the minute. Here Jesus uses the mustard seed and the mature plant to picture the contrast between very small beginnings and very large consequences. Such is the work in which he and his disciples are engaged. Surely Jesus is offering not simply a lesson in patience but a word of encouragement and hope. All of us need such encouragement when efforts seem to bear little fruit and "what's the use?" sets in.

The yeast in the flour (v. 33). Very likely, Jesus' auditors were surprised that his stories of God's work in the world were drawn from common and everyday experiences. Such surprise may have been greater here because yeast was sometimes the image of evil at work in a group (Matt. 16:6). Even so, Jesus converts the image to serve his point. Good also can gradually influence a group. A word here, a cup of cold water there, a firm stand on a matter of conscience—let them do their own work without forcing, without pushing. Drop the stone in the water; the ripples will spread beyond sight.

The treasure hidden in a field (v. 44). The one who discovers the kingdom, even accidentally, is so full of joy and anticipation that everything else is sold in the prospect of that one treasure. Let the interpreter avoid getting entangled in the legalities of hiding the treasure until the field can be bought. Likewise, talk of sacrificing for the kingdom should be eliminated. The highlights are the surpassing worth of the kingdom and the joy of finding it.

The pearl of great value (vv. 45–46). The message here is essentially the same. It is a judgment call as to whether this parable was intended to convey a small contrast with the preceding one. In the one case, the kingdom was discovered as though accidentally; in the other, the kingdom was found by one on a search. Whether or not such a distinction was intended, faith experiences confirm the difference.

The fish net (vv. 47–50). In several respects, the passage is similar to verses 24–30, 36–43: both the fish net and the weeds in the grain field are parables about the final judgment; both carry their own interpretations; both parables have an element of unreality in order to accommodate the interpretations. Some students of the parables are persuaded that Jesus' original parable consisted only of verse 47: "Again, the kingdom of heaven is like a net that was thrown in the sea and caught fish of every kind." Were such the case, then the parable would be similar to that of the sower, in which the word was sown indiscriminately with no intention of being selective. Or perhaps more exactly, it would correspond to Luke's parable of the banquet (14:16–24), in which all kinds of people were invited. However, the fish net is Matthew's parable, and we know Matthew's frequent reminders of a separating judgment. In fact, in Matthew's account of the parable of the banquet (22:1–14), both good and bad are invited, but the king tosses out the one without a wedding garment.

The householder's treasury (vv. 51–52). The comparison here is not with the kingdom but with "every scribe who has been trained for the kingdom." The disciples of Jesus say they have understood all these parables (v. 51; quite unlike Mark's portrait of them, 4:13, 34). In the statement that follows, Matthew has Jesus comparing his disciples to scribes, or perhaps implying that they should be as scribes trained for the kingdom. This favorable view of scribes is found elsewhere in Matthew (23:34: "Therefore I [Jesus] send you prophets, sages, and scribes") and has led some to speculate that Matthew was himself a scribe. Given this Evangelist's emphasis on teachings and the careful observance of them, it is reasonable to assume that a Christian scribal tradition would develop in this circle of Christianity. In any case, the kingdom scribe draws upon a rich treasure of the old and the new. Specifically, what is meant is unclear. Law of Moses (old) and Christ's word (new)? Christ's teachings (old) and Matthew's interpretations (new)? Perhaps both; at least the church has carefully preserved the tradition while continuing to hear and understand it anew.

Proper 13 [18]
(Sunday between July 31 and August 6 inclusive)

Genesis 32:22–32;
Psalm 17:1–7, 15; or
Isaiah 55:1–5;
Psalm 145:8–9, 14–21;
Romans 9:1–5;
Matthew 14:13–21

Themes of struggle, conflict, and transformation run through the Old Testament text and psalm in the *Common Lectionary.* In the Old Testament lection, Jacob struggles all night to realize that he has been wrestling with God, who gives him a new name. Psalm 17 is a complaint, or lament, song of a righteous individual crying for help against his adversaries.

Those using other lectionaries will find in today's Old Testament reading from the concluding chapter of Second Isaiah a set of invitations to participate in God's bounty and heed God's instructions. Similar reassurances, which affirm the Lord's goodness, mercy, and compassion, and acknowledge God as a bountiful provider who watches over the faithful, are expressed in the selections from Psalm 145.

The epistolary reading, the opening section of the lengthy section of Romans dealing with the relationship between Jews and Gentiles, expresses Paul's anxiety over Israel's general failure to accept Christ, yet reaffirms his solidarity with his ancestral tradition. The Gospel reading, Matthew's account of Jesus feeding the five thousand, also suggests God's ability—and willingness—to provide bountifully for those in need.

Genesis 32:22–32

In terms of context, Genesis 32:22–32 is the counterpart to the Old Testament lesson for Proper 11 [16], Genesis 28:10–19a. That story of Jacob at Bethel took place as he was leaving Canaan for northwest Mesopotamia, and the events in today's reading take place on the boundary of the land as he is returning. Both are at key turning points in the life of the patriarch, and in both instances he is the object of divine revelation at a dangerous time, and at night. Fear stands in the background of both accounts. In the first instance, he was fleeing from Esau; here, having escaped the wrath of his father-in-law, he

384

knows he is about to meet his brother. So the immediate context of Jacob's nocturnal struggle at the Jabbok is his conflict with his brother. A story of struggle with superhuman powers is framed by a confrontation between brothers.

Brief as it is, the story of Jacob at the Jabbok is strange and complicated. Some of its strangeness and complexity can be explained in terms of the history of its transmission and development. There is strong evidence that the tradition was passed down in the oral tradition in various forms. We begin to recognize that evidence when we attempt to identify Jacob's opponent. Initially we are told that "a man wrestled with him until daybreak" (v. 24), but later it appears that the opponent has the power both to put Jacob's thigh out of joint with a touch and to bless him. This confusion, along with the facts that the opponent fears the daylight and refuses to divulge his name, suggests a nocturnal demon. In the struggle, the opponent declares ambiguously that Jacob has "striven with God and with humans" (v. 28), and in the end the patriarch says he has "seen God face to face" (v. 30). It seems clear, then, that the narrator has taken over an ancient, pre-Yahwistic tradition that once talked of a nocturnal demon or deity and reinterpreted it as a confrontation between Israel's God and her ancestor.

The complex history of tradition is also revealed in the fact that the story has so many distinct resolutions or conclusions. Some of these points seem almost trivial when compared with the others. There are two distinct etiological conclusions, one explaining the name of the place as Peniel, "face of God," because Jacob saw the face of God there and lived (v. 30), and the other explaining the origin of a ritual practice. The Israelites do not eat "the thigh muscle that is on the hip socket" because the opponent struck the ancestor's hip socket at the thigh muscle (v. 32). This latter point is particularly curious, not simply because the taboo is unattested elsewhere, but because it was a human thigh that was touched and animal muscles that are therefore not to be eaten.

The two other resolutions to the story are more integral to the plot and to one another. One concerns the change of the ancestor's name to Israel or, more likely, the giving of an additional name. This emerges directly from the struggle. On the one hand, Jacob demands to know his opponent's name, but the antagonist refuses to disclose it. In the old oral tradition, to know the name of the nocturnal demon or deity was to obtain a measure of control over it. On the other hand, when the adversary asks, Jacob identifies himself and in turn receives the new name, Israel ("one who strives with God," or "God strives"). The other point concerns the blessing, a direct result of the conflict. The opponent demands to be released because daybreak is approaching, but Jacob refuses to release him until he is blessed (v. 26). This is the hinge upon which the drama turns. Who will win the contest? Jacob received his blessing (v. 29), but he did not escape without injury.

In all levels of the tradition, this is a story of strife and struggle. Our author, the Yahwist, and his audience would not have missed the corporate implications of the story and its results. The people of Israel, like their patronymic ancestor, had striven with powers both human and divine and, in the time of the monarchy, knew that they had prevailed and been blessed. Moreover, although the ancient tradition may have viewed the conflict as one with some demon, our narrator finally knows that behind the hidden visage is the face of God. As the old traditions have been incorporated into a theological interpretation of Israel's past, there is a skillfully developed ambiguity in the identity of the opponent.

Those who know struggle—and who does not?—will find it easy to identify with both the protagonist and the storyteller. Life entails strife, conflict, and struggle. Often we can neither see the face nor know the name of what confronts us in the night. The struggle may even be with the unfathomable mystery of God. The passage, however, goes further than holding up a mirror to life as struggle. By example it says: do not let go, but continue to struggle, even when God is experienced as threatening. Furthermore, by its resolution it concludes that struggle—even with God—may end with a blessing, even though one may limp on afterwards with the scars of the battle.

Psalm 17:1–7, 15

Psalm 17 is a psalm composed for use in legal hearings at the temple when a person felt or was falsely accused of some wrong. Old Testament laws concerned with the administration of justice allowed for cases to be appealed to Yahweh and the temple personnel when it was impossible to decide a case in the normal fashion, that is, when a jury of elders could not reach a verdict (see Exod. 22:7–8; Deut. 17:8–13; 19:15–21; 1 Kings 8: 31–23). Failure of the normal process might be the result of a lack of witnesses, the particularity of the case, or other reasons.

In the temple ritual or ordeal, the litigants in a case would appeal to God for a verdict, assert their innocence, and place themselves under an oath or curse. The priests sought to determine guilt and innocence, and where they could not, the participants' self-imprecation was assumed to bring condemnation upon the guilty. Frequently, the litigants spent the night in the sanctuary under the observation of the cultic officials. Apparently, verdicts in a case were declared in the morning.

The reason for selecting Psalm 17 for reading with Genesis 32:22–32 is its reference in verse 15 to seeing God's face, which bears some analogy to Jacob's experience at the ford of the Jabbok.

The following is an outline of the contents of the psalm: (1) an opening appeal to God for a hearing (vv. 1–2), (2) a statement of innocence (vv. 3–5), (3) a second appeal (vv. 6–9), (4) a description of the accusers (vv. 10–12), (5) a final appeal (vv. 13–14), and (6) a statement of confidence (v. 15). Note that the entire psalm consists of prayer addressed to the Deity. (The lection for this Sunday breaks off in the middle of the second appeal.)

In the initial appeal to Yahweh (vv. 1–2), legal and court terminology prevail: "just cause," "lips free of deceit," "vindication," and "the right." The case of the supplicant is laid at the feet of Yahweh, with an appeal that Yahweh would hear, give heed, and look upon (favor) the right or innocent one in the case. The specifics of the case are not laid out. Such psalms as this one were composed to be used over and over again by different persons as the need arose. Thus the statements about the case are made in general terms in order to cover a particular type of situation rather than a specific situation per se.

In verses 3–5, the worshiper, as a defendant, offers to the Deity a statement of innocence. If the psalms were written by temple personnel, then this statement could have served two purposes. On the one hand, it allowed the innocent person to affirm innocence in the strongest of terms. On the other hand, for one who was actually guilty but pretending innocence, this statement forced the litigant to lie in a strong fashion. Such statements of innocence may have forced the guilty into a crisis of conscience and thus confession. At any rate, it would have greatly intensified the sense of guilt and perhaps served to engender a reevaluation of one's status before God. The worshiper, in other words, was forced, in the context of a solemn service in the temple in the presence of Yahweh, to confront the reality of guilt and innocence. The worshiper was confronted with telling the truth or lying with a high hand. The cult was as committed as any other institution to truth telling!

Innocence is asserted in several ways in verses 3–5. References to the heart and testing at night (when asleep) indicate the total commitment of the person and the conscience to truthfulness. Reference to the mouth indicates a claim not to have participated in slanderous gossip or unsubstantiated accusations. Commitment to "the word of your lips" is a claim to have lived by the divine teachings as made known in the community. The supplicant claims that knowledge of God's will has kept him or her from participation in the ways of the violent. The paths of God have been where the supplicant's feet have trod.

In the appeal, the worshiper asks God to incline the ear, hear the words of appeal, and answer (v. 6). The matter, however, is not left at the level of a legal hearing and verdict rendering. There is also a request for divine mercy and love. Verse 15 expresses the worshiper's confidence of divine favor and, in a legal case, a favorable decision given in the morning.

Isaiah 55:1–5

This brief lesson is the first of two invitations to Israel (vv. 1–5, 6–11) to come to God for relief from all her woes and for renewal of life by the free offer of divine grace. In the second invitation, the voice is that of the prophet calling the people to meet God in worship; but in the text before us, the voice is the voice of God.

God's invitation is to Israel in exile in Babylon, but that exile is soon to end. Cyrus, ruler of Persia, has already defeated the Medes and the Lydians, and now Babylon lies on his path of conquest. Isaiah is quite hopeful about the future, seeing in Cyrus God's new instrument of liberation, God's shepherd, God's redeemer. All Israel should be roused to life by the promise of the immediate future.

However, many exiles no longer believe good news. Why? Perhaps they have grown weary with leaping to the window at every rumor of new and better political conditions, every whispered hope of improved economy, every passing story of going home soon to Jerusalem. Perhaps they have been too long exiled to permit themselves the brief joy of anticipation followed by the painful thud of dashed dreams. One way to protect oneself against disappointment is to abandon hope. By not flying too high, one does not have too far to fall. The prophet of promise has, therefore, the difficult task of gaining a believing ear. Hence Isaiah 40–66 is filled with the widest range of rhetorical strategies: the prophet calls, exhorts, sings, begs, shouts, cajoles, shames, mocks, laughs, and argues. He appeals to creation, the Exodus, the covenant with Abraham, the promise to David. Every sacred event in Israel's history is recalled in efforts to awaken memory as the key to imaging a bright future. Yesterday is hope as well as history. Such is the context of Isaiah 55:1–5.

God speaks, and the voice calls in free, unconditional grace. Three times God says, Come (v. 1). The invitation unfolds in some detail:

Come to a life of plenty, with sufficient food for both the body and the soul. The offer is to everyone, and it is to God's banquet table.

Turn away from a life that does not satisfy, a life of such compromises and accommodations among strangers in exile that the former life of the faith community haunts and disturbs by its absence. Eating at the exile table does not fill the void (v. 2).

Come again to hear God's word, the word that created and sustained Israel in all her life (v. 3a).

Enter again into a relationship with God that has again the quality of covenant. David has not been forgotten; God's love for David continues steadfast as always. The covenant with David was not with him alone but with his house forever (v. 3b).

Come and enjoy the favor God grants those in covenant. David was blessed, was elevated among the people, and was a testimony to the nations of the power and grace of God (v. 4). So will God again glorify Israel, but in ways beyond the favor bestowed on David. Now Israel will invite the nations to come and share in the blessing of God, and the world will come to Israel to hear, to believe, to receive (v. 5).

Of course, the message struck despairing ears as unbelievable, that a people languishing in exile far from home would not only return to Zion, but

> the mountain of the LORD's house
> shall be established as the highest of the mountains,
>   and shall be raised above the hills;
> all the nations shall stream to it.
> Many people shall come and say,
> "Come, let us go up to the mountain of the LORD,
>   to the house of the God of Jacob. (Isaiah 2:2–3)

Psalm 145:8–9, 14–21

Portions of this psalm were discussed earlier under Proper 9 [14]. This acrostic or alphabetic psalm interweaves petition and proclamation, prayer and praise, speech to God and speech about God into a well-integrated and articulate composition. Petition/prayer/speech to God is found in verses 1–2, 4–7, 10–13a, 15–16, and proclamation/praise/speech about God is found in verses 3, 8–9, 13b–14, 17–21. Verse 13b belongs with verses 14–21.

Verses 13b–20 may be said to describe the nature of the king who rules over his domain. One of the linguistic features of these verses is the word "all" (Hebrew kol), which appears over a dozen times in these verses. The term indicates the inclusiveness and universality of the actions and sentiments of God.

Two things should be noted, in general, about this latter part of the psalm. (1) The author of the psalm, and thus all who used it, speaks about God in a rather detached fashion. Theological speech is present in an almost unique form, but there is little passion, little sense of intense feeling. This fits in with the teaching and didactic quality and alphabetic form of the psalm. (2) The theology of the psalm is one based on extreme confidence, assurance, and certitude. That is, the psalm seems to breathe the air of success in life, to reflect the positive outlook of one secure in the world, confident in the operations of the cosmos and positive in outlook and perspective.

Verses 13b–21 may be viewed (and preached) in terms of two, almost synonymous, propositions that are stated and then further expounded and illustrated. The propositions are found in verses 13b and 17. God is "faithful [loyal] in [to] all his words, and gracious in all his deeds" and "just in all his ways, and kind in all his doings." Two characteristics of the Deity are emphasized: fidelity to justice in actions, and mercy (kindness) as the disposition, the motivating sentiment, behind divine actions.

Verse 14 illustrates the principle that justice is characteristic of divine actions. Such justice is shown in God's rescue of the falling, support of those bowed down. Those who suffer and are oppressed needlessly and without cause can find in God a defendant and one who rights the situations. (This is one of the reasons why the Old Testament, especially the psalms, contains so many laments and complaints, so many gripes about the human situation. The expression and articulation of the human hurt is viewed as therapeutic; it also is assumed that ultimate reality, God, is disposed to give justice.) That God upholds the falling and raises the fallen echoes one of the major themes of the Bible—God as the special protector of the weak and oppressed, God as the one who "reverses human fate," who brings to fulfillment and realization the unpromising. (This is the Cinderella theme that can be seen as a dominant motif in so much of the Old Testament: Abraham and Sarah with no children, Moses as a babe afloat in the Nile, the Hebrews in slavery, David as a shepherd lad.)

Verses 15 and 16 illustrate the principle that God is gracious. All living things (good and bad, Israelite and foreigner, human and animal) are dependent on God and are not disappointed. God's providence and care sustain the whole of existence.

In verses 17–20, 17a is illustrated in verse 18, and verse 17b is illustrated by verses 19–20. (Verse 21 is a sort of closing benediction.) In verses 17–20, a few modifications and conditions enter the picture and slightly modify the more sweeping claims in verses 13b–16. Note that "in truth" is a condition in verse 18b, and verse 20 claims that God preserves those "who love him" but destroys the wicked. Even in God's providence, moral factors are seen as playing their role.

Romans 9:1–5

Today's text introduces the long, self-contained section of the Epistle to the Romans (chaps. 9–11) in which Paul wrestles with the question of how the inclusion of the Gentiles within the people of God affects the destiny of Israel. The fact was that the gospel had been received more warmly by Gentiles than Jews; indeed, it had met outright rejection by many Jews. Not only the message about Jesus, but Jesus himself had been resisted and rejected by Israel.

This created a problem for Paul. If God had been revealed in a new way in Christ and if salvation was now more broadly defined to include both Jews and Gentiles, how did Israel's rejection fit into God's overall purpose? Surely God did not intend for the gospel to exclude Israel! Yet as a whole, Jews were not responding favorably, at least not to Paul's preaching. By contrast, Gentiles were accepting the good news. Does this mean that God has now tilted toward the Gentiles and turned away from the Jews? If so, what do we make of the many promises God made to Israel, such as the promise to form an *everlasting* covenant (Gen. 17:7–8)?

In short, the question was, What is the role of the Jews in salvation history? If they are no longer in a privileged position as *the* people of God and if Gentiles have now come to be included among God's elect, what are the respective roles of Jews and Gentiles in God's overall scheme?

In this section, Paul struggles with this dilemma created by Israel's rejection of the gospel. The divine promise was never intended to extend to Jews only, but was always meant to include everyone whom God chose, including Gentiles (9:6–13, 24). Even when the promise was directed to Jews, not all Jews responded (9:27–29), which shows that all along the promise came not through birth but through faith. Historically, God had called people to be obedient, and Israel was no exception. The same call now comes anew through Christ: respond to God in faith (10:1–13). But Israel has yet again failed to hear God's call (10:14–21).

Yet God is not willing to give up on Israel. There have always been pockets of fidelity among the people of God. A few have always been loyal to the divine purpose (11:3–4). So also now, the Gentiles serve as God's faithful remnant who will serve to call back disobedient Israel (11:11–16). This does not mean that the Gentiles can be arrogant toward disobedient Jews. Even if they are fresh branches that have been grafted onto the tree to bring it new life, the fact remains that the trunk is Jewish (11:17–24). Gentiles may witness to Jews, but they are bound to do so in humility and faith.

So God's unfolding plan is this: the acceptance of the gospel by the Gentiles will work to bring about the conversion of Israel. Once the Gentiles demonstrate their responsiveness to the gospel, the Jews will be responsive in their turn. As it turns out, the conversion of the Gentiles represents yet another extension of God's mercy to the Jews (11:30–32).

The words of today's text introduce an emotion-filled discussion of Israel's role in salvation history. At the outset, Paul asserts his own integrity, which suggests that the issues he is about to discuss are highly controversial and of deep import to him (cf. Gal. 1:20; 2 Cor. 11:31; 1 Tim. 2:7). These are also matters of conscience for him (cf. Rom. 2:15), and they have caused him considerable pain and anguish (cf. 2 Cor. 11:28–29). So important are the issues that he is willing to place himself under divine curse in behalf of his fellow Jews (cf. 1 Cor. 12:3; 16:22; Gal. 1:8–9). Even more, he is willing to sever his connection with Christ for the sake of his kinspeople. Here we see yet another form of being willing to lay down one's life for one's own people (1 John 3:16).

Earlier, Paul had asked, "What advantage has the Jew?" (3:1). We now have an elaboration of his answer, "Much in every way," as he enumerates the eightfold blessing of being Jewish (vv. 4–5): (1) Jews bear the distinguished name *Israelites,* after their forebear Jacob (Gen. 32:28; 35:10; cf. 2 Cor. 11:22); (2) their relationship with God is one of *being children by adoption* (Deut. 14:1; Hos. 11:1); (3) they basked in the dazzling presence of God, the divine *glory,* which provided protection in the wilderness (Exod. 16:10) and instruction through the law (Exod. 34:29–35; 2 Cor. 3:7); (4) they were partners with God in several *covenants* (Gen. 17:3–8; Jer. 31:31–34; Sir. 44:12, 18); (5) they are the distinct heirs of the *giving of the law* (Exod. 19–20); (6) their *worship* is in the temple, with its impressive liturgy (cf. 1 Kings 6); (7) they are the recipients of God's *promises* (4:13; 9:8–9; 15:8); and (8) they have a rich ancestry of *patriarchs* (Exod. 13:5).

The capstone of these blessings is that Christ was of Jewish lineage: "From them, according to the flesh, comes the Messiah" (v. 5). It had already become part of early Christian confession that Christ had descended from David according to the flesh (Rom. 1:3), and this was established through genealogies (Matt. 1; Luke 3:23–38). Even those who refused to accept Jesus as Messiah could hardly deny that he was of Jewish origin.

One important exegetical question here is whether Paul actually asserts that Christ was God. It depends on how one punctuates verse 5. NRSV and REB are less assertive, perhaps because Paul is elsewhere reluctant to apply the name "God" to Christ (cf. 1 Cor. 8:6; 15:27, 28; Phil. 2:6–11; also Eph. 1:20–23; Col. 1:15–20) and because such prayers of blessing are normally addressed to God (Rom. 1:25; 2 Cor. 11:31; Ps. 41:13). NJB, however, is more explicit: "Christ who is above all, God, blessed for ever"; similarly, NIV: "Christ, who is God over all, forever praised."

Obviously, today's text will have to be read in light of the entirety of chapters 9–11. But as brief as these verses are, they serve as a salutary reminder that talk about exclusion from God and being deprived of access to divine promises are always occasions of emotion and pain. They also show us someone who is struggling with the richness of his religious heritage, on the one hand, and the light of new revelation, on the other. Perhaps this is in itself a parable of the religious life—the new transforming, perhaps even surpassing, the old, but never quite able to live apart from it.

Matthew 14:13–21

Jesus feeding the five thousand is one of the relatively few stories recorded by all four Evangelists (Mark 6:30–44; Luke 9:10–17; John 6:1–14). In general, Matthew follows Mark's story. The feeding occurs at a lonely place, which Jesus and the disciples reached by boat but which the crowds reached on foot. The miracle is an act of compassion on the people who are away from home and without food, and the hour is late. The disciples favor dismissing the crowds, but later cooperate with Jesus in the feeding. From five loaves and two fish everyone eats to satisfaction, and there are twelve baskets of leftovers.

However, in some important details Matthew alters Mark's story. In Mark (6:30–31), the disciples have just returned from a mission, and Jesus invites them to withdraw and rest. Matthew tells of Jesus sending the Twelve on a mission but never reports their return. Because in Matthew Jesus has just received the news of the death of John the Baptist (14:1–12), we are left to assume that Jesus withdrew to a lonely place in response to that news. But why? To escape a similar fate? To grieve John's death? To reflect on what John's death portends for his own future? Matthew gives us no clue. The disciples are not mentioned until verse 15; Jesus alone is in Matthew's eye both when he enters the boat and when he arrives at the lonely place. Matthew also abbreviates the conversation between Jesus and the Twelve. They volunteer the information about five loaves and two fish and do not appear at all as being dull to the point of insolence, as in Mark ("Are we to go and buy two hundred denarii worth of bread, and give it to them to eat?" Mark 6:37b). Mark's harsh view of the Twelve is generally softened by Matthew.

But none of these details tells us what to make of the story. In its background lies the multiplication of loaves by Elisha (2 Kings 4:42–44), but that information still leaves us with the question, How did the church and how does the church understand Jesus feeding the multitude? Primarily in two ways.

First, the story is for Matthew as well as Mark and Luke (but not John) a compassion story. Jesus had withdrawn to a lonely place, but when met by a huge crowd he had compassion and ministered to their needs. Although holding the miracle to be unique to Jesus, the church has accepted the compassion as obligatory for all Jesus' followers. And there has been no scene more generative of compassion than that of hungry men, women, and children. Long-range programs as well as emergency relief have occupied followers of Jesus (not sufficiently or consistently, to be sure) for twenty centuries. In fact, Jesus said the question, What did you do in the face of human hunger? would be on the final exam (Matt. 25:35).

Second, the feeding of the multitude was and is understood as a eucharistic story. This is its primary meaning for the Fourth Gospel, but it is evident in the Synoptics as well.

Eucharistic language is used: he blessed, broke, and gave (v. 19). But just as significantly, notice how this story ends. One does not, as in other miracles, read of amazed crowds; no one is asking, Who is this? No one believes because of this, and there is no comment about the spread of Jesus' fame throughout the region. Why? Because the miracle was paltry compared to others? No. More likely it is because the story, by the time the Gospels were written, had become an inside story, a church story, an account of Jesus feeding his followers. In other words, it was recited when the church gathered at the Lord's Table.

Proper 14 [19]

(Sunday between August 7 and 13 inclusive)

Genesis 37:1–4, 12–28;
Psalm 105:1–6, 16–22, 45b; or
1 Kings 19:9–18;
Psalm 85:8–13;
Romans 10:5–15;
Matthew 14:22–33

The first of two Old Testament readings in the *Common Lectionary*'s semicontinuous reading of Genesis that deal with Joseph, today's text comes from the beginning of the Joseph saga. Relating the circumstances that led to Joseph's rejection by his brothers and his journey to Egypt, the text is filled with tension and strife. Portions of Psalm 105 overlap with the psalm reading from Proper 12 [17], although verses 16–22 are new and deal specifically with Joseph.

The Old Testament reading for traditions that do not use semicontinuous readings from the Pentateuch is the account of Yahweh's commission to Elijah at Mount Horeb. The psalm, the second half of Psalm 85, affirms God's faithfulness and commitment to peace and justice on earth.

The epistolary reading, which asserts (in the words of Deut. 30:11–14) the nearness of God's word, speaks exultantly of those who proclaim God's good news. The Gospel lesson, Matthew's account of Jesus' walking on the water, is a story of faith and endurance, presenting Peter as an enthusiast without staying power at a critical moment.

Genesis 37:1–4, 12–28

In the semicontinuous Old Testament readings for this season, we are now in the fourth generation of the ancestors of Israel, having moved from Abraham, Isaac, and Jacob to the sons of Jacob, or Israel. Jacob is still present until the end, but his children are the center of interest. The lessons for this week and the next are two texts from the story of one of those sons, Joseph. That story itself, which includes Genesis 37, 38–47, 50, is introduced by accounts dealing primarily with the children of Jacob in Genesis 34–36 and 38. In Genesis 48–49, Jacob blesses those sons as the ancestors of the twelve tribes of Israel.

393

The Joseph story, although similar in some respects to the other narratives in Genesis, is quite distinctive. The fact that it is a long, highly developed story, with a coherent plot from beginning to end, has led many scholars to compare it to the short story or novella. Most of the other patriarchal narratives are short, self-contained stories linked together like beads on a string. The Joseph story shows serious interest in human personalities and emotions, such subtle points as the awareness that foreigners may need to communicate through translators, carefully constructed subplots, and literary techniques such as foreshadowing. Moreover, unlike most of the other narratives in Genesis, this account shows the differences between the characters in their youth and their maturity. One needs only to compare the Joseph of our passage with the one of Genesis 45. A spoiled brat becomes a mature man who is generous and compassionate. The vigorous and aggressive brothers of chapter 37 are seen in chapter 45 as bent with age and the effects of their struggles.

Although the story as a whole is a unity with few major breaks or contradictions, it still bears the marks of the combination of the older sources of the Pentateuch, the Yahwist and the Elohist. Traces of those sources are visible in this reading. In verse 25 (J), it is the Ishmaelites who are seen on the horizon, but in verse 28 (E), the boys sell their brother to the Midianite traders. In verses 21 and 29, it is Reuben who wants to save Joseph, but it is Judah in verse 26. But for the most part, an editor has woven material from these sources and developed it into a coherent plot that moves toward a clear resolution. Genesis 37 is the introduction to the story as a whole.

Each of the episodes in this larger plot has its own exposition, development of tension, and climax, usually followed with some link to the next stage of the story. In Genesis 37, verses 1–2 come from the Priestly Writer's genealogical framework. But even here, the animosity between Joseph and the brothers is patent. He is a tattler who brought "a bad report" of the sons of Bilhah and Zilpah to their father. The exposition is in verses 3–4, introducing the characters and their relationships, both physical and emotional, to one another. It is a concise and masterful sketch of the spoiled brat and of sibling rivalry, interpreting the motives of the characters. Jacob loved Joseph because he was "the son of his old age," and Jacob had made Joseph a "long robe with sleeves." (The Hebrew here is quite uncertain. The traditional translation, "coat of many colors," is suggested by the Greek. NJPSV reads "an ornamented tunic." Clearly the attire is not appropriate for the kind of hard work his brothers do.) The brothers hated him because their father loved him more than he did them.

Verses 5–11, omitted from the reading, develops the tension between Joseph and his brothers with the reports of Joseph's dreams. Important as these reports are in this episode, they are even more important in the story as a whole as foreshadowing of the events to come. The parents and the brothers will, in the end, bow down to Joseph. The literary touch at the end of this episode, "but his father kept the matter in mind" (v. 11), is a hint to the reader that momentous events are to follow. Although the name of God is not mentioned at all, we will see in the end that a divine plan unfolds and that its results had been revealed to Joseph at the very beginning.

In verses 12–28, the action rises to a climax. The brothers are away, taking care of the flocks, and Jacob sends Joseph to check on their well-being and report back. Animosity rises to the level of a murder plot when the brothers see Joseph coming (vv. 18–20). But this danger is averted when Reuben proposes that instead of actually killing him they throw him in a pit. Again, Reuben's motives are explained—"that he might rescue him" (v. 22). When Joseph arrives, the first thing they do is strip off that cursed robe (v. 23), and then throw him into a pit. Obviously, they intend to let him die there. As the brothers are eating, they see a caravan coming, headed for Egypt. Judah's proposal that they sell him to the traders meets with agreement, so they take him out of the pit and deliver him for twenty pieces of silver (vv. 26–28). This explains how Joseph got to Egypt, and in the broader narrative it will account for the presence of the people of Israel in that foreign land.

The remainder of the chapter reports first how Reuben, who we must believe was not present when his brother was sold to the traders, returned to the pit to find it empty (vv. 29–30), and then how the brothers deceived their father by producing evidence that Joseph had been killed by a wild animal (vv. 31–33). Their motive, obviously, is to conceal their crime, to explain Joseph's absence. Here the special robe, now soiled with blood, plays its final role. This is followed by the poignant scene of the father mourning the loss of his favorite son and refusing to be comforted (vv. 34–35). The episode concludes with a transition of great importance, noting that Joseph had been sold to a certain Potiphar, one of the pharaoh's officers (v. 36). The narrative has come to a clear and definite conclusion, but this transition keeps it alive and opens the door to the next episode.

Family stories such as this one can be the occasion for reflection upon family relationships. Although it relates events long ago and far away, the presentation is thoroughly realistic. Family tensions—the preference of one sibling over others, jealousy—lead to family violence, which leads to suffering. Our narrator does not pass judgment on the characters, neither blaming the events on the father's preferential love for the youngest son nor even explicitly condemning the brothers for their crimes against their brother and their father. But we cannot miss the significance of differences in status and even material things such as clothes. Such factors can set into motion events that lead to tragic consequences. And that is how it ends, with only the hints in the boy's dreams that this family tragedy will play a role in a larger history.

Psalm 105:1–6, 16–22, 45b

Portions of this lection were the reading for Proper 12 [17]. What has been added here are verses 16–22, which supplement the reading from Genesis 37.

The famine mentioned in verse 16 was the occasion for Joseph's rise to power in Egypt. According to Genesis 41:54 and 42:5, the famine affected not only Egypt but also Palestine. In verse 17, Joseph is depicted as the one divinely sent by God to prepare a course for his kin in Egypt.

The description of Joseph's suffering in verse 18 supplements the material found in Genesis. According to verse 19, Joseph was tested by God. In postbiblical literature, Joseph becomes a central character in a number of stories. One of the most interesting is *Joseph and Aseneth*, which can be found in collections of the Old Testament pseudepigrapha (for Aseneth, see Gen. 41:45, 50–52; 46:20). References to Joseph's feet and neck being bound illustrate some of the ways the biblical text was expanded on.

Joseph's rise to power and his prominence at the pharaoh's court are noted in verses 21–22, which elaborate what is told about Joseph in the Bible. That the Hebrews were the source of learning for other nations is stressed in verse 22. The Joseph story bears many similarities to a widespread ancient near eastern story plot. This plot has an outsider brought to the court of a ruling monarch only to rise in prominence to the second highest position in the land. Daniel provides another example of this common narrative folk tale.

1 Kings 19:9–18

This lesson, the account of the epiphany of Yahweh to Elijah on Horeb, is rich in possibilities for theological and homiletical reflection. The awesome appearance of the Lord comes in the context of the collection of stories concerning the life and times of the prophet. The reading for the day brings us to an issue at the heart of those stories, the conflict between Yahweh and Baal, between Elijah and the followers of Baal—especially those in Israel's royal palace, Ahab and Jezebel. So it is part of a story of piety, politics, and prophetic succession, but the leading theme is the encounter between the prophet and the Lord.

The geographical setting of the story is important. Traveling forty days and forty nights into the wilderness, Elijah has arrived at "Horeb the mount of God" (19:8). What some of the Old Testament sources and traditions call "Horeb"—Deuteronomy in particular—others identify as "Sinai." Horeb was the location of Moses' call (Exod. 3:1). The mountain was the site of the establishment of the covenant and the revelation of the law through Moses. Historical geography has not been able to locate the place with certainty. The traditional site, Jebel Musa, is deep in the Sinai peninsula and far from any usual route between Egypt and Canaan. Some recent scholarship tends to set the site near Kadesh-barnea, much further to the north and nearer the boundaries of Israel. For our text, the important point is that the prophet has gone to the holy mountain of divine revelation and takes up residence in a cave.

What transpires is an epiphany of Yahweh to Elijah. The report has two distinct parts, verses 9b–13a and verses 13b–18. The opening formula, "Then the word of the Lord came to him" (v. 9b), introduces the first encounter, but it could just as well stand as the heading for the passage as a whole. We are not to forget that it was the *word* of the Lord that was decisive in the epiphany. Both sections of the account consist of dialogue between Yawheh and the prophet. Yahweh speaks (vv. 9b, 11a, 13b, 15–18) and Elijah responds (vv. 10, 14). The first two exchanges are divine questions and the prophet's responses. Finally, Yahweh's last word (vv. 15–18) is not a question but instructions, which Elijah obeys but does not answer.

The questions and answers are virtually identical. When the Lord asks Elijah what he is doing in this place, the prophet responds with words of self-defense and, perhaps, self-pity. He cites both his zeal ("I have been very zealous," vv. 10, 14) for Yahweh and the apostasy of the people of Israel. He insists that he is the only faithful one left and has had to flee for his life. Note that he accuses, not Ahab and Jezebel, but the people of Israel of violence against Yahweh's altars and prophets. The plural reference to altars is an accurate historical allusion, because worship was not centralized in Jerusalem and all other sanctuaries torn down until the time of Josiah in the seventh century. The reference to the slaughter of the prophets may allude to the persecution by Jezebel noted in 1 Kings 18:4, 13.

Between the first and second dialogue is the account of the epiphany itself (vv. 11–13a). It is parallel in some respects to the appearance of the Lord to Moses (Exod. 33:17–23). Both take refuge in the mountain (a cave or a "cleft in the rock"), and neither is allowed to see Yahweh directly. The account of the theophany to Elijah is consistent with a widespread Old Testament tradition. When the Lord appears, there are awesome and dangerous natural phenomena. Here it is first "a great wind" (v. 11) that even splits rocks; then an earthquake (v. 11) followed by fire (v. 12). In every case, there follows the refrain "But the Lord was not in the wind . . . the earthquake . . . the fire." Finally, there was "a sound of sheer silence" (v. 12; REB reads "a faint murmuring sound"). Only then does the prophet come to the mouth of the cave and hear the word of Yahweh. That "he wrapped his face in his mantle" (v. 13) reflects the deep awareness in the Old Testament tradition that no one can see God and live (cf. Exod. 33:21; Isa. 6:2–5).

The speech of Yahweh to Elijah, framed within the account of the theophany, concerns the conflict between Yahwism and Baalism. God's appearance leads to words of commission—similar in some ways to the vocation reports of other prophets—to the fugitive prophet. The prophet's complaints are answered by commands, first to return to the land where his life was in danger. Yahweh instructs him further to anoint two kings, one for Syria and one for Israel, and a prophet as his own successor (vv. 15–16). Then follows a somewhat cryptic, oracular interpretation of the purpose for which these three are to be anointed (v. 17)—bloodshed. The final sentence (v. 18) at once clarifies the death sentence—presumably for all who *have* "bowed the knee to Baal" and kissed him, that is, his image—and rebukes Elijah for his claim that he is the only one left who is faithful to Yahweh (19:10, 14).

There is a poignant note in this commission. Elijah, who has been at the center of the religious and political conflict, is not to see its resolution. That will be for his successor; Elijah's duty is to designate the instruments of the Lord's will. Like Moses, who was not allowed to enter the promised land, he lives with the promise and not its fulfilment.

The major issue in this passage is the nature of divine revelation. Although awesome and destructive natural phenomena (wind, earthquake, fire) may attend the appearance of Yahweh, the God of Israel is not to be identified with any of these. The story may even contain a polemic against the popular cultic view of the theophany (cf. Ps. 18:12; Ps. 68; Hab. 3:3). In any case, the perspective of this prophetic tradition is unmistakable: God reveals himself by means of the word, here the spoken word, and not fundamentally through the manipulation of natural forces; although those forces, to be sure, are set into turmoil by God's appearance. That word is calm, comprehensible, personal, and purposeful. The purpose of the epiphany is to commission the prophet to change history.

Thus, along with issues of the form of revelation and questions concerning the prophetic role and vocation, the passage raises but does not resolve for us the problem of the relation between faith and politics. Both those who feel that religious leaders should be involved directly in politics and those who feel that they should not are likely to find support in this text. On the one hand, Elijah, like all Israel's prophets, was deeply involved in politics, to the point of instigating rebellion. Without such zeal, it is questionable whether the Yahwistic faith would have survived. On the other hand, his fanatically held faith called forth a bloodbath, which at least one later prophet will condemn (Hos. 1:4–5). Today, in a very different culture, where political and religious institutions are more distinct, we are impelled to struggle with the issues of faith and culture, religion and politics.

Psalm 85:8–13

The proclamation of verses 8–13 is best seen in light of the psalm as a whole. Verses 1–3 recall an earlier time when God had restored the fortunes of the people, forgiving their sins and withdrawing the divine wrath. What this section talks about specifically remains uncertain. Does it refer to the return from exile proclaimed in glorious terms in Second Isaiah? Or does it revolve around features of Israel's great autumn festival season, when God was annually proclaimed as forgiving the people's sin on the day of atonement and providing for the people a new slate and a new fate for the coming year? Probably the latter should be seen as the context of this psalm's usage and the phenomenon described in verses 1–3. The prayer for God to revive and restore the people in verses 4–7 would thus be a plea that God would again, in the festival, put away divine indignation and anger and display instead his salvation and thus revive the people.

The lectionary text, according to the above interpretation, would be an oracle spoken in the service of worship by some cultic official (priest? prophet?) who already envisioned and anticipated what God's response would be and what consequences it would produce. (Note that v. 1–7 are addressed to the Deity and are thus prayers, whereas vv. 8–13 speak about the Deity and are somewhat similar to the preaching and proclamation of a prophet, like Elijah.)

Psalm 85:8–13 anticipates the appearance of God and already perceives its consequences. What God will speak is peace (*shalom!*). The consequences of Yahweh's speaking are described in a play on a number of terms—faithfulness, righteousness, peace, steadfast love. What these terms describe are all good qualities. They are depicted coming together as if they were two who meet and kiss or as if one springs from the earth and the other looks down from the sky. That is, because God speaks, full harmony and unity result. Here ideal qualities are merged.

Verse 12 returns to more mundane matters; God will give what is good, and the land will yield its increase. This again suggests the use of this psalm in the fall festival, when the old agricultural year ends and a new year begins. In Palestine, the rainy season, from October through April, is followed by a rainless season, from May through September. Thus the new agricultural year in the Bible began after the first rains in the fall, when new crops could be sown. The fall festival was celebrated as the hinge between the ending of the old and the beginning of the new. Thus the oracle of verses 8–13 closes with the promise of a good agricultural year. (Perhaps vv. 4–7 suggest that the previous year's harvest had not been good.) In the Elijah narrative, the coming of rain to break the drought is a prominent motif.

Romans 10:5–15

A portion of this text (10:8*b*–13) also serves as the epistolary reading for the First Sunday in Lent in Year C. The reader may want to consult our remarks in that setting.

The proper context for framing today's text is established in the opening verses, where Paul contrasts "the saving justice that comes by the Law" (v. 5, NJB) and the "saving justice of faith" (v. 6, NJB). The background to his exposition is provided by Deuteronomy 30:11–14, which emphasizes the nearness and accessibility of God's covenant with Israel. What God requires through the covenant is not remote. It is neither in the heaven nor beyond the sea, as if Israel had to go in search for it. Rather, "the word is very near to you; it is in your mouth and in your heart for you to observe" (Deut. 30:14). In establishing a covenant with Israel, Yahweh had graciously reached out in their direction, drawn near to them, had indeed come to be within them—on their lips and in their hearts (cf. Jer. 31:31–34).

Drawing on these words from Deuteronomy, Paul reads them in light of the Christ-event. Just as Israel was reassured that the covenant was not remote and far away, so Paul insists that Christ is to be sought neither in the heavens nor in the abyss of Hades. It is not as if we must go in search of Christ to find him. His presence is not spatial, but existential. We experience him not by gazing upward nor peering downward, but by looking (and listening) within. And how is this so? Through the "word of faith that we proclaim" (v. 8b). By putting the gospel into words, faith becomes articulated. God's promise becomes expressed in speech; and when we receive it in faith, we discover that "the word is near [us], on [our] lips and in [our] heart" (v. 8a, quoting Deut. 30:14). Here Paul is insisting that the living Christ, who is mediated to us through the preached word, is as near, as existentially present within us, as was the covenant Yahweh made with Israel.

As we receive the word of faith that is proclaimed—"that God raised [Christ] from the dead"—God's word actually comes to expression within us, and we in turn express this conviction by confessing with our lips that "Jesus is Lord." Salvation can thus be construed as our words responding to God's words. Through faith, God's word becomes articulate within us, and we in turn articulate the faith that saves us.

It is difficult to think of anything nearer or more existentially present than the very words on our lips or the convictions of our hearts. What is said and what is believed define who we are. Here, what is said is the Christian confession—"Jesus is Lord" (1 Cor. 12:3; 2 Cor. 4:5; Phil. 2:11; Col. 2:6)—and what is believed is the Easter faith: God raised Christ from the dead (Rom. 4:24; 1 Pet. 1:21). It is on the basis of this conviction and this confession that we experience salvation.

It follows rather naturally that salvation should be universally available. After all, every human being has heartfelt convictions that the lips put into words. Consequently, Paul cites Isaiah 28:16 to show that all who believe will find their faith coming to fruition. They will not be put to shame. They will not be disappointed. This applies to everyone—Jew and Gentile alike. Because there is only one Lord—that is, Jesus Christ (Acts 10:36; Phil. 2:9–11)—there cannot be two ways of being saved. Everyone is justified on the same grounds and in the same way—through faith. We should recognize that the Lord's bounty is extensive enough to accommodate everyone who is willing to yield in faith. Thus "every one who calls upon the name of the Lord will be saved" (v. 13; cf. Joel 2:32).

We should note the repeated insistence that everyone has access to God in faith. If we see ourselves as the elect of God, it is all too easy to conclude that we have a monopoly on God's riches. But God draws near through the preached word to everyone, and those who respond by calling on the name of the Lord for help and hope will not be disappointed; they will be saved.

From Paul's midrashic exposition of Deuteronomy 30:11–14 and his use of other Old Testament passages, we can make the following observations:

First, salvation is not so much a matter of our drawing near to Christ, as if we must seek him in order to find him at the end of a long search. It is rather that Christ has drawn near to us through the gospel. This means that the presence of God as mediated through Christ has become both universalized and localized. It is no longer necessary for us to go find Christ in a sacred place (cf. John 4), for now the word of God has become portable. Christ becomes present whenever and wherever the gospel is preached. Salvation is to be found here and now—within us—because God has drawn near.

Second, salvation belongs to the faithful—all the faithful, not to a select group who regard themselves as the most faithful or who see themselves alone as the faithful. The basis on which all of humanity comes to know God is now common to us all. We can be assured that our faith, if it is genuine, will not come to nought. We can also be assured that God's riches are bountiful enough to go around. We may believe that God is exclusively ours or that we relate to God in a uniquely close relationship, but here we are reminded that everyone who calls out to God for help, even as we do, can and will be heard.

The final section of today's text (vv. 14–15) might well be extended through verse 17, for it is the natural ending of this unit. Given the importance attached to the preached word in the previous unit, it is only natural that Paul would emphasize the crucial role of the messenger who bears the good news. As important as the proclaimed word is, it only comes to expression on the lips of human messengers—those whom God sends. As the final verse emphasizes, faith is finally a matter of hearing—listening to and listening for the word of God through the preached word. But even though it is the messenger's words that we hear, behind them, ultimately, and through them existentially, we actually hear the "word of Christ," both the message about Christ and the message that originated with Christ.

Matthew 14:22–33

The story of Jesus walking on the water is joined in Matthew, Mark (6:45–52), and John (6:16–21) to the feeding of the multitude. Perhaps the two stories were united earlier in the tradition and may echo Israel's experience of the sea and the wilderness feedings. The part about Simon Peter (vv. 28–31) is a Matthean addition; but even so, 14:22–33 is a distinct unit and can be treated as such in sermon and lesson. The lection begins with the disciples entering a boat and ends before they land at Gennesaret.

Jesus walking on the water may have served in some Christian circles as evidence of Jesus' cosmic power subduing the forces of nature. In biblical literature, the sea is often represented as the abode of demonic forces hostile to God. In the Apocalypse, the final reign of God will mean that the sea no longer exists (21:1). Matthew's picture of Christ standing on violent waves amid raging winds, saying to the fearful, "I am" (vv. 25–27), certainly affirms the lordship of Christ over the created world.

However, as it stands in Matthew, the story functions differently. It is a kind of epiphany, an appearance of Christ not unlike a resurrection appearance. On a dark night of fear and helplessness, Christ comes to his disciples. Until reassured, they think they see a ghost. Special attention to Peter recalls resurrection narratives (Luke 24:34; John 21; 1 Cor. 15:5). In John 21, Peter jumps into the water, but does not walk on it. Whatever may be the relationship, literary or historical, between this story and others, we must look to the story itself to hear what Matthew is saying.

Matthew has made two major changes in the story as received from Mark 6:45–52: the insertion of Peter's attempt to walk to Jesus and the radical alteration of the ending. Before looking at those elements, it is important to keep in mind that this is a story to and for the church. The scene, set between a crowd (14:12–21) and a crowd (14:34–36), involves only Jesus and the Twelve. For the disciples alone to be the beneficiaries of a miracle is very unusual in the Gospels and provides a rare glimpse inside the church of that time. The fact that many find it easy to preach on this text is due to Matthew's having already made this event a sermon. The church in the world is as the church in a storm: the disciples are in a boat without Jesus; a threatening storm arises; Jesus comes, bringing first fear and then assurance; the disciples, in the person of Peter, now feel strong enough to handle the storm as Jesus did, and the venture almost succeeds; Jesus again rescues them from the storm, which ceases when he enters the boat; the disciples now worship Jesus as Son of God.

Notice, then, how Matthew's vignette about Simon Peter functions. This small story is inserted between the description of the disciples as fearful (vv. 26–27) and as confessing and worshiping (v. 33). Simon Peter, the voice and heart of the group, is thus between fear and faith. He walks and he sinks; he trusts and he fears. His response enables Matthew to move the story along in three phases: "It is I," announces Jesus (v. 27); "Lord, if it is you," responds Peter (v. 28); "Truly you are," says the entire group (v. 33).

And finally, Matthew's altered ending allows him to join this story to his larger narrative in which the disciples respond to Christ's lordship with fear, doubt, and worship (28:16–18). Mark's insistence that the disciples never understood, here (6:52) and elsewhere, is modified by Matthew to a portrait of persons "of little faith" (8:26; 14:31; 16:8; 17:20). Jesus' followers have faith, but not enough, and so Jesus nourishes that little faith to the point of confession and praise. The continuing presence of Christ in the believing community is experienced as judgment, to be sure, but also as patience and grace.

Proper 15 [20]
(Sunday between August 14 and 20 inclusive)

Genesis 45:1–15;
Psalm 133; or
Isaiah 56:1, 6–8;
Psalm 67;
Romans 11:1–2*a*, 29–32;
Matthew 15:(10–20) 21–28

In the *Common Lectionary*, the Old Testament text comes from the end of the Joseph saga, when he is reconciled with his family and they then move to Egypt. In response to this moving story of family reconciliation, Psalm 133, a short responsorial psalm, appropriately proclaims the blessedness of families living together harmoniously.

In the other set of Old Testament and psalm readings, the first lesson is provided by a portion of the postexilic poem from Isaiah 56, which proclaims Yahweh's declaration of justice and willingness to accept non-Israelites and deal faithfully with them. Psalm 67 praises God as one who is both gracious and equitable in dealing with the nations.

In the second lesson, Paul continues to wrestle with the question of the role of Israel in the plan of God in light of the growth and development of the church, especially the inclusion of Gentiles within the people of God. The narrative in the Gospel reading addresses the question of who is properly excluded from God by defilement, and, fittingly, concludes with Matthew's account of the Canaanite woman whose persistent plea impinged on Jesus' exclusive mission to the house of Israel.

Genesis 45:1–15

For an introduction to the Joseph story as a whole, see the comments on Genesis 37:1–4, 12–28 for the previous week. Genesis 45:1–15 is a key episode in that narrative (Gen. 37, 39–47, 50). In fact, this account of Joseph's revelation of his identity to his brothers is the climax of the narrative, the point at which the main tensions of the plot are resolved and the purpose of the events disclosed. That purpose is not easy to understand without considering this episode in its larger context.

Although the Joseph story is a carefully crafted narrative, it has been composed of material from the older sources, J and E. Careful reading of our passage will reveal some evidence of the combination. It is not clear, for example, whether Joseph's display of emotion was private or heard by the Egyptians. He twice tells his brothers who he is, and—perhaps indicating that something has dropped out—he asks if his father is still alive (v. 3) but proceeds to give instructions to bring him to Egypt without hearing the answer.

The brothers, jealous of Joseph, had sold him into slavery, where he had not only survived but prospered. His special talents and skills had taken him, as he says, to the second highest office in Egypt. (The language of 45:8 and elsewhere indicates that the narrator sees him as the Grand Vizer, in effect, the prime minister under only the pharaoh.) Egypt and the entire region are suffering the period of famine foreseen by Joseph in his dreams, so the brothers come looking for food. The tension had been allowed to grow: how will the old conflict between Joseph and the brothers be resolved? Our text shows the answer and also makes it clear that the plot—the development of the story as a whole—had actually been taking place on a different level from that perceived by the participants in it.

Following an introduction (vv. 1–4a), most of the passage before us is a speech by Joseph to his brothers. It is filled with the emotion of the reunion. When Joseph reveals his identity, the brothers are "dumbfounded" (REB, v. 3) by fear and unbelief. Will Joseph, who now is so powerful, repay them with what they did to him? The brothers quickly learn what we, the readers, knew already—that he will forgive them. But, significantly, Joseph gives what amounts to a theological explanation for his attitude and his actions: "God sent me before you to preserve life. . . . God sent me before you to preserve for you a remnant on earth." (vv. 5, 7). That is the point of the Joseph story as a whole, expressed somewhat more comprehensively in Genesis 50:20: "Even though you intended to do harm to me, God intended it for good, in order to preserve a numerous people, as he is doing today."

Thus the movement of events, so transparent on the human level, is the expression of a gracious divine purpose, which only in the end becomes plain. The two main themes of the passage, human conflict and divine care, converge. One who, like Joseph, understands and has confidence in God's providential care is able to love and forgive one's enemies. Who knows, God may be in the process of using the wrath of human beings to praise him.

Psalm 133

The vocabulary of unity among kindred in Psalm 133 had led to the choice of this psalm to accompany the story of Joseph's reunion with his family.

As one of the pilgrim psalms (see the discussion of Psalm 122 for the First Sunday of Advent), Psalm 133 gives expression to the unity that the people felt in their journeying to and arrival at Jerusalem.

Two metaphors are used to describe the blessings of unity. The first, in verse 2, draws on the imagery of the anointing of a high priest when the holy oil was poured over the head of the new high priest (see Exod. 29:7; Lev. 8:12). To us this imagery may appear absurd, if not grotesque. For the ancient Israelites, the inauguration of a new high priest expressed the ongoing function of the ritual offices that stood between God and the people, and thus was an assurance of society's ongoing well-being. The high priest represented the unity of the people before God. The second metaphor describes the unity of the people as a blessing paralleling the "dew of Hermon." Mt. Hermon to the northeast of Jerusalem stands as a snow covered range over 9200 feet above sea level. Its melting snows feed the Jordan River. Perhaps "dew of Hermon" was the name given the extra heavy dew that falls in late summer and early autumn, which is sufficient to water small plants and produce some growth. Community unity is thus seen as life invigorating.

Isaiah 56:1, 6–8

For a quick review of the historical context for this lesson, turn back to the comments on Isaiah 55:1–5 found in Proper 13 [18]. Even though some scholars divide chapters 56–66 from 40–55 and designate the section Third Isaiah, the political situation may not be radically altered between chapters 55 and 56.

In these verses, it is God who is speaking. The reader should not be disconcerted by occasional shifts from first to third person and back to first; this is not an uncommon literary trait, especially in the prophets and the psalms. Even though verses 2–5 are not in today's reading, the whole of 56:1–8 needs to be kept in view in order to understand the literary structure and hence the message of the text.

Isaiah 56:1–8 has to do with enlarging the membership of God's redeemed community, at God's own invitation. This means, of course, that there must be some changes from Israel's pre-exile self-understanding. Verse 1 lays out very clearly the terms of membership, with no exceptions: maintaining justice and doing what is right. To be sure, the new community is God's to create and to sustain, but this does not mean that it is without standards of membership. That this is so is not a new idea from the prophet; Sinai was and is at the heart of shaping the people God calls. However, prophetic activity is reminding the listener of the old, too often forgotten covenant. Ethical, moral, and religious expectations are written into the covenant. And in fact, why would any persons, especially the oppressed and denied, even be interested in belonging to the community of God's people if justice and right relationships did not prevail there?

Verses 3–8 are specifically addressed to two groups widely regarded as outsiders—foreigners and eunuchs. With good reason, the foreigners said, "The Lord will surely separate me from his people" (v. 3). Ezra 10:18–44 is but one of many voices in Israel insisting on the separation of Jews and Gentiles. With good reason, the eunuch said, "I am just a dry tree" (v. 3). Deuteronomy 23:1 is quite clear in its exclusion from the assembly of God's people all males who by reason of accident or birth could not procreate. Structurally, verses 3–8 form a chiasm, a rather common literary pattern for expressing and remembering units of thought:

Foreigner, v. 3*a*

Eunuch, v. 3*b*

Eunuch, vv. 4–5

Foreigner, vv. 6–8

These verses taken together make one of the most radical statements about the generosity of grace and the universality of God's love to be found in all the Bible. God here embraces two groups clearly outside the commonly held definition of God's people.

Again, however, the enlarged borders of the community do not represent relaxed or abandoned demands on those who would live within it. Listen to these words to the foreigner who would join God's people: minister, love, serve, keep the sabbath, hold to the covenant, worship with offerings and sacrifices. But lest any think that they, by approved conduct, earn entrance, the word is repeated: "These I will bring to my holy mountain" (v. 7). Of course, some may be bothered that this passage contradicts others; for example, those texts that exclude foreigners and eunuchs. That is one way to view it, but it might be more helpful to learn again here how the Bible debates and argues with itself as God works with stubborn and prideful people to bring about a realm of love and justice that does not exclude. If the Bible did not mirror these very struggles of our own lives, how could we really hear it as God's word to us? But in the enthusiasm of inclusivity, the reader is reminded not to be so occupied with the distant foreigner that "the outcasts of Israel" (v. 8), the outsiders within, are overlooked. In fact, just in case someone begins to act as self-appointed host in God's house, God says not to try to calculate the guest list: "I will gather others to them besides those already gathered" (v. 8).

Although it is not necessary to turn to the New Testament to supplement this rich and full text, the fact remains that those familiar with its writings are already experiencing what Aristotle called "the joy of recognition." Isaiah 56 is most important for early Christian interpreters of the event of Jesus Christ. Simply to stimulate further reflection, three contacts with this text are called to remembrance. First, the ministry of Jesus as presented by Matthew, Mark, and Luke was primarily to "the outcasts of Israel." Second, on the occasion of Jesus cleansing the temple, Mark says that Jesus quoted Isaiah 56:7: "My house shall be called a house of prayer for all the nations" (11:17). And third, in the story of the Ethiopian eunuch (Acts 8:26–40), Luke joins into one person the two outsiders of Isaiah 56 who are embraced in God's new community, the foreigner and the eunuch.

Psalm 67

Psalm 67 contains both request to receive blessing and thanksgiving for blessing received. Verse 1 and verses 6–7 speak about God, whereas verses 2–5 directly address God and thus are in prayer form. Verses 3 and 5 are a refrain. Probably different groups of people or different choirs sang the prayerful requests of verses 2 and 4 and the refrains of verses 3 and 5.

Three elements, or emphases, in the psalm are of interest and could be developed in preaching. There is, first, the benedictory character of the opening verse. In this text, the congregation requests divine favor and blessing. For the "face to shine upon" someone was a way of saying "show favor toward." It is equivalent to our saying, "may God 'smile' on us." Both in terminology and concern, this opening verse is very similar to the great priestly blessing found in Numbers 6:24–26, truly one of the great texts of the Hebrew Scriptures.

Second, the psalm has a strong universal emphasis. This is expressed in three ways. (1) The request for divine blessing on the Israelite community has, as its rationale, a universal goal. Bless us, it requests, "that your way may be known upon earth, your saving power among all nations." Divine blessing on the worshiping community is thus seen as the means for God to bear witness to himself among other people. (2) The psalm petitions God to let the nations of the world (the Gentiles) join in the praise. This envisions others joining the chosen people in the worship of their God, but not necessarily their conversion. (3) God is declared ready to be the judge and guide for the nations, a role that the Divine exercises with equity. Such a declaration clearly affirms a universal rule for the Deity.

Finally, the psalm offers thanksgiving for the earth's increase. Verses 6–7 suggest that this psalm may have been used in conjunction with either the spring or the fall harvest seasons. The divine blessing is related, however, not to the worshiping community's own self-enjoyment but as an instrument for the universal acknowledgment and fear of God.

Romans 11:1–2a, 29–32

I n the concluding section of chapter 10, Paul cites Old Testament passages (Ps. 19:4; Deut. 32:21; Isa. 65:1–2) to underscore Israel's traditional pattern of disobedience to God's promise. But does this mean that God has rejected Israel unconditionally? This is the question with which chapter 11 opens (v. 1a), and Paul can only respond with an emphatic denial: "By no means! . . . God has not rejected his people whom he foreknew" (vv. 1–2).

What follows in chapter 11 is an extended discussion of Israel's rejection and how it fits into God's overall plan of redemption. Paul insists that even Israel's rejection of the gospel could be construed as a redemptive act. In refusing the gospel, the Jews might have "stumbled," but they had not fallen permanently (11:11). Their resistance was only a temporary stage in God's overall plan. It had provided the occasion for turning to the Gentiles, thus "through their stumbling salvation has come to the Gentiles" (11:11). Stage one, then, was Israel's rejection. This was to be followed by stage two, the Gentiles' acceptance. Stage three would be Israel's final acceptance.

Because it was Paul's unique vocation to serve as an "apostle to the Gentiles" (v. 13; Rom. 1:5; 15:16; Gal. 2:7–8), he could see his missionary work as the crucial middle stage in God's overall strategy for bringing about salvation for all people. Accordingly, he could "glorify [his] ministry" among the Gentiles, and in doing so accelerate God's purpose in the world.

He is quite pointed in conceding that his purpose in preaching to the Gentiles was to evoke the jealousy of the Jews (v. 14). The logic here seems to be that the Gentiles' acceptance of the gospel would testify to their reception of God's love. Seeing God's love redirected toward the Gentiles, the Jews would sense that they were out of favor with God and become jealous. Like a jilted lover, they would then return to God to regain full favor.

Paul's line of argument here may seem trivial to us, but he is informed by scriptural precedent. Divine jealousy is a prominent Old Testament theme. Just as Israel could stir Yahweh to jealousy by their flirtations with other gods, so could Yahweh provoke Israel to jealousy by accomplishing the divine will through other nations (Deut. 32:21; cf. Rom. 10:19). For Paul to conceive of his mission work to the Gentiles as provoking jealousy among the Gentiles, and thus prompting them to return to God, was merely to interpret his own work in light of God's past dealings with Israel.

It is in this sense that the rejection of Israel would mean the reconciliation of the world (v. 15; cf. 2 Cor. 5:19; Col. 1:19–20; Rom. 4:8). Their refusal would only be penultimate. It would allow opportunity for the Gentiles to respond to the gospel, and this in turn would trigger the Jews to respond in kind. In this way, God's reconciling work would reach its goal. Thus their rejection is but a middle stage toward God's ultimate reconciliation, and their final acceptance would be "life from the dead" (v. 15). For them finally to accept the gospel would be tantamount to the dead coming to life again!

And why should Paul hold out for such a redemptive role on the part of disobedient Israel? Because "the gifts and the calling of God are irrevocable" (v. 29). It was a matter of inviolable principle for Paul that God's integrity remained intact. The immutability of God's promise had become something of an axiom in Old Testament thought (Num. 23:19; 1 Sam. 15:29; Isa. 31:2; 54:10; Ps. 110:4). This confidence in God's truthfulness and fidelity had also become an ingrained feature of Christian faith (Rom. 15:8; 1 Cor. 1:9; 10:13; 1 Thess. 5:24). Once invited into the membership of God's elect, no one could be disinvited, at least not permanently. No matter how disobedient Israel might have been, it was inconceivable that God would turn away in an act of final, irrevocable abandonment.

Rather, God sought ways of working the divine will even in the midst of human mismanagement. Just as disobedient Gentiles had become recipients of God's mercy, so now would disobedient Jews become recipients of God's mercy. As Paul had shown earlier, all humanity—both Jews and Gentiles—is under the grip of sin (Rom. 1:18–3:21). Thus "God has imprisoned all human beings in their own disobedience" (v. 32, NJB), but not with a view to being vindictive. Rather, the universality of sin has become an occasion for the universality of divine grace: "that [God] may be merciful to all" (v. 32; cf. 5:9; 15:9; 1 Tim. 2:4; Ezek. 18:23).

One obvious homiletical possibility presented by today's text is the unequivocal faith in God's integrity (v. 29). The God who gives and the God who calls may be trusted to retract neither the gift nor the call. Our own refusal to receive or to listen may become profound disobedience, but even this cannot thwart the divine purpose. Indeed, in an odd sort of way, our disobedience may even extend the work of God.

Matthew 15:(10–20) 21–28

The preacher has the option of including verses 10–20 as background for dealing with the encounter between Jesus and the Canaanite woman (vv. 21–28). Relating the two stories may not seem natural or helpful. Different geographical locations are involved, different audiences encounter Jesus, and apparently different issues are addressed. But maybe not.

Pharisees and scribes from Jerusalem criticize Jesus because his disciples do not observe a tradition of ritual cleansing (vv. 1–3). In the course of the ensuing debate about rituals, tradition, and the will of God, Jesus makes a strong pronouncement: it is not what enters the stomach but what exits the heart that is of concern for him and for all seeking to be God's people (vv. 10–20). In principle, this became the position of the Christian community on food laws. In practice, however, the church struggled a long time over the matter, as the Acts of the Apostles testifies, because nonobservance of food laws meant opening table fellowship to persons excluded because of the food regulations. In effect, Jews and Gentiles could now eat together; a major barrier had fallen.

But had it? Did all followers of Jesus accept this inclusivity? To accept a principle and to engage in its practice are often in us and among us miles apart. Now attend to the story in verses 21–28.

Obviously, Matthew 15:21–28 and Mark 7:24–30 are telling the same story, but the differences are so marked that some have conjectured two traditions about Jesus' visit to the region of Tyre and Sidon. The preacher would do well to read the two accounts together as a part of preparation, not only to assure that Mark's record not bleed unintentionally into Matthew, but also by so doing, to fix Matthew's story more clearly in mind.

In the district of Tyre and Sidon, Jesus is met by a Canaanite woman. The use of this ancient term is strange. Perhaps it was used to serve as a contrast to Israel in verse 24. It is a dramatic way of portraying her as an outsider. But even more strange is her address to Jesus: "Lord, Son of David" (v. 22). She is not simply calling him an Israelite of David's family; she is using a title, in some quarters a messianic title. Considering that the people in Jesus' own country have not so perceived him, and even his disciples are yet to speak of him messianically (16:13–20), this title on the lips of a Canaanite living in another country is most unusual. But perhaps that is Matthew's point; in other words, Matthew may be saying that first from a Gentile, a foreign woman, came the confession of faith. Although the story is historically difficult, it may thus be theologically understandable.

Even so, there is a painful harshness in this event that will not go away. To the woman's plea, "Have mercy on me," Jesus is at first silent (v. 23). Then the disciples say, "Send her away," she is a nuisance to us (v. 23). When Jesus does speak, he tells her that his ministry is "only to the lost sheep of the house of Israel" (v. 24). The woman repeats her plea, falling on her knees before Jesus. Again, Jesus puts up an obstacle, saying it is not fair to give the children's bread to the dogs (v. 26). Her final response is to say, in effect, then treat me as a dog and let me have the crumbs that fall from the table. At this display of tenacious trust, Jesus commends her faith and heals her daughter (v. 28).

Commentators on this text make various attempts to relieve the story of its embarrassment. Jesus was testing her faith, say some; Jesus was struggling in his mind with the idea of a Gentile mission, say others; Jesus was bringing her to an appropriate humility, say yet others. All of these together do not smooth out the surprisingly harsh tones of this encounter between Jesus and the Canaanite woman.

That Matthew understood Jesus' mission during his lifetime to be confined to Israel is quite clear. Only three times in this Gospel does Jesus minister to outsiders: here, in Capernaum (the centurion's servant, 8:5–13), and in Gadara (8:28–34). After the resurrection, Christ commissioned his followers to preach to all nations (28:18–20). However, there were some in the early church who believed that the post-Easter church should continue to confine itself to Israel. Luke reports in Acts that even Peter, prior to the Joppa vision, believed Gentiles to be unclean (10:1–11:18). The first conference of the church, says Luke, was to debate the issue of admitting Gentiles who did not first become Jews (Acts 16). Paul's position was, to the Jew first, and then to the Gentile (Rom. 1:16; 2:9–10).

Matthew 15:21–28 registers this painful issue, forms of which still plague the church. Jesus healed the woman's daughter, but the blessing was hard won—the victory of a tenacious claim on the compassion of Christ.

Proper 16 [21]
(Sunday between August 21 and 27 inclusive)

Exodus 1:8–2:10;
Psalm 124; or
Isaiah 51:1–6;
Psalm 138;
Romans 12:1–8;
Matthew 16:13–20

Today's Old Testament reading from the *Common Lectionary* marks a shift in the semicontinuous reading of the Pentateuch, as the focus now shifts to Moses. This text sets the scene for the Exodus by characterizing the Egyptian oppression of the Israelite people and reporting the birth of Moses. The psalm is a corporate thanksgiving song, an appropriate response to the anticipated deliverance from Egypt.

Another text from Isaiah supplies the Old Testament reading for those who use other lectionaries. The opening section of Isaiah 51 serves as an invitation by Yahweh for Israel to recall the ways the divine promise was fulfilled through Abraham and Sarah, and to believe that Yahweh's power to deliver will continue. In response, Psalm 138, a psalm of thanksgiving, expresses gratitude for Yahweh's faithfulness and confidence that it will continue.

The epistolary lesson turns to the hortatory section of Romans, drawing on the opening section that calls for us to offer ourselves as renewed, transformed beings in sacrificial offering to God. In the Gospel reading, Matthew reports his version of the episode at Caesarea Philippi in which he includes Jesus' comments on Peter as the rock upon which he will establish the church.

Exodus 1:8–2:10

It is important to set these verses into their broader Old Testament context, for a great deal has transpired between last week's account in the semicontinuous pentateuchal reading concerning Joseph and today's lesson, and momentous events are yet to come. The lengthy and sophisticated account of Joseph and his brothers (Gen. 37, 38–47, 50) finally served to show how Jacob's family ended up in Egypt. Our reading for today describes the circumstances of Israel in Egypt and begins the preparation for their exodus under the leadership of Moses.

Our reading is preceded by the first paragraph of the Book of Exodus (1:1–7), which provides the transition from the Book of Genesis. When the Book of Exodus begins, the family of Jacob in the time of Joseph has "multiplied and grew exceedingly strong, so that the land was filled with them" (v. 7). Thus the first part of the promise originally made to Abraham (Gen. 12:1–3) and reiterated to his son and grandson has been fulfilled—the promise that their descendants would become a people great and numerous. The next unit (Exod. 1:8–22) reports the Egyptian oppression, the dark background for the Lord's rescue of his people. The third section (Exod. 2:1–10) is the story of the birth and deliverance of the baby who will grow up to lead Israel to freedom. A jealous and foolish tyrant fears a little baby and, it turns out, for good reason. Except for verses 1–7 and 13–14, which come from the Priestly Writer, this material comes from one of the older pentateuchal sources, most likely the Yahwist.

The account of the Egyptian oppression (1:8–22) provides the necessary narrative preparation for the Exodus in general and for the birth story of Moses in particular. The new (unnamed) Egyptian king fears the now numerous Israelites for hypothetical reasons (in case of war they might join the enemy side). He takes two steps to deal with the problem; both of them defy logic but are consistent with the habits of tyrants. First, he enslaves them and sets them to work on his construction projects, but mysteriously they thrive all the more, and the Egyptian fears the increase (vv. 11–12). Second, he takes one and then another step to kill the Israelite male babies. This was hardly the best way to assure himself of a good slave population, but tyrants are not known for their wisdom and good judgment, especially in the stories told by their subjects. After the Hebrew midwives refuse to cooperate by killing the males (1:15–21), the pharaoh commands that all the male babies be thrown into the Nile (1:22).

The story of Moses' birth and rescue, like that of the Hebrew midwives, is a woman's story. Chapter 2 begins abruptly as the report of perfectly ordinary events, marriage and birth, but by verse 2 the reader knows that the death threat stands in the background. The unnamed baby's mother manages to conceal him for three months but then must take other steps. What follows is a historically improbable sequence of events, full of irony. With great care the mother prepares a waterproof basket for the baby (v. 3), and the very river in which he was to be drowned bears him to safety. Now the central character appears on the scene, the boy's older sister. (The report of the baby's birth implied that he was the firstborn, but obviously he was not.) She and the mother watch while the princess and her attendants come to bathe in the Nile and discover the child. The princess has compassion on the baby and remarkably knows that "this is one of the Hebrews' children" (v. 6). Boldly, the sister comes forward and offers to find a nurse to care for the baby. Her offer is accepted, and she brings the child's mother.

One purpose of the story is to report how Moses got his name. Ordinarily, children would have been named at their birth, but here it comes later to serve as the narrative conclusion. The princess named him Moses (*mosheh*) because she "drew him out" (*mashah*) of the water. The etymology, like most such biblical accounts, is a popular, nontechnical one based on similarity of sounds. As many commentators have noted, our narrator probably did not know that the name "Moses" is actually the Hebrew form of a common Egyptian word meaning "son."

A second concern is revealed by the story's style and tone, and especially its irony. It is ironical that the future leader of the people is the adopted son of the princess—that is, he grows up in the very court of the one who sought to kill him—and at the same time is nursed by his own mother. The instrument of that reversal, that defeat of the pharaoh's scheme, is a simple slave girl. Doubtless, later children of those slaves must have laughed or at least smiled to hear how a girl and her mother outwitted the tyrant. Moreover, one way that slaves survive tyranny—and sometimes even overthrow it—is through ridicule. Note that the tradition is not unqualified in its criticism of foreigners, for success depended upon the compassion of the Egyptian princess.

Above all, this passage is a chapter in the story of the deliverance of Israel from slavery in Egypt. It sets the stage and introduces the central human character, Moses, and reports that he was on the one hand educated in the Egyptian court but on the other hand was nursed and guided by his Israelite mother. Although the name of God is not mentioned in the story of Moses' birth, we are to understand from the context that the will of God is being worked out in history, and in opposition to the will of the foreign king. God will save a people, but through human instruments—eventually Moses, but here through a girl and her mother, and even though unwittingly, a compassionate foreign princess.

Psalm 124

Psalm 124 is one of the "Songs of Ascents," or "Songs of Pilgrimage." It is a thanksgiving psalm that offers thanks for God's care during the past. Thus it is the type of psalm that would have been appropriate for the occasion when pilgrims looked back over the past year. Although no references in the psalm mention Moses or the plight of the Hebrews in Egypt, the conditions depicted in the psalm may be understood as analogies to the situation of Exodus 1:8–2:10.

Probably the opening of the psalm was sung by the pilgrim leader, who then called upon all the pilgrims to join the song. This explains why verse 2a repeats verse 1a and why verse 1b says, "Let Israel now say." The remainder of the psalm may have been sung by the leader line by line and then repeated by the pilgrims.

The psalm offers thanks for having survived the past. We would say for having survived the alienation and anarchy of life. Two main images are employed to give expression to the concepts—overwhelming waters (vv. 3–5) and bird traps (vv. 6–7). The opponents of the worshipers are simply described as "enemies" (v. 2b) and "their" (v. 6b). The actual opponents are not as significant as the sentiments expressed. The psalm allows the worshipers to express their feelings and give vent to their emotions.

The sense of alienation and being overwhelmed by life are described with strong pictures: swallowed up, anger kindled, floods sweeping over one, torrents overcoming, and "raging waters." Obviously, the idea is that of people struggling to retain their bearings and some stability in life. The threat is that of absolutely losing control. The minister could preach on this psalm and deal with the human effort required to stay in control of life. Much of every person's life is spent fighting anarchy. Paying bills, meeting schedules, and a whole range of activities are undertaken merely to clear a little space in which we feel at home. Sickness and, in this case, the actions of others always are potential "waters" that threaten to engulf life.

Verses 6–7 pay tribute to God's care. Just as verses 1–5 proclaim that having God on one's side gives life some tranquility, so God is here blessed for having offered rescue in the time of need. Again strong metaphors appear. The NJPSV translates these verses:

> Blessed is the Lord, who did not let us
> be ripped apart by their teeth.
> We are like a bird escaped from the fowler's trap;
> the trap broke and we escaped.

Here as is so frequently done in the psalms, the speakers seem to be paranoid to a certain extent. Whether or not this seems to reflect a situation bordering on the psychotic or not would depend on how one experiences and interprets life. There is a legitimate extent to which all people occasionally experience the world as a very hostile place, as if life were lived on a beachhead. At least, ancient Israel allowed its worshipers to give expression to this sense of life as enemy territory.

The psalm, of course, does not begin or end on a pessimistic note. At the beginning, one encounters the word *Yahweh* before meeting a description of life's problems. At the end, the psalm concludes with a strong affirmation. After all, if God who made heaven and earth is on our side, then we have hope. In the psalm, people offer thanksgiving for this bedrock of faith in the Divine.

Isaiah 51:1–6

That portion of the Book of Isaiah referred to as Second Isaiah (chaps. 40–66) is marked by comfort and hope for God's people. The Babylonian Exile is ending through the instrumentality of Cyrus, king of Persia. (See comments on Isa. 55:1–5 found in Proper 13 [18].) The exiles are asked by the prophet to imagine themselves back in their homeland and again able to worship in Zion. But the vigor of the prophet's language in 51:1–6 implies resistance or unbelief. Why? Is it unbelievable that God could or would give them a new beginning? Or have the people come to prefer the idea of going home, the hope of returning, to the actuality of going home? Looking forward to an event can become a way of life that one may hesitate to relinquish for the event itself. To paraphrase T. S. Eliot, between the hope and the reality falls a shadow. Or as Elie Wiesel once said in an interview, "Jerusalem is my favorite city in all the world, when I am not in Jerusalem."

Whatever the reason or reasons, Israel needs to be persuaded, and such is the general force of 51:1–8. Verse 9 begins a new literary move, a prayer very much like a communal lament. Verses 1–8 constitute an appeal or address to Israel consisting of four units or stanzas: verses 1–3; 4–5; 6; 7–8. All four begin with a plural imperative, the form for addressing all Israel. Our text for today includes the first three of the four units.

In the first unit (vv. 1–3), the prophet voices one of the most common appeals to Israel—remember. Sometimes memory recalls creation; sometimes memory evokes the Exodus; here it is the story of Abraham and Sarah, the rock from which Israel was hewn, the quarry from which they were dug. The point being served here by the recollection of the ancient couple is that the power of God is able to make many from one. Abraham and Sarah were as barren as a desert, and yet God has made them the forebears of countless thousands. (The thought here is analogous to Jesus' story of the mustard seed, which begins small but becomes a large plant.) What, therefore, God did God is able yet to do. God will comfort (as a man comforts his wife) Zion, and the barren will be fruitful, the desert will be a garden, the wasteland of Zion will flourish as Eden. Joy and gladness, gratitude and singing will fill the Holy City. And why should Israel believe it? God's power says I can; God's love says I will.

The second unit (vv. 4–5) enlarges on the first. Just as unit one moved from Abraham and Sarah to Israel, unit two moves from Israel to the nations. The image of God's word going out from Zion recalls 2:1–4 as well as other passages in Isaiah. In both Romans (chap. 4) and Galatians (chap. 3), Paul developed the theme of Abraham, the father of all those in every nation who believe. However, the most striking feature of the image of Israel as a light to the nations as offered by our text is the political context out of which it comes. A people long in exile, with every human reason to think revenge and retaliation, are told that they are to be the avenue of God's grace to the enemy nations and to all nations. After all, says the text, these peoples also wait and hope for God (v. 5). With God, who sends sun and rain on the just and unjust, there is not partiality.

The third unit (v. 6) changes the category for thinking about God's approaching deliverance. Units one and two cast the message in spatial terms: God's salvation moves out from Abraham and Sarah to Israel to the nations. Now the prophet speaks in temporal terms: "My salvation will be forever, and my deliverance will never be ended" (v. 6). In other words, what God is doing for Israel and the world is not contingent on any historical change, not subject to the shifting fortunes of politics. In fact, says the prophet, even the most apparently permanent factors of our existence are in comparison to the certain and eternal deliverance of God as temporary as an old garment, as transient as smoke, as brief of life as a gnat. Look at the heavens; permanent? No. Look at the earth; firm and fixed? No. Both are but a puff when measured against the sure and steadfast favor of God. Isaiah has already said as much: "The grass withers, the flower fades; but the word of our God will stand forever" (40:8). The psalmist has said as much: "As for mortals, their days are like grass: they flourish like a flower of the field; for the wind passes over it, and it is gone, and its place knows it no more. But the steadfast love of the Lord is from everlasting to everlasting" (103:15–17). And Jesus said as much: "Heaven and earth will pass away, but my words will not pass away" (Matt. 24:35). God works within our world of time and space, but God's work transcends all time and space.

Psalm 138

This psalm may be subdivided into three parts. Verses 1–3 thank and praise God; verses 4–6 extol the grace and glory of God and their impact on the rulers of the world; and verses 7–8 express trust in God.

The general tone of the psalm clearly identifies it as a thanksgiving. It differs, however, from most thanksgiving psalms in two ways: (1) there is no description of the trouble or the distress from which the person was rescued (see v. 3, which refers to an appeal to God at an earlier time of distress), and (2) the psalm is addressed directly to the Deity throughout (v. 8a is possibly an exception), whereas most thanksgivings are addressed to a human audience.

The person offering thanks in the original usage of this psalm was probably the king. This is suggested by the references to the kings of the earth in verse 4 who hear the words of Yahweh's mouth, perhaps words spoken by the Judean king. Also, the king was especially the one at God's right hand (v. 7; see Ps. 110:1).

Several elements in the psalm call for elucidation:

1. The reference to "before the gods" (v. 1) could mean one of several things. Ancient translations read "before the angels," "before kings," or "before judges." If the reference is to

pagan gods, then the worshiper could be saying no more than, "I sing your praise in an alien culture." If the reference is to heavenly beings (see Pss. 29:1; 82:1), then the phrase could denote worship before the heavenly council of God.

2. To bow down toward the temple does not imply that the worshiper is in some foreign land or away from Jerusalem. This could be a reference to worship or activity at the temple gate, near the main altar, or in the temple courtyard.

3. The lowly may not refer to a class—the poor, the downtrodden, or others in similar conditions—but could be a self-designation, even of a king—the lowly over against the Divine.

4. The verb translated "perceives" in verse 6b may mean, on the basis of an Arabic parallel, "to humble." Thus "the haughty he humbles from afar."

The statement of trust in verses 7–8 gives expression to a serene confidence—almost. Verse 8c still resorts to petition even after the statement of assurance. Note that the psalm does not assume that life will be free of distress and problems but only that God will preserve one through them all. Trouble and enemies are the givens in life; grace and preservation to endure and overcome them are the sustaining gifts.

Romans 12:1–8

Today's text is an appeal, a piece of moral exhortation: "I appeal to you therefore . . ." (v. 1). Nor is it a mere afterthought, a cushiony way to end an otherwise difficult theological argument. The use of "therefore" links it directly with all that precedes it in chapters 1–11. It is not added to, but *derives from*, what precedes.

We should understand the function of this passage and the remainder of the letter in light of what has been said earlier. The "gospel according to Paul" was not without its detractors. The interlocuter, Paul's imaginary dialogue partner throughout the argument, has consistently raised objections, and these have set the agenda for the unfolding argument (cf. esp. 3:1–9; also 3:27–31; 4:1, 9; 6:1–2, 15; 7:7, 13; 9:14, 30; 11:1, 11). What becomes clear is that these questions are real, not imagined. We are hearing the heated debates caused by Paul's preaching within the synagogues, churches, and streets.

One of the most serious objections to Paul's theology of justification by grace through faith was that it lacked an adequate ethical base. To insist that we are justified by faith and not by works of law, Paul's detractors argued, resulted in moral relativism. Take away law, and you remove all ethical boundaries. No rules, no ethics. Moreover, you create an open license to sin. Indeed, Paul's gospel would seem to encourage sin. If sin becomes an occasion for God to display grace, the more sin, the more grace. Ergo: sin more! (6:1–2).

To draw such conclusions, Paul countered, was sheer sophistry. It misunderstood the nature of baptismal participation in the death and resurrection of Christ (6:3–11). It also failed to recognize the moral transformation that occurs when one becomes united with Christ (6:12–23). Far from impelling one toward a life of sin, Paul's gospel found its motivating center in death *to sin* (6:10). If the cross meant anything, it signified the triumph of righteousness over sin in the person of Christ. In Christ, disobedience gave way to obedience, and it did so not because Christ was impelled to keep a law, or the law, but because he was bound to God in faith. Christ, then, becomes the central paradigm illustrating the compelling ethical power of grace.

What form would such a life take among believers? Today's text begins to sketch the profile for us. (A similar move is made in Gal. 5–6.) Far from leaving us afloat, drifting in the sea of moral chaos, Paul's gospel calls for a clearly ethical life-style.

Today's text may be treated in two parts: (1) the appeal (vv. 1–2); and (2) the nature of life together in community (vv. 3–8).

1. *The appeal* (vv. 1–2). At the heart of Paul's appeal is a single guiding metaphor—"living sacrifice" (v. 1). Paul uses not only cultic metaphors to interpret the work and death of Christ (3:25; cf. Eph. 5:2; 1 John 2:2) but also his own apostolic ministry (15:16; Phil. 2:17). Here, of course, believers are envisioned as sacrificial offerings made to God, not dead, however, but "living . . . holy . . . acceptable" (cf. 1 Pet. 2:5). This is to be done in a manner that befits "sensible people" (v. 1, NJB), or perhaps "in a spiritual way." Among Christians there is no official cultus with sacrificial offerings. Instead, there is the ultimate sacrifice of Christ himself and our "very selves" as "a living sacrifice" (REB). What this implies, of course, is that our lives are continually being offered up before God not as sacrifices to placate an angry God but as thank offerings in response to a gracious God.

Along with this sacrificial metaphor is the twofold injunction that provides the rubric for the various exhortations that follow—not being conformed to this world but being transformed by the renewal of our minds (v. 2). Moral transformation inevitably involves putting away certain forms of behavior and exchanging them for newer, more appropriate forms of behavior. Hence the standard scheme of "putting off—putting on" (cf. 6:13, 19; Col. 3:5–17).

The "pattern of this present world" (v. 2, REB) no longer provides the mold into which behavior is cast as it once did. For one thing, it is now seen to represent an old order that is passing away, that has been rendered obsolete by the Christ-event (Gal. 1:4; 1 Cor. 7:31; 2 Cor. 5:17). Here we have a clear call to nonconformity: "Do not model your behaviour on the contemporary world" (v. 2, NJB; cf. 1 Pet. 1:14).

What makes such nonconformity possible, however, is an inner transformation that encompasses the whole person: "Let your minds be remade and your whole nature thus transformed" (v. 2, NEB). The process is one of essential renewal: a new self (Col. 3:10), a new creation (2 Cor. 5:17), a new spirit (Eph. 4:23). The renewing agent is the Holy Spirit (Titus 3:5). Though the process begins now, it culminates in the Eschaton (Phil. 3:21; 1 Cor. 15:43, 49, 53; Rom. 8:29; 2 Cor. 3:18; 1 John 3:2).

2. *Life together in community* (vv. 3–8). What is striking about the instructions that follow is the way they define individual Christian behavior in the light of corporate responsibility. There is first the call to proper self-understanding, a warning not to overvalue our real importance (v. 3; cf. 1 Cor. 4:6). We should instead "form a sober estimate based on the measure of faith that God has dealt to each of [us]" (v. 3, REB). Fundamental here is the recognition that whatever we have is a divinely apportioned gift (cf. 1 Cor. 12:11; also Matt. 25:15; Eph. 4:7; 2 Cor. 10:13). This in itself will curb our tendency to take credit for what is essentially God's work or gift.

To underscore the proper relationship between the one and the many, Paul introduces the metaphor of the body (cf. 1 Cor. 12:12–13, 27; also 1 Cor. 6:15; 10:17). It has the effect of reminding us of the plurality of gifts and functions among us, and of the diversity as well. We may be plural and uniform, or plural and diverse. For Paul, the latter is the divine intention.

Especially strong here is the emphasis on being "members one of another" (v. 5). It is the difference between being a group and being a community, between being related and being a family. What is called for is active concern for, and involvement with, one another.

Consequently, the list of gifts in verses 6–8 is remarkable, because each gift is outwardly directed. Prophecy denotes utterances intended to edify others, not the self (1 Cor. 14:3). Similarly, teaching and exhortation are outwardly directed (1 Cor. 14:3; Phil. 2:1; Heb. 13:22; 1 Tim. 4:13). Serving obviously presupposes "others" as its object, thus eliminating behavior that is self-serving (Mark 10:45). Making contributions and doing acts of mercy also point away from the self, but the motive is crucial in each case—freely and cheerfully. Even being a leader, which calls for exerting oneself, should be an act done for the corporate good rather than for self-aggrandizement (v. 8; 1 Thess. 5:12; 1 Tim. 5:17; Heb. 13:17; esp. Mark 10:42–45).

In a word, the profile of behavior sketched here is a responsible sense of community, one that produces a form of living together that embodies the "second great commandment" (13:9).

One way of appropriating this well-known Christian text is for the preacher to focus on the corporate responsibility called for here. Presenting ourselves as living sacrifices may all too easily become an act of *personal* sacrifice without due regard to the active care for one another that this requires. To be sure, Christian ethics takes concrete shape in the profile of individual service, but Paul's remarks here follow directly on an extended exposition about the joining of two *peoples*—Jews and Gentiles—into a single family of God. That can hardly be done merely on an individual basis.

Matthew 16:13–20

In all three Synoptics, the events recorded in the readings for today (Mark 8:27–30; Luke 9:18–21) and next Sunday are crucial in the ministry of Jesus and in the disciples' understanding of who he was and what he was doing. In verses 13–16, Matthew follows Mark rather closely. Verses 17–19 are a Matthean elaboration and interpretation, relieving many readers of an uneasiness created by Mark's strange silence. In Mark, the confession of Peter is briefer; there is no indication of what Jesus being the Christ really means, and Jesus neither affirms nor rejects Peter's confession. At verse 20, Matthew rejoins Mark.

Although Luke seems uninterested in locating this event, both Mark and Matthew place it at Caesarea Philippi, twenty miles north of the sea of Galilee on the slopes of Mt. Hermon. Formerly known as Paneas, an ancient Greek worship center, the area was now a part of the tetrarchy of Philip, one of Herod's sons. Philip named the place for Tiberias, and it became known as Philip's Caesarea to distinguish it from the Caesarea on the Mediterranean that Herod had built, or rather rebuilt, to honor Caesar Augustus. The population was mostly Gentile.

A few interpreters of Matthew have taken the position that much should be made of the contrast between "Son of Man" (who do people say the *Son of Man* is?) and "I" (Who do you say I am?). This is to say, Jesus seems to be distinguishing between the eschatological figure who was to come and himself. This has been, however, a minority view, because the identification of Jesus with the Son of Man is clear and frequent in the Gospels. The more obvious contrast is between the public view of Jesus and that of the disciples.

Matthew's version of Peter's confession combines the title "Son of God," used earlier at 14:33, and "Messiah," used for the first time here. This elaboration of the confession beyond that of both Mark and Luke probably reflects the Christology of Matthew's church. We are not made privy to the full investment of meanings in this use of the two titles applied to Jesus. Two matters, however, are quite clear: first, Jesus approves of the confession (v. 17); and second, at least part of what it means for Jesus to be Christ and Son of God involves Jerusalem, suffering, death, and resurrection (vv. 21–28, the reading for next Sunday).

That Simon Peter was able to identify Jesus as Messiah and Son of God is not an indication that Peter was more perceptive or intelligent than others. His insight came by revelation (v. 17). That true understanding of Jesus' identity was and is a matter of divine revelation Matthew has already said (11:25–27), and in that view he is joined by Luke (10:21–22), John (6:45–46 among many such statements), and Paul (1 Cor. 1:26–29; 12:3). This revelation and hence this confession may be what is meant by the rock on which Christ builds his church (v. 18). However, the preacher will want to review the commentaries on verse 18 to recall the claims for Simon Peter as the foundation of the church. Much of the debate hinges on the interpretation of the two words *petros* and *petra* used in Jesus' response to Simon. In either case, we have Jesus' promise of a church that will be his church and that will not be overcome even by death itself. Only here and at 18:17 in the whole of the Gospels does Jesus refer to "church." Of course, in Matthew's own day the church as a distinct community had been formed by and for those who confessed Jesus as Christ. But the fact that here alone Jesus speaks of building his church has long generated debate as to whether Jesus as a preacher of the kingdom of God had in mind during his earthly ministry the formation of a separate community as a "church." Discussions of what Jesus had in mind have always fallen short of conclusiveness.

What is abundantly clear, however, is the New Testament's affirmation that the continuity between Jesus and the church was provided by the apostles. They were chosen by Jesus and given authority during his lifetime (Matt. 10:1 and parallels), an authority to be exercised in the church after Jesus' departure. The granting of authority to Simon Peter is obviously symbolic for all the apostles (v. 19), for elsewhere in Matthew (18:18) and John (20:23) this bestowal of power is on them all. Even those least appreciative of authority can imagine into what sentimental and errant paths the church would have wandered had not responsible persons preserved and passed on to the church what Jesus said and what Jesus did. The apostolic tradition gives the church the memory out of which it lives.

Proper 17 [22]
(Sunday between August 28 and September 3 inclusive)

Exodus 3:1–15;
Psalm 105:1–6, 23–26, 45c; or
Jeremiah 15:15–21;
Psalm 26:1–8;
Romans 12:9–21;
Matthew 16:21–28

The Old Testament reading for the *Common Lectionary* is the narrative of Moses' commission to return to Egypt and lead the Hebrews out of bondage, free them from Egyptian oppression, and lead them to the land of promise. The psalm, once again, is taken from Psalm 105, though the new section (vv. 23–26) relates Israel's coming to Egypt and God's call of Moses and Aaron.

For those confessional traditions using other lectionaries, the Old Testament reading is provided by Jeremiah's second lament, which strikes a note of protest yet concludes with Yahweh firmly resolving to vindicate the prophet's cause. In similar tones, the reading from Psalm 26 calls for Yahweh to vindicate the cause of the psalmist, who conducts himself uprightly and behaves faithfully.

In the Epistle lesson, Paul appeals to his readers to practice a particular style and way of life that is commensurate with the will and grace of God and that manifests the life of the Spirit in the Christian community. In the Gospel reading, Jesus teaches that following him involves the shaping of life according to the pattern of his ministry and thus suffering and being willing to die on a cross.

Exodus 3:1–15

This passage includes only the first parts of the report of the vocation of Moses, his call to lead the people of Israel out of Egypt. When the account begins, Moses is settled down in the land of Midian with a family and a livelihood, but when it ends he is headed for Egypt as the Lord's agent to rescue his people. It forms the essential prelude for Moses' confrontation of the pharaoh and the exodus from Egypt. Careful study of the first parts of the vocation report enables us to address questions important to all who reflect upon their divine vocations.

It is a long account, reflecting both the combination of literary sources and a complex history of tradition. The report of Moses' call is the combination of the older pentateuchal sources J (the Yahwist) and E (the Elohist), which in turn rest on oral traditions. In addition, there is the Priestly Writer's parallel account (Exod. 6:2–7:7), which reports that the vocation took place in Egypt. Evidence for the composite character of the account in Exodus 3–4 includes the different divine names, God and Yahweh (translated "Lord" in most translations except the *Jerusalem Bible*), repetitions of contents (vv. 7–8 parallel vv. 9–12), the different names for the sacred mountain ("Horeb" here, but "Sinai" in other texts), and the manner of divine revelation (through an angel or by direct address). Modern scholarship has rightly recognized that at least two old oral traditions have been combined in the written sources. One focused upon the theophany and accounted for the sacredness of the place. It would have been similar to the story of Jacob at Bethel (Gen. 28:10–22). That place was the mountain remembered as the site of the covenant (Exod. 19–24). In addition to the designation as "Horeb, the mountain of God" (v. 1), the Hebrew name for the burning bush (*sin*, v. 2) probably contains an allusion to "Sinai." The other tradition, that of the vocation of Moses, now dominates the record.

Within a slender narrative framework, our reading consists mainly of dialogue between God and Moses. The solitary shepherd finds himself in the wilderness at Horeb, which he probably does not know is "the mountain of God." Verse 2 serves as a general heading for what is to follow: "The angel of the Lord appeared to him." Seeing an astounding bush that burns but is not consumed, he approaches, only to hear the voice of God speaking first with a warning that he is on holy ground (v. 5), then with self-introduction (v. 6), and finally with a call (vv. 7–10). Moses' response (v. 11) is only the first of a series of objections, but God reacts with words of reassurance and promise (v. 12).

Three major themes are sustained in this passage, corresponding to some extent to the old traditions behind it. The first is the divine self-revelation in the form of a theophany to a particular individual. How does God make himself known? According to a great many Old Testament accounts, it is by means of a dramatic appearance at a holy place. Here that place is on or near "the mountain of God." As in most other such reports, the individual who witnesses the theophany did not choose the place, nor did he even set out to find such a place or such an experience. It is almost providential or fortuitous that Moses strayed where—it is clear—God wanted him to be.

Often reports of theophanies indicate that God "came down" (cf. Exod. 19:11), but in any case, the Lord's appearance is accompanied by a dramatic natural phenomenon or some "marvelous sight" (v. 3, NJPSV), such as the bush that burns but is not consumed. The theophany at Mt. Sinai included smoke and fire and the quaking of the mountain (Exod. 19:18; cf. 1 Kings 19:9ff.). Some of the prophetic vocation reports include allusions to such dramatic phenomena (Isa. 6:1–4; Ezek. 1–3). Furthermore, theophanies hardly ever are simple demonstrations of the awesome presence of God, but include direct address.

Moses stands in the presence of the Holy One, and the encounter is awesome and frightening. It is dangerous to approach the boundary between the Divine and the human. Obeying the command to remove his shoes because he is on holy ground, he hears God speak and hides his face. No one can see God directly and live (Isa. 6). God, however, deigns to identify himself as the personal God of the ancestors. If the theophany stresses God's transcendence, the words stress his identification with a particular people.

Closely related to the theme of the appearance of God is a second tradition, that of the revelation of the name of Israel's God. This is presented in Exod. 3:13–15, which in its immediate context functions to present Moses' second objection and the Lord's response to it. Note how indirectly Moses objects and poses the question, as if it is not his own query but that of the people: "If I come to the Israelites [he has not yet agreed to go!] and say to them, 'The God of your ancestors has sent me to you,' and they ask me, 'What is his name?' what shall I say to them?" (v. 13). The question is by no means a trivial one: Who is God, and how shall I address him? Such questions may be asked for a wide variety of reasons. Moses suggests a pragmatic and political concern—so the people will listen and follow. The question can come from the heart of faith: one wants to know how to begin a prayer of praise or thanksgiving. It can also come from the fundamental human desire to control—to call down the power of the heavens into one's own service. The intrinsic importance and urgency of the question explains why Jewish and Christian commentators and theologians from the earliest times have fastened upon this unit of Scripture. They wanted it to yield an answer to Moses' question. But the Christian preacher might very well make the question itself the focus of homiletical reflection.

The divine response to Moses is, to say the least, enigmatic: "I AM WHO I AM" (v. 14). This appears to be a popular etymology for the name Yahweh. Grammatically, "I am" (*'ehyeh*) is a first person singular imperfect form of the Hebrew verb "to be" and could with equal reliability be translated with a future tense, "I will be what I will be" (NRSV footnote). "Yahweh" could be a third—not first—person singular imperfect form of the same verb. It is not possible to determine whether or not the divine name itself actually originated from this verb, as a confession of faith in the God "who is," or "who will be," or even "who causes to be," but that seems unlikely. What we have here is a similarity of sounds and some reflection upon the meaning of the name, but only after that name had been in use for centuries.

The specific connection of the expression "I am who I am" with the name Yahweh comes only in verse 15, which in itself would have been a direct answer to the question posed by Moses. It seems likely that the response to Moses reflects more than one stage of development. In its present form, Moses' question is answered, but in an earlier stage it seems likely that God refused to answer directly. The answer "I am who I am" is similar to the answer a parent hears when he or she asks a child where he or she is going: "Out" or "I am going where I am going."

Particular concern with the disclosure of the name in the time of Moses comes from the Elohistic source, according to which the name was not known earlier. That interest is shared by the Priestly Writer, who also considered it anachronistic for the name to be mentioned before the time of Moses (Exod. 6:2–9). The Yahwist, on the other hand, obviously believed that God was known by that proper name even to the first human beings (Gen. 2:4bff.). Thus the sources presumed different doctrines of history and revelation. According to E and P, knowledge of the name Yahweh was not general and was revealed to Israel only in the time of Moses, just before the Exodus.

The third major theme is carried by the dialogue between the two parties, God's call and Moses' response. In fact, the major narrative tension of the report as a whole concerns whether or not Moses will accept his vocation to lead the people out of Egypt. The full substance of the call is stated at the very outset: God has heard the cries of his people in Egypt and will bring them out to a land of their own. Moses is to be the instrument of that will (vv. 7–10). Moses resists, not once but several times, and God patiently responds to his objections. Finally, armed with reassurance, the name of God, signs and wonders to perform, and the help of his brother Aaron, Moses obeys.

The reluctance of Moses requires special attention. Readers of this passage find it difficult to resist the temptation to analyze the personality of Moses or even speculate on physical limitations that might have made him a poor public speaker. This resistance, however, is not specific to Moses but is found in virtually all of the other Old Testament vocation reports. Gideon (Judg. 6), Isaiah (Isa. 6) and Jeremiah (Jer. 1:4–10) all resist the call on the grounds of unworthiness or inadequacy. Consequently, it is clear that a sense of unworthiness or inadequacy is inherent in being called by God. The resistance to the call is related to the experience of the Holy. One need not be especially timid, shy, or cowardly to feel unworthy to act on behalf of God.

Another aspect of the biblical understanding of vocation and the will of God is transparent here and in other reports of calls. It is God who will bring the people of Israel out of Egypt, but it is taken for granted that a human agent is required to effect that will. Moreover, the will of the one called is not subsumed completely into the will of God. Rather, he or she has—and is allowed to have—autonomy to continue to question, resist, or choose to obey the one who called.

Psalm 105:1–6, 23–26, 45c

Portions of this psalm were used at Propers 12 [17] and 14 [19]. The new element in the reading for this Sunday is the inclusion of verses 23–26, which introduce Moses and Aaron.

Verse 23 picks up the recital of Israel's past history with the reference to Jacob's move into Egypt during the famine and while Joseph is a ruler in pharaoh's court (see Gen. 46:1–7). The "land of Ham" is a synonym for Egypt. The Old Testament divided the nations of the world into groups traced back to the three sons of Noah—Ham, Shem, and Japheth. This division was based primarily on linguistic features and not along racial lines. Hamitic nations were understood as those speaking African as opposed to Semitic or Indo-European languages.

With poetic hyperbole, the Hebrews in Egypt are described as becoming stronger than the natives (v. 24). It is interesting to note that the hostile actions taken by the Egyptians against the Hebrews are said to have been caused by God (v. 25). The psalmist is eager to stress the absolute sovereignty of God throughout this psalm and thus ascribes the attempt to exterminate the Hebrews to divine action. (On Yahweh's hardening of pharaoh's heart, see Exod. 7:3; 9:12.)

Verse 26 introduces Moses into the drama as well as Aaron, whom God had chosen, that is, to be the mouthpiece or spokesman for Moses (see Exod. 4:14–17).

Jeremiah 15:15–21

The time of Jeremiah's prophetic activity is marked at the beginning of the book (1:1–3): from the thirteenth year of King Josiah (627 BC) until the eleventh year of King Zedekiah and the captivity of Jerusalem (597 BC). This dating means that Jeremiah experienced and perhaps helped launch the great religious reform under Josiah, a reform that bequeathed to Judaism and to us the literary legacy, the Book of Deuteronomy. Jeremiah preached during the political tensions in Judah created by the struggles between Babylon to the north and Egypt to the south. Jerusalem sat between those two great powers but was lulled to sleep by a false sense of security. After all, is not Jerusalem God's holy city? Is not the temple God's own house? It can never happen here. Jeremiah condemned this self-righteous illusion, but his words were laughed at and he was scorned, until Nebuchadnezzar captured the city. The prophet also condemned the corruptions among the priests and the syncretistic religious practices that blended Israel's faith and ritual with the cultic life of other religions of the territory.

Because Jeremiah condemned corruption at the temple, because he prophesied that Israel had no guarantees of divine protection and that because of her sins the city would fall, because he urged exiles being taken to Babylon to accommodate themselves to their new home, Jeremiah was regarded as unpatriotic, a traitor to his country and to his religion. When the leader of Nebuchadnezzar's invading army extended special privileges to Jeremiah, the gulf between him and his own people widened. Severely opposed, threatened, ridiculed, publicly condemned and punished, Jeremiah experienced anguish and suffering daily. At times he hated his own life and longed not to be a prophet; at other times he shook his fist at heaven, blaming God for a call he did not want and for a message the people certainly did not want to hear. Because of these painful reflections on his own life and ministry, we know more about Jeremiah than we do about the other prophets of Israel. There is a great deal in the book that is biographical and autobiographical.

There is, however, some debate among scholars as to whether all the self-referencing and apparently autobiographical statements are, in fact, to be taken as the prophet's comments about himself personally. For example, today's reading is a portion of the third of six "confessions" or "laments" of Jeremiah (11:18–23; 12:1–6; 15:10–21; 17:12–18; 18:18–23; 20:7–18). The studied opinions about the nature of these passages are basically three. First, some argue they are what they seem; that is, personal expressions of the prophet's own soul. Second, some regard these as from the soul of the nation cast in personal and private terms. This is to say, Jeremiah speaks not about or for himself but uses the first person to voice Israel's cry to God. As the person Abraham, or Moses, or David was at times a corporate image of the whole people, so is Jeremiah here. And finally, other scholars regard these confessions as liturgically formed and finished, and whatever may have been their historical value originally, that now is lost. These are now liturgical pieces useful for a variety of times and places. Those of this opinion point to the similarity between these passages and psalms of lament.

As for the confession in 15:15–21, it seems most appropriate to hear in it the voice of Jeremiah calling on God to regard his personal anguish and to respond. This perspective is strengthened when verses 15–21 are taken in conjunction with verses 10–14, the first of the two laments in 15:10–21.

Here, then, is the prophet, crying to God, asking not to be forgotten or left alone (v. 15). It is, after all, on God's behalf that he is being persecuted and insulted (v. 15). When God's words were found (perhaps a reference to the rediscovery of the law of Moses in the temple, 2 Kings 22:8), Jeremiah consumed them, making them his own, filled with delight to be God's person (v. 16). But now the whole experience has turned to pain: there is no social life for the prophet; he sits alone (v. 17). And why? God's word in him is indignation over the sins of Israel, and that word is a weight on his heart, a pain in his chest, an open wound, an unslaked thirst (vv. 17–18). He never dreamed that being God's prophet would carry such a price. Were his persecutors Babylonians or Egyptians or Canaanites, the suffering could be predicted and even borne with a measure of satisfaction, but it is God's own people who inflict the pain.

God's response to Jeremiah (vv. 19–21) is one of correction, challenge, and assurance. I can still use you as my mouth, says God, but you must not change your message to worthless words in order to be accepted. The response to you will be mixed, says God; some will turn to you, but others will continue to fight you. But the responses of the people are neither your fall nor your rise. The point is, says God, I am with you to save, to deliver, to redeem.

All who speak for God in every age and who experience the response Jeremiah received have embraced God's response just as personally as did the prophet of Israel.

Psalm 26:1–8

This text is best understood as a composition used to claim and affirm one's innocence when the falsely accused was charged with some crime or breach of sacral obligation. Three elements characterize the psalm: the desire to be judged, the affirmation of innocence, and the certainty of the outcome. The psalm thus makes a good parallel to Jeremiah's lament.

The opening section appeals to God for a legal decision or personal assessment ("Vindicate me . . . Prove me . . . try me . . . test my heart and my mind" [literally, "my kidneys and heart"]). Such terminology may suggest an actual religious court context, or it may be used metaphorically ("acknowledge my righteousness . . . see for yourself"), although the former seems more likely. The presence of a phrase referring to God in the third person in the context of direct address to God (v. 1c) can probably best be explained as a technical expression, "to trust in Yahweh," which came more easily than "to trust in you."

The statement of innocence found in verses 4–8 refers to the types of person whom the worshiper avoids. Verses 6–7 refer to what must have been part of the ritual involved in asserting innocence, washing the hands and walking around the altar, and to the events associated with being cleared of charges— a song (psalm) of thanksgiving and public testimony.

Verse 8 affirms the worshiper's devotion to Yahweh. The rather peculiar expression "I love the house in which you dwell" (or "the dwelling-place of Your glory," NJPSV) may be a circumlocution for saying, "I love Yahweh." The psalm composers did not have the worshipers frequently refer to loving Yahweh (see Pss. 31:23; 97:10; 116:1; 145:20) but used such expressions as to love God's name (Pss. 5:11; 69:36), God's law (Pss. 119:47, 48, 97, 113, 119, 127, 159, 163), or God's salvation (Pss. 40:16; 70:5). In Deuteronomy, where "to love God" is frequently employed, the expression seems to mean, primarily, to obey God's will.

Although it probably reads into the psalm more than was originally structured into it, the person's claims in the protestation of innocence can be seen as tenfold:

1. Walking in integrity (1a)
2. Trusting in the Lord (1b)
3. Remembering divine love (3a)
4. Walking in faithfulness (3b)
5. Not sitting with false men (probably idolaters) (4a)
6. Not consorting with dissemblers (probably members of some secret cult) (4b)

7. Hating evildoers (5a)

8. Not associating with the wicked (5b)

9. Proper worshiping of God (6–7)

10. Loving the temple (8)

Romans 12:9–21

Today's epistolary lection is a miscellany of moral exhortations, many of which extend the theme of the first section noted last week—responsible corporate behavior within the Christian community.

This is especially the case in the first section (vv. 9–13): loving "without any pretense" (v. 9a, NJB; cf. 2 Cor. 6:6; 1 Cor. 13:6); mutual affection (v. 10; cf. 1 Thess. 4:9; Heb. 13:1; 1 Pet. 1:22; 2:17; 2 Pet. 1:7); showing honor to one another (v. 10b; 13:7; 1 Pet. 2:17; 2 Pet. 1:7); active care for the needs of the saints (v. 13; Acts 6:3; 28:10; Phil. 4:14); showing hospitality to strangers (v. 13; 1 Tim. 3:2; 5:10; Titus 1:8; Heb. 13:2; 1 Pet. 4:9).

Some of the other activities that are commended, such as constant prayer (v. 12), are perhaps best understood as being done toward the common good (Col. 4:2; 1 Tim. 2:1). So practiced, the Christian virtues become less privatistic pieties and more corporate responsibilities.

The second section (vv. 14–21) contains several injunctions that echo sentiments found in Matthew's collection of Jesus' teachings otherwise known as the Sermon on the Mount.

"Bless your persecutors; never curse them, bless them" (v. 14, NJB). In the Matthean tradition, the command to pray for our persecutors is linked with love for our enemies, which reverses the normal pattern of loving our friends and hating our enemies (Matt. 5:44). Perhaps the most visible and memorable instance of this is the Lukan portrait of the crucified Christ, who asks the Father to forgive those who crucified him for acting in ignorance (Luke 23:34). The portrait of Stephen in Acts is clearly modeled on the earlier depiction of Jesus (Acts 7:60), Luke's way of indicating that the church is to emulate the example of Jesus in this respect. It is a form of reverse response that is enacted in the apostolic ministry of Paul (1 Cor. 4:12). In 1 Peter 3:9–12, blessing as the appropriate response to reviling is justified by appealing to Psalm 34:12–16, which eschews speech that is evil and full of guile.

"Rejoice with others when they rejoice, and be sad with those in sorrow" (v. 15, NJB). In the second Beatitude, those who mourn are promised solace (Matt. 5:4). The Jewish wisdom tradition also made it obligatory to minister to those in mourning: "Do not avoid those who weep" (Sir. 7:34). What is envisioned here in this double-pronged injunction is a level of genuine community where "not just the exceptional situation but everyday life with its alternation of laughter and tears summons us away from the Stoic ideal of *ataraxia* not merely to participation but beyond that to demonstrated brotherhood with all" (Käsemann, following Conzelmann). Not that a sense of community was absent among Stoics, for Marcus Aurelius insisted that one should be a "rational and civic creature" who fulfills social obligations: "That which is not in the interests of the hive cannot be in the interest of the bee" (*To Himself* 6.54).

"Live in harmony with one another" (v. 16a). This is the call to be of the same mind (cf. Rom. 15:5; 2 Cor. 13:11; Phil. 2:2; 4:2). "This does not mean that [we] must think the same thoughts, which is only seldom realized and not even desirable. It is rather a matter of orientation to the single goal of the community united in grace, which . . . enables us to be of one spirit in spite of tensions, and which comes to expression in unanimity" (Käsemann).

"Do not be haughty, but associate with the lowly; do not claim to be wiser than you are" (v. 16b). The flavor of this first injunction is expressed especially well by NJB: "Pay no regard to social standing, but meet humble people on their own terms." Arrogance and self-assertion are inappropriate forms of Christian behavior, not only because they reverse the true nature of the work of Christ (Phil. 2:5–11; cf. Mark 10:45), but because they reflect an egocentrism that becomes debilitating to any genuine form of community (1 Cor. 4:6–7; 11:22). We should also note that more is being called for here than mere change of attitude toward the lowly. We are enjoined to "associate with the lowly," which can only suggest community and solidarity at their most basic level (Mark 2:15–17; Luke 4:18–19).

The latter section (vv. 17–21), from various perspectives, addresses the natural urge to be vindictive. Once again, there are echoes of the Synoptic tradition (cf. Matt. 5:38–42; also cf. 1 Thess. 5:15; 1 Pet. 3:9). Instead of trying to avenge evil, we are urged, in the spirit of Proverbs 3:4, to try to "find favor and good repute in the sight of God and of people." An especially central motivation in this regard is the recognition that vengeance is an exclusive prerogative of God (v. 19, quoting Deut. 32:35). Rather than avenging our enemies, we are asked to fulfill the expectations of Proverbs 25:21–22 and give them "bread to eat . . . and water to drink" (cf. Matt. 5:44). Rather than buckling under the power of evil, we are instead to experience the overpowering force of good.

As we noted earlier, these various exhortations are intended as guidelines for "living in harmony with one another" (v. 16) and "living peaceably with all" (v. 18). In many fundamental respects, they call for reversing natural human inclinations, and thereby become expressive of the gospel in the basic sense.

Matthew 16:21–28

Y ou are the Messiah, the Son of the living God" (16:16). Whatever else may be involved in this identification of Jesus, at least it included the suffering, death, and resurrection of Jesus. We know this because Jesus approved of and accepted this confession (v. 17) and on the basis of it began to teach his disciples about his coming passion in Jerusalem. That Jesus "sternly ordered the disciples not to tell anyone that he was the Messiah" (v. 20) implies that Jesus did not regard the public, with its view of him as the forerunner of the Christ (v. 14, their view of Jesus is the same as our view of John the Baptist; that is, the one to prepare the Messiah's way), as ready to receive the announcement, "The Messiah has come and it is Jesus of Nazareth." The public would certainly not be ready for a suffering and dying Messiah; but then, as our reading reveals, neither were the Twelve.

Our lection consists of two parts: first, what his messiahship meant for Jesus (vv. 21–23), and second, what it meant for those who were his disciples (vv. 24–28). "From that time on" (v. 21) is Matthew's addition to Mark's account (8:31–9:1), indicating a clear turning point in Jesus' ministry. He now begins to prepare his disciples for his passion, which, says Matthew alone, will take place in Jerusalem (v. 21). Jesus' suffering will be at the hands of the supreme council of the Jews, the Sanhedrin (composed of elders, chief priests, and scribes). That Jesus must go is not a reference to the Greek notion of fate or destiny but to the will of God. As to the suffering, death, and resurrection on the third day, no further details are supplied. This is the first prediction of the passion.

Not unexpectedly, Simon strongly resists Jesus' words, finding them a contradiction to his being the Messiah, the Son of God. Mark says Peter rebuked Jesus but gives no content to the rebuke. Matthew tells us that Peter remonstrated to the effect, "This must never happen to you" (v. 22). Luke omits this exchange between Jesus and Peter (9:22–27). Although not as sharply stated as in Mark, Matthew still preserves what amounted to a shouting match (vv. 22–23). We are not dealing with a disagreement; Simon Peter is the voice of the tempter seeking to turn Jesus from the will of God, and Jesus feels the presence of Satan just as strongly as in the wilderness (4:1–11).

Verses 24–28 are addressed to the disciples, not to the crowds as in Mark (8:34). Verses 24–25 were anticipated at 10:38–39, and the references to the cross, which did not appear in Jesus' prediction of his death (v. 21), not only anticipate Jesus' death but also reflect upon the past fact of it. The two sayings about the value of one's life in verse 26 are rather loosely joined to verse 25 and probably existed originally in other contexts. They seem to have been clustered about the common phrase "his life" and not about common subject matter.

The passage concludes on an eschatological note, promising the coming of the Son of Man in judgment upon every person. We have come to expect the element of judgment as the conclusion to Matthew's record of Jesus' teaching on discipleship. Already in 13:36–43, 47–50, we are told that judgment will be carried out by the Son of Man and his angels. This emphasis will reappear dramatically at 25:31–46. And although Matthew will, in chapters 24–25, speak often of "the delay," here in our text the anticipation of the end within a short time has been preserved (v. 28). Because Matthew carries both perspectives, a delayed coming of the Son of Man and a coming very soon, perhaps it is best to remind ourselves that Christian behavior does not flow from the belief that the end is near but from the belief that God is near. All else is secondary.

Proper 18 [23]
(Sunday between September 4 and 10 inclusive)

Exodus 12:1–14;
Psalm 149; or
Ezekiel 33:7–11;
Psalm 119:33–40;
Romans 13:8–14;
Matthew 18:15–20

The Old Testament lesson for the *Common Lectionary* contains Yahweh's speech to Moses and Aaron that gives directions about the preparations to be made in anticipation of the coming Passover. A festive note is struck in Psalm 149, which also praises Yahweh for executing judgment against Israel's enemies—an appropriate theme that anticipates God's deliverance of Israel from the Egyptians.

In other lectionaries, the Old Testament reading is supplied by the oracle from Ezekiel where the prophet is appointed God's sentinel for the house of Israel and proclaims a theology of individual responsibility. In a responsive mood, the selection from Psalm 119 expresses the psalmist's willingness to accept instruction from Yahweh, to follow the divine laws and commandments faithfully, and thereby to experience the benefits of such obedience.

In the epistolary reading, we see how centrally the demands of Torah to love one another shape Christian moral expectations, but we also find a call to vigilance and moral purity that resonates with the Exodus reading. In the Gospel, Jesus discusses how broken relationships in human affairs can be handled.

Exodus 12:1–14

Between the call of Moses, reported in last week's reading, and the Passover night recorded in today's lection, the story has reported a series of confrontations between Moses and pharaoh, and nine plagues upon the Egyptians. Exodus 12 brings us very close to the center of the Exodus story, for the Passover was believed to have been instituted in the very night that Israel was brought out of Egypt. Each time the Passover was celebrated in Israel, the people of God remembered that they were slaves set free by their God.

Although the section before us is relatively straightforward, it is part of a very complex section in the Book of Exodus. Because it is the climax of the Exodus traditions, it has attracted a great many diverse elements. The unit, which reports the events immediately

427

surrounding the departure from Egypt, begins in Exodus 11:1 and does not end until Exodus 13:16. One can identify four distinct motifs within this section. The most important is, of course, the departure from Egypt itself. Although this is noted quite briefly (12:37–39), it is the focal point of all other motifs. Second is the report of the final plague, the killing of the firstborn children of the Egyptians. This plague is quite distinct from those that preceded it, both in the fact that it was effective and in the extensive preparations for it. The third and fourth motifs are the religious ceremonies connected with the Exodus, the celebration of Passover and the Feast of Unleavened Bread. Passover is linked to the final plague because it entailed a procedure for ensuring that the Israelite firstborn would not be killed, and it is connected in very direct ways with the immediate departure from Egypt. The final plague is what motivated the pharaoh to release Israel, and the Passover was to have taken place just before they left.

It is important to keep in mind that this passage is part of a narrative, a story more of divine actions than human events. Its setting is the history of salvation, the account of Yahweh's intervention to set his people free. In that context, Exodus 12:1–14 is a report of divine instructions to Moses and Aaron concerning the celebration of the Passover. Thus everything except verse 1 is in the form of a speech of Yahweh, a direct address to Moses and Aaron. These instructions have the tone and contents of rules established for perpetuity and thus reflect the perspective of Israelites centuries after the events. On the basis of the style and the technical terminology, this passage—with the possible exception of verse 14—comes from the Priestly Writer.

The instructions are precise and detailed with regard to both time and actions. The month in which the Exodus takes place is to become the first month of the year, and the preparations for the Passover begin on the tenth day of the month (vv. 2–3a). It is a family ceremony, with a lamb chosen for each household—that is, unless the household is too small for a lamb, in which case neighboring families are to join together to make up the right number to consume the lamb (vv. 3b–4). A lamb without blemish is to be selected and then killed on the fourteenth day of the month (vv. 5–6). Blood is to be smeared on the lintels and doorposts of the houses, and the meat is to roasted and eaten with unleavened bread and bitter herbs (vv. 7–9). The meal is to be eaten in haste, and anything not consumed by morning is to be burned (vv. 10–11).

After the instructions follows an explanation of the meaning of the meal and of the practices associated with it. The Lord will pass through the land of Egypt to destroy the firstborn, but will see the blood and "pass over" the Israelites (vv. 12–13). Verse 14, which comes from another writer, stresses that the day is a "day of remembrance," and forever, whereby later generations will remember the Exodus.

In both the present text and later practice, Passover was combined with the Feast of Unleavened Bread. The former was a one-night communal meal, whereas the latter was a seven-day festival. The combination was quite ancient, but the two originally were distinct. It seems likely that the Feast of Unleavened Bread was a pre-Israelite festival related to the agricultural year in Canaan. Passover, on the other hand, probably originated among semi-nomadic groups such as the Israelites as a festival related to the movement of their flocks from winter to summer pasture. The feast certainly was a family ceremony during the early history of Israel. In later generations, Passover was one of the three major annual pilgrimage festivals for which the people were to come to Jerusalem (Deut. 16:2–7). It is not difficult to imagine a priest reading the present text, in effect, taking the role of Moses in communicating the instructions for the festival.

The word "passover" (Hebrew *pesach*) is explained in this passage by connecting it with a verb for "to skip" or "hop over," but the actual etymology of the word is uncertain. Throughout the Old Testament, it refers either to the festival described here or to the animal that is killed and eaten. Many passages use the word in both senses (e.g., 2 Chron. 35:1–19). The ceremony had both sacrificial and communal dimensions, in that the animal was ceremonially slaughtered but then consumed as a family meal.

No ceremony was more important in ancient Israel or early Judaism than Passover. To participate in the ritual was to remember and become a part of the story it celebrated. In that story, God promised to set the slaves free. What were they to do in anticipation of that freedom? They were to gather together and eat a particular meal. In doing so, they acknowledged and celebrated both who they were and who their God was. Their God was the one who sets people free and makes them his own. The Passover celebration thus bound the people together and to their God.

Psalm 149

This psalm is a hymn celebrating victory and for this reason is read together with the Exodus account of Passover.

The first three verses are the introit to the hymn calling upon the community to praise God. The "assembly of the faithful" (v. 1) probably simply refers to the people assembled for worship. Reference to divine kingship in verse 2 could indicate that the psalm was used in the fall festival in which the kingship of God and the election of Zion were celebrated. The nature of the celebration is indicated in verse 3, which mentions dancing and music making.

The rationale for celebration or the reason for praise is given in verse 4. God takes pleasure in the people; God adorns or grants victory to the humble. The reversal of fate motif was a characteristic feature of the Passover celebration. Psalm 113, sung at Passover, has this as a basic theme. The Mishnah reports that in the father's retelling of the exodus from Egypt during the Passover seder, he "begins with the disgrace and ends with the glory."

Verses 5–9 calls on the community to celebrate their triumph over their enemies, singing "for joy on their couches," perhaps a reference to the reenactment of victory in battle during the course of a shared communal meal. The images in verses 6–9—singing praise to God with swords in their hands, executing vengeance on the nations, binding kings and nobles with chains, and carrying out the decreed judgment—may sound harsh to a modern ear, but one must realize that religious sentiments and national ambitions went hand in hand in most ancient cultures. Altruism would hardly be expected in rituals that celebrated victory over one's opponents and escape from the bondage of a foreign oppressor.

Ezekiel 33:7–11

This lesson is part of a unit that marks a major new section of the Book of Ezekiel. In the more or less chronological arrangement of the book as a whole, a decisive turning point comes in 33:21–22 with the arrival of the news that Jerusalem has fallen. Because Ezekiel received his initial call in Jehoiachin's fifth year (593 BC), this event would have been the second capture of the city in 587 BC. But the book's arrangement is also theological and likely reflects a change of emphasis in the prophet's role and message. Before 587, he proclaimed judgment and warning concerning the coming disaster. Now the words are more and more focused on the life and fate of those Judeans in exile in Babylon, calling for their obedience to the law and warning them of the consequences of disobedience. Moreover, the message increasingly focuses upon the announcement of salvation beyond the judgment.

Our reading comes from a unit that begins in 33:1 and is not concluded until 33:20. Following the introductory formula for the word of the Lord in verse 1, the entire section is presented as a speech of Yahweh directly to the prophet. The Lord addresses the prophet as "mortal" ("son of man," RSV; "man," REB). There are three distinct parts to the speech. In verses 2–7, Yahweh describes the case of a "sentinel" (better, "sentry") appointed in time of war. Verses 8–9 apply the case to Ezekiel, whom the Lord commissions to be a sentry. Verses 10–20 present the Lord's responses to questions posed by the people of Israel, queries concerning divine justice and the effects of sin.

The style of verses 2–7 is casuistic, like case law in presenting a series of connected conditions, from more general to more specific, with the results of each condition stated. The imagery comes from warfare. If, in time of war, the people elect a sentry, and if danger comes, and if the sentry warns someone by blowing the trumpet, and if that person heeds the warning, then life is the result. But if not, then the person who did not heed the warning, is responsible for his own death. But if the sentry does not sound the alarm and someone dies, then the sentry is held accountable. In fact, such a sentry is guilty of murder. Note that the ground is already laid for the theological application of the extended metaphor when the prophet points out that Yahweh is the one who brings the sword (v. 2; cf. Amos 3:6) and the one who imposes the death sentence on the negligent lookout (v. 6).

Verses 7–9 begin with the explicit commission of the prophet as a sentry for the house of Israel and then, literally, lay down the law to him, again in casuistic form. (Ezekiel 3:16b–19 is an exact parallel.) Instead of seeing the sword coming, however, this sentry hears a word of the Lord and must proclaim the warning. If the Lord announces death to the wicked, then Ezekiel must warn that person. If he fails to do so, he is guilty of a capital crime. But, like the sentry for the city under the threat of the sword, his responsibilities have their limits. The prophet does not cause the disaster, and once he has given his warning, he has saved his life.

Verses 9–20 are in the form of a disputation between Yahweh and the people. The dispute assumes that the people have heard and accepted the sentry's warning but now raise questions about what to do and what to believe. Their words mingle confession of sin with complaint. They are trapped in the effects of iniquity. Now the divine purpose is made plain. The threat of judgment and the sentry's warning are to provoke the repentance that lays the foundation for and leads to life.

The text evokes reflection on two distinct issues. The first concerns the vocation and role of the prophet as sentry for the people. Although other prophets as well had seen themselves as sentinels (Isa. 28:1; Jer. 6:17–19; Hab. 2:1), the role described here represents a development of earlier understandings of the prophetic role: (a) prophets had been called not primarily to warn but to announce, and thereby to set into motion the Lord's judgment (Amos 1:2; Isa. 6:1–13; Jer. 1:4–10); (b) most earlier prophets mainly addressed the people as a whole, but now Ezekiel is to warn individual sinners. His duty is pastoral, to shepherd persons to life. Most important is the combination of urgency and limits in the prophetic role. Faithfulness to the call to be a sentry is, quite literally, a matter of life and death. But once the prophet sounds the warning, his duty is done. There is no way that he is responsible for the sinner's failure to heed his cry.

Second, when the prophet reported what he had heard to the people—as he surely did—what kind of message was it? In reporting his call to be a sentry, he already begins to sound the warning. The purpose of the passage, then, is found in verse 11: the Lord, who has no pleasure in the death of the wicked, calls for the people to turn back and find life. What is God's purpose? God brings the sword upon the city and sets death before the sinner. But the one who brings judgment also provides the means to avert it, to frustrate his own plans. The Lord wants to be given every opportunity to repent. Thus announcement of judgment becomes warning to avoid it. The Lord's sentry, through sounding the warning and calling for repentance, is an instrument of divine grace.

Psalm 119:33–40

This reading was discussed previously as one of the lections for the Seventh Sunday After the Epiphany.

Romans 13:8–14

The second part of this epistolary lection (vv. 11–14) serves as the New Testament reading for the First Sunday of Advent in Year A, which has been treated earlier in this volume. The first part (vv. 8–10), which deals with the obligation to love our neighbor, continues the theme of corporate responsibility treated in the previous two weeks. We will focus our remarks on this first section.

It may strike us as odd to speak of love as obligation, but this is the tone of these remarks: "Leave no debt outstanding, but remember the debt of love you owe one another" (v. 8, REB; similarly, NIV). The sentiments are in keeping with the commandment we know from the Gospel tradition (Matt. 22:34–40; Mark 12:28–34; Luke 10:25–28). There is an oughtness to love: "Since God loved us so much, we also ought to love one another" (1 John 4:11).

But we misconstrue love if we try to remove any sense of ought from it. Certainly, love carries with it obligation, even though it is not knee-jerk obligation. To say that love does not obligate us renders it anemic. In fact, love in the biblical sense obligates in a compelling sense. It locks us into active concern for others.

We are even reminded that love encompasses the law: if we love our neighbor we have fulfilled the law (v. 8). The various commandments of the Decalogue dealing with mutual relationships with each other may be seen most properly as explicit formulations of the more fundamental obligation to love (v. 9; Exod. 20:13–17; Deut. 5:17–21). This conforms to Jesus' insistence that the whole law can be reduced to the twofold love for God and neighbor (Mark 12:18–34 and parallels; cf. Lev. 19:18). It is in this sense that the "whole law is fulfilled in one word—love (Gal. 5:14; cf. Col. 3:14; 1 Tim. 1:5). Thus "love is the one thing that cannot hurt your neighbor; that is why it is the answer to every one of the commandments" (v. 10, JB).

To preach from this text, it will be necessary to confront one of the most familiar demands of the gospel—the positive obligation to love our neighbor.

Matthew 18:15–20

We have today the first of two sessions on 18:1–35, the fourth major body of Jesus' teaching in Matthew (19:1 is the formal ending). The last place mentioned is Capernaum (17:24), but the location for these sayings is unimportant. In fact, chapter 18 is really a collection of diverse sayings, some of which are in Mark (9:33–50), some held in common with Luke (15:3–7; 17:3–4), and some in Matthew alone. The discourse falls into two parts: verses 1–14, the treatment of children (new disciples?) and verses 15–35, the relationship of church members to one another. Our readings today and next Sunday constitute the whole of part two.

In order to understand our text, it is necessary to realize that the setting is not the life of the historical Jesus but the life of the church that came into being after Easter. These sayings presuppose the existence of congregations that gather at times to handle disputes and offenses among members. Verses 15–20 contain instructions as to how to negotiate such matters. Such teachings to Jesus' disciples during his earthly ministry would have been useless and confusing. As the word of the risen and living Christ who is with his disciples whenever two or three are gathered (v. 20), our text speaks clearly to the very common problem of offenses among Christians.

Here, as in the Sermon on the Mount, the instructions are addressed to the victim: "If another member of the church sins against you" (v. 15). The offended are to take the initiative. There is no room in the teaching of Jesus or in the conduct of the Christian life for sitting around, licking wounds, and sighing, "Poor me." One cannot always avoid being a victim, but one can avoid the victim mentality. Finding oneself offended by a member of the faith community, the principle operative in the action one takes is respect, both for the offender and for the entire church. The matter is therefore settled privately, if possible, and if not, in the presence of "one or two others" (v. 16). Such use of witnesses echoes Deuteronomy 19:15. If this second step fails, then the whole congregation is to gather to hear and to resolve the dispute (v. 17). "Church" as used here refers to a local congregation. Paul called upon congregations to discipline members (1 Cor. 5–6; 2 Cor. 2:5–8), but the history of this procedure is not one of unambiguous success. It often is a case of pulling up the wheat with the tares. Matthew is assuming a small gathering of Christians pure in motive and objective in judgment. Not all congregations can be so described and therefore render the process questionable. What is without question, however, is the realism of the text: disputes do arise among believers, and it is important that the problems be addressed directly, as privately as possible, but always with care and respect.

The conclusion of verse 17 is quite a problem for the reader. That discipline by excommunication occurred is historical fact. (It was presumably temporary until reconciliation occurred.) However, the expression "as a Gentile and a tax collector" sounds more like something coming from a conservative Jewish Christian community than from Jesus. We know that some Jewish Christians had difficulty with the embrace of Gentiles (Acts 10:14, 28; 11:8; Gal. 2:1–16). But we also know that Jesus sent his disciples to all nations (Matt. 28:18–20) and during his earthly ministry defended his practice of accepting tax collectors (Matt. 9:10–13). In fact, one of the Twelve was a tax collector (Matt. 10:9). The whole of Jesus' ministry argues against Matthew's derogatory reference to Gentiles and tax collectors. The interpreter sometimes must use Jesus against statements in the name of Jesus. The entire matter of verses 15–20 is not a simple one or easy to translate into new settings.

The binding and loosing referred to here (vv. 18–19) has to do with discipline and reconciliation in the congregation. Even if the gathered community number only two or three, heaven is alert to the business being transacted, and the living Christ is present. The promise of Christ's presence, even if only two or three are gathered, has long since been extracted from the judicial context of making disciplinary decisions and extended as a general blessing upon every Christian community, whatever its size. Such a wider claim on verse 20 is not out of order and certainly accords with the church's experience everywhere.

Proper 19 [24]
(Sunday between September 11 and 17 inclusive)

Exodus 14:19–31;
Psalm 114 or Exodus 15:1b–11, 20–21; or
Genesis 50:15–21;
Psalm 103:(1–7) 8–13;
Romans 14:1–12;
Matthew 18:21–35

The Hebrew crossing of the Red Sea to escape from Egyptian oppression and to begin their trek toward the promised land is the theme of the Old Testament lesson in the *Common Lectionary*. In lilting praise, Psalm 114 recalls Yahweh's deliverance of Israel from Egypt, or alternatively, the response may be provided by the first half of the Song of Moses and the Song of Miriam in Exodus 15, both of which sing of God's mighty triumph.

In other lectionaries, the Old Testament reading is supplied by the touching story in Genesis 50 where Joseph extends forgiveness to his brothers. Yahweh's willingness to forgive freely serves as the major theme of Psalm 103, a bold statement of divine grace.

The epistolary reading comes from Paul's discussion of the "weak" and "strong," where relationships within the Christian community are placed before the universal reign of God. In the Gospel reading, we hear Jesus teaching about forgiveness and presenting us with the well-known parable of the unforgiving servant.

Exodus 14:19–31

This reading concludes the account of Israel's deliverance at the sea. The report of the episode began in Exodus 13:17 and is followed by the songs of Moses and Miriam in Exodus 15:1–21. It is an extremely important story in Old Testament tradition, but it is not—as some commentators have thought—the central point of the Exodus itself. Israel has already been released from Egypt (Exod. 12:29–51). Both in terms of the structure of the Book of Exodus and the motifs of the passage, the account of the rescue at the sea is part of the wilderness traditions.

The importance of the events reported here is seen in the rich and complex history of tradition that they evoked. The narrative account itself is the combination of at least two of the pentateuchal sources, and then there are the songs of Moses and Miriam that reflect further responses. Although the sources are combined into a complete story, and there is no scholarly consensus on all the detailed source division, recognition of the existence of older sources here enables one to hear the different religious and theological concerns in the passage.

There are first of all basic differences in the accounts concerning the method by which the rescue was effected. Did God divide the sea to allow Israel to cross, or did a strong east wind blow back the waters so that the Egyptian chariots became clogged in the mud? There are further repetitions, duplicates, and differences in style and perspective that lead to the conclusion that there is a more or less complete account from the Priestly Writer and another from the older sources J and E. They differ not only on the details of events but also concerning the purpose and meaning of those events.

According to the Priestly Writer (found mainly in 14:1–3, 8–10a, 15–18, 21a, 22–23, 26–27a, 28–29), the Lord hardened the heart of the pharaoh so that he pursued the Israelites, because the Lord had a purpose in mind from the outset: "I will gain glory for myself over Pharaoh and all his army; and the Egyptians shall know that I am the Lord" (v. 4). The deliverance appears to have taken place in the daytime. Upon instructions from God, Moses stretched out his hand, the sea divided, and the people of Israel crossed on dry land with the Egyptians in pursuit (vv. 16, 22–23). Then Moses lowered his hand and the waters returned, killing the Egyptians (vv. 26, 28–29). The divine intervention is dramatic, and the purpose is revelation—that the Egyptians may know that the Lord is God.

According to the older sources, the people flee, but when they see the Egyptians approach they become fearful and complain to Moses (vv. 10–12), who commands them to be still and see the deliverance that the Lord will perform for them (vv. 13–14). In this tradition, there is no report of an Israelite crossing of the sea. The angel of God keeps the camps apart, with the pillar of cloud that had led the Israelites moving between them and the Egyptians (vv. 19–20). The event seems to have happened at night. The decisive events transpire when Yahweh "drove the sea back by a strong east wind" (v. 21b). Then Yahweh "looked down on the Egyptian army through the pillar of fire and cloud, and he threw them into a panic" (v. 24, REB). The Egyptian chariots became clogged in the mud, and when the sea returned to its usual position they seem to have run into it (v. 27b). This imagery is very similar to the traditions of the holy war, when Yahweh fights for Israel against her enemies. The account concludes with a summary and a theological interpretation: "Thus the Lord saved Israel that day from the Egyptians. . . . Israel saw the great work that the Lord did against the Egyptians. So the people feared the Lord and believed in the Lord and in his servant Moses" (vv. 30–31).

Although preaching is hardly the place to display the source critical analysis of a biblical passage, recognition that diverse documents have been combined here calls attention to some of the different ways that this story can be recalled and interpreted. (1) One may stress the deliverance at the sea as unqualified good news, deliverance from trouble. That would be consistent with the JE account, which also makes it clear that the people of Israel by no means earned this deliverance through good works, but, to the contrary, they only complained. Then in that tradition, the result of the divine initiative is the faith of the people, not only in the Lord but in God's designated representative. (2) In the younger source P, the divine intention is to let the wider world, represented by the Egyptian pharaoh, know that the Lord is God. It is not surprising, therefore, that the saving event takes place in broad daylight and that it is an unmistakably miraculous intervention. (3) Finally, these diverse sources and traditions have been combined into the complete story before us now. The final editors probably knew the different theological emphases but saw no contradiction between them. They are complementary. Even the different pictures of the event itself agree about the agency. God acts dramatically to divide the sea, or God acts through the strong east wind and then throws the enemy into a panic. Whether directly and through Moses or through so-called natural phenomena, it is the God of Israel who acts to save.

Psalm 114

This psalm has been discussed in detail as one of the lections for Easter Evening.

Exodus 15:1*b*–11, 20–21

This alternative reading to Psalm 114 contains a portion of what is called "the Song at the Sea" (Exod. 15:1–18) along with the "Song of Miriam" (vv. 20–21), both celebrating the escape through the sea and the destruction of the pursuing Egyptian forces.

After the initial statement of singing praise to God (v. 1*b*, which parallels v. 21), the song of the sea may be divided into three stanzas: (1) verses 2–5 describe Yahweh in speech about the Deity, (2) verses 6–10 rehearse the actions of Yahweh in destroying the Egyptians (the negative pole), but in speech addressed directly to God, and (3) verses 11–18, which focus on God's care and guidance of the people (the positive pole), in speech addressed directly to God.

The emphasis in Moses' song stresses the warrior character of Yahweh with regard to Israel's enemies and his protective nature with regard to Israel.

At the turn of the century, the British Old Testament scholar Samuel Rolles Driver wrote: "The ode of triumph [Exod. 15:1–18] is one of the finest products of Hebrew poetry, remarkable for poetic fire and spirit, picturesque description, vivid imagery, quick movement, effective parallelism, and bright sonorous diction."

The ancient rabbis noted that this was the first song of salvation in the Bible: "God had saved men before, yet none had sung words of praise: not Abraham (the reference to Abraham in this context is explained in the Midrash) when saved from the fiery furnace; nor Isaac when saved from the knife; nor Jacob when saved from the angel, from Esau, or the men of Shechem. But as soon as Israel was saved they uttered their song. And God responded: 'I have been waiting from them.'"

The Song of Miriam, on the other hand, is short and to the point, with the emphasis falling as much on the women's behavior as on the content of the song. The actions of the women, dancing with tambourines, probably reflects some of the celebration associated with festivals. Although processions and dancing are not so much a part of contemporary worship, they were highly important in the Israelite cult (see 2 Sam. 6:12–16). Eleven different Hebrew words are used in the Old Testament denoting dancing, suggesting that ritual choreography was a major part of life.

The references to later events in the life of the Hebrews (vv. 14–16) and the allusion to the temple precinct in Jerusalem (v. 17) suggest that the song of the sea was not written by Moses but was a cultic hymn celebrating the occasion of the Exodus placed back into the narrative of the events.

Genesis 50:15–21

This lesson comes from the concluding paragraphs of the story of Joseph (Gen. 37, 39–47, 50). For an introduction to the Joseph story as a whole, see the comments on Genesis 37:1–4, 12–28 for Proper 14 [19] found earlier in this volume. In important respects, today's lesson is similar to Genesis 45:1–15, the text assigned for Proper 15 [20].

This text, like any other, can be read by itself, but its power and its compelling irony come through only when seen in its broader context. Although composed of materials from the Yahwist and the Elohist, the older pentateuchal sources, the story of Joseph and his brothers is such a carefully crafted piece that it has been compared with modern short stories or novels. It has a clear plot with characters who grow and develop as the events unfold. At the beginning (Gen. 37), the brothers, jealous of Joseph, had sold him into slavery, where he had not only survived but prospered. His special talents and skills had taken him, as he says, to the second highest office in Egypt. (The language of 45:8 and elsewhere indicates that the narrator sees him as the Grand Vizer, in effect, the prime minister under only the pharaoh.) Egypt, and with it the entire region, was suffering the period of famine foreseen by Joseph in his dreams, so the brothers come looking for food. The tension had been allowed to grow: how will the old conflict between Joseph and the brothers be resolved? The account in Genesis 45 of the meeting of the brothers shows the answer and also makes it clear that the plot—the development of the story as a whole—had actually been taking place on a different level from that perceived by the participants in it.

In the plot as a whole, the lesson from Genesis 50 is part of the denouement, or unfolding, following the story's climax, which had come in chapter 45. It recapitulates the interpretation of the story and of the meaning of Joseph's life with his brothers expressed in chapter 45. The immediate context is the account of the death of Jacob, Joseph's father. When the brothers had sold Joseph into slavery and deceived their father with evidence that he had been killed, Jacob, bowed in grief, had sworn that he would mourn the loss of his favorite son until the day he died. But he had come to Egypt to be reunited with Joseph, to pronounce his blessings on his children, and then to die (Gen. 49:29–32).

Genesis 50:15 revives the tension that had driven the plot, the conflict between Joseph and his brothers. Now that their father is dead, will Joseph still "bear a grudge" against them? In the scene that follows (vv. 16–21), the contrast between Joseph and the brothers is sharp. They are guilt-ridden, fearful, and in a position of weakness. He is wise, understanding, forgiving, and powerful. The thoughtful reader will remember, along with the narrator, what the brothers have forgotten: they are fulfilling the prophecy of Joseph's first dream (Gen. 37:5–8) that they would one day bow down to him. Thus, on the level of human relations and human conflicts, the arc of the narrative is complete. The brothers' anxiety, however, is understandable, on the one hand as the persistent effect of guilt, and on the other hand as a realistic assessment of Joseph's power over them. Benevolent he may be, but the last word is his.

Following Joseph's words of reassurance ("Do not be afraid," v. 19a), he makes two points. First, he responds to the request for forgiveness with a rhetorical question: "Am I in the place of God?" (v. 19b). Although it is enigmatic in the sense that he does not grant their request, the sentence certainly means to limit the authority of Joseph and to say that God is the one who grants—or refuses to grant—forgiveness. This perspective leads to the second point, the interpretation of the meaning of the story: "Even though you intended to do harm to me, God intended it for good, in order to preserve a numerous people, as he is doing today" (v. 20). God's ways may be hidden and mysterious, concealed even in human conflicts, active in and on human hearts, but God has guided the events of their lives to a salvific purpose.

Psalm 103:(1–7) 8–13

This hymnic psalm of thanksgiving comes very close to being a theological catechism enumerating the personal qualities and behavioral characteristics of the Deity. In expounding this psalm, the ancient rabbis, however, were interested in what it had to say about the human, that is, its anthropological dimensions. In speaking about "all that is within me," the Midrash (rabbinic commentary) on Psalms notes ten things within a person: "the windpipe for voice, the gullet for [swallowing] food, the liver for anger, the lungs for drink [to absorb liquids], the gall for jealousy, the maw [when full] for sleep, the stomach to grind the food, the spleen for laughter, the kidneys for counsel, and the heart for decision." Of interest here is the way various organs are associated with particular human emotions.

In speaking of the expression "bless the Lord," one ancient rabbi noted the following as the distinction between God as artisan and all other artisans: "A sculptor makes a statue; the sculptor dies, but his sculpture endures. But with the Holy One, it is not so. For the Holy One made man, and man dies, but the Holy One lives and endures. This neither the sculptor nor the silversmith can do. The silversmith casts an image; the silversmith dies; the casting endures. But the Holy One made man, and it is man who dies; it is the Holy One who lives and endures for ever and ever."

Although a thanksgiving, this psalm contains no direct address to the Deity; thus it is not a prayer of thanksgiving. In fact, the composition begins as a self addressing the self (v. 1). In the final stanza, the range of vision is greatly expanded, arching out to include the angels, the heavenly hosts, and all the works of creation.

If we include verse 6 with verses 1–5, and this is a possible although not an obvious division, then the first six verses speak of seven deeds of the Deity:

> forgives iniquity
>   heals diseases
> redeems from the Pit
>   crowns with steadfast love and mercy
> satisfies with good as long as one lives
>   renews youthful vigor like that of an eagle
> works vindication and justice for all oppressed

All of these actions are expressed through participial forms of the verbs. One might take such formulations, like participles in English, as describing states as being. Thus the actions denoted are taken as descriptions characteristic of the Deity.

Verses 8–13 have a second series, containing this time six items that describe the character of Yahweh, particularly with regard to the divine reaction to human error, wrongdoing, and rebellion. Verse 14 should be considered in conjunction with these verses, for it offers anthropological insight and rationale for divine behavior, offering reasons anchored in human existence for God's grace and mercy.

Throughout this section, descriptions of God's treatment of the sinner and explanations of divine behavior are interlaced. Each verse makes independent but interrelated points. (1) God's nature is oriented to mercy and grace. God is not easily upset, and when this is the case, there is mercy abounding (v. 8). (2) God does not perpetually torment or nag incessantly, for divine anger does not abide forever. The text does not deny that God has anger and that the Divine does react in wrath; however, the Divine is willing to let bygones be bygones (v. 9). (3) God does not operate on a tit for tat basis. The punishment is not made to fit the crime. God is free to reduce the penalty, to soften the shock of human actions (v. 10). (4) Divine mercy is compared to the greatness of the heights of the heavens above the earth (v. 11). (5) The vertical dimension used in verse 11 is replaced by a horizontal dimension in describing the removal of transgressions. East and west, or literally the rising and setting (of the sun), is a way of stressing the radical separation (v. 12). (6) The parent-child relationship and parental pity form an analogy by which to understand divine love. It should be noted that such pity is granted to those fearing (=obeying the will of) God (v. 13; note vv. 17–18). The human condition helps incline God to mercy: God knows the weakness of the human condition—people's dusty origin and their dusty destiny. In forgiving his brothers, Joseph's attitude has analogies to that of the Divine.

Romans 14:1–12

Religious communities are like all other social groups in at least one important respect—our members disagree. We "quarrel over opinions" (v. 1). What is different is that we disagree on matters we regard as of ultimate importance. To disagree on wages and benefits is one thing; to disagree on our final reward is quite another. It is the difference between welfare here and welfare hereafter.

The situation in view in today's epistolary reading has to do with differences in everyday religious practice—the appropriate way of being religious: whether to eat meat or just vegetables (vv. 2, 6); whether to drink or abstain from wine (14:21); whether to observe certain days as holy or whether to regard every day as holy (vv. 5–6). This is the stuff over which religious persons—Jews, Muslims, Christians, and others—have disagreed for centuries. They are the sand in the crankshaft.

Paul's treatment here is rather nonspecific and slightly distant. It is not clear whether the "day" is the sabbath day, some other (Jewish) feast day, or days in general. Elsewhere, observing certain days is linked with astral speculation, and Paul's response to those who would impose day keeping on all Christians is more direct (Col. 2:16; also Gal. 4:10). Maybe he knows the Roman situation less well, never having been there (Rom. 1:11). Maybe he is casting his theological net more widely in hopes that his teaching will be more widely applicable. As to the question of what to eat, we are clearly dealing with some form of religious asceticism, not the question of eating sacrificial meat offered to idols (cf. 1 Cor. 8–10).

What is striking here is that Paul does not take sides. He appears far less interested in the particular merits of each side's argument than with the impact of these arguments on the life of the community as a whole. In fact, he is remarkably tolerant, that is, if the dispute over religious holidays has anything at all to do with astrological speculation, which he clearly regarded as inimical to Christian practice (Gal. 4:8–10).

Yet he sees it in terms familiar from other discussions (cf. 1 Cor. 8–10)—how the weak (14:1–2) and strong (15:1) live together in community. We do not know precisely who the weak and strong are—Jewish Christians, Gentile Christians, neither, both? We do know that the weak are taking a narrow line, the strong a broader line. In this sense, the weak are rigorous in their insistence on vegetarianism, whereas the strong are less rigorous and "believe in eating anything" (v. 2). The weak are conservative in insisting that one day is better than another, whereas the strong are liberal in insisting that all days are alike (v. 5).

Thus one group insists on making sharp distinctions, whereas the other group sees shades of gray. One sees unbreakable principles at stake; the other sees principles as more flexible guidelines. One argues that to concede this point means that the whole house of cards collapses; the other argues that if the house is that fragile perhaps it should collapse. One sees a crucial point at stake; the other doubts whether this one point is the single axis on which the whole religious universe turns. Small circles versus larger circles. Narrow boundaries versus wider boundaries. Black and white versus shades of gray. Obedience versus freedom.

And how does Paul respond? First, he insists that even the eyes of faith can see things differently. The religious positions articulated here are polar opposites, mutually exclusive. He makes no effort to harmonize them or to impose uniformity. For Paul, "faith does not make all persons and things equal" (Käsemann).

In fact, he allows that radically different theological positions can stem from the same motive—honoring the Lord and giving thanks to God (v. 6). It is not that one is operating with sinister motives, the other with pure motives. Both are genuinely attempting to live properly before the Lord. Good and pure religious convictions can manifest themselves in radically different ways.

One thing that is important is for everyone to "be fully convinced in their own minds" (v. 5). One might have thought that Paul would call for loosening the bolts of religious conviction in this situation. Instead, he insists on firmly held, clearly conceived, intellectual positions. In the heat of religious controversy, they are asked to put their minds in gear, not out. The way forward is not through loosely formulated positions that one can flex on demand. Rather, what is called for is genuine conviction that remains open to God's future. "What the apostle has in view is the renewed reason of 12:2 whose critical capacity leads through the call into a circumscribed sphere to firm conviction and resolute action on the basis of insight into one's own situation, and from the perspective remains open to new situations and the assessment of the brother" (Käsemann). Before we can talk fruitfully, we must think clearly.

A second perspective is offered in verses 7–9, which is perhaps the central section of our text. It seems to provide a central, guiding principle that informs the whole discussion, both what precedes and what follows: "We do not live to ourselves, and we do not die to ourselves" (v. 7). With this sharply formulated principle, Paul says no to robust individualism. An individual Christian is an oxymoron. No one is an island. We are creatures of the whole, not of the part. Religiousness is not exclusiveness. Our personal existence is no city of refuge to which we can flee.

And why not? Because we live and die to the Lord (v. 8). The universal dominion of the Lord precludes the universal dominion of the individual. The whole spectrum of human existence, from death to life, lies outstretched before the risen Christ, who alone encompasses life in its fullest. He alone is the "Lord of both the dead and the living" (v. 9). We cannot be both "in the Lord" and "in ourselves." To be "in the Lord" is to recognize a larger dominion than the world of the self. Even more, we must recognize that we stand in solidarity with a host of others, dead and living, past, present, and future, who confess the universal dominion of the

Lord. Thus, however vital our own personal relationship with the Lord is, it is neither unique, solitary, nor exclusive.

A final perspective is offered in verses 10–12, one that derives from our acknowledgment of the universal dominion of the Lord: ultimate self-accountability before God relativizes our sense of others' accountability to us. Our ultimate reference point is God's future, when "we will all stand before the judgment seat of God" (v. 10; cf. 2:16; 2 Cor. 5:10; Matt. 25:31–46; Acts 10:42; 17:31; 2 Tim. 4:1; 1 Pet. 4:5). We must finally bow before God in worshipful praise (v. 11; cf. Isa. 45:23; 49:18; Jer. 23:24; Ezek. 5:11; also Phil. 2:10–11). But with praise comes responsibility—and accountability (v. 10).

So sobering is the thought that each of us is ultimately accountable to God that our own inclination and ability to "pass judgment" diminishes. The more concerned we are with our responsibility before God, the less concerned we become with others' responsibility to us. For one thing, in the presence of God we become painfully aware of our own inadequacies. The light of God makes us so transparent that we find it difficult to place others under the beam of our own investigative light. To recognize that God passes judgment on us makes us less ready to pass judgment on others, much less to despise them (v. 10).

Taken seriously, Paul's advice in today's text will make Christian individuals less judgmental and Christian communities more livable. It will also change our agendas from passing "judgment on one another" (14:13) to pursuing "what makes for peace and mutual upbuilding" (14:19; 1 Cor. 14:26). It will not make us any less variegated in the theological positions we take or in the religious life-styles to which those positions lead us. But it will place our diversity under the scrutiny of the Lord of the living and the dead rather than under the watchful eye of those bent on making us in their own image and in their own likeness; that is, those who think that the boundaries of life and death are theirs to define— and to guard. It will, in a word, place our destiny in the hands of God, not in the hands of those who think they can do God's work better and quicker than even God can do it. It will save us from those who make God's future their present and God's agenda their own.

Matthew 18:21–35

We complete today Jesus' teachings on relationships within the Christian community, the fourth of five major teaching sections in Matthew. The preacher may find it helpful to review the introductory comments on the lection for last Sunday.

After the rather detailed procedure outlined in verses 15–20 for seeking reconciliation with an offending brother or sister, verses 21–22 are most refreshing. In the final analysis, that which creates and sustains the Christian community is forgiveness. Forgiveness is not, of course, carelessness or indifference to wrong. It is not permissiveness or the absence of any sense of ethical standards. On the contrary, there can be no forgiveness without standards and values being violated, without persons and relationships being hurt, without a loss so deeply felt that efforts at restoration are pursued. From a distance, forgiveness may look like condoning or permissiveness, but in reality forgiveness takes the violators, the violated, and the violation most seriously. To be forgiven is to be taken seriously. Forgiveness does not abrogate but fulfills righteousness.

And how often should one forgive? A rabbinic tradition said three times. Simon Peter, in a generous gesture, suggested possibly seven times (v. 21). Jesus says forgiveness does not count the times. Who is keeping score? In saying seventy-seven times (ancient versions translated the expression "seventy times seven," which has continued in modern versions even though the word means "seventy-seven"), Jesus is simply dramatizing the point that forgiveness is unlimited. Very likely the number seventy-seven was intended as a reversal of Genesis 4:24, in which Lamech claimed revenge seventy-sevenfold.

Our lection closes with a parable intended to underscore the fact that the Christian community is a community of the forgiven and forgiving. To lay claim to the one without extending the other is to demonstrate an inability to live in and by the forgiveness of God. The preacher will not want to press the parable in detail to the point that forgiveness takes on an ugly face. For instance, the parable contains exaggerations. How could a slave owe anyone ten thousand talents (v. 24) when just one talent was the sum total for fifteen years of common labor? Some commentators suggest the slave in the story is a subservient prince or territorial governor who failed to pay taxes due the king. Maybe. Another detail not to be pressed is the statement about selling into slavery one who is already a slave (v. 25). Or again, being delivered to the jailers (literally, torturers) until all the debt is paid strains the reason (v. 34). It is much better to accept such elements as the furniture of the story, the force of which is to say, We have been forgiven much; let us not withhold forgiveness for the lesser offenses that creep into our fellowship.

The preacher will, of course, be disturbed by the Matthean comment following the parable (v. 35). We have grown accustomed to Matthew's manner of underscoring his point by making reference to a final judgment. But Matthew, in saying that God will likewise torture all who do not forgive from the heart, makes an appeal that falls short of effectiveness for most Christians. It is difficult to forgive "from the heart" with such a threat hanging overhead. But sometimes conditions in a congregation can so deteriorate that the preacher speaks louder than usual and appeals to God's final judgment more frequently than usual. Such may be Matthew's situation.

Proper 20 [25]
(Sunday between September 18 and 24 inclusive)

Exodus 16:2–15;
Psalm 105:1–6, 37–45; or
Jonah 3:10–4:11;
Psalm 145:1–8;
Philippians 1:21–30;
Matthew 20:1–16

In the final form of Israel's early history, now embodied in the Pentateuch, the theme of disobedience and murmuring in the wilderness plays a significant role. This week's Old Testament lesson in the *Common Lectionary* provides one of the first examples of this motif. Psalm 105 initially praises the wonderful works of God and finally recounts God's deliverance of Israel from Egypt.

For the Old Testament reading in other lectionaries, we have the account of Jonah's impetuous response to Nineveh's conversion, which prompts a defense by God for extending mercy to this great city. Jonah's description of God is echoed in Psalm 145, which extols God as compassionate and long-suffering.

The epistolary reading is the first in a series of semicontinuous readings from Paul's letter to the Philippians. Here occurs Paul's memorable confession that "living is Christ." The Gospel reading continues the teaching of Jesus from Matthew with the parable of the laborers in the vineyard who receive the same wage for different amounts of work. We hear the workers' understandable protest of inequity and Jesus' censure of them for questioning the master's right to determine wages and for being oblivious to his generosity in making it possible for them to work in the first place.

Exodus 16:2–15

According to all levels of Old Testament tradition, between the exodus from Egypt and the settlement of the land of Canaan, Israel wandered in the wilderness. As indicated in the discussion of last week's text, Exodus 14:19–31, the deliverance of Israel at the sea took place when the people were out of Egypt and in the wilderness. The scene that is played out in chapter 16 is one that will recur over and over along the way from Egypt to Sinai and from Sinai to the edge of the promised land: the people of Israel complain because of some real or imagined need, Moses remonstrates with them and intercedes with the Lord, and the Lord responds graciously but not always without anger. The most persistent themes concerning the wilderness wandering thus are expressed—the dramatic contrast between the people's persistent complaints and the Lord's gracious care and preservation.

Although the basic profile of the story as a whole is clear enough, Jewish and Christian commentators from the earliest times have recognized a large number of difficulties in the chapter. The rabbis in particular noticed (1) that in verse 8 Moses gives divine instructions regarding the observation of the sabbath that he did not receive until verses 11–12, but even so, the commandment was not given until later at Sinai, and (2) that there is an allusion in verse 34 to the tent of the meeting that was not built until later. Moreover, there are gaps, repetitions, and different descriptions of the manna. Only some of these difficulties are resolved by the recognition of different sources. Most of the chapter comes from P, but some verses (mainly vv. 4–5, 27–31) come from the Yahwist. The latter stresses the gift of the manna as a test, whereas the former emphasizes that the purpose was to demonstrate that it was the Lord who brought the people out of Egypt.

It would be difficult indeed for the modern preacher to develop a line of thought concerning the story of the manna and quails that has not already appeared in the history of the interpretation of this tradition, either elsewhere in the Old Testament, in the New Testament (see esp. John 6; 1 Cor. 10:1–13; 2 Cor. 8:15; Rev. 2:17), or in the history of the church and synagogue. The manna story has been used as the basis for moralistic homilies, it has been spiritualized, and there have been attempts even in the early Christian centuries to find a rational explanation for the miracle. Among the possibilities for homiletical reflection are the following:

1. Consider the murmuring or complaining of the people. The specific issue in Exodus 16 is food. Was the complaint legitimate or not, or—better—does the narrator of the story consider it a legitimate complaint? By his choice of words ("complained," or "grumbled," NJPSV) and by the way he phrases the complaint, our reporter disapproves of a whining people: "If only we had died by the hand of the Lord in the land of Egypt, when we sat by the fleshpots and ate our fill of bread." (v. 3). That is the dominant view in the tradition, that Israel's complaints were unfair. (There is an alternative tradition that seems to think of the time in the wilderness as the period of Israel's full obedience to and dependence upon the Lord. Cf. Hos. 2:14; 11:1; 13:4ff.; Jer. 2:1ff.) On the surface, the complaint concerns food, but it is actually far more serious. In effect, the Israelites are objecting to their election, to the fact that Yahweh brought them out of slavery into freedom! Small wonder that preachers have used the Israelites in the wilderness as bad examples!

The Old Testament view about complaining to God, however, is not so unambiguous. Although one may not see God and live, one could certainly complain to God in the strongest possible terms and not only survive but hope for relief. Such complaints are found not only in the Book of Job but in more than fifty psalms of individual or corporate lament. There the individual or the community petitioned God for help in time of trouble, confessing either sin or innocence (cf. Pss. 6, 17, 22). The context for such prayers was worship, from which no human emotion or feeling was prohibited.

2. Here the gift is a test. When the Lord responds to the complaint with a promise to "rain bread from heaven," he says it is in order "to test them, whether they will follow my instruction or not" (v. 4). What is the point, and what is the penalty for failure to pass? The instructions conceal a promise: "Each day the people shall go out and gather enough for

that day." The test is whether they will do just as they are told, no more and no less. Some of the people, however, fail the test, for they do not trust the promise that tomorrow there will be enough for that day. Contrary to the further instructions (v. 19), they tried to save some of the manna. What happens when one fails to trust in the promise of daily bread? How is punishment handed out to those who do not pass the test? Not without a sense of humor the narrator reports that the hoarded manna "bred worms and became foul" (v. 20).

3. Then there is the giving of the manna itself. At one level, the chapter is a popular etymology of the name of the wilderness food, a play on the sound of the question "What is it?" (Hebrew *man hu*). But above all, the manna, like all good things to eat, is a gift. Deuteronomy views the gift as didactic, God's means of teaching the people one of the most fundamental points about life: "He humbled you by letting you hunger, then by feeding you with manna . . . in order to make you understand that one does not live by bread alone, but by every word that comes from the mouth of the Lord" (Deut. 8:3). Here "every word that comes from the mouth of the Lord" has a double meaning. On the one hand, it is spiritual, calling attention to the divine law and teachings. On the other hand, it alludes to the creative power of the word of God, by which all good things are brought into being. Thus the manna is a test and it is a lesson, but above all it is God's graceful response to an ungrateful and even rebellious people.

Psalm 105:1–6, 37–45

Portions of this psalm have been used on several earlier occasions in Year A. Here the newly included text is verses 37–45, which stress the divine care of the Hebrews in their journey from Egypt to the promised land.

In the description of this period, Psalm 105 never mentions any trouble or disobedience by the people (cf. Ps. 106, which is a recital of the people's murmuring and disobedience). This illustrates the fact that traditions could be shaped to fit the occasion and the context of their usage. In Deut. 8:4, the people's clothes and shoes are depicted as not even wearing out during the forty years in the wilderness!

Here the Hebrews leave Egypt with wealth, and the Egyptians are glad to see them leave (vv. 37–38). The Hebrews are divinely fed, led, and watered in the wilderness because God remembers the promise made to Abraham (vv. 39–42). The people are given the land of promise and its wealth so that the people might possess a place in which they could live according to the laws and statutes of God (vv. 43–45).

Jonah 3:10–4:11

The presence of the Book of Jonah in the prophetic canon is remarkable, for it is unlike all the other prophetic books. The others consist primarily of collections of the speeches of and the traditions about the prophets, but Jonah is a prose narrative about a prophet. The only prophecy in the book is a single line, Jonah's announcement of judgment in the name of the Lord: "Forty days more and Nineveh shall be overthrown" (3:4). The themes and the message of the book, however, are consistent with the heart of the prophetic tradition, especially as represented in Jeremiah and Second Isaiah (Isa. 40–55).

Although it is impossible to date the book's composition with any precision, it is clear that it arose in the postexilic period, most likely in the fifth century. The writer contributed to a debate among the people in Judah concerning the mercy of God and the relation of the chosen people to other nations. The story is by no means presented as history or biography but as a didactic short story or an instructive tale. The writer has a very serious message, but presents it with humor bordering on the farcical.

Our lesson consists of the final scenes in the narrative and is best understood in the plot as a whole. In fact, the preacher may well allow the story to tell itself. The story begins suddenly with the notice that "the word of the Lord came to Jonah . . . ," commanding him to go to Nineveh and "cry out" against the city. Just as suddenly, and without any explanation by the narrator, Jonah fled "from the presence of the Lord" by ship to Tarshish. But the Lord's presence could not be escaped so easily, and the Lord brought a storm that threatened to destroy the ship. After casting lots and determining that Jonah was the cause of their trouble, the sailors quite reluctantly threw the prophet overboard. The storm ceased, and Jonah was rescued by a divinely appointed fish. In the next scene, we find the prophet writing and singing poetry in the belly of the fish, which then vomited Jonah out onto dry land. Jonah then obeyed the Lord's second command to go to Nineveh, pronouncing that the city would be destroyed in forty days. But the people and even the king repented, saying, "Who knows, God may relent and change his mind; he may turn from his fierce anger, so that we do not perish" (3:9). God indeed repented, leading to the book's final scene in which Jonah complains about God's mercy but sits down to see what will happen to the city. The book concludes with God's rebuke to the prophet: "And should I not be concerned about Nineveh, that great city, in which there are more than a hundred and twenty thousand persons who do not know their right hand from their left, and also many animals?" (4:11).

Although it is a single story, it is composed in two distinct and parallel parts, chapters 1–2 and chapters 3–4, each of which has three scenes. God's commission and the prophet's response in 1:1–3 parallels that in 3:1–4; the account of the storm and the pagan sailors (1:4–16) parallels the report of repentance in Nineveh (3:5–10); the account of Jonah's prayer in the belly of the fish in chapter 2 parallels his prayer and God's response in chapter 4. Such literary balance cannot be accidental but is the result of careful creative writing.

Jonah is hardly a hero. Reluctance to respond to God's call is not unusual, but is typical in Old Testament reports of vocations. Jonah's flight from God, however, reveals something distinctive about this character; he obviously presumes that God's power is limited to his little land. Above all, there are the sharp contrasts between Jonah and the foreigners. First, during the storm each of the sailors is praying to his own god, and our prophet is fast asleep. They are reluctant to throw him overboard, and he expresses self-pity. The people of Nineveh repent on the strength of his one-sentence announcement, and he resents God's reversal of his decision to destroy the great city on the grounds that his prophecy is now proven wrong.

The book is above all a rebuke of a narrow understanding of God's mercy. God's elect can be foolish, and outsiders can be pious. Narrow parochialism is ridiculed and rebuked. Many have rightly seen in this story an argument for the view that God's elect are called to be a light to the nations. The book is a parable of God's grace, of the wideness of God's mercy. If it concerns repentance, it emphasizes God's willingness to repent (3:10; 4:2; cf. RSV). God is more willing to forgive than his prophet can understand. Finally, the text reflects indirectly on the role of the prophet. The prophetic word must be proclaimed, but the prophet should not be surprised at the way God uses that word.

Psalm 145:1–8

Aportion of this psalm was earlier one of the readings for Proper 9 [14]. These verses have been selected to accompany the reading from Jonah because of verse 8, with its emphasis on Yahweh's mercy and kindness.

Verse 8 has the quality of a liturgical formula and may have been used in worship as a communal response. It occurs not only in Psalms 86:15 and 103:8 but also in Exodus 34:6; Joel 2:13; and Jonah 4:2.

Philippians 1:21–30

Because this is the first of four semicontinuous readings from Paul's Epistle to the Philippians, some introductory words are in order.

We should first note that the letter reflects a long-standing relationship between Paul and the church at Philippi. He can look back to the time when this church began active financial support of his ministry, and their generosity has been repeated (4:14–16). This letter is prompted in part by yet another financial contribution (4:17–18) and thus takes the form of a letter of thanksgiving (1:3–11; 4:10). The mood is intimate between Paul the missionary and his supporting church, and the tone is deeply moving and personal.

The letter is written from prison (1:7, 13) and serves to allay the church's anxiety about Paul's welfare. There is an apologetic tone noticeable in the first chapter as Paul seeks to reassure the church that in spite of his imprisonment the gospel is making progress (cf. 1:12). He still has his detractors, but he can still report that "Christ is proclaimed in every way" (1:18).

From his repeated mention of "joy" and "rejoicing" (1:4, 18–19; 2:2), we should not conclude that all is necessarily well within this relatively well-established church. Signs of internal tension surface early in the letter (2:1–4, 14), and by the end he is mentioning by name persons who should be encouraged to get along with each other (4:2). Opponents from the outside also pose a threat (1:28), and the tone becomes especially polemical in chapter 3, which originally may have existed as a separate letter to the church.

Paul's pastoral concern is evident throughout the letter. Exhortation is combined with direct instruction. Warnings stand alongside ethical imperatives.

Today's text opens with some of the most familiar words of Paul: "For to me, living is Christ and dying is gain" (v. 21). How one construes this will dramatically affect one's understanding of the whole passage. One option is to read it as the classic expression of Paul's mysticism, his complete identification with the risen Christ as it came to be expressed in the Pauline formula "in Christ" (cf. 2 Cor. 5:17). Reciprocally, of course, this could be understood as the living Christ present within Paul, and by extension to all Christians (Rom. 8:10; Gal. 2:20; Col. 1:27; 2 Cor. 13:5; cf. John 17:23). Thus Christ could be spoken of as the one "who is our life" (Col. 3:4).

But there's another way of reading it. The immediate context is a discussion of Paul's imprisonment and its impact on his apostolic work (1:12–14). His main concern is to reassure his supporting church that the gospel has not been hindered by this. Rather, Paul insists that "now as always" (1:20) Christ is being magnified in his body; that is, the message of Christ continues to be echoed through his word and person (cf. 2 Cor. 4:11–12). He is confident that this will be the case whether he lives or dies. Thus, for him to live means that Christ gets preached. Life in the flesh means "fruitful labor" for the sake of the gospel (v. 22). To remain alive would expedite their "progress and joy in the faith" (v. 25). Yet even if he dies, the gospel "gains" as well. His death would become a sacrificial offering that helped make possible their triumph in the day of Christ (2:16–17). Either way, the cause of the gospel is served.

This interpretation in no way reduces the tension presented by the two options. Nor does it dull Paul's desire to "depart and be with Christ" (v. 23). Clearly, he would prefer to experience the fullness of the presence of Christ that is possible beyond death to the partiality and fragility of human existence this side of death. To be "away from the body and at home with the Lord" (2 Cor. 5:8) is much to be preferred. Yet duty calls. Apostolic responsibility to his churches presses upon him, and he knows it (v. 24).

The second section of our text (vv. 27–30) shifts emphasis away from Paul's own situation to that of his readers. It opens with a call for them to adopt a life-style appropriate to the gospel (v. 27; cf. 1 Thess. 2:12; Eph. 4:1; Col. 1:10). His chief concern is the solidarity of his pastoral charge, regardless of whether he can be present physically or must be absent (v. 27). Above all, he wishes for their strength and unity of spirit (v. 27; cf. 2:2; also 1 Cor. 16:13; Gal. 5:1; Phil. 4:1; 1 Thess. 3:8; 2 Thess. 2:15) and for their continued partnership with him in the struggle for the gospel (cf. 4:3; Rom. 15:30). Such a show of unity is the best defense against their detractors (v. 28; cf. esp. chap. 3).

The Philippians are reminded that their salvation is "God's doing" (v. 28; cf. Eph. 2:8), a theme reemphasized later (2:13). There is also an indication that they are suffering on behalf of the gospel in a manner comparable to that of Paul (vv. 29–30). Elsewhere, Paul insists that suffering is part and parcel of living the gospel (Rom. 5:3; cf. 2 Thess. 1:5; also Acts 5:4; Matt. 5:12; 1 Pet. 4:13).

One homiletical task will be to expound what it means to say, "Living is Christ and dying is gain." At least one possibility, however, is to plump for the practical over the mystical. "Life is Christ" (v. 21, REB) may mean that Christ is seen and heard through us as much as it means the merging of ourselves with Christ in mystical union.

Matthew 20:1–16

Last Sunday's Gospel lesson was a parable; so is today's and the lessons for the next three Sundays. If the preacher did special study of the nature and function of parables when our texts were from Matthew 13 (Propers 10–12 [15–17]), then it would be helpful to review that material. C. H. Dodd said parables are drawn from nature or common life, but their exact meanings are left in sufficient doubt so as to tease the mind into active thought. Some parables have a surprise turn at the end, which not only teases the mind into active thought but also shocks or even offends some listeners. Such, for example, was the parable of the loving father (prodigal son), and such, certainly, is the parable of the generous employer.

The parable of the generous employer, sometimes called the parable of the workers in the vineyard, is clearly drawn from common life. The elements in the story are quite normal.

When grapes are at their prime, the vineyard owner needs extra workers to harvest them quickly. Unemployed men were available in the marketplace. A deal is struck with some workers, who agree to the usual wage of one denarius for a full day's work, sunrise to sunset. Concern that the harvest might not be completed that day sends the owner back for more workers at nine, at noon, at three, and at five, one hour before the close of the day. The owner promises to pay what is fair, presumably an appropriate portion of a denarius. There is no hint that any of the later workers deliberately delayed their availability so as to presume upon the employer's goodness. In fact, the workers who began at five in the afternoon said they were unemployed because no one had offered them a job (v. 7).

So far all is normal. The surprise jolt comes in the payment at the end of the day. There is no evidence that payment was usually made beginning with the last. Matthew has preceded (19:30) and followed (20:16) this parable with the often-used saying of Jesus to the effect that the last will be first and the first last. This saying may have influenced the order of payment, but it certainly does not capture the heart of the story. The last first and the first last expresses a reversal of fortunes, but such is not the case here. The first receive the agreed upon wage. Very likely, we can account for the order of payment so that all can witness the owner's generosity and hence heighten the drama. This is simply good story-telling. It is also good storytelling to tell of the payments to the last and the first. That contrast provides the issue; details about paying the nine-, noon-, and three-o'clock-workers would have dragged the story to a halt.

The grumbling on the part of the full-day workers was natural. The answer to the question "Are you envious because I am generous?" (literally, Is your eye evil because I am good?) is in all honesty, yes. No one has been denied, no one cheated, no one given less than what was agreed upon. The offense lies in the generosity to others. The offense of grace is not in the treatment we receive but in the observation that others are getting more than they deserve. Jonah was offended that God accepted the people of Nineveh. Forgiveness and generosity do not seem fair. God sends sun and rain on the just and the unjust, the good and the bad (Matt. 5:45). That offends some of us. God is kind to the ungrateful and the selfish (Luke 6:35). That offends some of us. The generosity of God quite often cuts across our calculations of who deserves what. For all our talk of grace, the church still has trouble with it.

In the course of interpreting this parable, sometimes the first and last workers have been understood as Pharisees and sinners in Jesus' day. At other times, commentators have seen in the first and last the Jews and the Gentiles. But always and everywhere the parable addresses those of us who have difficulty celebrating the gift someone else receives.

Proper 21 [26]
(Sunday between September 25 and October 1 inclusive)

Exodus 17:1–7;
Psalm 78:1–4, 12–16; or
Ezekiel 18:1–4, 25–32;
Psalm 25:1–9;
Philippians 2:1–13;
Matthew 21:23–32

In the continuous reading from Exodus, the week's *Common Lectionary* Old Testament lesson reports the story of Moses striking the rock to supply water for the murmuring, faultfinding Hebrews. The psalm selection rehearses the story of God's acts, with special attention given to the Exodus.

The Old Testament text from Ezekiel expounds the theme of individual responsibility, thereby challenging Israel to take responsibility for their resistance and misdeeds before the Lord. The sentiments of the psalm selection illustrate what Ezekiel calls for: acknowledging individual guilt and responsibility while praising God for being good and upright.

If obedience is reflected in both sets of texts just mentioned, this theme receives its classic statement in the New Testament lesson, where Paul quotes an early Christian hymn centrally focused on Christ's obedience. The Gospel reading from Matthew shows Jesus teaching about doing the will of God. Here we have the parable of the two sons, one who said, "I will," but doesn't; the other who said, "I won't," but does.

Exodus 17:1–7

Like last week's Old Testament lesson in the semicontinuous readings from the Pentateuch, this text presents an episode from the account of Israel's wandering in the wilderness. This story of water from the rock follows immediately after the account of the manna and is followed by the report of a war between Israel and Amalek (Exod. 17:8–16). The stories are linked on the chain of the wilderness itinerary that lists the stopping places along the way (17:1; cf. 16:1; 17:8). Although this itinerary has the appearance of precision, it is impossible to reconstruct an actual route of the travels from Egypt to Canaan. (Note that there is a parallel to Exod. 17:1–7 in Exod. 15:22–25.)

Exodus 17:1–7 presents the two major motifs of the wilderness tradition in sharp contrast. On the one hand, there was the almost continual grumbling and complaining of the people. They complained out of fear because the Egyptians pursued them to the edge of the sea (Exod. 14:10–12). They complained because they were hungry (Exod. 16:2–3). Then, after feasting on the manna for years, they complained that their diet was boring (Num. 11:4–9). Here they complain for lack of water (17:2–3). On the other hand, the time in the wilderness was remembered as a time of God's gracious and miraculous care for the people. When the people were needy, the Lord provided manna, quails, and water.

Although there are duplicates and tensions that show the presence of different documents or traditions (cf. vv. 2–3), the story that follows the itinerary in verse 1 comes mainly from the Yahwist and presents a plot that can be followed easily. Finding themselves at a place without water, the people found fault with Moses and uttered the by-now familiar complaint: "Why did you bring us out of Egypt in the first place?" Moses in turn complains to Yahweh in words that are at once accusation and petition (v. 4). The Lord, answering Moses' prayer by instructing him to strike the rock with his rod, promises that water will flow for the people to drink (vv. 5–6a). Moses does as he is told, and, presumably, the water appeared (v. 6b). The story concludes (v. 7) with the naming of the place in memory not of the miracle of the water but of the contentious people: Massah ("trial" or "proof") and Meribah ("contention" or "argument").

Particular points that require brief comment are the references to Moses' rod, to Horeb, and to Yahweh's standing on the rock. The writer reminds us that Moses' rod is the one he used to strike the Nile (v. 5), recalling the miraculous plagues against Egypt. The power for the miraculous action is not in the rod itself but in the word of the Lord. It, like Moses, is an instrument of the divine power. The reference to "Horeb" (v. 6) is out of place, for the people are not yet at the sacred mountain. The allusion is one of those tensions that show a complex oral tradition behind the story. The reference to Yahweh's standing on the rock (v. 6) is difficult to understand, but likely simply indicates the presence of the Lord as Moses carries out the instructions.

Were the people's complaints legitimate or not? The story of the manna in Exodus 16 (see the commentary for last week) had made it clear that the complaints were unnecessary grumbling. The passage before us today is ambivalent on that point. On the one hand, the Israelites found themselves at a place without water (v. 1), not unusual in the desert. Small wonder, then, that they should complain because of thirst. Yahweh grants the request and provides water, thus acknowledging the need. On the other hand, the complaint is seen to go far beyond a prayer for water. As in most other cases, the people blame Moses for their problems and call their very election and salvation into question (vv. 2–3). Moreover, their contentiousness is emphasized in the names of the place of the miracle (v. 7). The complaint, finally, amounts to a denial of the presence of the Lord among them (v. 7). Most Old Testament use of this tradition (Pss. 78:15–16, 20; 95:8–9) reprimands the people for their complaints, uses the people as bad examples, and recalls that Yahweh punished the people of that generation by not letting them enter the promised land.

The contrast between Israel's complaints and God's response is dramatic. The Lord neither reprimands nor threatens those who complain so bitterly. With Moses as the agent, God acts to meet the need. The Lord will not allow the unfaith of the chosen ones to frustrate the fulfillment of the promise to make of Abraham's descendants a great nation in their own land. Thus the story is a parable of God's patient grace. Grace comes here through miraculous means, but its form is as simple as it is essential—life-sustaining water.

Psalm 78:1–4, 12–16

Psalm 78 is one of the few psalms concerned with the history of Israel and Judah. Other examples are Psalms 105 and 106. The intentions of Psalm 78 are (1) to show that the people's—especially the northern tribes'—history was one of disobedience and lack of faith (vv. 9–66) and (2) to claim that God had forsaken the Northern Kingdom and chosen the (southern) tribe of Judah, the city of Jerusalem (Zion), and the family of David (vv. 67–72). As with Psalms 105 and 106, this psalm illustrates how the people's historical traditions could be used for particular purposes in the people's later history.

The opening of the psalm is rather unique in that it begins with someone calling the people to listen to the recital of a historical presentation. (Ps. 49 is somewhat similar, but there it is an autobiographical rather than a national history that is the concern.) The sense of verses 1–4 is better represented in the NJPSV than in the NRSV:

> Give ear, my people, to my teaching,
>> turn your ear to what I say.
> I will expound a theme,
>> hold forth lessons of the past,
>> things that we have heard and known,
>> that our fathers have told us.
> We will not withhold them from their children,
>> telling the coming generation
>> the praises of the Lord and His might,
>> and the wonders He performed.

Who the "I" is who speaks is unknown. Was it the king, an officiating priest, some prophet preaching in a temple service? We cannot know. At any rate, the psalm shifts to the first person plural in verse 4, and the first person address does not occur again in the psalm.

Some features of Israelite faith are evident in these opening verses: (1) the people constantly drew upon their past in order to understand the present; (2) the past was frequently understood and interpreted in terms of the interests of the present (just as today we are reexamining history in light of the civil rights and feminist movements); and (3) a very judgmental and condemnatory attitude was taken toward the past. Much of the history in the Old Testament debunks Israel's past and the people's life and practices. Such an attitude creates the ability of a culture to look at itself critically in the present without such an examination being considered "unpatriotic." Such an attitude not only allows but also engenders changes.

Verses 5–11, which are skipped in this reading, describe the giving of the law and testimony as a depository of the will of God to be transmitted to every new generation with the hope that that generation would have a steadfast heart and a spirit faithful to God (v. 8). Note that in this text, a primary role of the older generation is the transmission of the law and lessons from the past to the next and new generation. The fathers must teach their children. The NJPSV catches the tone of verses 5–7.

> He established a decree in Jacob,
>> ordained a Teaching in Israel,

> charging our fathers
> to make them known to their children,
> that a future generation might know
> —children yet to be born—
> and in turn tell their children
> that they might put their confidence in God,
> and not forget God's great deeds,
> but observe His commandments.

Such an attitude produces a culture that is past-oriented and ideally one that is neither overly fascinated by the fads of the present nor unrealistically wooed by promises of the future.

Verses 10–11 tick off the disobedience of the past: they did not keep God's covenant; they refused to walk according to God's law; they forgot the things God had done and the miracles that God had shown them. The text then expounds on these miracles, marvels, or wonders in verses 12–16: the plagues (v. 12), the crossing of the sea (v. 13), divine guidance by day and night (v. 14), and the giving of water in the desert (vv. 15–16). (In later rabbinic tradition, the rock that gave water to the Hebrews in the wilderness was understood as having followed them throughout the forty years of wandering. Paul was familiar with this tradition and quotes it in 1 Cor. 10:1–5, identifying Christ with the Rock.)

Ezekiel 18:1–4, 25–32

In Ezekiel we meet a prophet who was active in Babylon during the Babylonian Exile. That he was taken in the first group of exiles with King Jehoiakin and the nobles in 597 BC suggests that he was among Jerusalem's aristocracy, a conclusion borne out by what we learn of him from the book. He received his call in Jehoiakin's fifth year (Ezek. 1:2), that is, 593 BC. Although Ezekiel was a prophet, especially in the tradition of Hosea, Isaiah, and Jeremiah—whose works he seems to know—his message has affinities on the one hand with priestly concerns and on the other hand with apocalyptic expectations. He was deeply steeped in Israel's legal tradition, including the substance of the laws in Exodus 20–24, the Book of Deuteronomy, and the Holiness Code (Lev. 17–26). His vision reports, in terms both of style and imagery, suggest those of later apocalyptic literature.

Ezekiel 18 records a disputation of the prophet with an audience composed of Judean exiles. He addresses them directly throughout and frequently cites their own words as he opposes them. On the surface, the occasion for the dispute is their repetition of the proverb "The parents have eaten sour grapes, and the children's teeth are set on edge" (v. 2). But the saying, just the tip of the iceberg, reflects some deep problems. The exiles are dispirited, believing themselves caught in the cycle of sin and judgment, living under a curse set into motion by their ancestors. Ezekiel uses the form of debate to correct their views, thereby teaching a different understanding of sin and punishment. We should not, however, allow his repetitious and legal arguments obscure the main goal of the chapter. He holds out "life"—the full, abundant life in the presence of God (vv. 9, 21, 22, 27, 28, 32)—to the despairing people. He argues that the sins of the parents are not visited upon the children and that even the sinner can repent.

The passage presents three distinct but related themes, any one of which merits consideration by the preacher:

1. The most obvious point is Ezekiel's reaction to the proverb, which amounts to an assertion of individual responsibility. The proverb (see also Jer. 31:29), of course, comes from a tradition often expressed in the Old Testament, including in the Decalogue: "punishing children for the iniquity of the parents, to the third and the fourth generation" (Exod. 20:5; Deut. 5:9). Harsh as it is, there is some truth to the saying. Children do, indeed, often suffer for the sins of their parents. But the legal tradition also held individuals responsible for their own behavior. The problem is that Ezekiel's compatriots have taken the proverb as the full interpretation of their situation in exile and thus live in resignation, bearing the iniquity of their ancestors. Thus, for all the warnings about death to the individual sinner, the news is good: you are set free from the effects of the sins of your parents.

2. Then there is Ezekiel's description of the life of the righteous person. More than a dozen points are listed (vv. 5–9) in the form of case law, "if he does . . . ," and most of them are negative in form, noting what the righteous person does not do. The catalogue is not meant to be exhaustive, but it is well worth pondering. None of these provisions is new. Most of them can be found in the Old Testament legal corpus, especially Leviticus 17–26 and Exodus 21–23. They concern a wide range of matters, from false worship to cultic purity to matters of social justice, including generosity to the poor. All are summed up at the beginning and end (vv. 5, 9) in the word "righteous." As Psalm 15 clearly shows, such righteousness was the criterion for admission to the house of the Lord, and thus to the full life.

3. Next there is the call to repentance. The disputation of which our reading is a part does not reach its goal until Ezekiel 18:30–32. Throughout the argument stressing individual responsibility, the prophet has indicated that both the righteous ones and sinners may turn from their ways and have the consequences of that new direction (vv. 26–27). In the concluding paragraph, this motif becomes an explicit call to repent. Herein also the justice of God is manifest, that sinners may turn and have that full life. Not only are the effects of sin held in check, limited to the effects for the individual, but even a sinner is called to get "a new heart and a new spirit" (v. 31). In answer to the challenge to God's justice (v. 25), Ezekiel hears God affirming, "For I have no pleasure in the death of anyone. . . . Turn, then, and live" (v. 32).

Psalm 25:1–9

Two general features should be noted about this psalm. First, like a few other psalms (Pss. 9/10, 34, 37, 111, 112, 119, 145), this one is an alphabetic poem, sometimes called an acrostic. This means that the psalm flows through the alphabet, with each successive verse commencing with the next letter of the Hebrew alphabet. Second, the composition is a lament of an individual; that is, it was originally written to be used in worship services in which an individual's needs were the focus of attention.

The psalm moves back and forth between the individual's petitions to the Deity (vv. 1–7, 16–22), the priest or worship leader's address to the worshiper (vv. 8–10, 12–14), and the worshiper's statement to the priest/worship leader (v. 15). Thus the psalm contains three types of material: petitionary prayer, confession, and priestly proclamation.

The lection for today is comprised of two of the psalm's components: a prayer or petition addressed to the Deity (vv. 1–7) and theological proclamation probably addressed by the priest to the worshiper (vv. 8–9).

Two verbs are of fundamental importance in verses 1–7: "wait" and "remember."

The term "wait" appears in verses 3 and 5. In the former, it appears in a petitionary intercession on behalf of a group—"those that wait for you." In the latter, it appears in a confessional statement expressing trust. Intercession and confession may thus be seen as two ways of waiting.

In the melody of the waiting there lies, however, a dissonant chord. The time of waiting is not simply the idle passing of the hour; it is a time of misery and trouble. Note, in verses 16–19, the cacophony of unharmonious notes: loneliness, affliction, a troubled heart, distresses, sin, innumerable foes, and violent hatred. The psalmist waits for God when all the evidence suggests that the waiting may be long and the pain and misery deep. Mere endurance, however, is not the goal of waiting. Note the counterbalance of requests over against the terms depicting misery: "turn," "be gracious," "relieve," "bring me out," "consider," "forgive," "guard," "deliver," and "let me not be put to shame."

The psalmist also speaks about remembering. Three times the verb occurs in verses 6–7. (The first occurrence, the NRSV translates "be mindful.") The request for remembrance here takes two forms: remembering and remembering not. The psalmist asks God to remember mercy and steadfast love, those divine qualities that predispose the Deity toward human redemption. These are seen as the qualities possessed by God "from of old." On the other hand, there is the request to "remember not," that is, forget, the human past with its youthful sins (inadvertent errors and wayward faults) and more adult transgressions (more deliberate and premeditated wrongs).

The final plea to remember is in verse 7b, where the psalmist asks that God should, on the basis of divine love and goodness, "remember me." Remember me, not my past, just me, as I am, waiting and remembering.

Philippians 2:1–13

So accustomed are we to hearing this profound christological text within the liturgical setting of Holy Week that it may take some doing to appropriate it into the Season After Pentecost as yet another epistolary reading from the Epistle to the Philippians. The Christ-hymn (2:5–11) has, of course, justly earned a place as the New Testament reading for the Sixth Sunday in Lent, which may be observed as Passion or Palm Sunday. Consequently, it is heard in this setting every year, and comments are provided in this context in each of our three volumes. Also, this passage (2:5–11), which focuses on the exalted name "Lord" that Jesus received by virtue of his resurrection and ascension, serves as the second option for the New Testament reading for Holy Name of Jesus: Solemnity of Mary, Mother of God, in all three years. The reader may want to consult our remarks in that setting as well.

Thus once again the church hears this classic Pauline text, but this time within the context of the whole Philippian letter from which selections are read over a four-week period. Accordingly, we can look at the passage within its concrete setting.

It will be recalled from our remarks last week that this was no young, fledgling church. It had existed long enough to endear itself to Paul because of its continued support of his apostolic work. But with age had come the perennial congregational enemies: internal dissent and external threat. Today's text addresses the former concern as focal.

It has a twofold structure: (1) the appeal for unity and solidarity (vv. 1–4), and (2) the basis for the appeal (vv. 5–11).

1. *The appeal* (vv. 1–4). First there is a series of "ifs": "If then our common life in Christ yields anything to stir the heart, any consolation of love, any participation in the Spirit, any warmth of affection or compassion" (v. 1, REB). Could we but assume a capacity for mutual encouragement within the fellowship where Christ is present (cf. Rom. 12:8; 1 Cor. 14:3); or the presence of a compelling power to love (1 Cor. 13:4–7); or a genuine sense of community where the Spirit is the prime mover and actor (2 Cor. 13:13); or the presence of "warmth or sympathy" (NJB; 2 Cor. 6:12; 7:15; Philem. 7, 12, 20; Col. 3:12; 1 John 3:17), then we could become one. We should note the "if-then" structure. First the community must possess a certain character informed by the presence of Christ. Then comes the capacity to respond in faith to the demands of the gospel.

In this case, the demands are for unity and solidarity: being "united in your convictions and united in your love, with a common purpose and a common mind" (v. 2, JB). Elsewhere, Paul conceives congregational harmony as a gift from God (Rom. 15:5; cf. 12:16), yet it can be commanded (4:2; 1 Cor. 1:10; 2 Cor. 13:11; 1 Pet. 3:8). It is this that makes the preacher's "joy complete" (v. 2) in the sense that it provides one a true source of joy (cf. 1:4, 18; 2:17; 4:1, 10).

And how is this achieved, this community where there is "no competition . . . no conceit . . . ," where everyone is "self-effacing" (v. 3, JB; cf. Gal. 5:26; 1 Pet. 5:5; Rom. 12:16)? By adopting a single, fundamental perspective within our congregational life; by considering the other person better than ourself; by thinking of the interest of others before we think of our own interests (vv. 3–4). This becomes something of a cardinal principle in Paul's theology of the congregation (1 Cor. 10:24, 33; also 1 Cor. 13:5). Whether intentional or not, this paraenetic advice is the concretization of Jesus' teaching (Matt. 7:12; 22:34–40).

2. *The basis for the appeal* (vv. 5–11). The form of the imperative is clear enough. Not only is it clear, it is also difficult. How then can one translate imperative into indicative, apostolic theory into congregational practice? Paul's answer: christologically.

He proceeds to buttress his appeal with the magnificent two-part christological hymn with its "V-shaped Christology" that rehearses the descent of Christ from above (vv. 6–8) and the ascent of Christ from below (vv. 9–11). But how is this hymn intended to function? Does it present Christ as *exemplar* or *enabler*? If the former, the ethical move is one of imitation, conforming our lives to the example of Christ. If the latter, the ethical response is one of appropriation, being empowered by God's work in Christ.

Here, of course, we meet a crucial exegetical choice, and it depends on how we render verse 5. One option is clearly expressed by NJB: "Make your own the mind of Christ Jesus," hence imitation (similarly, NRSV, NIV, REB). The other option is given by NEB: "Let your bearing towards one another arise out of your life in Christ Jesus," hence appropriation through empowerment (similarly, note in NRSV). In the one case, we take our cue from Christ and accordingly conform our life to his. In the other case, we become what we already are, allowing our conduct toward each other to become the concrete realization of what we have already experienced in Christ. The critical difference is that the one accents our achievement, the other accents God's achievement. The one sees Christian behavior as our "conforming to" an external example, whereas the other sees Christian behavior as our "being transformed by" an act of God.

Analysis of the structure of the hymn itself and the various claims that are made on behalf of Christ receive treatment in our comments elsewhere on this passage. We would refer the interested reader to those discussions.

The preacher will find much here that addresses the hard realities of congregational life. We all know the fragility of church life and the delicacy required to maintain some sense of harmony. We also know the price of harmony and unity and the trade-offs that must occur for the common good. We also know the intransigence even of the converted soul and our resistance to thinking first of others' interests. We know the sheer difficulty of translating this Pauline vision of unity, harmony, and solidarity into real-life form. Perhaps this is why Paul finally moves beyond the language of human imperative to transcendent, divine action.

Matthew 21:23–32

Between the reading for last Sunday and that for today, Matthew records two events that provide the context and atmosphere for 21:23–32. The first is Jesus' entry into Jerusalem (21:1–11), as a result of which, says Matthew, "all the city was stirred." The second is the cleansing of the temple (21:12–13), the event that precipitated the crisis between Jesus and those who will plot his arrest and death (21:15–16, 45–46).

Our text, then, is to be read and understood in a context of controversy and tension. We are to understand, of course, that argument and debate were common in the discussions of Scripture and tradition among religious leaders of Judaism. In fact, at one time in the rabbinic tradition, teachers worked in pairs, one liberal and one conservative, arguing before the students the fine points of the law. Even today, Judaism tends to be more vigorous and open to polemic in its conversations with God and with itself than is Christianity. In the text before us, however, the reader of Matthew is aware that the debates between Jesus and the religious authorities will have far more serious consequences. Three times Jesus has predicted his death in Jerusalem (16:21; 17:22–23; 20:17–19).

The controversies in which our text is couched are recorded in 21:23–22:14. The opposition to Jesus consists of "the chief priests and the elders of the people" (v. 23). The substance of this entire section consists of Jesus' responses to the question put to him: "By what authority are you doing these things, and who gave you this authority?" (v. 23). Although we may, out of faith in Jesus as Son of God, consider the question out of order, it was not. It was an appropriate question by those responsible for the faith, morals, and institutional life of Judaism. The "these things" of their question is best taken as referring not solely to the disruption of the temple but to the whole of Jesus' ministry in Jerusalem, which had stirred the city and attracted to Jesus large favorable crowds (vv. 14, 46).

Jesus' response to his opponents consists of two parts. First, he counters with a question about the authority of the ministry of John the Baptist (vv. 24–27), a question his interrogators were unwilling to answer. Their unwillingness to answer is portrayed as an act of political expediency thinly veiled under the response "We do not know" (v. 27). Jesus, then, is unwilling to answer their question about his authority. The issue is important; credentials are important. Any responsible community leader, any shepherd of a believing flock, would ask it of the new charismatic figure in town. But it is not a question to be answered if asked as a trap, if asked to make the other vulnerable, if prompted by self-interest, if no answer will really be heard, if the issue is not truth and a desire to pursue it but rather position and power. Those unwilling to answer questions should not ask them. Second, Jesus took the offensive, offering three parables (21:28–32; 33–43; 22:1–14). These three parables will occupy us today and the next two Sundays.

The first parable (vv. 28–32) is found in Matthew alone. The parable proper ends at verse 31a, with verses 31b–32 serving as commentary not only on the parable but on the real issue embedded in verses 23–27. This is to say, Jesus' opponents had already demonstrated who and what they were in their response to John the Baptist. They had resisted and rejected John's proclamation of the kingdom and call for repentance; there is no reason to expect any different answer now that Jesus is the preacher. The issue is not Jesus' authority; the issue is how one responds to God's call to repentance and invitation into the kingdom. Before such urgent preaching, ecclesiastical debates over clerical roles and credentials are treated as so much smoke screen.

The parable says that responses to God are of two kinds: that of the person who has said no but who repents and whose life says yes; and that of the person who says yes but whose life says no. Jesus' opponents represent the latter; tax collectors and harlots, the former (vv. 31b–32; see Luke 7:29–30). By admitting that those who say no but then repent are the ones who do the Father's will, the chief priests and elders indict themselves (v. 31a). They know the necessity of repentance; they know God accepts the penitent. Their resistance to John and to Jesus is not due to lack of knowledge but to lack of trust. They did not believe the truth about themselves and the truth about God. Those who do believe, regardless of past behavior, enter the kingdom of God first.

Proper 22 [27]
(Sunday between October 2 and 8 inclusive)

Exodus 20:1–4, 7–9, 12–20;
Psalm 19; or
Isaiah 5:1–7;
Psalm 80:7–15;
Philippians 3:4b–14;
Matthew 21:33–46

The Old Testament reading for today's *Common Lectionary* consists of the Priestly version of the Decalogue and might profitably be read alongside the Deuteronomic version (cf. Deut. 5:6–21). The psalm reading, with its lyrical praise of the "law of the Lord" as more desirable than gold and sweeter than honey, is an appropriate response to the Old Testament reading.

For confessions using the other first lesson and psalm, the song of the vineyard in Isaiah 5 supplies the Old Testament text, with the section from Psalm 80 portraying Israel as a vine as an appropriate complementary text.

The New Testament reading comes from the polemical section of Philippians where Paul stresses the unrealized dimension of the Christian calling, urging the people to pursue the heavenly calling of God in Christ. The Gospel reading presents us with the parable of the vineyard in which the tenants mistreat the servants of the householder, finally kill his son, and reap the consequences of their misguided actions.

Exodus 20:1–4, 7–9, 12–20

The main body of today's reading comes from the Decalogue, but the initial and concluding verses that provide the immediate narrative framework stress the importance of considering these laws in their context. On the broadest level, the communication of these laws is part of the story that begins with creation and runs at least to the Israelite occupation of the land of Canaan. More specifically, the revelation of the law takes place at Sinai, where the story reaches one of its high points, and is part of a covenant ceremony reported in Exodus 19 and 24. Exodus 20:18–20 alludes to the theophany of chapter 19 and anticipates the conclusion of the ceremony in chapter 24. It is hardly possible to exaggerate the importance of the immediate narrative setting as indicated in Exodus 20:1–2. The laws are

459

understood as direct expressions of the will of God (v. 1), who introduces himself in a special way: "I am the Lord your God, who brought you out of the land of Egypt, out of the house of slavery" (v. 2). This means that the law is given in the context of and with the precondition of God's grace. The people to whom these commandments are given have already been saved—quite literally, redeemed from slavery and chosen by God to be God's own. At least in this passage, there is no room for works righteousness, because grace and salvation precede the requirement of obedience.

Laws were collected and handed down in ancient Israel, as in most cultures, in collections. The Decalogue is followed in Exodus 21–23 by a longer collection, the Book of the Covenant (Exod. 24:7). That collections of ten laws were a traditional genre is seen in the existence of a parallel to Exodus 20 in Deuteronomy 5:6–21 and a so-called ritual decalogue in Exodus 34. "Decalogue," or "Ten Commandments," is even an Old Testament term (Exod. 34:28; Deut. 4:13–10:4).

All ten laws in Exodus 20:3–17 are apodictic in form; that is, they are brief statements of general expectations in the form of direct address in the second person. This contrasts with many of the laws in Exodus 21–23 that are case laws that give a legal condition and its consequence: "When someone steals an ox or a sheep, and kills it or sells it, the thief shall pay five oxen for an ox, and four sheep for a sheep" (Exod. 22:1). All but the fourth and fifth laws are prohibitions, that is, they are formulated in the negative.

Because the form of the individual laws is so clear, one can easily distinguish between the laws themselves and their elaborations. As elsewhere in the Old Testament, especially Deuteronomy, the elaborations include both commentary and preaching. The comments explain the law and urge the hearers to obey. Thus, lest there should be any question about the meaning of the prohibition of graven images in the second commandment, the elaboration specifies that there are to be no images of anything in heaven, or on earth, or in the sea (v. 4b) and that such are not to be worshiped at all (v. 6a). The remainder of the elaboration goes on to urge obedience in terms of threat (v. 5b) and promise (v. 6). The elaboration of the sabbath commandment explains its meaning—no one is to work (vv. 9–10)—and gives the reason for its sacredness in terms of the days of creation (v. 11). By contrast, Deuteronomy 5:12–15 explains the reason for the sabbath rest in terms of the history of the Exodus: You and all your servants are to rest, remembering that you were slaves in Egypt and the Lord brought you out.

In terms of contents, the last five commandments (vv. 13–17) clearly belong together as regulations of social relationships in the community. Likewise, the first three specify directly the relationship between the people and their God. The fourth commandment, the sabbath law, is related to the first three, and the fifth is more closely akin to the final five, although it directly concerns the family instead of the community as a whole.

A few comments concerning some of the individual laws may be helpful. There can be no doubt that the first commandment is the most important one. Its expectation of exclusive devotion to Yahweh makes all the other requirements possible. The command to have no other gods is not an expression of monotheism, but to the contrary assumes the possibility of worshiping other deities. Likewise, the second commandment (vv. 4ff.) assumes a real problem in ancient Israel's culture, the creation and worship of idols. The meaning of the third commandment (v. 7) is not so self-evident. "Wrongful use" refers to the abuse or misuse of the divine name. The translators of the NJPSV go further and read, "You shall not swear falsely by the name of the Lord your God." The fundamental concern is with the attempt to manipulate Yahweh by invoking his name for evil or selfish purposes, as in curses or even

prayers. The prohibition against killing (v. 13), in the wider Old Testament context, is neither limited to murder nor absolute. Because ancient Israel understood that killing in
wartime and capital punishment could be in accord with the will of Yahweh, it is killing that
is not in the interest of the community that is prohibited. The prohibition of bearing false
witness (v. 16) does not refer to lying in general but to perjury in particular.

What is the preacher to do with a rich and full text such as this? There can be no doubt
about the importance of the entire list. John Calvin considered the text so significant that
he had it read regularly in the Geneva liturgy. One could hardly hope to expound all Ten
Commandments in a single sermon! Consider also the fact that in recent polls of the American public, although the majority affirmed that the Bible is in some way the word of God,
only a small percentage could name as many as four of the Ten Commandments.

Certainly, a major issue concerns the place of the law in the Christian faith. One form
of that question, as discussed in the sayings of Jesus and then debated by Paul, his contemporaries, and his successors, relates specifically to the Old Testament law. Did one have to
become a Jew first or obey all the laws of Judaism? That particular form of the question is no
longer alive, but continues in another form: Because God saves by grace, what is the place of
works of the law? An answer is already indicated in the Old Testament Sinai pericope.
Obedience is not what moves God to save, but it is the grateful response to God's saving
actions. God's gracious deeds evoke a response of obedience.

Above all, the law defines what it means to be a covenant people. Verse 2 states God's
part of the covenant: "I am the Lord your God." Verses 3–17 define the other side, stating in
summary fashion what it means to be a covenant people and how they will behave toward
God and one another.

Psalm 19

Psalm 19 forms an appropriate parallel to the reading of the Decalogue, for much of it
is concerned with the law. This psalm is generally divided into two parts and sometimes even seen as the secondary combination of two separate psalms. Verses 1–6
declare that nature and creation, especially sky and sun, proclaim the glory of God and
testify to his will. Verses 7–14 praise the law (Torah) of God, which has been made known
in commandment, precept, and ordinance. The character of the psalm is further complicated, however, because the "law" section, verses 7–14, can be further subdivided.
In verses 7–10, the law is praised and God spoken about in the third person, whereas
verses 11–14 are a prayer addressed directly to God.

In spite of its complexity, the psalm can be seen as a unity. The nature portion, verses
1–6, declares that creation, without normal words, voice, or speech, points to divine will
and control and thus prompts expressions of praise. The law portion, verses 7–10, focuses on
the written law formulated in words that elicit attitudes of praise. Verses 11–14 are a prayer
that one might be aware of sins, faults, and errors in order to live a life that is without great
transgressions. The final plea, in verse 14, requests that not only the words but also the
unspoken meditations of the heart be acceptable to God. Thus the psalm moves from describing the unarticulatable expressions of nature, which proclaim God's work and fill the
whole expansive realm of creation, down to the inarticulated meditations of the heart. Thus
the thought of the psalm moves from the outer reaches of the natural world to the inner
recesses of the human personality, the human heart.

Verses 7–14 are primarily concerned with the praise and glory of the law and the worshiper's petition offered in light of the will of God manifest in nature and law. The antiphonal praise of the law, verses 7–10, knows the Torah as an object of praise and not as a burden or a yoke to be borne in grumbling servitude. Six synonymous terms are used to speak about the Torah: law, testimony, precepts, commandment, fear, ordinances. Perhaps these six terms were used to express the fullness and completeness of the known will of God. The adjectival descriptions of the Torah are extremely positive in their affirmations: perfect, sure, right, pure, clean, true, righteous. Four aspects, or benefits, from the Torah are noted. The Torah revives the soul; it is life giving and sustaining. It makes wise the simple by providing them with understanding. It rejoices the heart, making one glad to know the will and way of the Lord. It enlightens the eyes by providing a perspective within which to view the world and one's own life. Thus the law of God is a nobler and finer possession than gold and is sweeter than honey. The law is to be more desired than the most precious of human treasures or the most reviving of foods.

This praise of the law and its life-giving qualities was characteristic of much Israelite and Jewish thought about Torah. Christians, viewing matters from the Pauline perspective on the law as found in Galatians, frequently have difficulty affirming the value and goodness of law. Yet the positive aspects of the written Torah should be emphasized, because Torah provides persons with specific directions, allows us to locate ourselves with regard to the understood will of God, and thus provides a sense of security. The law provides not only a general map for human living but also specific directions along the highway of life.

With verse 11, the focus of the psalm moves from the world of creation and the praise of the law to the sentiments and concerns of the individual worshiper. The law, which like the sun is perfect, sure, and faithful, also like the sun at noontime touches all so that "nothing is hid" from its purview. In light of this judging and quickening aspect of the law, the worshiper recognizes that the law not only warns but also calls into question human adequacy and constancy. Thus the psalmist prays to be kept from hidden faults, that is, those things one might do without realizing they are faults (v. 12); as well as presumptuous sins, that is, grave sins of arrogance or pride (v. 13). If one can be kept from hidden faults and presumptuous sins, then surely one is blameless, for these represent the two extreme poles.

The praise of God's glory in creation and the meditation on the law, in this psalm, led naturally to critical self-examination and to a focus on the whole range of disobedience—from secret, hidden sins to overt, callous acts of open transgression. In the concluding petition, verse 14, the psalmist requests full acceptance from the words of the mouth, the external articulated word, to the meditation of the heart, the internal unarticulated thought.

Isaiah 5:1–7

This famous passage, the song of the vineyard, is a self-contained unit, quite distinct from what precedes and what follows in terms of both form and content. It begins with a distinct introduction, moves to a clear conclusion, and is followed in 5:8ff. by a series of indictments.

Although the fundamental point of this unit is clear and relatively simple, the route to that point is circuitous and complicated. Initially, the speaker announces that he will sing a song, but when one examines the unit as a whole, it becomes clear that the song is limited to verses 1b–2. If it is not a song, then what is it, and how does the prophet reach that powerful conclusion? In order to understand just what kind of literature this is, we have to note the shifts of speaker or role and the outline of the poem.

The speaker who issues the call obviously is the prophet Isaiah of Jerusalem in the eighth century BC. But what role does he assume? In verses 1 and 2, Isaiah speaks as the friend of the bridegroom. Decisive here is the translation of *dodi* ("beloved" in the NRSV) as "friend," as well as the realization that in the song he is not speaking of his own "vineyard" but about that of another. As is common in Hebrew love poetry, the vineyard represents the beloved. In verses 3–6, the prophet assumes another role—that of the owner of the vineyard, who speaks now for himself. That owner brings charges against his vineyard, reporting as if in court that he had done everything necessary to promote growth. However, the vineyard had failed him, so he announces the punishment. In verse 7, Isaiah speaks as prophet, indicting Israel on behalf of Yahweh. This application makes transparent what only had been hinted at in verse 6 ("I will command the clouds . . .")—that the owner is Yahweh and the vineyard is Israel. Thus, in the initial love song, Isaiah has spoken as friend of Yahweh.

Once he has the attention of the audience, the prophet begins a love song, perhaps even singing one already known in Israel. But already in verse 2, the tone and contents of the song have changed to suit his purpose, ending in an accusation against the "vineyard": "He expected it to yield grapes, but it yielded wild grapes" (v. 2). Then, in the role of the owner of the vineyard, the prophet addresses the audience directly. First (vv. 3–4), he asks that they "judge between me and my vineyard" (v. 3), that is, determine which of the two is guilty of failure. Second (vv. 5–6), the owner, assuming that the verdict is against the vineyard, pronounces judgment on the vineyard. He himself will execute that judgment, returning the land to a waste and even prohibiting the clouds from raining on it.

It appears, then, that what began as a song, and a love song at that, has now become a trial in which Isaiah, on behalf of the owner of the "vineyard," argues a case before an Israelite audience. The closest parallel to this passage, 2 Sam. 12:1–15, is the prophet Nathan's confrontation of David with the parable of the poor man's lamb. After David has taken Bathsheba and had her husband Uriah killed, Nathan comes to David with the tale of a rich man who stole a poor man's favorite lamb. David responds in anger against the criminal, and when he pronounces judgment on him, Nathan says, "You are the man" (2 Sam. 12:7). Likewise, in Isaiah 5:1–7 the accused hear a parallel that leads them to pronounce judgment upon themselves. Both texts are juridical parables.

Isaiah 5:1–7 thus has two uneven parts. Verses 1–6 contain the parable of the vineyard, and verse 7 gives the conclusion. In that conclusion, the identity of the partners is revealed: the vineyard is Israel, and the "owner" is the Lord of hosts. Then the indictment implied in the parable is made explicit: "He expected justice, but saw bloodshed; righteousness, but heard a cry!" These concluding lines contain plays on words, determined by the Hebrew words for "justice" and "righteousness." He expected *mishpat* ("justice") but saw *mispah* ("bloodshed"), *sedeqah* ("righteousness") but heard *seaqah* ("a cry"). The conclusion does not go as far as the parable did. In the parable, the owner moved on from indictment to the pronouncement of judgment, but the conclusion stops with the indictment. That leaves the final emphasis on the accusation, but the implications are not forgotten. The hearers are left, like David in 2 Samuel 12, to apply the judgment upon themselves.

The indictment is against the people of Israel and Judah. It is a sweeping accusation, but it lacks details. The failure of justice and righteousness is a frequent theme in the early prophets in particular (Amos 5:21–24; Mic. 6:6–8; Isa. 1:10–17, 21–22). "Justice," particularly in Isaiah, refers to fair and equitable relationships within society grounded in the justice of the Lord and established through honest procedures. When such justice fails, it is because the economically and/or politically powerful have taken advantage of the weak. "Righteousness" refers to that relationship with the Lord from which springs loyalty to the Lord's expectations of justice. Isaiah implies that the failure of justice and righteousness will lead to disaster for the Lord's elect people.

Psalm 80:7–15

Psalm 80 is a community lament composed for use when the people had suffered humiliation, probably at the hands of a foreign enemy. As such, it is a request for revival, renewal, restoration. Portions of this psalm have been discussed earlier as a lection for the Fourth Sunday of Advent.

In the psalm, two images are used for the Divine and simultaneously two images for the people. In verses 1–2, God is depicted as a shepherd; in verses 8–18 as a vine grower. Israel is thus God's sheep and his vineyard. The two professions, shepherding and viticulturist, require of the shepherd and vineyard keeper great concern and tender care. The shepherd must direct the flock, look for its pasture, defend it from its predators, care for its injured and sick members, ensure the succor and nurture of its young, and search for and return its wayward members. The vineyard keeper must prune the vines in season, fertilize the plants, weed the fields, and protect the crops from marauders and plunderers.

This psalm accuses God of failure on both accounts. As a shepherd, God has not cared for his sheep. As a vineyard keeper, God has functioned foolishly so that the vineyard is left without protection, to be used as public property and a haven for wild beasts. The appeal of God throughout the psalm requests a favorable response in which the troubled people would be redeemed and God would show himself a concerned shepherd and a competent viticulturist. That is, the psalm is a supplication for a return to normal in the Divine-Israel relationship.

Two expressions in verses 1–7 need elucidation for the average reader. The description of God as "You who are enthroned upon the cherubim" (v. 1) draws upon the imagery of early Israelite warfare. The ark was originally conceived as a movable throne upon with the Deity sat. The presence of the ark in battle represented the presence of the Divine. The cherubim were mythological flying guardian figures that were artistically represented on the ark (for this view of the ark, see the story in 1 Sam. 4). (Another interpretation of the ark, which had probably disappeared before much of the Old Testament was written, saw it as a container for the law; see Deut. 10:1–5.) The reference to Yahweh as the one enthroned on the cherubim was a way of recalling the times of bygone warfare and better days and a means of reminding the Deity of divine militancy, now neglected. "To let the face shine" was a metaphorical way of saying "to show favor" or "to be favorably deposed toward." So the refrain in verses 3, 7, and 19 contains parallel requests: "restore us" and "let your face shine."

Philippians 3:4b–14

Today's text also serves as the epistolary reading for the Fifth Sunday in Lent in Year C. The reader may want to consult our remarks in that setting.

As part of the semicontinuous reading of the Epistle to the Philippians, however, this text should be set within the overall context of chapter 3. With 3:1, there is a clear break in the literary structure of the letter ("Finally, my brothers and sisters . . ."). With this comes a radical change in both mood and theme. Even though there are earlier references to detractors (1:15–17) and opponents (1:28), the caricature here (3:2, 4, 18–19) is especially harsh. The theological exposition of a "righteousness from God based on faith" (v. 9), as opposed to self-achieved righteousness "that comes from the law" (v. 9), introduces a new theme into the letter that is strongly reminiscent of the Epistles to the Romans and Galatians (however, cf. 1:11). The entire chapter (3:1–4:1) may even have existed as a separate letter or a fragment of a Pauline letter that was sent to the Philippians on a separate occasion when Paul sought to address directly the threat of outside opponents. The mood, then, is thoroughly polemical, though the section ends on a note of affectionate reassurance (4:1).

Today's text consists of the central portion of this larger section and is prompted by Paul's polemical reference to those who put their "confidence in the flesh" (v. 4a; cf. Gal. 6:13; 2 Cor. 11:18).

The rehearsal of his religious pedigree (vv. 4b–6) highlights his Jewish heritage and does so in a way that points to his pride in this heritage and the confidence it justifiably provided him. "Circumcision on the eighth day" (v. 5) suggests strict conformity to Torah (Gen. 17:12; Lev. 12:3) and aligns the observance of Paul's parents with that of the parents of John the Baptist (Luke 1:59) and Jesus (Luke 2:21). His mention of his status as an Israelite and member of the tribe of Benjamin suggests that he still sees himself as essentially Jewish (similarly, Rom. 11:1; also 2 Cor. 11:22). The same is true of his Pharisaic loyalties, a motif echoed in Luke's portrait of Paul (Acts 23:6). His persecution of the church provided irrefutable proof of his zeal (cf. Acts 8:1–3; 9:1, 21; 22:4, 19; 26:10–11; 1 Cor. 15:9; Gal. 1:13, 23).

Then the "great exchange" occurred "because of Christ" (v. 7). It was a trade between two conceptions of righteousness: between a way of being religious that was measured by one's capacity to keep the law, hence a self-generated, self-measured righteousness, and one that comes from God as a gift to those with faith in Christ (vv. 8–9). It was a trade between righteousness construed as human achievement and righteousness experienced as divine gift, between righteousness that finds confidence in past performance and righteousness that finds confidence in future possibility (vv. 10–11). The language of "gain and loss" may echo the Synoptic tradition, where Jesus speaks of "selling all one has" in order to purchase something infinitely more valuable (cf. Matt. 13:44–46; also 16:26).

Especially worth noting is Paul's emphasis on futurity in this text. Even though he has already abandoned what formerly gave him confidence, he still speaks of "gaining Christ" as a future hope (v. 8). To be sure, he has already experienced the presence of Christ to an undeniably present degree. Yet his "knowledge of Christ," which entails both identifying with him as a coparticipant in his sufferings and experiencing the "power of his resurrection," is something he is still in the process of attaining—all with a view to eventual full attainment of "resurrection from the dead" (v. 11).

Thus the dominant theme of these verses is "not yet," the perspective of unrealized existence. Here Paul eschews all claims to full attainment and realized perfection (v. 12). His experience of the fullness of Christ is still partial and incomplete, even though Christ's "seizure" of him is complete and final (v. 12). What Christ has done, he has done completely and finally: Christ's work upon Paul is one of full comprehension, absolute knowing, complete ownership. Consequently, it is an "upward call" (v. 14); it comes from without, from beyond, as a result of what God has already done in Christ (cf. Heb. 3:1). To be sure, we are caught up in our pursuit of Christ, just as the sprinter strains "forward to what lies ahead" (v. 13; cf. 1 Cor. 9:24). The thrust can only be forward toward future realization, not backward toward past achievement (vv. 10–11). The one who plows with a backward glance is not fit for the kingdom of heaven (Luke 9:62).

This is the perspective of the genuinely "mature," the "perfect" (*teleioi*, v. 15). This is likely a slap against those self-professed "perfect" who know only the life of "already" and are uncomfortable before the "not yet" (cf. 1 Cor. 3:1–3; 14:20). There were those in the early church for whom resurrection had to be a present reality, fully experienced here and now, something to be clutched, not attained (cf. 2 Tim. 2:18; cf. 1 Cor. 15:12). The genuinely mature recognize their own partiality (1 Cor. 13:9–10). The way to "perfect" wisdom and knowledge is to admit to our own folly and ignorance (1 Cor. 3:18). To know truly is to confess that God can still reveal more truth to us (v. 15). There does exist a higher Christian wisdom, but it comes from God, not ourselves (1 Cor. 2:6–16).

Yet maturity of this sort does not lapse paralysis of the will: "Only let us hold fast to what we have attained" (v. 16). Even though we may not have attained everything, we have at least experienced something of the fullness of Christ. Here we are called to live within our own partiality, recognizing the "not yet-ness" of our existence. As Paul insists elsewhere, "We have this treasure in clay jars" (2 Cor. 4:7). Finally, we must see that God's transcendent power works amidst the fragility of human existence. Imperfection is the crucible within which the work of God is carried out.

The critical perspective offered in today's text, then, is that "the righteousness from God based on faith" (v. 9) is a process, not an achievement. It moves toward the fullness of God's future. It does not rely on the fullness of past human performance. To be "mature in Christ" is to recognize the incompleteness of our own existence.

Matthew 21:33–46

Our text falls within the controversy section, 21:23–22:14. As we have already seen, the controversy is between Jesus and the chief priests and elders of the people (21:23). Jesus is quizzed about his authority and his credentials, and he responds with a question concerning their opinion of John's authority (vv. 24–27). Following this counter, Jesus takes the offensive, pointing out that the real issue is not his authority but the response of his interrogators to his preaching and that of John, which called for repentance and the bearing of fruit appropriate to the kingdom of God (3:7–10; 7:20–21, 24–27; 35:31–46). Jesus' indictment of his critics is presented in three parables (21:28–32, 33–43; 22:1–14). Our lection is the second of the three.

Matthew has placed the parable immediately after the parable in verses 28–32. Both are vineyard stories and concern obedience, and so have natural kinship. However, both Mark (12:1) and Luke (20:9) separate this parable from preceding material. Matthew has not only given the story a thematic context, but added commentary. Verse 43 makes it clear that the subject is not a vineyard but the kingdom of God. The reader had known this from the outset, however, because the parable opens with direct use of the image of Israel as God's vineyard from Isaiah 5:1–7. In other words, the story of a vineyard is not really a story of a vineyard; the issue is God and the people of God. This is made even more clear by the insertion of a quotation from Psalm 118:22–23 (v. 42), which concerns not a vineyard but a building, and the rejected stone that God made the head of the corner. Why this insertion, which evokes a different image? Because, the change of image notwithstanding, the quotation corroborates the parable's climax: the tenants cast out and kill the owner's son (v. 39). By this time, of course, it is clear to the reader that the story is about the rejection and killing of Jesus, preceded by the beating and killing of the prophets whom God had sent, calling for fruitfulness among God's people.

With these comments we have as much as called verses 33–40 an allegory and not a parable. A parable is a self-contained story, the meaning of which is found within its own actions and characterizations. An allegory has its meaning in events and actions outside itself to which it refers. Our text clearly is referring to the rejection of the prophets, the killing of Jesus, the punishment of the tenants (destruction of Jerusalem), and the transfer of the vineyard to the Gentiles. Because this involves developments dated years after Jesus' lifetime, apparently Matthew has taken a parable of Jesus, interpreted it in light of post-Easter developments and the shift from a Jewish to a Gentile mission, and given to his readers this story. Many scholars believe that Luke (20:9–18) preserves a version closer to Jesus' own telling, and perhaps the Gospel of Thomas (Logion 65) is even closer to what Jesus said. Whatever the case may be, Matthew here clearly shows us what Scripture and preaching are all about—bringing the tradition forward to address a new condition facing the church.

But the question now is, Why did Matthew tell this? Is this an antisynagogue polemic? Is this gross triumphalism, dancing over the grave of those who lost their tenancy in God's kingdom by fruitlessness and efforts at taking over the arena of God's rule? Is the reader to applaud (we now have the kingdom) or weep (others have lost the kingdom)?

There is no cheap shot here. There is, to be sure, some encouragement to those who have, at great price, followed a crucified Messiah. But beyond that is a warning; unless the new tenants (and Christians are tenants, not owners) bear fruit, the vineyard may again be transferred. The owner of the vineyard is still expecting righteous living, human caring, and courageous witnessing, these three being Matthew's understanding of "fruit." The preacher of this text is not to be a teller of stories about disobedient Jews but a listener to stories told to disobedient Christians.

This may, in fact, be the force of verse 44. (Note: The ancient Greek manuscripts are not of one mind on this verse. Some contain it, others do not. The RSV of 1971 put it in a footnote; the NRSV includes it but with a notation. But we know from Luke 20:18 that the statement is firmly within the sayings of Jesus.) Verse 44 has the quality of a proverb and as such carries its truth to all people without distinction. In other words, followers of Jesus need to heed the truth it expresses as much as the original audience did. If it speaks the truth, it is true for all. And what is its truth? Jesus is the stone of God, the cornerstone of God's work. His role is decisive; he is, in a sense, the crisis of the world. He is not to be dealt with casually as just another religious figure. To encounter him is to face a moment of truth; life's Yes and No are at stake. Who more than the churches needs to ponder this proverb?

Proper 23 [28]
(Sunday between October 9 and 15 inclusive)

Exodus 32:1–14;
Psalm 106:1–6, 19–23; or
Isaiah 25:1–9;
Psalm 23;
Philippians 4:1–9;
Matthew 22:1–14

In the Old Testament lesson from the *Common Lectionary*, we have one of the most well-known instances of Israel's infidelity—the golden calf incident. Along with Israel's breaking the covenant occurs Moses' intercession on behalf of the people. The reading from Psalm 106 rehearses the same incident, albeit in the form of a prayer of confession rather than biblical narrative. In retrospect, Israel realizes the stupidity of their exchanging the glory of God for the image of an ox; they realize the enormity of their amnesic act—forgetting the great things God had done in Egypt.

An opening song of thanksgiving from Isaiah, followed by an eschatological vision, supplies the Old Testament reading for other lectionaries. Reassurance of God's care for the poor and needy in the Isaiah text is reinforced by the familiar lines of the Twenty-third Psalm.

The New Testament lesson is the last of four semicontinuous readings from the Epistle to the Philippians. It consists of concluding exhortations that lay special stress on rejoicing, the nearness of the Lord, and the reassuring nature of God's peace. In the Gospel reading, we have Jesus' parable of the marriage feast in which the host's invitation is refused by the invited guests and is thus extended to a wider, more receptive audience. It concludes on a note of rejection as the man dressed in improper attire is turned away.

Exodus 32:1–14

The frame of reference within which this passage must be understood is the covenant between Yahweh and Israel. Hardly had the people agreed to bind themselves in covenant before they violated one of its most fundamental stipulations. Murmuring and complaining about needs both real and imagined were one thing, but the rebellion reported in the story of the golden calf is quite another matter, rupturing the covenant relationship and threatening the life of the community. This account of the making and

468

worshiping of the golden calf is the initial part of a coherent unit of material that includes Exodus 32–34 and leads finally to the renewal of the covenant.

Our assigned reading contains three distinct units of narrative, each one of them dominated by dialogue between the main parties. In the first unit, verses 1–6, the dialogue is between the people of Israel and Aaron. While Moses is on Mt. Sinai receiving the revelation of the law, the people become impatient and resentful of their leader's absence, so they demand that Aaron "make gods for us, who shall go before us" (v. 1). Without visible resistance, Aaron calls for all the gold ear rings and fashions them into a golden calf, declaring it to be the "gods" (!) who brought Israel out of Egypt (v. 4). When the people worship the image, he builds an altar and proclaims a festival.

In the second unit (vv. 7–10), the scene shifts to the mountain, and a dialogue between Yahweh and Moses begins with a lengthy divine speech. The Lord tells Moses to go down immediately, for "*your* people, whom *you* brought up out of the land of Egypt have acted perversely" (v. 7, italics added). He then informs Moses of the people's actions and declares his intention to let his wrath "burn hot against them" and destroy them (v. 10).

The third unit (vv. 11–14) consists primarily of Moses' response to the Lord. It is a prayer of intercession on behalf of the rebellious people. Moses pleads the case for forgiveness by pointing out that the Egyptians would consider Yahweh's intentions evil from the outset, and he reminds the Lord of the promise made to the ancestors to multiply their descendants and give them the land of Canaan. The passage concludes with the report that the Lord "changed his mind about the disaster that he planned to bring on the people" (v. 14, or "repented of the evil which he thought to do," RSV).

If one reads no further in chapter 32 than verse 14, the tensions in the story as a whole would not be obvious. When Moses returns down the mountain to the people, he hears the sound of the festival and apparently is surprised to learn what Yahweh had already told him in verses 7–10. He initiates punishment, having the Levites kill three thousand men, and then tells the people that he will go up to the Lord and attempt to make atonement on their behalf. When he pleads for forgiveness, the Lord assures Moses that his angel will lead the people to the promised land, but he will punish the guilty parties. He does so by sending a plague. The themes of the sin and Moses' intercession continue into the next two chapters. These various perspectives on the events indicate that although there is thematic unity, the section has been composed of more than one source or tradition. The basic story line comes from one of the older pentateuchal sources, most likely the Yahwist. Verses 7–14 almost certainly are a later deuteronomic addition to the story.

The story of the golden calf probably has been influenced by the memory of the events reported in 1 Kings 12:25–33. When Jeroboam rebelled after the death of Solomon and established the Northern Kingdom, he set up golden calves in Bethel and Dan, saying, "Here are your gods, O Israel, who brought you up out of the land of Egypt" (v. 28; cf. Exod. 32:4). In the deuteronomic tradition of the seventh century and following, if not earlier, one of the functions of the story of the golden calf in the wilderness was as polemic against a concrete problem, the corruption of worship in the Northern Kingdom.

Three important themes for theological and homiletical reflection emerge from this reading:

1. The first, the sin of the people, is the one that has received the most attention in the history of Christian interpretation of the text. Note, above all, that in Stephen's speech in Acts, those sinful people are accepted as "our ancestors" (Acts 7:38). Specifically, the

making and worship of the golden calf violated the second commandment, but in doing so it violated the first one as well. What was the calf, or what did it represent? In Exodus 32:1, the people seem to ask for a replacement for Moses, but in verse 4 the calf clearly is identified with Yahweh. In the Canaanite culture surrounding Israel, the calf must be related to the bull that symbolized the god Baal. Aaron as religious leader responds to a religious need with a religious solution: a cult object, an altar, and a festival. But especially according to the deuteronomic tradition, less religious activity is better than more of questionable form. Even if people should construct an image only to make their worship of Yahweh more concrete, there is the danger that they will confuse the symbol with the reality that is beyond all symbols. Thus our narrator holds the people up to ridicule for their actions.

And what of the role of Aaron in this affair? At best, his character is weak, for he gives the people what they ask for. It is a wonder that he is not among those punished by death. Compare the report of his construction of the idol in verse 4 with his own explanation in verse 24: "I threw it [the gold] into the fire, and there came out this calf!"

2. The second theme concerns the role of Moses as mediator. He stands between the people and God, and communicates in both directions. His immediate response to the Lord's report of the people's sin and the threat of punishment is to intercede. Although there is no threat to him (v. 11b), he identifies with the people, the same ones who have grumbled about his leadership so many times. As he pleads and argues, he neither offers excuses for the people nor insists that they deserve forgiveness. Rather, he appeals to the faithfulness and mercy of God.

3. The third theme, the capacity and willingness of God to repent, is noted only briefly, but it runs like a thread through the entire story. It is the foundation for the prayer of intercession, and the factor that makes a renewal of the covenant possible. Even as the Lord is announcing his decision to destroy the people, he is leaving room for change by indirectly inviting Moses to interfere (v. 10).

Psalm 106:1–6, 19–23

The selections for this reading have primarily to do with the incident of the golden calf produced in the wilderness and thus parallels the reading from Exodus.

Verses 1–6 contain four elements: a call to praise God (vv. 1–2), a pronouncement of happiness upon the ones who observe justice and do righteousness (v. 3), an appeal by an "I" (the king, the community, or individual worshiper?) (vv. 4–5), and the beginning of a confession of wrongdoing (v. 6), which continues through verse 46. Note that although the recital of wrongdoing concerns the ancestors that come out of Egypt, verse 6 places the contemporary community in the company of the rebellious earlier generations.

Note that verses 7–8 place the original murmuring against Moses and God already in Egypt itself. Probably what is referred to here is the incident noted in Exodus 14:10–13. In the story of the flight from Egypt, when the people faced the sea and were being pursued by the Egyptian army, they, out of fear, complained that it would have been better to find a grave in Egypt than in the wilderness. In making their complaint against Moses, the people refer to the fact that already in Egypt they had said to Moses, "Let us alone and let us serve the Egyptians" (Exod. 14:12). Ezekiel develops this tradition of rebellion in Egypt claiming that the people refused to give up the detestable things and idols of Egypt (Ezek. 20:8).

The latter rabbis suggested that when their fleeing ancestors went down into the sea, they complained: "Out of mud and mire [their brickmaking work] we come forth, and now we come back to mud and mire." Another way the rabbis had of explaining the rebellion of the sea was as follows. When the tribes got to the sea, none of them wanted to go first down into the waters. Eventually, Judah did and for this reason was rewarded with having the king (the Davidic family) come from its number.

The incident of the golden calf is the concern of verses 19–23. The psalm describes three wrong acts in the episode: (1) they made an image, thus breaking the second commandment (see Exod. 20:4–6); (2) they worshiped an image of an ox in place of God; and (3) they forgot God and his great acts in Egypt (in the land of Ham) and the awesome things he did at the Red Sea.

The psalm emphasizes the intercessory role of Moses, who places himself between the people and God to turn away the divine wrath. This intercessory role of Moses shows up frequently in the murmuring in the wilderness episodes. For an example of Moses' standing in the breach, see Numbers 11:10–15. In a very late rabbinic text, it is even suggested that Moses died by the hands of his own people.

Isaiah 25:1–9   *Tucker*

This text falls within the body of material assigned by most scholars to the eighth century prophet, Isaiah of Jerusalem (1:1). Chapters 1–39 are, in a number of ways, different from chapters 40–66, the section usually called Second Isaiah. In these earlier chapters, Assyria, not Babylon, is the dominant world power; the Exile is a future threat, not a now-ending experience; and punishment, not redemption, is the overriding message. However, the themes of punishment and redemption should not be too sharply separated; there is some of both in the two sections. In fact, one should not claim too much literary or theological unity for either chapters 1–39 or 40–66. There is evidence of editing and reediting, with some passages bearing marks of being historically and theologically later, being inserted (for reasons not clear to us) into earlier materials.

Our text for today seems such a case in point. Chapters 24–27 may be some of the latest additions to the book. Although containing themes from earlier chapters, the images of restoration resemble chapters 40–66. Consisting primarily of promissory eschatological oracles, chapters 24–27 reflect the interest in the catastrophic end of the present world order that characterized much of postexilic Judaism. Given this apparent disjuncture between chapters 24–27 and the remainder of chapters 1–39, probing the political, social, and religious context for the ministry of Isaiah of Jerusalem would not be particularly helpful at this point.

That 25:1–9 is concerned with the world order and not solely with Judah and Jerusalem is repeatedly evident in the text: strong peoples (v. 3), ruthless nations (v. 3), aliens (vv. 2, 5), all peoples (vv. 6, 7), all nations (v. 7), all faces (v. 8), and all the earth (v. 8) are some of the terms that express the scope of God's activity. The passage gains its focus, however, by centering on two cities. One is an unnamed city, perhaps representative of the unbelieving world. This city is called "city of chaos" (24:10), "the fortified city" (25:2), "the palace of aliens" (25:2), "the lofty city" (26:5), and is the object of God's wrath (25:2). In contrast is the city on God's mountain, the place of God's splendid favor (25:6–9). This most certainly is Jerusalem.

It is important, however, to hear this recital of punishment and restoration in the canticle of praise set forth in unusual symmetry. Verses 1 and 9 frame the recital. In verse 1, God is praised for being faithful to the plan of God laid down ages ago. In other words, what will happen to the world, both punishment and salvation, is the unfolding of God's will. Ultimately, it is not military promise, political shrewdness, or any chance turn of events that provides history's final chapter, but God's "plans formed of old, faithful and sure." In verse 9, God is praised for keeping the promises, for carrying out the plans formed in the beginning. There was long waiting, to be sure; more than one generation asked the question "How long, O Lord, will you tarry?" But on the day of deliverance, the faithful will say, "This is the Lord for whom we have waited; let us be glad and rejoice in his salvation" (v. 9).

Between the framing words of praise in verses 1 and 9, the passage does not fall simply into two divine acts, punishment of the wicked and redemption of the faithful. God does act in behalf of the poor and needy and oppressed, and the imagery used to portray God's benevolent intervention is movingly beautiful: a refuge, a shelter in the storm, shade from the heat, and welcomed quiet (vv. 4–5). God does refresh and nourish the Holy City as with a banquet of unimagined plenty (v. 6). But the effect of God's gracious activity is positive even among the ruthless and unbelieving. Before the demonstration of God's faithful love, "strong peoples will glorify you; cities of ruthless nations will fear you" (v. 3). God does not desire that any should perish (2 Pet. 3:9). In the Revelation to John, even the fall of the wicked city of Babylon is sung as a lament (chap. 18).

Because Isaiah 25:1–9 is eschatological in nature, it is not surprising that early Christian writers drew from it in portrayals of the final victory of God. One hears verse 7 in Paul's triumphant shout, "Death has been swallowed in victory" (1 Cor. 15:54). And the prophet of the Apocalypse who, like Isaiah, envisions God's redemption of the Holy City, draws on verse 8 in assuring the reader of God's tender presence: "He will wipe every tear from their eyes" (21:4).

Psalm 23

This psalm was discussed earlier as a lection for the Fourth Sunday in Lent.

Philippians 4:1–9

Portions of today's epistolary lection also serve as the New Testament lesson twice in Year C: the Third Sunday of Advent (4:4–7) and Thanksgiving Day (4:4–9). The reader may want to consult our remarks in those settings as well.

Today's text consists of "last words," final reminders from the apostle to his beloved readers. The tone of the passage is endearing and reassuring, yet it is filled with straight talk and clear directives. We are hearing Paul the father, pastor, and teacher give words of lasting advice. As is often the case in words of farewell, we have a miscellany of exhortations, and homiletical possibilities are as numerous as the advice is diverse. Any attempt to systematize is somewhat artificial. Hence we can treat the passage generally following the paragraph divisions in the NRSV.

Standing firm in the Lord (v. 1). This call for steadfastness and fidelity arises directly from the preceding remarks and may in fact be taken with 3:12–21. The language is intimate. Paul is unabashed in his love and yearning for the church with whom he has had a long-standing relationship. They are his "joy and crown," to be counted among his fondest memories (1:3–4, 8; cf. 1 Thess. 2:19; 3:9). The tone here resonates with the effusive language of the opening thanksgiving (1:3–11).

His advice is simple and straightforward: "Stand firm in the Lord." It is the advice he commonly gives his churches, often as a parting word. It may suggest being alert and courageous (1 Cor. 16:13), faithful in the pursuit of Christian freedom (Gal. 5:1), steadfast in the face of suffering (1 Thess. 3:7–8), responsible and obedient to the received tradition (2 Thess. 2:15), and unified in purpose (Phil. 1:27). In this particular context, especially when taken with what precedes, it probably suggests being resistant to the advances of opponents who live as "enemies of the cross of Christ" (3:18–19).

Agreeing in the Lord (vv. 2–3). Within the space of two verses, we are introduced to four persons, three of them named, who belong to Paul's circle of co-workers. It is well known, of course, that he carried out his apostolic work assisted by a large number of such colleagues (cf. Rom. 16). What becomes clear, however, is that working together in the Lord has put a strain on the relationship between two of them, Euodia and Syntyche. We do not know any more than this, nor need we, for it is a situation we all know: two colleagues striving together soon find themselves disagreeing, then pulling against each other, finally at odds. Their common task that once bound them together has given way to their separate agendas. They are no more two working as one, but two working as two.

Paul's response is, "Be of the same mind in the Lord" (v. 2). Find common ground again in your mutual participation in the One who transcends both of you. Such harmony is, after all, a gift from God (Rom. 15:5), yet it can be enjoined as a form of appropriate Christian behavior (Rom. 12:16; 1 Cor. 1:10; 2 Cor. 13:11; 1 Pet. 3:8).

Rejoicing in the Lord (vv. 4–7). Once again, the exhortation is anchored "in the Lord." We first hear the familiar call to rejoice (2:18; 3:1; cf. 1 Thess. 5:16). Then comes the call for "good sense" (NJB), "consideration for others" (REB), or "gentleness" (NRSV, NIV). One test of the righteous person is whether he or she can be rattled by the insults and taunts of the ungodly (Wisd. of Sol. 2:19; cf. Titus 3:2).

Part and parcel of such rejoicing is being able to pray, which includes giving thanks as well as making petitions to the Lord (v. 6). To be "in the Lord," that is, to be Christian, is to pray. Prayer is the earmark of Christian existence (Acts 2:42; Rom. 12:12; 1 Thess. 5:17–18; Eph. 6:18; Col. 4:2; 1 Tim. 2:1). Here it is seen as the antidote to anxiety (Matt. 6:25–34; Luke 12:22–34; 1 Pet. 5:7; 1 Tim. 6:6, 8).

And what provides the basis of our confidence? Reassurance that "the Lord is near" (v. 5)—temporally (1:10; James 5:8–9; Heb. 10:37) and spatially (Ps. 145:18). The Lord's presence is experienced as peace, understood not merely as the absence of strife, but as the state of positive well-being and fullness—an eschatological gift that we begin to experience now (John 14:27; Col. 3:15).

The contours of the Christian mind (v. 8). The sentiments commended here are as Stoic as anything we find in Paul. They represent the finest aspirations of pagan thought. "Excellence" (*arete*, v. 8) is unusual here because it is Paul's single use of a term that abounds in Greek thought. What is called for here is to "think about these things" (v. 8). Seen one way, this appears to be rationality pure and simple, but taken with Paul's thought as a whole it suggests a way of thinking that goes hand in glove with moral transformation in Christ (Rom. 12:1–2; 2 Cor. 10:5).

Embodying the tradition (v. 9). Once again, Paul calls on his readers to imitate him (cf. 3:17; cf. 1 Cor. 4:6; 11:1). But the notion is expanded here to include "learning and receiving" what is taught *as well as* emulating what they have heard and seen him do. Passing on the tradition must finally occur at both the intellectual and moral level, combining both message and messenger. The witness must finally come to life in the witnesses (2 Tim. 2:2). Teaching and doing, word and deed, are interlocked in the genuine transmission of the faith (Acts 1:1).

As noted earlier, this text is a sampler. The advice is diverse, yet there are some common themes that the preacher may profitably explore. Among other things, one might explore what is possible "in the Lord" and the difference this stance makes as opposed to other stances not directly anchored in one's experience of Christ.

Matthew 22:1–14

Craddock

The parable of the marriage feast (22:1–13; v. 14 is a typical Matthean proverb of the type used to conclude stories but which do not deal precisely with the messages of the stories) is the last of three parables against Israel's leaders that are set by Matthew in the context of Jesus' final days in Jerusalem.

This parable is strikingly similar to the one preceding it, the story of the wicked tenants (vv. 33–43). The king parallels the vineyard owner, the guests refusing the invitation parallel the wicked tenants, and so on. In both, waves of servants are sent; in both, servants are mistreated and killed; in both, severe punishment is meted out; and in both, something is expected of the newly invited. Both stories conform to historical events: Israel's mistreatment of the prophets, Israel's rejection of early Christian missionaries, the destruction of Jerusalem, and the movement of the church toward a Gentile constituency. Today, as last Sunday, we are listening not to a parable but to an allegory. The meaning lies outside the story in those persons and events to which it refers. As is true of most allegories, the story loses its lifelike qualities in order to make evident its point; for example, troops execute guests and burn a city while a prepared meal is waiting. Those brought in off the street are described in moral terms—the bad and the good (v. 10). And the man thrown out is not simply rejected; he is cast into outer darkness, the place of weeping and the gnashing of teeth (v. 13). Matthew is not being subtle at all; the man lands not in the street but in hell. In other words, Matthew is not talking of a banquet and guests but of God, the kingdom, Jews, Gentiles, and the demands of the kingdom life.

Both Luke (14:16–24) and Thomas (Logion 64) tell simpler and perhaps earlier versions of the banquet story. This is not to say that they preserve exactly Jesus' own telling of it. On the contrary, Luke's fingerprints are on his version as Matthew's are on his. For example, Luke is in character when he invites to the banquet "the poor and the crippled and the blind and the lame" (14:21), just as Matthew is when he refers to those off the streets as the "bad and good." Those who argue that the parable originally ended at verse 10, verses 11–14 being Matthew's addition, miss the fact that the entire story, verses 1–14, is now Matthew's story. His concerns are evident in the telling from beginning to end, not only in the ending.

Whatever may have been the focus of the story when first told, in Matthew it is the final, the eschatological banquet. The story assumes the banquet occurs *after* the Jewish rejection, *after* the destruction of Jerusalem, *after* the Gentile ingathering. Here as in other parables (the weeds, 13:24–30; the ten maidens, 24:1–13; the talents, 25:14–30, and others), Matthew calls attention to the final judgment, no minor theme for this Evangelist.

And what is the basis of judgment? It is not simply whether one says yes or no to the invitation. The invitation is most gracious; all are invited, both bad and good. But just because all are invited does not mean there are no standards, no expectations of the guests. A wedding garment (kingdom talk for new life, righteous conduct) is expected. (The preacher will want to avoid dipping into Luke's guest list of the poor and crippled and then raising the issue of those who could not afford a wedding garment. Luke's guest list and Luke's concerns are not Matthew's.) Matthew knew how easily grace can melt into permissiveness; he knew that for those who presume upon grace, forgiveness does not fulfill righteousness but negates it. Matthew apparently is addressing a church that had lost the distinction between accepting all persons and condoning all behavior. Those who tend to wallow in grace, to sever sanctification from justification, may be startled by the king's question, "Friend, how did you get in here without a wedding robe?" (v. 12).

"How Did You Get in here?"
... a strange feast...

"putting on Christ"

Proper 24 [29]
(Sunday between October 16 and 22 inclusive)

Exodus 33:12–23;
Psalm 99; or
Isaiah 45:1–7;
Psalm 96:1–9 (10–13);
1 Thessalonians 1:1–10;
Matthew 22:15–22

The Old Testament reading in the *Common Lectionary* for today records the conversation between Moses and Yahweh after the golden calf incident in which Moses asks for confirmation of Yahweh's leadership. It also reports the intriguing episode where Moses asks to see God's glory and is given divine protection in the crevice of a rock. Psalm 99 is an enthronement psalm celebrating Yahweh as ruler of the earth, yet one who responds to the calls of those who cry out for help and guidance.

The Old Testament lesson in other lectionaries consists of Yahweh's address to Cyrus, "his anointed." Reaffirming Israel's elect status, Yahweh proclaims his uniqueness and creative power. Psalm 96, an enthronement psalm, also ascribes unique status to Yahweh and calls upon Israel's worshipers to acknowledge his universal dominion.

The passage from First Thessalonians is the introductory section of the epistle, which consists primarily of the opening prayer of thanksgiving. In the Gospel text we have the Matthean version of Jesus' conversation with the Pharisees and Herodians, where he responds to their question concerning paying taxes to Caesar.

Exodus 33:12–23

Today's reading is part of the longer composition in Exodus 32–34, the account of Israel's violation of the covenant by building and worshiping a golden calf, God's forgiveness, and the renewal of the covenant. Viewed in that context, Exodus 33:12–23 serves two main purposes. First, it continues the theme of Moses' intercession with Yahweh on behalf of the people. Second, just as the theophany on the mountain in Exodus 19 set the stage for the revelation of the law and the conclusion of the covenant in Exodus 20–24, so the appearance of the presence of God to Moses in this passage prepares the way for the laws and the covenant renewal in Exodus 34.

The passage consists entirely of reported dialogue between Moses and Yahweh. It contains two relatively distinct units, verses 12–17 and verses 18–23. (The paragraph division in the NRSV is misleading.) In the first section, Moses intercedes successfully on behalf of the people, and he asks for and is granted a special revelation of the presence of God.

What is it that Moses requests on behalf of the people? It is difficult to understand the point of the dialogue in the first unit in particular without reading the first three verses of the chapter. There the Lord, having forgiven the people for the episode with the golden calf, promises to send an angel before them to drive out the inhabitants of the land. However, he says that he himself will not "go up among you, or I would consume you on the way, for you are a stiff-necked people" (v. 3). Having successfully pleaded with the Lord to forgive the people and not kill them, and to remember the promise of descendants and the land, Moses wants more! He will not let the Lord go until there is a full restoration of the covenant relationship. The election of Israel, he insists and the Lord agrees, entails the presence of God with the chosen people (vv. 14–16). (Notice that there is some disorder in the report, for in vv. 15–16 Moses continues to ask for what had been granted in v. 14.)

If there is a moral to verses 12–17, it is a familiar one: "Ask and it shall be given you." That is particularly the case when one asks on behalf of another. God seems here only to be waiting for the request. Thus the role of mediator is recommended to the readers.

The second unit, verses 18–32, is one of the most familiar passages in the Old Testament. The sequence of request and response is simple enough. Moses asks to be shown the Lord's "glory," and the Lord gives a three-part response: (1) He will make all his "goodness" pass before Moses and make known his name, Yahweh (v. 19; cf. Exod. 3:13–15). (2) But Moses will not be allowed to see Yahweh's face, lest he die (v. 20). Notice, however, that Exodus 33:11 had reported that the Lord "used to speak to Moses face to face, as one speaks to a friend." (3) Yahweh instructs Moses to stand on a rock, and when his glory passes by Yahweh will put Moses in a cleft of the rock, cover him with his "hand," and take away his hand so that Moses can see Yahweh's "back" (vv. 21–23).

The vocabulary of this passage and its meaning have occupied the attention of interpreters for centuries. Usually, in the Bible human beings encounter God through God's voice, but here the experience is visual as well. The mystery and the danger of the scene, combined with the striking anthropomorphic language in reference to God, produce an encounter that is both intimate and distant. God has a "face," and a "hand," and a "back." But it is God's "glory" that Moses had asked to see, the side of God that is revealed to and experienced by human beings. Interpreting his powerful inaugural vision, Ezekiel stressed God's transcendence: "Such was the appearance of the likeness of the glory of the Lord" (Ezek. 1:28).

Human language reaches its limits when it attempts to describe God or even to capture the experience of the encounter with the One who is both radically other and immediately present. Anthropomorphic language is fitting because God is encountered as personal, but it must not be taken literally as descriptive, and it must be balanced with the language of otherness. Even Moses, who communicated more directly with God than any other Old Testament figure, could only catch a fleeting glimpse of the Lord's "back."

Psalm 99

One of the so-called enthronement psalms, this reading, like the others in its class (Pss. 93, 96–98), begins with the expression "Yahweh reigns," or "Yahweh is king," or, perhaps better translated, "Yahweh has become king."

Several features in the structure of this psalm are noteworthy. Three times Yahweh is affirmed as holy (vv. 3, 5, 9; note Isa. 6:3). In the first two, the expression is "Holy is he," whereas in the last occurrence the form is "Yahweh our God is holy." This affirmation tends to divide the psalm into three units (vv. 1–3, 4–5, 6–9).

In addition, verses 5 and 9 have the quality of a refrain. In both, the first four words in Hebrew are the same: "Extol the Lord our God; [and] worship." This refrain would subdivide the psalm in two units (vv. 1–5 and vv. 6–9).

Another way of looking at the psalm structurally is in terms of the addressee. The Deity is spoken to in verses 3–4 and verse 8, whereas the rest of the psalm speaks to a human audience.

From the perspective of its content, the psalm may be divided into the topics "Yahweh's universal kingship" (vv. 1–5) and "Yahweh and God's people" (vv. 6–9).

In the opening verses (vv. 1–2), we have three parallel assertions made about the Deity: (1) Yahweh has become king or reigns as king, (2) Yahweh sits enthroned upon the cherubim, and (3) Yahweh is great in Zion. The emphasis here is on Yahweh as the ruler of the universe who sits enthroned in the city of Jerusalem on Mt. Zion where the temple was located. The expression "enthroned upon the cherubim" draws upon the old imagery of the ark as being decorated with cherubim (see 1 Sam. 4:4; 2 Sam. 6:2; and Exod. 25:10–23, esp. vv. 18–20). Two large cherubim with outstretched wings were placed in the Holy of Holies of the Jerusalem temple (see 1 Kings 6:23–28; 8:6–8). Cherubim, in the Middle Ages, came to be considered innocent, round-faced babes. In the ancient world they were celestial-type flying figures, probably composite in character, with animal bodies, human faces, and bird wings (see Gen. 3:24; Ezek. 41:18–20). In mythology, the cherubim provided transportation for the deities. In the temple, it was assumed that God "sat enthroned" over the cherubim with the ark as his footstool.

To return to the psalm, the three assertions about the Deity are the bases for two exhortations and an affirmation. All three emphasize the universal dominion of Israel's God. The peoples of the world are called upon to tremble and the earth to quake. In verse 2b, the psalm affirms that Yahweh is exalted over all peoples.

This psalm, like the other psalms of enthronement, was used in the great fall festival, the Feast of Tabernacles (or booths; Succoth). This feast, held following the time of the autumn equinox in late September or early October, celebrated the creation of the world and God as king and ruler over the universe. It marked the end of the old agricultural year and the beginning of the new (see Exod. 23:16b; Deut. 16:13–15; Zech. 14:16–19).

Verses 3–4 ask God to let or declare that all peoples praise God's great and awesome name. (The Hebrew allows either translation.) Yet at the same time, God is declared to be one who loves justice and establishes equity in Jacob (=Israel). The three terms used in verse 4—justice, equity, and righteousness—emphasize the establishment of just and equitable orders in society. Yahweh is not only the ruler and monarch reigning over nature but also the author and custodian of justice in society. Yahweh's holiness is reflected in this area as much as in the world of nature. If the minister wants to analyze what Yahweh's holiness required in human life, an ideal way to handle this would be to examine Leviticus 19, where holiness is the theme of the chapter. Special note should be made that it is within the context of the proclamation of God's holiness that one finds laws on social justice and an emphasis on love of the stranger as well as the neighbor (Lev. 19:17–18, 33–34).

The rehearsal of Israelite history in verses 6–8 mentions three heroes, Moses and Aaron as priests and Samuel as prophet (though the text does not here call him a prophet). The emphasis here is on the role of the people as intercessors. (For descriptions of their intercessory functions, see Exod. 14:15; 17:11–13; 32:11–14, 30–34; Num. 12:13; 14:13–25 for Moses; Num. 16:44–48 for Aaron; and 1 Sam. 7:8–11; 12:16–25 for Samuel.)

Verse 8 emphasizes the forgiving character of Yahweh but at the same time speaks of God's role as avenger or punisher of wrongdoings. If the "them" in this verse is still Moses, Aaron, and Samuel, then these three had wrongdoings attributed to them that were unforgiven or were at least avenged (Moses and Aaron in Num. 20:12; Aaron in Exod. 32; Samuel in 1 Sam. 8:1–3, where the disobedience of his sons demands changes in the people's mode of government and the requests for a king).

Worship and bowing down before the Deity are called for as the appropriate human response (vv. 5, 9). "At his footstool" and "at his holy mountain" are synonyms meaning at the temple housing the ark in Jerusalem.

Isaiah 45:1–7

Isaiah 44:24–45:13 is a lengthy speech in three sections in which God addresses Israel in an effort to persuade the exiled people that Cyrus, king of Persia, will be God's instrument to effect the return to their homeland. In 45:1–7, Israel overhears God speak to Cyrus, surprisingly referred to as God's "anointed," or "messiah" (v. 1). In this speech, God tells Cyrus that he will be doing God's service even though he does not know God (vv. 4–5). God will go before Cyrus, open doors, assure military success, and finally cause Cyrus to recognize his debt to the God of Israel (v. 3). In fact, the turn of political events in Israel's favor will be a persuasive argument to the world that Israel's God is the one true God: "There is no one besides me; I am the LORD, and there is no other" (v. 6). Cyrus of Persia did, in fact, conquer Babylon and institute the policy of permitting exiles to return home and providing assistance in reconstruction (see comments on Isa. 55:1–5 found in Proper 13 [18]).

As to be expected, Israel resists the prophet's interpretation of international affairs, even though a theological rendering of world politics is not new to them. In 10:5, the eighth-century prophet Isaiah of Jerusalem had spoken of Assyria as the rod of God's anger, the instrument God would use to punish a corrupt and disobedient Israel. Resistance to such pronouncements occurs on at least three levels. On the historical level, Israel did not accept the idea that international politics and warfare really affected their life as the people of God. They did not read the signs of the times in the eighth century, when Assyria arose as a dark threat. Now they do not read the signs in the impending war between Babylon and Persia. Either despondent over long exile or living in comfortable accommodation in Babylon, Israel seems not to be stirred by a changing political map. On the theological level, Israel resisted the interpretation of Cyrus as God's servant because her religion was too closely joined to nationalism. When God and country are allowed to become one value rather than two, it is very difficult to acknowledge God's favor on another country and almost impossible to concede that God could be using another nation either to punish or to save one's own. In fact, any prophet who preached such a message would no doubt incur the public wrath as a traitor, politically and religiously. And finally, on a personal level, God's people, even when confessing to lapses of faith and acts of disobedience, tend to regard themselves as superior to other peoples of other religions. Comparatively speaking, are we not morally and ethically head and shoulders above Assyrians, Babylonians, Persians, or any other society of the world? It would, then, be personally offensive to hear a prophet refer to Cyrus as God's anointed one.

No religious community is immune to the kind of blindness for which Isaiah indicts Israel. It is a blindness to the full meaning of one's own confession of faith. If one confesses that there is but one God and there is no other, then is it not true that God is the God of other peoples, other nations, other cultures in addition to one's own? That other cultures do not acknowledge the one God as such does not mean that they are "godless." Cyrus did not know the very God who was making use of him for redemptive purposes. And if one confesses God to be Creator of heaven and earth, can any place or people be dismissed as lying beyond the reach of God's benevolent concern? If any doubt existed in Israel's mind on the subject of monotheism, Isaiah addresses it clearly in words offered as God's own words (v. 7):

> I form light and create darkness,
> I make weal and create woe;
> I the Lord do all these things.

Psalm 96:1–9 (10–13)

This psalm was discussed as one of the lections for the First Proper for Christmas.

1 Thessalonians 1:1–10

For this day and the next four Sundays (Proper 25 [30]–Proper 28 [33]), the New Testament lessons are drawn from Paul's first letter to the Thessalonians. A few words about this letter are in order.

A brief narrative account of Paul's establishment of the church in Thessalonica is given in Acts 17:1–10. Several details of this account are worth noting because they are echoed in Paul's letter to the church. Even though Paul preached first to the Jews in the synagogue at Thessalonica (Acts 17:2), the positive response among Gentiles was especially noteworthy (Acts 17:4; cf. 1 Thess. 1:9–10; note Aristarchus in Acts 20:4; 27:2). The church was born amidst conflict as the young church met fierce opposition from Thessalonian Jews (Acts 17: 5–9, 13; cf. 1 Thess. 1:6; 2:14–16; also Phil. 4:16). We should also note the prominent role of Silas, Paul's loyal co-worker (Acts 17:4; cf. 1 Thess. 1:1; 2 Thess. 1:1; also Acts 15:22–35, 40–18:5; 2 Cor. 1:19; 1 Pet. 5:12), as well as the less conspicuous role of Timothy (Acts 17: 14–15; cf. 1 Thess. 1:1; 2 Thess. 1:1; also Acts 16:1; 18:5; 19:22; 20:4; Rom. 16:21; 1 Cor. 4:17; 16:10; Phil. 2:19–24; Heb. 13:23; 1 and 2 Timothy).

Paul wrote the first letter to the Thessalonians only a few months after he had established the church (1 Thess. 2:17–20), though he had remained in contact with them through Timothy, his emissary (1 Thess. 3:1–3). Now that he had received from Timothy a positive report about their faith (1 Thess. 3:6–8), he is refreshed and able to continue his apostolic teaching through the medium of letter writing. Much of the letter recalls his time among them (1 Thess. 2:1–3:13) and serves as an occasion for reflecting on the nature of his apostolic ministry. These reflections also become an occasion for thanksgiving (1 Thess. 2:13; 3:9–10), and as it unfolds the letter takes the form of a pastoral prayer (1 Thess. 3:10–13; 5:23–24).

Because the Thessalonians have been Christians for only a short time, they are still in need of exhortation in the life of faith (1 Thess. 4:1–2; 5:12–22) and instruction concerning questions that puzzle them, most notably the fate of those who die before the Lord's coming (1 Thess. 4:13–5:11). The tone throughout the letter is that of moral exhortation, and hence it should be read as a paraenetic letter.

Today's text consists of two parts, the salutation (v. 1) and the opening prayer of thanksgiving (vv. 2–10).

This opening prayer is reminiscent in both form and function of other Pauline thanksgivings that serve to introduce his letters (cf. Rom. 1:8–15; 1 Cor. 1:4–9; Phil. 1:3–11; 2 Thess. 1:3–4; Philem. 4–7). Like the others, it introduces some of the main concerns of the letter and thus functions as a loosely conceived table of contents. In addition, it sets the mood of the letter.

This particular prayer is marked by reminiscence, as it recalls Paul's work in founding the church and the nature of its response to the gospel. It, like his other churches, is a source of constant concern to Paul and hence is repeatedly in his prayers (v. 2; 2:13; cf. Rom. 1:9; also 2 Cor. 11:28). Several features are worth noting, though they overlap in certain respects.

1. The Thessalonians' exemplary commitment is summarized as Paul recalls their "work of faith and labor of love and steadfastness of hope" (v. 3). They have come to embody the familiar Christian triad of virtues (cf. 5:8; also 1 Cor. 13:7, 13; Rom. 5:1–5; 12:6–12; Gal. 5:5–6; Eph. 1:15–18; 4:2–4; Col. 1:4–5; 1 Tim. 6:11; Titus 2:2; Heb. 6:10–12; 10:22–24; 1 Pet. 1:3–9). The form of expression used here, however, makes it clear that these are by no means abstract virtues but aspects of living action: "your work produced by faith, your labor prompted by love, and your endurance inspired by hope" (v. 3, NIV). Faith, love, and hope have come to expression within the Thessalonian church. Paul is thankful "because [their] faith is growing so wonderfully and the mutual love that each of [them] has for all never stops increasing" (v. 3, NJB).

2. They came into being as the result of divine election: "[God] has chosen you" (v. 4). This emphasis on divine initiative is recurrent (2 Thess. 2:13–14). Behind these words we hear echoes of election as understood in Old Testament terms (Deut. 7:6–11; 1 Chron. 16:8–13; Jer. 33:19–26; Amos 3:2; Hos. 11:1–2), but the summons of God is now focused more specifically in Jesus Christ.

3. The gospel is seen more as divine power than persuasive word (v. 5). As noted earlier, the call of God is now heard through the gospel (2 Thess. 2:13–14). The form of the message is inescapably human; it is articulated through human speech, even persuasive speech, but we are mistaken to think that its power to convict arises from the preacher's way with words. Rather, the gospel should be construed as the Divine Voice resonating through the human voice, as the Word of God reverberating through the human word. The preached word of the messenger of God provides an occasion for the Spirit to act and to do so in the power of God (v. 5; cf. 1 Cor. 2:4–5; Rom. 15:18–19; also Acts 1:8). So construed, the act of preaching is a moment of divine empowerment that leads to conviction.

4. The Thessalonians "in spite of persecution received the word with joy" (v. 6). Their response to the gospel was met with stout resistance and became an occasion for suffering (Acts 17:5–9; 1 Thess. 2:14–16). Yet in this respect they were merely following in the path of Paul (1 Thess. 2:1–2), becoming his imitators (cf. 1 Cor. 4:16; Phil. 3:17; 4:9; 2 Thess. 3:7, 9; Gal. 4:12). More important, their suffering in behalf of the gospel made them imitators of the Lord (1 Pet. 2:21–24).

5. Their faith and steadfastness became exemplary to other believers (v. 7). The gospel is preached not only by rehearsing the story of Christ, the kerygma, but also by rehearsing the story of the faith of others (Rom. 1:8; 16:19). This is illustrated through the emergence of the two-volume work of Luke-Acts, which links the words and deeds of Christ in the gospel with those of the church in Acts—clear testimony that the story of the church (and churches) has kerygmatic value along with the story of Christ. The steadfastness of the Thessalonians in the face of persecution had enabled the gospel to "spread rapidly and be glorified everywhere" (2 Thess. 3:1).

6. Theirs had been a conversion from the worship of idols to the worship of the one God, who is "living and true" (vv. 9–10). In these concluding words of the opening prayer of thanksgiving, we have an embedded kerygmatic summary of missionary preaching to Gentiles. It consists of several elements: (1) the call to turn away from the worship of idols (Acts 14:15; 1 Cor. 12:2); (2) the acceptance of one God, confessed as "living and true" (cf. Heb. 9:14; John 17:3); (3) faith in Jesus as the One whom God raised from the dead (cf. Acts 3:15; 4:10; 5:30; 10:40; 13:30, 37; Rom. 1:4) and as the Son of God expected to return and deliver from the coming wrath (1 Thess. 5:9; Rom. 5:9; also Matt. 3:7).

This suggests that the conversion of Gentiles entailed repentance, or turning away from a false form of worship, and faith. We should observe, however, that faith for Gentiles had two prongs: belief in a monotheistic God and belief in a Christ who was raised from the dead and expected to return in the future to redeem his own from a coming judgment. As we know from the latter part of this epistle, Gentiles could find notions of resurrection and eschatology befuddling. Thus we find Paul continuing to expound the kerygma to them and explaining its full implications.

Matthew 22:15–22

The lection for today is the first of four question-and-answer encounters between Jesus and Jewish leaders in Jerusalem during the closing days of Jesus' life. Of these four (22:15–22, 23–33, 34–40, 41–46), all but the second involve the Pharisees. These four confrontations are set by Matthew between the three parables against Israel (21:2–22:14) and Jesus' scathing word against scribes and Pharisees (23:1–36).

The form of our text is that of a "pronouncement story," a unit of material that consists of a pronouncement of Jesus cradled in a simple narrative relating the barest essentials as framework for the pronouncement. These stories probably circulated in a variety of contexts as the church looked to the authority of Jesus' words to address opponents and critics. Matthew 22:15–22 follows the basic outline of Mark 12:13–17: questioners come to Jesus with flattering lips and hostile intent; they pose the question of paying taxes to Rome; Jesus perceives their evil design; Jesus asks for a coin and poses a question; Jesus answers their question; they marvel and go away.

The interrogators of Jesus are Pharisees, the major party to survive the wars with Rome. Because the Pharisees were the principal representatives of Judaism in Matthew's day, because they were concerned with interpretation of Torah, and because they operated out of the synagogue, debates between them and Jesus had direct transfer value for Matthew's church in its debate with the synagogue. Their plan to entrap Jesus involved sending to Jesus a delegation of their own disciples accompanied by Herodians. This union of forces is strange, found only here (v. 16; Mark 12:13) and in Mark's record of an attempt to destroy

Jesus (3:6). The Pharisees smarted under Roman taxes (here probably referring to the poll tax levied in AD 6 and sparking many Roman-Jewish clashes) and other such intrusions into Jewish life. Herodians, however, supported the Rome-endorsed Herod dynasty and, therefore, the tax. The delegation thus represents both yes and no on the tax issue; Jesus will surely displease someone in his answer.

"Is it lawful [permitted, proper] to pay taxes to the emperor, or not?" In verse 18, the word translated "malice" in the RSV can also be translated "evil," as in "rescue us from the evil one" (Matt. 6:13). And "put me to the test" can be translated "tempt me," as in the traditional translation of the Lord's Prayer and Jesus' experience in the wilderness (Matt. 4:1–11). If one uses the words "evil" and "tempt" in understanding verse 18, then it is clear that Jesus perceived the occasion as something more than a game of wits, a mental trap. If Jesus is being tempted, then the evil one is, through these questioners, seeking to lure Jesus into the political power struggle. The scene is reminiscent of the wilderness offer of the kingdoms of the world. In other words, Jesus understands that he is being confronted by evil, not just "a tough question."

On one level, therefore, one can cheerfully conclude that Jesus is of a keen mind and again outwits his opponents. On another level, one can see that evil is very real; it often approaches through flattery (v. 16); its agents may be religious leaders, and the issue most often is complex, demanding discernment. It is difficult to believe Matthew preserved this story to show how clever Jesus was. In Matthew's world, Caesar was still Caesar, the tax was still due, and Christians were still struggling with the place of Caesar if Jesus Christ is Lord.

Jesus' response to the question did not and does not solve the problem but simply defines the nature of the struggle. For Jesus, discerning what is God's and what is Caesar's was a test or temptation. For the early church, the task of interpreting Jesus' statement continued: how is the Christian to relate to political structures (Rom. 13:1–7; 1 Pet. 2:13–17; 1 Tim. 2:2; Titus 3:1; Rev. 13:1–18; 18:1–24)? For those who call Caesar "Lord" and for those who call Caesar "Satan," answers are simple. But if the church can at times support and at times must resist the state, then the answers are never simple nor are they final; the struggle resumes with every new situation.

From this wrestling Jesus was not exempt. In fact, in his decisions he was finally alone, with church and state conspiring against him. One can hardly imagine a heavier demand— called upon to obey God, not simply in the face of political wrath but without the support of the community of faith. But it still happens.

Proper 25 [30]
(Sunday between October 23 and 29 inclusive)

Deuteronomy 34:1–12;
Psalm 90:1–6, 13–17; or
Leviticus 19:1–2, 15–18;
Psalm 1;
1 Thessalonians 2:1–8;
Matthew 22:34–46

Forest Park Sunday

I n the *Common Lectionary* for this week, the Old Testament selection from Deuteronomy is the account of the death of Moses. The account is accompanied by a fitting obituary of Moses as Israel's peerless prophet and the passing of the torch to Joshua. The psalm, a communal lament, opens by reflecting on the transience of life and concludes by calling on God to show compassion on the faithful.

Selections from the Levitical Holiness Code supplies the Old Testament lesson for other lectionaries for today, and the first psalm in unforgettable images contrasts the lives of the righteous and the wicked.

In the New Testament lesson from First Thessalonians, Paul reflects on his missionary preaching among the Thessalonians, giving us a profile of exemplary ministerial service. In the Gospel lesson, we have the Matthean account of Jesus' teaching concerning the two great commandments of loving God and neighbor and his biblical exposition concerning Christ as the Son of David.

Deuteronomy 34:1–12

T he events described in this passage, the death and burial of Moses, define the Book of Deuteronomy as a whole. In its final form, the book is the report of the last words and actions of Moses. Most of Deuteronomy is thus the last will and testament of the one who led Israel out of Egypt, through the wilderness, and to the border of the land promised to the ancestors. And what a testament it is: the law, the covenant, and a series of sermons on the law.

By no means did all this material attributed to Moses arise at the same time and in the same place. Some of the individual laws are indeed quite ancient, but it is difficult if not impossible to establish their provenance. The core of the book, chapters 12–26, is identified with the reform of King Josiah in 621 BC, but some of the materials arose earlier in the oral tradition. The initial and concluding chapters of the book come from the latest strata, associated with the deuteronomistic historian(s) who composed the account of Israel's past from the time of Moses to the Babylonian Exile. Chapter 34 comes from the latest strata of the book, from the deuteronomistic historian who worked about 560 BC. Verses 9–12 are perhaps an even later addition to the book. Thus our passage was composed centuries after the events it reports, by and for people who had experienced a long history of living with the heritage they believed Moses had left them.

Deuteronomy 34 is the immediate narrative continuation of Deuteronomy 32:48–52, in which Yahweh commands Moses to ascend Mt. Nebo and survey the promised land. The blessing of Moses in Deuteronomy 33 has been inserted into the previously established story. Although a new era in the history of Israel begins with the death of Moses, there is no sharp break at the end; Joshua 1 continues directly where our passage ends.

The Book of Deuteronomy mentions over and over again the point that Moses was not to be allowed to enter the promised land (Deut. 1:37; 4:21; 3:27) and that he died in Moab "at the Lord's command" (Deut. 34:5). Given the author's presupposition that this fact was punishment for sin, it was considered an act of grace that Moses was allowed to see the land, an act not to be shared by the original wilderness generation of sinners (Deut. 1:34–39). In order to view the land, Moses ascends a mountain in the land of Moab in Transjordan, opposite Jericho; verse 1 contains two traditions about either the place or its name, Mt. Nebo or Mt. Pisgah. Recalling his promise to the ancestor (v. 4), Yahweh shows Moses the sweep of the land, generally to the north, the west, and then the south. Actually, there is no mountain in Moab from which one can see all the way to the Mediterranean, the "Western Sea" of verse 2. Some commentators have seen in this visual survey an allusion to a form of legal conveyance of the land (cf. Deut. 3:27; Gen. 13:14ff.).

In the initial and brief notice of Moses' death, the reporter gives a relatively modest epitaph that describes him when he died: he was one hundred and twenty years old, and "his sight was unimpaired and his vigor had not abated" (v. 7). Both the literal and figurative meaning of the first phrase is relatively clear; his eyesight and "vision" were strong. The reference to undiminished vigor ("natural force," RSV) is unusual and probably refers to sexual power, and is thus a figure of speech for vitality. To some extent, this characterization conflicts with what Moses said on his one hundred and twentieth birthday, "I am no longer able to get about" (Deut. 31:2).

It is a curious note that "he was buried" or "he [that is, the Lord] buried him" (RSV, v. 6). This tradition must be based on the fact that there was no knowledge of the place where Moses was buried.

The final paragraph (vv. 9–12) marks the transition from Moses to Joshua and makes a final comment upon the special relationship between Yahweh and Moses. Joshua successfully assumes the reigns of leadership because the gift of the spirit had been transferred to him by Moses (v. 9); that is, Joshua has authority indirectly through Moses. What had been identified only as "the spirit" in Numbers 27:18 is now called "the spirit of wisdom."

Moses is both identified with and distinguished from the usual prophetic role: "Never since has there arisen a prophet in Israel like Moses" (v. 10). His functions were quite different from the classical prophets such as Amos, Hosea, Isaiah, Jeremiah, and the others, who announced the word of God concerning the immediate future. What such prophets shared with Moses was the fact that they were mediators of the divine word and will to their people. Thus Deuteronomy 18:15–22 can anticipate future prophets who will be like Moses.

What was different was the mode of revelation to and through these figures. Although ordinary (!) prophets would see visions and have auditions of the word of God, Moses was the only one "whom the Lord knew face to face" (v. 10; cf. Deut. 33:11). Not only that, the mighty power of God was manifest through him in "all the mighty deeds and all the terrifying displays of power that Moses performed in the sight of all Israel" (v. 12).

In no sense, then, does our reporter recommend Moses as an example to be followed. Because of his special and direct relationship with God, that is impossible. All this praise of Moses is rather to commend the words attributed to him as authoritative and to be followed. Thus even the report of the death of Moses serves for these writers a homiletical purpose—to urge faithfulness to the covenant that Moses established and obedience to the laws that he taught.

Psalm 90:1–6, 13–17

This psalm is a communal lament in which the community offers its complaint to the Deity about the transience and the brevity, the toil, and the trouble of life.

Two basic contrasts are drawn in the psalm between the Deity and humanity. The one contrast, and the most overt, is that between the eternal, everlasting nature of God and the transitory, dying character of humankind. The second contrast is that between the holy God, who reacts with anger and wrath against disobedience, and humanity, with its overt iniquity and secret sin, its unholiness and rebellion.

There is a certain undercurrent of animosity toward God in this psalm. Although it doesn't stand out starkly revealed, nonetheless it is there. The psalm writer must have felt, even if it is not said, that there seems to be some injustice to the way things are. On the one hand, God exists forever and is in no way conditioned by the calendar or subservient to time. On the other hand, human life is so fleeting, so time-bound, so insubstantial. In spite of his disparity between the human and the Divine, the psalmist, however, is not led to despair. Instead, the writer sees the one eternal God as the dwelling place for the endless generations of human beings (v. 1) and asks for divine assistance in coming to terms with the length and shape of human existence (v. 12).

The opening invocation, hymnic in style, anchors human and communal life with its everflowing generations in the embrace of the eternal God (v. 1). The eternity of God is expressed by affirming divine existence prior to the earth's giving birth to the mountains and even prior to the divine formation of the earth and the world (v. 2). When compared to God, the earth and the mountains that watch the generations come and go are but youngsters. These symbols, which stand for continuity and endurance, are but the creations of the Everlasting.

The first stanza (vv. 3–6) laments the brevity and frailty of human life, which ends in death. God is described as the timeless one, for whom a millennium, a thousand years, seems like a yesterday to humans or passes as quickly and quietly as a (four-hour) watch in the night to a sleeping person. Yet the everlasting, hardly conscious-of-time God has decreed that humans should return to the dust from whence they came (Gen. 3:19). The One who bestowed life is the One who withdraws it. Human life must be lived knowing that death is awaiting. (The minister preaching on this or similar texts should make it clear that they were written at a time in Israel's history before the people believed in resurrection from the dead or in the doctrine of immortality.)

Even life itself—the dash between two dates—is subject to dissipation. Like a dream, like grass in the morning, life has a fading quality (v. 6). Life at its peak, its best, here symbolized by the morning grass covered with the invigoration of the dew, soon encounters the noonday heat and by evening has faded and withered. The psalmist here gives expression to the recognition that once we pass the child-producing, child-rearing phase of life, nature or God has a way of sweeping us away. Strength, vitality, and spirit atrophy and wither.

Only this psalm is attributed to Moses (see the psalm's heading). Such attribution probably stems from a period in Jewish exegesis of the psalms when there was an effort to relate at least some of the psalms to individual persons. One can imagine that the heading was added so that interpreters might look at this psalm against the background of the events in Deuteronomy 34. Moses stands on Mt. Pisgah, viewing the promised land and knowing that he will never enter it. Death awaits him (cf. Deut. 34:7 with Ps. 90:10). The pains and disappointments of life torment him. Failures bring life to an end without full fruition. In such conditions, he exemplifies the general thrust of Psalm 90. Such is at least one way of looking at the psalm.

Leviticus 19:1–2, 15–18

This is virtually the same text assigned for the Seventh Sunday After the Epiphany in this liturgical year (that reading includes vv. 9–14). For commentary, see our remarks in that setting.

Psalm 1

Psalm 1, which opens the Psalter, might just as well be an introduction to the Pentateuch, for it focuses on legal piety and Torah observance. The psalm opens in beatitude form, although the actual content of the psalm expands such a form beyond its bounds and becomes a poem of admonition.

The psalm profiles two types of persons, the righteous and the wicked, and thus reflects a pattern frequently found in the Old Testament. Obviously, the intention of the text was to encourage emulation of the righteous and to discourage imitation of the wicked. As such, the psalm is a sharp call for commitment to a certain pattern of life, a pattern based on study and meditation on the Torah and observance of its commandments.

In such depictions of opposite attitudes of life, there is no neutral ground, there are no neutral corners. The two ways lead in two different directions, and one cannot walk in both paths. The decision for Torah is the decision to take upon oneself the shield and protection, the ordering and regulation of the Torah. To refuse Torah is to choose chaos, impermanence, the lack of a mooring for life.

In depicting the righteous person, the psalm does so in a series of negative characteristics (v. 1). The righteous does not follow the counsel of the wicked, does not take the path of sinners or join the company of the insolent. The positive description (v. 2) describes the righteous as making the law a fundamental concern of life, an object of meditation day and night.

Verse 3 may be read as the promise conditional upon the Torah piety described in verse 2. The righteous becomes like a tree—fruitful, productive, predictable.

The description of the wicked, on the other hand, presents them as unstable, insecure, open to the whims and winds of the moment, carrying in themselves no weight of character (v. 4). Thus sinners, or the wicked, will be unable to stand in judgment; that is, they either will be unable to serve as judges and participants in legal suits or else cannot survive the judgment of their (righteous) peers.

Finally, the two ways are summarized. The way of the righteous God knows (cherishes, upholds, aids), but the way of the wicked is on its own—doomed, perishing, headed for chaos.

1 Thessalonians 2:1–8

With the memory of his founding visit still fresh in the minds of his readers, Paul recalls the circumstances in which the Thessalonian church was born. By virtue of their existence as a "church of the Thessalonians in God" (1:1), they bore witness to the productivity of his first visit. It had not been in vain (v. 1).

They are asked to recall that the opposition he met at Thessalonica was typical rather than exceptional. Prior to coming to Thessalonica, Paul had preached the gospel in Philippi (Acts 16:11–40). There too he had met stiff resistance, even to the point of being beaten and jailed (Acts 16:20–24). It was in this respect that he "had already suffered and been shamefully mistreated at Philippi" (v. 2), and this had apparently become common knowledge. His reputation had preceded him.

The preaching of the "gospel of God" (v. 2; cf. Mark 1:14; Rom. 1:1; 15:16) had called for courage "in our God." On other occasions, he had experienced a failure of nerve when he reflected on the odds against the gospel (cf. 1 Cor. 2:1–5; Acts 18:9–10). It was not a question of dipping into his inner, human resources and finding the strength to speak, but rather of relying on the power of God (1 Cor. 2:5; 2 Cor. 4:16; 5:5–8). Such confidence and boldness became an earmark of apostolic witness (Acts 4:13, 29; 28:31), and it characterizes Paul's ministry (2 Cor. 3:12; Phil. 1:20; Philem. 8; cf. 1 Tim. 3:13).

At this point, Paul begins to depict some of the features of his ministry among them. The tone is slightly apologetic, as if he is defending himself against the charges of opponents. In other settings, Paul encountered opposition from those who accused him of behaving in ways unbecoming to an apostle (cf. esp. 2 Cor. 2:17–3:2; 4:2–3; 10:7–12). No such explicit reference to opponents occurs here, however.

In any case, we are assured of the purity of his motives: "Our appeal does not spring from deceit or impure motives or trickery" (v. 3; cf. 2 Cor. 12:16). He further denies having gained entry among them through the use of flattering words, insisting that his aim was not human but divine approval (Gal. 1:10). He carried out his work before God as his witness (v. 5; cf. Rom. 1:9), as the One who "tries the heart and mind" (Jer. 11:20).

Nor did he ever use his speeches as "a cover for trying to get money" (v. 5, JB). The wandering preacher, or itinerant philosopher, whose speeches were followed by requests for money, was commonplace in the Greco-Roman world, and Paul constantly had to distance himself from such charlatans. His consistent practice was to preach free of charge, working to support himself (1 Cor. 9:12–18), and in this way he excluded himself from the "peddlers of God's word" (2 Cor. 2:17; 2 Pet. 2:3).

He also chose gentleness over harshness as the form in which to couch his ministerial practice (vv. 6–7). As an apostle of Christ, he might have made it his practice to pull rank and appeal to his authority as a common ministerial device. And sometimes he does lay express claim to apostolic authority and the power that comes with it (cf. 1 Cor. 4:19–21; 2 Cor. 10–13, esp. 10:8; 13:3–4, 10; Gal. 1:6–9). But more often than not, we see Paul placing limits on his apostolic authority, restraining himself in his use of power rather than unleashing harsh threats (Philem. 8–9).

The image used here to capture this mode of ministry is that of the wet nurse who cares for her children (v. 5; cf. 1 Cor. 3:2; Eph. 5:29). This same image was also used by Greco-Roman authors to depict the proper way of philosophical instruction—nurturing rather than intimidating. What is suggested here is a level of genuine commitment, a willingness to give of himself completely in the work of ministry (v. 8).

Today's text is first and foremost a statement about the nature of ministry. It provides us with a sort of catalog of characteristics of authentic ministry, both negatively and positively: not error, uncleanness, guile, flattery, greed, but courage, gentleness, affection, and self-giving. It may well provide an appropriate occasion for the preacher to explore the dynamic between church and ministry.

Matthew 22:34–46

Two tables; Two Commands.

Today we conclude the question-and-answer encounters between Jesus and leaders of Judaism as these encounters are recorded in Matthew 22:15–46. Three units deal with questions posed by these leaders to Jesus (two by Pharisees, one by Sadducees), and one, the concluding unit (vv. 41–46), consists of a question by Jesus to the Pharisees. Jesus and these leaders can argue because they have a common heritage and embrace common sacred texts. It is in interpreting that heritage and those texts that tension arises. At verse 46, a major section of Matthew closes. In chapter 23, the audience changes; Jesus now talks to the crowd and to his disciples about the religious leaders. In these closing chapters of Matthew, Jesus moves from the leaders, to the crowds, to his disciples, to the cross.

The reader will notice immediately that this lection consists not of one unit but two (vv. 34–40; 41–46). Each unit begins with the Pharisees coming together (vv. 34, 41), but in the one the Pharisees ask the question; in the other it is Jesus who is the interrogator. Verse 46 concludes not only the unit begun at verse 41 but the entire section begun at 22:15. The decision facing the preacher is whether or not to embrace both units in one message. After all, the first part concerns Old Testament commandments, the second concerns Christology. Understandably, some lectionaries conclude the reading at verse 40. One suggestion is to focus on verses 34–40, using verses 41–46 as a christological affirmation to conclude the debates and conflict. It would be most appropriate to declare who the Christ is as a climax to a period of grueling interrogation.

Matthew 22:34–40 has parallels in Mark 12:28–34 and Luke 10:25–28. Luke agrees in some detail with Matthew but locates the story earlier as preface to the parable of the Good Samaritan. Mark has the question about the great (first) commandment come from a sincere scribe whom Jesus commends. The question itself is neither unusual nor new. Rabbis had long engaged in classifying commandments, sometimes according to weight (light or heavy). It was inevitable—both in the context of a classroom and in the common struggle to keep, if possible, the weightier laws—that the question arises, Which one is greatest, first?

Jesus' answer is not surprising. He joins the Shema of Deuteronomy 6:5 (Matthew uses the Septuagint but substitutes "mind" for "might." Mark and Luke have both "mind" and "might") to Leviticus 19:18, the command to love one's neighbor. That Luke says it was the lawyer who cited the Old Testament texts (10:27) and that Mark says the scribe approved of Jesus' citation of these two texts should remind us that Jesus and the Pharisees had much in common. These two commandments had been joined by rabbis long before Jesus. Too often Christians want everything good to originate with Jesus, and much too often assume an "over against" posture in relation to all leaders of Judaism mentioned in the New Testament. The message of Jesus' response to the question is clear: love God totally, and the love of God is expressed in love of neighbor. This is vital, not simply as a discussion topic with the synagogue but for the church as well. As Matthew has repeatedly said, love toward all, without partiality, is a distinguishing mark of life in the kingdom (5:43–48; 7:12; 9:13; 12:1–8; 18:12–35; 25:31–46).

The second unit of our lection, verses 41–46, has parallels in Mark 12:35–37a and Luke 20:41–44, but with noticeable differences. Only in Matthew is Jesus' question confrontational, "What do *you* think?" Earlier the Pharisees had said to Jesus, "Tell us . . . what you think" (v. 17). Now the roles are reversed. That the Christ was son of David was supported by numerous texts (Isa. 9:2–7; 11:1–9; Jer. 23:5–6; 33:14–18; Ezek. 34:23–24), and Matthew clearly accepts the view (1:1–17, 18–25; 9:27; 12:23; 15:22; 20:30–31; 21:9, 15). The answer of the Pharisees is not wrong, but it is incomplete. The Christ is also David's Lord. Psalm 110 is used to enlarge the Pharisees' view of the Messiah. This text, Psalm 110:1, was understood messianically by the early church, and is, in fact, the most used Old Testament citation in the New Testament to affirm the exaltation and enthronement of Christ. Just as the record of Jesus' baptism ends with heaven's affirmation (3:17), just as the Transfiguration ends with heaven's affirmation (17:5), so here, following a period of intense conflict, Matthew concludes with a triumphant note. After that, no one asked any more questions.

"Sit at my right hand, *until* . . ." (v. 44, italics added). The preacher would do well to pause over the word *until*. Christ is Lord; Christ is becoming Lord. The exaltation of Christ is our song, but it is also our assignment.

Proper 26 [31]
(Sunday between October 30 and November 5 inclusive)

Joshua 3:7–17;
Psalm 107:1–7, 33–37; or
Micah 3:5–12;
Psalm 43;
1 Thessalonians 2:9–13;
Matthew 23:1–12 ——————

"Sitting in Moses' seat"

The *Common Lectionary*'s Old Testament reading for today relates the story of Joshua's leading Israel through the waters of the Jordan. The responsorial psalm, a communal psalm of thanksgiving, expresses gratitude for the redemptive power of God, but in the second section employs images illustrating God's ability to reverse the natural course of things, thereby echoing God's action described in the Old Testament reading.

Prophets who frame their words to receive a favorable response rather than speak God's truth directly and who pursue their calling in order to profit rather than prophesy are roundly condemned in the other Old Testament lesson. In Psalm 43, the psalmist begs God for vindication against ungodly people and calls for God's light and truth to work their irresistible attraction in bringing him to worship in Jerusalem.

In today's epistolary reading, Paul relates how he sought to "parent" the house (family) of God in Thessalonica. In the Gospel reading from Matthew, Jesus instructs his followers that it is not by privilege, place, and preference but by obedience, humility, and service that the community of faith is established.

Joshua 3:7–17

With this text we have moved, in the semicontinuous readings for the season, beyond the Pentateuch, from the time of Moses to the period of the settlement of Israel in the land of Canaan. This continuation of the Pentateuch into the Hexateuch makes sense because it is only in the Book of Joshua that the promise to Abraham in Genesis 12:1–4 is fulfilled. Thus the history set into motion in Genesis continues here. But the Book of Joshua, the first of the so-called historical books, is also the second "chapter" in what has been identified as the deuteronomistic history, consisting of the Books of

Deuteronomy, Joshua, Judges, 1 and 2 Samuel, 1 and 2 Kings. It is so-called because it provides a more or less continuous account of events from the time of Moses to the Babylonian Exile and bears the marks of editors who worked in the style and from the point of view of the Book of Deuteronomy. In the end, the purpose of that history is to explain the disaster of the Babylonian Exile as the result of a history of sin. The authors and editors have organized the history in various ways, including the division of the past into a series of eras in terms of Israel's leaders: Moses, Joshua, the judges, the kings.

The previous reading in this series from the Book of Deuteronomy had alluded to the ordination of Joshua as Moses' successor. Although ancient Israel believed that no other leader was comparable to Moses, Joshua comes closer than any others, and the editors of the Book of Joshua stress that he was Moses' legitimate successor (1:5, 17). One of the functions of the miracle at the Jordan, says the Lord, is "to exalt you [Joshua] in the sight of all Israel, so that they may know that I will be with you as I was with Moses" (3:7). Many of his actions are drawn as parallels to those of Moses. The account of the crossing of the Jordan in our reading in particular is parallel in some ways to the account of the rescue at the sea in Exodus 14–15. In both cases, the leader acts on Yahweh's instructions to divide or hold back the water as the people of Israel pass through.

The full account of Israel's entrance into the land by means of a miraculous crossing of the Jordan requires two chapters, Joshua 3 and 4. Complex and diverse traditions have been combined. In the reading for today, evidence for some of that complexity is seen in the fact that first "twelve men," one from each tribe, were chosen (v. 12), but it is the priests (v. 13) who carried the ark. Some modern interpreters have seen behind this account evidence for an ancient liturgical commemoration of Israel's entrance into the land, an event once held annually out of the sanctuary at Gilgal. In the final form of the text, this and other oral traditions have been preserved and shaped to serve the interests of the deuteronomistic editors.

Joshua 3 presents three distinct scenes related to Israel's entrance into the promised land. First, verses 1–13 report the arrival at the edge of the land and the preparations for the crossing of the Jordan. Liturgical features include the careful statement of the time (v. 2), probably to coincide with the celebration of Passover, the presence of the ark of the covenant, the procession of the ark carried by the priests, and Joshua's specific instructions to the people to "sanctify" themselves (cf. Exod. 19:10) for the dramatic and sacred events to follow. The "prophetic" role of Joshua is visible in the preparations as he functions to mediate between the Lord and the people, including the priests (vv. 5–6, 9–13). The central theological if not dramatic point in the text comes in Joshua's sermon to the people: "By this you shall know that among you is the living God" (v. 10).

The second scene (vv. 14–16a) describes the miracle of the water. Following Joshua's instructions, the priests set out at the head of the procession carrying the ark. The narrator pauses to point out that the river overflows its banks at "the time of harvest" (v. 15), otherwise no miracle would be required, because all readers know that the Jordan can be forded easily when the water is low, as it is most of the year. When the feet of the priests touch the water, its flow is stopped well upstream of the crossing (v. 16a). In the third scene (vv. 16b–17), continued into chapter 4, the people crossed while the priests with the ark stood in the river bed.

This story contains the only mention of the ark of the covenant in the stories of the settlement of Israel in the land. The sacredness of this symbol of the throne of Yahweh is indicated in several ways. It could be carried only by priests, and the people were to keep their distance, about two thousand cubits (v. 4). In the account of David's movement of the ark to Jerusalem, Uzzah was struck dead because he touched the ark to keep it from falling (2 Sam 6:6–11).

The central purpose of this text is to tell how the people of Israel got into the land, how the promise to Abraham and the other ancestors was fulfilled. The emphasis upon the miraculous intervention of the Lord makes it clear that the events to follow in the Book of Joshua are not stories of Israel's conquest of that land's inhabitants. Rather, they are accounts of the Lord's granting of the land to Israel.

Here the miracle is to evoke belief in the living God (v. 10). Can one believe without seeing such miracles? Certainly the ancient participants in the rituals that celebrated the events believed without seeing the miracle. They reenacted it. Their belief in that living God must have stemmed from experiences other than seeing waters stopped. Can one believe in the living God without believing that this text presents a reliable account of actual events? Some commentators have explained the events in terms of natural phenomena, for more than once in historical times the flow of the Jordan has been interrupted for short periods by earthquakes or landslides. The text, however, makes no reference to natural or "secondary" causes, such as the "strong east wind" in Exodus 14:21. So we are left to struggle with the text's fundamental claim—that it was the Lord who brought Israel across the flooding Jordan and into the land.

Psalm 107:1–7, 33–37

Psalm 107 is an all purpose thanksgiving psalm for communal usage. Thanksgiving psalms were used after a period of trouble or distress had passed and thanks was given for redemption. The plight and redemption of various groups are reflected in this psalm: trouble in travel (vv. 4–9), imprisonment (vv. 10–16), illness (vv. 17–22), and danger at sea (vv. 23–32).

The choice of the verses for this reading is to provide parallels to Joshua 3:7–17, with its account of the crossing of the Jordan River. Verses 1–3 of the psalm are a general call to thanksgiving. Verses 4–7 describe the condition of distress experienced by those lost in the desert but who are then led to safety by God. In the Pentateuch, the Hebrews spend from Exodus 14 to the end of Deuteronomy "lost in the desert." Finally in Joshua 3, they reached their desired goal—entry into the land. The condition of the lost desert traveler in the psalm is thus an analogy to the lost people of God in the wilderness.

Verses 33–37 speak of God as one who reverses the fate of people and as one who transforms conditions. Rivers and farmlands can become deserts and salty wastes (vv. 33–34), but deserts may be transformed into their opposites as well (v. 35). The transformation of existence—when the last shall be first—is held out as an expectation when God grants the hungry food, the homeless a place to live, and those who wander a homeland and a city to inhabit (vv. 36–37).

Micah 3:5–12

The message of the Book of Micah is to be distinguished from that of the prophet himself. The prophet Micah was active in the eighth century BC; he was a contemporary of Isaiah of Jerusalem, Amos, and Hosea. Micah was a Judean whose theological perspective closely paralleled that of Isaiah in his belief in the dynasty of David as

God's means of care for the people and in the city of Jerusalem as God's holy place. The heart of his message is expressed in this Old Testament lesson. It stressed judgment upon the people, and the city of Jerusalem in particular, because of social injustice, especially in high places.

On the other hand, the message of the *book* of Micah is more complicated: God will indeed judge the people and punish them with military defeat and exile; but later, as an act of grace, the Lord will bring them back and establish a reign of perpetual peace, with its center in Jerusalem and its leader a king in the line of David. The most vivid statement of that promise is Micah 4:1–5, which is virtually identical to Isaiah 2:2–5. This message, with salvation as the last word, is the result of the history of the book's use and growth through the centuries after the time of the original prophet. Consequently, the book as we have it is the product of generations who heard the word of God in ever new circumstances.

Virtually all commentators are agreed that the material in chapter 3 comes from Micah himself. It consists of three distinct prophetic addresses that are closely related to one another thematically. The lesson for the day contains two of those addresses, verses 5–7 and verses 8–12. They are preceded by the comprehensive indictment of and announcement of judgment upon the political leadership in Jerusalem (3:1–4). Because those who are responsible for justice (v. 1) hate good and love evil, thus destroying God's people, they will cry to God, but he will refuse to hear them (v. 4).

Micah 3:5–8 is another announcement of punishment that continues the indictment of Jerusalem's leadership, turning specifically to the prophets. In some respects, this speech concerning—and directed to—other prophets is typical, and in one respect it is unique. It is a prophecy of punishment that includes the indictment, or reasons, for punishment (v. 5) followed by the announcement of judgment (vv. 6–7). The punishment fits the crime. There will be no vision, divination, or light for such prophets, and they will be disgraced (vv. 6–7). What is unique is the conclusion in verse 8, a dramatic and unequivocal declaration of self-justification by the prophet concerning his own mission and message. This conclusion makes obvious what is implied in the rest of the speech—that the prophet is engaged in a controversy with other prophets. The issue is quite simple, the answer is not easy to discern, and the stakes are high. Who is the true prophet? The one who cries "Peace"? Or the one who declares to "Jacob his transgression and to Israel his sin"?

Micah himself has no doubt. The other prophets in Jerusalem are corrupt because their word can be bought. Therefore such prophets, seers, and diviners will be disgraced, put to shame, left in the dark without vision or answer. But Micah is convinced that he is filled with power and the Spirit of the Lord, which corresponds to justice and might. The true word, at least in his time and place, is one of sin and judgment.

This is by no means the first time such an issue arose in ancient Israel. Jeremiah, always a controversial figure, was challenged by another prophet, Hananiah. Jeremiah prophesied disaster, whereas Hananiah, speaking in the name of the same Lord, prophesied peace (Jer. 27–28). For a while at least, Jeremiah entertained the possibility that he was wrong and Hananiah was right. The word of God, because it comes through human perception, is no dogma; it is always the same and always known. First Kings 22 reports the story of Micaiah ben Imlah, who accused some four hundred prophets of giving a false and misleading word.

How is one to know who is true and who is false? It is an indication of how widespread the problem was that the Old Testament proposes several different ways of resolving the question. Among others, Jeremiah suggests that the true prophet is the one who announces disaster, and the prophet of peace is the false one (Jer. 28:5–9). There are other suggestions, including this passage in Micah and possibly Amos 7:10–17, that professional prophets are false, and those called directly by the Lord are true. Still other texts resolve the matter by observing that subsequent events will reveal the true prophet. He is the one whose words come true. This is accurate, perhaps, but hardly useful in the moment when one has to decide how to act. The Book of Deuteronomy has yet another way of resolving the matter. Anyone who leads the people away from the true and uncompromising worship of the Lord is a false prophet. This is a theological criterion that can be applied to our own situations. Is the word of the "prophet" consistent with the heart of the faith, with what one knows about God?

The second part of our lesson, verses 9–12, contains the most comprehensive of Micah's prophecies of punishment concerning the leaders in Jerusalem and brings the message of chapter 3 to its horrible climax. The indictment (vv. 9–11) includes all political and religious leaders. They combine corruption and greed with a false confidence that the Lord is on their side. Moreover, the announcement of judgment (v. 12) is not limited to the punishment of the leaders but includes Mt. Zion, where the temple stands, and the entire city, thus sweeping up the entire population. Once again, with this announcement we encounter the powerful and difficult notion of corporate guilt and punishment. Because of the actions of some, the entire people will suffer.

Micah is particularly critical of the view popular in his time that because the Lord has chosen Zion as a dwelling place, the people of Jerusalem and Judah have nothing to fear (Mic. 2:6ff.; 3:9–12). On the contrary, the prophet constantly calls attention to the failure of the people, and their leaders in particular, to act with justice. It is the sense of that justice which comes from God and which God expects that stands at the heart of his own vocation (3:8). No holy city, no temple, however sacred, can save a people whose political and religious leaders fail to embody such divine justice. The Lord, says Micah in these chapters, will act to balance the scales. And in this case, such balancing means judgment upon the nation. Because of the corruption of its leadership, the city will become "a heap of ruins," and the place where the temple stands will be "plowed as a field" and become "a wooded height."

Such uncompromising indictment of unjust and self-serving political and religious leaders as the cause of national disaster could be the occasion for serious reflection on the importance of justice in high places.

Psalm 43

Psalm 43 is actually the third strophe or section of a single composition now designated Psalms 42–43.

Psalm 43 is composed of a plea addressed to the Deity (vv. 1–4) and the self-address or refrain (v. 5). The petition addressed to God is quite aggressive, punctuated by a number of imperatives: vindicate (judge), defend, send out, let them lead/bring. There is, in other words, a move away from the character of passivity found in Psalm 42 to a more extroverted, demanding posture. The responsibility, or at least some of it, for the psalmist's welfare and status is shifted to the Deity, who is "commanded" or requested to rectify matters. In addition, God is even accused of dereliction of duty, for not being the adequate source of refuge that God should have been or for even casting away the one who would seek solace in divine protection (v. 2).

What the worshiper desires is God's light and truth, that is, for the worshiper and others to see and understand things as they really are (v. 3a) and to move in pilgrimage to the temple where God dwells (v. 3*b*). The final goal, the ultimate request, is to go to the altar (to offer sacrifice) and there to praise God (v. 4). In spite of life's troubles, worship is seen as the means for confronting and overcoming them.

It is possible that we overpersonalize such a psalm as this and try too hard to discover some individual's face beneath the poetic mask. It is entirely possible that this psalm (Pss. 42–43) was written to be used by worshipers and sung antiphonally as pilgrims set out on their way to some pilgrimage in Jerusalem. The portrayal of the present discontent with life thus forms the backdrop for the expectations of coming worship (see Pss. 84 and 120).

1 Thessalonians 2:9–13

Today's epistolary lection continues directly from last week's New Testament lesson. The topic is still Paul's reflections on the nature of his ministry among the Thessalonians when he was first with them.

The first item mentioned in today's text is his practice of working to support himself financially in his apostolic work. "Labor and toil" often refer specifically to work done for the sake of the gospel, what we would call "church work" (1 Thess. 1:3; Rom. 16:6, 12; 1 Cor. 3:13–15; 15:10; Phil. 2:30). To be sure, Paul has in mind his work of ministry in the broadest sense, but especially in view is his "secular" work as a tentmaker (1 Cor. 4:12; Acts 18:3). His justification for this practice has several elements: providing for the necessities of himself and others (Acts 20:34) and avoiding being a burden on his churches (2 Thess. 3:8). Also related to this was his theological principle of preaching the gospel free of charge (1 Cor. 9:18). To support oneself while preaching the gospel conformed to the more general expectation that Christians would not only work at their jobs but be diligent in doing so (2 Thess. 3:10–13; Eph. 4:28).

A further item is his exemplary behavior. He reminds them of "how pure, upright, and blameless our conduct was toward you believers" (v. 10). The importance of personal examples was well understood in the Greco-Roman world, as seen in the remarks of Julian the Apostate (d. ca. AD 363), in reflecting on the Cynics of an earlier era: "Deeds with them came before words, and if they honoured poverty they themselves seem first to have scorned inherited wealth; if they cultivated modesty, they themselves first practised plain living in every respect; if they tried to expel from the lives of other men the element of theatrical display and arrogance, they themselves first set the example by living in the open market places and the temple precincts, and they opposed luxury by their own practice before they did so in words (*Oration* 7.214, as cited in A. J. Malherbe, *Moral Exhortation: A Greco-Roman Sourcebook* [Philadelphia: Westminster, 1986], p. 39).

To give his remarks more specific point, Paul compares his relationship with his church to that of a "father with his children" (v. 11). Though the image shifts from that of wet nurse (2:7–8), it has the same effect of rendering his relationship with his church as intensely personal and intimate. It was common for him to view himself as the father of the churches he established and of Christians whom he converted (1 Cor. 4:14–15, 17; 2 Cor. 6:13; Gal. 4:19). Like a parent, he could be stern in rebuking immature behavior (1 Cor. 3:1–4), but also tender in nurturing growth (1 Cor. 4:14).

In presenting himself as an exemplary father, Paul conforms to the well-established practice within the Graeco-Roman moral tradition. This is illustrated especially well in the remarks of Pseudo-Isocrates (ca. fourth century BC): "Nay, if you will but recall your father's principles, you will have from your own house a noble illustration of what I am telling you. For he did not belittle virtue nor pass his life in indolence; on the contrary, he trained his body by toil, and by his spirit he withstood dangers. Nor did he love wealth inordinately . . . neither did he order his existence sordidly, . . . I have produced a sample of the nature of Hipponicus (the father), after whom you should pattern your life as after an example, regarding his conduct as your law, and striving to imitate and emulate your father's virtue; for it were a shame . . . for children not to imitate the noble among their ancestors" (*To Demonicus* 9–11).

Several elements of Paul's fatherly ministering are mentioned: exhorting, encouraging, and charging (v. 12). The first two refer to the positive, more gentle work of guidance and nurture, whereas the third has a sterner element. The sense is captured especially well by NEB: "appealing to you by encouragement, as well as by solemn injunctions." Both the softer and harder, the positive and negative, dimensions of the task had a single purpose—to get them "to live lives worthy of the God who calls you into his kingdom and glory" (v. 12, REB). To live "upward" in response to the noble calling of God and to conform one's life in an appropriately "high" manner is to adopt a life-style worthy of the kingdom (2 Thess. 1:5; 2:14; Eph. 4:1; Phil. 1:27; Col. 1:10; 1 Pet. 5:10).

At this point, the *Common Lectionary* breaks off the epistolary text, doubtless because of the severity of the language Paul uses in verses 13–16 to describe the opposition of the Jews to the gospel. It is commonly read as one of the most anti-Jewish texts in the New Testament, and for this reason it has figured prominently in Jewish-Christian dialogue and in ecumenical efforts in this regard. Some scholars have argued that this section is a later interpolation.

The final section of the chapter (vv. 17–20) turns again to personal concerns—Paul's anxiety at not being able to see the Thessalonians and his justified pride in their steadfastness and fidelity to the gospel (vv. 17–20). It is the concern of an anxious parent who is unable to see her or his children and the recognition that there is no substitute for a face-to-face visit (3:6, 10; Rom. 1:11; 2 Tim. 1:4). We are also hearing a father boast about his children, who are for him a source of constant joy (3:9). His hope for their acceptance and vindication "before our Lord Jesus at his coming" (v. 19; 3:13; 4:15; 5:23; 2 Thess. 2:1, 8; 1 Cor. 15:23; James 5:7–8) also expresses the inmost desire of the Christian parent.

As was the case in last week's epistolary lection, the primary focus here is on the nature of ministry. Yet the concerns expressed here loom larger than this. The worthwhileness of a parental example obviously has vast import for Christian moral teaching. Parents can be charged to be worthy examples, and children can be charged to be grateful for parents whose lives are exemplary.

Matthew 23:1–12

Matthew 23:1 begins the fifth and last of the major sections of teaching in this Gospel. This section ends at 26:1 and has at its center the apocalyptic speech of chapter 24. Because the Synoptic apocalypses are traditionally read the First Sunday of Advent, the lessons from Matthew during this season after Pentecost will not include chapter 24. This teaching section is a compilation of sayings and, like the other four, is not to be regarded as a single discourse. Some of these teachings are paralleled in Mark; more are found in Luke; but clearly, they are gathered here from a variety of settings.

It is not possible to recover the original contexts, but obviously, Matthew did not regard that as important. Jesus' teachings have been brought forward to address the Matthean situation.

In 23:1, the crowds are included in the audience for the sayings that follow. Perhaps Matthew is joining this section to the preceding, picturing the multitude that gathered during Jesus' debates with religious leaders. However, it is quite clear, at least beginning at verse 5, that the real audience consists of the disciples, for it is to them the warnings and instructions are addressed. In other words, in Matthew 23:1–12 Jesus is talking to his church, and especially to its leaders. At 24:1, that the disciples are the intended audience for Jesus' discourse becomes even more explicit.

And what is Jesus saying to the church? In general terms, Jesus warns against arrogance and self-exaltation among leaders in the faith community. The method of the warning is to point to the scribes and Pharisees as negative examples. That the scribes and Pharisees were skilled in and devoted to the precepts of Moses is not questioned. That they were successors to Moses as teachers of Israel is accepted and affirmed (vv. 2–3). This endorsement is in accord with 5:17–18. The warning, however, points elsewhere to two glaring weaknesses among the scribes and Pharisees: the failure to practice their teaching and the love of place and honor. Matthew's rebuke seems general, as though all scribes and Pharisees were guilty. Actually, the rabbis themselves lamented and condemned these evils among their number, just as Christian leaders do within their ranks. That the law was loved and followed by many is amply testified (Pss. 1:2; 119:97).

Our lection is reminiscent of 6:1–18 which addresses the same problems of love of chief seats, special greetings, and titles of honor. The phylacteries and fringes refer to special attire worn especially at prayer time. Phylacteries were leather boxes containing Scripture verses (Deut. 6:6, 8; 11:18), and fringes were tassels on the corners of prayer shawls (Deut. 22:12). The charge here is that they had become quite ornate and decorative. The titles—rabbi, father, and master (vv. 8–10)—are to be rejected because all are brothers and sisters before one teacher, father, and master. The closing verses (vv. 11, 12) are appropriate in principle but are clearly independent sayings of Jesus found in other contexts in the Gospels. For example, see Matthew 20:25–28 and Luke 22:25–27.

It is quite clear that Matthew is not simply reciting the flaws to be found among synagogue leaders so the Christian leaders can say, "I thank God I am not as they are," thereby revealing that they are. Matthew is addressing the problem that infected Judaism, early Christianity, and the church ever since— the love of place and preference among the servants of God. The restrictions in our text are severe and allow no titles, a practice followed by some groups. In some such groups, pride and love of recognition show up even in humble terms such as "Brother." But the point of the text is clear and is found repeatedly in the teaching of Jesus. Neither the problem nor its solution lies in clothing and terms designating one's place in the community. Until the model of Jesus' ministry is embraced, games such as prizes for the most humble will continue.

Proper 27 [32]
(Sunday between November 6 and 12 inclusive)

Joshua 24:1–3*a*, 14–25;
Psalm 78:1–7; or
Wisdom of Solomon 6:12–16 or Amos 5:18–24;
Wisdom of Solomon 6:17–20 or Psalm 70;
1 Thessalonians 4:13–18;
Matthew 25:1–13

The narrative account of Joshua's conquest supplies the Old Testament reading for the *Common Lectionary* for today. The opening section of Psalm 78, a historical psalm, recalls God's injunction to Israel to teach their children so that future generations would remember the marvelous works done by God in the past.

In other lectionary traditions, there are two options for the Old Testament. The first option is the description of Wisdom personified as a woman, whereas the second option is the prophetic warning where Amos confronts Israel with the reality of the impending day of the Lord, criticizes empty, ritualistic practices, and calls instead for justice and righteousness to be realized in Israel's community life. For the response, there are also two options. The first is the sequel to the Wisdom of Solomon text just mentioned, where the pursuit of wisdom is presented in the most attractive terms imaginable. Alternatively, Psalm 70, a lament, unfolds a prayer of desperation in which the psalmist urgently calls on God for rescue and help.

Eschatological themes are prominent in today's epistolary text, where Paul clarifies puzzling features of his preaching about the coming of Christ, thereby reassuring the community of Thessalonian believers. The Gospel reading from Matthew, the parable of the wise and foolish bridesmaids, is the first of three eschatological sections in chapter 25. Although similar in tone to the epistolary text, it especially emphasizes the need to be alert.

Joshua 24:1–3*a*, 14–25

This reading consists of selections from the account of the covenant made at Shechem under the leadership of Joshua. In the wider biblical narrative that runs from Genesis through 2 Kings, Joshua 24 is a pivotal chapter. On the one hand, it looks back, concluding the account of the fulfillment of the promise of progeny and land to Abraham (Gen. 12:1–4); having become a great nation, the descendants have now completed the occupation of the promised land. On the other hand, the chapter looks forward, establishing the basis for the life of the people in that land in a covenant with the God who gave it to them. Will Israel be faithful to the God who has been faithful to them? Will they keep their promises as Yahweh has kept his?

Within the Book of Joshua, our lesson is part of a second farewell address by Joshua, the first coming in chapter 23. The setting for both addresses is established by 24:29–31, the account of the death and burial of Joshua. The fact that we have two versions of the last will and testament of Joshua indicates something of the complex literary history of the book. Chapter 23, which comes from the deuteronomistic editors who put together the history contained in the books of Deuteronomy through 2 Kings, contains a sermon concerning the forms of Israel's worship of Yahweh in the land. Chapter 24, which also bears the marks of deuteronomistic editing, preserves ancient traditions concerning the establishment of a covenant. Its major concern is Israel's exclusive worship of Yahweh.

The full account of the covenant ceremony includes an introduction (vv. 1-2a) in which the people are summoned to Shechem, Joshua's speech recounting Yahweh's saving acts as the basis for Israel's faith (vv. 2b–13), Joshua's challenge and the response of the people (vv. 14–24), and the account of the covenant ceremonies, concluding with the dismissal of the people to their assigned territories (vv. 25–28).

Although the text presents itself as an account of an event that happened once just before Joshua died, there is strong evidence that it reflects a rite that was reenacted periodically if not regularly in ancient Israel. Internal evidence for this conclusion consists of the liturgical features of the account, including the solemnity and the location of the gathering, the leader's questions and the people's responses (vv. 15–24), the concluding description of what has happened (v. 25), the setting up of a monument (vv. 26–27), and the dismissal (v. 28). The external evidence that this is the reflection of a recurrent ceremony, the renewal of the Sinai covenant (Exod. 19–24), is seen in the other reports of such events (2 Kings 23; Neh. 9–10), including the parallel report in Joshua 8:30–35 and the covenantal structure of the Book of Deuteronomy.

Joshua begins the ceremony with a recital that is common to covenant rituals, the account of the history of salvation (vv. 2b–13). The purpose of this account is to identify the God with whom the covenant is made, to indicate that (and how) Yahweh has chosen a people, and to testify that this God keeps promises. The shortest form of that history is the prelude to the Decalogue in Exodus 20:1: "I am the Lord your God who brought you out of the land of Egypt." Various forms of this confession appear throughout the Old Testament (see esp. Deut. 6:20–25; 26:5–9). The covenant is established with a free decision of the people, affirmed solemnly (vv. 16–18, 21). Like a contractual agreement, it is sealed by witnesses (v. 22; cf. Ruth 4:9–11). The contents of the covenant are the laws (here "statutes and ordinances," v. 25) that define the lives of those bound to Yahweh (Exod. 20–24). Lest there be any doubt about the contents of the laws that bind the people to Yahweh, the covenant is written down (vv. 26–27). The tone of the report about the inscribed stone implies what is explicit in other accounts of covenants: those who obey will be blessed, and those who disobey will be cursed (Josh. 8:34; Deut. 27–28).

Behind this passage stand at least two quite distinct situations for the people of God, corresponding to the final editorial stage and the older covenant traditions. The material was given its final form in the time of the Babylonian Exile, when the descendants of Joshua's generation no longer possessed the promised land, when the blessing had turned to curse. The older traditions relate to an unknown era—and very likely more than one period—after the time of Joshua, perhaps as early as the time of the judges. In both situations, the central point, the most pressing concern, is expressed in Joshua's challenge: "Choose this day whom you will serve . . . but as for me and my household, we will serve the Lord" (v. 15).

In the earlier situation, reflecting the crisis for Israel in the land, the people are faced with the choice between Yahweh and the gods of either their ancestors or of the native inhabitants of the land. Behind this language (vv. 2, 14) stands the old perspective that deities are limited geographically and that every land has its god or gods. Joshua insists that the people must renounce allegiance to all other gods for this one, Yahweh. Verse 14 contains the only reference in the Pentateuch to the gods worshiped in Egypt.) Thus the center of this covenant is the substance of the first commandment, the radical and uncompromising requirement that worship of Yahweh must be undivided. Moreover, the older traditions indicate that the covenant not only binds people to God but also people to people.

In the time of the Babylonian Exile, when the deuteronomistic history was completed, the call to exclusive and unswerving fidelity to Yahweh would be the same, now heard by people living far beyond the bounds of the land, even in the region from which their ancestors came. They could see around them powerful alternatives, specifically the gods of Babylon, and must have wondered if the Lord was present in foreign lands. Beyond that, this text served one of the central themes of the full history of Israel, namely, the explanation of the reasons for the Exile. Like the Book of Deuteronomy, this covenant states the faithfulness to Yahweh as the requirement for Israel's continued existence in the land. The Exile is thus understood as punishment for a history of apostasy. Finally, this passage contains good news, even for exiles in Babylon. The covenant can be renewed once again if Israel is willing and responds positively, just as her ancestors did in the time of Joshua.

Psalm 78:1–7

Portions of Psalm 78 were read for Proper 21 [26]. Like Psalms 105, 106, 135, and 136, Psalm 78 is one of the few "historical" psalms in the book. Like Joshua 24, the opening of Psalm 78 is a call to observance of the law.

Verses 1–4 give the impression of an individual speaker who sets out to instruct an audience on the lessons of the past. The form of the material in these verses is perhaps patterned after a model used by wisdom teachers in instructing their students. The NRSV translation, perhaps influenced by the use of verse 2 in Matthew 13:35, gives the impression that what is being taught is a dark secret previously unknown. As verse three makes clear, what is being expounded is something already known. The NJPSV translates verses 2–3 as follows:

> I will expound a theme,
>   hold forth on the lessons of the past,
> things we have heard and known,
>   that our fathers have told us.

The psalm stresses the need and the desire to make known the past to the future generation (see Deut. 6:4–9). The present generation stands as the link between past and future. To serve as a transmitter of the traditions is depicted as a divinely ordained requirement. For this reason, Judaism has always been a tradition-oriented religion.

Three factors are associated with the need to make ever present the traditions of the past to the children that are our responsibility. (1) The new generation learns the tradition so they may pass it on to the children yet unborn. (2) The tradition provides the basis for hope in life by stressing the correlation of past and future events. (3) Only the possession of the tradition will allow for knowledge and observance of the divine requirements. Each generation must view itself as an indispensable link in the chain of tradition, a chain to be broken only with disastrous consequences.

Wisdom of Solomon 6:12–16

In this first option for the Old Testament lesson, we have a highly poetic presentation of Wisdom personified. In many ways, the passage encapsulates major themes of the book as a whole, for it presents wisdom as an eminently worthwhile pursuit, something of inestimable benefit to every human being. Even though this outlook characterizes much wisdom literature, it receives specially poignant treatment in Wisdom of Solomon.

For one thing, wisdom is not simply regarded as a quality of life we should pursue or embody. Nor even is it heralded as a virtue in the same sense that the Greeks did, who placed it at the head of the list of cardinal virtues, followed by justice, courage, and self-control. Instead, it is personified as Lady Wisdom, thus taking on a much more realistic, substantial nature.

Among the elements of wisdom that are especially treated in today's text are its unqualified desirability and irresistible attractiveness. Wisdom's unfading radiance calls to mind images of glowing brightness that are welcome in any setting, especially where darkness reigns and ignorance and misunderstanding abound. The text also insists that Wisdom seeks out seekers of wisdom, taking the initiative in trying to find those worthy of her delights. But we are also reminded that seekers of wisdom will not be disappointed, that the true quest for wisdom will not be an intellectual, moral wild goose chase. The benefits of this fulfilled search are tranquillity, greater understanding, and a calming sense of satisfaction.

Although today's text offers little help in specifying what constitutes wisdom, it does have the salutary effect of presenting it as eminently worth striving for. So at the very least, it serves as an invitation.

Amos 5:18–24

With the readings for today and next Sunday, we prepare to meet the end of the liturgical year with our faces turned toward the future. Two prophetic texts with eschatological themes, from Amos for today and from Zephaniah for next Sunday, begin to set the stage for the conclusion of the season and the year that ends with the festival of Christ the King.

This reading from the Book of Amos, brief as it is, contains two distinct units of prophetic discourse, verses 18–20 and verses 21–24. Each is a different form of prophetic speech, and each has its own particular message.

Amos 5:18–20, like many other prophetic addresses, begins with the cry traditionally translated "woe" (RSV), rendered more neutrally in NRSV "Alas." Typically, what follows this exclamation is a description of the prophet's audience in terms of their sinful actions. Thus Amos 6:4ff. reads:

> Alas for those who lie on beds of ivory,
>   and lounge on their couches . . . " (See also Isaiah 5:8–22.)

In this case, however, the prophet accuses those "who desire the day of the Lord." With a series of rhetorical questions and metaphors, he then attacks and corrects some unspecified false expectations concerning the day of the Lord.

The day of the Lord, which later becomes an apocalyptic expectation of the end of history, is a persistent and important theme in the message of Amos. Obviously, however, expectation of the day of the Lord was already well-established when this prophet came onto the scene in the middle of the eighth century BC. Although it is not possible to know for certain what Amos' audience expected, it seems most likely that the day of the Lord was associated in their thinking with the ancient tradition of the holy war. As in the holy war, on that day the Lord would arise to defeat his enemies, usually believed to be also the enemies of the Lord's people. In the thought of Amos, the day of the Lord is still the day of the Lord's warfare against his enemies. The difference, however, is that his own people, Israel, have become the enemy!

So Amos 5:18–20 is filled with reversals and irony. The people who look forward to the day will see it, but it will be darkness and not light. Just as one escapes from a lion and is met by a bear, or escapes into a house to be bitten by a snake, so will be the day of the Lord for Israel. The little discourse is thus an announcement of judgment upon the people, not of the end of history, but of their military defeat and exile.

In the second unit, verses 21–24, the prophet quotes the Lord directly. The speech is not an announcement of the future, like most of the individual discourses in the Book of Amos, but a prophetic torah (law, instruction) speech, like the ones found in Isaiah 1:10–17 and Micah 6:6–8. Following the pattern of a priest's response to a question from the laity concerning a particular matter of sacrifice, worship, or the distinction between clean and unclean, the prophet hears Yahweh give an answer that is quite contrary to what is expected. The purpose of the speech is thus to instruct people in the actions God expects from them.

The torah speech has two unequal parts, verses 21–23 specifying what Yahweh does not want, and verse 24 stating what Yahweh wishes. The matters rejected include most of the important aspects of the cult: worship gatherings (v. 21), various forms of sacrifice (v. 22), and the lyrics and music of worship (v. 23). We cannot be certain whether Amos means to reject all forms of established cultic practice or simply to insist that such things are no substitute for right behavior. Taken in themselves, however, these lines amount to a radical indictment of established religion.

What God expects is the full and regular outpouring of justice and righteousness. These two powerful words frequently are linked in prophetic address, as elsewhere in the Old Testament. To Amos, justice refers to what we would call due process (cf. 2:6–7; 5:10–12) and the fair and equitable distribution of resources. The prophet is particularly concerned about the oppression of the poor by the rich (4:1–3; 5:10–13; 6:4–7), about equity and fairness in human society. But the substance of justice stems from the fact that the God of Israel is just and will not tolerate unfair actions. Righteousness refers more to the internal characteristics of devotion and piety that are the sources of just behavior.

When these two units are considered together, they point to the fuller message of Amos. Because of the failure of justice and righteousness, and the arrogant reliance upon ritual practice, the people of God are doomed to destruction at the hand of a foreign invader. Looking beyond Amos to the belief in the reign of God as expressed in this liturgical season, this text reminds us that the day of the Lord is to be defined by justice and righteousness. The kingdom of God is that time and place when God's justice reigns among all.

Wisdom of Solomon 6:17–20

Wisdom as a female figure is presented as a path to the good and faithful life. Probably verse 21 was the conclusion to this section, which indicates that the instruction was especially addressed to rulers and would-be monarchs.

The form of this text is what the ancients called a sorites, a form especially employed by the Stoic teachers. In a sorites, the predicate of the preceding statement becomes the subject of the next statement so that the thought is built accumulatively. The path is thus laid out from the initial impulse to the final, full realization. Desire for instruction leads to love of wisdom, love of wisdom is expressed by living according to wisdom, living according to wisdom provides the assurance of immortality, and immortality brings one into the presence of God, into the divine kingdom. Thus if one's final goal is to be achieved, the steps along the way must be carefully observed.

Psalm 70

For all practical purposes, Psalm 70 is identical with Psalm 40:13–17. In the latter psalm, this material forms one of the pleas in the psalm for deliverance and salvation in a time of trouble (see also Ps. 40:11). The content of Psalm 70 would suggest that the psalm was composed for use by persons who were under attack and threatened by opponents, perhaps false accusers bringing charges of wrongdoing or, on the basis of Psalm 40, perhaps national enemies attacking the Judean king.

Psalm 70:1–3 provides a good example of what has been called the double wish of the lament psalms, because the request to be saved is balanced by a request for the destruction of one's enemies or opponents. Frequently, the calamity that is requested to befall one's enemy is very similar to the condition that the one praying faced. Thus numerous psalms reflect something of that attitude, so widely felt, namely, that those who plan evil should have a corresponding evil beset them. Christians often shy away in horror from the prayers in the psalms that request a destruction or a calamity to fall on one's enemies. Such sentiments seem contrary to the teaching and life of Jesus. We must, however, understand that the psalms sought to give full and appropriate outlets for people to express their true feelings and sentiments. It may be that only by verbalizing such sentiments and expressions can they be overcome or transcended. Expressions of one's truest and deepest feelings may be necessary before a person can release them and replace them with better feelings. In many ways, some of the psalms probably allowed persons to vent their anger and hostility to such a degree of animosity and with such a degree of revenge that the mere recital of such cursing wishes relieved the anxiety and pent-up emotions of the worshiper (Ps. 109).

The opening verse of Psalm 70, with its plea for God to hasten and to deliver, is followed by two verses asking that the enemies be put to shame and turned back; that is, make their plans go awry so they will end up being shamed. If the prayer was originally offered by the king, then the adversaries could be foreign powers or nations who were threatening hostile military action.

Verse 4 is an intercessory prayer, although the worshiper is included in the group being prayed for. The intercessor requests that all those who seek God and love his salvation rejoice and proclaim forever that God is great. This is obviously a prayer asking that the king and his subjects be victorious over the enemy or that they be spared a possible impending conflict.

In the final verse, the worshiper reverts to an appeal in his or her own behalf. The fact that the one praying is described as poor and needy does not mean that the person was destitute and poverty-stricken. Such expressions are metaphorical statements characterizing the person in the most sharply drawn and the humblest terms in order to evoke God's aid.

1 Thessalonians 4:13–18

There were a conspicuous number of Gentile converts among the membership of the Thessalonian church (Acts 17:4; 1 Thess. 1:9–10). With little or no familiarity with the Jewish apocalyptic tradition, especially as it developed during the Hellenistic period, the so-called intertestamental period (e.g., Isa. 26:19; Dan. 12:2–3; 2 Macc. 7:9–14), many of them were understandably puzzled about certain features of Christian eschatology. In some traditions of Greek thought, it was possible to conceive of the immortality of the soul. By this was meant that the soul had an eternal existence, but could take up residence periodically and temporarily within a human body; that is, be reincarnated. In this view, the body was thought of as a tomb in which the soul was captured. Although Greeks could look forward to a time when the soul would be released from the body and return to its eternal state, they did not find the notion of a resurrected, or revivified, body attractive. When Christian preachers spoke of the resurrected body of Christ and the time when the bodies of the dead would be raised, the Gentiles were bound to have questions.

Today's text points us to some of these questions raised by young converts to the faith. From remarks by Paul in this passage, it appears that one of their questions was not so much *whether* there would be a resurrection (cf. 1 Cor. 15:12) or even *what form of existence* they would experience. Their question was rather what would happen to those who died prior to the coming of Christ.

It is an understandable query. Paul had been with them only a short time during his founding visit, and he doubtless was able to introduce them to only the barest essentials of the early Christian kerygma. Perhaps Timothy had followed through with his instruction (3:1–10). But as we have seen, a central element of the early missionary preaching to Gentiles was the proclamation of the risen Christ, who would come at a future date to rescue the saved from the coming wrath of God (1:10). The natural expectation was that this would occur soon, certainly within their lifetime (Rom. 13:12; 1 Cor. 7:29, 31; 16:22; Heb. 10:37; James 5:8; 1 Pet. 4:7; Rev. 22:20). Indeed, Paul himself at one point expected that he would be alive at the coming of Christ (4:17), although he apparently finally came to reckon with the possibility that even he might die prior to the Lord's coming (2 Cor. 4:16–5:10).

Assume, then, that a person has responded to the gospel, becomes a Christian, and fully expects to be rescued from the coming wrath by the returning Son of God. Then assume that this person dies, or falls asleep (v. 13). The natural question is, Does that person lose out on the promised deliverance of the coming Messiah?

Paul's response is to reassure those Christians who are troubled about their fellow Christians who have died: "God will bring with him [Christ] those who have died" (v. 14). They are reminded that the destiny of the dead lies with the God who raised Jesus from the dead. God, like Jesus, should be seen as the "Lord of both the dead and the living" (Rom. 14:9).

Paul goes even further in his answer to their question. He establishes the sequence of events at the end time. For comparison, one might recall a similar sequence in 1 Corinthians 15:23: "each in his own order: Christ the first fruits, then at his coming those who belong to Christ." Here no distinction is made between the dead and the living who belong to Christ at his coming. This, however, is precisely the distinction made in today's text: first the dead in Christ will rise (v. 16); then in a second stage those in Christ who are alive "who are left, will be caught up in the clouds together with them to meet the Lord in the air" (v. 17). Thus, according to Paul's vision of the end time, the dead in Christ will be resurrected and will be joined by those who are still alive, so that a single host of believers will join Christ in the heavens. It is interesting to note that Paul does not address the point here whether those who are alive in Christ will be transformed into another form of existence, although this can be inferred from his discussion in 1 Corinthians 15:35–50.

What precipitates this is the "coming of the Lord" (v. 15; cf. 2:19; 3:13; 5:23; 2 Thess. 2:1, 8; 1 Cor. 15:23; James 5:7–8). His coming is described in terms drawn from Jewish apocalyptic: the Lord descends from heaven, the archangel calls, and the trumpet of God sounds (v. 16; cf. Matt. 24:30–31; Mark 13:26–27; 2 Thess. 1:7).

The intention of this set of instructions is paraenetic: "Therefore encourage one another with these words" (v. 18). This is worth noting because eschatology often functions in Christian preaching to terrify rather than comfort. It is also worth noting that Paul leaves much unanswered. The focus of his remarks is on those who are "in Christ," and thus he leaves unanswered the question of the fate of those outside of Christ. Neither does he in this context discuss the agenda that he follows in 1 Corinthians 15, namely, the kind of body with which we will be raised. In a word, he responds directly to the questions posed by his hearers and attempts to answer them simply and directly, without complicating their understanding even further. In this instance, less is better.

As we approach this text homiletically, we do well to note the concrete setting in which these eschatological questions arose. The questions of the Thessalonians were quite specific, and they arose because of their expectation of an imminent return of Christ. Naturally, our situation is different, and our questions will also be different. Even so, it is a common Christian concern to wonder about "those who have fallen asleep," even more, to grieve over them. But Paul calls us not to grieve "as others do who have no hope" (v. 13). Like everyone else, Christians die. This is inescapable. But what distinguishes the Christian understanding of death is our fundamental belief that "Jesus died and rose again"(v. 14) and that the God in whom Jesus placed his own destiny is the God in whom we have placed ours. From this cardinal element of our faith does Christian hope spring. It is this that renders Christian exhortation as reassuring rather than unsettling (v. 18).

Matthew 25:1–13

On these last three Sundays before Advent, we will attend to Matthew 25: two parables and the vision of the coming of the Son of Man. This chapter not only concludes the fifth major teaching section begun at 23:1 but also marks the end of Jesus' ministry to the public (26:1). From this point on, Jesus will move toward his passion in the presence of close friends and disciples.

Matthew 25:1–13 contains the parable of the ten maidens, found only in the first Gospel but with fragments of similar parables in Luke 12:35–36 and 13:25. Matthew offers very brief commentary on the parable. In verse 1, the word "then" tells the reader that the story concerns the future, and in this case, the future that governs the discussion from 24:36 to 25:46—the certain but uncertain final day and hour. In verse 13, the exhortation to "watch" is commentary on the entire section and not particularly on the parable of the maidens. In this parable, it is not watchfulness that is being enjoined; after all, the wise maidens slept also. The issue is preparedness in the face of uncertainty. The major commentary on this story, as we will see, is offered by the context.

Gospel parables are basically of two types: those that offer a surprise of grace at the end (a party for a prodigal, a full day's pay for one-hour workers, a tax collector justified, and others) and those that follow the direct course from cause to effect as surely as the harvest comes from what is sown. There are no gifts and parties. Together the two types present justice and grace, either of which becomes distorted without the other. Today's parable moves straight from cause to predictably painful effect; the door is shut and will not be opened.

The preacher will find in the commentaries ample discussion of wedding practices in the writer's time and place, clarifying for modern readers the text's attention on the groom and on the movement of the groom's wedding party. In this brief space, we need to attend to Matthew's emphasis in the story: "The bridegroom was delayed" (v. 5). When one looks at the larger context, the delay theme is seen more clearly as the key to the story. This parable is one of three successive stories bearing this theme: "My master is delayed" (24:48); "As the bridegroom was delayed" (25:5); and "After a long time the master of those slaves came" (25:19). It may have been that on the lips of Jesus the parable was designed to speak of preparation in view of the kingdom having arrived at the door, but in the Evangelist's hand, the story is in the futuristic mode. Perhaps Matthew's church faces the problem of how appropriately to live and work as Christians in view of a delayed Parousia. As the parable has it, the delay created the crisis for some of the maidens; the delay was the circumstance about which some proved wise and some foolish; the delay triggered the series of events ending in the final exclusion of those unprepared.

We do not know how widespread and how intense the expectation of the imminent return of Christ really was. However, because many New Testament writers devote attention to the delay (Mark 13:7; 2 Pet. 3:3–10), we may surmise that such an expectation lay at the heart of the faith of many. But in the face of the problems created by the delay, Matthew refuses to abandon eschatological fulfillment. Whatever the nature and extent of present realizations of the kingdom, the future remains the time of completion and reckoning.

Matthew presents, then, a theology for the delay, for the ongoing life of the church in the world. The maidens who calculated an immediate arrival of the groom were the ones in trouble. But accurate or inaccurate calculating is not at all the issue. The issue has to do with responsible behavior *in the meantime*. After all, it is not the coming of the bridegroom that makes some wise and some foolish; it merely reveals who is.

Proper 28 [33]
(Sunday between November 13 and 19 inclusive)

Judges 4:1–7;
Psalm 123; or
Zephaniah 1:7, 12–18;
Psalm 90:1–8 (9–11) 12;
1 Thessalonians 5:1–11;
Matthew 25:14–30

For today's *Common Lectionary* Old Testament reading, we have the opening section of the Deborah story (Judg. 4:1–5:31), where she emphatically states the command of the Lord to Barak, son of Abinoam. The response is provided by Psalm 123, a brief communal lament expressing despair for having to experience insults from the arrogant and proud but also hope that God will extend help.

The other Old Testament reading is supplied by portions of Zephaniah 1 that especially stress the impending day of the Lord. Reminders of the transience and unpredictability of life are repeated in Psalm 90, a communal lament, and thus serve as suitable preparation for pondering God's coming.

In the New Testament lesson, Paul instructs the church that the proper way to prepare for the Lord's return is not by calculating the time and place but by conducting oneself properly and establishing meaningful relationships within the community of believers. So also speaks Jesus in the parable of the talents, where he concedes that the end may not occur until "after a long time," but insists that the question of how one has handled one's position of trust will eventually be raised.

Judges 4:1–7

This text brings us to the conclusion of the semicontinuous Old Testament readings for the season. All but three of those lessons came from the Pentateuch. Those for the previous two Sundays from the Book of Joshua concerned Israel's occupation of the land of Canaan and the beginning of its life in the promised land. This single reading from the Book of Judges summarizes the circumstances of Israel in the first era after Joshua, the period of the judges before the establishment of the monarchy.

This periodization of biblical history is one of the characteristics of the deuteronomistic history (Deut. through 2 Kings), which interprets the time from the death of Joshua to the Babylonian Exile as a history of apostasy. The main periods are defined in terms of the leaders of Israel, from Moses and Joshua to the judges to the kings. In that scheme, the period of the judges is viewed as a time of chaos, making it patently obvious that a stronger government would be required. After reporting the death of the Levite's concubine and war among the tribes (Judg. 19–21), the deuteronomic editor concludes the book with the observation: "In those days there was no king in Israel; all the people did what was right in their own eyes" (Judg. 21:25).

The reading for today comes from the central part of the book (Judg. 3:7–16:31) that includes a series of stories of individual "judges," charismatic political and religious leaders. Preceding those stories is a section reporting the completion of the taking of the land (1:1–2:5) and a summary of the era (2:6–3:6). That summary interpretation, which is reflected in our lesson for the day, addresses a historical and theological problem: If Yahweh gave Israel the land in the time of Joshua, why did the people continue to struggle with the native inhabitants? The answer is twofold: enemies were left in order to punish Israel for its apostasy (2:1–3), and they were left in order to test Israel, to determine whether or not they would be faithful (2:21–23). So a cycle recurred through the period: Israel sinned, Yahweh gave them into the hand of one of their enemies, who oppressed them for a number of years; Israel cried out to the Lord, who sent a deliverer to save them from the enemy; and the land had rest for a period of years. Then Israel again did what was evil in the sight of the Lord, and the circle turned again.

Our reading is a selection from one of the more extended accounts of this cycle of sin and deliverance, the stories of Deborah and Barak. Judges 4–5 contains two quite distinct traditions of these heroes, one prose and the other poetry. Judges 5, the poetic Song of Deborah, is generally accepted as one of the most ancient pieces of biblical literature. The prose narrative in chapter 4 contains another old tradition that is framed by the deuteronomistic editors in verses 1–3 and verses 23–24. That framework puts the story of the war into the typical pattern: "The Israelites again did what was evil in the sight of the Lord. . . . So the Lord sold them into the hand of King Jabin of Canaan. . . . Then the Israelites cried out to the Lord for help" (vv. 1–3). By the time the story ends, God has put an end to the threat (v. 23, cf. also 5:31b).

Following the introduction, verses 4–10 report Deborah's preparation for the war, including the call of Barak. Against Jabin, Sisera, and their mighty army, including "nine hundred chariots of iron" (v. 3), stand Deborah, Barak, two Israelite tribes, Yahweh, and, surprisingly, a Kenite woman. Behind the story stand the traditions and rituals of the holy war, in which Yahweh is the one who defeats the enemy.

This text will serve to remind preachers and congregations that although the Bible emerged in a patriarchal culture, it is a story of women as well as men. Deborah performs several distinct roles and fills more than one office. She is initially introduced as "a prophetess" (v. 4). The term, which might have designated more than one function in early Israel, is the same as that applied to Miriam, the sister of Moses (Exod. 15:20). It is the feminine form of the same term applied to the classical prophets. In this context, she performs the prophetic function by communicating the word of Yahweh to Barak (vv. 6b–7); this prophetic function repeats a frequent pattern in accounts of holy wars. But she is also identified as a judge. This term fits her in two different senses. Initially she is seen to be performing a legal, juridical function, settling disputes among the Israelites (vv. 3–4). More commonly in the stories of the judges, however, the designation refers to a political or military leader. She acts in this office as well when she goes into battle with Barak, and never as his subordinate but as the one through whom the Lord delivered Israel.

Our lesson breaks off with Deborah's communication of the word of the Lord to Barak. It is followed by Barak's expression of reluctance and Deborah's agreement to go with him. When she prophecies that Barak will not get glory for the victory but Sisera will be turned over to a woman (v. 9), the reader will think the woman to be Deborah. But it will turn out that Jael, another heroic woman, will kill the enemy general with a tent peg through his temple, after he has escaped from Barak.

It is an exciting and bloody tale, but it bears a heavy theological burden, mainly in the editorial framework. It may provide the occasion for reflection on the ways of God in history. Human beings, even heroic ones, act, but finally it is the Lord, in response to prayer, who delivers. The Lord is seen to have delivered the people into the power of their enemies because of their sins. Moreover, it is not only men but women—including powerful charismatic leaders and ordinary ones such as Jael—who serve as instruments of the Lord. Finally, the modern interpreter should reflect for a moment on modern warfare before contrasting this ancient heroic tale with contemporary civilization.

Psalm 123

This is one of the pilgrim psalms (see the discussion of Psalm 122 for the First Sunday of Advent). The psalm begins with a first person singular speaker ("I" in v. 1) but shifts to the plural in verse 2 following. This perhaps suggests that the psalm was sung antiphonally by the pilgrims as they made their way to a festival. Verse 1 and verses 3–4 are expressed as a prayer to God, but verse 2 is a confessional statement of human to human address.

In verse 2, the hope is expressed that one's concentration will be so focused on God that one can obey the Deity like a servant who obeys the commands of another merely by receiving hand signals without verbal communication having to take place.

The pleas for divine mercy in verses 3–4 speak of a situation of distress caused by being held in contempt by others. The lack of anything specific in the description makes it impossible to sense anything about the trouble other than its creation of a feeling of alienation.

Zephaniah 1:7, 12–18

This reading continues and expands one of the main themes of last week's Old Testament lesson from Amos, the announcement of the day of the Lord. In fact, Zephaniah must have had the Book of Amos before him as he composed this announcement, for 1:15 picks up the language of Amos 5:18 and 8:8–14 characterizing the day as one of darkness, and 1:13 is a paraphrase of Amos 5:11.

According to the first verse of the book, Zephaniah was active during the reign of King Josiah of Judah, which we date 640–609 BC. Other seventh century prophets were Jeremiah, Nahum, and Habakkuk. One of the most important international events during the time of Josiah was the fall of the Assyrian city of Nineveh in 612 BC. Whether the conflicts that led to the fall of Nineveh or some earlier international crises have influenced the message of Zephaniah is not known. The prophet sees disaster on the horizon, but his interpretation is moral and theological: Judah and Jerusalem will be punished for their sins.

Our assigned reading comes from the first major section of the book, 1:2–2:3, a graphic announcement of judgment against Judah and Jerusalem. Except for the occasional messenger formulas (1:2, 3, 7, 10) and the concluding paragraph (2:1–3), in which the prophet calls for the humble among the people to assemble and seek the lord, the speaker throughout is the Lord. The doom announced is so total that it is almost apocalyptic. It alternates between a cosmic destruction of all living things (1:2–3a, 18) and the destruction of the wicked inhabitants of Judah and Jerusalem, or some particular group among the people (1:3b–6, 8–9). In particular, the Lord singles out those who have led or participated in idolatrous worship and refuse to inquire of the Lord (1:4–6), the officials and even the sons of the king (1:8). In addition, the Lord condemns people for their attitudes as well as their actions, especially those who say in their hearts, "The Lord will not do good, nor will he do harm" (1:12). Whereas Amos had accused people of religious arrogance, Zephaniah attacks religious cynicism.

As today's reading begins, the prophet is commanding the people to be silent before the Lord God (1:7). In the end, he is calling for a solemn assembly, for those who are willing to humble themselves to seek righteousness so that they might "perhaps" escape the wrath of God (2:3). What stands between these prophetic injunctions is the description of the sounds and sights of the day of the Lord as judgment day. The sounds and sights are those of warfare, for the day is the time when the Lord will arise to defeat his enemies, not beyond but among the chosen people. (For further discussion of this point, see the comments on last week's Old Testament lesson from the Book of Amos.)

The sound of the day is "bitter," and even the mighty warrior cries out (v. 14). One hears the war trumpet and the battle cry, not of the defenders but of those who attack the fortified cities (v. 16). The sights are visions of attacking armies, plundering hordes (v. 13), of people stumbling about like the blind and blood spilled on the ground (v. 17). Above all, the imagery of darkness and gloom is used both literally and figuratively (v. 15). The message focuses upon the dark side of the intervention of God in history.

As in Amos, this announcement of judgment is directly related to the justice of God. The Lord will bring about the day of wrath because of the sinfulness of the people, especially of their officials, priests, princes, and all those who look cynically upon the Lord's willingness to act in history. As far as the reading for today goes, the prophet's purpose is to make the will of the Lord clear and—through the creative power of the word—to set the future into motion. However, in the paragraph that immediately follows (2:1–3), he holds out the bare possibility that some may escape the wrath to come. In the broader context of the book as a whole, the day of the Lord is to be the initial step in the establishment of the kingdom of God, the reign of the Lord in justice. The punishment is to be purging and cleansing, leaving Jerusalem inhabited by those who are humble, seek the will of God, and do justice and righteousness.

Psalm 90:1–8 (9–11) 12

Portions of this psalm were discussed earlier at Proper 25 [30]. In this psalm, the end of human life can be associated with the theme of judgment and the day of the Lord found in the reading from Zephaniah.

When this psalm sets out to speak of God, in verses 3–6, it presents the Deity as the one who, unhindered and untouched by time, nonetheless places human life under severe strictures of time. God is the one who "uncreates" humans and returns them to the dust from which they came. It is God who sweeps humans away and cuts human life so short. The brevity of people's lives is seen as the work of one for whom there was no beginning and for whom a thousand years of evenings and mornings are no more than a still clearly remembered yesterday or a watch in the night—something that passes while one sleeps without even awareness that it has come and gone. Unlike humans, when time passes, God doesn't. (The minister should be aware of and give expression in preaching to the human feeling of hostility toward God that permeates this psalm.)

Two or perhaps three depictions metaphorically describe the shortness of human life in verses 3–6. Life ends in the dust from which it emerged (v. 3). Its stay and span are like the grass that grows and flourishes only to fade and wither. While it is here, it is somewhat like a dream, insubstantial, experienced but unabiding, fleeting, raising questions of its reality, not forgotten but soon gone, impermanent, and once gone, irretrievable.

In speaking about human beings, in verses 7–10, the psalm cannot avoid speaking about God. Life, with its short span, is lived under divine scrutiny. This means, according to the psalmist, that people experience God's consuming anger and overwhelming wrath (v. 7). It also means that humans live their lives as sinners; open iniquities and secret sins are known to God, who reacts against them in wrath and anger (v. 8). Even if life has the benefit of longevity and one lives out the normal ideal span of seventy years—or beyond the normal, eighty years—these will be full of toil and trouble, soon gone, soon forgotten (probably the connotation of "to fly away").

The pessimism (or extreme realism) of verses 3–10 are somewhat muted by the opening confession of the psalm (vv. 1–2) as well as the petition in verses 10–12. The opening lines confess and affirm God as dwelling place ("home" or "refuge" are also possible as translations). That is, God is home. The frailty and mortality of dying humans can lose some of their threat in the shadow of the everlasting and undying God. Perhaps all of verses 3–10 should be read in light of the affirmation of verses 1–2. If so, it would mean that the great divisions between God and humans—God as everlasting and undying, humans as created and mortal; God as holy, humans as beset with public and private sins—still remain, but confidence in God as home allows the worshipers to live with some security and assurance.

In spite of the psalmist's rather dark and realistic reading of life, the writer does not end in absolute discouragement, or counsel despair, or contemplate suicide, or encourage hedonistic abandonment. Verse 12 is, of all things, an appeal for instruction. To be taught! As if life itself were not a lesson hard enough! The psalmist prays for wisdom so that we will be able to number our days, to calculate our calendars, to live aright so that we may not die awry.

1 Thessalonians 5:1–11

Like last week's epistolary text, today's New Testament lesson addresses an eschatological question. If it was natural to wonder about the fate of those who died before Christ came, it was only natural to wonder *when* Christ would come. It was common to speculate about the "times and seasons" that would presage the coming of Christ (cf. Matt. 24:36; Acts 1:7).

Paul's opening remark is to reassure his readers of the futility of constructing eschatological timetables (v. 1). Much more important than speculating *when* it would come is to know *how* it would come—suddenly and unexpectedly. The image of a thief coming in the night is frequently used to illustrate the unpredictability of the time of the day of the Lord (Matt. 24:43; 2 Pet. 3:10; Rev. 3:3; 16:15; cf. Wisd. of Sol. 18:14–16).

Another favorite image used to depict the sudden coming of the Lord is the woman expecting a child (v. 3). It can be used differently. In Isaiah 13:6–8, the day of the Lord is said to be near, and those unprepared for it are promised that pain and agony will seize them and that they "will be in anguish like a woman in labor" (cf. also Jer. 6:24; Hos. 13:13). In today's text, however, the point of the image is the suddenness with which a woman can go into labor and a child be born (cf. Mark 13:17 and parallels). At the critical moment, the process is irreversible: "There will be no escape" (v. 3).

Both of these images—the stealthy thief and the pregnant woman—serve as vivid reminders that we cannot pinpoint precisely when the moment of crisis comes. We are cautioned against reading false signals. When we hear "peace and security" (v. 3; cf. Jer. 6:14), rather than relaxing our guard we should put our systems on alert. The message here is not to try to calculate the hour, but to be alert so that we are prepared at any hour.

After this first set of warnings about the unpredictability of the time of the Lord's coming, Paul urges us to be in a constant state of preparedness—not that this requires us to be something we are not, or do something we do not normally do. Instead, he instructs us about the true character of Christian existence: "You are all children of the light and children of the day" (v. 5). Christian conversion can be conceived as a transition from darkness to light (1 Pet. 2:9; 1 John 1:5–7). The dualistic outlook reflected here is also common in Jewish apocalyptic thought. But the point of this reassuring knowledge is that "children of light" need not be frightened by enemies who flourish in darkness, most notably Satan and his denizens.

Because we "belong to the day" (v. 8), we are expected to behave accordingly. The two activities that are excluded are sleeping and drunkenness, both of which presuppose that one is not fully conscious, at least not to the point of being able to make rational, clear-headed decisions. We are urged, then, "to keep awake and be sober" (Rom. 13:11; Eph. 5:14). The proper mood in which to prepare for the day of the Lord is alertness (Mark 13:37; Acts 20:31; 1 Cor. 16:13; 1 Pet. 5:8).

Yet another image is introduced with the mention of "the breastplate of faith and love . . . and for a helmet the hope of salvation" (v. 8). Here we are to think of the soldier fully equipped for battle, ready to engage the enemy, on call rather than asleep or drunk in a stupor. Although the metaphor is not developed in as much detail as it is in Ephesians 6:14–17, it is vivid nevertheless as it recalls the image of God as a fully equipped soldier (Isa. 59:16–17; cf. Wisd. of Sol. 5:18). What is striking in the New Testament appropriation of this metaphor is that the Christian is being asked to take on the very attire that God wears!

We should also note the occurrence here of the familiar triad of virtues: faith, love, and hope (1:3; cf. Rom. 5:1–5; 12:6–12; 1 Cor. 13:7, 13; Gal. 5:5–6; Eph. 1:15–18; 4:2–4; Col. 1:4–5; 1 Tim. 6:11; Titus 2:2; Heb. 6:10–12; 10:22–24; 1 Pet. 1:3–9).

If we are properly equipped with the soldier's armor, we can expect to be protected by God from the coming wrath (v. 9; cf. 1:10; Rom. 5:9). It is not God's intention that anyone should be condemned to stand under the divine wrath, especially those who are called through the gospel "to obtain salvation through our Lord Jesus Christ" (v. 9). This is possible because he "died for us" (v. 10; cf. 4:14; Rom. 14:9; 1 Cor. 15:3–4, 12). As he stressed earlier, regardless of whether we "wake or sleep," that is, whether we are still alive when the Lord comes or whether we die before he comes, "we [will] live with him" (v. 10; cf. 4:17; also Rom. 6:8; Phil. 1:23).

As before, the eschatological discussion concludes with exhortation: "Encourage one another and build up each other" (v. 11). Part of the Christian's ongoing responsibility is to engage in mutual encouragment (cf. 4:18; Heb. 3:13) and corporate edification (cf. Rom. 14:19; 1 Cor. 10:23; 14:12, 26; 2 Cor. 12:19; also Jude 20).

In spite of the span between Paul's time and ours, his words are surprisingly modern, considering the continued apocalyptic speculation that goes on around us. Those who would circle the calendar and predict the date of the Lord's coming are still with us. Their fixation on "times and seasons" continues. Paul's advice is as sage now as it was then: the important question is not *when* but *how* the Lord will come. The proper response is not frenzy but preparedness that comes from knowing that "we are of the day." It is this, after all, that translates into mutual encouragement and upbuilding, not the feverish fits of the clock watchers.

Matthew 25:14–30

Matthew's parable of the talents and Luke's parable of the pounds (19:12–27) are sufficiently similar to have come from the same story. However, they are sufficiently different to alert the preacher to avoid trying to interweave them. The parable before us is enough for the sermon. The early church historian Eusebius reported on a third version in a work referred to as the Gospel of the Nazarenes, a second-century writing. In that version, there were three servants: one multiplied, one stored, and one wasted. Upon his return, the master received one with joy, rebuked one, and put one in prison.

This is a story of financial activity. A talent was not the ability to sing or paint but a large sum of money, approximately the amount a laborer would receive for fifteen years of hard work. A capitalist wants his money to be working while he is away, and so he entrusts sums of money with servants, expecting a return on his investment. According to the third servant's description of him, the master loves deals without risk and without hard work (v. 24). The preacher will want to beware of making the parable an allegory, having the talents represent one thing, the journey another, the servants another, and the master another. To do so could lead to making the master a representation of Christ, which would, of course, be a misrepresentation. It was not unusual for Jesus to use persons of less than admirable qualities to provide lessons in other parables, the dishonest steward and the unjust judge being two examples. All this assumes the truth of the third servant's portrayal of the master, a description not denied in the master's response.

Having been warned against allegorizing the parable, the reader will, of course, notice that Matthew himself has inserted into the story language that belongs not to a story of financial dealing but to the kingdom. Notice at verses 21 and 23 the reward extended to the first two servants: "Enter into the joy of your master." This is not business talk. Likewise, in the conclusion (v. 30) the reference to outer darkness where there is weeping and gnashing of teeth has no meaning in the financial world but is very much a part of Matthew's description of eternal judgment. Matthew uses the expression eight times, most recently occurring in the conclusion of the parable of the marriage feast (22:1–14).

After these many Sundays with Matthew, we have become familiar with two characteristics of the first Gospel: the insertion of "spiritual truths" into parables and frequent reminders of the final judgment. And we must acknowledge that at times Matthew's sermonic insertions, no doubt prompted by conditions being addressed, do not seem to flow naturally from the story itself. We saw this in verse 13 as a comment on the parable of the ten maidens, and we see it here in verse 29. This is a proverbial saying, sometimes spoken in cynicism, very much like, "Them that has gets" or "The rich get richer and the poor get poorer." Here Matthew probably means to moralize to the effect that gifts unused atrophy, but gifts exercised increase. Many sermons on this parable take verse 29 as the central thrust of the story.

However, to do so is to miss the high-risk activity of the first two servants. They doubled the money entrusted to them, hardly a possibility without running the risk of losing the original investment. (Recall Luke's story of a shepherd leaving ninety-nine sheep "in the wilderness" to go in search of one that was lost, 15:3–7.) The major themes of the Christian faith—caring, giving, witnessing, trusting, loving, hoping—cannot be understood or lived without risk. To take verse 29 as the total thrust of the parable is also to miss the problem of the third servant. He was motivated by the opposite of faith; he was afraid (v. 25). Although some degrees and occasions of fear are not inappropriate, this is a case of being immobilized at the very center of one's responsibility and purpose. Fear of failure, fear of punishment, fear of loss have not only paralyzed this servant but many servants and many congregations.

Finally, notice again verse 19: "After a long time." As discussed in last Sunday's lection, this and the two preceding parables deal with Christian living in view of the delay of the return of Christ. Faithfulness in service is neither determined by nor destroyed by the time of the Parousia.

Proper 29 [34]

(Christ the King or Reign of Christ Sunday between November 20 and 26 inclusive)

Ezekiel 34:11–16, 20–24;
Psalm 100; or
Psalm 95:1–7*a*;
Ephesians 1:15–23;
Matthew 25:31–46

The Season After Pentecost concludes with the festival of Christ the King. In this respect, this Sunday anticipates Epiphany, which also celebrates the lordship of Christ. The dramatic vision of Christ coming to reign on his glorious throne (Matt. 25) governs all the texts for today. The subtheme of Christ as shepherd separating sheep and goats has attracted Ezekiel 34 as a companion passage.

In the *Common Lectionary*, Psalm 100 sounds the note of God's universal glory, but also depicts God as shepherd of his people. These dual emphases also occur in Psalm 95, which is preferred in other lectionary traditions.

The New Testament reading is provided by the majestic text with which the Epistle to the Ephesians opens; the reading concludes by exalting Christ to universal dominion.

Ezekiel 34:11–16, 20–24

This passage from Ezekiel is a highly appropriate reading for the last day of the liturgical year, the celebration of Christ as King. On the one hand, the text calls attention to important Old Testament roots of New Testament images and ideas concerning Jesus Christ and the kingdom of God. On the other hand, it has its own particular contributions to make to the Christian proclamation of messianic and eschatological themes.

Ezekiel was a prophet of the period of the Babylonian Exile. He was taken with the first of the deportees, when the Babylonians captured Jerusalem in 597 BC, and reports that he received his call to be a prophet in Babylon in the fifth year of the Judean king Jehoiachin, that is, 593 BC. He emerged as one of the leaders of the exiles in Babylon, although he was frequently in conflict with them concerning the Lord's plans for their future. He clearly stands in the tradition of his prophetic predecessors, such as Hosea, Isaiah, and Jeremiah, but in many ways he is a transitional figure. On the one hand, he shows clear priestly interests, and his thought is related in some ways to the Priestly Document of the Pentateuch. Moreover, he is deeply aware of the legal traditions for which the priests were primarily responsible. On the other hand, both the form and the content of many of his messages move in the direction of apocalyptic literature. Although his visions are not as extended as, for example, those in Daniel, some of his dramatic images are almost as bizarre as are those of later apocalyptic books. Although he does not look to an end of history, his expectations for transformation tend to go beyond those of earlier prophets.

Ezekiel's discourses include the full range of announcements known to the prophets. There are vision reports, narratives of symbolic actions, prophecies of punishment—especially from his earlier period—prophecies against foreign nations, and announcements of salvation. The assigned reading for today is part of a larger collection (Ezek. 33–39) consisting mainly of announcements of the return of the exiles and the restoration of the nation with its center in Jerusalem. Most of this material comes from the later period of his activity, after the second fall of Jerusalem and the total destruction of the city in 586 BC (cf. Ezek. 33:21–22).

Ezekiel 34, either as a single lengthy discourse or as a collection of several smaller ones, employs the imagery of the shepherd to recapitulate the history of Israel—past, present, and future. The prophet persistently introduces and quotes the words of Yahweh. The chapter begins (vv. 1–6) with an indictment of "the shepherds of Israel," the kings who did not feed the sheep, that is, the people of Israel. Then comes an announcement of judgment against those shepherds, the Lord vowing that he himself will take charge of the sheep (vv. 7–11). The chapter concludes with an announcement of the restoration of the people and the promise of a "covenant of peace" (vv. 25–31).

Within that framework, the verses assigned for today contain two distinct units, verses 11–16 and verses 20–24. Both employ the metaphor of the shepherd in proclaiming the Lord's concern for his people, but they use it differently. In the first case, the "shepherd" is Yahweh himself (v. 15). Like a shepherd, the Lord will search out the sheep that have been scattered, "bring them out from the peoples, and gather them from the countries, and will bring them into their own land" (v. 13). This clearly is a promise of a return from the Babylonian Exile and restoration in the promised land. The Lord further promises to provide the main elements necessary for life: food—and in abundance—and security (vv. 14–15). He will take particular care of the lost, the strayed, the crippled, and the weak (v. 16).

There are two distinctive elements in verses 20–24. First, the "one shepherd" is not Yahweh but "my servant David, and he shall feed them" (v. 23). The promise of a future David is not to be taken literally, but is a messianic hope, the expectation of a new and righteous king from the Davidic line. Second, the prophet's expectation of a restored nation includes the element of judgment, as in Matthew 25:31–46. The Lord will judge the sheep, punishing the "fat sheep" who have pushed aside the others, thus making them "lean sheep" (v. 20). These fat sheep he accuses of scattering the flock abroad, that is, of being responsible for the exile of the nation. Remarkably, no specific punishment is noted. Rather, the emphasis falls upon the Lord's provision of proper and just leadership for the nation.

In the concluding line, the tension between the Lord as shepherd and David as shepherd would appear to be resolved. Employing the language of covenant, Yahweh affirms: "I, the Lord, will be their God, and my servant David shall be prince among them" (v. 24). The passage is an announcement of salvation, especially for those who have suffered under bad leadership. The kingdom of God envisioned here is not beyond history but within it. God is concerned that his people have food to eat and security with justice (v. 16).

Psalm 100

This psalm was discussed above as one of the readings for Proper 6 [11].

Psalm 95:1–7a

This psalm may be divided into the following components: (1) Verses 1–2 are a communal call to offer praise to God. (2) Verses 3–5 stipulate, in hymnic fashion, the reasons why God should be praised. (3) Verse 6 reissues the call to praise, with verse 7a offering the reason for praise. (4) Verse 7b calls on the people to listen to God's address. (5) Verses 8–11 are an oracle delivered as a speech of God.

The opening call to praise (vv. 1–2) speaks of four sentiments or actions that manifest devotion to God: sing (or "shout for joy"), make a joyful noise (or perhaps "pay homage"), come into his presence with thanksgiving (or "greet him" or "approach his presence [enter the temple] with thanksgiving"), and acclaim him with songs. In these verses, only one metaphor is used to describe God—the rock of salvation, a rather common description in the Old Testament (see Pss. 18:2, 31, 46; 19:14; Isa. 44:8) that denotes God's reliability and stability.

The reasons offered for praising God focus on God's status as Lord over the world and the status of the world as divine creation (vv. 3–5). God is *the* great God (see Ps. 77:13) who rules as king over the other gods. Verse 3 thus clearly presupposes a polytheistic background. God is not the only god but is the greatest of the gods. The whole of creation belongs to him. The concept of the totality of creation is expressed in the employment of opposites—the depths of the earth and the heights of the mountains, and the sea and the dry land. The world is God's because the Divine made it (v. 5) and controls it (v. 4).

The second call to praise (v. 6), actually a call to worship, employs three synonymous expressions: worship, bow down, kneel. The image of God as creator is carried over in the expression "the Lord, our Maker" in verse 6. In verse 7, the emphasis is not so much on God as creator as much as caretaker; God is the shepherd, and the people are the sheep, a point of contact with the reading from Ezekiel 34.

Ephesians 1:15–23

This text also serves as the epistolary reading for the Ascension of the Lord, which has already been treated in this volume. A longer form of today's epistolary lesson (1:11–23) provides the second lesson for All Saints Day in Year C. Additional comments on this text are provided in that setting.

Matthew 25:31–46

The festival of Christ the King concludes the post-Pentecost Season and immediately precedes Advent. One could hardly imagine a more appropriate text than Matthew 25:31–46. With this teaching, Jesus concludes his public instruction, and if the principle of end stress is at work here, then Matthew wants this to be the lingering lesson in his auditors' ears. These verses have no parallel in Mark or Luke; their kinship is with the throne scene in Revelation 20:11–15 and with Son of Man passages in the Old Testament (Dan.) and in extracanonical writings such as Enoch.

This text is not a parable but an apocalyptic vision of the last judgment. The purpose of the vision is not speculation about the end or for the fascination of the community. Rather, the vision is the vehicle for ethical instruction. The heart of it is the coming ("Parousia," 24:3) of the Son of Man. His coming is not to the earth, but to the throne in heavenly glory. The scene is an enthronement, the Son of Man being installed as King and Judge (Son of Man appears only in v. 31; thereafter the term is "King," vv. 34, 40). The "coming" has been dealt with already: it will be sudden as the lightning (24:27); it will be on clouds of glory and with great power (24:30–31); the day and hour are unknown (24:36–42); it will be as a burglar entering at night (24:43); it will be a time of reckoning and woe to the unprepared (24:45–51). Three parables have dealt with the delay of the coming (24:45–25:30). But now comes the full vision, glorious in appearance, cosmic in scope, and yet personal in that every life must appear before the judgment seat.

Terms used to describe the event are drawn from the treasury of Jewish thought. "Right" and "left" (v. 33) were common terms in both Jewish and Gentile culture for the favored and unfavored position. "Inherit the kingdom" (v. 34) comes from Israel's tradition about the promised land. "From the foundation of the world" (v. 34) draws upon the view that all that was essential for God's eternal purpose was created before the world was made. In other words, all that pertains to God's will is not contingent upon anything in the created order.

Three elements in the vision draw special attention. First, the basis for the final judgment is one's response to human need (vv. 35–36). These needs are not unusual but present themselves in the ordinary coming and going of one's life. Second, both those at the right and at the left are surprised that they have so served or failed to serve Christ (vv. 37–39, 44). This touch of being surprised is a beautiful portrait of those saints whose service to others is so much a part of their behavior that they are embarrassed at the recital of their deeds and amazed that service to those in need is service to Christ. And the element of surprise also describes vividly those who, in Matthew's community, were busily religious in attention-getting ways but who bypassed the scenes of human anguish. Recall 7:21–23 and those who are rejected even though they make valid claims to having prophesied, cast out demons, and performed miracles. What could be more religious, Matthew says, than attending to those who need care?

And finally, the vision reminds the reader that service to another is service to Christ. Matthew said this earlier (10:40–42), but here the point is dramatized and elevated to ultimate importance. However, the reader will want to avoid turning this truth into a strategy for assuring one's salvation. That is to say, one must avoid reading this text and then concluding, "From now on, every time I see a person alone or in prison or hungry or thirsty I will not see that person but I will see Christ." Such behavior would render every needy person faceless and nameless by those joyfully "serving Christ" rather than human need. Most likely these, too, would be surprised at the final judgment.

All Saints, November 1, or on First Sunday in November

Revelation 7:9–17;
Psalm 34:1–10, 22;
1 John 3:1–3;
Matthew 5:1–12

All the readings for today announce the blessed estate of the saints of God. Both the Gospel and the psalm describe the nature of this happiness and those to whom it is given. The Epistle quietly and modestly extends the thought: if we are children of God now, consider how it will be with us when Christ appears and we share in his likeness. The Apocalypse, replacing the Old Testament lection, envisions that future glory of the saints who have endured, purified by having been bathed in the suffering of Christ.

Revelation 7:9–17

Even though this text is normally associated with All Saints' Day, it serves as the New Testament lesson for the Fourth Sunday of Easter in Year C. In that setting, it occurs as part of the semicontinuous reading of the Book of Revelation from the Second Sunday through the Sixth Sunday of Easter. In order to place the passage in its wider literary context, the reader may want to consult our remarks on the passage in the volume treating Year C.

As the first lesson for All Saints' Day, this is a most impressive reading. One of several visions of the heavenly court in the Book of Revelation, it recalls the earlier vision of God sitting enthroned, surrounded by the twenty-four elders, the four animals, and the angelic host (4:1–5:14). The focus of their attention is the Lamb who had been slain but vindicated by God as the one with "power and wealth and wisdom and might and honor and glory and blessing" (5:12).

In the heavenly scene depicted in today's lesson, the audience around God's throne is further extended to include a vast host of people, an innumerable multitude "from every nation, from all tribes and peoples and languages" (v. 9). We should imagine a truly universal audience that includes people from every part of the globe. When first introduced, they are all "robed in white, with palm branches in their hands" (v. 9). As we envision this sea of white stretching out through the heavens, we recall an earlier scene when the Lamb opened the fifth seal and saw underneath the altar "the souls of those who had been slaughtered for the word of God and for the testimony they had given" (6:9). They are easily recognized as the slain martyrs who cry out to God for vindication: "Sovereign Lord, holy and true, how long will it be before you judge and avenge our blood on the inhabitants of the earth?" (6:10). Although their cry for vindication is not immediately answered, they are given white robes, the attire of those who have been sanctified through their martyrdom. It is the proper attire of the heavens, as the elders around the throne are similarly described (4:4).

In addition to wearing white robes, they are described as holding palm branches in their hands (v. 9). This may serve to underscore the celebrative atmosphere, given the use of palm branches in festal celebrations (Lev. 23: 40–43). This was certainly part of the symbolism associated with the triumphal entry of Jesus, which was accompanied by the spreading of palm branches (John 12:13; cf. Matt. 21:1–11 and parallels).

All the angels surround the throne and ascribe blessings of glory and honor to God (v. 12); but as yet, the multitude of people is unidentified. To this point, we know that it is an innumerable multitude, international in scope. The mention of white garments causes us to reflect on the earlier vision of the martyrs in chapter 6, but no direct link is made with that earlier vision.

As we ask ourselves who they are, one of the elders puts the question for us: "Who are these, robed in white, and where have they come from?" (v. 13). In almost the same breath, he tells us their identity: "These are they who have come out of the great ordeal; they have washed their robes and made them white in the blood of the Lamb" (v. 14). In apocalyptic thought, "the great ordeal" signified the time of unprecedentedly fierce persecution that would precede the end time (cf. Dan. 12:1; Matt. 24:21; cf. Joel 2:2). These, then, are not merely those who have undergone suffering in behalf of the kingdom, but intense suffering and violent death.

By now, the identity of this innumerable host is known to us: they are the martyred saints, those who have died in behalf of the faith. The vindication that they sought in the vision in chapter 6 is now achieved (vv. 15–17). It is described in terms of almost unimaginable bliss: worshiping God in the temple night and day; free of hunger, thirst, and scorching heat; sheltered by the Lamb, their shepherd, who guides "them to springs of the water of life" (v. 17); without tears.

As the vision unfolds, it is easy to understand why this text is chosen as the first lesson for All Saints' Day. It is a heavenly vision focused on those who have died for the faith and whose cause is finally vindicated in the heavenly court. Such a clear focus on the martyred saints takes us close to the original significance of All Saints' Day as a day celebrating unnamed martyrs who died in persecution. Yet we should recall that the word "saints" (*hagioi*) in the New Testament is used in a much broader sense. It may have been the most common self-designation of the early Christians (cf. Rom. 1:7; 8:27; 12:13; 1 Cor. 1:2; 14:33). In certain traditions, the celebration of this wider circle of faithful Christians occurs on the following day, All Souls' Day.

Whether this day is observed in the narrow or broad sense, it serves as a day of remembrance and celebration. Technically, today's text focuses more narrowly on the martyred saints, but the Book of Revelation eventually extends the heavenly host to include all the redeemed (21:1–22:5). Given the usage of "saints" within the New Testament as a whole, we are justified in making it a more inclusive celebration, a time to remember all those who have preceded us in the life of faith—and all those who will succeed us.

Psalm 34:1–10, 22

Psalm 34 is an individual thanksgiving psalm intended for use by persons who have moved through trouble and distress and now enjoy security on the "redeemed" side of the turmoil. Like most thanksgiving psalms, this composition has a strong autobiographical or testimonial quality about it. Such psalms were used to look back on the trouble from which one had been freed.

The use of this psalm on All Saints' Day shifts the focus from a this-worldly to an other-worldly orientation. That is, the original usage of the psalm was concerned with offering thanks for redemption from some "ordinary" predicament in this life. It was not concerned with giving thanks for having passed through life in its entirety and having gone to one's final state or having died in the faith.

Verses 1–10 contain an opening affirmation of thanks (vv. 1–2), an invitation to others to join in the thanksgiving (v. 3), an autobiographical statement (vv. 4–7), and an appeal to the human audience to learn from the worshiper's experience and to share in the sentiments expressed (vv. 8–10).

Several points can be noted about this psalm: (1) Even though cast in general terms and stylized language, the autobiographical section shows that rehearsing one's story was considered a valuable and therapeutic experience; this is a basic element in modern therapy just as it has been in testimonial meetings throughout church history. (2) Persons can learn from the experiences of others; the mutual sharing of burdens and triumphs is thus encouraged. (3) The psalm assumes that life, even for the good and the faithful, is filled with its own troubles and distresses. (4) The psalm testifies to the encouragement that faith gives to life. (5) The optimism of the psalm, especially in verses 7–10, may seem a bit idealistic, but such sentiments help set the pace and orientation of people who share them and thus contribute to particular attitudes with which they face life and its problems and triumphs. Verse 22 affirms Yahweh as redeemer and promises that trust in the Divine will not go unrewarded.

1 John 3:1–3

This epistolary lection is also included in the longer reading (1 John 3:1–7) that serves as the second lesson for the Third Sunday of Easter in Year B. The reader may want to consult our remarks in that setting.

There is some merit in reading today's text closely with what immediately precedes (2:28–29). Even though NJB makes a decisive break between 2:28 and 2:29–3:2 (similarly, NRSV), NIV treats 2:28–3:3 as part of a single division. REB treats 2:28–29 and 3:1–3 as separate units. What favors the editorial decision of NIV is the occurrence of "children" in 2:28 and the use of the image of divine begetting in 2:29: "Everyone who does what is right has been born of him." An eschatological thread also runs through the entire section (cf. 2:28 and 3:2).

In any case, the main theme of today's text as defined by the *Common Lectionary* is the status we enjoy as God's children. The notion of divine paternity, which is introduced in 2:28, is rendered specific with the mention of "Father" (v. 1). To understand God through this image is a pervasive Johannine theme (1:2–3; John 1:14, 18; 5:17; 10:30; cf. Matt. 11:27). It is axiomatic that the Father loves the Son, and by extension every child (John 3:35; 5:20; 10:17; 15:9; 16:27). The opening note of today's text is the incredible lavishness of the Father's love:

"You must see what great love the Father has lavished on us" (v. 1, NJB). A similar note is struck by Paul, who insists on our inseparability from God's love in Christ (Rom. 8:38–39; cf. 8:14–17; Gal. 3:26; also Eph. 1:5).

Several angles of this rather incredible status are explored. On the one hand, it is present reality—"and this is what we are" (v. 1). "Here, and now, dear friends, we are God's children" (v. 2, NEB). Yet the full realization of this gift is still a future hope—"what we shall be has not yet been disclosed" (v. 2, REB). The tension between the "already" and "not yet" is vividly present within our text. And this conforms to our own experience. As children, we have some vague notion of our relationship to our parents, but it becomes more concrete as they grow older, even more so when we become parents. Yet as undefined and elementary as our understanding is, it is no less real and meaningful. In a similar fashion, today's text projects our filial relationship into the future; and as the future unfolds, our awareness of the true significance of being God's children compounds geometrically.

We are struck by how our text hammers home this present reality. We are told in the most emphatic terms that we are children. At one level, this should appear obvious to us; yet at another level, we have to be reminded of our true identity primarily because it is called into question by "the godless world" (v. 1, NEB). This sharp distinction between the children of the world and the children of God is typical of Johannine dualism (4:4–6; John 8:23; 15:19; 17:16). It seems to reflect a sectarian outlook that not only defines the church against the world but also understands Christ as an alien figure, a "stranger from heaven," who is misunderstood and finally rejected by the world (John 1:10–11). Here we see how ecclesiology is reinforced by Christology: the church's own fate becomes an extension of the fate of Christ. It goes unrecognized because he was unrecognized. In Johannine theology, the world was oblivious to the way in which the Father was at work in the world through the Son (John 7:28; 8:55; 14:7; 15:21; 16:3; 17:25; also Acts 13:27; 1 Cor. 2:8). The world's ignorance of the divine mystery was its failure to see the unfolding revelation of God before its very eyes (John 9).

The danger of having our identity constantly called into question by the world is that it may not only skew our present understanding but undermine our future hope. We are thus assured that being God's children opens us to a future when even fuller recognition occurs: "What we shall be has not yet been disclosed, but we know that when Christ appears we shall be like him, because we shall see him as he is" (v. 2, REB). The future disclosure is the coming of Christ, before whom God's children will be able to stand "confident and unashamed" (2:28, REB). It is presented here as a moment of transparent vision, when our view of Christ is completely unobstructed.

But more is promised than a clear view of Christ: "We will be like him" (v. 2). With full revelation comes transformation, what Paul refers to as an exchange of "our lowly body" for "his glorious body" (Phil. 3:21; cf. Rom. 8:29; 2 Cor. 3:18; Col. 3:4).

The effect of this vision of the future is moral purification: "All who have this hope in him purify themselves, just as he is pure" (v. 3). Moral purity is commonly understood as a prerequisite for seeing God (Matt. 5:8; Heb. 12:14; also 2 Cor. 7:1).

This second lesson serves as a useful complement to the first lesson, where the heavenly hope is sketched in such vivid terms. In a sense, the first lesson is maximalist, the second lesson minimalist. In one instance, we see the saints exalted, vindicated, clothed in white, equipped with palm branches, gathered around an elaborately configured throne. They join the twenty-four elders, the four living creatures, the angelic host in giving praise and honor to God and the Lamb. Little is left to the imagination. In the other instance, the promise is

"We will be like him . . . we will see him as he is." Here much is left to the imagination. Much is left unsaid. Yet we are no less reassured of the hope that awaits us.

On All Saints' Day, the preacher may want to contrast these very different ways of conceiving the future hope, perhaps consider the relative merits of the more graphic depiction over against the one impressionistic one. Or another possibility is to explore the tension within our text between present reality and future hope, what we know to be our present identity, the way it can be called into question, and the kind of expectation it shapes within us. How other saints have lived in this tension and how their lives have been empowered by their vision of the future may provide valuable clues.

Matthew 5:1–12

All Saints' Day is an occasion for remembering with gratitude those whose lives bear witness to the blessing of God. It will be with them in mind that the Beatitudes are said and heard.

The Sermon on the Mount is the first of five major sections of Jesus' teachings recorded in Matthew. All five sections conclude with the same formula (7:28; 11:1; 13:53; 19:1; 26:1), giving the impression of careful structuring. Most likely, Matthew has the memory of Moses in mind as he portrays Jesus bringing God's instruction from the mountain. However, given the wide range of subject matter in these three chapters, plus the fact that portions of this material are found in parallels scattered through Mark and Luke, one is persuaded that the "sermon" is a compilation of teachings from Jesus, the original audiences and occasions now being lost to us. Such a view does not rob any of the sayings of their authority or meaning, but it does free the interpreter from having to discover or construct a single audience for all the material. Matthew's audience, of course, is the church. Were a title to be given to this collection of sayings, it could well be "Life Under the Reign of God."

Matthew has these teachings of Jesus addressed to an audience that is described as a crowd (4:23–25; 5:1; 7:28) and yet as a group of his disciples (5:1). Does this mean that he taught the crowds or that he taught those from the crowd who were his disciples? Luke's parallel offers little help, speaking of a great crowd of his disciples and a multitude of people (6:17), concluding with the words "in the hearing of the people" (7:1). This question is important. Is the Sermon on the Mount for the church or for society as a whole? It seems safe to say that Jesus is not offering a way of reordering society regardless of one's faith in or relationship to Jesus. Rather, these teachings are for those who are the community gathered around Jesus. However, the presence of the crowd keeps the invitation open. Speaking to his followers in the presence of the public keeps all of them honest about who they are and where their commitments lie. The church is a community but not a ghetto; meetings are aware of and open to the world.

The Sermon on the Mount begins with blessings, or Beatitudes. Instruction is prefaced with blessing, just as the Ten Commandments were prefaced with a recital of God's favor toward Israel (Exod. 20:1–2). In other words, God's imperative is couched in and surrounded by grace. Obedience is thus to be understood as response to, and not an effort to gain, God's favor. The Beatitude says, "Blessed are those who"; that is, it gives its blessing; it is not a formula for happiness such as "If you want to be happy, this is what you do." Neither is a Beatitude an exhortation. The preacher will want to avoid giving the impression that Jesus said, "We ought to be poor in spirit" or "Let us be meek." He pronounces his blessing, and the language is performative, conferring the favor in the very saying of it.

The preacher cannot in one sermon give detailed word studies and exegetical analyses of all the Beatitudes. And on All Saints' Day there will be no desire to do so. There will be occasions for that. In this sermon, several accents might be helpful. First, brief attention to what a blessing is (Pss. 84:5–6, 12; 128:1; Ecclus. 25:7–10) and the powerful dynamic of saying and receiving the blessing can give life to the passage. Second, notice that these Beatitudes completely reverse the values of most societies, including our own. No doubt many in Jesus' audience were upset, preferring to take the kingdom into their own hands, and by force if necessary. These blessings elaborate on the description in Isaiah 61:1–3 of those to be visited with God's favor. The meek, the poor in spirit, the peacemakers, those who mourn—these need to be seen and heard as persons, not merely defined and described. And finally, the preacher would do well to distinguish between Jesus extending his blessing to victims and Jesus calling people to be victims. The former he does; the latter he does not do. Even victims do not have to have a victim mentality. Blessed victims take initiative to claim a life appropriate to the blessing. Those who give the coat, turn the cheek, love the enemy, and go the second mile are no longer victims. They are kingdom people.

Thanksgiving Day

Deuteronomy 8:7–18;
Psalm 65;
2 Corinthians 9:6–15;
Luke 17:11–19

A first reading of these texts will fix in mind one sentence: God is a God of abundance. The Deuteronomist, the psalmist, and Paul all sing of God's overflowing gifts. But dangers to the human spirit lurk, and prosperity casts its own kind of shadow. One can soon forget the source of all things (Deuteronomy); one can fail to express gratitude to God for creating and sustaining life (Luke); and one can refuse to match God's generosity with a cheerful generosity toward those in need (2 Cor.). Although Thanksgiving is not a traditional festival of the church, these texts help build an altar on what is otherwise a national holiday.

Deuteronomy 8:7–18

The Book of Deuteronomy is full of excellent texts for Thanksgiving Day. This is because the book, presented as the last words of Moses in the plains of Moab just before the entrance of the people of Israel into the promised land, anticipates the life of those people in a rich land given to them by their God. The book actually was written in the centuries after the time of Moses by preachers and writers who had experienced the land as a gift. They knew and wanted to remind others that their wealth was not the fruit of their own strength, but had been given to them.

Today's reading includes most of a sermon (Deut. 8:7–20) on the attitude of the people of God toward the gift of a rich land and the behavior that results from that attitude. It is preceded by another sermon on a similar theme (Deut. 8:1–6). Like virtually all of the Book of Deuteronomy, it is in the form of second person address, looking toward the future. By using the logic of rhetoric, the speaker appeals to the audience in order to promote the right attitude and actions. There are also implied and expressed (v. 19) threats and promises. It is dangerous to ignore these injunctions to respond in gratitude, but to follow them leads to the abundant life.

One of the most important elements of thanksgiving is to count one's blessings. This the preacher invites his hearers to do in verses 7–10, giving a catalogue of the good things in and of the land. The style of that description is almost poetic. The land is well-watered (v. 7), a factor that certainly could not be taken for granted in the terrain in and around

Canaan. It is agriculturally rich, producing all kinds of good things to eat (v. 8), and in fact the people will lack for nothing in it (v. 9a). Its resources even include the metals that were most important in the Old Testament period, iron and copper.

In order to be properly thankful, one must cultivate a good memory. Thus the preacher warns his hearers not to forget (v. 11). In this context, as elsewhere in Deuteronomy, "forget" refers to two different matters. On the one hand, it refers to the commandments of the Lord, which must not be forgotten, that is, ignored (vv. 1–6, 15–16). On the other hand, it refers to God and what he has done and continues to do for Israel: Do not forget the Lord your God. If you do, you might assume that you have brought yourself into the land and provided all the good things in it (vv. 11a, 12–14, 17–18). Memory is an essential element in the theology of the Book of Deuteronomy. It is an active remembrance, the recital of the mighty acts of God that then defines and shapes behavior. One who remembers what the Lord has done will obey the stipulations of the covenant and thus live the abundant life in the land (v. 18).

With its two major sections, then, this sermon urges that one be thankful for the natural resources of the land (vv. 7–10) and for the acts of God in the past (vv. 11–18). Behind the sermon is the preacher's concern that the wealth of the land can be dangerous. A people who are rich certainly will be tempted to be self-sufficient. Those who have plenty of food, "fine houses," herds and flocks, and even gold and silver (vv. 12–13) may become arrogant (v. 14) and even say in their heart, "My power and the might of my own hand have gotten me this wealth" (v. 17). Such persons have short memories. The way to avoid that corrupting attitude and its attendant behavior is to remember. Remember that the Lord brought you in and gave you the land, and even gave you "power to get wealth" (v. 18). Finally, in the allusion to the "covenant that he swore to your ancestors" there is an allusion to the promise of the land and descendants to the ancestors, reminding the hearers that they stand at the end of a long line of other persons who have made their good life possible.

Psalm 65

This reading was discussed above at Proper 10 [15].

2 Corinthians 9:6–15

The context in which today's epistolary lection occurs is Paul's discussion in 2 Corinthians 8–9 of the contribution for the Jerusalem poor. At an early stage in his ministry, Paul had agreed not to forget the poor in Jerusalem (Gal. 2:10). During the period of his Aegean mission, collecting money for this relief fund became an important priority for him (1 Cor. 16:1–3). Besides the way it would provide relief for the impoverished in Palestine, it would also serve as an expression of solidarity between the newly founded Gentile churches in the Aegean area and the largely Jewish church in Palestine (Rom. 15:25–27).

At a critical stage, the Corinthians seem to have dragged their feet. We do not know the reasons, but we do know that their reluctance did prompt the longest discussion of this topic we have in Paul's writings. Some scholars have plausibly suggested that this two-chapter section of Second Corinthians actually consists of a series of shorter notes sent to the church at different times, later compiled into a separate letter and finally redacted into what we now know as "Second Corinthians."

In these remarks, Paul appeals to the Corinthians to complete their part of the relief fund, reminding them that the churches of Macedonia, their northern neighbors, had already given generously (2 Cor. 8:1–7). He makes a number of appeals: the example of Christ (2 Cor. 8:8–9), the need for equal distribution of resources (2 Cor. 8:13–14), his own reputation as one who had testified to their generosity (2 Cor. 8:24–9:5). Today's text continues these appeals.

We do know that his appeal was finally successful. The Corinthians finally came through, and Paul was able to complete the project. As he concludes the Letter to the Romans, he is en route to Jerusalem with the gift, even though he is apprehensive about how it will be received (Rom. 15:14–33, esp. vv. 30–31).

The first appeal in today's text is *the principle of return*: sow sparingly and you will reap sparingly; sow bountifully and you will reap bountifully (v. 6). It was common in moral exhortation to cite examples from nature to reinforce one's case (Gal. 6:7–8; cf. 1 Cor. 15:35–41). The Jewish wisdom tradition offered similar advice: "Some give freely, yet grow all the richer; others withhold what is due, and only suffer want" (Prov. 11:24).

A second observation is the *need for voluntary rather than forced generosity* (v. 7). Paul makes a similar distinction in his Letter to Philemon in calling for kindness that is "a matter not of compulsion . . . but of [his own] free will" (Philem. 14, REB). It would be kindness in either case, and doubtless it would have salutary effects, regardless of the motivation; but Paul is more interested in the motivation that gives rise to the act than the consequences that result from the act. What especially pleases him about the generosity of the Macedonian churches is that they gave voluntarily (2 Cor. 8:3). When Israel was commanded to provide for the poor, they were enjoined to give freely, not begrudgingly (Deut. 15:10). The Old Testament attested God's love for cheerful givers (v. 7).

Third, our text mentions the *generosity of God* (vv. 8–10). We are reminded of God's capacity to provide for our needs—to do so abundantly—so that we can be equipped for good works (v. 8; cf. Eph. 2:10; Col. 1:10; 2 Thess. 2:17; 2 Tim. 3:17; Titus 2:14). Again, Scripture supplies the warrant for this claim: God provides rain and snow to water the earth, making it productive to give "seed to the sower and bread to the eater" (Isa. 55:10).

This is an important point, for it suggests a close correlation between faith and generosity. We may withhold our goods and money as an act of self-protection and self-preservation, but to do so implies that our preservation is in our own hands. To let go of our possessions, by contrast, becomes an expression of faith because it symbolizes the commitment of ourselves and our future to someone other than ourselves—God. To cling to our possessions symbolizes our doubt in God's ability to provide.

Fourth, *generosity produces thanksgiving* (vv. 11–13). Any act of charity obviously benefits the one in need. In this case, the Corinthians' contribution would "supply the needs of the saints" (v. 12). Benefit also accrues to the free-hearted giver: God's abundance is opened up even more. But, in addition, God will be honored: acts of generosity "produce thanksgiving to God" (v. 11); they "overflow with many thanksgivings to God" (v. 12). In mind here are prayers of thanksgiving that occur on the lips of the recipients, those who benefit from the generosity of others. Paul further adds that the Corinthians' generosity would "glorify God" because it would be an expression of "obedience to the confession of the gospel of Christ" (v. 13).

It matters to Paul that acts of generosity result in more prayers being offered to God, not because God needs our prayers and acknowledgments but because such acts express the right kind of faith—faith in God as Creator (Rom. 1:18–25). For Paul, the sure mark of being pagan is the inability, or refusal, to give thanks. Those incapable of thanksgiving are those who have exchanged the creature for the Creator, and in doing so have forfeited "the truth about God" (Rom. 1:25). By contrast, the capacity to give thanks becomes the earmark of true faith, for it recognizes who is creature and who is Creator.

Not surprisingly, his remarks end with a thanksgiving: "Thanks be to God for his inexpressible gift" (cf. Rom. 6:17; 7:25; 1 Cor. 15:57; 2 Cor. 2:14; 8:16).

This is an important text to read and hear at Thanksgiving because it properly anchors thanksgiving in theological reflection. There is much here about God's generosity and God's ability to provide for us in abundance. There is also the call for generosity of heart. Our text says no to the zipped pocket. It calls nature as a witness against the sparing sower. Above all, it sees thanksgiving as an expression of faith in God the Creator.

Luke 17:11–19

On the way to Jerusalem." With this phrase (v. 11), Luke reminds the reader that the story that follows occurs in the travel narrative begun at 9:51. Therefore, the preacher need not struggle to join the story of the healing of the lepers with what precedes it. Verse 11 is a clear transition. This account is found only in Luke, with vague similarities to Mark's account of Jesus healing a leper (1:40–45). One is impressed with the realistic details of the account. Lepers tended to live in groups (2 Kings 7:3), and they avoided contact with nonlepers (v. 12; Lev. 13:45–46; Num. 5:2), but they kept close enough to populated areas to receive charity. Jesus' command that they show themselves to the priest (v. 1) was according to the law of Moses (Lev. 14:2–32). However, one is also struck by elements in the story that raise questions. For example, the location between Galilee and Samaria (v. 11) is a bit confusing in view of the fact that Jesus is on his way to Jerusalem and had much earlier entered Samaria (9:52). Very likely, Luke uses the Galilee-Samaria border as a literary avenue for introducing a story involving Jews and a Samaritan (v. 16). Another uncertain element is the command to go and present themselves to the priest. Did that apply to the Samaritan? Also, why reproach the nine for not returning when they had been commanded to go (vv. 17–18)? In fact, their healing occurred in their going; their obedience was apparently the expression of faith essential for their healing (v. 14). One can understand why some commentators believe that Luke has idealized an event in order to join faith, obedience, and gratitude.

However, it seems more natural to understand this passage as a two-part story: verses 11–14 and verses 15–19. The first part is a healing story—a case of evident need, a cry to Jesus for help. Jesus treats the lepers as already healed, sending them to the priest, and their healing occurs in their response of faith. (In Mark 1:40–45, the leper is sent to the priest after the healing.) The second part (vv. 15–19) is a story of the salvation of a foreigner. It is the foreigner who praises God and gives thanks to Jesus. It is the foreigner to whom Jesus says, "Your faith has made you well" (v. 19). The verb translated "made you well" is a form of the verb "to save." There is more given to the Samaritan than the cleansing that they all received. This additional blessing is termed "salvation."

The story makes two points vital to Luke: the faith of foreigners (7:9; 10:25–27; Acts 10–11) and Israel's blindness to what is available in Jesus (Acts 28:26–27). It is important to note that Jesus did not reject the nine Jewish lepers; they were blessed with healing.

Neither did Jesus set aside Jewish law; he sent them to the priest for the postcleansing rituals. But the Gentile responds in ways beyond that of the Jews. Probably by the time Luke was written, such stories noting the differences between Jewish and Gentile responses to Jesus were told in abundance. Very likely this story was inspired by the one to which Jesus had referred earlier (4:27), the healing of a leper, a foreigner, who was converted to Israel's faith (2 Kings 5:1–14).

We cannot suppose that Luke told this story simply to paint a favorable picture of a Gentile and an unfavorable one of the Jews. Some condition is being addressed in Luke's church. Possibly some Christians were seeking benefits from Jesus' ministry but not salvation. Perhaps some were taking their blessings for granted, without gratitude. If so, again it was, and is, the outsider who reminds the church what faith is, what praise is, and what thanksgiving is.

Presentation of the Lord, February 2

Malachi 3:1–4;
Psalm 84 or 24:7–10;
Hebrews 2:14–18;
Luke 2:22–40

This special service commemorates the presentation of the child Jesus in the temple in the rite of dedicating him to God. The temple is important in Luke's story of Jesus and the early church, and there is no shortage of Old Testament texts to join him in that affirmation of the temple as central in the life of God's people. Malachi pictures the awful day of the Lord's coming to the temple to cleanse and purify. The psalmist sings not only of the Lord's coming to the temple but also of the beauty and attractiveness of the temple for all those who trust in God. The Hebrew text shifts the image, portraying Christ as the meeting place of the eternal and holy God and the people who are but flesh and blood. In order to be for us a place to meet God, Christ, who came from God to be one of us, was made in every way like his brothers and sisters.

Malachi 3:1–4

The Book of Malachi originated in the postexilic period, between 520 BC, when the temple was rebuilt, and 400 BC, when the law was instituted by Ezra. Sacrifices and offerings in the temple seem to have become a regular part of the life of worship. Judah would have been a province of the Persian Empire, with its own "governor" (Mal. 1:8).

Nothing is known about the life of the prophet himself, not even his name. "Malachi" is not a proper name but the title "my messenger," apparently taken from the passage before us (3:1). The person responsible for the book continues the ancient prophetic tradition of speaking in the name of the Lord concerning the immediate future, and he is willing to challenge current beliefs and practices. He was deeply interested in priestly matters and likely was identified with the Levites (Mal. 2:4–9).

The reading for today is part of a unit that begins in 2:17 and concludes with 3:5. It is a disputation between the prophet, speaking on behalf of the Lord, and persons whose words he quotes. They have "wearied" the Lord by saying, "All who do evil are good in the sight of the Lord, and he delights in them," and by asking, "Where is the God of justice?" (2:17). In short, because evildoers prosper, these opponents question the presence of a God of justice.

Malachi 3:1–4 is the prophetic response to such objections. The prophet hears the Lord announcing the arrival of a messenger, the messenger of the covenant, who will prepare for the appearance of the Lord himself in the temple. The day of arrival, elsewhere called the day of the Lord, will be a terrible time, for no one can stand before him. It will be a day of refining and purification, particularly of the Levites, who will then present offerings that "will be pleasing to the Lord" (v. 4).

Next, the Lord himself will appear in judgment, punishing "all who do evil" (2:17), including sorcerers, adulterers, and those who deal unjustly with the weak, such as hirelings, widows, orphans, and resident aliens (3:5). Where is the God of justice? God is sending a messenger to prepare the way, cleansing the priesthood and the temple worship, and then God himself will approach as judge. Sinners may prosper, but not for long.

The passage has reverberated in various ways throughout Christian tradition. Mark took the messenger to be John the Baptist and quoted the initial line of verse 1 to introduce the account of John's appearance and his baptism of Jesus. On the commemoration of Presentation, read with Luke 2:22–40, the ambiguities of verse 1 take on added significance. Is Jesus the messenger or the Lord himself, who "will suddenly come to his temple"? The somber, apocalyptic tone of the passage from Malachi underscores the threatening aspects of the presentation of Jesus in the temple (Luke 2:34–35). Behind this serious note, however, the good news of Malachi is unmistakable. God will establish justice, and the arrival of his messenger will restore the means of communion with God (3:4).

Psalm 84

The two psalms selected for reading in celebration of Jesus' presentation at the temple are concerned with devotion to the temple. Psalm 84 may have been once used in conjunction with pilgrimages made to Jerusalem at festival time, although verse 9 seems to suggest it was used by the king. Psalm 24 contains words spoken at the time when pilgrims entered the sanctuary precincts.

Psalm 84:5–7 probably talks about the route to Zion taken by pilgrims as they made their way along the roads to the city. At the time of the fall festival, some of the early autumn rains may already have fallen, reviving the parched land. "Strength to strength" could be translated "stronghold to stronghold"; that is, the people move from one village outpost to another.

The piety of the worshiper and the psalm composer can be seen in various ways in the text. One way of analyzing the materials is to note the three groups whom the writer declares "blessed" (or "happy," which is a better translation of the Hebrew word used in all three cases).

1. First, a happy company is the birds that dwell continuously in the temple (vv. 3–4). The sparrows and swallows that nest in the sacred precincts have the advantage of constantly dwelling in the house of God, where they can sing God's praise forever.

2. Happy are those who go on pilgrimage to Jerusalem (vv. 5–7). To visit the temple and Zion is to experience happiness and to see "the God of gods."

3. Happy are those who trust in God (v. 12), who find their confidence in him. Here we have a sort of generalizing pronouncement that moves beyond the specificity of temple piety.

Verse 10 may be taken as embodying the overall sentiment of the psalm: to visit the temple and worship in its courts were some of the supreme experiences for the ancient Hebrews.

Psalm 24:7–10

Of all the psalms, Psalm 24 probably illustrates most clearly the fact that the psalms were used as the spoken part of cultic rituals. Throughout verses 3–10, the material is comprised of a series of questions and answers probably recited by pilgrims and priests. The psalm opens (vv. 1–2) with a hymnic praise of Yahweh that identifies the God of Israel as the possessor of the world and all that is in it. The ownership of the terrestrial kingdom is Yahweh's by right of creation. Yahweh is the one who anchored the earth in the midst of the seas and established it firmly upon the rivers (or streams) of the deep that ancients believed lay underneath the dry land. (Such a belief is partially based on the presence of springs and wells that suggest that water lies beneath the earth.)

The questions in verse 3 were addressed by the pilgrims to the priests inside the temple as the pilgrims arrived at the gates of the temple. The questions concern the qualifications demanded of those allowed to enter the sacred precincts: "Who shall ascend the hill of the Lord [who can enter the temple precincts]? Who shall stand in his holy place [in the temple in the presence of God]?" The priestly answer in this catechism of admission (vv. 4–5) brings together two pairs of ethical qualifications: purity of outward deeds (clean hands) and purity of thought or inward truthfulness (pure heart) followed by purity of religious practice or unadulterated faith (not lifting up the soul to what is vain) and purity in speaking (not swearing deceitfully). These four principles in themselves provide a rather comprehensive perspective of ethical demands and requirements. If such demands as these were made as part of the worship, then one surely cannot condemn ancient worship services of being devoid of ethical interests and demands.

Verse 6 provides the worshipers' response to the requirements for entrance: "Those are the kind of people we are." Thus they claim the promises of verse 5—blessing and vindication from God.

With verse 7, the focus shifts from humankind and the moral values of living to God himself. The pilgrims or choir outside the sanctuary address the temple gates demanding that they be lifted up so that the King of glory may come in. But how could God enter the sanctuary? No doubt, the ark, the symbol of God's presence, had been carried out of the temple to reenter with the pilgrims on a high holy festival day. The choir or priests within offer a response in the form of a question, "Who is this King of glory?" God is then described as the one strong and mighty, mighty in battle. Perhaps part of the festival involved the proclamation of God's triumph over the forces of evil.

Hebrews 2:14–18

At one time, especially in the Western church, this feast day was oriented toward Mary, and this was reflected in its name "Purification of the Blessed Virgin Mary." But because this appeared to threaten the doctrine of the sinlessness of Mary, in modern times the Roman church reverted to the more ancient understanding of the Easter church that celebrated this day as the "Presentation of the Lord." This more nearly conformed to its various designations in the East: "Coming of the Son of God into the Temple" (Armenian); "Presentation of the Lord in the Temple" (Egyptian); "The Meeting of the Lord" (Byzantine). The shift in title reflects a shift in emphasis: it is intended to be a feast of the Lord and not a feast honoring Mary.

With this focus on the presentation of the Lord, which, according to scriptural prescription, took place forty days after this birth (Lev. 12:2–8), this feast day has an incarnational cast. Celebrated on February 2, the fortieth day after Christmas, it serves to mark the end of the Christmas Season. Although the Gospel reading provides an account of the Lukan story of the presentation of Jesus in the temple (Luke 2:22–40), the epistolary reading serves to anchor the redemptive work of Christ in his incarnation. This text should not be forced into a false harmony with the Gospel reading, because each reflects a different theological interest. Nevertheless, there is a certain irony in the fact that the child who is presented in the temple "according to the law of Moses" finally becomes the merciful and faithful high priest officiating in the heavenly temple, making expiation for the sins of the people.

Several features of today's epistolary lection are worth noting:

First is the solidarity between Christ, "the one who sanctifies," and all humanity, "those who are sanctified" (v. 11). In the previous verses, several Old Testament texts are placed on the lips of Christ to show that he identifies completely with all of God's children (Ps. 22:22; Isa. 8:17–18). As such, he was born a member of the human family, sharing completely in our nature as "flesh and blood" (v. 14; Rom. 8:3, 29; Phil. 2:7). Just as it is the lot of every member of the human family to die, so did Christ experience death.

The effects of his death, however, were far from ordinary. For one thing, it was God "for whom and through whom all things exist" who made Jesus the "pioneer . . . perfect through sufferings" (v. 10). In addition, through death he passed through the heavens and became the exalted Son of God (Heb. 4:14). Because his death was both uniquely exemplary and triumphant, he destroyed death as the stronghold of Satan (v. 14; John 12:31; Rom. 6:9; 1 Cor. 15:55; 2 Tim. 1:10; Rev. 12:10). In his death, he delivered "those who all their lives were held in slavery by the fear of death" (v. 15). The incarnation of Christ eventually meant the freedom of all humanity from the fear of death.

Second is Christ as the merciful and faithful high priest (3:1; 4:14; 5:5, 10; 6:20; 7:26; 8:1; 9:11; 10:21). Because of his complete obedience, Christ demonstrated his true fidelity as the Son of God (5:8–9; cf. 1 Sam. 2:35). Because of his complete identification with the entire human family through his becoming "flesh and blood," he can be thoroughly sympathetic with the human condition. His own suffering and testing qualifies him to assist us in our sufferings and testing (v. 18; 5:2; cf. Matt. 4:1–11 and parallels; 26:36–46 and parallels).

In his role as high priest, Christ makes expiation for our sins (v. 17). His unique experience as one of God's earthly children makes it possible for him to plead in our behalf (5:1; Rom. 3:25; 1 John 2:2; 4:10; cf. Exod. 4:16).

Christ as a heavenly high priest, officiating in the heavenly temple and pleading in our behalf, can easily become a lofty image, far removed from the world we know and live in. Oddly enough, Christians have always found it easier to worship such an elevated Christ, enthroned high above the heavens. It is far more difficult for us to envision a Christ who became like us *in every respect* (v. 17, italics added). Yet today's epistolary text makes this unqualified claim about Christ, who was concerned not with angels but with the descendants of Abraham (v. 16). Given a choice between the company of angels and the company of humans, Christ plumps for flesh and blood. Why shouldn't we?

Luke 2:22–40

The text that provides a Gospel basis for the service of the Presentation of Jesus is found only in Luke (2:22–40). In fact, Luke places between the nativity (2:1–20) and Jesus beginning his public life at age thirty (3:23) three stories: the circumcision and naming when the child was eight days old (2:21; see the special service for January 1);

the presentation in the temple when he was about forty days old (2:22–40; Lev. 12:1–4); and the visit to the temple at age twelve (2:41–52). All this is to say that the Jesus who began his ministry at age thirty was thoroughly grounded and rooted in his tradition, that observance of the law and attendance to temple duties were very important, and that although he was a Galilean, neither he nor his disciples scorned Jerusalem. In fact, says Luke alone, Jesus' disciples were to remain in Jerusalem after his ascension and from Jerusalem were to launch their mission (24:47–48). "And [they] returned to Jerusalem with great joy; and they were continually in the temple blessing God" (24:52–53). It is no wonder that Jesus, the true Israelite, went to the synagogue on the sabbath, "as was his custom" (4:16). Jesus and some of the religious leaders disputed over the tradition, to be sure, but it was a tradition he knew and kept from childhood.

When one looks at the presentation account itself, it is evident that there is the story line (2:22–24, 39–40) into which two substories have been inserted: that of Simeon (vv. 25–35) and that of Anna (vv. 36–38). The principal story line seems to have as its basic purpose the demonstration that in the life of the Christ Child the law of Moses had been meticulously observed (vv. 22, 23, 24, 27, 39). In the course of making that point, Luke has conflated two regulations: a mother was to be ceremonially purified after child-birth (Lev. 12:1–4; in cases of poverty, Lev. 12:6–8 was applied), and a firstborn male was to be dedicated to God (Exod. 13:2, 12–16). Of course, provision was made for parents to redeem their son from the Lord (Num. 18:15–16) so they could keep him as their own. Luke says nothing about the redemption of Jesus; perhaps his silence serves to prepare the reader for the next story in which Jesus in the temple at age twelve said to his parents, "Did you not know that I must be in my Father's house?" (v. 49). That story, along with verses 40 and 52, makes it evident that Luke is echoing the story of the boy Samuel, who was dedicated to God and who lived in the temple (1 Sam. 1–2).

In the persons of Simeon (vv. 25–35) and Anna (vv. 36–38), Luke tells how the Israel that is true, believing, hoping, devout, and temple-attending responded to Jesus. Simeon's acknowledgment of Jesus as "the Lord's Messiah" was inspired by the Holy Spirit (v. 26), and Anna's was that of a true prophet who fasted and prayed continually (vv. 36–37). Simeon longed for "the consolation of Israel" (v. 25), a phrase referring to the messianic age. The Nunc Dimittis (vv. 29–32) may have been a portion of a Christian hymn familiar to Luke and his readers. Simeon's words make it clear that Israel's consolation would not be a time of uninterrupted joy; hostility and death would be aroused by the appearance of the deliverer. Good news always has its enemies. Mary herself would pay a heavy price: "And a sword will pierce your own soul too" (v. 35). Devout and obedient Israel, as portrayed in the old prophet Anna, also saw in Jesus "the redemption of Jerusalem" (v. 38). Her thanks to God and her witness concerning Jesus provide a model of the Israel that accepted Jesus and saw in him the fulfillment of ancient hopes. Luke will write later of that portion of Israel which rejected Jesus and turned a deaf ear to the preaching of the early church. But in Luke's theology, they are thereby rejecting their own tradition and their own prophets as it was interpreted to them by one who was a true Israelite, Jesus of Nazareth. He not only kept the law, held Jerusalem in great affection (13:34), and was faithful to the synagogue, but also his teaching was in keeping with all that was written in Moses, the prophets, and the writings (24:44). No prophet is so powerful and so disturbing as the one who arises out of one's own tradition and presents to the people the claims of that tradition.

Annunciation, March 25

Isaiah 7:10–14;
Psalm 45 or 40:5–10;
Hebrews 10:4–10;
Luke 1:26–38

March 25, exactly nine months prior to the date for celebrating Jesus' birth, is observed in some traditions as the day of the Annunciation. Central to the observance is Luke's story of the visit of the angel Gabriel to Mary in Nazareth of Galilee (1:26–38). However, the other readings gather around Luke 1 in strong support and in meaningful elaboration. Isaiah 7:10–14 prophesies the birth of a child to be called Immanuel. Hebrews draws on both Psalm 40:5–10 (10:4–10) and Psalm 45 (1:8–9) for its portrait of the preexistent Son, crowned, sceptered, and anointed, coming from his eternal home into the world to become as we are that we might become as he is. So even though March 25 comes during Lent, it is a day of joyful anticipation.

Isaiah 7:10–14

This passage from the Book of Isaiah provides important background for the Lucan account of the Annunciation. Central here is the prophecy of a birth as a sign of God's intentions towards God's people. Moreover, the name of that child, "Immanuel," which means "God is with us," is an interpretation of the Lord's will. Although we now recognize that Isaiah had in view a particular woman and child in his own time, and not Mary and her son Jesus, the ancient promise still has its contribution to make to Christian worship and to the Christian life.

Some of the literary and historical questions concerning our passage can be answered with relative certainty. It is one of a number of reports of encounters in Jerusalem between Isaiah and King Ahaz at a particularly critical moment in the history of Judah. The historical situation is summarized in Isaiah 7:1–2 and spelled our further in 2 Kings 16:1–20. When the Assyrian king Tiglath-pileser III started to move against the small states of Syria and Palestine, the leaders of those states began to form a coalition to oppose him. Apparently because Ahaz of Judah refused to join them, the kings in Damascus and Samaria moved against Jerusalem (ca. 734 BC) to topple Ahaz and replace him with someone more favorable to their policies. In the passage (7:1–9) that immediately precedes our reading, Isaiah counseled nonresistance based on faith in the ancient promise to David that one of his sons would always occupy the throne in Jerusalem. The fact that our unit begins with the expression "Again the Lord spoke to Ahaz" (v. 10) indicates that it is a continuation of the prophet's actions in the same situation.

Isaiah 7:10–14 is good news in the form of a prophetic symbolic action, especially to the king but also thereby to the people as a whole. Note that the entire section is presented as if the Lord himself is speaking directly to King Ahaz, but it would have been the prophet who conveyed the message. In the previous unit, Ahaz had been afraid; here he refuses even to inquire of the Lord, even when Isaiah instructs him to do so (vv. 11–12). It was common for kings or other leaders to inquire of the Lord, often through prophets, before deciding to go to battle (see 2 Kings 13:14–19). When Ahaz refuses to ask for a sign, the prophet becomes impatient and says that the Lord himself will give a sign: "Look, the young woman is with child and shall bear a son, and shall name him Immanuel" (v. 14). He goes on to interpret the sign, promising that before the child knows how to "refuse the evil and choose the good"—that is, within a short time—the present military threat will have ended. Although the means are not stated, the prophet promises that God will intervene to save his people.

Few textual and translation problems in the Old Testament have generated more controversy than those of Isaiah 7:14. However, there can be little doubt about the meaning or translation of the crucial word. The Hebrew word 'almah is correctly rendered by the NRSV and almost all other modern translations "young woman." The term is neutral with regard to her marital status. It was the Greek translation of the Book of Isaiah, the Septuagint, that read "virgin" (Greek parthenos), thus setting the stage for the particular messianic interpretation of the passage expressed in the New Testament. The bridge between the eighth century and the early church is thus yet another historical and theological context, that of the translation of the Hebrew Scriptures for Jews in a Hellenistic, pre-Christian culture. It is equally clear that the Book of Isaiah originally read here "young woman" and that the Evangelists inherited a translation of Isaiah that read "virgin."

As in most other prophetic announcements or symbolic actions, Isaiah has the immediate future in view, and thus the woman and child are his contemporaries. As the NRSV (see also REB) indicates, he indicates to the king a woman who is already pregnant. But the identity of the woman is difficult if not impossible to establish. In view of a context that stresses the significance of the Davidic dynasty, many commentators have taken the child to be the crown prince, and the woman as the wife of Ahaz. Others, seeing the passage in some ways parallel to Isaiah 8:1–4, have argued that the woman was the wife of the prophet, and the child his son. It is quite likely, however, that the "young woman" was simply a pregnant woman whom Isaiah saw as he was addressing the king.

One of the keys to the meaning of this passage is the word "sign" (Hebrew 'oth). It is the same word used in the tradition about the "signs and wonders" performed in Egypt before the Exodus and thus has come to be associated in our minds with the so-called miraculous. However, such signs may be ordinary events as well as extraordinary ones. The decisive point in the Old Testament view is that a "sign" is revelatory, that it communicates God's word or will or nature. Thus it is not remarkable that in Isaiah 7 something as common—and also as wonderful—as the birth of a baby boy is a message from God, and for the future. The name embodies the promise of God's saving presence.

To be sure, it is hardly possible for Christians to hear this passage and not think of the coming of Jesus. But in addition to directing our attention to the Incarnation, Isaiah 7:10–14 has its own good news. It is a message that sees pregnancy and birth—even when not understood as miraculous—as signs of God's concern for God's people. Furthermore, this message is directed to a people living in chaos and fear, faced with such specific problems as international politics and the threat of destruction. Even in such a situation, the word of God offers hope.

Psalm 45

Psalm 45 is clearly a wedding psalm. The references to the king and the bride in the text, however, are the source of differences in interpretation. Four approaches are worthy of note.

1. One line of interpretation is what might be called the metaphorical approach. This assumes that the marriage described is simply a conventional wedding. The normal, everyday groom is described in metaphorical language as a "king" and the bride as a "princess."

2. A second approach can be called the mythological. This assumes that the wedding partners are actually the male deity, played by the king, and the female goddess, played by the queen.

3. A third approach is the allegorical. The king in the text stands for Yahweh, and the bride is his chosen people. What is said in the text is not to be taken literally but allegorically.

4. A fourth interpretation is the historical. This assumes that the text was composed for an actual wedding for an actual ancient Israelite or Judean king. Because the text refers to Tyre, it has sometimes been assumed that the psalm was composed for the marriage of King Ahab of Israel to the Phoenician princess Jezebel, who was from the city of Tyre.

The association of this text with the Annunciation strains any reading of the text unless one wants to understand the king in the text as God and the bride as the Virgin Mary. The more common Christian interpretation is to relate the figure of the king to that of Jesus, as is already done in Hebrews 1:8–9. If Jesus is identified with the groom, the bride, however, is best understood as the church, not as Mary. At any rate, any exegesis of the text that Christianizes the interpretation forces the imagery considerably.

Of the four interpretations noted above, the most likely original reading is that which sees the psalm as a composition from an actual wedding of a Hebrew king, though it is doubtful if we can identify which king was the groom.

The following is the outline of the psalm: (1) a statement about the poet and the purpose of the poem (v. 1), (2) the glorification and praise of the king (vv. 2–9), (3) the glorification and praise of the bride (vv. 10–15), and (4) a statement to the king, which promises him great and famous progeny (vv. 16–17). The psalm allows us some insight into the opulence of the royal court and a glimpse at some of the flattery of the king that must have characterized court life.

Although the poet praises and flatters the king, he may also have engaged in some "preaching" to the monarch by making frequent reference to the king's responsibilities. The ruler is described as the fairest of men, one blessed with grace. The king, gloriously garbed in regal splendor with girded sword, can be visualized in the imagery of verse 3. The king, whose arrows destroy his enemies, is portrayed as the defender of the right and the cause of truth. The throne of the king is proclaimed as eternal and his rule as one of equity and righteousness. The status and well-being of the king are reflected in the perfumes that scent his royal robes, in the ivory palaces where he is entertained by instrumental music, in the daughters of royalty who inhabit his mansion, and in the golden splendor of his queen.

The bride is addressed and admonished to forget her family and country (Tyre) and to give her affection and attention to her new husband. The bride in her wedding finery and her attendants and ladies-in-waiting are described as being led in procession to the palace of the king.

The psalm concludes, like many modern Near Eastern weddings, with a statement expressing the hope and assurance of numerous offspring. Because fertility—numerous offspring—was considered a blessing from God (see Ps. 127:3–5), such a promise or blessing was especially appropriate for the king, whose offspring would share in the rule of the Davidic dynasty to whom God had promised eternal rulership.

Psalm 40:5–10

This lection is excerpted from the thanksgiving portion of a psalm probably originally used by the king. Verses 5–10 comprise the worshiper's thanksgiving spoken directly to the Deity in response to having been redeemed from some great distress (described in vv. 1–3). The association of this text with and its appropriateness for the Annunciation are its emphasis on willingly submitting to the divine will (see esp. v. 8), as was the case with Mary.

Several statements in the text require explanation. Verse 6 declares that God does not desire sacrifice. Four different types of sacrifice are referred to, some of the free-will type and others mandatory. What the verse intends to emphasize, however, is that what God really requires is a faithful, hearing attitude. The expression "ears thou hast dug for me" probably was a proverbial way of saying "I am really hearing you."

The book referred to in verse 7 may have been the Book of the Law, especially if this was written for use by the king (see Deut. 17:14–17), perhaps an official record or court document, or maybe a heavenly book in which it was believed were recorded all the activities of a person's life. At least, the book seems to give a favorable opinion of the worshiper (see v. 8).

In verses 9–10, the worshiper testifies to having proclaimed the salvation of God. In these verses, the same point is made with two positive affirmations (vv. 9a, 10b) and three denials (vv. 9b, 10a, 10c). The psalmist declares that the story he or she made known in public worship in the life of the congregation has thus borne testimony to God's salvation.

Hebrews 10:4–10

What qualifies this epistolary lection as a suitable text for Annunciation is the phrase in verse 5 "when Christ came into the world." This is a remarkable text within the Epistle to the Hebrews, where the stress lies less on Christ's incarnation than on his exaltation to the heavenly sanctuary, where he officiates as our great high priest. There are, however, some allusions to his "coming," for example, 9:11: "when Christ came as a high priest of the good things that have come."

But our text is concerned with more than the fact of Christ's coming into the world. It intends to explain for us the motive for his coming as well as expose the interior of that motive. To achieve this, the author makes an unusual move. He attributes the words of Psalm 40:6–8 to Christ himself. We have no indication in the Gospel tradition that Christ actually quoted this psalm or that the church interpreted him in light of it. Certainly, some of the sentiments of the psalm are expressive of Christ's teachings, most notably the denigration of sacrificial offerings as the way to God's heart (cf. Matt. 9:13; 12:7). Another motif that seems to echo sentiments of Jesus as known through the Gospel tradition is the statement in verse 7: "See, God, I have come to do your will, O God." To be sure, in this form the phrase sounds Johannine (cf. John 4:34; 5:30; 6:38–39). There is also some correspondence with the words attributed to Jesus in the tradition relating to the Gethsemane experience (cf. Mark 14:36).

But what especially intrigues the author of our text is the relationship between these two sentiments: the inefficacy of sacrifice and the primacy of obedience. The conclusion that is drawn is "He abolishes the first in order to establish the second" (v. 9). Christ's coming is thus interpreted as a critique of the sacrificial system that results in its abolition. In its stead, he establishes the obedient will as that which pleases God. It is for this reason that our passage opens with the outright assertion "For it is impossible for the blood of bulls and goats to take away sins" (v. 4). Why? Because they represent a form of worship that is intrinsically displeasing to God. Not only are animal sacrifices ineffective in doing what they are intended to do—take away sin; they are fundamentally the wrong kind of response to God, who is more interested in obedience than sacrifice.

It is finally the obedient will of Christ that results in his self-sacrifice, the offering of his own body "once for all" (v. 10; cf. 9:26; 10:14). This is the event in which our own purification, or sanctification, has been achieved (10:29; 13:12; cf. 1 Thess. 4:3; Eph. 5:2).

As we can see, today's epistolary lection takes us well beyond reflection on the single event of Christ's birth or of its Annunciation. But it does direct our attention to the central purpose of his coming into the world. It was a mission of one who came to do the will of God. So motivated, he was not concerned with the proper protocol of making sacrificial offerings. Instead, he himself became the preeminent sacrificial offering.

Luke 1:26–38

It would be a mistake to think that the early church's sole interest in the calendar was in various attempts to ascertain the time of the end and the return of Christ. Although such calculations have waxed and waned throughout the life of the church, the calendar has held other interests for Christians. Quite early there was a desire to structure the disciplines of worship and prayer on the significant hours and days in the life of Christ. Christian calendars were developed and framed primarily around the seasons of central importance, Easter and Christmas. Once a date was set for the celebration of Jesus' birth, it was only a matter of time until the day nine months earlier would be observed as the Annunciation, the day of Gabriel's visit to Mary. By thus observing March 25, the church was able to focus upon the beautiful text of Luke 1:26–38 outside the already rich and full season of Advent.

Luke says that Mary received the word of God's favor from the messenger (the meaning of the word "angel") Gabriel. In later Judaism, angels, both in the service of God and in the service of Satan, came to figure prominently in theology and in popular religion. Such beings were common in religions of Persia and may have found a welcome in Jewish thought in a time when the distance between a transcendent God and human beings required mediators. Angels carried messages and performed other functions in God's dealings with creation. In some literature, important angels were given names, Gabriel being one of the most familiar (Dan. 9:21). In the New Testament, Luke's stories are the most populated with angels, with the obvious exception of the heavenly scenes in the Apocalypse. Christians have differed in their ways of appropriating the conversation between Mary and an angel: some literally, others by means of literary, psychological, or sociological categories. The story has survived all interpretations.

Luke apparently has no need to speculate on the choice of Mary as the mother of the Christ. The point is, God has chosen her, and as in any act of divine grace, the reasons are enfolded in God's purposes and not in the recipient. The angel's message that Mary's child will be Son of God and son of David is a composite of phrases and lines from Isaiah, Genesis, 2 Samuel, Micah, Hosea, and Daniel. It is possible that this hymnlike expression of praise (vv. 32–33) came to Luke from an early Christian liturgy. Many scholars believe that the church quite early put together Old Testament verses that were useful in worship, preaching, and teaching new members.

Mary wonders, quite naturally, how she, without a husband, can conceive and bear a son. She is given no answer that approaches biology. Rather, she is given an announcement and a bit of information that functioned as a sign of the truth of the promise. The announcement was that the birth would be the work of the Holy Spirit and the power of the Most High (v. 35). In other words, Jesus of Nazareth is God's act of grace and power. The information that encourages Mary's faith is that her kinswoman Elizabeth, old and barren, is in her sixth month of pregnancy. Echoed in the Elizabeth story is that of Abraham and Sarah (Gen. 18:14). But behind the stories of Mary's, Elizabeth's, and Sarah's conceptions is the creed beneath and behind all other creeds: "For nothing will be impossible with God" (v. 37). It is to this word that Mary responds in trust and in obedience.

Visitation, May 31

1 Samuel 2:1–10;
Psalm 113;
Romans 12:9–16b;
Luke 1:39–57

This service focuses on Mary as God's servant and not on the advent of the Christ Child. Luke's account of Mary's visit to Elizabeth does, of course, anticipate Advent, and so the preacher will want to keep the camera on Mary, who is for Luke the model of humble obedience to God. Mary's song makes much use of the Song of Hannah (1 Sam. 2), both of which speak of God's favor upon those who serve with little attention and less praise. This theme naturally attracts Psalm 113 and Romans 12.

1 Samuel 2:1–10

This text has found its place as the Old Testament lesson on Visitation primarily because Hannah, the mother of Samuel, has been seen as a type of Mary, the mother of Jesus. In addition, the occasions of the Song of Hannah and the Magnificat are quite similar. Both concern the birth of babies who are divine gifts, and both of the babies are dedicated by their mothers to the service of God. Moreover, several themes in Hannah's song parallel those of the Magnificat, especially those that focus upon God's care for the lowly.

Hannah's song, like Mary's, comes at a critical point in history. In the lengthy history of Israel from the time of Moses to the Babylonian Exile, Samuel is an extremely important figure who spans two distinct eras, the end of the period of the judges and the beginning of the monarchy. The baby whose birth Hannah celebrates will be the last and most significant judge, but he will be more, serving both priestly and prophetic functions as well. Finally, he will be the one to preside over Israel's debate about whether or not to have a king and will designate first Saul and then David as kings.

None of this is told in the account of the birth of the boy Samuel, but it is made clear from the outset that he is a child of destiny. In his birth, the devotion of a woman and the graciousness of God work hand in hand. Long past the age of childbearing, Hannah goes to the sanctuary at Shiloh, presided over by Eli the priest, to pray for a son, vowing that he would be dedicated to serve the Lord. The Lord heard her prayer, and when the child was weaned she took him to Shiloh to hand him over to service in the sanctuary.

The Song of Hannah is presented as part of the service for the consecration of Samuel. However, its relationship to the context is quite loose. Within the song there are no specific allusions to the persons or the period, but, on the other hand, an anachronistic allusion to the king (v. 10). It is likely that the song itself is a later addition to the narrative, supplied as an appropriate expression of Hannah's piety, and a typical part of a service of worship.

Hannah's song is similar in many respects to other Old Testament lyrical poetry that arose and was used in worship. In particular, it is a song of thanksgiving that has, like many such songs, features of hymns of praise. The thanksgiving song typically was part of services of worship not found on a liturgical calendar. When an individual or the nation found itself in trouble, a prayer service was held in which the central part was a prayer of complaint. When the individual or the nation was delivered from the distress, they called a service of thanksgiving. When Hannah first went to the sanctuary at Shiloh, she went to complain about her barrenness and ask the Lord's help. Now, fulfilling the vow made as part of that prayer, she gives thanks.

Songs of thanksgiving and praise spring from the human experience of God as both powerful and caring. Hence they are filled with the mood of joy and confidence. Because that experience takes many forms, the themes of such songs are almost unlimited. They may celebrate the world as God's creation, or particular acts of salvation in history or in one's life. Among the themes of the Song of Hannah are the following: (1) there is joy and rejoicing because of the Lord's help (v. 1); (2) the Lord is incomparable as a sure support (v. 2); (3) the Lord chooses the weak over the powerful (v. 4); (4) the Lord cares for the needy, whether they are hungry or barren (vv. 5, 8a); (5) the Lord's power extends to all things, over life and death and to the foundations of the earth (vv. 6, 8b); (6) the Lord protects the faithful against the wicked, defeating his adversaries, and his reign will extend to the ends of the earth (vv. 9–10).

Psalm 113

Three general considerations about this psalm should be noted initially: (1) It, along with Psalms 114–118, was employed in both temple services (at the time of the slaughter of the lambs) and home celebrations (as part of the meal ritual) during the Passover festival; thus the imagery of the psalm came to be associated with the events of the Exodus, which was commemorated in the Passover ritual. (2) The psalm has many similarities to the Song of Hannah in 1 Samuel 2:1–10, with which it may profitably be compared; the similarity of both of these to Mary's Magnificat in Luke 1:46–55 has led to their connection with Visitation. (3) The psalm shares in a common biblical motif, which might be called the "reversal of fate" or the "from rags to riches" sentiment.

The genre and structure of the psalm are clear. It is a hymn used to express and instill faith and particular beliefs by and in the congregation. The initial verses (1–4) are a summons to praise God, temporally in all time and forever (v. 2), and geographically in all places and everywhere (v. 3). Verses 5–9 provide the motivations, the reasons why God should be praised. These are presented in the form of a question (vv. 5–6) and an answer (vv. 7–9).

The psalm develops a dialectic in the Divine and thus speaks about God in contrasting ways. In the question (vv. 5–6), God is highly exalted; God sits above looking far down upon earth and even far down upon the heavens. If such a transcendent God must squint to see the earth, then surely the course of events and the status of individual persons must be beyond divine purview. The answer given to "Who is like Yahweh?" comes, however, as unexpected in its content. Yahweh is the one who reverses the fate of the unfortunate, who

transforms the status of those whom society judges as failures. Yahweh is not an unconcerned transcendent Deity but the caretaker of the dispossessed and the unpossessing. The
heavenly Lord is involved in earthly human existence.

Verses 7–8 concern the reversal of status of the male. The poor and the needy would
have been those condemned by fate and fortune to marginal participation in the life of the
community. These would have been forced to live in poverty at the peripheries of society.
Perhaps they had gotten in that condition by the accident of birth, misfortune, poor harvests, illness, or debt. The dust and the ash heap refer to the city garbage dump, where the
dispossessed and unpossessing as well as the sick and leprous (see Lam. 4:5; Job 2:8;
Lev. 13:45–46) made their domicile, grubbed for survival, begged for a handout, and got
food and clothing from family and friends if they had any. Such places of last resort are
similar to modern old folks' homes and public shelters as well as dump hovels where the
world's refugees congregate. A male living under such conditions in ancient times would
have been without social standing and without self-respect and confidence. So much for
verse 7, the "before" in the psalmic commercial.

The "after" we find in verse 8. The ones suffering deprivation and ostracism are made
to sit with the nobles/princes, that is, with the rich and the powerful. To "sit with" implies
acceptance by others and self-assurance by the new participant. (Remember the difference
between standing integration and sitting integration in the South. "Sit-ins" marked a new
state in the civil rights movement because to "sit with" is to share.) For the ideal of one who
sits with the nobles, see Job 29:1–25.

The transformation of the unfortunate female is noted in verse 9. The mother was not
really "at home" in the extended family of her husband; that is, she had no real security or
sense of fully belonging and participating until she and her children created their own space
and place in the family. The wife, always brought into the husband's family, was an outsider
to her in-laws until children transformed her into an insider and made her "at home." It
must have been lonely in such a situation for the barren wife—so much so, that barrenness
could be understood as a disgrace if not a curse from God (see Gen. 16:2; 20:18; 1 Sam. 1:5;
Luke 1:25). Many of the matriarchs of Israel, however, were barren (Sarah, Rachel, Hannah)
for a long time before they produced a child viewed as the result of divine intervention.

Romans 12:9–16b

Today's epistolary lection consists of a catalog of Christian exhortations notable for
their proverbial form. Among them is the charge not to be haughty, but to associate
with the lowly, which picks up on a major theme from today's Gospel reading, the
Magnificat (cf. esp. Luke 1:52). In a similar vein, Psalm 113 praises Yahweh as one who
favors the humble.

Even though this is but one motif of the epistolary reading, it is part of a larger set of
concerns that give thematic unity to Paul's instructions here. He opens by insisting that love
should be genuine, literally "without hypocrisy" (v. 9), and many of his remarks that follow
are but variations on this theme. In his own apostolic ministry, he was motivated by genuine
love (2 Cor. 6:6), and elsewhere the New Testament insists that love should issue from a
pure heart (1 Tim. 1:5; cf. 1 Pet. 1:22).

"Hate what is evil, hold fast to what is good" (v. 9). These words are reminiscent of
Amos 5:15: "Hate evil and love good, and establish justice in the gate." And as the psalmist
reminds us, "The Lord loves those who hate evil" (Ps. 97:10).

"Love one another with mutual affection" (v. 10). Here the general injunction to love is given specific content, as Paul urges Christians to model themselves after the family, where siblings experience mutual love and concern (cf. 1 Thess. 4:9; Heb. 13:1; 1 Pet. 1:22; 2:17; 2 Pet. 1:7).

"Outdo one another in showing honor" (v. 10). Later, Paul urges that honor be given to those to whom honor is due (13:7).

"Do not lag in zeal, be ardent in spirit" (v. 11). It is quite possible to grow fainthearted even in doing good works, or perhaps especially in doing good works (cf. Gal. 6:9). Accordingly, one should look to the Spirit as the source of strength (cf. Acts 18:25).

"Serve the Lord" (v. 11). The object of Christian service is the Lord Christ (Col. 3:24; cf. Acts 20:19).

"Rejoice in hope, be patient in suffering" (v. 12). This continues Paul's instruction introduced in Romans 5:2–3. The object of Christian hope was the resurrection hope: this enabled early Christians to develop patience in facing tribulation. Earlier he stresses that one can face suffering creatively by seeing in it an occasion to strengthen one's character (Rom. 5:4).

"Persevere in prayer" (v. 12). Vigilance in prayer is held out as a common expectation for Christians (Acts 2:42; Eph. 6:18; Phil. 4:6; Col. 4:2; 1 Thess. 5:17; 1 Tim. 2:1). Here is another theme that relates directly to today's Gospel reading. It is, after all, a prayer in which Mary magnifies the Lord. In fact, one should note the number of prayers that occur in Luke 1–2.

"Contribute to the needs of the saints; extend hospitality to strangers" (v. 13). At the outset of his ministry to the Gentiles, Paul had agreed to "remember the poor" (Gal. 2:10) and thus devotes considerable time, energy, and space to the relief fund for the Jerusalem saints (cf. 1 Cor. 16:1–3; 2 Cor. 8–9). Extending hospitality was but another form of this, and in fact was so important that it became a criterion for judging the worthiness of potential church leaders (1 Tim. 3:2; 5:10; Tit. 1:8; Heb. 13:2; 1 Pet. 4:9).

"Bless those who persecute you" (v. 14). The language echoes the teachings of Jesus (Matt. 5:44; cf. Luke 23:34; 1 Cor. 4:12; Acts 7:60; 1 Pet. 3:9; Luke 6:35; Eph. 4:32).

"Rejoice with those who rejoice, weep with those who weep" (v. 15). Here is another point of connection with the Gospel reading, for we recall that when she had given birth, "they rejoiced with her" (Luke 1:58). This also echoes the sentiments of Sirach 7:34: "Do not avoid those who weep."

"Live in harmony with one another" (v. 16). Christian community implies living together in harmony and love (cf. Rom. 15:5; 2 Cor. 13:11; Phil. 2:2; 4:2; cf. 1 Cor. 1:10; 1 Pet. 3:8).

"Do not be haughty, but associate with the lowly; do not claim to be wiser than you are" (v. 16). In keeping with Old Testament warnings against pride and conceit (Prov. 3:7; Isa. 5:21), Paul excludes arrogance from permissible Christian behavior (cf. Rom. 11:20, 25; 1 Tim. 6:17).

Luke 1:39–57

The service of Visitation recalls Mary's visit to her kinswoman Elizabeth in the hill country of Judah. This celebration not only provides the occasion for the church to anticipate Christmas yet six months away, but also the opportunity to hear Luke sing and expound on that beautiful moment. Before the births of either John or Jesus, the reader of Luke is made privy, through their mothers, to the profound Christian themes yet to be lived out and proclaimed.

Elizabeth and Mary are not nameless and faceless women who are no more than the wombs that carry great sons. They are persons with names, addresses, beliefs, hopes, and joy in service. Such is Luke's treatment of women in the Gospel story. Mary will reappear in trust and devotion (Acts 1:14), as will other women who join in the mission (Luke 8:1–3), and to them is entrusted the one sustained hallelujah of the Christian faith: He is risen (Luke 24:1–12).

Mary's visit to Elizabeth provides the occasion for the two women to celebrate the angel's word to Mary, which was also the angel's word to Abraham and Sarah: "For nothing will be impossible with God" (1:37; Gen. 18:14). As Paul was to express it, God gives life to the dead and calls into existence things that do not exist (Rom. 4:17). It does not matter whether it is a case of an old and barren couple or a virgin without a husband. The Visitation is, therefore, a double celebration of the power of God to give life.

The Visitation is also a study in contrasts. Elizabeth is old, the wife of a priest who was part of an ancient order of things in Israel. Having a child in her old age is a reminder of the past: Abraham and Sarah, Manoah and his wife, Elkanah and Hannah, from whom came Isaac and Samson and Samuel. The promises of God survived and continued through the unlikely births to the old and barren. But Mary was young, a life new, virgin, and all promise. She and her child do not remind one of the past; in fact, in them begins a new history. Mary's child is continuous with the past, to be sure, the fulfillment of a promise, but in him God is doing a new thing. So radically new is this act of God that the only appropriate means was a woman young, and a virgin.

The Visitation is also a beautiful reflection, through the women, of the futures of their unborn sons. As Elizabeth is humbled by the visit of "the mother of my Lord" (v. 43), so John was witness and servant to Jesus. As John leaped in Elizabeth's womb when Mary entered the house (vv. 41, 44), so John's joy was that of a groomsman when the bridegroom arrived (John 3:29–30). As Elizabeth blessed Mary not only for her child but also because Mary believed the word of God (vv. 42–45), so John would come calling for faith in Jesus as the means of life in the kingdom. There is never any question for Luke that Jesus and not John is the Messiah, but neither is there any question that both Elizabeth and Mary are servants of God's purpose, both their sons are gifts of God, and both sons have appointed ministries in God's plan for the ingathering of the nations.

The Visitation is also a preview of reversals yet to come. The ordinary structures of history, the usual cause and effect sequences of events, could not sustain or contain what God would be doing. The empty will be full and the full, empty; the poor will be rich and the rich, poor; the powerless will reign and the powerful will be dethroned. In a close approximation of the Song of Hannah (1 Sam. 2:1–10), Mary sings of the eschatological reversal of stations and fortunes in the realm where and when God's love and justice rule supreme.

Holy Cross, September 14

Numbers 21:4*b*–9;
Psalm 98:1–5 or Psalm 78:1–2, 34–38;
1 Corinthians 1:18–24;
John 3:13–17

The "lifting up" of Jesus is a frequent reference in the Fourth Gospel to Jesus' death on the cross and to his exaltation to God's presence. In John 3, the expression is joined to the analogy of the brazen serpent story in Numbers 21. In the Epistle, Paul speaks of the preaching of the cross as God's weakness and foolishness, which is stronger and wiser than all human accomplishments. In a similar vein, both readings from the Psalms praise the triumph, not of God's power, but of God's forgiving goodness.

Numbers 21:4*b*–9

Like many other Old Testament readings for special days, this one has been connected with the particular occasion on the basis of typological exegesis. The association of this passage from Numbers with the cross of Jesus comes from New Testament times. "Just as Moses lifted up the serpent in the wilderness, so must the Son of Man be lifted up" (John 3:14). It continues to be instructive to reflect on the ways the story of the serpent in the wilderness is like the story of the cross.

It seems as if Moses had nothing but trouble from the people of Israel in the wilderness. On other occasions in the readings for this season, we have encountered those people complaining against Moses and the Lord, even objecting to the burdens of their election, the fact that they were set free from slavery in Egypt.

Although this story of complaint begins like most of the others, its results are quite different from the previous ones. There is the general observation that the people "became impatient on the way" (v. 4). The reader familiar with the story of Israel's travels from Egypt will already find this remarkable; they had been impatient and dissatisfied almost from the first day! Then follows the grumbling that is a summary of all the things they have complained about from the beginning. They grumble against God and Moses about being in the wilderness, about the lack of food and water, and—inconsistently—about the food they do have. This doubtless is an objection to the manna, never especially appealing, and certainly boring after the traditional forty years in the desert.

Usually what has happened at this point in the stories of Israel's complaints is Moses' intercession with the Lord, who graciously meets the needs of the people, either for food,

547

water, or security. But we hear without explanation that the Lord sent "fiery serpents among the people and they bit the people, so that many people of Israel died" (v. 6). Now the people do two things: they confess their sin of rebellion against the Lord and the leadership of Moses, and they ask Moses to intercede with the Lord to remove the serpents (v. 7).

When Moses prays for the people, the Lord responds but does not "take away the serpents." Instead, the Lord instructs Moses to make a fiery serpent and set it on a pole so that those who are bitten may look at it and live (v. 8). Moses did as instructed, setting up a bronze serpent, and it functioned as promised (v. 9).

The religious background of the traditions in this passage is complex. The belief is widespread that the image of a dangerous animal can function as protection against it, and the image of the snake in particular is associated with healing rituals in various religions. But does not the very fashioning of such an image violate the second commandment (Exod. 20:4) and thus threaten to violate the first commandment (Exod. 20:3)? Perhaps that is why the text mentions cautiously that the people were only to "look at" the bronze serpent. It is not an idol but a gift of the Lord. There must have been such an image in the temple in Jerusalem, for 2 Kings 18:4 reports that when Hezekiah purified the worship, he destroyed "the bronze serpent that Moses had made." Even healing symbols can become objects of idolatry.

Theologically, the most important factor here is the pattern of sin, punishment, and God's means of grace. Once the people sin, experience the punishment, confess their sin, and pray for relief, the Lord responds. On the one hand, it appears that the Lord was eager to respond almost before they asked. On the other hand, the prayer is not granted in the form requested. Sin has—and will continue to have—its effects. The dangers remain, and the people continue to suffer from the potentially death-dealing snakes. However, now there is healing from the Lord, although the scars of the snake bites—the effects of sin—doubtless will remain.

Psalm 98:1–5

One of the enthronement hymns, Psalm 98 praises Yahweh as the sovereign reigning over the world of creation and as the special benefactor of the house of Israel. Thus both the universal and the particular domains of Yahweh are noted.

Much of this psalm consists of calls or summons to praise/worship as well as reasons why God should be worshiped and praised. Those called upon to praise God are the community of Israel (implied; vv. 1–3), all the earth (all humanity; vv. 4–6), and various elements in the world of nature (sea, world, their inhabitants, floods, and hills; vv. 7–9). The ancient rabbis, in commenting on verse 8, noted that there are only three references in Scripture (Old Testament) to the clapping of hands: the peoples clapping hand in hand (Ps. 47:1), the trees of the field clapping branch against branch (Isa. 55:2), and the floods clapping against the banks of the river (Ps. 98:8).

The reasons for praise in the first section (vv. 1–3) are all associated with the word "victory." God has won victory for himself (v. 1), God has made known his victory (v. 2), and the ends of the earth have seen his victory (v. 3). The marvelous things God has done, which are not spelled out, are related to his vindication ("His triumph"; NJPSV) in the sight of the nations and to the manifestation of his steadfast love and faithfulness to Israel. The reason for praise in the second section (vv. 4–9) is the coming of God to judge the world, not simply to judge but to judge with (establish) righteousness and equity (v. 9).

Psalm 78:1–2, 34–38

This psalm is a long composition offering a recital of the historical epochs of Israel's past. The following epochs are covered: (1) the patriarchal period (vv. 5–11), (2) the Exodus and wilderness wanderings (vv. 12–53), (3) the settlement in the land of Canaan (vv. 54–66), and (4) the election of David and Zion (vv. 67–72). These epochs and the events associated with them are used as points of departure for preaching and proclamation. In this psalm, most of the past is interpreted as times of disobedience and is used to engender a sense of guilt and shame from those addressed in the psalm.

The two sections selected for this lection are part of the introduction (vv. 1–2) and a portion of the psalmist's interpretation and preaching on the wilderness theme (vv. 34–38). The opening verses present the historical synopsis and interpretation that follow as a teaching or a parable, that is, not as a pure recital of history but as an interpretative reading of the past intended to speak to the present.

Verses 34–38 are a portion of the homily on Israel's behavior in the wilderness. Although cared for, preserved, and fed in the desert, the Hebrews are described as having constantly sinned. The people are depicted as demurring and demanding, unappreciative and uncooperative. Over and over again, God has to act to reprimand them. Verses 34–38 proclaim two things about the people. First, they were not repentant until they were punished; they did not turn toward God until God had turned against them. Their repentance was the product of divine coercion. Second, their devotion was superficial and temporary. Their mouths and their tongues were committed to religious expression, not their hearts. Flattery and lies, not fidelity and loyalty, were their hallmarks.

In spite of the people's behavior and their transient faith, they depicted God as their refuge and redeemer (v. 35). Long-suffering and forbearing, God forgave and did not destroy; God withheld his anger and did not give vent to his wrath (v. 38).

1 Corinthians 1:18–24

It is a tribute to this celebrated Pauline passage that we hear it read every liturgical year. It is featured prominently each year when 1 Corinthians 1:18–31 serves as the New Testament lesson for Tuesday in Holy Week. In Year A, the same text is heard on the Fourth Sunday After the Epiphany. In Year B, a slightly longer version of this text (vv. 18–25) is heard on the Third Sunday in Lent. And for the celebration of Holy Cross each year, verses 18–24 serve as the New Testament lesson. How it is heard and read will obviously differ at each of these times, for each liturgical setting creates its own nuance and causes us to attune our ears accordingly. The preacher may want to consult our remarks on this passage in these other settings, because its full implication can hardly be grasped with any one reading or set of interpretive comments.

We should first read the passage—and understand it—in its own context, within Paul's first letter to the church at Corinth. It occupies a prominent position toward the beginning of the letter, immediately following his appeal for unity (1 Cor. 1:10–17). Its placement here is crucial, for it introduces a theological perspective that serves as an important corrective. Within the Corinthian church there was an emerging theological position, if not a position at least an outlook, that placed a high premium on wisdom and knowledge. Paul had already begun to see the debilitating effects this viewpoint was having on the church, creating pockets of loyalty and rivalry, stratifying the community into levels—levels of knowledge and ignorance, levels of gifts, levels of concern or lack of concern for one another, levels of strength and weakness. Some scholars have characterized the viewpoint as "gnostic," and perhaps it was in the sense of an amorphous outlook but not in the sense of a developed theological system such as we find in the second century.

In the face of the situation as he perceived it, Paul casts anchor at the very outset. The point at which he pitches the battle for the hearts of the Corinthians is "the message about the cross" (v. 18). With these words we are close to the heart of Paul's gospel. In his original missionary preaching among the Corinthians, he had made an intentional choice to focus primarily, if not exclusively, on "Jesus Christ, and him crucified" (1 Cor. 2:2). If asked to define his own psychological center of gravity, Paul would answer: the cross. Somehow the cross had become for him more than a narrative event, more than a story dramatically unfolded in the passion story (Mark 15:16–47; Matt. 27:27–44; Luke 23:26–56; John 19:1–42). Doubtless, when he preached about the cross he rehearsed this story, if not in whole at least in part. The "message about the cross" was preaching whose content, as well as motivation, was the story of the crucified Christ. In this sense, it was a past event, for he could speak of those who had "crucified the Lord of glory" (1 Cor. 2:8).

But just as surely as the cross was for Paul a past event, it was more than this. It was narrative, but it was also symbol. Somehow the word "cross" captured the essence of God's dealings with humanity. Somehow it became for Paul a riddle, an inescapable enigma. His word for it is "stumbling block," or "scandal" (*skandalon*, v. 23; Gal. 5:11). We know some of the reasons why. The notion of a crucified Messiah created a severe hermeneutical problem. Deuteronomy 21:22–23 stated that "anyone hung on a tree is under God's curse," and given the undeniable nature of Jesus' death by crucifixion, he was implicated by this passage. We know how incredible Peter found the notion of a suffering Messiah (Matt. 16:21–23).

There was also the sheer incredibility of the "message about the cross." Paul insists that Jews found it offensive and Greeks found it irrational. Or, in the words of today's text, "a stumbling block to Jews and foolishness to Gentiles" (v. 23). Judged in the arena of public opinion, the "message about the cross" did not fare that well. It came as a minority opinion, voted down by the majority.

Yet as Paul understood the cross, it revealed something unique and fundamental about God. The sheer fact that humans found it difficult to accept, if not an inconceivable way for God to act, was itself revelatory, for in this way the cross illustrates God's capacity to confound us. Our tendency is to rationalize the work of God so that it conforms to our own expectations. We make it fit, or else we implicate God; but this is the height of human arrogance, Paul insists, this inclination to call God's hand. God needs no human consultants! (vv. 19–20).

Rather than repelling Paul, the cross attracted him, but not because of the beauty of the passion story. It was neither beautiful nor powerful. If anything, it was a story of human savagery, of misguided human motives, of human conspiracy and human ignorance. It was an unfolding drama of powerlessness, of events turning in on themselves, of the inability of divine intervention. Yet it was precisely in and through an event, or series of events, where human weakness reigned, where divine power was conspicuously absent rather than dramatically present, that Paul saw God most visibly revealed. The cross was a vacuum where neither "signs" nor "wisdom" was present to save the day. It was its own sign, its own peculiar symbol, its own form of wisdom, its own revelatory word. And if we look closely, we see God at work in a way that "makes sense" of the world as we know and experience it.

The cross as event, symbol, and enigma thus becomes the clue to who God really is. It reveals a God who is made known in weakness rather than strength, in suffering rather than robust health, in powerlessness rather than in shows of force, in moments of darkness rather than in shafts of dazzling sunlight. It is the God who is experienced in the underside of life, in the shadows, not in the sun.

So construed, the cross becomes for Paul a point of psychological redefinition. "May I never boast of anything except the cross of our Lord Jesus Christ, by which the world has been crucified to me, and I to the world" (Gal. 6:14). His angle of vision on the world was radically altered by the cross. From this vantage point, the world's values were reversed (Phil. 3:4–7). Indeed, the "world" became crucified in the sense that it ceased to lay hold on him in the way it once did. It died. It ceased to exist. It no longer had the finality it once had. After the cross, "the form of this world [began to pass] away" (1 Cor. 7:31; 2 Cor. 4.16–5:5).

The reverse was also true. Just as the "world" died, so had Paul "died." The "I" that figured so prominently in his self-understanding died. Through the cross, and his coparticipation with Christ in the crucifixion, the form of his personal existence radically shifted from an "egocentric" to a "Christocentric" form of existence (Gal. 2:19–20).

Paul was the first to admit that such an understanding of the cross was reserved for "those who are called" (v. 24). It was, after all, a matter of being summoned by God. In this sense, the cross beckons, and its beckon must be heard over the objections of scandal and irrationality.

John 3:13–17

As a magnet, the subject of the cross has been held over the text for the day, drawing to itself those verses pertaining directly to that event. Fairness to the subject and to the text demands, however, that verses 13–17 be set back into the context in order to extract them again.

John 3:1–21 is usually regarded as a conversation between Jesus and Nicodemus. However, where the Evangelist ends the conversation and where his own comments begin is not clear. One had but to look at different red-letter editions to see this uncertainty illustrated: Do Jesus' words end at verse 15, at 16, or at 21? The question is, however, a moot one, because the text reveals clearly that John is doing more than reporting a conversation. Such a shift begins at verse 7 with a change from the singular to the plural "you." The message from Jesus, says the writer, is to all and not to Nicodemus alone. The plural continues in verses 11 and 12. In addition, at verse 11 the "conversation" becomes more openly a debate between the church and the synagogue over the subject of life in the kingdom. Note the "we" versus "you" (plural). Furthermore, at verse 13 the passage becomes even more obviously a post-Easter Christian message by the statement in the past tense: "No one has ascended into heaven except the one who descended from heaven, the Son of Man." The earthly sojourn of the Savior is viewed as a completed event. It would be unfair, therefore, to treat this text within the confines of a private conversation at the beginning of Jesus' ministry, and it would be grossly unfair to be critical of Nicodemus for not understanding it. The Evangelist, by means of Nicodemus, is addressing the reader.

And what is the Evangelist saying to the reader? Let us confine ourselves to the bearing of the text on our subject, the cross of Christ. If the cross is not mentioned in verses 13–17, how is it to be discerned here? To be sure, in traditional church art, music, and theology,

John 3:16 is associated with Golgotha. It is as though it were to be translated, "For God so loved the world that he gave his only Son *on the cross.*" That the cross is a part of the Johannine understanding of salvation is beyond question. Jesus lays down his life for the sheep (10:11); he lays down his life for his friends (15:13); he dies as the Passover lamb providing the freedom of a new exodus for the people of God (19:31–37). But the cross in this Gospel is the means of glorifying the Son (12:23–28), that is, of returning the Son to the presence of God. Hence the double meaning of being "lifted up" (v. 14; 8:28; 12:34)— up on the cross and up into glory. This being lifted up is as surely an act of God's grace and love as was the provision for salvation in the camp of Israel when they suffered God's judgment and punishment for their unbelief and disobedience (v. 14; Num. 21). Jesus' being lifted up was an act of love from God toward the world; and to be understood as this Evangelist presents it, that act needs to be seen in the full movement of the descending and the ascending of the Son of Man (v. 13).

In summary fashion, John's message may be stated this way: the Son came into the world to reveal God (1:18), whom to know is life eternal (17:3). That revelation is not only in signs and discourses but also in the cross.

The God revealed in the Son is a God who loves, who loves the whole world, and who desires none to perish but that all have life eternal. God does not simply wish this; God sends the only Son to offer this life as a gift.

However, the cross refers not only to Jesus' death but to his being lifted up to God. This also is a part of the salvation event in that the glorified Christ sends the Holy Spirit to his church (7:39): "Nevertheless I tell you the truth: it is to your advantage that I go away, for if I do not go away, the Advocate will not come to you; but if I go, I will send him to you" (16:7).

Index of Texts

INDEX